Aegean Sponge Fishing and the Island of Kalymnos (19th–20th Centuries)

Brill's Studies in Maritime History

The titles published in this series are listed at *brill.com/bsmh*

Aegean Sponge Fishing and the Island of Kalymnos (19th–20th Centuries)

By

Evdokia Olympitou

Edited by

Joyce Goggin

Translated by

Michaela Stergiopoulou

BRILL

LEIDEN | BOSTON

Originally published as *Σπογγαλιευτική Δραστηριότητα και Κοινωνική Συγκρότηση στο νησί της Καλύμνου (1905–2005 αι.)* [*Sponge Fishing Activity and Social Construction on the Island of Kalymnos (19th–20th c.)*], Institute of Historical Research, National Research Foundation, Athens, 2014.

Cover illustration: The town of Pothia, 1950s. Photograph by Dimitrios Harisiadis. Source: Photographic Archive of the Benaki Museum.

Library of Congress Cataloging-in-Publication Data

Names: Olympitou, Eudokia, 1962–2011, author. | Goggin, Joyce, 1959–
   editor. | Stergiopoulou, Michaela, translator.
Title: Aegean sponge fishing and the island of Kalymnos (19th–20th
   centuries) / Evdokia Olympitou ; edited by Joyce Goggin ; translated by
   Michaela Stergiopoulou.
Other titles: Spongalieutikē drastēriotēta kai koinōnikē synkrotēsē
   sto nēsi tēs Kalymnou (1908–2008 ai.). English
Description: Leiden ; Boston : Brill, 2025. | Series: Brill's studies in
   maritime history, 2405-4917 ; volume 17 | Includes bibliographical
   references and index.
Identifiers: LCCN 2024018022 (print) | LCCN 2024018023 (ebook) |
   ISBN 9789004701939 (hardback) | ISBN 9789004701946 (ebook)
Subjects: LCSH: Sponge divers—Greece—Kalymnos (Municipality—History. |
   Sponge fisheries—Greece—Kalymnos (Municipality—History. | Kalymnos
   (Greece : Municipality)—Social conditions.
Classification: LCC HD8039.S55552 G76513 2025 (print) | LCC HD8039.S55552
   (ebook) | DDC 331.7/63970949587—dc23/eng/20240514
LC record available at https://lccn.loc.gov/2024018022
LC ebook record available at https://lccn.loc.gov/2024018023

Typeface for the Latin, Greek, and Cyrillic scripts: "Brill". See and download: brill.com/brill-typeface.

ISSN 2405-4917
ISBN 978-90-04-70193-9 (hardback)
ISBN 978-90-04-70194-6 (e-book)
DOI 10.1163/9789004701946

Printed by Printforce, the Netherlands

To my father because ... he is Kalymnian.

∵

Contents

Foreword

Vassilis Panagiotopoulos

"Barren, rocky, arid Kalymnos". The birthplace of Evi Olympitou's father, and a place of particular emotional involvement for Evi herself; the island ultimately proved to be her solace. It is with great satisfaction we read her exclaim, "I, too, became Kalymnian", at the close of the book's introduction. To be precise, she wrote: "The study of the sponge fishery made me Kalymnian". The island of Kalymnos, a land of extreme and eternal poverty, was not only a local refuge in Evi's search for her cultural identity, but also the place where the Gordian knot of a personal, scientific dilemma was cut. There, on the island, and here, in this book, Evi answered the question "history or folklore?" This question pre-occupied her in a dynamic and, I believe, completely rational way: History and Folklore.

The dilemma may sound commonplace; however, the result is exciting because it no longer concerns the conventional co-existence of history and folklore, whereby a chapter of an historic introduction, or historic context, albeit sufficient, informs the reader of the "other" historic details of the land and its society. This, however, is not the place to examine the relation of history to folklore. There are serious scientific issues to address, arising from the institutional status of folklore, including the issue of historic material segmentation, and the conversion of history into methodology; issues which the Greek scientific community tends to avoid. In this brief preface, I will approach history and folklore, and their conventional content, as they have been experienced by both my generation and, I think, the younger generation of Greek researchers to which, of course, Evi belonged.

In the present book, history and folklore are intermingled to such an extent that the two areas – the two itineraries for discussion – are seemingly indistinct. If the two methodologies, those of history and folklore, remained separate in the preparatory phases of Evi's research, in the work itself they have been distilled into a shared, common endeavour with internal difficulties, both on the abstract methodological level, as well as on the level of execution. The organization of the themes addressed in the book, the distribution of content, the analogies drawn from factual data and research findings, were only some of the considerable difficulties that had to be conquered.

Moreover, in every Greek research area one encounters local peculiarities and a plethora of obstacles that must be overcome. Among other things, the Greek researcher has to cope with diverging cultural traditions; various, successive foreign occupations; proximity to and osmosis with foreign-speaking populations; radical and profound geographical particularities and peculiarities. Working in Dodecanesian history, multiple difficulties arise, even where conducting straight-forward research is concerned. For example, prior to the incorporation of the islands in the national core in 1947, two successive foreign occupations – the Ottoman, followed by the Italian occupation – created additional bibliographic issues, and necessitated specialized research and information. The Greek community of Kalymnos, although it never lost the idiosyncratic characteristics of its internal organization, had to be studied first through the administrative apparatus imposed by the prolonged Ottoman administration, and second, that which was imposed in the thirty-year Italian occupation before Greek state regulations came into force on the island. During foreign occupations, and most significantly the Ottoman occupation, the community of Kalymnos might have had serious room for autonomy and acting on its own behalf – a point which this book often showcases – but communal acts had to comply with the more general policy of the central state power; this was a restriction that affected the range of autonomy and margins of communal administration on the Greek islands.

On this point as well, Evi Olympitou's method of addressing the topic is one of the best examples of a modern historical-anthropological approach available. Aside from the fact that she does not veer off into a separate, self-contained narrative of community actions, or state rulings of the time, Olympitou monitored and investigated the conditions of social and economic life on Kalymnos, to the degree to which, and interconnected with, how she addresses sponge fishing. Moreover, in the spirit of historical anthropology imbued with the concept of prolonged, Mediterranean duration, Evi neither treated the profound changes that foreign sovereigns brought in as absolute, nor did she underestimate their importance and the consequences of the changes they put in place for the economic life of the island. This is of particular significance given that the core of the Kalymnian economy is the sponge fishing industry, which is particularly fragile because it relies on a single technique.

However, the need to respect the ruling presence, first Ottoman, later Italian, and then Greek, becomes imperative because new methods and means imposed on the archaic art of sponge fishing, from the mid-19th century onwards, were truly game-changing. New technologies in sponge fishing such as the scaphander diving suit, not only exceeded the limits of the enforcement of community power, they also exceeded the intentions and the will of state sovereigns. The introduction of the scaphander diving suit was not, however, the only occurrence that reversed long-standing labour and life practices. Indeed, the introduction of new national restrictions on the once-free sponge beds of the Mediterranean; the appearance of new types of enterprise, the arrival of labour forces from neighbouring islands, and so on, are some of the issues that called for strong interventions and required a state presence, or its upgrading. During the second half of the 19th century and the first decades of the 20th century, old community and guild provisions were no longer able to deal with the complexity of relations that arose from technological change (i.e. the scaphander diving suit) and, more generally, from what was, at the time, the new economy.

Anyone undertaking research into the sponge fishery – an old but renewed economic activity, especially in the late phase of its development – is called upon to monitor state interventions, given their absolutely vital role at the central level where decisions are made (Constantinople, Rome, Athens), as well as on the local level of their implementation on Kalymnos. Thus, we return to our initial thoughts on the dual methodology of this book, that is, to the fact that this peculiar professional activity – sponge fishing – cannot be studied outside the scope of general conditions of that period and, in particular, not outside the scope of state interventions, both on a national and on a local level. The result of such state interventions functioned in a complementary, as well as in a decisive or paradigm-changing way, with long-standing methods of fishing for sponges, which are resistant to change. Ultimately, this is related to the traditional, long-standing Kalymnian lifestyle, which is likewise resistant to change. Evi, I believe, knew and understood the meaning of the "paradigm shift" that took place with the arrival of the scaphander diving suit on the island of Kalymnos along with other modern changes, and she attempted to fathom the new historical conditions in which industrial-era sponge fishing, with its "man-eating machines", was destined to be part of a cycle of rebirth, evolution, and decay.

For folklorist Evi Olympitou, the emergence of the scaphander diving suit was the critical point in her deliberation on and treatment of folklore and history. The diving suit is at the crux of the longtime of folklore, and the short-time of history; a point at which societies are tested, and new kinds of relationships and organizational forms emerge. Through this moment in the mid-19th century at which Kalymnian society was tested, Olympitou saw the before-and-after versions of the life of sponge fishermen. She "read" the century-old, sponge-fishing adventure through the transition – the schism, or shift – brought about in the community by the scaphander diving suit. In an innovative approach to her own disciplinary orientation, Evi was as interested in the ancient method of diving with the "skandalopetra", as she was in the modern use of the scaphander diving suit and the "novel" violation of security limits that came with it for investors and crews. In other words, Olympitou engaged with a wide range of topics, and this involved spiritual courage and personal integrity, both of which are present throughout the book.

Sponge fishing is a professional activity that requires specialized skills, and which is characterized by high risk. Evi Olympitou studied technological change in the form of the scaphander diving suit from the point of view of an historian, while she continued to see the life and behaviours of sponge fishermen from the point of view of a folklorist. This methodological rapprochement of history and folklore in Evi's approach to the world of sponge fishing provides answers to a number of questions, such as that of social equilibrium, which does not appear to have been practically disrupted on the island. During the prolonged period of traditional sponge fishing with naked divers and the skandalopetra, a balance of risk-benefit was established, however, as Evi points out, there is a certain tendency to euphemistically under-report this balance, ignoring the fact that naked diving also had its victims. In the era of the scaphander diving suit, this did not seem to give rise to an aversion to the profession of sponge fishing. Without a doubt, losses (increased deaths and disability) were painful yet accepted, much as warrior societies accept danger. And, where one might expect a change in the game with the use of the scaphander, yet another new balance of risk-benefit came to dominate, and to complicate (or even cancel) the work of well-intentioned opponents of the new machines. It is this new risk-benefit balance that Evi sought to understand. Although the deaths and unprecedented disabilities caused by the technological innovation of the scaphander diving suit increased, this was not sufficient to significantly disrupt the social fabric of the island. This was a time of high expectations and incomes as a new logic of risk-benefit took shape, which affected all of the social groups on the island.

The new conditions were: more intense monetisation leading to bank loans, greater visibility and commercialisation of the product, the introduction of seasonal workers from other islands to the island's sponge-fishing labour force, less-specialized workers and, of course, reduced remuneration. All things considered, this is a miniature version of the beginnings of the industrial revolution, including various iterations and images of the period. This insight is one more important contribution offered by Evi's book.

Another crucial and ever-present topic present in this study is the issue of accidents. The dimension of danger for the people involved is perhaps an inconspicuous axis in this book, however in the chapters containing Olympitou's more specialized research, she carefully attempts to illuminate all sides of the issue, and here her moderation and restraint become even more evident. The intensification of labour, driven by new economic conditions, underwrites the sacrifice of the divers "to the Minotaur of sponge fishery", but

Evi's detailed approach to the phenomenon results in a complex narrative, the minutia of which Evi helps us to discover. Such details include the small number of scaphander diving suits per vessel, which meant that the shipowners demanded shorter periods of under-water decompression for divers working with the scaphander suit; imperfect knowledge and inept use of machinery on the part of the so-called "specialized" staff; the divers' failure to obey to the technical staff's commands in their attempt to increase their yield and thus their remuneration; and, lastly, largely at the close of the period addressed in this book, the employment of under-specialized staff as noted above.

While this book is rich in documentation, bibliography, legal provisions, oral testimonies, and so on, the key issue of accidents is elucidated by means of arguments from all sides and all players, which are, in my opinion, less conflicting than what one might expect. "Stories of these darkest moments in the history sponge fishing tell of the just and the unjust, the innocent and the guilty alike" (current volume, p. 257), she concludes. And Evi does not play favorites:

> The health risks from lengthy dives at great depths – paralyses and sudden death – may well have been attributable to a lack of knowledge of decompression procedures, although these procedures do indeed appear to have been followed as required. Risk taking was, however, the only way to repay debts [and the platika paid in advance], and to generate profits for investors in the sponge fishery, as well as for those practicing it. Moreover, the time required for decompression, which necessitated a gradual, prolonged ascent to surface, would have been an impossible luxury for sponge-fishing vessels equipped with just one breathing device, one scaphander helmet, and two suits at most. (current volume, p. 257)

A little further on she speaks of "the intoxication of the deep" "when they espied rich sponge-bearing areas" and the accidents that it caused (current volume, p. 259). In other words: the more intense the work pace, the more acute the benefit problem for shipowners (businessmen-investors), the greater the tendency to neglect safety rules in pursuit of greater gains. These factors combined all dramatically increased risks and losses. And, along with these vital elements, secondary – albeit not negligible occurrences – such as professional shortfalls in auxiliary staff, exacerbated the already high-risk conditions of the profession.

With her boundless love for the people of the sponge fishery, Evi Olympitou examines, in a thorough and deliberative fashion, economic mechanisms and human behaviours, synthesized against the background of the island of Kalymnos, largely over the years of transition from structural stagnation to the abrupt shifts of the 19th and 20th centuries. Investors and captains; divers and mechanics – they were all children of a society that struggled desperately to survive on that small Dodecanesian island, on which poverty and "dangerous living" are ever-present. Sponge fishing deaths and disabilities were not uncommon on the island, and the pages of Evi Olympitou's book are filled with the resulting tensions and human emotions. The dignity of her ancestors – also a constant in Evi's own brief life – prevented her from being swept up in inappropriate and unproductive sentimentality. Evi did not feel pity for Kalymnian sponge fishermen. She shed no easy, unfelt tears for anyone. She understood Kalymnian sponge fishermen honestly, both them and their time.

Foreword to the English Publication

Joyce Goggin

For most people, the word "sponge" suggests little beyond mundane household objects such as mops, insulation or cosmetic applicators. It is also doubtful that visitors to Greece who purchase "natural" sponges give them much thought apart, perhaps, from thinking that "natural" means not synthetic, and therefore somehow "good for the environment". And the vintage photograph of a sponge diver wearing an antique scaphander helmet reminiscent of Jules Verne on the label for packaged sea sponges sold in shops all over Greece, does little to alert customers to the environmental damage and the historic human cost of the industry.

This is an accurate description of my own interest in and knowledge of sponges, until I was invited to participate in a conference hosted by SOAS, London, and held on the island of Hydra in 2018. It was at *The Global Life of Sponges*, that Gelina Harlaftis presented a paper on Evdokia Olympitou's ethnography and industrial history of sponge diving and the island of Kalymnos, which Olympitou completed shortly before her untimely death in 2011. It was also at that conference that the idea arose to translate Olympitou's remarkable book into English, so that her meticulous account of Aegean sponge fishing could be made available to a wider public.

Thus a translation project was created at the Centre of Maritime History at the Institute for Mediterranean Studies, of the Foundation of Research and Technology in Rethymnon, Crete, that provided the funds and technical support, from 2019 to 2023. The project was coordinated by Gelina Harlaftis, Joyce Goggin undertook the editing of the volume, and Michaela Stergiopoulou was hired to translate the text. In 2019, Michaela Stergiopoulou began translating Olympitou's book into English and sending the manuscript, chapter by chapter, to Joyce Goggin to be edited. With that process completed, from 2020 to 2022 Gelina, Michaela and Joyce began meeting regularly on what they fondly called "Sponge Fridays", to painstakingly review the text, line by line, as they revised the edited English translation with the original Greek text in hand to compare for accuracy. The result, *Aegean Sponge Fishing and the Island of Kalymnos, 19th–20th Centuries*, is a faithful translation – as faithful as possible – of Evdokia Olympitou's highly detailed, foundational work on sponge fishing and the island of Kalymnos.

Importantly, Olympitou's *magnum opus* is about the island from which her family came, and the legacy with which she was raised. From a long line of

Kalymnians involved in the sponge trade such as investor Ioannis Emmanouil Olympitis, or merchant and outfitter Themelis Olympitis in the 19th-century, as well as the 20th-century warehousing sponge merchant Vouvalis Olympitis, Evi had remarkable access to both text-based archives as well as to living memories of the industry, which she recorded from interviews with members of the local population.

The publication of Evi's book in Greek was made possible by a group of devoted friends. All of them have given their support at various stages for this book's production. We are most grateful for their help and encouragement. In particular, we would like to thank Katerina Dede who selected the photographs published in this book from the photographic archives of the Benaki Museum.

Olympitou's *Aegean Sponge Fishing and the Island of Kalymnos*, studies the island and its inhabitants, as well as the industry and its multifarious impacts on the island's population and ecosystems from multiple disciplinary perspectives, such as anthropology, ethnography, industrial history, economic history, human geography and cultural studies. This is, moreover, a work of rich and remarkable detail. Yet while Evdokia Olympitou offers us an important archive in the following pages, there are still gaps to be filled, and that job must be passed on to future researchers. At the same time, while some of the detail provided here might seem superfluous, we believe that Evi also intended this book as a resource for people who will hopefully carry on her research and take it in new directions.

It is our hope that this book will be of service to readers interested in our seas and oceans and their history, and we affectionately dedicate it to the memory of Evdokia Olympitou, in thanks for her important and invaluable work.

Tables, Maps and Images

Tables

Maps

Images

Evdokia Olympitou, 1962–2011

Kalymnos 30 July 2005, during a scientific mission for the classification of the Kalymnos Municipal Archive

PHOTOGRAPH TAKEN BY NIKOS ALEVYZAKIS

Evdokia Olympitou was born in 1962. She studied at the University of Athens, where she wrote her PhD thesis titled «Η οργάνωση του χώρου στο νησί της Πάτμου (16ος–19ος αιώνας) ["The Organisation of the Space on the Island of Patmos (16th–19th century)"]. From 1994 to 2003 she was an Associate Researcher at the Centre for Neo-Hellenic Research of the Institute for Historical Research of the Hellenic National Research Foundation, and in 2003 she was appointed Assistant Professor of Ethnology in the Department of History at the Ionian University. Her research interests were the insular communities of the Aegean Sea, where she studied the history of inhabited areas and pre-industrial societies, the socio-economic effects of proto-industrialisation on maritime populations, demographics, labour history and history of fishing, based on archival sources and fieldwork. She was a member the Greek Commission of TICCIH (The International Committee for the Conservation of Industrial Heritage); of the Greek Contemporary Modern History Archives (ASKI); of the Society for the Study of New Hellenism, *Mnimon*. She published a large number of articles and books. Some of her books are: *Ψαρεύοντας στις ελληνικές θάλασσες. Από τις μαρτυρίες του παρελθόντος στη σύγχρονη πραγματικότητα* [*Fishing in the*

Greek seas. From the Testimonies of the Past to the Modern Reality] (in collaboration with Dimitris Dimitropoulos), Athens 2010; *Γυναίκες του Αγώνα* [*Women of the Greek War of Independence*], Athens 2010; *Άνθρωποι και παραδοσιακά επαγγέλματα σε νησιά του Αιγαίου* [*People and Traditional Professions in the Aegean Islands*], Athens 2003; *Αρχείο του Κεντρικού Συμβουλίου της ΕΠΟΝ. Συλλογή Αρχείων Σύγχρονης κοινωνικής Ιστορίας. Κατάλογοι και Ευρετήρια* [*Archive of the Central Council of EPON. Collection of Greek Contemporary Modern History Archives. Catalogues and Indexes*], (in collaboration with Dimitris Dimitropoulos) Athens 2000.

The present volume is her last book published by a group of her friends and loved ones, three years after she passed away. Her family, friends and colleagues were devasted by her sudden death in Corfu on 17 May 2011, at age 49. Evi, as she was known, was an exceptional and charismatic person and an outstanding teacher. As one of her colleagues at the Ionian University wrote: "For us you were above all a person with a rare ethos, somebody who possessed both an intellectual and innate mental kindness and modesty that characterized all aspects of your personal and professional life. You were distinguished for your broadness of mind, your critical thinking, your deep democratic beliefs, the constant urge to think and always research, examine and compare ... Always humane, modest, never indifferent or arrogant, you were open to the concerns and problems of others to carefully listen, understand, sympathize and help."[1]

---

1 "Εύη Ολυμπίτου (1962–2011): Αποχαιρετισμός σε έναν δικό μας άνθρωπο"["Evi Olympitou (1962–2011): A Goodbye to One of Our Own People"] in https://enthemata.wordpress.com /2011/05/22/olympitoy/.

Publishing Team's Note for the Greek Publication

This book is the fruit of Evi Olympitou's final, prolonged scientific endeavour. All of us who loved Evi took part in the lengthy preparation for this study, and we knew her tireless research spirit, her frequent trips to unearth material, her hours-long interviews with informants, her endless hours of working in libraries and archives, and her all-nighters in front of the computer. We knew her passion to discover, to document and to understand every aspect of the subject she was researching; we knew her deep respect and love for the people she studied, her constant attentiveness to the text, and her wish that it be perfectly written and understandable for her readers.

Although Evi thought the text needed further processing, following her sudden death the question spontaneously arose as to whether this work could be published. Our response was positive and effortless because, as we realized while reading Evi's text, the writing had almost reached its final stage, in spite of the fact that some sections were not yet fully completed. While this may be the case, this study constitutes an important contribution to ethnography and history writing, in part because brings to light previously unknown documentary material. It goes without saying however, that this version of Evi's book is not the one she had envisioned, given that she did not have time to finish it, and shape it into its final form.

During the publishing process, it was necessary to proceed with modifications, which were made by Evi's partner, Kostas Efthimiou, who had observed the writing process and had a clear picture of the book; Evi's friends Sophia Laiou, Dimitris Dimitropoulos, Lina Venturas and Katerina Dede were also involved. Any changes made were largely concerned with omissions and repetitions and, in a very few cases, the text was restructured based on Evi's own outline. In all cases, an effort was made to preserve the style and content of the book completely unaltered. It is also worth noting that the text's extensive documentation required no further additions or editing.

All references to the Municipal Archive of Kalymnos follow the system of classification established by the author and a team of her students (the catalogue of the Archive was submitted to the Municipality of Kalymnos). When completing the preparations for publishing the manuscript, we were informed that a new system of classification had been introduced into the archives through a local initiative, which may change the numbering of some folders. It is our hope that, with the publication of this study, which makes a significant contribution to the history of the Kalymnian sponge fishery, the Municipality of Kalymnos will commission a table of equivalents for the old filing system in the archive's new numbering system.

This publication owes greatly to the contribution of Vassilis Panagiotopoulos and Triantafyllos Sklavenitis, who attentively read the text; of Vallia Rapti – Evi's former student at the Ionian University who stepped up to proofread the text and create the index; as well as the contributions of Konstantina Simonetatou, who took great care with the layout of the text. We also extend our gratitude to the Director of the Institute of Historical Research, Professor Taxiarchis Kolias, who agreed to include this book in the publications of Institute of Historical Research (IHR) of the National Hellenic Research Foundation (NHRF). Evi had worked closely with the IHR/NHRF for several years, either on contract or as a volunteer in its research programs.

This book is the product of Evi's rare and remarkable scientific ethos, her training and the consistent quality of her research. Evi's selflessness, together with her compassionate character, and her unflagging will to share and to be generous with everyone, defined her as someone who served science and loved life. Evi was passionate about everything she believed in, and she connected with the people around her with such a generous soul that she left her mark on her scientific and professional communities, and of course, to an even greater extent, on all the people who loved her.

The Publishing Team

Introduction

The exploitation of marine resources, a task undertaken by maritime populations, does not appear to be an easy feat. For centuries, on islands like the rocky
island of Kalymnos, most island dwellers tenaciously and patiently endeav-
oured to tame arid lands. Such environments demand hard, systematic labour
to be made arable, and to yield what is ultimately a small production, vulnerable to the fluctuations of the island climate and weather adversities. Despite
intensive exploitation, the sloping and often rocky soil of islands like Kalymnos
have not been able to meet the nutritional needs of the populations they support; populations whose needs steadily evolve against the meagreness of food
sources. Hence such environments, adverse to production, have prompted
inhabitants to search for complementary means of survival: the exploitation
of all possible natural resources, the promotion of new technical know-how
and, ultimately, naturally outward-looking movements.

In the mid-17th century, along with perhaps somewhat imposed self-
sufficiency, some islands began developing the communicative potential that
the sea had to offer. All of the risks that this entailed aside, navigation turned
out to be a profitable means of transportation for goods and people, creating a
strong, resiliant tradition for several coastal populations. Yet diving for sponges
belonged to an unfamiliar and eerie world, brimming with real and mythical
dangers, as the practice was inextricably linked with the depths of the sea, and
required that the diver be experienced and skillful, and work in confrontation
with both the unfamiliar environment and time.

The development of a technical skill, the local productive specialization,
and the exclusive connection of the resulting product to export and trade are
phenomena that may be familiar artisanal activities in mountain and island
spaces. Although an activity may attract a labour force which shapes a technical tradition, leading to a favourable estimation of the activity, it does not
necessarily suffice to guarantee the viability of an activity, or to provide a stable rate of development for the groups engaging in said activity. The peculiar
structural characteristics of primary and manufacturing activities, which bore
the archaic qualities of the Ottoman world, rendered them particularly sensi-
tive to the challenges and competitiveness at the dawning of the industrial era.

All of these local "mono-professions" present similarities with, as well as
differences from, the Greek sponge fishery. Here too, there were specific
boundaries, transitory demand, scarce available capital, limited technical
renewal, and the capacity to deal with crises was inexistent. Sponge fishing is
a rural, "small-scale industry", conducted mostly on the barren islands of the

Aegean Sea, which are somewhat analogous to mountain spaces. Such singular community professions begin with the product, which requires rudimentary processing, and concludes with the product's introduction into the market, while engaging a large segment of the local population. Analogies could also be sought in the case of itinerant craftsmen with their specialized expertise and travel routes.

Sponge fishing, however, is not an evolved form of a prior, self-sustaining cottage industry that had raw material and experience to hand. In this case, the know-how involved in the production and processing of the raw materials required specialized knowledge of the water, the sea currents, the weather, the depths, and the sea bottom; these competences, perhaps, were similar to those of fishermen, who needed to know maritime areas and seasonal passages, in order to catch substantial "prey".

Moreover, even though both sponge fishing and fishing activities had formed local densities, and unique technical traditions with significant historical depth, they remained insecure and unstable. One substantial difference was, however, the fact that sponges had to be found and collected, one by one, from the seafloor. Therefore, timely access to and the safeguarding of fishing spots from anyone else who might try to claim a copious catch was an important part of the profession. In fact, the seabed amounted to a mental image, an informal allotment of the sea space, which perhaps, to some degree, bears a resemblance to the distribution of pasture lands in continental Greece.

Another singularity of sponge fishing is the fact that the product was not consumed by the populations who fished and processed it. On the other hand, industrial development increased demand, as well as the intensification and technological support of the sponge fishery, which was conducted in an environment that remained pre-industrial.

The industrialized West's search for raw materials also found productive fields in various areas, with rich subsoil and natural resources. In the second half of 19th century, sponge fishing was perhaps at least partially correlated with other forms of colonial exploitation, where new technological achievements were imposed on "native" populations, whose familiarization with the new technology was minimal. Similarly, sponge fishermen, were generally not well acquainted with the possible outcomes and risks involved in using the new diving equipment but were willing or forced to take risks in order to survive, as well as to strike it rich from the "sea-bottom gold".

Those who took advantage of this new supply of employment had to submit to the conditions of the job, and organize their family and social life based on the periodicity of the fishery. A nexus of transactions and specializations took shape around sponge fishing, which imposed an evident professional hierarchy and pronounced stratification of social groups, while the quantitative and qualitative characteristics of sponge fishing prompted various demographic, economic, and cultural realignments on all of the sponge-fishing islands of the Dodecanese. Changes in the composition of the population, the accumulation of wealth, as well as disputes within the island's community, are some features of sponge-fishing societies at the industry's peak period. The sponge fishery also acted as an enabler that provided the island populations and settlements with a new physiognomy, forming hubs of economic prosperity and cultural efflorescence, meeting the modern social standards of those who financed the activity and traded the product. However, in spite of the contrasts and financial opportunities to which the profession gave rise, employees did not manage to escape their common fate, that is, "worker of the sea".

The history of Kalymnian sponge fishing is similar to that of the rest of the sponge-fishing islands of the Dodecanese – that of Symi, Chalke, and Kastelorizo. The distinguishing feature of sponge fishing is its duration and development, or perhaps its constant presence, which continues throughout at least the 19th and 20th centuries. At that time, sponges were the most important source of livelihood for the island of Kalymnos, which is mountainous and barren, with very few natural resources and little productive capacity.

Furthermore, the Kalymnian sponge fishery appears to combine a number of factors and speculations that fostered its impressive growth. For over a century, the sponge fishery managed to channel its production; to connect to the network of international markets; to maintain robust trading houses abroad; to maintain its labour force, and attract even more workers from neighbouring islands; to cope with crises, and develop active diaspora settlements in Tunisia and on the coasts of Florida, USA; and, ultimately, to adapt to the technological innovations that were imposed on the profession. The most important part, however, is the fact that the island developed an exclusive specialization in sponge fishing, which played a primordial role in its social composition and physiognomy, as well as in the formation of a singular local culture; of an identity with multiple versions and depictions; and of a material and immaterial culture which might even be called a "culture of the sponge".

On the other hand, inevitable and coincidental, or unexpected, game-changing circumstances led to the gradual restriction and disappearance of sponge fishing, reinforcing, however, its cultural representation. For all the reasons above, I believe the sponge fishery of Kalymnos constitutes a particularly privileged historical and ethnographic case.[1]

---

1 On the uniqueness of every ethnographic example, see Bernard Russell, "Paratsoukli: Institutionalized Nicknaming in Rural Greece", *Ethnologia Europaea* II–III (1968–1969), pp. 65–74.

My goal was to tell the story of Kalymnian sponge fishing over the course of its prolonged existence, with brief attention to what came before and what came after, on a factual and symbolic level. My subjects of study are the local social and cultural realities and interrelations over the entire period in which the scaphander diving suit dominated the professional environment; that is, from the moment that the "machine" made its appearance in 1860s until the end of its use in 1970s, when the last sponge-fishing vessel equipped with scaphander diving suit set sail from the port of Kalymnos, with a nine-member crew. The examination of this long journey brings both stability and inconsistency to light, both "internal" and "external". It is easy to trace the complications that political and economic shifts on the map of the Eastern Mediterranean, and in international markets, caused for fishing and trading sponges; surviving official sources, however, are usually lacking when it comes to social upheaval relating to changes or crises in the sponge fishery.

In this study, I sought to follow the topic in three main directions in which I refer to the past and the present selectively. The first direction follows the business behaviours and employment relations prevalent when the scaphander diving suit dominated the industry, and gave rise to its expansion and intensification. I refer here to sponge fishing at great depths, and its accompanying professional competitiveness. I refer here also to the disputes of involved parties, and the transformation of what had previously been a seasonal, supplemental activity – (i.e. sponge fishing by "traditional methods") – into an organized undertaking and profession.

As noted, this rapid process was not devoid of conflict, and the study of this specific employment landscape requires the search for and understanding of various institutional and social stances against the "violent" introduction of technological innovation. These come together in what is known as the (in)famous "sponge-fishery issue", which unsettled the sponge-fishing populations of the Aegean during the final decades of the 19th century, and the first decades of the 20th century, when the demand for sponges from industries in the West was particularly great. It was at this point in time that seasonal activity was reshaped into an organized endeavour. This began with the introduction of the first diving apparatus, as a response to the new state of affairs (i.e., increased demand for sponges), which generated a series of changes and set up a chain of reactions in a professional field that, until then, only knew of "archaic" diving and sponge-fishing methods. Public debate on the fatal accidents that resulted became the order of the day during that period; a field of confrontation that would fuel conflicts between crew members over the course of time – mostly between divers and captains.

The second direction pursued in this book is related to the ways in which the physiognomy of the labour force took shape, and a local elite made itself known through the sponge fishery. These developments consolidated the social stratification of the population, and shaped the residential and social organization of the island. Included here are the unique professional groups of the sponge fishery, their internal hierarchy, and the various survival mechanisms developed by the people who left the island, as well as by those who stayed. I refer here mainly to the female population, and the wives of sponge fishermen in particular. Given the exclusively man-dominated nature of the activity, I explore how responsibilities were distributed based on gender, and how everyday life was organized, which had to be condensed into the seasonal presence and absence of a significant portion of the male population. Working mostly with ethnographic material, I also attempted to describe facets of the work aboard the vessels and of the life of crews during their six to seven month long stay at sea; the "tyranny", as the sponge fishermen themselves used to call sponge-fishing voyages.

In my search for factual material, and particularly in my search for traces of culture and ideology in pieces of evidence and testimonies retrieved from the archives, I tried to understand people's lives and attitudes towards the sponge fishery prevalent in that particular working environment, in that period of time. This included the culture of business groups, the cultural traits of the labour force that coalesced around the activity, as well as various depictions of sponging in literary texts and film. This material is rich and diverse, and offers insights into cultural expressions of social protest, as well as into expressions of a more or less ethnographic or political nature. The study concludes with an attempt to record and interpret some of the symbolic representations and established stereotypes that fuel the various versions of Kalymnian identity to this day.

My intention was neither to reconstruct a continuous thread through the industry and how it is conducted, nor to attempt to provide an historical review of sponging and the sponge fishery. From antiquity and through the Ottoman period in its entirety, sources old and new, here and there, mention fishing methods and uses of sponges; however, these topics are not part of my research interests. Neither are natural history, or sponge physiology of interest here; moreover, both of these fields fall far outside my own competence. However, the ways in which sponge fishermen named and described sponges, the quality-based classification of sponges and how sizes dictated price, as well as the remuneration of sponge fishermen, are indeed of interest here, along with the impact of occasional diseases of the sponges, which obliterated sponge beds for years on end.

On a related note, the primary content of this study is drawn from various sources, both written and oral. The lengthy time span addressed here justifies their combination, while their time in sequence links the past with the present. It is obvious that oral and written narratives, and individual and institutional discourses, are generally the products of different moments in history and capture events and memories that may not always be congruent, although they function in a complementary fashion. In my analysis and interpretation of this material I do not attempt to construct a linear narrative. Rather, I have tried to formulate a synthetic account in which I focus on a different subject in each chapter, in dialogue with the argument of the book in its entirety, so that these topics come together as part of a unified whole.

In this context, the institutional discourse contained in official documents, press publications, contemporary and older literature, popular and eponymous lyrics of popular songs and so on, were all taken into account. The field is, however, incomplete without the protagonists of the activity; those who left behind written evidence that narrates the story of their work, or those who wished to offer their personal testimonies – their own version of the story. Various pieces of archival evidence, with their monotonous, unvarying phrasing in the form of hundreds of sponge-fishing agreements and the lacunary transcriptions of the decisions of local notables – all of these served to condense or hush incidents, express social alliances and hierarchies, and often mitigate local controversies. Nevertheless, hints and innuendos surface and suffice to suggest that prosperity was often fragile, especially for some of the island's inhabitants, hence unanimity and unity were not always a given.

Many of the testimonies contained here are personal biographies, wherein the subjects recall their own perceptions of the past, and usually highlight the most heroic or tragic moments of the sponge fishing. A number of narratives describe the life of the divers as particularly cruel and unbearable; as a sequence of episodes and examples that centre on danger, disease and death. Under the sea anything could happen or seemed to become possible: the depths were filled with money, glory, and better luck, as well as bankruptcy and death. Yet, without sponge diving, there was no life. Some confessed that they were afraid of the job, and that they trembled with terror when they descended, alone, to great depths where they might encounter some unforeseen event, be it natural or supernatural. But most of all, they were afraid of being "hit by the machine", that is, being afflicted by "the bends" or decompression sickness resulting in paralysis or death. Moreover, the testimonies of male and female narrators has great potential to contribute to our understanding of the data; more importantly however, they reveal the how the collective local culture dealt and deals with its sponge-fishing past.

I would also like to explain here that, in the case of oral testimonies, when processing and documenting material, I specify whether interviews were conducted by me, or recorded by others and kept in collections of relevant material. Frequently, the views presented are regarded as common knowledge among Kalymnians. Where this occurs, the names of informants are not always provided, thereby eliminating the necessity of constantly citing the same names. In some other cases, informants' names have been omitted at their request.

The Archive of the Elders' Council and the Municipality of Kalymnos holds 309 registers which contain only copies of outgoing documents, but no copies of incoming documents. References to the Archive's documents are not, in fact, uniform, as many registers do not have numbered pages, whereas other files do not have numbered documents. Where possible, the document number is provided, otherwise the citation is accompanied by the page number of the register. Date and year are always included in the citation. Some topics that appear in the text recur in the archival sources. In these cases, citations are indicative and not detailed. Where quotations are taken from pieces of archival evidence are concerned, I based my transcription on the Greek monotonic system, with no further changes to spelling.

It is impossible to pinpoint the thought or "trajectory" that drew me into the study of the Kalymnian sponge fishery which began in 2002. Memories, narratives, and images have been powerful motivators, and have however, also worked in a limiting capacity. This is why the work lay incomplete and dormant for several years, and it may still be, at least in terms of what my thorough research brought to the surface. At times when my pace and the work slowed down, my interest was rekindled by moments of fruitful debate, the exchange of ideas, and criticism. I refer here to seminars and lectures that took place at the University of Thessaly, the University of the Aegean, and the Panteion University. Here, I would like to thank Christine Agriantoni, Yannis Yannitsiotis, Eleni Gara and Eva Kalpourtzi.

My research in the Municipal Archives of Kalymnos was long and labourious. An important step to my familiarization with the organizational structure of local administrations and their archival records was, therefore, cataloguing and classification, which was conducted under my direction with the valuable contributions of five senior – at the time – students of the Department of History, Ionian University: Nikos Alevizakis (2005, 2006), Alexandra Papadopoulou (2005, 2006), Aristeidis Marantos (2005), Giorgos Pagonakis (2005) and Eleni Renesi (2005). I would also like to extend my warm thanks to Ms. Fani Kapella-Koutouzi and the then mayor of Kalymnos, Mr. Giorgos Roussos.

In all of the years that this work has been in progress, I have come to owe a debt of gratitude to friends, colleagues, family members and compatriots. Omitting, for the moment, the names of people for whose more general understanding I am grateful, I would like to mention my former colleagues, teachers, interlocutors, and friends from the Institute of Historical Research of the National Hellenic Research Foundation (IHR/NHRF). In particular, Vassilis Panagiotopoulos, Dimitris Dimitropoulos, Leonidas Kallivretakis, and Katerina Dede who read versions of this text and, for years, discussed the issues and concerns arising from it, both before and during the writing process.

My colleagues from the Ionian University, Sophia Laiou and Gelina Harlaftis, offered new ideas, books and references, and heartily supported this endeavour.

Alexis Politis, Lina Venturas, Manos Zacharias, Eva Kalpourtzi, and Ilias Nikolakopoulos engaged with me in fruitful discussions, helped me solve problems, and provided me with bibliographic and cinematic material, some of which was difficult to find and rare.

Family and friends from Kalymnos – a hospitable human network – assisted me in any way possible with my various and sometimes demanding research queries. Without my Kalymnian family, this task would not have been possible. Therefore, I extend my special thanks to my cousins Sofia and Takis Glynatsis, my uncles Argyro and Giannis Glynatsis, as well as to Kalymnians: Giorgos Proestakis, Niki Reisi, Lena and Mickes Kalikazaros, Nikos Magkos, and Fani Kapella-Koutouzi of the Reading Room.

There were numerous informants; most of them were Kalymnians. Some however, originated from Leros and worked on the sponge-fishing vessels of Kalymnos for many years: Antonis Kampourakis, Nikolas Kampourakis, Vassilis Kampouris, Giannis Koutouzis, Vassilis Konstantaras, Michalis Lambos, Giannis Loulourgas, Lefteris Mamouzelos, Petros Marthas, Konstantinos Nomikarios, Dimitris Peros, Thrasyvoulos Politis, Nikolaos Sdregas, Giannis Tsoulfas, Manolis Chilas. My research was conducted over a long period of time, which means I must express my thanks to some people who are no longer with us.

Lastly, Kostas Efthimiou participated, listened, and read.

And now, at the close of this long journey, it feels as though the study of sponge fishing has made me Kalymnian!

CHAPTER 1

The Land and the Activities of Its Inhabitants

Have you seen the island where the fig tree blossoms, and
the gnarled olive tree spreads its silvery leaves? Have you seen the
daughter of Sun and Sea, the mother of the Sponge, who whelps
cubs, gives birth to brave lads, and raises giants and kings of Pontus?
Have you seen Kalymnos?

SKEVOS ZERVOS[1]

∴

1.1 "Our Island Is Rocky, Arid, and Barren"

In 1884, the Elders [*Demogerontes*][2] of Kalymnos wrote the following to Nazif
Pasha, the Governor-general of the Ottoman Archipelago: "Kalymnos, a barren, rocky, jagged and extremely arid island, does not produce anything to feed
its hapless inhabitants, whom necessity has always forced to take up the highly
dangerous practice of fishing for sponges in order to feed their poor families".[3]
Another memorandum drawn up early in 1894 "by sponge-fishing parties
of the Mighty Ottoman Empire", and addressed to the Governor-general of
the Imperial Archipelago, Abedin Pasha, reiterated the reasons set forth by the
populations of the Southeastern Aegean for their long-standing involvement
with sponge fishing. "Because their lands", the Elders of Kalymnos wrote on
the inhabitants' behalf, "are entirely arid, rocky and barren, and it is therefore
impossible for the people to live off of them. Necessity and divine economy
have compelled them for some centuries now to turn to sponge fishing".[4]

---

1 Θεμελίνα Καπελλά, *Ιστορικές μνήμες Καλύμνου* [Themelina Kapella, *Historical Remembrances of
   Kalymnos*], Athens 1997, p. 116.
2 The *Demogerontes* [Elders]: The Ottoman governing apparatus was a combination of
   Demogerontes or administrators who controlled things such as public order, the military, and
   central taxes, and members of the local population who enjoyed limited power and controlled less crucial matters as well as some local taxation. The members of the Elders' Council
   were all elected from the local population. More on this topic in the following sections.
3 Excerpt from a report to Nazif Pasha, 20/2/1884, pp. 17–20, *Elders' Council Minutes and
   Correspondence 1884–1885*, Municipal Archives of Kalymnos [MAK].
4 Doc. 1, 4/1/1894, Correspondence *1894–1895*, MAK.

© KONSTANTINOS EFTHYMIOU, 2025 | DOI:10.1163/9789004701946_003

The same complaint is repeated in various texts from that period, such as official documents and testimonies. Although it is perhaps obvious why letters sent to the Ottoman administration by the Elders commonly open with such vivid descriptions, these laments are not far from reality.[5] On the rocky, barren island of Kalymnos, fishing for sponges and the activities involved in the sponge trade were the only – albeit extremely profitable – productive resource for the population, from at least the early 19th century onwards.

Although "sponge hunting" was developed and honed out of necessity, it nevertheless became an activity that could sustain a large number of families in sponge-fishing areas. The abundance of sponge-bearing beds in the Mediterranean, and in rather shallow depths at that time, required a sizable workforce and offered a means of survival for the entire population. Thus "the inhabitants of those sponge-fishing areas – young and old alike – as well as highly skilled and less skilled sponge divers, were able to work and earn a living from sponging".[6] Although, in the Elders' opinion, Kalymnians had a seemingly natural, innate ability to harvest sponges, the sponge fishermen also had to take on farming activities in order to meet their basic needs.

The inhabitants of Kalymnos, like those of even the most arid and barren of the Aegean islands, did indeed engage in agricultural activities such as farming and raising livestock on a regular basis. The arable land on the island was divided into small parcels, and production was limited in quantity and variety. Small quantities of grain were sown – mostly wheat and barley – on mountain slopes where terraces (the so-called "σπορίδια" – i.e. sporidia, or small, infertile parcels of land) had formed. Based on the data, which we must assume is accurate, provided in the *Yearbook of the Archipelago Province* [*Ημερολόγιο της Νομαρχίας του Αρχιπελάγους*], the official bilingual publication of the prefecture's printing office in Chios, at the end of the 19th century, wheat was cultivated over 22 hectares and barley over 140 hectares,[7] and this ratio in the number of hectares of wheat, to hectares of barley, does not appear to change

---

5 The reasons for this are clear, as these documents in which the island's scant natural resources were enumerated specifically targeted the administration and were sent to ask that various privileges be preserved. On the same topic see also Kalymnian lawyer Miltiadis Caravokyros' brief study of the topic in his *Étude sur la pêche des éponges. Les pays spongifères de l'Empire et le scaphandre*, Constantinople 1886, p. 4 and p. 7.

6 Doc. 1, 4/1/1894, Correspondence 1894–1895, ΜΑΚ.

7 *Ημερολόγιον της Νομαρχίας Αρχιπελάγους* [*Yearbook of the Archipelago Province*], 1304 ΑΗ [1886/1887], p. 116. See also Μιλτιάδης Ιάκ. Λογοθέτης, "Πληροφορίες για την οικονομία και κοινωνία της Δωδεκανήσου στα τέλη του 19ου αιώνα από τα ημερολόγια της Νομαρχίας Αρχιπελάγους", *Δωδεκανησιακά Χρονικά* 11 [Miltiadis Iak. Logothetis, "Information on the Economy and the Society on Dodecanese Islands in the Late 19th Century Retrieved from the Yearbooks of the Archipelago Province", *Dodekanisiaka Chronika* 11], 1986, pp. 91–117.

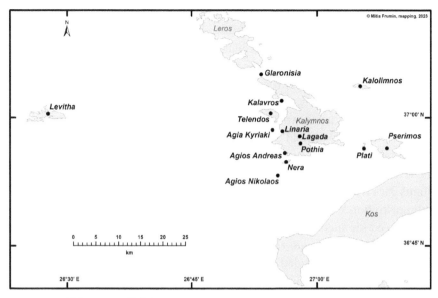

MAP 1.1   Kalymnos and Islets

until the end of ww II.[8] To the above, one should add small vegetable crops
for the population's own consumption, including potatoes, as well as a few citrus fruits and garden vegetables cultivated in the Pothia area and Brosta. In
the fertile valley of Vathy on the island's north side, there were orchards with
orange, lemon, and tangerine trees and, although production was limited, it
does appear that some of the total yield was also exported. Figs and almonds
comprised the remainder of the farming production.[9]

8   Δωδεκάνησος. Τετράτομος μελέτη του Υπουργείου Ανοικοδομήσεως και συνεργατών του υπό την διεύθυν-
     σιν του κ. Κ. Α. Δοξιάδη, Σειρά Εκδόσεων του Υπουργείου Ανοικοδομήσεως [Dodecanese. Study in
     four Volumes by the Ministry for Reconstruction Under Mr K. A. Doxiadis, Publication Series of
     Ministry for Reconstruction], Athens 1947, pp. 98–117.

9   Doc. 44, 45 and 46, 23/2/1894, Correspondence 1894–1895, ΜΑΚ; Doc. 823, 4/1/1894, Minutes
     of Administrative Council – Correspondence 1884–1885, ΜΑΚ. See also Doc. 210, 25/12/1925,
     Correspondence 1925–1927, ΜΑΚ, and Κάρολος Φλέγελ, Η νήσος Κάλυμνος [Carl Flegel, The
     Island of Kalymnos], Constantinople 1896, p. 10. As reported in the Yearbook of the Archipelago
     Province (p. 116) there were 600 orange trees and 316 lemon trees. G. Reisis reported exports
     to Russia of about 2,000,000 units; See Διονύσιος Ν. Ρείσης, Περιγραφή της νήσου Καλύμνου
     [Dionysios N. Reisis, Description of the Island of Kalymnos], Athens 1913, p. 30. The same infor-
     mation is found in Γεράσιμος Δ. Δρακίδης, Λεύκωμα των Δωδεκανήσων [Gerasimos D. Drakidis,
     Almanac of the Dodecanese], Athens 1913, p. 69, but also in [Anonymous], "Τα Δωδεκάνησα",
     Ημερολόγιον Σκόκου ["Dodecanese", Skokos' Journal] 29 (1914), p. 329. See also report of the
     Consul N. Souidas, 15/6/1910, Consulate in Rhodes, Folder 43 (1912), Subfolder, 3, Historical

During the long period leading up to WWII under consideration here, Kalymnians were also involved in the cultivation and processing of tobacco, although there is not enough available information to provide an accurate assessment of its significance. As with other agricultural products, tobacco production was exempt from taxation, as long as it was not channeled into the market. Be that as it may, there were still frequent disputes between cultivators and local authorities, as well as with the Régie Company, an Ottoman concern founded in 1883 that held a tobacco monopoly. The company claimed that illegal tobacco was being trafficked, and demanded that an appropriate tax be levied, while the company's violent behaviour towards the island's inhabitants gave rise to strong protests and appeals made by the community to the administration.[10]

Tobacco production continued on a more regular basis during the Italian occupation and, in 1938, the Italian Governor of the Dodecanese, Cesare Maria de Vecchi, expanded the monopoly of TEMI Company [*Tabacchi Egei Manifattura Italiana*], which was headquartered in Rhodes, to the entire Dodecanese. The 23 small-scale cigarette manufactures on the island of Kalymnos, where about 150 male and female tobacco workers and cigarette makers were employed, were forced to cease their activities.[11] Following WWII in 1947, Kalymnians resumed production by tapping this expertise with two workshops that employed 22 people,[12] and a craft industry founded in 1950, for the importation of unprocessed tobacco from tobacco-producing areas of Greece.[13]

Archives of the Greek Foreign Ministry [IAYE]. During the period from 1935–1941, production amounted to 10,000 oranges, 700,000 tangerines and 15,000 lemons. In 1939, Kalymnos had 6,000 orange trees, 30,000 tangerine trees and 3,000 lemon trees; Δωδεκάνησος. Τετράτομος μελέτη του Υπουργείου Ανοικοδομήσεως [*Dodecanese. Study in Four Volumes by the Ministry for Reconstruction*], Tables 8 and 9.

10 Doc. 167, 22/6/1894, Correspondence 1894–1895, MAK; *Resolutions* 18/1/1894 and 14/2/1894, *Minutes and Resolutions 1893–1907*, MAK. See also the *Report of the Elders of Kalymnos*, 21/2/1905, Consulate in Rhodes, Folder 44 (1911), Subfolder 2, Historical Archive of the Greek Ministry of Foreign Affairs (IAYE). It seems that the situation on the neighbouring island of Leros was similar. See Ηλέκτρα Κωστοπούλου, *Η Λέρος στην Οθωμανική Αυτοκρατορία. Σελίδες από τα βιβλία της Δημογεροντίας* [Ilektra Kostopoulou, *Leros in the Ottoman Empire. Pages from the Books of the Demogerontia*], Athens 2005, pp. 148–157.

11 See Γεώργιος Μ. Σακελλαρίδης, "Antonio Ritelli", *Καλυμνιακά Χρονικά* [Georgios M. Sakellaridis, "Antonio Ritelli", *Kalymniaka Chronika*] 6 (1986), pp. 151–169.

12 National Statistical Service of Greece, General census in the Dodecanese carried out on October 19th, 1947; p. 68.

13 Testimony of Argyro Glynatsi to E.O., 4/2/2011.

When sponge fishing was slow as, for example, during one particular period in 1893, some Kalymnians also tended livestock, although raising sheep and goats was a less urgent undertaking – as opposed to farming – for the survival of the population at such times.[14] Indeed the Elders' and the inhabitants' councils periodically opted to remove all sheep and goats from the island, although such decisions were rash and were most likely not carried out with great rigor, or remained in effect for short periods of time only.[15] Testimonies from the late 19th century and the first decade of the 20th century attest to the presence of a small, stable number of farmers and livestock farmers on the island: about 50 farmers, 100 families raising livestock, and 8,000 sheep and goats.[16] This number probably remained largely unchanged in the following decades, as a record of 7,813 sheep and goats on Kalymnos in December 1941 would indicate.[17]

Small olive groves and vineyards that produced limited quantities of olive oil and wine, as well as household silk weaving, beekeeping,[18] and fishing of limited significance, constituted the primary activities of the island's inhabitants. Basic food products (meat, olive oil, flour, pulses such as beans, and wine) were imported during the Ottoman era, mainly from the opposite coast of Asia Minor and from other areas of the Greek state.[19] The municipality also

14   Doc. 671, 21/12/191, Correspondence 1910–1913, MAK. According to Carl Flegel's reports, there were about 50 shepherd families with a total of 5,000 sheep and 3,000 goats. Φλέγελ, *Η νήσος Κάλυμνος* [Flegel, *The Island of Kalymnos*], p. 39.

15   Resolution 30/6/1893, Minutes and Resolutions 1893–1907, MAK.

16   Κάρολος Φλέγελ, Η Α.Θ. "Παναγιότης ο Οικουμενικός Πατριάρχης Άνθιμος ο Ζ' εν Καλύμνω" [Carl Flegel, "His Holiness the Ecumenical Patriarch Anthimos VII in Kalymnos"], Samos 1896, p. 24; Ρεῖσης, *Περιγραφή τῆς νήσου Καλύμνου* [Reisis, *Description of the Island of Kalymnos*], p. 11.

17   Δωδεκάνησος. Τετράτομος μελέτη του Υπουργείου Ανοικοδομήσεως [*Dodecanese. Study in Four Volumes Carried out by the Ministry for Reconstruction*], Table 10.

18   See Michael D. Volonakis, *The Island of Roses and Her Eleven Sisters, or, The Dodecanese from the Earliest Times to the Present Day*, London 1922, p. 65; Κωνσταντίνος Γ. Καταγάς, "Το καλύμνιο μέλι", *Καλυμνιακά Χρονικά* [Konstantinos G. Katagas, "Kalymnian Honey", *Kalymniaka Chronika*] 17 (2007), pp. 21–28.

19   See Ἱπποκράτης Ταυλάριος, "Περί τῆς νήσου Καλύμνου", *Πανδώρα* [Hippocrates Tavlarios, "About the Island of Kalymnos", *Pandora*] 12 (1861–1862), p. 518–522. The text is republished by Δανιήλ Ζερβός, "Μια περιγραφή της Καλύμνου του 1862 και ένα πολιτικό κείμενο του 1908", *Καλυμνιακά Χρονικά* [Daniil Zervos, "A Description of Kalymnos in 1862 and a Political Text from 1908", *Kalymniaka Chronika*] 18 (2009), pp. 85–125. Newton notes that all necessary commodities for the population's survival, even stones for building houses, were imported, and that the inhabitants manually carried various goods and foodstuffs from the harbour to the Chora settlement. C. T. Newton, *Travels and Discoveries in the Levant*, vol. 1, London 1865, p. 297. There are many relevant mentions of the same in the archives. See for example doc. 579, 25/2/1911, Correspondence 1910–1913, MAK.

obtained stationery, school books, medicines, building materials, and various
industrial products from Smyrna, Syros and Piraeus on a regular basis.[20] Along
with the above, colonial products such as coffee and spices, as well as rice,
potatoes, and sugar also arrived on the island. Contact with the coast of Asia
Minor was, moreover, steady and frequent both to and from Bodrum since
many Kalymnians were born in Bodrum and owned farmlands there.

In 1862, Kalymnian lawyer Hippocrates Tavlarios, who lived and worked
in Constantinople, described the island's scant resources while emphasizing
that its inhabitants "acquired all cereals and other of primary products from
Asia Minor at the most distant remove".[21] Butcher shops, fishmongers, grocery
shops, flour shops, traditional coffee shops, and wine shops are a few of the
commercial enterprises that were established in the Pothia area in the late 19th
century. Manufacturing and artisanal activities were limited to a few necessary
sectors producing and trading in various utility products, and a number of people were employed in professions and facilities such as sawmills, smithies and
shipyards, which provided support for the sponge-fishing industry.[22]

Unquestionably, however, the fruits of Kalymnos (the so-called *frutta
di Kalymno*)[23] did not come from the land, but from the sea. Indeed, in the
mid-19th century, just before the introduction of the scaphander diving suit[24]
to Greek sponge fishing, Tavlarios wrote that,

> [a]lmost all Kalymnians are sponge fishermen except for a few merchants
> and farmers, travelling throughout summer (i.e. from May to October),
> along the coasts of Greece, Syria, Barbary, Benghazi, Crete, Rhodes,
> Cyprus, and Athos up to the Dardanelles in order to harvest sponges. The
> main and foremost export trade is in sponges, mostly of three different

---

20   There are constant reports and relevant correspondence in the Municipal Archive. See
      Doc. 141, 24/8/1883, Minutes of Administration Board 1882–1883, MAK; Doc. 22, 19/1/1894,
      Correspondence 1894–1895, MAK.
21   Ταυλάριος, "Περί τῆς νήσου Καλύμνου" [Tavlarios, "About the Island of Kalymnos"],
      pp. 518–522.
22   Collas' study is the only source we found wherein mention is made that, in the early
      19th century, Kalymnos had important shipbuilding facilities. However, the prohibition
      on timber exportation from the East brought this manufacturing activity to a standstill.
      See M. B. C. Collas, *La Turquie en 1861*, Paris 1861, p. 224.
23   Newton reports that this is how locals referred to sponges in his *Travels and Discoveries*
      (1854), p. 295.
24   The "scaphander" helmet is discussed in detail in Chapter 2. Briefly, the scaphander,
      (Greek σκάφος [*skáphos*, "hollowed"] + ἀνήρ [*anér*, "man"]), French [*scaphandre*], is the
      name for the helmet with a water-tight diving suit.

types: *psilos* [ψιλός], *tsimoucha* [τσιμούχα], and *hondros* [χονδρός].[25] These
sponges are traded in Germany, France, and the United Kingdom by competent merchants, resulting in the influx of some million *kuruş* into the
island. Europe was the trailhead of various commodities both for local
use as well as for trading with Asia Minor, which in exchange obtained
woolen products and coffee. The only source of wealth for the inhabitants
is the sponges. These are sought after and quite expensive; a top-quality
sponge being sold for more than 100 drachmas in Kalymnos, and a
hondros [sponge] fetching more than 20 drachmas per oka.[26] Almost 450
boats called *skaphe* [σκάφαι] harvest sponges along the above-mentioned
coasts. The fishermen dive up to 35 fathoms or often up to as much as
40 fathoms below the sea and remain at the bottom for 2 to 4 minutes.
Each boat carries 5–10 men and the best sponges are found around Crete,
Barbary and Cyprus. These boats are quite small.[27]

In the 19th century, the administrative structure of Kalymnos was comprised
of two main axes; the relatively autonomous status granted by the Ottoman
administration; and an evolving municipal institution, which replaced the
community system that existed prior to the revolution. Beginning in
the 1860s, this institution evolved into the Elder's Council [*Demogerontia*].
In the mid-19th century, Kalymnos' sub-district or commune [*nahiye*][28] was
part of the Province [*eyalet*] of the White Sea Islands [*Cezayr-i Bahr-i Sefid*],
under the District Administration [*kaymakamlik*] of Rhodes.[29] Following the
introduction of the Tanzimat, that is, the administrative reorganization of the
Ottoman domain in the Aegean, and the 1867 "Law on Provinces" [*vilayet* law],
Kalymnos remained in the district [*sanjak*] of Rhodes.[30] When Cyprus was
handed over to the British in 1878, the White Sea Province [*eyalet*] was restructured on an administrative level, resulting in the incorporation of Kalymnos'
sub-district [*kaza*] (along with the islands of Kos, Psara, Patmos, Leros, etc.)

---

25   For more on the various kinds of sponges, see Chapter 2.
26   The oka, okka, or oke [Ottoman Turkish وقّه‎] was an Ottoman measure of mass, equal to
      400 Ottoman drams [*dirhems*]. Its value varied, but it was standardized in the late empire
      as 1.2829 kilograms.
27   Ταυλάριος, "Περί της νήσου Καλύμνου" [Tavlarios, "About the Island of Kalymnos"],
      pp. 518–522. Themelis Kindynis [Θέμελης Κινδύνης] shares a similar report in Η νήσος
      Κάλυμνος [*The Island of Kalymnos*], Athens 1879, pp. 24–26.
28   There are many terms in Turkish for Ottoman subdivisions (i.e. *vilayet, eyalet, beylerbeylik,
      sancak, nahiye, kaza*). We translate all of these as "district" and supply the specific Turkish
      term in square brackets.
29   Ali Fuat Oreng, *Yakindonem Tarihimizde Rodos ve Oniki Ada*, Istanbul 2006, p. 68.
30   *Oreng, Yakindonem Tarihimizde Rodos*, p. 112.

into the district [*sanjak*] of Chios.[31] In 1879, Kalymnos had risen to district governance [*kaymakamlik*] status while still under the administrative authority of Chios. Together with the sub-district or commune [*nahiye*] of Astypalaia, the district governance [*kaymakamlik*] of Kalymnos was home to 16,000 inhabitants.[32]

In March 1912, shortly before the Italian occupation of the Dodecanese, the capital of the general government, or of the Archipelago Province [*vilayet*], was Rhodes, which consisted of four districts [*sanjaks*]: Rhodes, Chios, Mytilene and Lemnos. The sub-district [*kazas*] of Icaria, Leros, Kalymnos and the sub-district/commune [*nahiyes*] of Patmos and Astypalaia fell under the district [*sanjak*] of Chios.[33] In the same period, Kalymnos shared common metropolis headquarters with Leros and Astypalaia.[34]

In 1835, the community of Kalymnos began paying an annual lump-sum tax [*maktu*] to the Ottoman state, and was exempt from any other contribution, be it per capita or based on the island's agricultural production. This privileged status was maintained until the end of the Ottoman rule over the Dodecanese. On numerous occasions however, the Ottoman administration attempted to revoke or restrain these privileges as, for example, by means of an attempted population census in 1888, at a time when the empire's relations with the Greek state were tense. Likewise, an Ottoman harbour master was put in office on the islands of the southern Sporades, beginning with Kalymnos, and this occurred again in 1908 with the Young Turks.[35] The Ottomans also put increasing pressure on Symi and Kalymnos, the two islands whose population had increased

31   Oreng, *Yakindonem Tarihimizde Rodos*, p. 120.; Martin Strohmeier, "Economy and Society in the Aegean Province of the Ottoman Empire, 1840–1912", *Turkish Historical Review* 1 (2010), p. 167. G. Koukoulis claims that, in 1836, the four islands in the north of the southern Sporades were removed from the administrative district [*moutasarrifate*] of Rhodes and annexed to the administrative district [*moutasarrifate*] of Chios. See Γιώργης Κουκούλης, "Δύο έγγραφα της Δημογεροντίας Καλύμνου προς τη Δημογεροντία Σύμης", *Καλυμνιακά Χρονικά* [Giorgis Koukoulis, "Two Documents of the Elders of Kalymnos to the Elders of Symi", *Kalymniaka Chronika*] 6 (1986), p. 46, note 3.

32   Oreng, *Yakindonem Tarihimizde Rodos*, p. 121.

33   Report 3/1912, Consulate of Rhodes, Folder 43 (1912), Subfolder 3, IAYE.

34   Ηλέκτρα Κωστοπούλου, *Η Λέρος στην Οθωμανική Αυτοκρατορία* [Ilektra Kostopoulou, *Leros in the Ottoman Empire*], pp. 181–182.

35   On the Port Authority, see Κυριάκος Κων. Χατζηδάκης, "Από τον αγώνα για την προάσπιση των προνομίων στις Νότιες Σποράδες. Το λιμεναρχικό ζήτημα στην Κάλυμνο (1897–1899)", *Καλυμνιακά Χρονικά* [Kyriakos Kon. Chatzidakis, "From the Fight for the Defence of the Privileges of Southern Sporades. The Port Authorities Issue on Kalymnos" (1897–1899), *Kalymniaka Chronika*] 17 (2007); Γεώργιος Μ. Σακελλαρίδης, "Αυτοδιοίκηση στα χρόνια της σκλαβιάς", *Καλυμνιακά Χρονικά* [Georgios M. Sakellaridis, "Self-Government in Times of Servitude", *Kalymniaka Chronika*] 6 (1986), pp. 61–68. For more on the challenge

rapidly and whose sponge export trade income was considerable.[36] Slightly adjusted, this tax system was retained throughout Italian rule until 1930, which means that Kalymnos paid 7,692 Italian lira in tax, while Karpathos and Symi paid 11,143 and 8,800 lira respectively. However, after 1930, a single tax system was established for the entire Dodecanese, while a series of new taxes and duties was imposed based on declarations made on behalf of tax-paying inhabitants and local financial administration.[37]

The Elders represented the island's population to the Ottoman, and later Italian authorities.[38] The mandate of the Elders' council – elected indirectly up to the 1890s when universal male suffrage was established – was annual and

       to the privileges of the Dodecanese by the Young Turks, viz. inter alia C. D. Booth, Isabelle B. Booth, *Italy's Aegean Possessions*, London 1928, pp. 208–209.

36   See Jeanne Z. Stephanopoli, *Les îles de l'Égée. Leurs privilèges*, Athens 1912, pp. 118–120; Αλέξανδρος Καρανικόλας, "Νότιες Σποράδες. Σελίδες από την ιστορία των προνομίων τους", *Παρνασσός* [Alexandros Karanikolas, "The Southern Sporades. Pages from the History of Their Privileges", *Parnassos*] 13 (1971), pp. 3–29 (reprint); Μιλτιάδης Ι. Λογοθέτης, "Το εμπόριο στις Νότιες Σποράδες (Δωδεκάνησα) κατά τα τελευταία χρόνια της Τουρκοκρατίας", *Δωδεκανησιακά Χρονικά* [Miltiadis I. Logothetis, "Commerce in the Southern Sporades (Dodecanese) in the Last Years of Turkish Rule", *Dodekanisiaka Chronika*] 9 (1983), pp. 139–140; Γιώργης Κουκούλης, "Η συμβολή της Καλύμνου στους αγώνες για τα προνόμια", *Καλυμνιακά Χρονικά* [Giorgis Koukoulis, "The Contribution of Kalymnos in the Struggle for Privileges", *Kalymniaka Chronika*] 4 (1984) p. 24. The author refers to previous sovereign edicts [*firmans*] and, in particular, to the 1755 sovereign edict [*firman*], which set out the fiscal status of the southern Sporades. See also Γ. Ν. Κουκούλης, "Η Κάλυμνος στους αγώνες κατά της απογραφής του πληθυσμού (1885–1888)", *Καλυμνιακά Χρονικά* [G. N. Koukoulis, "Kalymnos in the Struggles against the Population Census (1885–1888)", *Kalymniaka Chronika*] 7 (1988), pp. 39–62, Ηλέκτρα Κωστοπούλου, Η Λέρος στην Οθωμανική Αυτοκρατορία [Ilektra Kostopoulou, *Leros in the Ottoman Empire*], pp. 51–52, Κυριάκος Κ. Χατζηδάκης, "Η Κάλυμνος στα τέλη της Τουρκοκρατίας", *Καλυμνιακά Χρονικά* [Kyriakos K. Chatzidakis, "Kalymnos at the End of Turkish Rule", *Kalymniaka Chronika*] 8 (1989), pp. 59–90. In 1851, Niven Kerr, British Consul in Rhodes, reported that the annual tax amounted to 31,000 *kuruş*, and that Kalymnians paid another 5,000 for the island's local Governor [*mudir*]. Χατζηδάκης, "Από τον αγώνα για την προάσπιση των προνομίων" [Chatzidakis, "From the Fight for the Defense of Privileges"] p. 101. Ali Fuat Oreng reported that after 1856 and the substitution of a per capita tax with a *bedel-i askeriye*, Kalymnos, together with Ikaria, Leros and Patmos, continued to be exempted from the per capita tax (and, consequently, from the *bedel*) in exchange for a lump sum. Efforts were made to increase the sum, because it was considerably lower than the tax paid by the rest of the islands, but local Governors protested. See *Oreng, Yakindonem Tarihimizde Rodos*, pp. 540, 551; Strohmeier, "Economy and Society in the Aegean Province", p. 175.

37   *Δωδεκάνησος. Τετράτομος μελέτη του Υπουργείου Ανοικοδομήσεως* [*Dodecanese. A Study in Four Volumes Carried out by the Ministry for Reconstruction*], p. 251.

38   Upon the arrival of the Italians, the jurisdiction of the Elders council, still elected by the inhabitants in the same way, was restricted, and it no longer maintained its prior administrative autonomy.

its members were paid a regular stipend.[39] The renewal of council members, even with their short-lived mandate in community offices, was less frequent than what might be expected. Moreover, while the existence of opposing parties and of their influence is not evident, it is clear that the members of the council came from wealthy groups with social standing and influence, either as a function of their occupation (doctors, teachers), or their business activities (merchants, sponge merchants, investors in sponge-fishing expeditions).[40]

The Elders were assigned the task of collecting revenue and the annual lump-sum tax. The community's revenue originated from levies on sponge-fishing (sponges imported and sold on the island); from imported commodities; from agricultural products; from a tithe on vineyards and orchards; from sheep and goat taxes; from the rent on monastery lands; and from notarial deeds.[41] The community also managed and rented sheep and goat pastures through public auctions on the nearby uninhabited and populated islets of Pserimos, Telendos, Plati, Nera, Gaidouronisi, Kalavro, Agios Nikolaos, Agios Andreas, Agia Kyriaki, Glaronisia, Kalolimno, which were viewed as Kalymnos' peripheral territories. The community had also levied a sort of municipal tax – the "local welfare tax" – to finance public works, the construction of the port, the operations of communal institutions, educational establishments, and so on.[42]

From at least the mid-19th century onwards the community managed education, supported by contributions from the wealthiest social groups, whether they lived on the island or abroad.[43] The municipal archive abounds in documents on such concerns as school organization, the recruitment of teachers, and ordering books. A 1911 census records the operation of two elementary schools in the island's capital for at least 50 years – one of which was an all-girl

---

39   According to the 1884–1885 record book, the 32 voters from Chora and Pothia elected the 12-member council. The first to receive a majority vote was elected President of the Council, and the recipient of the second largest number of votes was named Second Elder and Kalymnos' Municipal Treasurer. *Minutes of Administrative Council, Correspondence, Various 1884–1885*, pp. 1–3, ΜΑΚ. See also Γιάννης Θ. Πατέλλης, "Ο θεσμός της Δημογεροντίας στα Δωδεκάνησα. Το παράδειγμα της Καλύμνου", *Καλυμνιακά Χρονικά* [Giannis Th. Patelis, "The Institution of Demogerontia in the Dodecanese: The Example of Kalymnos", *Kalymniaka Chronika*] 15 (2003), pp. 61–64.

40   For more on the financing of the sponge fishery, see Chapter 2 of the present volume, pp. 126–138.

41   See the 1902 budget in Financial Committee Minutes-Correspondence 1902–1904, ΜΑΚ; See also Doc. 129, n.d. 1921, 4/1/1894, Correspondence 1920–192.2, ΜΑΚ. Carl Flegel writes that its revenues amounted to an average of 100,000 francs per year. See Φλέγελ, "Η Α.Θ. Παναγιότης ο Οικουμενικός Πατριάρχης Άνθιμος" [Flegel, "His Holiness the Ecumenical Patriarch Anthimos"], p. 30.

42   Doc. 13, 12/1/1894, Correspondence 1894–1895, ΜΑΚ.

43   See also Volonakis, *The Island of Roses and her Eleven Sisters*, p. 549.

school – two municipal town schools founded in 1887 and 1890, two private schools, the Vouvaleio School for Girls, and the Nikiforeios Greek School in Pothia, founded in 1906 and operating as a secondary school.[44]

The Elders had financial, administrative, and judicial responsibilities. They served as registrar, market overseer, notary, and regulated sponge-fishing related issues and disputes.[45] They were responsible for the implementation of public works, the administration of education, public health, and sanitation. Having organized a system of social care, they oversaw and maintained the operation of schools, municipal medical practices, and pharmacies, and they paid the salaries of teachers, doctors, pharmacists, and the Elders' council staff. They were also responsible for the financial management of churches, whereas they appointed church overseers and sacristans in concert with the Metropolitan.[46]

By the mid-19th century, there were few Ottoman officials appointed in Kalymnos, however there is evidence of the existence of a local Governor [mudir], either selected by the local notables or appointed by the Sublime Porte.[47] He had ten gendarmes [zaptiyes] at his command and was in charge of the tax [maktu] collection.[48] At that time, the island underwent an important

---

44 Doc. 667, 23/11/1911, Correspondence 1910–1913, MAK. See also Κινδύνης, *Η νήσος Κάλυμνος* [Kindynis, *The Island of Kalymnos*], p. 27.

45 See also the Elders' Regulation in Doc. 1, 20/12/1894, Minutes and Resolutions 1922–1948, MAK. See also Volonakis, *The Island of Roses and her Eleven Sisters*, p. 299; C. D. Booth, Isabelle, *Italy's Aegean Possessions*, pp. 210–212; Γιάννης Θ. Πατέλλης, "Η δημόσια υγεία στην Κάλυμνο την εποχή της Δημογεροντίας", *Καλυμνιακά Χρονικά* [Giannis Th. Patelis, "Public Health on Kalymnos in the Time of the Demogerontia", *Kalymniaka Chronika*] 13 (1999), pp. 159–164.

46 Ιωάννης Π. Χαλκίτης, "Συμβολή στην ιστορία της Εκκλησίας της Καλύμνου. Η ουσιαστική συμμετοχή του λαού της Καλύμνου στη ζωή της ορθοδόξου τοπικής εκκλησίας του", *Καλυμνιακά Χρονικά* [Ioannis P. Chalkitis, "Contribution to the History of the Kalymnian Church: The Meaningful Participation of the People of Kalymnos in the Life of their Local Orthodox Church", *Kalymniaka Chronika*] 6 (1986), pp. 127–137.

47 The terms "Sublime Porte", "Ottoman Porte" or "High Porte" have all become metaphors for the central government of the Ottoman Empire. These terms refer to the old practice whereby rulers announced their official decisions and judgements at their palace gates.

48 C. D. Booth, Isabelle Booth, *Italy's Aegean Possessions*, p. 205, Oreng, *Yakin-donem Tarihimizde Rodos*, p. 87, note 383. In 1842, the local Governor's [mudir] salary paid by the inhabitants of the sub-district [kaza] of Kalymnos amounted to 350 kuruş, as in Patmos and Leros. In 1853, Mahmud Bey was appointed local Governor [mudir] to Kalymnos and was a notable figure from Kos. He held the office of Chief Chamberlain [kapuj-bash] for the Sublime Porte and received a salary of 1,500 kuruş, whereas in the past the salary totalled 400 kuruş, and was paid by the inhabitants. In 1860, the local Governor [mudir] of Kalymnos was Halil Efendi of Rhodes, while in 1865 this role was filled by Ismail Agha who received a salary of 800 kuruş. A man named Kostakis was responsible for quarantines and earned a salary of 300 kuruş.

administrative change when, at the end of the Cretan revolt and beginning in 1869, a high ranking Ottoman official, the District Governor [*Kaymakam*], was stationed on the island.[49] He oversaw the implementation of legislation and imperial orders, collected taxes and delivered them to the state treasury, and carried out administrative and policing tasks. His arrival was met with distrust and protests by the local population, worried that the self-governing privileges that they had been granted would be restricted. Moreover, relations between the Elders and the District Governor [*Kaymakam*] were often less than harmonious, and whenever he attempted to act against the inhabitants' interests, or to interfere in the Elders' mandate, tensions would rise, and local authorities would protest loudly. Indeed, there were several protests and grievances concerning the infringement of the limits of District Governor's [*Kaymakam*] responsibilities, the misuse of powers by his staff, and the violent behaviour of his soldiers. Greek national N. Symeon, who served as honorary Vice-consul of the Greek consular agency in Kalymnos beginning in 1880, addressed a long letter to Ioannis Kaloutsis, the Greek consul of Rhodes, in which he offered an exaggerated account of the island's tragic situation that did not seem to improve, despite the resolution of the Cretan revolt. He reported that the military guard remained on the island and caused unjustifiable incidents, attacked the population, and terrorized the women while the male population was away sponge fishing.[50]

Under the new administrative regime, and despite constant friction, the Governor [*Kaymakam*] was the sole competent person who could enforce order. Given that he maintained an armed force on the island, his contribution was necessary to the implementation of various decisions made by the

---

49   It was first implemented in Symi and then the rest of the southern Sporades followed. Most of these populations reacted strongly because they considered this administrative modification to be a violation of their privileges: Καρανικόλας, "Νότιες Σποράδες. Σελίδες από την ιστορία των προνομίων τους" [Karanikolas, "The Southern Sporades. Pages from the History of their Privileges"], pp. 8–11; Γιώργης Ν. Κουκούλης, "Νικόλας Θ. Τηλιακός, Το χρονικό του 1869 (τον καιρό των Τουρκώ)", *Καλυμνιακά Χρονικά* [Giorgis N. Koukoulis, "Nikolas Th. Tiliakos, The Chronicle of 1869 (in the Time of the Turks)", *Kalymniaka Chronika*] 3 (1982), pp. 7–21; Χατζηδάκης, "Η Κάλυμνος στα τέλη της Τουρκοκρατίας" [Chatzidakis, "Kalymnos at the End of Turkish Rule"], pp. 61–64; Σακελλάρης Ν. Τρικοίλης, *Νεότερη ιστορία της Καλύμνου. Κοινωνική διαστρωμάτωση* [Sakellaris N. Trikoilis, *Modern History of Kalymnos. Social Stratification*], Athens 2007, pp. 352–356; Χατζηδάκης, "Από τον αγώνα για την προάσπιση των προνομίων" [Chatzidakis, "From the Fight for the Defence of the Privileges of the Southern Sporades"], pp. 101–102. Ali Fuat Oreng however, claims that a *Kaymakam* was put in place earlier – in 1867 – and that this was followed by fierce reactions and an increase in military measures on Kalymnos and Symi. Oreng, *Yakindonem Tarihimizde Rodos*, p. 132.

50   Letter from Consular Agent N. Symeon of Kalymnos to Ioannis Kaloutsis, Consul in Rhodes, 1/9/1896, Consulate in Rhodes, Folder 44 (1911), Subfolder 2, ΙΑΥΕ.

Elders, mainly where issues concerning policing were concerned. The Elders' continuous letters and reports make clear that debtors who refused to pay, law breakers, all types of troublemakers and criminals, as well as fugitive sponge fishers could not be arrested without the mobilization of Ottoman gendarmes [*zaptiyes*]. Arrests, however, were carried out following decisions made by the local authorities.

1.2   The Population of Kalymnos

Diffuse data on the number of the island's inhabitants in the 19th century does not tally, and the reliability of this data cannot easily be confirmed. According to a memorandum from Ioannis Kapodistrias, prior to 1821 Kalymnos had 6,000 residents, whereas by 1828 the population had decreased to 4,800,[51] a figure that comes close to the 5,000 residents noted by S. Agapitidis and G. Sakellaridis.[52] Nevertheless, in a census conducted by the local authorities, with the encouragement of Ioannis Kapodistrias, there were fewer residents in the period from 1828 to 1830: 3,853 residents (1,853 men and 2,000 women) divided over 850 houses.[53] In 1850 the island's population totalled 7,600 residents according to S. Agapitidis,[54] or 9,500 souls as Niven Kerr, the British

---

51   See Δημήτρης Δημητρόπουλος, *Μαρτυρίες για τον πληθυσμό των νησιών του Αιγαίου, 15ος–αρχές 19ου αιώνα, Τετράδια Εργασίας* KNE/EIE [Dimitris Dimitropoulos, *Testimonies on the Aegean Islands' Population from the 15th to Early 19th Century, Research Notebooks* INR/NHRF] Athens 2004, p. 303.

52   Σωτήριος Αγαπητίδης, "Ο πληθυσμός της Δωδεκανήσου", *Δωδεκανησιακή Επιθεώρησις* [Sotirios Agapitidis, "The Population of Dodecanese", *Dodekanisiaki Epitheorisis*] 2–4 (1948), p. 88; by the same author, "Ο πληθυσμός της Δωδεκανήσου", *Νισυριακά* ["The Dodecanesian Population", *Nisyriaka*] 3 (1969), p. 7; by the same author, "Πληθυσμιακές εξελίξεις στα Δωδεκάνησα", *Δωδεκανησιακά Χρονικά* ["Population Developments in the Dodecanese", *Dodekanisiaka Chronika*] 11 (1986), p. 12. Γιώργιος Μ. Σακελλαρίδης, "Η πληθυσμιακή εξέλιξη της Καλύμνου και τα αίτιά της", *Καλυμνιακά Χρονικά* [Giorgos M. Sakellaridis, "The Population Increase in Kalymnos and its Causes", *Kalymniaka Chronika*] 4 (1984), pp. 69–73.

53   Κώστας Δαφνής (Kostas Dafnis) (ed.), Ioannis Kapodistrias Archive, vol. VIII, *Society for Corfiot Studies, Corfu* 1987, p. 305.

54   Σωτήριος Αγαπητίδης, "Ο πληθυσμός της Δωδεκανήσου", *Δωδεκανησιακή Επιθεώρησις* [Sotirios Agapitidis, "The Population of Dodecanese", *Dodekanisiaki Epitheorisis*] 2–4 (1948), p. 88; by the same author, "Ο πληθυσμός της Δωδεκανήσου", *Νισυριακά* ["The Dodecanesian Population", *Nisyriaka*] 3 (1969), p. 7; by the same author, "Πληθυσμιακές εξελίξεις στα Δωδεκάνησα", *Δωδεκανησιακά Χρονικά* ["Population Developments in the Dodecanese", *Dodekanisiaka Chronika*] 11 (1986), p. 12; see also Γεώργιος Μ. Σακελλαρίδης, "Η εξέλιξη και διαμόρφωση του πληθυσμού της Καλύμνου", *Καλυμνιακά Χρονικά* [Georgios M. Sakellaridis, "The Development and Configuration of the Population of Kalymnos", *Kalymniaka Chronika*] 9 (1990), p. 395.

Consul of Rhodes, noted in a report dated June, 1851.[55] In his own survey, conducted in 1860, M. B. C. Collas reported that Kalymnos had 5,500 inhabitants.[56] In 1888 there were 9,000 residents on the island; in 1894 Kalymnos' population exceeded 12,000 residents,[57] whereas in 1900 that number appears to have increased to 19,400 residents.[58] In the 1886–1887 *Yearbook of the Archipelago Province*, the total island population and facilities are recorded as follows:

> The island of Kalymnos has 1,950 houses, a population of 10,400 residents, 45 shops, 13 cafés, 1 hotel, 1 administrative centre, 2 pharmacies, 15 churches, 2 tanneries, a 10-room leper house, 116 sponge-fishing diver boats, 19 boats of the *zipkin* type [ζηπκήν], 4 all-boys' and 2 all-girls' schools, with 400 male students and 120 female students.[59]

According to Lithuanian scholar Carl Flegel, by the end of the 19th century, of the 16,000 residents of the entire island, Pothia's population had increased to 9,000 or 9,500 residents, whereas the population of Chora totaled 5,000 or 5,500.[60]

Despite contradictions and reliability issues connected with available sources, they do illustrate impressive demographic growth over the 20-year period from 1880 to 1900. This growth may be traced to the migration of workers from the surrounding maritime costal area and Asia Minor, which workforce

---

55 Kerr's report is a summary description of Kalymnos, its administrative organization, and the inhabitants' activities. The report is addressed to Stratford Canning, Ambassador of the United Kingdom to Constantinople; Κυριάκος Κων. Χατζηδάκης, "Κάλυμνος, 1851", *Καλυμνιακά Χρονικά* [Kyriakos Kon. Chatzidakis, "Kalymnos, 1851", *Kalymniaka Chronika*] 12 (1997), pp. 38–44. The number of residents – 9,500 – probably remained stable throughout the 1850s. See Κυριάκος Κων. Χατζηδάκης, "Η σπογγαλιεία στις Νότιες Σποράδες στα μέσα του 19ου αιώνα", *Καλυμνιακά Χρονικά* [Kyriakos Kon. Chatzidakis, "Sponge Fishery in the Southern Sporades in the Mid-19th Century", *Kalymniaka Chronika*] 13 (1999), p. 236.

56 Collas, *La Turquie en 1861*, p. 224.

57 Doc. 88, 20/4/1894, Correspondence 1894–1895, MAK.

58 Emile Kolodny, *La population des îles de la Grèce. Essai de géographie insulaire en Méditerranée orientale*, vol. 1, Aix-en-Provence 1974, p. 312. The information is probably extracted from the publications of Sotirios Agapitidis.

59 *Yearbook of Archipelago Province*, 1304 AH, p. 115. It is thought that this census does not depict the situation accurately because the people of Dodecanese resisted its mandatory enforcement by the Governor of Rhodes, Kemal Bey. The population was, therefore, most likely considerably larger. See Λογοθέτης, "Πληροφορίες για την οικονομία και κοινωνία της Δωδεκανήσου" [Logothetis, "Information on the Economy and Society of the Dodecanese Islands"], pp. 111–112.

60 Κάρολος Φλέγελ, Η νήσος Κάλυμνος [Carl Flegel, *The Island of Kalymnos*], Constantinople 1896, p. 12; The same, "Η Α.Θ. Παναγιότης ο Οικουμενικός Πατριάρχης Άνθιμος" ["His Holiness the Ecumenical Patriarch Anthimos"], p. 10.

was employed on sponge-fishing vessels with scaphander diving gear, all of which required large crews.[61] However, questions concerning the exact number of non-natives involved, their places of origin, the duration, and conditions of their stay in Kalymnos, cannot be answered with available sources.

In June of 1911, in response to a request from the Greek Foreign Ministry, the Consul of Rhodes compiled a series of tables with statistical data on the population and education in the Dodecanese. Based on that data, in 1910 the population of Kalymnos totaled 18,000 residents, and there were 11 schools.[62] In the Greek Consul's opinion "together with Symi, this island competes for the leading place among the islands of Sporades, since they are indeed the most populous and most advanced in terms of growth, commerce and welfare".[63]

Various documents and surveys contemporary with this report, and some written shortly thereafter, do not appear to agree on the population of Kalymnos, while the archive itself sheds no further light on the topic. In 1912, when Italy seized the Dodecanese, Kalymnos had a population of 18,500 residents according to the Greek Consul of Rhodes, and a total of 20,855 or even 23,200 residents according to Jeanne Z. Stephanopoli and Charles Vellay.[64] According to another source,[65] there were 25,000 inhabitants, 7 elementary schools, 1 Greek school and 4 private schools in Pothia.[66] If the 1912 population figures are accurate, it would appear that in the first years of the Italian occupation, there was a noticeable decrease, with the population dwindling to 14,950 inhabitants in 1917.[67] Available sources for 1918, when Kalymnos is reported to

---

61   See, for example, the of list surnames based on the place of origin presented by Σακελλαρίδης, "Η εξέλιξη και διαμόρφωση του πληθυσμού της Καλύμνου" [Sakellaridis, "The Development and Configuration of the Population of Kalymnos"], p. 397.

62   Reports of Consul N. Souidas, 1/6/1910 and 2/6/1911, Consulate in Rhodes, Folder 43 (1912), Subfolder 3, IAYE.

63   Report of Consul N. Souidas, 15/6/1910, Consulate in Rhodes, Folder 43 (1912), Subfolder 3, IAYE.

64   Jeanne Z. Stephanopoli, *Les iles de l'Egée. Leurs privilèges*, Athens 1912.

65   Consulate in Rhodes, Folder 43 (1912), Subfolder 3, IAYE; C. D. Booth, Isabelle B. Booth, *Italy's Aegean Possessions*, London 1928, p. 317; Χατζηδάκης, "Η Κάλυμνος στα τέλη της Τουρκοκρατίας", *Καλυμνιακά Χρονικά* [Chatzidakis, "Kalymnos at the End of Turkish Rule", *Kalymniaka Chronika*] 8 (1989), pp. 59–90; Αγαπητίδης, "Πληθυσμιακές εξελίξεις στα Δωδεκάνησα" [Agapitidis, "Population Developments in the Dodecanese"], pp. 12 and 15–16; Αγαπητίδης, "Ο πληθυσμός της Δωδεκανήσου", *Νισυριακά* [Agapitidis, "The Dodecanesian Population", *Nisyriaka*] 3 (1969), p. 7.

66   See also Ρεΐσης, *Περιγραφή της νήσου Καλύμνου* [Reisis, *Description of the Island of Kalymnos*], p. 10.

67   According to the Italian census; C. D. Booth, Isabelle Booth, *Italy's Aegean Possessions*, p. 318; Σακελλαρίδης, "Η πληθυσμιακή εξέλιξη της Καλύμνου" [Sakellaridis, "The Population Progress on Kalymnos"], pp. 69–73. On the same topic, see Χρ. Γ. Τσιγάντες, "Η Δωδεκάνησος. Μετά την ενσωμάτωσίν της, τα ζητήματα και αι υποχρεώσεις του κράτους", *Ελευθερία* [Chr. G. Tsigantes, "The Dodecanese Following its Annexation: The Issues and the Obligations

have had 18,000 residents, are likewise relatively vague.[68] As the period under study offers scant official census data, we rely on population estimates from community reports, scholarly and council testimonies, and travel narratives.

In 1922, the population of Kalymnos increased to 15,500 according to S. Agapitidis, perhaps due to the arrival of refugees from Asia Minor.[69] In contrast, according to the official Italian census, Kalymnos had 14,000 residents in 1922, while in 1931 the population had risen to 16,512, including the Italian settlers. Throughout this period, the population of Kalymnos was second only to that of Rhodes.[70] With a total of 14,872 inhabitants recorded in 1941, Kalymnos' population then decreased to 12,227 in 1947. After the emancipation of the Dodecanese, however, the population increased again; a fact that may be partially attributable to the resettlement of Kalymnians in their homeland.[71]

1.3   Pothia, a 19th-Century Town[72]

By the mid-19th century, Pothia had not yet assumed the characteristics and functions that would identify it as a "town"[73] or, more importantly, as the island's "capital".[74] Iakovos R. Ragavis referred to Pothia as the port of Chora,

---

of the State", *Eleftheria*], 13/6/1948, p. 1. The writer of the article estimates a decrease from 25,000 to 11,000 inhabitants.

68   A table showing the population of the Dodecanese islands was first published by Theodore D. Moschonas, "Irredenta Dodecanesius filia Grecia est", *Near East* 21/12/1918. The article is published in Skevos Zervos and Paris Roussos, *White Book. The Dodecanese. Resolutions and Documents Concerning the Dodecanese 1912–1919*, London 1919, p. 14. Note however that we are discussing a period during which official census data are scant, and we therefore rely on population estimates from community reports, scholarly and consular testimonies, and travel narratives.

69   See tables published by Σακελλαρίδης, "Η πληθυσμιακή εξέλιξη της Καλύμνου" [Sakellaridis, "The Population Progress on the Island of Kalymnos"], p. 72.

70   See the census data as they were published in *Αθηναϊκά Νέα* [*Athinaika Nea*], 23/5/1932, p. 1 and in Ελεύθερον Βήμα [*Eleftheron Vima*], 19/11/1931, p. 6.

71   Σακελλαρίδης, "Η πληθυσμιακή εξέλιξη της Καλύμνου" [Sakellaridis, "The Progress of Population in Kalymnos"], p. 72.

72   A first version of this text was published under the title "Από την ορεινή χώρα στην παραλιακή Σκάλα. Παρατηρήσεις για τη διαμόρφωση μιας νησιωτικής πόλης", *Ιόνιος Λόγος* ["From the Mountainous Chora to the Seaside Skala: Observations on the Configuration of an Island Town", *Ionios Logos*] 1 (2007), pp. 151–179.

73   The sources referring to Kalymnos' residential arrangement are scant and not very enlightening. The oldest surviving record book of the Municipal Archive has only a few entries for 1863, and most of the surviving archival material dates back to 1880. It is also notable that, during the period in question, few travelers took any notice of Kalymnos.

74   More on the difficulties in elucidating the traits that define a town in Νίκος Σβορώνος, "Κοινωνικές δομές και πολιτιστική ανάπτυξη των πόλεων στον ελληνικό χώρο κατά την

and the only town on the island – and indeed 2,000 inhabitants of Kalymnos resided in Chora and at the port.[75] German classical archaeologist Ludwig Ross (1806–1859) described the island in 1841 in similar terms. He first came upon 50 to 60 houses located along the waterfront, and from there he walked towards the town, located about 45 minutes from the port. Once there, Ross attended a residents' meeting at the Church of the Virgin Mary.[76]

In 1864, British archaeologist C. T. Newton (1816–1894) estimated the population of Kalymnos at 10,000 inhabitants residing in the town at the foot of the mountain, but it took several decades for the population to gather more concentratedly in the coastal area. "This town", he wrote, "is situated on the neck of land half-way between Linaria and the harbour of Pothia. At this younger location [Linaria], a second town is growing up, which will probably someday be the capital".[77] A few years later, according to the chronicle of Nicolas Tiliakos, resident assemblies continued to be held at Chora given the incidents of 1869, and the arrival of the Ottomans who set up a District Governor [Kaymakam] on the island.[78] In his 1878 writings about the island, Kalymnian medical student Themelis Kindynis estimated that the total population of Kalymnos was more than 10,000, residing in 2,000 houses in Chora and 1,800 houses in the new town of Pothia, although he reckoned that most of the residents lived in Pothia.[79]

In this attempt to briefly retrace Kalymnos' settlement history, we discovered that the shift that we have been attempting to describe here is not the only shift that occurred. For example, as Newton also noted, the island's byzantine settlement, "Pera Kastro" [i.e. faraway castle] was situated in a naturally fortified position on the top of a rocky, steep hill in the middle of the island's largest plain, and at an almost equal distance from the coasts of both Pothia

Τουρκοκρατία" [Nikos Svoronos, "Social Structures and Cultural Development of Towns in the Greek Area under Turkish Rule"], in *Αμητός εις μνήμην Φώτη Αποστολόπουλου* [*Amitos: In Memory of Fotis Apostolopoulos*], Athens 1984, pp. 330–337.

75 Ιάκωβος Ρ. Ραγκαβής, *Τα Ελληνικά ήτοι περιγραφή γεωγραφική, ιστορική, αρχαιολογική και στατιστική της αρχαίας και νέας Ελλάδος* [Iakovos R. Ragavis, *Greek: Geographical, Historical, Archaeological and Statistical Description of Ancient and Modern Greece*], vol. 3, Athens 1854, pp. 392 and 395.

76 Γεώργιος Χρ. Χαραμαντάς (επιμ.), "Λουδοβίκος Ρος (Ludwig Ross), "Νησιωτικά ταξίδια. Κάλυμνος-Τέλενδος. Εικοστή πρώτη επιστολή"", *Καλυμνιακά Σύμμεικτα* [Georgios Chr. Charamantas (ed.), Ludwig Ross, "Island Trips: Kalymnos-Telendos Twenty-first Letter", *Kalymniaka Symmeikta*] 1 (1993), p. 72.

77 C. T. Newton, *Travels and Discoveries in the Levant*, pp. 295–296.

78 Κουκούλης, "Νικόλας Θ. Τηλιακός" [Koukoulis, "Nikolas Th. Tiliakos"], pp. 7–21.

79 Κινδύνης, *Η νήσος Κάλυμνος* [Kindynis, *The Island of Kalymnos*], pp. 13 and 21.

and Linaria.[80] Moreover, it is impossible to pinpoint the precise moment at which the population relocated in the foothills and created a new residential nucleus at Chora. Possibly, though, these developments coincide with the relative stability brought about by the definitive Ottoman conquest of the Aegean, and the increase in population noted above.[81] Nevertheless, Chora was the only settlement on the island until the mid-19th century, when a second residential centre formed on the island's southeast coast, namely[82] Pothaia ["Πόθαια", now Pothia], named after the ancient municipality of Pothaion.[83] It was established at the level end of the aforementioned plain, along the entire coast, and on the two facing steep slopes that encircle the settlement. Neighbourhoods were built and formed on these hills – the so-called "Marassia" – with small

80   C. T. Newton, *Travels and Discoveries in the Levant*, p. 296. See also Ζαχαρίας Ν. Τσιρπανλής, *Η Ρόδος και οι νότιες Σποράδες στα χρόνια των Ιωαννιτών Ιπποτών (1405–1605 αι.): συλλογή ιστορικών μελετών* [Zacharias N. Tsirpanlis, *Rhodes and the Southern Sporades in the Time of the Knights of the Order of Saint John (14th–16th Century): Collection of Historical Studies*], Rhodes 1991, p. 180.

81   For more on this topic, see Τρικοίλης, *Νεότερη ιστορία της Καλύμνου* [Trikoilis, *Modern History of Kalymnos*], pp. 191–214. More about Chora on pp. 219–229. See also Κ. Μιχαηλίδης, "Παρατηρήσεις πάνω σε τρεις πόλεις νησιών του Αιγαίου", *Αρχιτεκτονικά Θέματα* [K. Michailidis, "Observations on Three Towns of Aegean Islands", *Architektonika Themata*] 8 (1974), p. 140.

82   Sources and testimonies generally concur in terms of the timeline of the new town's formation. See Newton, *Travels and Discoveries*, p. 296. Ρεΐσης, *Περιγραφή της νήσου Καλύμνου* [Reisis, *Description of the Island of Kalymnos*], p. 13. Carl Flegel reports that the coastal settlement had been inhabited since 1836; Φλέγελ, "Η Α.Θ. Παναγιότης ο Οικουμενικός Πατριάρχης Άνθιμος" [Flegel, "His Holiness the Ecumenical Patriarch Anthimos"], p. 11. More recently, researchers such as Maria Magkli and Themelina Kapella also date the foundation of Pothia to c.1850, and they state that the first settlers were the island's "notable large-scale merchants". They report that, at the beginning of the 19th century when Pothia was considered the island's capital, the Metropolis was transferred to the Church of the Transfiguration of the Saviour: Μαρία Μαγκλή, Θεμελίνα Καπελλά, *Λαογραφικά Καλύμνου*, Λύκειο των Ελληνίδων [Maria Magkli, Themelina Kapella, *Kalymnos Folkore*, Lykio ton Ellinidon], n.d., pp. 17–19. See also Αθηνά Ταρσούλη, *Δωδεκάνησα* [Athina Tarsouli, *Dodecanese*], vol. 2, Athens 1948, p. 200. A. Tarsouli suggests that Pothia's coastal development took place sometime after the mid-19th century.

83   For the Municipality of Pothea and the ancient inscriptions that mention it, see Γιώργης Ν. Κουκούλης, *Η Κάλυμνα των Επιγραφών* [Giorgis N. Koukoulis, *Kalymna of Inscriptions*], Athens 1980. Sak. Trikoilis reports that they referred to Pothea [now Pothia] as the ancient town of Telendos. See Τρικοίλης, *Νεότερη ιστορία της Καλύμνου* [Trikoilis, *Modern History of Kalymnos*], p. 231. There is speculation as to whether the adoption of the name "Pothea", rather than the original "Limen" [λιμήν – port], is an allusion to the ancient Greek past in the name of Pothia/Pothaia. It is interesting to note the popular etymology of this name, given that "Pothia" suggests *Pothiti* [Ποθητή – desired] and the desire for or delirium of the deep that overcomes those who practice the dangerous profession of diving.

IMAGE 1.1   The town of Pothia, 1950s
SOURCE: PHOTOGRAPHIC ARCHIVE OF THE BENAKI MUSEUM, DIMITRIOS
HARISIADIS PHOTOS, AG.154–2.JPG

properties laid out in amphitheatrical form.[84] These densely-built neighbourhoods were mostly inhabited by workers on sponge-fishing boats as divers
or auxiliary staff, and were known as "σφουγγαρομαχαλάδες" or *sphoungaromakhaládes*, for the sponge workers who lived there.

---

84   Maria Bogdanou-Iliopoulou and Angeliki Fetokaki-Sarantide suggest that, over the course
      of the gradual formation of Pothia, the development of these areas preceded the zone in
      which larger properties at the rear of the harbour were located, and where the upper eco-
      nomic strata also lived. See Μαρία Μπογδάνου-Ηλιοπούλου, Αγγελική Φετοκάκη-Σαραντίδη,
      Κάλυμνος, Ελληνική Παραδοσιακή Αρχιτεκτονική [Maria Bogdanou-Iliopoulou, Angeliki
      Fetokaki-Sarantide, *Kalymnos*, Elliniki Paradosiaki Architektoniki], Athens 1984, pp. 10–11.

IMAGE 1.2   The town of Pothia, 2015
SOURCE: PHOTOGRAPH BY GELINA HARLAFTIS

There is further testimony by Hippocrates Tavlarios which may not be objective, but which conveys a picture of the settlement in Chora in the final decades of the 19th century:

> The town, as we said, lies in the middle of a valley and bellow the rocky hill of the fort, with almost 2,500 houses, or even more than the existing estimate. It is shabby and squalid, with narrow streets, like all Turkish towns, and there are hardly any buildings worth mentioning.[85]

In *The Island of Kalymnos* (1903), Carl Flegel compared the two settlements, writing that,

> there are hardly any new houses built in Chora today; the rather inaccessible ones situated in the foothills of Kastro and the entrance of the two gorges, Lagada and rear Lagada, are collapsing, because most activities

---

85   Ταυλάριος, "Περί της νήσου Καλύμνου" [Tavlarios, "About the Island of Kalymnos"], pp. 518–522.

and life itself tend to take place near the port in Pothaia [Pothia]. As a result, plots of land are sold at exorbitant prices, just like in the City of London.[86]

Perhaps it was not only this Lithuanian scholar who associated the old Chora with Ottoman rule on the island, given that the association was persistent. However, while this may be the case, Hippocrates Tavlarios has also observed that "[a]t the port, there are buildings in a more European style, and they are already trying to embellish it. The island has more than 15,000 inhabitants who reside mostly in the town, whose name is Chora, and at the port".[87] Moreover, in the first decade of the 20th century, Kalymnos attracted residents from neighbouring islands and the opposite coast of Asia Minor, the majority of whom lived in the port area. As G. Reisis estimated, of the 25,000 island dwellers, 20,000 resided in the town of Pothia.[88]

As the 19th century drew to a close, the focus seems to have shifted from the old to the new residential areas in just a few decades. While Chora had the look and feel of a "Turkish" town, the port developed in the "European" style and became associated with the financial life of the island, hosting the production activities that support sponge fishing. Shipyards, small-scale industries, sponge storage and processing facilities, machine shops, as well as cafés, taverns and various commercial shops catered to the needs of both locals and foreigners during the impressive period of growth in sponge-fishing activities that took place beginning in the early 1870s. Thanks to the advent of the scaphander diving suit in this period, deep-water sponge fishing, involving large crews, journeys that lasted many months, and long distances, dominated. However, in spite of these uneven developments in Chora and the port, the Elders' council [*Demogerontia*] itself appears to have taken a conciliatory approach to the two developing areas, declaring that "our island's town consists of two neighbourhoods, Pothia and Chora".[89]

---

86   Φλέγελ, *Η νήσος Κάλυμνος* [Carl Flegel, *Kalymnos Island*], pp. 22, 24. See also by the same author, "Η. Α.Θ. Παναγιότης ο Οικουμενικός Πατριάρχης Άνθιμος" ["His Holiness the Ecumenical Patriarch Anthimos"], p. 10.

87   Ταυλάριος, "Περί της νήσου Καλύμνου" [Tavlarios, "About the Island of Kalymnos"], and Γεώργιος Χρ. Χαραμαντάς (επιμ.), "Ιπποκράτη Δ. Ταυλάριου, "Περί της νήσου Καλύμνου"", *Καλυμνιακά Σύμμεικτα* [Georgios Chr. Charamantas (ed.), Hippocrates D. Tavlariou, "About the Island of Kalymnos", *Kalymniaka Simmikta*] 1 (1993), p. 77.

88   Ρείσης, *Περιγραφή της νήσου Καλύμνου* [Reisis, *Description of the Island of Kalymnos*], p. 13.

89   From a letter to Kalymnos' Kaymakam about the outbreak of small pox on the island; Doc. 3/1/1897, Correspondence 1896–1898, Folder 45.

The study of an inhabited area's planning and development often raises questions about its origins, the reasons behind the selection of a specific site for settlement, as well as the random or planned patterning, and the expansion of the construction and functions of any given urban space. Historical research has also addressed continental and island settlements, most often focusing on inaccessible mountainous regions for the establishment of residential sites under Ottoman rule. Various approaches to understanding the settlement of populations in a given area, or their withdrawal into the mountains, invariably gives prominence to a particular line of argumentation. However, valid conclusions on the origins of mountainous settlement locations cannot be reached based on the available evidence for the study of more recent settlements in Greece, namely those resulting from population movement, which necessitates more general observations. At the same time, each case may require special examination.

The case studied here is, however, not entirely unique. Since the mid-19th century, the structure of settled space on the island of Kalymnos has undergone significant rearrangements, as coastal areas gradually became inhabited in a more systematic way than they had been in the past. The once-uninhabited harbour of the mountain Chora was transformed over time into a dynamic settlement, which became the hub of financial and social life as noted above. In some cases, the population abandoned the mountain and settled by the sea. Clustered for centuries in an extremely narrow space – usually in a single settlement on small islands[90] – the inhabitants and habitation progressively expanded outside the fortified limits of the nucleus as bygone dangers disappeared, and while new activities and communication improved populations' living conditions. Traditional centres, like Chora in Kalymnos, characterized by their fort-like structure and typical scarcity of space, could no longer accommodate their populations. Indeed, for the most part, such settlements did not allow for new activities that gravitated toward the sea, and which depended directly on maritime communications.

---

90   In fact, insular towns such as Chora gradually accumulated some of the features and functions of urban centres. In some cases, the creation of a second structured settlement brought about the decay of the initial one. See Δημήτρης Δημητρόπουλος, "Αστικές λειτουργίες στις νησιωτικές κοινωνίες των Κυκλάδων (17ος–αρχές 19ου αιώνα)", Πρακτικά Επιστημονικού Συμποσίου Ελληνικός Αστικός Χώρος, Εταιρεία Σπουδών Νεοελληνικού Πολιτισμού και Γενικής Παιδείας [Dimitris Dimitropoulos, "Urban Functions in the Insular Societies of Cyclades", Minutes of Scientific Symposium "Greek Urban Space", Etaireia Spoudon Neoellinikou Politismou kai Genikis Paidias – Society for Neohellenic Culture and General Education Studies], Athens 2004, pp. 101–118.

For similar reasons, Symi and Chalki, the other two sponge-fishing islands of the Dodecanese, saw significant coastal settlements develop from the beginning of the 19th century onwards as their populations rapidly grew. At the same time in the Eastern Aegean, which was still under Ottoman rule, the growth of various seaside settlement sites was directly linked to the local manufacturing activities that channeled their production into the markets of Asia Minor, Egypt, and Europe. Moreover, while coastal locations such as these grew to accommodate new populations and activities, they also witnessed the creation and assembly of new administrative, economic, and social functions.[91]

1.3.1   Toward a Public Space

The "conquest" of space and the "modernization" of its physiognomy requires planning; the organization and allocation of diverse institutions and functions; and the construction of public works and buildings, as well as the creation of symbols that announce the presence of a new industry and the people supporting it.[92] The commercial port cities of the 19th century dominated the economic life of the new Greek state, as the centre of gravity shifted from the countryside and antiquated land transportation, to the sea and to maritime communications. With a number of activities pivoting on agricultural products that originated from farming in the hinterland, towns began turning to their ports in order to direct their production abroad. The money and time saved in transporting raw materials and finished products resulted in light and heavy industrial units being set up along the coastal zone.[93] Hermoupolis, Piraeus, Patras, Volos, and Smyrna, for example, developed along the seashore where the heart of economic and social life beats. Indeed, postcards and images of Smyrna from the 19th century often depict the port, thereby evidencing its importance and centrality for the city's development.[94]

---

91   Cf. Βασίλης Παναγιωτόπουλος, "Από το Ναύπλιο στην Τριπολιτσά: Η σημασία της μεταφοράς μιας περιφερειακής πρωτεύουσας τον 18ο αιώνα", Ο Ερανιστής [Vassilis Panagiotopoulos, "From Nafplio to Tripolitsa: The Importance of the Transfer of a Regional Capital City in the 18th Century", O Eranistis] 11 (1974), pp. 41–56.

92   The case of Nafplio is a typical example of planned interventions into built space as the capital of the newly founded Greek state. See Ελένη Καλαφάτη, Η πολεοδομία της Επανάστασης [Eleni Kalafati, The Urban Planning of the Revolution], pp. 265–282.

93   See Χριστίνα Αγριαντώνη, "Βιομηχανία" [Christina Agriantoni, "Industry"], in Κώστας Κωστής, Σωκράτης Πετμεζάς (επιμ.), Η ανάπτυξη της ελληνικής οικονομίας κατά τον 19ο αιώνα (1830–1914) [Kostas Kostis, Sokratis Petmezas (ed.), The Development of the Greek Economy in the 19th Century (1830–1914)], Athens 2006, p. 225.

94   N. Bakounakis offers an interesting view of the various illustrations of the city of Patras before and after 1830. See Νίκος Μπακουνάκης, Πάτρα, 1828–1860. Μια ελληνική πρωτεύουσα

At the same time, smaller coastal towns of the insular area were also formed as miniatures of larger ports. As lifestyles changed, moreover, traditional self-sufficiency was set aside, and local economies became more and more outward-looking and dependent on their surroundings. Where maritime activities and commercial relations developed, new social requirements arose, which are reflected in the construction of space and its organization. Coastal settlements organized their wharfs, incorporated neoclassical elements in their buildings, and gathered administrative, social, and cultural activities in the coastal zones.

A place of worship of imposing dimensions commonly dominates the centre of any given town, giving expression to the religiosity of the inhabitants, the town's material and symbolic importance, and its residents' prosperity.[95] In Kalymnos, the relocation of a number of inhabitants from Chora, and the accumulation of old and new populations in the coastal area, called for the construction of a larger church, given that the existing small churches could not accommodate the spiritual requirements of the local population. In a letter of 1892 to Chrysanthos, the Metropolitan of Leros and Kalymnos, the Elders of Kalymnos provided a list of the island's churches: "The Church of the Transfiguration of Christ. This one too, also constructed many years ago as a little church, was reconstructed three decades ago and enlarged so that it could meet the needs of its parish".[96] Likewise, in Symi, the other important sponge-fishing centre in the Southeastern Aegean, the reconstruction of the small church of Agios Ioannis from 1836 to 1838, was carried out to meet the needs of the population's concentration in Gialos.[97]

When, on 19 January 1877, the Elders of Kalymnos assigned the construction of the iconostasis for the Church of the Transfiguration of the Saviour in Pothia to sculptor Ioannis Chalepas, the church had not yet become the Metropolis

στον 19ο αιώνα [Nikos Bakounakis, *Patra, 1828–1860: A Greek Capital City in the 19th Century*], Athens 1988, pp. 27–29.

95   See, for example Κώστας Τριανταφύλλου, "Ο νέος μεγάλος ναός στην Πάτρα του Πολιούχου της Αγίου Ανδρέα", *Πελοποννησιακή Πρωτοχρονιά* [Kostas Triantafyllou, "The New Large Church of the Patron Saint of Patra, Saint Andrew", *Peloponnisiaki Protochronia*] (1962), pp. 306–309.

96   The letter of 21/1/1892 is published in Κυριάκος Κ. Χατζηδάκης, "Από την έρευνα των αρχείων της Δημογεροντίας Καλύμνου", *Καλυμνιακά Χρονικά* [Kyriakos K. Chatzidakis, "From Research in the Archives of the Elders of Kalymnos", *Kalymniaka Chronika*] 5 (1985), pp. 276–278.

97   Σωτήριος Αλ. Καρανικόλας, *Τα σεβάσματα της λατρείας των Συμαίων* [Sotirios Al. Karanikolas, *The Objects of Worship of the People of Symi*], vol. A, Piraeus 1962, pp. 13–28.

of the island. Built at the seaside's midpoint around 1860,[98] it was one of the four existing churches of the settlement at the time.[99] Agios Nikolaos, the other large church by the sea, was built after the demolition of the previous small chapel on the same site, and the construction there of a larger church three decades later.[100] Christos [Χριστός], as the locals commonly called it, was to become "the most beautiful church of all [...] with a lead-covered dome, marble ambo and Bishop's cathedra, and remarkable icons by the Kalymnians Sakellarios Magklis and Georgios Oikonomou", as Carl Flegel wrote in 1896.[101]

Nevertheless, when sculptor Ioannis Chalepas of Tinos was carving the iconostasis for the Transfiguration of the Saviour church, Pothia had perhaps not yet become the island's most important settlement. However, available sources suggest that, in the decades that followed, Pothia was indeed making strides in that direction. Therefore, collaborating with one of the most significant marble-carving businesses of that time, and inviting a renowned sculptor to construct it, must have been deliberate choices. The new settlement was, moreover, organized according to relevant planning for and anticipation of future needs. The Church of the Saviour was one of those undertakings, or perhaps the prelude to projects that would give prominence to this developing use and awareness of urban space.

---

98   According to most sources, the Church of the Transfiguration of the Saviour in Pothia was built in 1866, however it may be older. According to a surviving document in the Municipal Archive of Kalymnos, on 12 November 1863, Nikolaos Chatzithemelis was appointed to the position of unsalaried administrator of the church. The document is published in Ιωάννης Ρ. Χαλκίτης, "Συμβολή στην ιστορία της Εκκλησίας της Καλύμνου. Η ουσιαστική συμμετοχή του λαού της Καλύμνου στη ζωή της ορθοδόξου τοπικής εκκλησίας του", Καλυμνιακά Χρονικά [Ioannis R. Chalkitis, "Contribution to the History of the Kalymnian Church. The Meaningful Participation of the People of Kalymnos in the Life of Their Local Orthodox Church", Kalymniaka Chronika] 6 (1986), p. 130. The existence of a church of "Kato Christos" ["Lower Christ"] in Pothia is also mentioned in this document. Perhaps, in its place they built the larger church, as in the case of the church of Agios Nikolaos; Χατζηδάκης, "Κάλυμνος, 1851" [Chatzidakis, "Kalymnos", 1851], p. 40.

99   The four reported churches were Virgin Mary of Kouvousi, Virgin Mary Kalamiotissa, Transfiguration and Agios Nikolaos. See Φλέγελ, Η νήσος Κάλυμνος [Flegel, Kalymnos Island], p. 25 and by the same author, "Η Α.Θ. Παναγιότης ο Οικουμενικός Πατριάρχης Άνθιμος" ["His Holiness the Ecumenical Patriarch Anthimos"], pp. 11–12.

100   Citation from a letter to the Metropolitan Council of Leros and Kalymnos, Chrysanthos, of 21 January 1892. The document was published in Χατζηδάκη, "Από την έρευνα των αρχείων της Δημογεροντίας Καλύμνου" [Chatzidakis, "From Research in the Archives of the Elders of Kalymnos"], pp. 275–282. As K. Chatzidakis notes, District Governor [Kaymakam] Hasan Bey had tried to hinder the completion of the church, which was also used as a cemetery until 1898, when burials in the churchyard were prohibited. Ibid., p. 277.

101   Φλέγελ, Η νήσος Κάλυμνος [Flegel, The Island of Kalymnos], p. 25.

Erecting and decorating a new, large church appears to have been part of broader plan. Up to the end of the 19th century, a series of architectural initiatives, public works and urban planning projects turned Pothia into a small-scale urban centre. Public and private buildings for educational and social purposes, charitable institutions, a courthouse, an administrative centre, a prison, and a customs house were built. The area surrounding the wharf was designated as a marketplace, and various public works, mainly port-related, were carried out there.[102] Meanwhile, houses were constantly being built, the regulation of which often gave the Elders trouble.

In the mid-1860s, the planning and organization of new urban spaces began to absorb a significant portion of municipal revenues. In principle, it was the Elders who allocated municipal and administrative services for the two settlements, while financing the creation and establishment of various social services at the port. For instance, in 1864 six soldiers were assigned to police duty on the island, three for each settlement.[103] In addition, two schools[104] and two municipal pharmacies[105] (at least after 1884) were established, whereas from 1896, three out of four public doctors – who, according to the 1894 charter of the Elders, were elected each year by universal suffrage[106] – were based in Pothia.[107] In 1908, the Elders decided to hire an engineer [δημομηχανικός], to manage public works in Pothia – mainly the construction of the all-girls' school.[108] This practice was discontinued due to the community's financial slowdown in 1922.

The local authorities intervened in the new city's urban landscape rather early on. The Elders council's records document a series of institutional

---

102   It appears, though, that the sheds belonging to various professionals and merchants would soon become a threat to public health given that, from the late 19th century onwards, the Elders [*Demogerontia*] made constant efforts to impose a clean-up of the area, whereas in 1902 they decided to remove the sheds altogether. Decision No 69, 18/4/1902, Correspondence 1902, MAK.
103   Minutes of Administrative Council 1, Minutes of Administrative Board 1863–1884, Folder 2.
104   On the schools of Pothia and Chora see Χατζηδάκης, "Η Κάλυμνος στα τέλη της Τουρκοκρατίας" [Chatzidakis, "Kalymnos at the End of Turkish Rule"], pp. 80–81.
105   Doc. unnumbered, p. 10, Minutes and Correspondence of the Elder Council 1884–1885, MAK.
106   See *Κανονισμός της Δημογεροντίας της νήσου Καλύμνου 1894, εκδ. Αναγνωστήριον Καλύμνου "Αι Μούσαι"* [*Regulation of the Elder Council of the Island of Kalymnos 1894*, ed. Anagnostirion Kalymnou "E Mousse"], Kalymnos 2000, p. 53.
107   Resolutions of public assemblies 8/1/1893–4/1/1907, Minutes of Administrative Council 10, MAK.
108   Doc. 274, 7/3/1908 and doc. 277, 11/3/1908, Minutes of Administrative Council 1908–1909, MAK.

interventions into the organization and management of the space, as well as the imposition of building and urban planning rules.[109] Beginning at least as early as 1879, the Elders took an interest in delineating and securing the public areas at the seashore, because of constant attempts by various individuals to polder land and build dwellings.[110] In spite of the fact that the decision to designate this new strip of land as public land was renewed in 1884,[111] this issue would again require the attention of the Elders a few months later, before it was finally resolved. At that time, the coastal area extended from "the southeast corner of the Transfiguration of Christ Church wharf, near the public toilets, in a straight line up to the seaward-facing corner of Michail Kampourakis' house".[112]

This decision also determined the parts of the twenty properties infringing on the public domain and called for their expropriation. It appears moreover that, in addition to urban planning which included the configuration of a free coastal zone and a wharf, the land was viewed as a marketable commodity when illegal construction and trespassing were restricted. However, in the next few years, the organization of space; the distribution of housing zones; the rezoning of commercial areas and areas where commercial and productive activities were conducted; along with the removal of illegal sheds from the coastal area, met with strong opposition from the locals. Archival research shows that the same decisions were repeated in the following decades,[113] while the Elders asked for the Ottoman District Governor's [*Kaymakam*] protection from the insults and threats they received from affected citizens. Attempts were also made to restrict the number of taverns and wine shops by prohibiting their activity in residential areas.[114] At the same time, the Elders attended to the construction of bridges, and the maintenance and clean-up of the road connecting Chora with Pothia.[115]

The 1885 census of inhabitants and properties on the islands of the southeastern Aegean conducted by the Ottoman administration describes its strategy, while presenting a picture of the new town's expansion. For example, the conflicting interests of the Ottoman authorities and the local Elders

---

109   See, for instance, Doc. 85, 21/9/1879, Minutes of Administrative Council 1879–1884, MAK.

110   Doc. 465, 29/3/1884, Minutes and Correspondence 1884–1885, MAK.

111   Decision of March 29th, 1884, Minutes and Correspondence of Administrative Council 1884 1885, p. 103, MAK.

112   Doc. 639, 15/6/1884, Minutes of the Administrative Council 5, Minutes and Correspondence of Administrative Council 1884–1885, pp. 200–202, MAK.

113   See, for instance, doc. 69, 18/4/1902, Correspondence 1902, MAK.

114   Doc. 671, 11/6/1884 and Doc. 700, 24/8/1884, Minutes of the Administrative Council – Correspondence 1884–1885, MAK.

115   Doc. 51, 14/3/1879 and doc. 84, 26/8/1879, Minutes of Administrative Council 1879–1884, MAK.

gave rise to various disputes concerning issues of administrative responsibility. One cause of constant friction was the draining of the wetlands, or lake Limni, located in the southwestern section of Pothia. The construction of houses had already begun there, when the District Governor ordered their demolition, putting forward the argument that drained wetlands and filled beach areas were public property and not private.[116] This occurred at a time in which the Ottoman state carried out administrative reforms and institutional changes through the *Tanzimat* [period and movement 1839–1876], attempting to impose construction and urban planning reforms, not only in the large urban centres, but also in smaller settlements under its dominion.[117] Despite the fact that the Greek administration was annoyed by the Ottoman authority's interventions, they shared the same vision: the proper organization of the urban fabric and the curtailment of the settlers' illegal activities.

Once more, Carl Flegel, an eyewitness of the island's developments, described the coastal area as well as the social stratification of the town's districts:

> For some time now, although the plain widens to almost one kilometer, there is insufficient space for the houses, which therefore now reach up to a considerable altitude on the pumice strata and on the rocky hill slopes of the middle and southern mountain range. Pothia's houses are more ostentatious than those in Chora, with some of them having red-tiled roofs instead of flat roofs covered in clay earth, whereas others have marble balconies with iron rails.
>
> Only the town's Southern half features a large wharf; the northern half is more densely built up with houses and storage facilities, except for a sandy parcel of land where the shipyard is located. In some parts of the wharf, which they started paving with square tiles, mainly close to the Church of Christ, a market takes place daily. At the widest end of the wharf, there is a range of public buildings, commercial shops and cafés.[118]

---

116   See Κουκούλης, "Η Κάλυμνος στους αγώνες κατά της απογραφής του πληθυσμού" [Koukoulis, "Kalymnos and the Struggle against the Population Census"], pp. 39–62.

117   On institutional changes introduced to issues of administration and the organisation of space, see Αλέκα Καραδήμου-Γερόλυμπου, *Μεταξύ Ανατολής και Δύσης. Βορειοελλαδικές πόλεις στην περίοδο των οθωμανικών μεταρρυθμίσεων* [Aleka Karadimou-Gerolympou, *Between East and West. Northern Greek Cities in the Era of Ottoman Reforms*], Athens 1997, pp. 29–79.

118   Φλέγελ, *Η νήσος Κάλυμνος* [Flegel, *The Island of Kalymnos*], pp. 24–25 and the same, "Η Α.Θ. Παναγιότης ο Οικουμενικός Πατριάρχης Άνθιμος" ["His Holiness the Ecumenical Patriarch Anthimos"], pp. 10–11.

It would have been interesting to document the value of real estate in Pothia and compare it with that of Chora, had we the relevant data at our disposal. However, on the topic of the comparative value of properties, Carl Flegel also noted that,

> Sixty years ago, one could have purchased the entire land mass of Pothia for a very low price, whereas today the value of the land without build-ings is estimated in the millions. The lots located close to the sea next to the port are, of course, more expensive, and somewhat more sought-after. Such is the case with the plot of land where Mr. Nomikos Christodoulakis built his residence of fine marble, estimated at 1,000 Ottoman lira or 24,000 gold francs.[119]

Here Flegel is referring to a lot situated just behind the Transfiguration of the Saviour Church. Furthermore, as he writes, "families with pretentions to wealth and modernity in Pothia rejected small-scale agricultural activities by turning fields into gardens or renting them".[120]

The concentration of the population, the expansion of artisanal, manufac-turing, and various commercial activities, along with the unsanitary wetlands area seems to have generated complex problems. One of the measures imple-mented along the coastal area, where mostly commercial and administrative activities took place, was the removal of potential sources of infection. In fact, one after the other the island's administrative authorities settled there – first the Ottoman administration, followed by the main Church and the district Elders' headquarters. Although there is little available information on the new town's sanitary organization, some surviving regulations and decisions show that it was a topic that preoccupied the local authorities.[121] For instance, public doctors issued recommendations and guidelines on cleanliness on a regular basis, and on taking preventive measures against epidemics, which appear to have broken out rather frequently on the island.[122] We also know that fines were levied on butchers who slaughtered animals in the street or who did not

---

119   Φλέγελ, *Η νήσος Κάλυμνος* (Flegel, *The Island of Kalymnos*), p. 24.

120   Φλέγελ, "Η Α.Θ. Παναγιότης ο Οικουμενικός Πατριάρχης Άνθιμος" [Flegel, "His Holiness the Ecumenical Patriarch Anthimos"], p. 23.

121   See Πατέλλης, "Η δημόσια υγεία στην Κάλυμνο" [Patellis, Public Health in Kalymnos], pp. 159–164.

122   See, for instance, Doc. 55, 1/8/1883, MC Minutes 1882–1883, MAK, on the town's cleanli-ness and the absence of public and private toilets, or the instructions on how to avoid cholera in Doc. 57, 3/8/1883, MC Minutes 1882–1883, MAK. On the street cleaners of Pothia and Chora and the settlements' cleaning, see doc. 2, [1/1897], Minutes of Administrative Board 1896–1897, MAK.

clean the area surrounding their shops, which were located on the wharf next to the Church of Christ.[123] Residents allowing pigs to wander freely on the street were also fined.[124] In addition, rubbish was collected regularly in carts which were ordered from Syros.[125]

To ensure the inhabitants' health, the Elders also decided to isolate lepers, as well as those thought to be suffering from the disease, and to relocate the leper colony from the Northeastern edge of the city to a remote uninhabited area. When Ludvig Ross visited Kalymnos in 1841, he recorded his impressions of the island's first residence for lepers:

> The first thing we saw on right side of the port was a small garden with trees and some houses, and the leper hospital, where eleven men and four women now reside. When they saw us, they quickly sent two of their own to our ship on a boat, which they had been granted, to ask for charity.[126]

This was in fact, a large infertile area that individuals had donated to the Elders and local authorities saw to it that the area was surrounded by walls. They also planted "fig and other trees", and built "small houses, a church, a cistern and other useful facilities for the lepers".[127]

1.3.2   Port Development

The wetland area, the stream that often overflowed in winter, the strong winds that hampered access to the seashore and damaged the numerous wooden sponge-fishing boats, called for important modifications to the port. Sources

---

123   There were repeated complaints over a long period of time. We note only, by way of illustration, doc. 129, 26/6/1895, Correspondence 1895–1986, MAK; also doc. 30 and 31 to the Governor [*Kaymakam*] of Kalymnos dated 21/2/1902 and the letter 145, 10/7/1902, Correspondence 1902, MAK.

124   Doc. 44 to the Governor [*Kaymakam*] of Kalymnos, 12/3/1902, Correspondence 1902, MAK.

125   Doc. 141, 2/6/1894, doc. 187, 14/7/1894, Correspondence 1894–1895, MAK.

126   Λουδοβίκος Ρος, "Νησιωτικά ταξείδια" Κάλυμνος-Τέλενδος. "Κατά μετάφρασιν υπό M. Μιχαηλίδου Νουάρου", *Δωδεκανησιακή Επιθεώρησις* [Ludvig Ross, "Island Travels: Kalymnos-Telendos". Trans. by M. Michailidou Nouarou, *Dodekanisiaki Epitheorisi*] 8 (1947), p. 334.

127   Doc. 24, 22/1/1894, Correspondence 1894–1895, MAK. See also Doc. 28, 12/2/1897, Correspondence 1896–1898, MAK. On the removal of the lepers see also Doc. 32, 13/6/1883, Minutes of the Administrative Council 1882–1883, MAK; Doc. 203, 3/8/1894, Correspondence 1894–1895, MAK. For the configuration of the area see also Κινδύνης, *Η νήσος Κάλυμνος* [Kindinis, *The Island of Kalymnos*], p. 14.

are not particularly illuminating on the port development and Kalymnos' port traffic for the period we are studying,[128] However, according to Tavlarios:

> The port consists of a large open bay, facing the East and located directly opposite some villages of the island of Kos, which gives the impression of narrowing bay. It is a handcrafted but excellent port, built with state funding and peoples' contributions. Here official trade takes place based on the importation of various products and the exportation of sponges.[129]

The Elders claimed that "life on our land depends on the port, so that the ships of our poor sponge fishermen may be protected", and deemed it necessary to repair the existing old mole or breakwater in order to shelter small vessels from southerly winds. In order to do so, gunpowder was required from the local government to mine the stones needed for repairs.[130]

Other documents from the period often note that the coastal area was not entirely suited to docking vessels because it had a shallow side, and a large section of the wharf was exposed to strong winds. However, the increased sponge-fishing activity from the 1860s also saw a rise in the number of vessels kept on land during winter. In 1865 for example, 352 sponge-fishing vessels must have docked at Pothia,[131] as well as an unknown number of supply boats [deposita] carrying tanks, and fishing boats.

---

128   For developments carried out on large ports of the Eastern Mediterranean, mainly from the second half of the 19th century, see Μαρία Συναρέλλη, Δρόμοι και λιμάνια στην Ελλάδα, 1830–1880 [Maria Synarelli, Roads and Ports in Greece, 1830–1880], Athens 1989. See also Βίλμα Χαστάογλου, "Από τις "Σκάλες" του Λεβάντε στις σύγχρονες εμπορικές προκυμαίες" [Vilma Hastaoglou, "From the 'Skalas' of Levante to the Modern Commercial Docks"], in the Minutes of the 2nd International Convention: "Η πόλη στους νεότερους χρόνους" ["The City in Modern Times"], Athens 2000, pp. 51–68. On the motivation for the construction of a port on Nisyros, and works at the port of Mandraki carried out concurrently with those on Kalymnos, see Μιλτιάδης Λογοθέτης, Οι πρωτεργάτες του λιμανιού της Νισύρου στα τελευταία χρόνια της Τουρκοκρατίας (1885–1912) [Miltiadis Logothetis, The Pioneers of Nisyros Port in the Final Years of the Turkish Rule (1885–1912)], Athens 1981.

129   Ταυλάριος, "Περί της νήσου Καλύμνου" [Tavlarios, "About the Island of Kalymnos"], pp. 518–522; Ζερβός, "Μια περιγραφή της Καλύμνου" [Zervos, "A Description of Kalymnos"], p. 99.

130   Doc. 636, 15/6/1884, Doc. 637, 15/6/1884, Minutes-Correspondence of the Administrative Council 1884–1885, ΜΑΚ.

131   The annual total number of ships employed in sponge fishing was not stable. Available information is based on the number of annual sponge-fishing permits (see below), as well as on the aggregate table included in a report of the Elders' Council to the Ottoman administration. See Ευδοκία Ολυμπίτου, "Η εισαγωγή του καταδυτικού σκαφάνδρου στη σπογγαλιεία της Καλύμνου", Τα Ιστορικά [Evdokia Olympitou, "The Introduction of the Scaphander Diving Suit in the Sponge Fishery of Kalymnos", Ta Istorika] 38 (2003), pp. 174–175.

The community's economic difficulties along with its administrative dependence on the Ottoman government dictated that necessary public works were implemented gradually. Port improvement projects are implicitly mentioned in documents from 1863, contained in the oldest surviving record book of the Elders,[132] while in 1879, sponge-fishing vessels were employed to remove sand from the area.[133] In a letter to the District Governor [*Kaymakam*] dated 1884, the Elders of Kalymnos' requested a supply of stones for small-scale works at the port. They wrote:

> Life on our land depends on the port, so that the ships of our poor sponge fishermen, who must scour the depths of the sea off the shores of Africa to earn their own and their poor families' living, may be protected. But, because the Municipal Treasury is in a difficult financial situation at the moment, which does not allow us to proceed with the cleaning of our island's port, and because that would require an amount of money exceeding our own material powers, we approved a limited repair of the existing mole of the bay, which is located on the north side of the town next to the leper residence. This breakwater, which was already old, was damaged both by age and the force of the waves due to southerly winds. With a low-cost repair, part of the mole will facilitate dragging small vessels onto the beach and to the land, and protecting them when they are in the sea.[134]

In another letter dated on the same day, they demand the expulsion of "immigrants from Patmos working as porters and muleteers, and the stone carriers from Karpathos", because they refused to carry stones and to work on this particular project, in spite of the fact that they were to be paid by the community.[135]

In the 1890s, residents made contributions to the Elders on a regular basis for the completion of works at the port of the so-called Skala.[136] In 1893,

---

132 For example, in a document on the payment of customs taxes by captains and merchants dated 18/2/1864 in the Minutes-Correspondence of the Administrative Board 1863–1884, MAK.

133 Doc. 54, 26/8/1879, MC Minutes 1879–1884, MAK. Other testimonies on the repair and improvement of port facilities can be found in Doc. 615, 14/3/1879 and doc. 618, 5/6/1884, Minutes-Correspondence of the Administrative Board 1884–1885, MAK.

134 Doc. 636, 15/6/1863, Minutes-Correspondence of the Administrative Board 1884–1884, MAK.

135 Doc. 637, 15/6/1863, Minutes-Correspondence of the Administrative Board 1884–1884, MAK.

136 See, for example, a list of debtors of the contribution in letter 135, 12/6/1896, Correspondence 1895–1896, MAK.

they again went to work removing sand,[137] while in 1895 and 1896 the Elders submitted insistent requests to the Ottoman administration for a dredging machine that was housed on the island of Kos, to deepen the harbour's sandy seabed.[138] However, since their efforts did not appear to yield results, they turned to their compatriot Nikolaos Petalas, a Suez resident, asking him to inquire as to whether the Suez Canal Company owned any similar machines.[139] A second-hand machine for this purpose was acquired several years later from Symi.[140]

In 1902, a wharf was constructed for loading and unloading commodities,[141] with the further purpose of dredging the harbour, thus facilitating access for steamships.[142] In this same period, the entire area got the necessary lighting while they carried out works to improve the port, to fill in various sites, and to build roads.[143] In the late 19th century, the Elders also expressed their desire to relocate the shipyard from the central area of the beach to its northeastern edge, given the large number of small ships and sponge-fishing boats that were pulled out and onto the shore for maintenance in the winter.[144]

There is no doubt that the increased sponge exports of that period boosted the growth of coastal shipping and played a part in the expansion of commercial relations and the import of various goods. In January 1884, in a letter to Em. Magklis, a local agent of the coastal shipping company "Asia Minor", the Elders of Kalymnos requested that he not issue tickets without their permission, because otherwise the relevant municipal tax was not being paid.[145] At the beginning of the 20th century, Kalymnos became connected with regular routes to Piraeus, the islands of the Aegean Sea, as well as to Cyprus, Beirut, and Smyrna.[146]

---

137   Doc. 189, 26/8/1892, MC Minutes 1879–1893, MAK.
138   Doc. 22, 24/1/1896, Correspondence 1895–1896, MAK.
139   Doc. 58, 12/3/1896, Correspondence 1895–1896, MAK.
140   Doc. 156, 16/8/1902, Correspondence 1902, MAK.
141   Letter No 128 to the Kaymakam of Kalymnos, 18/6/1902, Correspondence 1902, MAK.
142   To do that, the Elders brought a specific machine from Symi. The information originates from a letter in which the Elders protested to the local Governor against the levy of a customs tax on this machine, that had been applied as if it were new. Letter No 156 to the Kaymakam of Kalymnos, 16/8/1902, Correspondence 1902, MAK.
143   No 39, Folder 20, MC Minutes, MAK.
144   Folder 102–103, 8/8/1897, Correspondence 1896–1898, MAK.
145   Minutes-Correspondence of the Administrative Board 1884–1885, p. 13, MAK.
146   Γιάννης Γεράκης, Σφουγγαράδικες ιστορίες από την Κάλυμνο του 1900 [Giannis Gerakis, Sponge-Fishing Stories from Kalymnos in 1900], Athens 1999, p. 27. The author notes two ships on the Smyrna-Atalia route, the "Roumeli" and the "Olympia", which carried mostly Kalymnian minors to Smyrna and from there to Russia, to work in various branches of manufacturing. See also related announcements published in newspapers of that

1.4   Administrative and Social Organization of the Island

In October 1888, the Elders of Kalymnos submitted a request to the Holy Synod of the Ecumenical Patriarchate to elevate the Diocese of Lerni to the status of Metropolitanate, advancing the argument that "lately our homeland Kalymnos has seen a substantial increase in size and importance".[147]

In 1889, the first Metropolitan of Leros and Kalymnos, Chrysanthos Byzantios, (1888–1894) transferred the seat of the Metropolitanate from Chora to the new island capital Pothia, and more specifically to the Church of Christ our Saviour.[148] In addition, he appointed two episcopal overseers for a one-year period, in a clear attempt to soften the transition and garner favour.[149] When Anthimos, the former Metropolitan of Leros and Kalymnos, was elected Ecumenical Patriarch an official doxology was held at the church of the Transfiguration of Christ, while on the same day (January 25, 1895) they inaugurated a new, all-boys elementary school in Pothia.[150]

---

period, for example: Σκριπ [Skrip], 23/8/1908, p. 2, 9/11/1908, p. 6, 15/10/1909, p. 2 et al. On Kalymnian children working in Russia in this period, see also Chapter 4 of the present volume, pp. 264–268.

147 The decision of Dionisios V, Patriarch of Constantinople, is formulated in a similar manner: "Their homeland, composed of the islands Leros, Kalymnos, and Astypalaia, has recently seen a substantial increase in size and importance due to its commercial location". See the full text of the decision in the Patriarchal and Synodal Tome of 1888, in which it was published Γεώργιος Χρ. Χαραμαντάς, Επισκοπική Ιστορία της Εκκλησίας της Καλύμνου [Georgios Chr. Charmantas, Episcopal History of the Church of Kalymnos], Kalymnos 1983, pp. 22–24.

148 Χαραμαντάς, Επισκοπική Ιστορία [Charmantas, Episcopal History], p. 51; by the same author, Χώρα, η πρωτεύουσα της νήσου Καλύμνου. Κομμάτια και σελίδες από την ιστορία της και την παράδοσή της [Chora, the Capital of Kalymnos Island. Pieces and Pages of its History and Traditions], Athens 2000, p. 46. The same information is found in Χριστίνα Κομπιτσάκη, "Ο ναός της Κοίμησης της Θεοτόκου Χώρας Καλύμνου", Καλυμνιακά Χρονικά [Christina Kompitsaki, "The Church of the Assumption of Mary in Chora, Kalymnos", Kalymniaka Chronika] 9 (1990), pp. 196–203. For the elevation of the Diocese of Lerni to Metropolis of Leros and Kalymnos in 1888, see Μανουήλ Γεδεών, "Η Μητρόπολις Λέρου και Καλύμνου" Εκκλησιαστική Αλήθεια [Manouil Gedeon, "The Metropolis of Leros and Kalymnos", Ekklisiastiki Alitheia] 8 (1888–1889), p. 10; Ιωάννης Π. Χαλκίτης, "Συμβολή στην ιστορία της Εκκλησίας της Καλύμνου. Α΄ εκατονταετηρίς από της ανυψώσεως της Επισκοπής Λέρνης εις Μητρόπολιν Λέρου και Καλύμνου Νοέμβριος 1888–Νοέμβριος 1988", Καλυμνιακά Χρονικά [Ioannis P. Chalkitis, "Contribution to the History of the Church of Kalymnos. 1st Centenary from the Erection of Lerni Diocese as Metropolis of Leros and Kalymnos", November 1888–November 1988, Kalymniaka Chronika] 7 (1988), pp. 106–111.

149 Χαραμαντάς, Επισκοπική Ιστορία [Charmantas, Episcopal History], p. 51.

150 Ibid., p. 80.

By the end of the century, the headquarters of the Elders had been relocated in the port.[151] In 1902, they laid the cornerstone of a new Elders' building near the Church of Christ,[152] where they would also build the town's clock tower. For the ceremony, they availed themselves of Sultan Abdul Hamid Han II's 25-year rule celebrations, since on that day the District Governor [*Kaymakam*] of Kalymnos, Mahir Bey, and other representatives of the Ottoman regional administration, attended the official ceremony. It seems, however, that financial issues hampered the building's construction, which was ultimately completed thanks to the contribution of sponge merchant Nikolaos Vouvalis.[153]

In the same year, it was decided that a building should be erected, which would house the administrative centre in the coastal area.[154] This time however, the Elders managed to meet expenditure and the construction of the centre was completed in the space of one month except for the woodwork, which was completed shortly thereafter.[155]

As an administrative and financial centre, Pothia was at the heart of the island's political and social life and, in the yard of the Transfiguration of the Saviour church, elections were held for local authorities, as well a public assemblies.[156] In January 1884, according to available sources, voters from both Pothia and Chora participated in the elections of the island's Elders; however, there is no mention of how many voters turned out from each settlement.[157]

---

151 Πατέλλης, "Η δημόσια υγεία στην Κάλυμνο" [Patellis, "Public Health in Kalymnos"], p. 159.

152 Letter No 48 to the Kaymakam of Kalymnos, 16/3/1902, Correspondence 1902, MAK. Unfortunately, no surviving building plan can be found in the archives, a copy of which is said to have been submitted for approval to the local Kaymakam (Document 71, 22/4/1902).

153 Letter No 93 to the Kaymakam of Kalymnos, 13/5/1902, Correspondence 1902, MAK. It was common practice in Kalymnos – and elsewhere – for local or national benefactors to assist in works that benefited the public. An alternative motivation for this funding is presented in Αγγελική Φενερλή, "Ο καλλωπισμός της πόλης. Ένας πρωτότυπος συμμετοχικός τρόπος χρηματοδότησης δημοσίων κτιρίων στην Ερμούπολη (19ος αι.)" [Angeliki Fenerli, "Beautification of the Town: An Innovative Participatory Means of Funding Public Buildings in Hermoupolis (19th century)"], in *Minutes of the 2nd International Convention* "Η πόλη στους νεότερους χρόνους" ["The Town in Modern Times"], Athens 2000, pp. 173–182, which does not however appear to have been used in Kalymnos.

154 Letter No 126 to the Kaymakam of Kalymnos, 17/6/1902, Correspondence 1902, MAK.

155 Letter No 148 to the Kaymakam of Kalymnos, 29/7/1902, Correspondence 1902, MAK.

156 On the convocation and conducting of "general assemblies of the people", at least those organized by the Elder Council, see *Κανονισμός της Δημογεροντίας της νήσου Καλύμνου 1894* [*Regulation of the Elder Council of Kalymnos Island 1894*], p. 55. The Agios Ioannis Cathedral in Yalos at Symi enjoyed a similar honorary privilege. See Καρανικόλας, *Τα σεβάσματα της λατρείας* [Karanikolas, *The Objects of Worship*], p. 22.

157 Minutes of Administrative Board 5, Minutes and Correspondence of Elder Council 1884–1885, pp. 1–2, MAK.

The sources also reveal that the port of Pothia was the scene of various gatherings, and assemblies, as well as turmoil and confrontations between members of the population and the local authorities, both Ottoman and Greek.[158] Such instances occurred for example, when the Ottoman government attempted to constrain the privileges of the Four Islands [*Tetranesos*] after the Cretan revolt,[159] or when the "sponge-fishing issue" agitated the inhabitants of Kalymnos. At the same time, however, the municipal tax auctions of the "local sponge fee" and "Skala fee", with which the Elders paid community debts for school maintenance and healthcare, took place at a cafe on the seaside for several decades.[160]

The establishment of a "reading room", the proposal for which the Elders of Kalymnos began considering in 1877, serves as an interesting indicator of the new town's social and cultural choices.[161] In 1904, when Kalymnos' reading room "The Muses" [Αι Μούσαι] was finally founded, it was housed in a rented building on the shore of the Limni area.[162] However, only a few months after it was established, the Kaymakam of Kalymnos threatened to disrupt the reading room's operation. In their written protest, the Elders described its creation,

158 See, for example, the resolutions of the people's assemblies included in Resolutions of Public Assemblies 8/1/1893–4/1/1907, Minutes of Administrative Board, MAK.

159 The Tetranesos is comprised of Kalymnos, Leros, Patmos and Ikaria. For the formation and status of the Tetranesos see for example, Ε. Πρωτοψάλτης, "Η τύχη των Νοτίων Σποράδων κατά την Επανάστασιν και μετ᾽ αυτήν", *Καρπαθιακαί Μελέται* [E. Protopsaltis, "The Fortune of Southern Sporades During the Revolution and Thereafter", *Karpathiakai Meletai*], 2 (1981), pp. 306–307; Παναγιώτης Σαβοριανάκης, *Νησιωτικές κοινωνίες στο Αιγαίο. Η περίπτωση των Ελλήνων της Ρόδου και της Κω* (1805–1905 αι,) [Panagiotis Savorianakis, *Insular Societies in the Aegean: Greeks on Rhodes and Kos* (18th–19th century)], Athens, n.d. pp. 115–125.

160 Doc. 39, 17/2/1879 and Doc. 20, 2/5/1881, MC Minutes 1879–1884, MAK; Doc. 190, 18/5/1893, Minutes of Administrative Board 1892–1893, MAK; Folder 4, Minutes and Correspondence of the Kalymnos Financial Committee 1902–1904, MAK; Doc. 77, 1/7/1915, Doc. 86, 6/7/1915 etc., Minutes of Administrative Board 1915–1916, MAK.

161 See Θεμελίνα Καπελλά, "Η ιστορία του Αναγνωστηρίου", *Καλυμνιακά Χρονικά* [Themelina Kapella, "The History of the Agnostirion Reading Room", *Kalymniaka Chronika*] 1 (1982), pp. 26–28. Σακελλαρίδης, *Η εξέλιξη και διαμόρφωση του πληθυσμού της Καλύμνου* [Sakellaridis, *The Development and Configuration of the Population of Kalymnos*], p. 401–402; Χατζηδάκης, *Η Κάλυμνος στα τέλη της Τουρκοκρατίας* [Chatzidakis, *Kalymnos at the End of Turkish Rule*], p. 82.

162 The residence of doctor Sp. Caravokyros. See the Demogerontia's 9/12/1904 letter of protest addressed to the Kaymakam of Kalymnos, as published in the 6th volume of *Kalymniaka Chronika* (1986), pp. 14–18. In Symi, they had established a reading room called "Aigli" ["Splendor" – "Αναγνωστήριον: Η Αίγλη"] in 1872, in which a combination of educational and other activities were carried out. Γεώργιος Θ. Βεργωτής, "Περί την ιστορίαν του Αναγνωστηρίου Σύμης η Άιγλη᾽", *Τα Συμαϊκά* [Georgios Th. Vergotis, "On the History of Symi's Reading Room "Aegli᾽", *Ta Symaika*] 1 (1972), pp. 123–138.

while invoking its lawful operation, and the devotion of the Kalymnian people to the imperial throne.

> Many of the teachers, scientists and merchants and many young people of our best families – all of them sensible, decorous, law-abiding, loyal, and devoted to our cherished Emperor and lover of the arts – wish to avoid frequenting our inconvenient, noxious, and noisy cafés. More accurately, they feel the need to frequent a place with healthier conditions, and to make use of their time in a more decent, pleasant, and constructive manner. After consideration, they thus rented the house close to the beach on that portion of the Limni which belongs to the doctor Sp. Carabokyros, who currently resides in Rhodes. Our fellow citizens and members of the reading room gather and spend their free time there, reading newspapers published in Constantinople and Smyrna, or conversing quietly, in a lawful and orderly manner, on moral topics worthy of virtuous young men, fond of the arts and letters. Moreover, some of them get up amateur plays which are approved by the esteemed Sub-Governorate, such as moral and educational dramas on a small theatre stage set up in the reading room. Until yesterday, the money collected from these activities, after covering the costs of the play, were given to Elders' treasury, for distribution to the poor. In fact, this is what happened a few of days ago, when the reading room committee presented us with the sum of 400 *kuruş* which they had collected.[163]

However, in 1909 when the reading room ceased its operations, the community owed Sp. Carabokyros a total 3,000 *kuruş* in rent. To prevent the him from seizing the reading room's property, the Elders decided to pay the rent owing out of the municipal treasury. In their decision, it was pointed out that the owner's threat to keep whatever was found in the reading room was "undignified and insulting to our land, and disadvantageous because the property of the reading room holds far more value than the rent owed". They went on to note for example, specific property such as "the library of Pantaleon and a book donated

---

163   The document is published in "Έτος πρώτο – 1904 – του Αναγνωστηρίου", *Καλυμνιακά Χρονικά* ["First Year – 1904 – of the Reading Room", *Kaymniaka Chronika*] 6 (1986), pp. 11–18. For the founding members of the reading room, see also Θεμελίνα Καπελλά, "Η ιστορία του Αναγνωστηρίου" [Themelina Kapella, "The History of Agnostirion" (Reading Room)], pp. 26–29; by the same author *Ιστορικές μνήμες Καλύμνου* [*Historical Memories of Kalymnos*], pp. 98–106; Σακελλαρίδης [Sakellaridis], "Antonio Ritelli", pp. 159–160. The Italians forced the reading room to shut down in 1935 (see *Αθηναϊκά Νέα* [*Athinaika Nea*], 25/1/1935, p. 5). It resumed its activities in 1979.

by the late Maraslis, another by William Paton and various others [...]".[164] It
seems, though, that those frequenting the reading room were not simple newspaper and book readers, but came from the island's social and financial elite,
who were involved in politics, or were suspects in political conspiracies under
investigation by the island's foreign authorities.[165]

With approximately 19,000 inhabitants by the beginning of the 20th century, Kalymnos[166] had become an island with an organized market and
artisanal workshops directly or indirectly connected with the exclusive occupation of sponge fishing. The island also housed a labour force that consisted
of locals and foreigners employed on boats, along with a group of smaller and
larger-scale entrepreneurs, investors, and merchants. Importantly, the long
chain of activities and agents necessitated by the booming sponge fishery of
that era shaped the island's physiognomy.

In 1912, when Kalymnos was under Italian occupation, Pothia was the indis-
putable capital with 20,000 inhabitants, and Chora was the second settlement
in order of importance with a population that grew to 3,000 residents. "Its
capital, Pothaia, built in a semicircle on the island's eastern side, offers those
arriving on the island a magnificent view", writes Gerasimos Drakidis in 1913.
As he goes on to explain, "all the houses are stone-built, many of which are
two-storey and three-storey, and they have a simple, standard architectural
style, with furniture of mostly English origin".[167]

While the introduction of the scaphander diving suit marked the transition from the pre-industrial era to the "mechanisation" of sponge fishing, the
settlement of Pothia is evidence of a rejection of traditional, inward-looking
attitudes and cohesion, which prevailed for centuries among the island populations of the Aegean. Kalymnian society in that period was characterized by
changes in the composition of the population, the accumulation of wealth,
and the emergence of a local literate, cosmopolitan, elite that divided its time

---

164   Doc. 78, 9/5/1911, MC Minutes 1910–1912, MAK. The decision was not unanimous. For
      example, I. Ampelas advocated for the debts to be paid by the members of the reading
      room, and that rent be "paid by its board members" until its suspension.

165   Under Italian rule, the reading room ceased its operations and became known as "Café
      Italia". See Σακελλαρίδης [Sakellarides], "Antonio Ritelli", pp. 159–160.

166   In 1896, Carl Flegel reported that there were 5,000 inhabitants in Chora, 9,000 in Pothia,
      as well as others scattered in smaller settlements. Φλέγελ, Η νήσος Κάλυμνος [Flegel, *The
      Island of Kalymnos*], p. 12. See also Σακελλαρίδης, "Η πληθυσμιακή εξέλιξη της Καλύμνου
      και τα αίτιά της" [Giorgos M. Sakellaridis, "Population Growth on Kalymnos and its
      Causes"], pp. 69–73; by the same author, *Η εξέλιξη και διαμόρφωση του πληθυσμού της
      Καλύμνου* [Sakellaridis, *The Development and Configuration of the Population of Kalymnos*],
      pp. 395–405.

167   Δρακίδης, *Λεύκωμα των Δωδεκανήσων* [Drakidis, *Almanac of the Dodecanese*], p. 66.

between Kalymnos and European capitals, and by a labour force with a distinct internal hierarchy.

In the final decades of the 19th century, new conditions in sponge production and the organization of the international sponge trade also changed the structure of exports and resulted in Kalymnians setting up robust businesses headquartered in the most important European trade centres. On the one hand, the operation of commercial shops abroad put Kalymnians in touch with the culture of the Greek diaspora and, on the other hand, these developments also entailed a more efficient organization of their activities in their place of birth. The development of port works, and the improvement of maritime transport and urban infrastructures were essential components of a properly functioning sponge-trading business. At the same time however, the proactive presence of Kalymnians in public life and the administration of public affairs was not motivated by their business needs alone. Lenders, investors, captains, and sponge traders formed a dynamic group that expanded the limits of their activities, materially improving life on Kalymnos, while adopting "modernizing" behaviours, attitudes and consumer standards. The population's distribution in space was, moreover, straightforward with the sponge fishery's *nouveau riche* building massive two-storey properties in a unified architectural style on the settlement's lowlands behind the harbour, whereas on the surrounding hill slopes, the "Marassia", as well as the old Chora, remained working-class neighbourhoods where sponge fishermen grew up and dwelled.

1.5   Sponge Fishery: Kalymnos' Source of Livelihood

There was no other job here in Kalymnos. This was what I had to do.[168]

For Kalymnians, sponge fishing and the sponge trade are part of inherited technical expertise and a tradition that existed long before the 19th century, and probably in a systematic form,[169] favoured by the morphology and cli-

---

168   Testimony of Nikolas Kampourakis to E.O., 28/7/2005.
169   Sakellaris Trikoilis traces the involvement of Kalymnians with sponge fishing back to the 3rd and 2nd centuries BC, arguing that the island's inhabitants worshipped Apollo Delphinios, the patron of seafarers and, in Kalymnos, of sponge fishermen. In fact, he substantiates his claim with his interpretation of a dolphin in sculpted relief, which was brought to light through archaeological research at the ancient settlement of Damos in Kalymnos. See Σακελλάρης Ν. Τρικοίλης, "Το δελφίνι του Δάμου Καλυμνίων'. Ο διπλός συμβολισμός: Απόλλων-Θάλασσα", *Καλυμνιακά Χρονικά* [Sakellaris N. Trikoilis, "'The Dolphin of Damos Kalymnou' and its Double Symbolism: Apollo-Sea", *Kalymniaka Chronika*] 14

mate of the surrounding maritime area.[170] Although occasional mentions of sponge-fishing practices appear in various documents in the 18th century, we have no quantitative or any other type of information at our disposal to support research on the propagation and range of sponge fishing in the 19th century.[171] We must, therefore, content ourselves with the testimony of Kalymnian medical student Themelis Kindynis who, in 1878, wrote that "the practice of sponge fishing was introduced 150 years ago, according to the present-day Elders".[172] In 1885, Miltiadis Caravokyros also noted that sponge fishing was as old as time and that, according to tradition, it had reappeared in the past century.[173] Likewise, Carl Flegel also notes that "the elder inhabitants of Kalymnos recall that their ancestors were sponge fishermen".[174]

Kalymnos was, however, not the only sponge-fishing island in the Aegean. In the 19th century, there were various island and coastal areas involved in sponge fishing, in different styles and using different means, all of which are apparently typical of sponge fishing. The most important sponge-fishing centres were based in the Dodecanese (Kalymnos, Symi, Chalki, Kastellorizo), as well as on islands of the Argosaronic Gulf (Aegina, Hydra). At the same time, sponge fishing had also developed on other islands and coastal areas of the Greek territory, such as on Lemnos, Ermioni, Gythio, and Trikeri in Magnesia, where sponges had been one of the main products for export since the 18th century.[175] In those long-established maritime lands, they put their expertise

---

(2001), pp. 9–21. It has also been reported that the inhabitants' first contact with sponges was collecting them from the beach. Γεώργιος Ελευθ. Γεωργάς, Μελέτη περί σπογγαλιείας, σπόγγων και σπογγεμπορίου από των αρχαιοτάτων χρόνων μέχρι σήμερον [Georgios Elefth. Georgas, *Study of the Sponge Fishery, Sponges and the Sponge Trade from Ancient Times to the Present*], Piraeus 1937, p. 18.

170   Emile Y. Kolodny, *La population des îles de la Grèce*, p. 310.

171   Although older documents on this subject are rare, it seems that, throughout the Ottoman era, some Aegean populations were familiar with sponge fishing, and that this activity engaged a sizeable group of inhabitants in several areas, while the products of their occupation were exported and linked to external trade. Perhaps one of the oldest reports of sponge fishing in the Dodecanese dates to the mid-17th century. See Ιπποκράτης Φραγκόπουλος, *Ιστορία της Καλύμνου* [Ippokratis Fragopoulos, *History of Kalymnos*], Athens 1995, pp. 55–56.

172   Κινδύνης, *Η νήσος Κάλυμνος* [Kindynis, *The Island of Kalymnos*], p. 23.

173   Caravokyro, *Étude sur la pêche des éponges*, p. 5.

174   Φλέγελ, "Η Α.Θ. Παναγιότης ο Οικουμενικός Πατριάρχης Άνθιμος" [Flegel, "His Holiness the Ecumenical Patriarch Anthimos"], p. 13.

175   See Α. Τζαμτζής, *Η ναυτιλία του Πηλίου στην Τουρκοκρατία* [A. Tzamtzis, *Maritime Shipping in Pelion under Turkish Rule*], Athens, n.d., p. 31. See also Τάσος Ζάππας, "Γύρω από τον κόσμο της θαλάσσης. Στο κάβο με την κονταρομαχία της τσέτας", *Αθηναϊκά Νέα* [Tassos Zappas, "About the Sea World. At the Cavo with the Tseta Jousting", *Athinaika Nea*], 11/10/1938, p. 5.

in navigation to good use, along with their experience in maritime transport and trade. Likewise, the workforces in these other centres were also mobilized, thus turning sponge fishing into a regularized occupation and a professional specialization.

The Kalymnians, despite being "warriors of the sea",[176] were not however qualified seafarers; the island had no commercial fleet, and Kalymnians were not systemically involved in transit trade. In fact, near the middle of the 19th century, when the centre of gravity for sponge fishing shifted to the coasts of North Africa, there is documentation to the effect that Kalymnians chartered larger ships from Symi, Kassos or Leros, aboard which they placed their smaller

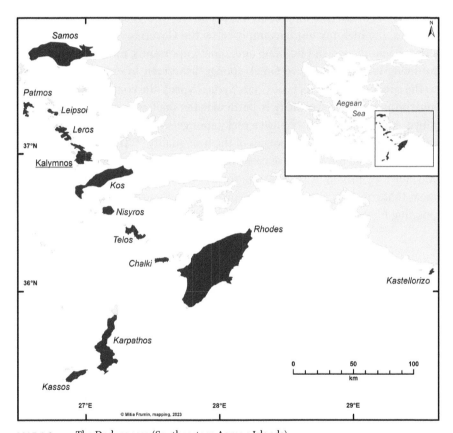

MAP 1.2   The Dodecanese (Southeastern Aegean Islands)

---

176   This expression is repeated in 19th-century texts. See, for example, Κινδύνης, Η νήσος Κάλυμνος [Kindynis, *The Island of Kalymnos*], p. 29.

sponge-fishing boats, and then transported them to distant sponge-fishery sites.[177] Beginning in the early 1860s however, this method of boat transportation was gradually abandoned, and workers in the industry took to travelling on larger ships to the coasts of North Africa.[178] Much later still, it was again reported that Kalymnian captains of sponge-fishing boats were not able to pilot their own sailing ships over such long distances, and they made special agreements to hire experienced seafarers to take charge of navigation.[179]

At least until the beginning of the 20th century, the geographical area in which the sponge-fishing populations of the Aegean islands and the coastal areas of Greece were active was chiefly the Eastern Mediterranean. Moreover, although, sponges continued to be harvested in the Aegean area until the mid-19th century, the depletion of resources, the increased demand for sponges, the high tax burdens imposed by the Governors of the Archipelago Province, improved shipbuilding and, most importantly, improvements made in diving technology, drove Greek sponge fishermen to expand Southwards to the sponge-bearing reefs of Crete, Syria, Cyprus, the coasts of North Africa, and the maritime area of Sicily. In particular, the shallow, warm waters of Egypt, Libya, and Tunisia, with extensive rocky sponge-supporting areas, were home to the largest quantities of sponges of the best quality.[180] Thus, a voyage of several months and the sojourn of crews aboard the boats for long periods of time was, for Kalymnians, a prerequisite for the discovery of rich sponge-bearing areas that could provide satisfactory production. Boats with naked divers, harpooning boats and gagavas set sail every spring from Kalymnos, Symi, Chalki

177 Louis Figuier, *Les merveilles de la science, ou déscription populaire des inventions modernes*, vol. 4, Paris 1870, p. 624; "Φλέγελ, Η Α.Θ. Παναγιότης ο Οικουμενικός Πατριάρχης Άνθιμος" [Flegel, "His Holiness the Ecumenical Patriarch Anthimos"], p. 13.

178 Caravokyro, *Étude sur la pêche des éponges*, p. 4.

179 Testimony of Giannis Tsoulfas to E.O., 3/2002.

180 See Αδαμάντιος Ε. Παχουντάκης, *Η σπογγαλιεία εν Αιγύπτω* [Adamantios E. Pachountakis, *Sponge Fishing in Egypt*], Alexandria 1905, p. 3; Γεωργάς, *Μελέτη περί σπογγαλιείας* [Georgas, *Study of the Sponge Fishery*], p. 24. On sponge fishing off the coasts of Tunisia, see *Ministère de la Marine, Revue maritime et coloniale*, vol. 101, Paris 1900, p. 704. On the topic of the Mediterranean sponge production more generally, see Jean-Pierre Boude, "Les pêches méditerranéennes", *Études Internationales* 18 (1987), pp. 83–105. In this period, sponge fishing had not yet encountered the problems that would arise from the restriction and prohibition of fishing in the sponge-bearing areas of North Africa. For more detail on this topic, see Σωτήριος Αγαπητίδης, "Η οικονομική οργάνωση των σπογγαλιευτικών συγκροτημά-των – ειδικότερα στη Σύμη", *Τα Συμαϊκά* [Sotirios Agapitidis, "The Economic Organization of Sponge-Fishing Groups – Particularly on Symi", *Ta Symaika*] 3 (1977), p. 181. The articles on this topic which appear in the Athens' press at the time are highly informative. See, for instance, *Εμπρός* [*Empros*], 14/3/1902, p. 1 and 31/3/1902, p. 1; *Σκριπ* (Skrip), 10/3/1902 etc.

and Kastellorizo, and stayed out fishing until early autumn, on an area stretching from the coasts of Egypt to the shores of Algeria. In a report by Robert Campbell, the English consul in Rhodes, to Stratford Canning (1786–1880), the United Kingdom's ambassador in Constantinople, it was noted that, of the 600 sponge-fishing boats that sailed from the islands of South Sporades in the summer of 1858, 70 worked along the coasts of Rhodes, 150 in the maritime area of Crete, while 180 boats were headed to Syria, and 200 to the coasts of North Africa. That year's production was estimated at 89,052 okas, sold for 350,000 pounds sterling.[181]

Beginning in 1860, several sponging ships ventured even farther to Derna and Benghazi and, beginning in 1884, many of those headed to Tripoli, Sfax and occasionally to Tunis and Alger. Flegel reports that the first sponge-fishing boat to arrive in Benghazi, in about 1860, was piloted by captain Georgios Antonellos from Leros, whose example Kalymnians promptly began imitating.[182] However, by the late 19th century the sea, that had seemed like an inexhaustible gold mine, was already giving cause for concern about overfishing.[183] At the beginning of the 20th century, Greek sponge fishermen preferred an area that stretched from Bombah up to Zeytoun Bay in Benghazi, the southwest cove of Greater Syrtis, the shores of Tripoli, the coasts towards the border with Tunisia, and especially Zoara and the coastal areas, which the Kalymnian sponge fishermen also called the "Benches of For" [Μπάγκοι του Φόρου].[184] In the meantime, new seas, rich in sponges, were being discovered at the Gulf of Mexico, in the Antilles and Cuba.

At the same time, constant market expansion was also fueling intense sponge fishing, thus attracting a labour force from neighbouring areas. Indeed,

---

181 An "oka" is a unit of measurement used in Turkey equal to about 2.75 pounds or 1.24 kilograms. Χατζηδάκης, *Η σπογγαλιεία στις Νότιες Σποράδες* [Chatzidakis, *Sponge Fishing in the Southern Sporades*], pp. 232, 234.

182 Φλέγελ, *Η νήσος Κάλυμνος* [Flegel, *The Island Kalymnos*], p. 28. Miltiadis Caravokyro mentions that, from the early 1880s, sponge fishing expanded off the coasts of Tripoli up to Tunisia and Algeria. Caravokyro, *Étude sur la pêche des éponges*, p. 4. On sailing ships' owners from Leros G. Antoniou or Antonello, see Ηλέκτρα Κωστοπούλου, *Η Λέρος* [Ilektra Kostopoulou, *Leros*], p. 91.

183 A. N. Bernardakis, *Le présent et l'avenir de la Grèce*, Paris 1870, p. 37.

184 [Π. Ζώτος], *Έκθεσις περί της ανά τας αφρικανικάς ακτάς διά σκαφάνδρου σπογγαλιείας* P. Zotos, *Report on Sponge Fishing by Diving Suit along the African Coasts*, Athens 1904, p. 3. With respect to the USA, it is worth noting that, at this historical juncture, the intensification and modernization of its fishery was partly due to Greek sponge fishermen who settled in Florida at the beginning of the 20th century, an era during which adverse circumstances in the Mediterranean forced Greek sponge fishermen to seek new lands and better working conditions.

there was steady, seasonal mobility towards Kalymnos, Symi and the other sponge-fishing islands of the Aegean, which often resulted in the permanent settlement of foreigners and their families in sponge-fishing lands. Whether or not these sponge-fishing populations stayed and settled, depended on the profits from sponge fishing. In periods of slowdown in the international demand for sponges, workers either suffered from unemployment and the resultant difficulty in sustaining a livelihood, which compelled them to seek employment in the sponge-bearing regions of Africa and the USA, or they turned to other types of employment, usually far from Kalymnos. By the time the Italo-Turkish war (1911–1912) broke out in Libya there were already communities of Kalymnians in Florida, Marseilles, and Buenos Aires.[185]

War operations, along with the political and diplomatic developments of the period from 1912 to 1922, created extensive problems for the practice of sponge fishing. During the first years of Italian rule, sponge fishing in the Dodecanese went into sharp decline.[186] Changes to the political map of the Mediterranean gave rise to a subsequent reorganization of the available sponge-bearing regions. As of 1912, fishing and sponge fishing off the coast of Turkey was permanently prohibited, whereas the access of Dodecanesian ships to the seas of Libya was gradually facilitated. At the same time, competition with the ships of sponge fishermen from Hydra and Aegina declined because they encountered difficulties in traveling to what was then the Italian coast of Africa. New competitors, however, mainly Italian sponge fishermen, could now fish freely in areas to which they earlier had only limited access due to Turkish control of the largest area of sponge-bearing beds in the Mediterranean.

Italy's Ministry of the Colonies, local governments, the port, as well as customs and consular authorities, exerted control over the organization of sponging activities by imposing tariffs, taxes, monopoly fees, or a deduction of part of the catch, while they imposed restrictions or occasional bans on sponge fishing, mainly on scaphander diving suits and boats with gagavas. In 1913, for instance, in order to preserve the wealth of sponge-bearing seabeds, a ban on sponge fishing on Eastern Syrtis was introduced, while conflicts between Italy and France about the extent of the maritime jurisdictions of Libya and Tunisia occurred on a regular basis. These conflicts had serious

---

185   Doc. 623, 1/7/1915, doc. 639, 1/7/1915, doc. 640, 17/2/1879 and Doc. 661, 4/1/1894, Correspondence 1910–1913, ΜΑΚ.

186   Γεωργάς, *Μελέτη περί σπογγαλιείας* [Georgas, *Study of the Sponge Fishery*], p. 42. During this period, the unstable financial and commercial policy of the Italians, as well as the restriction of local self-government, hampered all business activities of the Greek population.

repercussions for sponge-fishing boats in the area, provoking disputes over permits and the confiscation of catches.[187]

This forced "internationalization" of the sponge-fishing profession generated constant volatility given that fishing areas were often largely inaccessible. In times of political instability, turmoil and wars, the activity was abandoned or simply prohibited, as was the case, for example, in 1914 in Cyrenaica [the Bay of Benghazi, Libya]. Seeking alternative ways out, and safe sponge-bearing areas, Kalymnos remained one of the most important sponge-fishing regions during the 1920s and 1930s,[188] benefiting from the renewal of sponge-bearing beds after their involuntary 'fallow' in periods during hostilities. In contrast, Chalki, which equipped more than 30 groups with scaphander diving suits at the end of the 19th century, had at its disposal only 8 ships in 1912, and shortly thereafter it gave up permanently on sponge fishing.[189]

After the declaration of World War I, sponge fishing was banned in order to accommodate military operations,[190] even though a minimal number of ships was maintained; about 40 over the entire Mediterranean.[191] In its 1916 accounting, the Municipal Council informed the inhabitants of Kalymnos of the municipality's grave financial situation, owing to the fact that the only productive resource of the population, as well as its safest source of revenue, the "local sponge fee", had been handicapped.[192] There are no surviving documents from 1916–1917 on sponge-fishing activity in Kalymnos and, throughout

---

187 Report by the Minister of Finance, L. Koromilas to the Minister of Foreign Affairs G. Streit, Embassy of Tripoli – Libya, Folder 19 (1914), Subfolder 5, ΙΑΥΕ. The competition between the two countries had, on other occasions, a positive impact on Greek sponge fishermen working on Greek and Dodecanesian vessels, since opponents were forced to back down to attract more sponge fishermen. For more on this topic, see the report of the Minister of Finance, L. Koromilas, as well as the letter of the Consul of Tunis to his homologue in Tripoli (22/4/1914). According to Koromilas, rather than renewing the 14 permits that were issued up to 1913, they decided to grant an unspecified number of permits, but they banned scaphander diving suits and gagavas from 1 April to 31 May, while also prohibiting fishing in a depth of less than 20 meters. The relevant documents are found in the Embassy Tripoli-Libya, Folder 19 (1914), Subfolder 5, ΙΑΥΕ. However, before long, the depth restriction for scaphander diving suits was abandoned (26/5/1914).

188 Joseph Sl. Roucek, "Economic Geography of Greece", *Economic Geography* 11 (1935), pp. 100–101.

189 Kolodny, *La population des îles de la Grèce*, p. 313.

190 Roger E. Kasperson, *The Dodecanese. Diversity and Unity in Island Politics*, Chicago 1966, p. 7; Νίκη Γρ. Μπιλλήρη, *Της θάλασσας και της στεριάς* [Niki Gr. Billiri, *Of Sea and Land*], Athens 1986, p. 82.

191 Γεωργάς, *Μελέτη περί σπογγαλιείας* [Georgas, *Study of the Sponge Fishery*], p. 42.

192 Doc. 168, 1/7/1915, doc. 175, 17/2/1879 and Doc. 193, 9/5/1911, MC Minutes 1915–1916, ΜΑΚ.

the war, the local community appears to have been concerned with its financial and food deficit problems, and with handling threatening epidemics. At
the same time, continued immigration flows to the USA and Marseilles were
sizable.[193] Given that all activities had been brought to a halt, the issuance of
permits for sponge fishing with naked divers in several neighbouring sea areas
appears to have held particular interest for the opposing parties in the 1917
municipal elections.[194] The barren island of Kalymnos, with approximately
15,000 inhabitants – second largest island population of the Dodecanese, after
Rhodes – was confronted with famine.[195]

In 1919, the inhabitants of Kalymnos had run out of oars for small boats,
and requested permission to have a boat to bring them from Constantinople.[196]
Here, it is perhaps worth noting that "nowadays, life itself has become difficult" was the response of the municipal authorities that same year, when they
were petitioned to provide municipal servants with shoes so that they would
not have to go barefoot, or when they lent one rural policeman the money he
needed to buy shoes.[197] In 1920, the population of Kalymnos totaled 25,000,[198]
and it is reported that the island also accommodated more than 5,000 refugees from Asia Minor.[199] In spite of the measures that the municipal authority
attempted to adopt in 1920, "circumstances continue[d] to deteriorate [...]
since sponge-fishing activities encounter[ed] major obstacles and the people
[were] not able to carry on fishing".[200] At the same time, there were 1,500 poor
families eligible for free health care.[201]

On 22 January 1921, the Municipality of Kalymnos sent a letter to the
Minister of Finance for the Greek state, emphasizing, among other points of
interest, the following:

> It is well known that our island, like the other sister islands of Symi, Chalki
> and Kastellorizo, as well as the Greek sponge-fishing islands of Aegina,
> Hydra, Spetses and Ermioni, have for centuries now been making a living
> exclusively from sponge fishing, and thereby feeding their poor families.

---

193   Doc. 1000, 23/11/1916 and 1001, 24/12/1916, Correspondence 1915–1917, MAK.
194   Doc. 1071, 16/2/1917, Correspondence 1915–1917, MAK; 13th Conference, 15/6/1917, Minutes
      of Administrative Board 1917–1922, MAK.
195   See scattered reports in MC Minutes, 1917–1922, MAK.
196   Doc. 44, 19/9/1919, Correspondence 1918–1920, MAK.
197   Doc. 27, 24/8/1919, MC Minutes 1919–1922, MAK; Doc. 61, 12/11/1919, MC Minutes 1919–1922,
      MAK.
198   Doc. 19, 16/9/1920, Correspondence 1920–1922, MAK.
199   Doc. 70, 9/10/1920, Correspondence 1920–1922, MAK.
200   Doc. 73, 23/1/1920, MC Minutes 1919–1922, MAK.
201   Doc. 77, 5/2/1920, MC Minutes 1919–1922, MAK.

However, since the eruption of the war across Europe, and prior to it, witnessing their industry's steady decline, the poor inhabitants found themselves compelled to expatriate and to pursue other employment, in order to provide for their poor families. Last year, a few repatriated sponge fishermen, who did not want to see the long-established industry completely ruined, and because they thought that they would achieve the recovery of the once booming traditional industry, volunteered to repeat this toilsome undertaking, and traveled to the shores of Africa. Unfortunately, the results of this sponge-fishing season were unjustifiably unpleasant; as regards the following year, significant disillusionment and complete discouragement are expected where the resumption of the activity is concerned. This disillusionment is the result of numerous causes. The predominant cause, however, is the introduction of exorbitant and irregular tax measures by the governments of the different sea regions: for example, in Cyprus a 25% tax is levied, in Egypt they plan on introducing a similar tax, in Cyrenaica a tax of 3.75 French francs was also introduced by the Italian Trade Union, plus another 5 French francs per kilogram, and in Tunis they impose a heavy lump-sum tariff, whereas in Greece no tax is levied at all.

On this account, they asked for the Greek government's intervention in favour of a more moderate, uniform taxation system so that sponge fishing could continue.[202]

In the wake of the Asia Minor catastrophe, many refugees took shelter in Kalymnos.[203] In November 1922, when the Italian administration prohibited the import and export of commodities, ship departures, and even assemblies, the inhabitants of Kalymnos, having convened in small groups, drafted a resolution, with which they pledged their support to the Municipality, which refused to carry out the population census ordered by the Italian authorities.[204]

In the winter of 1922, only one sponge-fishing ship, with a 54-member crew, worked off the coasts of Libya.[205] Apart from difficult political circumstances, fishermen in Libya encountered various obstacles due to a limited number of permits, delays, and bureaucracy, along with the security deposits that captains paid to local Port Authorities by way of compensation in case of accidents. Many ships had to choose Sfax in Tunisia, even though Libya's fishing areas

---

202   Doc. 110, 29/1/1921, Correspondence 1920–1922, MAK.
203   84th Meeting, 27/9/1922, Minutes of Administrative Board 1917–1922, MAK.
204   Doc. 100, [11/1922], Minutes of Administrative Board 1917–1922, MAK.
205   Embassy Tripoli-Libya, Folder 29 (1923–1924), Subfolder 17, IAYE.

offered more sponges, and of higher quality.[206] Mussolini's policy moreover, significantly deteriorated the lives of the Italian state's Dodecanesian citizens, creating constant problems for their professional and business activities, and the years that followed were particularly difficult for sponge fishing, despite the international increase in the demand for sponges. With the limited fishery of previous years, production prices skyrocketed in 1923, reaching their highest point since the beginning of Italian rule.[207]

Notwithstanding an apparent normalization of the situation in the following years, the number of poor families registered in Kalymnos rose to 120 in 1926, while the Municipality feared that it would soon see a more considerable increase.[208] One of the reasons for the predicted increase was the continuous restriction of sponge fishing, and the high cost of sponge-fishing permits. As stated in the 1926 Greek-Italian trade agreement, half of the sponge-fishing permits for the coasts of Cyrenaica and Tripoli were granted to Greek sponge fishermen, and the other half to Dodecanesian citizens of the Italian state. The annual total number of permits granted was proportionate to the wealth of the area's sponge-bearing beds, which was to be determined by means of an examination.

Despite the equal distribution of permits granted, Dodecanesian sponge fishermen dominated the Libyan area and, in 1926, of the 411 Greek sponge fishermen working around Tripoli, and 360 came from the Dodecanese. However, there was a limited number of permits: in 1927, 12 permits were issued for the Cyrenaica, and 10 for Tripoli, Libya.[209] Given this, Dodecanesians could fish sponges in Greek seas and in the maritime area of Cyprus. Permits issued by the Egyptian authorities were also limited, whereas Turkey sustained its ban on sponge fishing off the coasts of Asia Minor.[210] Nevertheless, the tax levied by the Italian state in 1928 on Dodecanesian sponge-fishing vessels caused new problems for the practice of this activity.[211] Hence by 1929, Kastellorizo manned only two sponge-fishing groups, and the sponge-fishing fleet of Symi

---

206   Report 20/12/1924, Embassy Tripoli-Libya, Folder 29 (1923–1924), Subfolder 17, IAYE.
207   Embassy Tripoli-Libya, Folder 29 (1923–1924), Subfolder 17, IAYE.
208   Doc. 367, 3/6/1926, Correspondence 1925–1927, MAK.
209   Letter of the Greek Consul in Rome to the Vice-Consul in Benghazi, 16/3/1927, Embassy Tripoli-Libya, Folder 34 (1927–1929), Subfolder 1, IAYE.
210   Ελεύθερον Βήμα [Eleftheron Vima], 18/10/1926, p. 1 and 30/10/1926, p. 4; Οικονομικός Ταχυδρόμος [Oikonomikos Tachydromos], 7/11/1926, p. 8; 21/11/1926, p. 8 and 12/12/1926, p. 7. See also Θεόδωρος Α. Κριεζής, "Η σπογγαλιεία", Οικονομικός Ταχυδρόμος [Theodoros A. Kriezis, "Sponge Fishing", Oikonomikos Tachydromos], 14/8/1932, p. 5.
211   Ελεύθερον Βήμα [Eleftheron Vima], 11/2/1928, p. 5.

had shrunk to 14 actively engaged scaphander diving suits, 15 boats with gagavas, and approximately 12 naked divers' boats.[212]

The Italian state's systemic lack of support for the Dodecanese sponge fishery pushed the business into a constant state of recession, especially following
the financial crisis of 1930–1931 when, despite a drop in price, sponges were left
unsold in sponge traders' warehouses.[213] In 1936, the crisis reached a peak with
the sanctions imposed on Italy due to the Italo-Abyssinian War. Yet, in that
same year, about 600 Greek seamen, in addition to Dodecanesians, were working in the Greek maritime area and in the area of Libya.[214] In 1938, estimates
based on Italian statistics placed the unprocessed production of sponges in the
Dodecanese at 55,000 okas (1.282 kilograms).[215] Moreover, the consumption
of natural sponges had already begun to decline, while their price constantly
rose.[216] The declaration of WWII, and especially the German invasion of the
Dodecanese in September 1943, interrupted all sponge-fishing activities.

1.6   Post-War Sponge Fishery

The situation on Kalymnos was dire by the end of WWII. The island's scarce
agricultural resources, commerce, and the few manufacturing activities carried out there had been abandoned, whilst shipbuilding, whose existence was
directly interlinked with sponge fishing, had fallen into desuetude. The withdrawal of the Germans from the Dodecanese in May 1945 was followed by an
almost two-year-long British military administration. Some sponge-fishing
boats did work for a short period of time, from late July to late October 1945,[217]

---

212 Kolodny, *La population des îles de la Grèce*, p. 313–314.
213 Κριεζής, "Η σπογγαλιεία" [Kriezis, "Sponge Fishing"], p. 4. See also comparative data on the
      Greek sponge fishery production in *Οικονομικός Ταχυδρόμος* [*Oikonomikos Tachydromos*],
      7/5/1933, p. 5.
214 *Οικονομικός Ταχυδρόμος* [*Oikonomikos Tachydromos*], 31/5/1937, p. 1.
215 According to Greek sources, it amounted to 68,500 okas. *Δωδεκάνησος. Τετράτομος μελέτη του
      Υπουργείου Ανοικοδομήσεως* [*Dodecanese. Study in Four Volumes Carried out by the Ministry
      for Reconstruction*], pp. 88, 258.
216 Ν. Π. Πιζάνιας, *Φυσικό και τεχνητό σφουγγάρι* [N. P. Pizanias, *Natural and Artificial Sponges*],
      Kalymnos 1952, p. 13.
217 See Γεώργιος Μ. Σακελλαρίδης, "Το λυκαυγές της λύτρωσης. (μεταβατική περίοδος 8.9.1943–
      31.3.1947)", *Καλυμνιακά Χρονικά* [Georgios M. Sakellaridis, "The Twilight of Salvation.
      (Transitional Period 8/9/1943–31/3/1947)", *Kalymniaka Chronika*] 7 (1988), p. 91. By the
      same author see also, "Η οικονομική εξέλιξη της Καλύμνου στα σαράντα πρώτα χρόνια του
      ελευθέρου μας βίου (Διαπιστώσεις και προοπτικές)", *Καλυμνιακά Χρονικά* ["The Economic
      Evolution of Kalymnos in the First Forty Years of Our Free Life (Observations and
      Perspectives)", *Kalymniaka Chronika*] 8 (1989), pp. 127–149.

TABLE 1.1   Sponge-fishing boats (1946)

Islands	Scaphander diving suits	Fernez	Gagavas	Harpoons with hooks	Revera	Total
Kalymnos	20	15 (20)*	5	20 (24)	(10)	60 (54)
Symi	7	–	15	10		32
Astypalaia	2	–	1	1		4
Chalki	1	–	–	4		5
Kastellorizo	–	–	–	–		–
Kos	–	–	7	10		17
Leipsoi	–	–	1	8		9

* The figures in parentheses are taken from a local newspaper article from that time. See «Η εξόρμησις των σφουγγαράδων μας», *Η Κάλυμνος* ["Our Fishermen's Expedition ", *Kalymnos*], Folder 1 (30/8/1946), p. 4.

SOURCE: *ΔΩΔΕΚΑΝΗΣΟΣ. ΤΕΤΡΑΤΟΜΟΣ ΜΕΛΕΤΗ ΤΟΥ ΥΠΟΥΡΓΕΙΟΥ ΑΝΟΙΚΟΔΟΜΗΣΕΩΣ ΔΩΔΕΚΑΝΗΣΟΣ. ΤΕΤΡΑΤΟΜΟΣ ΜΕΛΕΤΗ ΤΟΥ ΥΠΟΥΡΓΕΙΟΥ ΑΝΟΙΚΟΔΟΜΗΣΕΩΣ [DODECANESE. STUDY IN FOUR VOLUMES CARRIED OUT BY THE MINISTRY FOR RECONSTRUCTION]* P. 135

even though part of the 1940–1942 production was amassed and left unsold in the sponge merchants' warehouses, together with the new catch.[218]

The 1945–1947 transitional period was critical for the Dodecanesian island complex on political, social, and financial levels. Commercial activities remained at a standstill, except for sponge fishing and the sponge trade, which enjoyed a prompt and brisk recovery. In 1946, with the unofficial aid of the Agricultural Bank of Greece [Αγροτική Τράπεζα της Ελλάδος, henceforth ATE], Kalymnos manned 60 ships with 1,000 people in total, far exceeding the crews of other islands.

All ships worked in North Africa, Crete, and the Aegean islands; but while the production of 1946 was absorbed by international markets, and at high prices, a new strong competitor arrived on the scene, namely the synthetic sponge which had started winning over consumers and replacing natural sponges in various aspects of manufacturing and in numerous household tasks. What is

---

218   Ν. Ρ. Πιζάνιας, *Για μια καινούργια Κάλυμνο. Σκοπός και καθήκοντα μιας συγχρονισμένης δημοτικής διοικήσεως* [N. R. Pizanias, *For a New Kalymnos: Objectives and Duties of a Synchronized Municipal Administration*], Athens 1950, p. 36.

more, synthetic sponges are much cheaper to produce than fishing for natural sponges.[219]

From 1946 to 1948 Greek sponge producers were able to sell both reserves and new harvests, even though sponges ranked fourth on the list of Greece's exported products.[220] In 1947, based on official calculations, the Greek sponge fishery accounted for about 83% of total Mediterranean sponge production.[221] Harsh post-war financial conditions led to an increase in the workforce involved in sponge fishing and, in a period during which the scaphander diving suit continued to dominate, sponge-fishing expeditions were organized from Kos, Astypalaia and Rhodes, while many natives of Leros sought employment among Kalymnian groups.[222]

In 1947, the ATE facilitated the efforts of Kalymnian sponge fishermen by granting loans of 765,000,000 drachmas, with an interest rate of 8%. In that summer, the fleet's size grew considerably, adding 51 scaphander diving suits, 42 diving suits with Fernez respirators, and 51 boats staffed by a total of 1,441 men. 90% percent of the divers worked on deep-water boats [*vathytika*][223] along the coasts of North Africa,[224] and the sponge catch amounted to 61,252 okas, of which 70% was sold on the American market and 30% on the British and the European markets, yielding a total of 8,500,000,000 drachmas.[225] In 1948, a total of 46 sponge-fishing ships – 27 from Kalymnos, 7 from Symi, and 12 from the remaining Greek sponge-fishing areas – sailed to Libya. Their production

---

219   Πιζάνιας, *Φυσικό και τεχνητό σφουγγάρι* [Pizanias, *Natural and Artificial Sponges*], p. 14.

220   Σωτ. Ι. Αγαπητίδης, "Γενική Εισήγησις εις το Α' Σπογγαλιευτικόν Συνέδριον", Γενική Διοίκησις Δωδεκανήσου. [Sot. I. Agapitidis, "General Statement to the First Colloquium on the Sponge-Fishery", Rhodes 24–27 February 1949. *Papers and Minutes*, General Administration of the Dodecanese] Rhodes 1951, p. 22.

221   *Το Βήμα* [*To Vima*], 17/10/1947, p. 1.

222   Ν. Ρ. Πιζάνιας, *Διά την ανασυγκρότησιν της σπογγαλιείας της Δωδεκανήσου* [N. R. Pizanias, *For the Reform of the Sponge Fishery in the Dodecanese*], Rhodes 1950, p. 5; Testimony of diver Giannis Koutouzis to E.O., 25/8/2003; Testimony of diver Dimitris Peros to E.O., 24/8/2004; Testimony of diver Giannis Loulourgas to E.O., 23/8/2004; Testimony of diver Thrasyvoulos Politis to E.O., 18/8/2004; Testimony of diver Vassilis Konstantaras to E.O, 17/8/2004.

223   For more on "*vathytika*" boats, see below.

224   E. Papataxiarchis, "A Hypothesis on the 1965–1977 Transition in the Socioeconomic Structure of the Sponge-Fishing Industry in Kalymnos", Department of Social Anthropology, London School of Economics, (PhD thesis), p. 15.

225   The data are drawn from an article published in the newspaper *Εθνικός Κήρυξ Νέας Υόρκης* [*Ethnikos Kirix Neas Iorkis*], 21/10/1948, p. 3; Γεώργιος Μ. Σακελλαρίδης, "Η Ελληνική Επαρχία. Η σπογγαλιεία εις την Κάλυμνον", *Καλυμνιακά Χρονικά* [Georgios M. Sakellaridis, "Greek Provinces. Sponge Fishery on Kalymnos", *Kalymniaka Chronika*] 6 (1986), p. 207–208 (article republication from *Εθνικός Κήρυξ Νέας Υόρκης* [*Ethnikos Kirix Neas Iorkis*] 21/10/1948, p. 3). See also the information published in *Βήμα* [*Vima*] 17/10/1947, p. 1.

amounted to a total of 62,943 kg, of which 35,436 kg were caught by Kalymnian caique fishing boats.[226] In October 1948, the ATE made 765,000,000 drachmas in funding available to the sponge fishery, while loans continued to be offered at a favourable interest rate of 8%. The ATE also provided fuel and other supplies at prices fixed by the state.[227] According to a report from 1949, written by the Greek Port Consul[228] at Benghazi, 46 sponge-fishing ships worked off the coasts of Cyrenaica, of which 34 came from the Dodecanese; 15 Fernez boats from Kalymnos, 7 gagavas from Kalymnos and Symi, 14 boats for divers with harpoons with hooks from Hydra and Ermioni, and 6 boats with naked divers from Kalymnos and Symi. In that year, in total 1,302 people were employed: 518 divers and 784 crew members.[229]

During the first decade following WWII this productive sector, in which the Dodecanese played a vital role, constituted a significant source of foreign exchange for the Greek state. In 1950, 25 sponge-fishing ships (of which 2 Kalymnian), 25 gagavas (of which 3 from Kalymnos), 25 boats equipped for sponge fishing with hooks (of which 16 were from Kalymnos), went fishing in Greek territorial waters. In the same year, 47 sponge-fishing vessels (40 from Kalymnos), 14 vessels with Fernez equipment from Kalymnos, and 10 boats with naked divers all from Kalymnos worked in the maritime area of Libya.[230] In 1952, 17 scaphander diving suits and 13 auxiliary ships were employed in Libya; of which 7 (all of them "vathytika") and 4 others that originated from Kalymnos.[231] In 1952, the overseer of sponge fisheries in Libya justified the fleet's increase based on loans granted by the ATE. In fact, he wrote that "this [increase] should be attributed to the fact that the ATE, by widely granting loans for sponge-fishing expeditions, stimulated the formation of new groups, especially in Kalymnos, where the number of the sponge-fishing boats

---

226 Embassy Tripoli-Libya, Folder 45 (1947–1948), Subfolder 3, IAYE.

227 Γιώργης Μ. Σακελλαρίδης, "Μιχαήλ Νεοκλέους Καλαβρός", *Καλυμνιακά Χρονικά* [Giorgis M. Sakellarides, "Michail Neokleous Kalavros", *Kalymniaka Chronika*] 7 (1988), pp. 133–135. Σωτήριος Αγαπητίδης, "Μεταπολεμικαί εξελίξεις εις την ελληνικήν σπογγαλιείαν", *Δωδεκάνησος* [Sotirios Agapitides, "Post-War Developments in the Greek Sponge Fishery", *Dodekanissos*] 6 (1957), p. 39; and Αντ. Παπακωνσταντίνου, "Σπογγαλιευτική και αλιευτική δραστηριότητα (Από τη σκοπιά της Αγροτικής Τράπεζας)", *Καλυμνιακά Χρονικά* [Ant. Papakonstantinou, "Sponge Fishing and Fishing Activity (From the Perspective of the ATE)", *Kalymniaka Chronika*] 2 (1981), p. 164–167; Σακελλαρίδης, Η Ελληνική Επαρχία [Sakellaridis, "Greek Province"], pp. 207–208.

228 Editors' note: "Port consuls" were Greek port authorities' officials in Greek Consulates established in ports around the world, to provide services to Greek vessels.

229 Report 25/10/1949, Embassy Tripoli-Libya, Folder 45 (1947–1948), Subfolder 3, IAYE.

230 *Αθηναϊκά Νέα* [*Athinaika Nea*], 30/12/1950, p. 6.

231 Embassy Tripoli-Libya, Folder 46 (1952), Subfolder 4, IAYE.

manned each year has doubled since 1948".[232] In the 1954 sponge-fishing season, Greek sponge production yielded a total of 81,311 kg, mostly harvested along the coasts of Cyrenaica, where 43 sponge-fishing boats and 35 auxiliary boats were operating.[233]

In the post-war era the Dodecanesian contribution to overall sponge-fishing activities did not undergo significant change when compared with the pre-war period. In 1938, for example, 2,395 people were employed in 237 ships, whereas in 1949 there were 2,405 employed aboard 221 ships.[234] Although pre-war figures were higher in total,[235] the change that occurred after WWII amounted to a gradual decline in activity in most sponge-fishing areas (such as in Chalki and Kastellorizo), and the simultaneous growth of Kalymnian sponge fishing. Throughout this period, Kalymnos yielded two thirds of the entire Greek sponge production (a total of 100–115 tons), which employed 1,000–1,500 men in Kalymnos, as well as 250–300 more men and women who were involved in sponge processing.[236] At the same time, Kalymnian sponge merchants continued to control European markets.

Given that sponge fishing constituted a dynamic sector of the Greek post-war economy, especially after the Dodecanese islands' annexation by the Greek state, various institutions made systematic efforts to stimulate productivity, and to streamline organization. In Rhodes in 1949, the General Administration of the Dodecanese organized the first and only Pan-Hellenic conference on the sponge fishing industry. Participants included executive members of the National Bank of Greece, the Commercial Bank of Greece and the ATE, representatives from the political sphere, specialized scientists, representatives of

---

232   "Έκθεσις εν σχέσει με την διεξαγωγήν της σπογγαλείας εις τα παράλια της Λιβύης κατά την θερινή περίοδον 1952" ["Report on Sponge Fishing off the Coasts of Libya in the Summer Season of 1952"], Lieutenant Commander Em. A. Koutsikopoulos, Sponge Fishery Overseer, Tripoli 28/11/1952, Embassy Tripoli-Libya, Folder 46 (1952), Subfolder 4, IAYE.

233   Οικονομικός Ταχυδρόμος [Oikonomikos Tachydromos], 6/1/1955, p. 12.

234   "Η σπογγαλιεία έχει εγκαταλειφθεί", Η Μάχη ["The Sponge Fishery Has Been Abandoned", I Machi], 25/3/1950, p. 6. For more on the dynamics of the pre-war and post-war sponge fishery, see Πιζάνιας, Διά την ανασυγκρότησιν της σπογγαλιείας [Pizanias, For the Reform of the Sponge Fishing Industry], pp. 5–6.

235   Greek pre-war production amounted to 200 tons, 26–27 tons of which were caught in Libya, whereas the annual production of the Dodecanese islands amounted to approximately 80 tons. See "Η σπογγαλιεία έχει εγκαταλειφθεί", Η Μάχη ["The Sponge Fishery Has Been Abandoned", I Machi], 25/3/1950, p. 6.

236   Αγαπητίδης, "Μεταπολεμικαί εξελίξεις εις την ελληνικήν σπογγαλιείαν" [Agapitidis, "Post-War Developments in the Greek Sponge Fishing Industry"], p. 39; Μιλτιάδης Λογοθέτης, "Επιβάλλεται η λήψις σειράς μέτρων διά την ενίσχυσιν του εμπορίου σπόγγων", Οικονομικός Ταχυδρόμος [Miltiadis Logothetis, "The Adoption of a Number of Measures to Boost the Sponge Trade", Oikonomikos Tachydromos], 12/11/1959, p. 9.

captains', divers', and sponge merchants' unions from all over Greece, as well as Dodecanesian dignitaries.[237]

The topics discussed during the conference were funding, organization and the staffing of sponge-fishing ventures; terms of employment for crews; sponge-fishing areas; and the embargo on Greek sponge fishing along the coasts of North Africa. According to press reports, contrary to expectations, and in spite of plans for the conference, a number of participants claimed that sponge fishing was a barbaric labour sector, albeit necessary for the survival of the population, and that it ought to be eradicated or at least modernized and restricted.[238] More specifically, the conference concluded with a series of proposals for the improvement of working conditions for sponge fishing, and the performance of related activities. Cited here, along with other documents, is the introduction to a professional diver's personal documentation and certification, the contents of which include an outline of the diet aboard sponge-fishing vessels, the creation of a divers' fund, the inclusion of sponge-fishing crews in the Seamen's Pension Fund [Ναυτικό Απομαχικό Ταμείο – NAT], the promotion of a cooperative organization, and the securing of long-term, low-interest loans by the ATE, and so on. Finally, with regards to sponge-fishing areas, there was a general request put forward for free, tax-exempt access to all Mediterranean sponge-fishing beds.[239]

In order to address the concerns just outlined, an advisory council on sponge fishing was set up in 1951, with Sotirios Agapitidis and Nikolaos Pizanias, who were employees of the Ministry of Coordination at the time, in the roles of chairman and secretary respectively. Their mission was to coordinate the various bodies managing the organization of the sponge fishery, namely the Ministries of Foreign Affairs, Maritime Affairs, Agriculture, and Commerce, as well as the NAT and the ATE. In addition, beginning in 1950, an inspection of the Dodecanese islands' sponge-fishing vessels by a special coast guard committee was scheduled, and sponge fishermen were required to take a medical examination prior to departure.[240]

---

237 Α´ Πανελλήνιον Σπογγαλιευτικόν Συνέδριον [The First Colloquium on the Sponge Fishery, Rhodes 24–27 February 1949, *Papers and Minutes*] Γενική Διοίκησις Δωδεκανήσου [General Administration of the Dodecanese], Rhodes 1951. See also Αγαπητίδης, "Μεταπολεμικοί εξελίξεις εις την ελληνικήν σπογγαλιείαν" [Agapitidis, "Post-War Developments in the Greek Sponge Fishery"], p. 39.

238 *Το Βήμα* [*To Vima*], 24–26/2/1949; *Ελευθερία* [*Eleftheria*], 15/3/1949, p. 4; *Τα Νέα* [*Ta Nea*], 24/2/1949, p. 4 and 25/2/1949, p. 4.

239 *Το Βήμα* [*To Vima*], 27/2/1949, p. 6 and 1/3/1949, p. 5.

240 *Η Μάχη* [*I Machi*], 23/3/1950, p. 3.

A handful of press articles and studies about the "reorganization" of sponge fishing were written about these initiatives of the 1950s, mainly by local employees of the bodies and organizations just mentioned. It is also worth noting that loans from Marshall Plan capital were also issued for the technological modernization of the sponge-fishing fleet.[241]

The most acute problem that the Greek sponge fishery encountered after WWII was securing adequate, favorable conditions for sailing and operating in sponge-bearing areas. Indeed, with efforts to restructure the sponge-fishing fleet, and in spite of an obvious bias for the African coasts, crews from the Dodecanese islands occasionally undertook sponge fishing in the Greek seas[242] and, in the years that followed, sponge fishers came up against restrictive or prohibitive measures introduced by the Mediterranean countries in possession of the richest sponge-bearing areas. Turkey had prohibited fishing in its waters since 1923, whereas other states, such as Egypt and Cyprus, imposed a restriction on the number of sponge-fishing permits granted, and issued them at high prices.

It should, moreover, be born in mind that these restrictions were not temporary. They were continuous and severe, and soon created insurmountable problems for the Greek sponge fishery. Hence, beginning in the 1950s, the Egyptian government issued a limited number of permits at a high price. As a result, many of the permits were leased by speculators, who took up to 40% of the sponge haul.[243] Furthermore, Egypt demanded that Greek crews employ local sailors and divers; pay a 5% levy on the sponge yield; and process sponges on site. These demands led to the curtailment of sponge fishing in the Egyptian seas,[244] and even their removal, for a number of years from the list of possible destinations for Greek sponge-fishing boats.[245] What is more, the Egyptian Sponge-Fishing Company, founded in 1947, held the exclusive rights to exploit the country's sponge-bearing beds, and forced Greek

241 *Τα Νέα* [*Ta Nea*], 27/3/1952, p. 4 and 1/4/1952, p. 1.

242 Captain Lefteris Mamouzelos reports that, in 1953, everyone worked in the Greek seas at the "upper part". In particular, he had worked around Serifos. Testimony of Lefteris Mamouzelos to E.O. 3/9/2004.

243 Π. Πιζάνιας, "Η σπογγαλιεία της Δωδεκανήσου" [P. Pizanias, "The Sponge Fishery of the Dodecanese"], *Ελευθερία* [*Eleftheria*], 1/7/1944, p. 3; Αγαπητίδης, "Γενική Εισήγησις εις το Α' Σπογγαλιευτικόν Συνέδριον" [Agapitidis, "General Statement to the First Colloquium on the Sponge Fishery"], p. 19.

244 Πιζάνιας, *Διά την ανασυγκρότησιν της σπογγαλιείας* [Pizanias, *For the Reform of Sponge Fishery*], p. 16. See also *Το Βήμα* [*To Vima*], 19/6/1949, p. 3 and 8/5/1952, p. 4.

245 Report of Ministry for Foreign Affairs, 7/11/1951, Embassy Tripoli-Libya, Folder 46 (1952), Subfolder 4, IAYE.

sponge fishermen to sell their catch there.[246] In 1951, the Greek government
and the Egyptian Sponge-Fishing Company signed an agreement under which
they granted 20 sponge-fishing permits. The fee for a permit was either 17.5%
of the catch or 1,750 Egyptian lira and, in that same year, it was also required
that the entire sponge haul remain in Egypt until 30 November. Only that
portion of the haul that was not sold by that date could be transferred and distributed to other markets.[247] Finally, in 1967, Egypt banned Greek boats from
fishing sponges in its seas all together.

Beginning in the mid-19th century, sponge fishers also operated in Libyan
seas on a regular basis, given the Ottoman, followed by Italian, rule over the
Dodecanese and Libya. Here again however, their leeway was restricted after
1946 and,[248] when Libya was recognized as an independent state in 1953, it
set restrictive conditions, especially for the Cyrenaica area. Following negotiations, a four-year agreement (1954–1958) was concluded, authorizing
40 Greek sponge-fishing groups per year in exchange for 500 lira per group. The
Greek state also assumed the obligation to purchase 1,500 tons of slaughtered
livestock annually, as a means of boosting local animal husbandry,[249] and then,
in 1952, a sponge-fishing monopoly company was established, that obliged
sponge fishermen to sell part of their catch in Libya.[250] Along with the above
requirements and the difficulties in acquiring permits, a mandatory recruitment scheme was also put in place in 1952, whereby local sailors and divers
had to be taken aboard Greek boats in order to learn sponge fishing, and this
came with a temporary restriction on access to Cyrenaica for Greek sponge-
fishing ships.[251]

---

246   Report of the Governor of the ATE to the Ministry for Foreign Affairs, 29/10/1951, Embassy
       Tripoli-Libya, Folder 46 (1952), Subfolder 4, IAYE.
247   Doc. dated 9/4/1951, Embassy Tripoli-Libya, Folder 46 (1952), Subfolder 4, IAYE.
248   Δωδεκάνησος. Τετράτομος μελέτη του Υπουργείου Ανοικοδομήσεως [Dodecanese. Study in Four
       Volumes Carried out by the Ministry for Reconstruction], pp. 76–78.
249   Αγαπητίδης, Μεταπολεμικαί εξελίξεις εις την ελληνικήν σπογγαλιείαν [Agapitidis, Post-War
       Developments in the Greek Sponge Fishery], p. 40. See also the relevant information for
       the period 1947–1950 discussed in Πιζάνιας, Για μια καινούργια Κάλυμνο [Pizanias, For a New
       Kalymnos], pp. 37–38.
250   Embassy Tripoli-Libya, Folder 46 (1952), Subfolder 4, IAYE.
251   Report of the Vice-Consul, 19/12/1951 and 15/2/1952, Embassy Tripoli-Libya, Folder 46
       (1952), Subfolder 4, IAYE; "Έκθεσις εν σχέσει με την διεξαγωγήν της σπογγαλιείας εις τα παρά-
       λια της Λιβύης κατά την θερινή περίοδον 1952", ["Report on the Sponge Fishery off the Coasts
       of Libya in the Summer Season 1952"], Lieutenant commander Em. A. Koutsikopoulos,
       Sponge Fishery Overseer, Tripoli 28/11/1952, Embassy Tripoli-Libya, Folder 46 (1952),
       Subfolder 4, IAYE.

Due to these adverse conditions, the results usually fell short of expectations, while sponge-fishing fleets and production were gradually decreasing,[252] so that by the late 1950s, crews employed 500 divers and 250 seamen. The number of ships also decreased in the 1960s[253] and sponge production declined to 70–85 tons per year.[254] It is also notable that Hydra, which island possessed two thirds of the Greek sponge-fishing fleet by the close of World War II, and boasted more than 60% of sponge-fishing crews, ended up almost abandoning sponge fishing by the end of the 1950s.[255] During that same period, the Greek press often featured articles on high fees and the expulsion of sponge fishermen from the fishing areas of Tunisia and Libya.[256]

Kalymnian sponge production continued to decline and, by 1961, two thirds thereof originated in the seas of Libya. The Greek government continued to pursue negotiations with Libya up until 1964, however, the terms proposed by Libya, namely that the recruitment of a local captain for the Greek ships would be conducted at the ship owner's expense and that 20–25% of the catch was to be held back, were considered particularly harsh.[257] By 1965 there were 511 people involved in sponge fishing, including 261 divers,[258] and negotiations were conducted again in 1968, resulting in a new agreement with the government of Libya.[259] In 1972 however, Libya followed Egypt in prohibiting sponge fishing in its maritime territory.

The British administration in Cyprus similarly created serious obstacles for Greek sponge fishermen, by allowing sponge harvesting on its coasts every four years only, while it withheld 25% of the catch.[260] Sponge fishing in Cypriot maritime territories was also temporarily discontinued in 1955[261] and, by means of a law enacted in 1968, the Democracy of Cyprus forced all those sponge fishing

252 Τὸ Βῆμα [To Vima], 29/1/1955, p. 4; Οἰκονομικός Ταχυδρόμος [Oikonomikos Tachydromos], 8/11/1956, p. 10.

253 See Οἰκονομικός Ταχυδρόμος [Oikonomikos Tachydromos], 17/12/1959, p. 7 and 7/3/1957, p. 10, as well as Ἐλευθερία [Eleftheria] 12/2/1967, p. 3.

254 Ν. Παπαδημητρίου, "Οἱ κυνηγοί τῶν βυθῶν" [N. Papadimitriou, "The Hunters of the Bottom of the Sea"], Ἐλευθερία [Eleftheria], 12/2/1967, p. 3.

255 Kolodny, La population des îles de la Grèce, p. 314.

256 See also Οἰκονομικός Ταχυδρόμος [Oikonomikos Tachydromos], 6/8/1959, p. 10.

257 Ταχυδρόμος [Tachydromos], 1/4/1964, p. 1.

258 Bernard Russell, "Kalymnos: The Island of the Sponge Fishermen", Annals of the New York Academy of Sciences 268 (1976), p. 303.

259 Οἰκονομικός Ταχυδρόμος [Oikonomikos Tachydromos], 16/5/1968, p. 11.

260 Τὸ Βῆμα [To Vima], 17/10/1947, p. 1.

261 Ἀγαπητίδης, Μεταπολεμικαί ἐξελίξεις εἰς τὴν ἑλληνικήν σπογγαλιείαν [Agapitidis, Post-War Developments in the Greek Sponge Fishery], p. 40.

in its territorial waters to have previously acquired special authorization, and forbade the use of the gagava.[262]

Furthermore, the Western European demand for sponges declined, prices dropped, and part of the Greek sponge production was channeled to USA markets at low prices. Nevertheless, large quantities of the 1949, 1950 and 1952 sponge harvest remained unsold.[263] Although the sponge was an entirely exportable product, particularly important to the Greek economy, sales and employee figures showed a downward trend in this period[264] while, beginning in the mid-1950s, the highest rate of population emigration to elsewhere (i.e. Australia) was from the Dodecanese.[265] In spite of a temporary recovery in the Greek sponge fishery – and only in specific years – up to the end of the 1950s, in the years that followed, the trend was downward because production costs remained high and the artificial sponge constantly seemed to win out over natural sponges.[266] This synthetic product, which was already being manufactured from viscose in the early 1930s, threatened Greek sponge fishery, as it served as a natural sponge substitute for most household and industrial purposes. In response to a similar downward trend in the 1960s, Symi gave up all sponge-fishing activities and at the end of the same decade, the sponge fishery also declined drastically on Kalymnos.

Moreover, each year permits for Egypt and Tunisia took longer to be issued, and Kalymnians' interest in the trade was also waning in spite of the fact that international markets were still interested in natural sponges.[267] In the 1960s and 1970s, it was the coastal populations of Libya and Tunisia that invested in sponge fishing on a regular basis, and later Croatia, whereas production in Syria and Turkey was also significantly declining in the same period.[268]

---

262 The "Law on Sponge Fishing" of the Republic of Cyprus, 1968.

263 Πιζάνιας, *Διά την ανασυγκρότησιν της σπογγαλιείας* [Pizanias, *For the Reform of the Sponge Fishery*], p. 18–19; Γιάννης Μαρίνος, "Πώς άρχισε η μετανάστευση από την Κάλυμνο στην Αυστραλία", *Καλυμνιακά Χρονικά* [Giannis Marinos, "How Immigration from Kalymnos to Australia Began", *Kalymniaka Chronika*] 15 (2003), p. 429.

264 See also the tables published in *Οικονομικός Ταχυδρόμος* [*Oikonomikos Tachydromos*], 30/1/1964, p. 7.

265 B. Kayser, *Ανθρωπογεωγραφία της Ελλάδος* [*Anthropogeography of Greece*], Athens 1968, p. 85.

266 *Οικονομικός Ταχυδρόμος* [*Oikonomikos Tachydromos*], 19/6/1944, p. 1 and 21/8/1944, p. 1. See also the idea for the 1960s production in *Οικονομικός Ταχυδρόμος* [*Oikonomikos Tachydromos*], 7/5/1964, p. 5 and 7/4/1966, p. 150.

267 *Το Βήμα* [*To Vima*], 12/5/1964, p. 6 and 11/3/1966, p. 8.

268 E. Voultsiadou, T. Dailianis, C. Antoniadou, D. Vafidis, C. Dounas and C. Chintiroglou, "Aegean Bath Sponges: Historical Data and Current Status", *Reviews in Fisheries Science* 19 (2011), p. 42.

In the face of these considerations, which led to a steady decline in the industry in other sponge-fishing centres, Kalymnos was the only island that seemed able to maintain its sponge-fishing activities and significant annual production until the 1970s.[269] Many Kalymnian sponge merchants also purchased sponges from various areas of the Mediterranean, transported them to Kalymnos for processing, and then exported them from there. Nevertheless, due to numerous difficulties and a slowdown in demand, those involved in the pre-war activity could no longer be employed, although some were already unemployed or had been under-employed for several years. Internal and transatlantic migration, along with offers of employment in Belgian mines, opened new prospects for Dodecanese spongers.

In April 1960, 35 sponge-fishing vessels with 682 men sailed from Kalymnos,[270] whereas in May 1961, that number had shrunk to 28 boats with 800 men, working off the coasts of Cyrenaica and in the Greek seas.[271] Sponge production in 1962 amounted to 68,400 kg, and Kalymnos with, 45,800 kg, was the largest single producer in the overall annual production, followed by Lemnos with 14,500 kg. However, the total number of 944 people employed in 1952 had decreased to 457 by 1962, for a total reduction of more than 50%.[272] By the end of the decade, that number had decreased to 229, while the importance of sponge fishing, as well as that of fishery in general, was very limited in national production, as well as in exports of the Greek state.

After 1970, all the aforementioned problems multiplied and were joined by others, such as the exhaustion of sponge beds or illnesses that killed sponges, rendering sponge-bearing areas defunct. Ongoing restrictions to fishing off the coasts of North African countries, competition with American sponge production, as well as the wide use of artificial sponges, pushed the Greek sponge fishery into further decline.[273] The islanders themselves also opted for other ways to earn a living – including emigration – rather than take on the particularly dangerous profession of sponge diving.

Since 1972, Kalymnos' sponge fishery had been restricted to the Greek maritime territory and, in spite of the financial slowdown after the crisis of 1974,

---

269   Μαρία Ζαΐρη, "Οι αποθήκες των σφουγγαριών", *Καλυμνιακά Χρονικά* [Maria Zairi, "Sponge Storehouses", *Kalymniaka Chronika*] 15 (2003), p. 418.

270   Kolodny, *La population des îles de la Grèce*, p. 315. Other sources mention 24 boats. See *To Βήμα* [*To Vima*], 21/4/1960, p. 5.

271   *Το Βήμα* [*To Vima*], 7/5/1961, p. 6.

272   *Οικονομικός Ταχυδρόμος* [*Oikonomikos Tachydromos*], 30/1/1964, p. 7.

273   For more on artificial sponges, see Πιζάνιας, *Φυσικό και τεχνητό σφουγγάρι* [Pizanias, *Natural and Artificial Sponges*], Kalymnos 1952; Αγαπητίδης, "Γενική Εισήγησις" [Agapitidis, "General Statement"], p. 22.

spongers still made up 10% of the island's workforce.[274] With the aid of loans and subsidies, the industry was maintained in Kalymnos in the following years and, in 1981, 60 Kalymnian vessels, of a total of about 80 vessels, were engaged in sponge fishing.[275] In 1983–1984, there were 50 to 60 active sponge-fishing boats in Kalymnos, employing a total of 200–250 men, and yielding an annual production of about 30 tons. However, by the end of 1983, only 60% of the production had been sold, due to stiff competition from Cuba and the USA, which were much larger producers, and their prices were more competitive.[276] Many believed that the sponge fishery's sole remedy lay in securing permits for the unexploited North African coasts still rich in sponges.[277]

1985 appears to have been a good year for the few remaining Kalymnian spongers – and probably their last good year. As stated in various reports, sponge prices ranged from 8,000 drachmas per kg, whereas each diver's share exceeded 1,000,000 drachmas for a 4-to-5-month working period in Greek waters.[278] At the same time moreover, the three artificial sponge manufactures operating on the island mostly exported their products to the USA.[279] In 1986, a serious disease ravaged the remaining Aegean Sea reserves, and only four ships continued to work in the maritime area of Sicily, where they harvested 8 tons of sponges. In the following year, on account of an agreement concluded with Egypt, only 10 sponge-fishing boats were granted a permit with a 30% share demanded from the catch.

In addition, sponge prices dropped yet further hence, if one considers that prior to WWII, a family could live for one month on the price of one oka [1.2829 kilograms, see footnote 26] of sponges, in 1950 the same amount sufficed for only 15 days.[280] Moreover, production had shrunken considerably in comparison with previous years: in 1975 production amounted to 25.5 tons,

---

274   Bernard Russell, "The Fisherman and His Wife", in William Mernard, Jane Schieber (ed.), *Oceans: Our Continuing Frontier*, California 1976, p. 304; Τὸ Βῆμα [*To Vima*], 13/11/1984, p. 6.

275   Γεώργιος Μ. Σακελλαρίδης, "Ἀλιεία, Σπογγαλιεία", *Καλυμνιακά Χρονικά* [Georgios M. Sakellaridis, "Sponge Fishery", *Kalymniaka Chronika*] 2 (1981), p. 172. Τὸ Βῆμα [*To Vima*], 14/3/1982, p. 13.

276   Γεώργιος Μ. Σακελλαρίδης, Προβλήματα καὶ προοπτικές ἁλιείας καὶ σπογγαλιείας, *Καλυμνιακά Χρονικά* [Georgios M. Sakellaridis, *Problems and Perspectives of Fishery and Sponge Fishery*, *Kalymniaka Chronika*] 3 (1982), p. 168; Γ. Ρ., "Μανόλης Ἀριστοτέλη Μαγκλῆς", *Καλυμνιακά Χρονικά* [G. R., "Manolis Aristotelis Magklis", *Kalymniaka Chronika*] 4 (1984), p. 262.

277   Σακελλαρίδης, Προβλήματα καὶ προοπτικές ἁλιείας [Sakellaridis, *Problems and Perspectives of Fishery*], pp. 168–169.

278   Γ. Μ. Σακελλαρίδης, "Σχολιάζοντας τὴν ἐπικαιρότητα. Ἀπόλλων-Θάλασσα", *Καλυμνιακά Χρονικά* [G. M. Sakellaridis, "Commenting on Current Affairs: Apollo-Sea", *Kalymniaka Chronika*] 6 (1986), p. 407–21.

279   Σακελλαρίδης, "Σχολιάζοντας τὴν ἐπικαιρότητα" [Sakellaridis, "Commenting on Current Affairs"], p. 412.

280   Πιζάνιας, *Γιὰ μιὰ καινούργια Κάλυμνο* [Pizanias, *For a New Kalymnos*], p. 11.

when 300 families on the island were involved in sponge fishing.[281] In 1977, of the 118 divers working on Kalymnos' sponge-fishing boats, 60 were Egyptian, according to data from the local Port Authority.[282]

From the 1970s on, the decline in the industry also led to a decrease in the duration of fishing voyages so that, of the sponge-fishing vessels that would previously have returned to the island in August for the feast of the Virgin Mary and stayed, a few left again for a brief autumn expedition in early September, when weather on the Greek seas was milder. Although the ATE increased the maximum amount of funding available to improve the equipment on sponge-fishing boats, the Greek sponge fishery was almost extinct.[283] In 1981 and 1982, sponge fishing was restricted to the Greek seas with 55 vessels; in 1983, the sponge-fishing fleet of Kalymnos had decreased to 25 vessels, while part of the previous years' production remained unsold.[284]

A comprehensive picture of sponge-fishing vessel departures from the port of Kalymnos in the period from 1975 to 2003 may be found in the Table 1.2, which was compiled with processed data from the "Master Muster Roll of the Port Authority" of Kalymnos.[285] The figures do not provide an accurate account of the number of ships, as only departures are listed,[286] but they do attest to the decline of the Kalymnian sponge fishery. The disease that afflicted sponges in 1986–1987 caused extensive damage to the sponge-bearing beds of the Aegean and put sponge fishing on hold for almost two years.[287]

---

281 Papataxiarchis, "A Hypothesis on the 1965–1977 Transition in the Socioeconomic Structure of the Sponge-Fishing Industry in Kalymnos", Department of Social Anthropology, London School of Economics, p. 3; Roxane Caftanzoglou, " Kalymnos: Contribution à la connaissance d'une société ", Honours MA thesis in Ethnology, (unpublished), Paris, 1978, p. 26.

282 Roxane Caftanzoglou, Kalymnos, p. 26.

283 *Οικονομικός Ταχυδρόμος* [*Oikonomikos Tachydromos*], 12/8/1971, p. 10.

284 *Το Βήμα* [*To Vima*], 6/5/1981, p. 11; *Τα Νέα* [*Ta Nea*]. 8/4/1982, p. 10 and 28/4/1983, p. 5.

285 Logs kept at the "Master Muster Roll of the Kalymnos' Port Authority", found at the Port Authority of Kalymnos.

286 In "Ναυτιλιακές δραστηριότητες στην Κάλυμνο", *Καλυμνιακά Χρονικά* ["Maritime Activities on Kalymnos", *Kalymniaka Chronika*] 8 (1989), pp. 195–212, Maria Zairi provides the following information on the year 1988: From January to April 1988, 23 sponge-fishing vessels sailed from the island, 17 equipped with the nargile system and the rest with revera. From May to October 1988, 27 ships departed in total: 14 with narghile and 13 with revera. Of these, only 5 were employed in sponge fishing in both fishing sessions. It is reported that Kalymnos' sponge-fishing fleet consisted of a total of 45 vessels, whereas the number of divers is estimated at 80 men. Other sources indicate that, in the same year, the sponge-fishing fleet totalled 60 ships, with crews totalling 150. See E. Voultsiadou et al., "Aegean Bath Sponges", p. 38.

287 Elda Gaino, Roberto Pronzato, "Epidemie e pesca intensive minacciano la sopravvivenza delle spugne commerciali del bacino mediterraneo", *Bollettino dei musei e degli istituti biologici dell'Universita di Genova*, 56–57 (1992), pp. 209–224; Roberto Pronzato, "Sponge

TABLE 1.2   Sponge-fishing vessels departing from the port of Kalymnos

Year	Nargiles	Revera	Harpoons with hooks	Deposito (auxiliary vessel)	Fernez	Scaphander diving suit	Gagava	Autonomous device
1975	19	13	2	1	1	1	3	
1976	22	16			2		2	1
1977	14	25			1		3	
1978	21	44					3	
1979	25	29			1		2	
1980	1	1			1			
1981	16	18					2	
1982	23	38					2	
1983	39	42					2	
1984	23	14					2	
1985	28	23					1	
1986	34							
1987	31							
1988	45							
1989	41							
1990	54							
1991	26							
1992	20							
1993	11							
1994	18							
1995	2							
1996	9							
1997	11							
1998	11							
1999	21							
2000	5							
2001	3							
2002	6							
2003	5							

SOURCE: PROCESSED DATA FROM THE "MASTER MUSTER ROLL OF THE PORT AUTHORITY" OF KALYMNOS

Although it is widely attributed to the Chernobyl nuclear accident,[288] there is no proof to support this hypothesis, given that "sponge disease" has afflicted various maritime areas all over the Mediterranean multiple times. Its typical symptoms are the white spots on the sponge's surface, which then loses its consistency and crumbles easily. As one would expect, the disease impacted the local economy, while giving rise to migration flows to the USA and Australia, while the sponge businesses turned to imports from Florida and the Caribbean.

At the same time, a shift to tourism was stimulated by the arrival of small family businesses. By way of illustration, in 1992 sponge production was reduced to 3,000 tons, from the 30,000 tons harvested in 1986.[289] In 1999, the disease cropped up again without, however, destroying most of the sponge-bearing beds the Mediterranean,[290] while some areas remained unaffected. The cause of the disease's reappearance is still unknown although it has been widely attributed to the pollution of the Mediterranean, severe earthquakes in 1986 and 1999, and the increase in the temperature of deep waters.[291]

The shift to alternative activities necessitated making unwelcome choices for Kalymnians, such as migration and tourism and, as early as the 1980s, various municipal authorities and the local community began to focus on the promotion of diving for tourists. At the same time, given the difficult and dangerous work of sponge fishing, from which one could expect only an unsteady income, it now seemed a less than optimal career choice and a profession that was doomed to disappear. The fishing sector replaced sponge fishing and absorbed part of the sector's crews, hence by the mid-1990s, 1,200 people, about 25% of the island's workers, turned to organized fishing, especially tuna fishing, regularly exporting their product to the European Union and Japan.

Mediterranean sponge-bearing beds are no longer rich in sponges. Intensive overfishing over the course of roughly two centuries, as well as persistent diseases that afflict sponges, make their further harvesting unsustainable. Moreover, climate change and sea pollution create constant problems and

Fishing, Disease and Farming in the Mediterranean Sea", *Aquatic Conservation: Marine and Freshwater Ecosystems* 9 (1999), pp. 487–488; Roberto Pronzato, Renata Manconi, "Mediterranean Commercial Sponges: Over 5000 Years of Natural History and Cultural Heritage", *Marine Ecology* 29 (2008), p. 150.

288   Faith Warm, *Bitter Sea: The Real Story of Greek Sponge Diving*, London 2000, pp. 92–93; Testimony of Nikolas Kampourakis to E.O., 25/8/2002.

289   David E. Sutton, *Memories Cast in Stone: The Relevance of the Past in Everyday Life*, Oxford, New York, 1998, p. 24.

290   Roberto Pronzato, "Sponge-Fishing Disease", pp. 488–489.

291   E. Voultsiadou et. al., "Aegean Bath Sponges", p. 35.

dramatically decrease healthy sponge reserves. It is not surprising therefore that, by the early 2000s, only about 10 sponge-fishing caiques were left in Kalymnos, with crews of 25–30, many of the members of which crews were already retired and did not have official permits. In 2005, the Diving School that began operating on Kalymnos in 1956 shut down. As of 2010, based on data provided by the Union of Kalymnos' Sponge Fishermen, there are 15–17 vessels with 100–120 people, and an annual production of about 4 tons. Sponges are harvested chiefly with nargile, and a very few with revera, in the maritime area of the Dodecanese islands, the Cyclades islands, off the coasts of Crete and the southeastern coast of Italy.[292]

---

292   *Η Ροδιακή* [*I Rodiaki*], 7/4/2010, p. 1 and E. Voultsiadou et al., "Aegean Bath Sponges" p. 38.

The Sponge-Fishing Industry

2.1   "Traditional" Sponge-Fishing Methods

Until roughly the middle of the 19th century, technical means for sponge fishing were scant and include three methods – naked diving, the gagava, and hook fishing from a boat – all of which are described in various documents from that period as being "old", or "ancestral".[1] The costs as well as the yields using these methods were limited.

2.1.1   Naked Diving

As archival evidence reveals, until the 1860s "naked diving" or "natural sponge fishing" was undertaken using the apnea method, that is, with the divers holding their breath. Various testimonies as well as subsequent descriptions provide us with information on the basic features of naked diving. Spongers "in Adam's [birthday] suit" dove down to the seafloor grasping the "*skandali*" or "*skandalopetra*" [trigger stone] as they called it on Kalymnos, in their left hand. This tool was also known as a "*kambanelli*" or "*kambanellopetra*" [bell-stone] on Symi and consisted of a flattened stone, often from a ground and smoothed block of marble, weighing roughly 12–14 kilograms or more, which was then tied to the vessel with a 30-meter-long rope. It is said that a Symiot diver, Michail Karanikas, arrived at the idea of using the *skandalopetra* in 1840, and was the first person to attempt a dive carrying a heavy stone *kambanelli* in his hand.[2] In preparing for their task, divers would stand on the side of the ship

---

1   See Κάρολος Φλέγελ, "Το σπογγαλιευτικό ζήτημα της Μεσογείου (Χανιά, 1903)", *Καλυμνιακά Χρονικά* [Carl Flegel, "The Sponge-Fishing Issue of the Mediterranean Sea (Chania, 1903)", *Kalymniaka Chronika*] 5 (1985), p. 205.

2   It is notable that pearl fishers in the Pacific Ocean were already diving in exactly the same way at this time. Δημοσθένης Χαβιαράς, *Περί σπόγγων και σπογγαλιείας από των αρχαιοτάτων χρόνων μέχρι των καθ᾽ ημάς* [Dimosthenis Chaviaras, *On Sponges and Sponge Fishing from Ancient Times to Today*], Athens 1916, p. 36. And by the same author "Τινά περί σπογγαλιείας", *Συμιακός* ["On the Sponge Fishery", *Symiakos*] 5 (2010), p. 5 (republished in Κωνσταντίνος Σκόκος, *Εθνικόν ημερολόγιον, χρονογραφικόν, φιλολογικόν και γελοιογραφικόν* [Konstantinos Skokos, *National Journal: Chronological, Philological and Satyrical*], vol. XII, 1903, pp. 411–415). It is reported that the pearl fishers of the Pacific Ocean were poor young divers, mostly black. See Leon Sonrel, *Le fond de la mer*, Paris, 1880, p. 182; Louis Figuier, *Les merveilles de la science, ou Description populaire des inventions modernes*, vol. 4, Paris 1870, pp. 630–631. According to P. A. Hennique, Tunisians used the same method of sponge fishing. See, *Les Caboteurs*

© KONSTANTINOS EFTHYMIOU, 2025 | DOI:10.1163/9789004701946_004

holding the *skandalopetra* with its narrow edge facing forwards.[3] The "fishermen swimmers" thus descended speedily to the bottom of the sea and, having
trained from a very early age, they could dive to depths of 12 to 18 meters, where
they stayed for a maximum of one to two minutes, that being as long as they
could hold their breath.[4]

Using the *skandalopetra* as a rudder with which to navigate through sea currents, as well as to accelerate or slow down, divers swam to specific areas on
the seafloor and harvested sponges at great speed, keeping them in a fishnet
bag attached to their waist or neck known as the "*pochi*" ['πόχη, fishnet]. A man
on the boat held one end of a thin cord, the "*gassa*" [γάσα], while the other end
was tied to the diver's arm. By means of coded tugs on the *gassa*, divers would
signal when they were almost out of breath and in urgent need of being hauled
to the surface. The *skandalopetra*, which was tied to another rope, also had to
be hauled to the surface with the diver to be used by the next diver.[5]

A good diver could dive multiple times per day[6] and their success greatly
depended on the discovery of sponge-bearing beds in shallow waters. As part

_____

    et pêcheurs de la côte de Tunisie: Pêche des éponges, Paris 1888, p. 23. See also the testimony
    of Symiot diver Manolis Giampakakis to Rodoula Louloudaki published in the newspaper
    Σαμιακός [*Samiakos*], Folder 213 (2008), p. 5.

3   It is reported that the older and more experienced divers threw it into the sea and, after
    reaching the seafloor, they looked for it and used it as a reference point. Χαβιαράς, *Περί σπόγ-
    γων και σπογγαλιείας* [Chaviaras, *On Sponges and Sponge Fishing*], p. 36. See also C. T. Newton,
    Travels and Discoveries in the Levant, vol. 1, London 1865, p. 292 (a translation in Greek was
    published in the 6th volume of *Καλυμνιακά Χρονικά* [*Kalymniaka Chronika*] (1986), p. 201–206);
    Αδαμάντιος Ε. Παχουντάκης, *Η σπογγαλιεία εν Αιγύπτω*, [Adamantios E. Pachountakis, *Sponge
    Fishing in Egypt*] Alexandria 1905, p. 7. By the mid-20th century people were familiar with
    naked diving in fishing communities all over the world. The use of a large stone to steer the
    divers to the seafloor was also common practice. For more on this topic, see Jacques Henri
    Coriol, *La plongée en apnée*, Paris, 2006, p. 9.

4   Although there are many reports of dives of up to 3 and 4 minutes, they seem rather exag-
    gerated. Flegel, however, notes that a few divers could remain underwater for ½ up to ¾ of
    a minute more. Carl Flegel, "The Abuse of the Scaphander in the Sponge Fishery", *Bulletin of
    the Bureau of Fisheries*, 28 (1908), Washington 1910, p. 516.

5   See Louis Figuier, *Les merveilles de la science*, p. 626; "Sponge Fishing", *Scientific American* 5
    (1849), p. 34. See also more recent testimonies: Manuscript 1838/1973, *Ευαγγελία Λαμπαδαρίου*
    [*Evangelia Lampadariou*], pp. 65–66, and Manuscript 2728/1976 *Μαρία Σεβαστοπούλου* [*Maria
    Sevastopoulou*], p. 58, *Center for Folklore Studies* [hereafter CFS].

6   It is reported that the men usually dove 8 to 10 times per day. M. B. C. Collas, *La Turquie en 1861*,
    Paris 1861, p. 225. According to Méricourt, they dove 5 to 10 times. Alfred Leroy de Méricourt,
    "Considérations sur l'hygiène des pêcheurs d'éponge", *Annales d'hygiène publique et de méde-
    cine légale* 31 (1869), p. 277. Here it is claimed that a good diver could descend 20 and 30 times
    to a depth of 30 or 40 meters: *Δωδεκάνησος. Τετράτομος μελέτη του Υπουργείου Ανοικοδομήσεως*

of the mission of finding new sponge-bearing beds, captains would inspect the seafloor ahead of the dive by pouring oil or "*gala*" ["γάλα", "milk"] on the surface of the sea, which acted as a lens and helped make the seafloor visible.

In larger groups, naked divers' vessels were accompanied by boats equipped with *yiali* [γυαλάδικες βάρκες], or crew members who guided the naked divers to sponge-bearing areas.[7] The naked divers' vessels had a capacity of 1–2 tons and their crews included a captain and 5 to 7 divers, up to 40 years of age, in excellent physical condition. In addition, there were 1 or 2 rowers to monitor the diving, and to carry out various auxiliary tasks.[8] In the early 20th century,

---

και συνεργατών του υπό την διεύθυνσιν του κ. Κ. Α. *Δοξιάδη, Σειρά Εκδόσεων του Υπουργείου Ανοικοδομήσεως* [*Dodecanese. Study in Four Volumes by the Ministry for Reconstruction Under Mr K. A. Doxiadis*, Publication Series of Ministry for Reconstruction], Athens, 1947, p. 136.

7   See Méricourt, "Considérations sur l'hygiène", p. 277; Αδαμάντιος Ε. Παχουντάκης, *Η σπογγα-λιεία εν Αιγύπτω* [Adamantios E. Pachountakis, *Sponge Fishery in Egypt*], p. 7. On the "marks of the sea bottom" see also Φανερωμένη Χαλκιδιού-Σκυλλά, *Ή σφουγγάρι ή τομάρι. Η ζωή των σφουγγαράδων της Καλύμνου μέσα από αληθινές μαρτυρίες* [Faneromeni Chalkidiou-Skylla, *Either Sponge or Corpse. The Life of the Sponge Fishermen of Kalymnos through Real Testimonies*], Kalymnos 2009, pp. 256–258.

8   The account given by Carl Flegel is particularly vivid in "Η Α.Θ. Παναγιότης ο Οικουμενικός Πατριάρχης Άνθιμος ο Ζ' εν Καλύμνω" "[His Holiness the Ecumenical Patriarch Anthimos VII in Kalymnos"], Samos 1896, p. 15, or Κάρολος Φλέγελ, *Η νήσος Κάλυμνος* [Carl Flegel, *The Island of Kalymnos*], Constantinople 1896, p. 29, as well as the description of Αλέξανδρος Λεμονίδης, *Το εμπόριον της Τουρκίας* [Alexandros Lemonidis, *The Commerce of Turkey*], Constantinople 1849, p. 157. See also earlier and more recent descriptions of this system and its organization in Milt. Caravokyro, *Étude sur la pêche des éponges. Les pays spon-gifères de l'Empire et le scaphandre*, Constantinople 1886, p. 5; Σκεύος Ζερβός, "Η νόσος των γυμνών σπογγαλιέων ή "νόσος Σκεύου Γ. Ζερβού"", *Καλυμνιακά Χρονικά* [Skevos Zervos, "The Disease of Naked Sponge Divers or 'Skevos Zervos Disease'", *Kalymniaka Chronika*] 18 (2009), p. 241; Χαβιαράς, *Περί σπόγγων και σπογγαλιείας* [Chaviaras, *On Sponges and Sponge Fishing*], p. 40; Θεόδωρος Αντ. Κριεζής, *Η σπογγαλιεία* [Theodoros Ant. Kriezis, *The Sponge Fishery*], Athens 1937, pp. 7–8; Νικήτας Χαβιαράς, "Συμαίων γυμνών σπογγαλιέων φρικτά επεισόδια", *Τα Συμαϊκά* [Nikitas Chaviaras, "Horrible Accidents Suffered by Symiot Naked Sponge Divers", *Ta Symaika*] 3 (1977), pp. 285–293; Σωτήριος Αγαπητίδης, "Η οικονομική οργάνωση των σπογ-γαλιευτικών συγκροτημάτων – ειδικότερα στη Σύμη", *Τα Συμαϊκά* [Sotirios Agapitidis, "The Financial Organization of Sponge-Fishing Groups, Particularly in Symi", *Ta Symaika*] 3 (1977), p. 185; Νικόλαος Ρ. Πιζάνιας, "Η οργάνωσις της σπογγαλιευτικής επιχειρήσεως (τεχνικώς-οικονο-μικώς)", Α' Πανελλήνιον Σπογγαλιευτικόν Συνέδριον (Ρόδος 2427 Φεβρουαρίου 1949). Εισηγήσεις και Πρακτικά, Γενική Διοίκησις Δωδεκανήσου [Nikolaos R. Pizanias, "The Organization of the Sponge-Fishing Enterprise (on a Financial Technical Level)", The First Colloquium on the Sponge Fishery, Rhodes 24–27 February 1949, *Papers and Minutes*, General Administration of the Dodecanese], Rhodes 1951, pp. 29–30; *Δωδεκάνησος. Τετράτομος μελέτη του Υπουργείου Ανοικοδομήσεως* [*Dodecanese. Study in Four Volumes by the Ministry for Reconstruction*], pp. 136–137; Bernard Russell, "Η σπογγαλιεία της Καλύμνου", *Σπουδαί* ["The Sponge Fishery of

Michail Kalafatas of Symi wrote a poem in which he described the work of naked divers:

> Our old ancestors, to sink deep
> beneath the waves and currents,
> invented a stone, white, oblique,
> tied to a thin rope through its core.
> The Bellstone, as today it's known,
> by which to plumb the deep.
> Hugging it tightly divers sink,
> steering by underwater leaps,
> alighting where they want.
> the bellstone firmly in his hands
> until he touches rock.
> His left hand leans the bellstone by
> and, crouching, feels for sponges.
> He leaves the bellstone if he finds
> good cutting place, uprooting
> as many as will fill his sack.
> Two guards stand ready on the prow,
> tied to him by a long rope.
> His breath gone, he tugs the rope,
> and feeling it, they raise him –
> these guards are known as Oars.
> If either Oar suffers a lapse
> of his complete attention,
> the diver suffers too.
> And if the lapse becomes too long,
> he bids his health farewell.
> But the two Oarsmen keep their heads
> and stand with full attention.[9]

In his chronicle of 1703, British traveler Aaron Hill provided valuable information on the life of islanders, and was greatly impressed by sponge fishing on the island of Symi:

Kalymnos", *Spoudai*] 1 (1970), pp. 13–14; Michael N. Kalafatas, *The Bellstone: The Greek Sponge Divers of the Aegean. One American's Journey Home*. Hannover: Brandeis University Press, 2003, pp. 9–10.

9 Μητροφάνης Καλαφατάς, "Χειμερινός Όνειρος" [Mitrofanis Kalafatas, "Winter Dream"] in Michael N. Kalafatas, *The Bellstone: The Greek Sponge Divers of the Aegean. One American's Journey Home*. Hannover: Brandeis University Press, 2003, pp. 109–110.

Half the Sponge, as I have said, is soak'd in Oyl, the other half is dip'd before in certain Stiptic Waters, to prevent the Oyl from Penetrating farther than it ought to go, when so prepar'd, they take the Sponge, and thrusting it within their Mouths, the Oyl'd part outward (but of that, almost an Inch within the Lips) they press their Teeth a little hard upon it, and by that means force the Oyly Sponge to close the Entrance of their Mouths against the Water. [...] THUS they Dive, and with a little difficulty in a Streighten'd Suction make a Shift to tarry under Water a considerable time. They sink the Baskets by the help of Stones, which they contrive to fasten at the Bottom, and with Instruments, they carry down on purpose, cut the Sponges from the sides of Rocks, till having fill'd the Baskets, they take off the Weights, and then they rise with ease, by reason of the Cork about them. How long they tarry under Water. By constant Practice many of these Divers are arriv'd at such Perfection in the Art, that they can tarry under Water till the Oyl corrupts, which it will always do in less than two hours time. There is a Law among the Divers of this Island, that no Man shall be allow'd to Marry, till he can demonstrate by a Tryal, he is qualify'd to Dive for one continued quarter of an Hour.[10]

A number of such reports exist and, although they come to us from the early 18th-century and attribute legendary skills to the naked divers, they are worth revisiting for their accounts of the scarce means that sponge fishers had at their disposal, as well as for their descriptions of divers' techniques for undertaking this activity in a challenging environment with rudimentary technical support.[11]

Simplifying, or perhaps glorifying, this working landscape, and drawing on the extent to which locals were familiar with the technical aspects of sponge diving, Kalymnian, Themelis Kindynis wrote:

Regarding the origins of sponge fishing: in the beginning inhabitants gathered sponges that storms had cast up on the beach and took them to Smyrna for sale. Gradually, they began entering the sea up to their chests and collecting sponges from this depth. In due course they

---

10 See Aaron Hill, *A full and just account of the present state of the Ottoman empire in all its branches: with the government, and policy, religion, customs, and way of living of the Turks, in general.* London: John Mayo, 1709: https://quod.lib.umich.edu/e/ecco /004869666.0001.000/264?page=root;size=100;view=text. Also qtd. In Κυριάκος Σιμόπουλος, Ξένοι Ταξιδιώτες στην Ελλάδα 1700–1800 [Kyriakos Simopoulos, *Foreign Travelers in Greece 1700–1800*], vol. II, Athens 1995, pp. 59–61.

11 When they got back from the voyage and sold the catch, they used pebbles for their calculations. See Caravokyro, *Étude sur la pêche*, p. 5.

were able to train and swim up to 5 fathoms and, lately, with the help of the accoutrement invented by the people of Symi, commonly called a '*skandalopetra*', they dive up to 35 fathoms and stay on the seafloor for 2–3 minutes. They train for this activity from childhood. [...] The overall number of sponge-fishing ships, commonly called '*skaphe*' [σκάφαι] amounts to 200, of which 60 carry diving suits with the scaphander, commonly called the 'machine' [μηχαναί], which is procured from Europe for sponge fishing.[12]

The naked diving methods practiced mostly by Kalymnian and Symiot spongers required familiarity with the sea, adeptness, and tremendous physical stamina to be effective. It appears, however, that naked diving as practiced in Kalymnos and Symi was safer than diving with the apparatus, although these divers had to face a number of dangers in the water. These dangers included those associated with sudden descent and surfacing, the lack of oxygen and the "terrible elements of nature – the sea, the wind, very high temperatures and even the beasts of the sea".[13]

In 1854, a few years before the introduction of the diving suit and scaphander to the Dodecanese sponge fishery, and while naked diving still prevailed, Kalymnos had 200 vessels at its disposal, harvesting sponges for a net worth of 16,949 pounds sterling. In 1858 – according to Robert Campell in the report of the British Consul to Rhodes – Kalymnos accounted for 254 of the total 600 sponge fishing-vessels of the southern Sporades, and 2,000 spongers of the overall 4,600 in the area.[14]

The data presented by M. Collas in his *La Turquie en 1861*, concur with the figures cited here above, noting the distribution of the number of vessels for the same year as follows: Kalymnos 254, Symi 190, Chalki 65, Kastellorizo 40, Leros 30, Astypalaia 12, Telos 7, Kassos 2.[15] Collas also noted of a small increase in the number of Kalymnian sponge-fishing vessels, and estimated that the island had 260 vessels in 1860; he added that many of them were transported

12   In Θέμελης Κινδύνης, *Η νήσος Κάλυμνος* [Themelis Kindynis, *The Island of Kalymnos*], Athens 1879, pp. 24–26.

13   Letter dated 1 August 1885 from the Demogerontia of Kalymnos to the Demogerontia of Symi regarding the privileges of the southern Sporades islands. The document was published in Γιώργης Κουκούλης, "Δύο έγγραφα της Δημογεροντίας Καλύμνου προς τη Δημογεροντία Σύμης", *Καλυμνιακά Χρονικά* [Giorgis Koukoulis, "Two Documents of the Elders of Kalymnos to the Elders of Symi", *Kalymniaka Chronika*] 6 (1986), pp. 45–60.

14   Newton, *Travels and Discoveries*, p. 293; Κυριάκος Κων. Χατζηδάκης, "Η σπογγαλιεία στις Νότιες Σποράδες στα μέσα του 19ου αιώνα", *Καλυμνιακά Χρονικά* [Kyriakos Kon. Chatzidakis, "Sponge Fishing in the Southern Sporades in the Mid-19th Century", *Kalymniaka Chronika*] 13 (1999), p. 231. See also "Sponge Fishing", *Scientific American* 5 (1849), p. 34.

15   Collas, *La Turquie en 1861*, p. 232.

IMAGE 2.1   Kalymnian naked diver with *skandalopetra*, 1930s
SOURCE: PHOTOGRAPH BY ELLI PAPADIMITRIOU, KALYMNOS 1932–36
© BENAKI MUSEUM/PHOTOGRAPHIC ARCHIVES

IMAGE 2.2   Kalymnian naked divers, 1930s
SOURCE: PHOTOGRAPH BY ELLI PAPADIMITRIOU, KALYMNOS 1932–36
© BENAKI MUSEUM/PHOTOGRAPHIC ARCHIVES

to the coasts of Crete, Syria and Barbary by larger ships, where they engaged in sponge fishing.[16] In the period between 1863 and 1866, M. Aublé, a French merchant on Rhodes, estimated the sponge-fishing population in the southern Sporades at 4,000 and the annual value of their sponge catch at 3,000,000 francs.[17]

In 1894, in a memorandum to Abedin Pasha, Kalymnians attempted a brief stocktaking of the activity up to 1866. They reported that Syria had more than 800 sponge-fishing vessels, Kalymnos and Symi 370 each, Chalki more than 200, and Kastellorizo around 50, whereas the islands involved in this activity at a later date commanded a smaller number of vessels.[18] According to Skevos Zervos, at the beginning of the 20th century, 9 out of 10 naked sponge divers lived on the island of Kalymnos, and he estimated that there were several thousands of them.[19] As Themelis Kindynis wrote,

> Cruising in summer, from early May to early October, here and there off the coasts of Africa, Cyprus, Crete, and Greece, they fish sponges. [...] Their ships are very small, piloted by native captains and with crews of 10–12 men. Kalymnians, nevertheless, as if they were present-day Delians,[20] working bravely and in dangerous conditions, they do not hesitate to venture forth with these small ships into the seas of Africa.

Although divers made use of various techniques to facilitate and prolong diving, as well as for the collection and storage of sponges, this method of sponging had little room for improvement. In fact, the time spent on the seafloor was limited to a few minutes, no matter how trained and resilient the diver was, and naked diving remained a widespread method employed in all sponge-fishing regions. And indeed, even after the appearance of diving apparatuses including the scaphander, the practice of naked diving was carried

---

16   Ibid., p. 224.
17   Méricourt, "Considérations sur l'hygiène", p. 276.
18   Doc. 1, 4/1/1894, Correspondence 1894–1895, MAK.
19   Ζερβός, "Η νόσος των γυμνών σπογγαλιέων ή "νόσος Σκεύου Γ. Ζερβού'" [Zervos, "The Disease of Naked Sponge Divers or 'Skevos Zervos Disease'"], pp. 246–247. Even though his estimate is rather exaggerated, it does seem that most of the naked sponge divers were found on Kalymnos and Symi. See Ιωάννης Αντ. Χειλάς, "Που να σε φάει το ψάρι", Καλυμνιακά Χρονικά [Ioannis Ant. Cheilas, "May the Fish Eat You", Kalymniaka Chronika] 18 (2009), p. 277.
20   Κινδύνης, Η νήσος Κάλυμνος [Kindynis, The Island of Kalymnos], pp. 24–26. Delians are residents of the island of Delos. Historically, the name is associated with the Delian League, founded in 478 BC, as an association of Greek city-states under the leadership of Athens. The League's purpose was to continue fighting the Persian Empire after the Greek victory in the Battle of Plataea at the end of the Second Persian invasion of Greece.

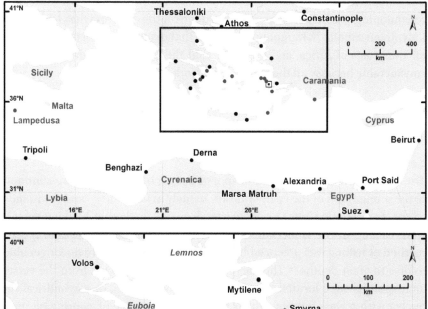

MAP 2.1   The sponge-fishing network

on in many sponge-fishing areas until the mid-1950s, albeit known by various names and subject to small variations.

Even after 1950, free diving continued with the "revera" method whereby the diver was no longer naked, but wore a wetsuit and fins, as well as weights around his waist. Crews were small, generally consisting of the captain and 1 to 5 divers. They worked all day for 4 to 5 months from May to late August or early September, depending on the distance of the fishing area and the yield. Crews fished along coastal areas and, when in Greek maritime territory, they were able to make regular stops for provisions of food, water, and fuel from the coastal areas, transport their catch there, and contact their families. The same happened off Africa's coasts but more rarely. Such opportunities for re-equipping also helped to increase the depth of the dives and the yield, hence Kalymnian captain N. Kampourakis recalls that many dove with the revera suit off the coasts of Africa, and he claims that the total yield of the vessels was considerable because all the divers could work simultaneously.[21]

2.2　Sponge Fishing from Aboard the Ship

2.2.1　*The Hook*
The simple, "primitive" method of sponge fishing by hook was more common in the sponge beds of the Peloponnese – namely in Ermioni[22] – and the islands of the Argosaronic Gulf. This, however, does not imply that hooking vessels were lacking in the Dodecanese.[23] According to M. Aublé's testimony, this method of fishing was practiced by elderly spongers who were no longer able to dive to great depths.[24] The harvest was usually conducted from the vessel after sponges were located the with the help of a mirror, or a cylindrical tin bucket with a glass bottom, which replaced the practice of pouring oil onto the water's surface in order to better view the seafloor. The hook's tip, fixed on a metal or wooden shaft about 10–15 meters long, had 4 pointed iron prongs, and weighed 2 to 3½ kilograms.[25] If the removal of the sponge proved difficult, the hookers would dive to the bottom of the sea or use a "gagava" or trawl.[26] It

---

21　Testimony of Nikolas Kampourakis to E.O., 23/7/2005.

22　According to T. Zappa, Ermioni "produces the well-known hook spongers" fishing off the Cyrenaica coasts. Τάσος Ζάππας, "Ξεκίνημα των σφουγγαράδων για τα αφρικανικά παράλια", *Αθηναϊκά Νέα* [Tassos Zappas, "Sponge Fishermen Setting Sail for the Coasts of Africa", *Athinaika Nea*], 4/5/1938, p. 3.

23　Fishing by hook was practiced in Kalymnos from 1885 onwards and the last two hooking vessels worked in 1975 with two crew members each, whereas the last gagava departed from Kalymnos' port in 1985. Information from the Port Authority of Kalymnos.

24　Figuier, *Les merveilles de la science*, p. 626.

25　Wooden or metal extensions could be attached to the apparatus by which means spongers could reach a depth of up to 25-meters; Δωδεκάνησος. Τετράτομος μελέτη του Υπουργείου Ανοικοδομήσεως [*Dodecanese. Study in Four Volumes by the Ministry for Reconstruction*], p. 139.

26　Hennique, *Les Caboteurs et pêcheurs*, p. 46–47; Παχουντάκης, *Η σπογγαλιεία εν Αιγύπτω* [Pachountakis, *Sponge Fishery in Egypt*], p. 8; Jules Toutain, *La Tunisie au début du xxième siècle*, Paris 1904, pp. 164–166; Χαβιαράς, *Περί σπόγγων και σπογγαλιείας* [Chaviaras, *On Sponges and Sponge Fishing*], p. 41; Κριεζής, *Η σπογγαλιεία* [Kriezis, *The Sponge Fishery*], p. 8; Τάσος Ζάππας, "Ξεκίνημα των σφουγγαράδων για τα αφρικανικά παράλια", Αθηναϊκά Νέα [Tassos Zappas, "Sponge Fishermen Setting Sail for the African Coasts", *Athinaika Nea*] 4/5/1938, p. 3; Αγαπητίδης, "Η οικονομική οργάνωση" [Agapitidis, "The Financial Organization"], p. 184; Χατζηδάκης, "Η σπογγαλιεία στις Νότιες Σποράδες" [Chatzidakis, "Sponge Fishing in the Southern Sporades"], p. 230.

is also said that experienced *"yialades"* (the men handling the "yiali" or looking glass) could pick out sponges in the seaweed at great depths any time of the year, and especially when the sun was not shining vertically on the water.[27]

Each vessel was equipped with 4–6 hooks and manned by a crew of 2–6 crew members. According to Alexandros Lemonidis "fishing by trident is less dangerous, but it is only practiced in calm weather and on smooth seas so that when oil drops fall on the surface of the water, fishermen are able to see sponges at the bottom of the sea, and spear and remove them with their tridents. The sponges are, however, lacerated due to the use and force of this weapon."[28] Often torn by the hook's pointed spikes, sponges harvested by means of this technique were less valuable and, in any event, capital and profit were limited given that catches ranged from 40 to 150 sponges per day for 4 people.[29]

2.2.2   *Gagava, Gagamo, Grypos or Draga*[30]
The gagava or dragnet used in sponge fishing consisted of a large net sack, 4 to 8 meters in length and about 3.5 to 4 meters in circumference. Its opening was sewn onto a heavy rectangular iron frame that hung from the vessel with ropes and chains that dragged it slowly along the seabed. Assisted by a winch on the ship, the net sacks removed sponges at great depths while sweeping up whatever else lay at the bottom of the sea.[31] As soon as the crew saw that the bag was full, they would haul it up on the boat, clean the net and return it to the seafloor. The use of the gagava and massive fishing net required vessels with a capacity of 5 to 10 tons such as the *"trechandiri"* type or lateen rigged *"skaphe"* which were capable of withstanding the weight of the metal mesh

---

27   See Kostas Fanouris' testimony to Faneromeni Chalkidiou-Skylla in Ἡ σφουγγάρι ἠ τομάρι [*Either Sponge or Corpse*], pp. 257–258.

28   Λεμονίδης, *Τὸ ἐμπόριον τῆς Τουρκίας* [Lemonidis, *The Commerce of Turkey*], p. 157.

29   Δωδεκάνησος. *Τετράτομος μελέτη τοῦ Ὑπουργείου Ἀνοικοδομήσεως* [*Dodecanese. Study in Four Volumes by the Ministry for Reconstruction*], p. 139. Τάσος Ζάππας, "Ξεκίνημα των σφουγγαράδων για τα αφρικανικά παράλια", *Ἀθηναϊκά Νέα* [Tassos Zappas, "Sponge Fishermen Setting Sail for the Coasts of Africa", *Athinaika Nea*], 4/5/1938, p. 3.

30   These are all names for small sponging vessels.

31   Φλέγελ, *Ἡ νῆσος Κάλυμνος* [Flegel, *The Island of Kalymnos*], p. 28; Ζώτος, *Ἔκθεσις περὶ τῆς ἀνὰ τὰς ἀφρικανικὰς ἀκτὰς διὰ σκαφάνδρου σπογγαλιείας* Zotos, *Report on Sponge Fishing by Diving Suit along the African Coasts*, Athens 1904, p. 4; Χαβιαράς, *Περὶ σπόγγων καὶ σπογγαλιείας* [Chaviaras, *On Sponges and Sponge Fishing*], p. 42; Flegel, "The Abuse of the Scaphander", p. 517; Κριεζής, *Ἡ σπογγαλιεία* [Kriezis, *The Sponge Fishery*], p. 8; Ν. Πιζάνιας, *Ἡ Κάλυμνος ἀπό πλουτολογικῆς, δημογραφικῆς, ἰδία δὲ δημοσιονομικῆς ἀπόψεως* [N. Pizanias, *Kalymnos from the Perspective of Plutology, Demography, and Especially Finance*], Athens 1935, p. 26; Ἀγαπητίδης, "Ἡ οἰκονομικὴ ὀργάνωση" [Agapitidis, "The Financial Organization"], p. 184; Δωδεκάνησος. *Τετράτομος μελέτη τοῦ Ὑπουργείου Ἀνοικοδομήσεως* [*Dodecanese. Study in Four Volumes by the Ministry for Reconstruction*], pp. 139–140.

sacks and dragging them across flat sea beds with clay bottoms.[32] However, as old spongers recount, this fishing method, for which a smooth seabed was a prerequisite, resulted in a limited yield amounting to 15 to 30 kilograms per day.[33] "It didn't come with great costs, but it didn't make great profits either", they note.[34] Moreover, the crew was small – the captain and 2–3 more men – and voyages were brief.[35]

Dragnets in sponge fishing are reported to have been systematically used on the island of Symi since 1877.[36] Despite the lack of fierce opposition when compared with the case of the scaphander diving suit which aroused much protest, the use of dragnets was also subject to recurrent restrictions and prohibitions beginning in the 19th century, and continuing into the first decades of the 20th century, because it was believed that they destroyed the sea beds and the spawning areas of fish.[37] To protect the sea bottom, the governments of sponge-producing states limited the number of permits issued, or banned dragnets from fishing in shallow waters.[38] In the post-war era, the declining use of this sponge-fishing method is attributed to its low effectiveness on one

---

32   A lateen or lateen rigging refers to a triangular sail set on a long yard mounted at an angle on the mast, and running in a fore-and-aft direction. Παχουντάκης, *Η σπογγαλιεία εν Αιγύπτω* [Pachountakis, *Sponge Fishery in Egypt*], p. 8.

33   The total haul of vessels fishing with gagava off the coasts of Tunisia amounted to about 400 kilograms in 1875; Toutain, *La Tunisie*, p. 166. A detailed description of the gagava is provided in relevant Hennique, *Les Caboteurs et pêcheurs*, pp. 68–69.

34   See also the testimony of Lefteris Mamouzelos to E.O., 3/9/2004.

35   Πιζάνιας, "Η οργάνωσις της σπογγαλιευτικής επιχειρήσεως" [Pizanias, "The Organization of the Sponge-Fishing Enterprise"], p. 30; Αγαπητίδης, "Η οικονομική οργάνωση" [Agapitidis, "The Financial Organization"], p. 184.

36   Χαβιαράς, "Τινά περί σπογγαλιείας" ["On the Sponge Fishery", *Symiakos*], p. 5. The use of dragnets began on Kalymnos in 1891: see Κυριάκος Κων. Χατζηδάκης, "Η Κάλυμνος στα τέλη της Τουρκοκρατίας", *Καλυμνιακά Χρονικά* [Kyriakos Kon. Chatzidakis, "Kalymnos towards the End of Turkish Rule", *Kalymniaka Chronika*] 8 (1989), p. 83.

37   The fight against the use of the scaphander diving suit, which often resulted in the diver being paralysed, as well as in over-fishing, is the topic of this chapter in what follows here below, as well as chapter 4 of the present volume. Opposition to the dragnet was the subject of a letter from the Minister of Foreign Affairs Th. Diliyiannis to the Vice Consul in Tripoli, 18/4/1891 and Letter of D. Forou, Vice Consul in Tripoli to the Greek Ambassador to Constantinople, 9/4/1891, Embassy in Tripoli-Libya, Folder 4 (1875–1897), Subfolder 4, IAYE. The ban was finally lifted because they imposed a special issuance permit for an annual total of 3 Ottoman lira per year. The same occurred in 1913, according to official telegrams on the topic. See Doc. 16/5/1913, Archive of the Vice Consulate in Benghazi, Folder 28, Subfolder 4, IAYE. See also Φλέγελ, "Το σπογγαλιευτικό ζήτημα" [Flegel, "The Sponge-Fishing Issue"], p. 209.

38   Letter from the Consul in Tunis to his homologue in Tripoli (22/4/1914), Embassy in Tripoli-Libya, Folder 19 (1914), Subfolder 5, IAYE. Note also that in 1914, the Italian government set a limit beginning at 20 meters.

hand, and on the other to the fact that the Agricultural Bank of Greece (ATE) discouraged the funding of dragnet harvesting because of the extensive damage dragnets inflicted on the seafloor.[39]

The dynamics of sponge fishery in the eastern Mediterranean were depicted in a table published by Miltiadis Caravokyros just before the diving suit with scaphander was introduced in 1866 (see Table 2.1). He estimates that, of a total of 100,000 inhabitants, 11,280 were involved in sponge fishing with 1,800 vessels. Kalymnians in particular contributed considerable revenues to the coffers of the Ottoman state, as well as to the island's community and their families.[40]

Despite rudimentary technology and scant fishing means, the sponge-fishing performance of the Dodecanesian populations up to the mid-1860s was certainly not negligible. With this "ancient method", as it is now known on Kalymnos, sponge fishing was practiced on a regular and systematic basis by

TABLE 2.1   Sponge fishing in the eastern Mediterranean (1886)

Sponge-fishing areas	Ships and boats	Divers and auxiliary staff	Permits	Customs office	Sponges	Imports
Kalymnos	370	2,600	18,000*	4,000*	500,000*	200,000*
Symi	370	2,600				
Chalki	100	800				
Kastellorizo	80	640				
Patmos, Leros and Astypalaia	50	400				
Bodrum	30	240				
Coasts of Karamania and Syria	800	4,000				
Total	1,800	11,280	18,000	4,000	500,000	200,000

*   In Turkish lira
SOURCE: MILTIADIS CARAVOKYROS, *ÉTUDE SUR LA PÊCHE DES ÉPONGES. LES PAYS SPON-GIFÈRES DE l'EMPIRE ET LE SCAPHANDRE*, CONSTANTINOPLE 1886

39   On Kalymnos, the sponges uprooted by the gagava that did not end up in the net were called "ha(ta)ides" ["χα(τα)ήδες"], because they were swept by the currents. See Γιάννης Χειλάς, "Χα(τ)ζής – Χα(τ)ζή(δ)ες και Χα(τ)ζήαινες", *Καλυμνιακά Χρονικά* [Giannis Cheilas, "Cha(t)zis, Cha(t)zides and Cha(t)ziaines", *Kalymniaka Chronika*] 13 (1999), p. 95.
40   Caravokyro, *Étude sur la pêche des éponges*, p. 8.

a significant portion of the island's population, while it established the social and financial conditions for the later mechanization of the activity.

2.2.3   First Diving Apparatuses

As captain Nemo of Jules Verne's *Voyage to the Bottom of the Sea* explains to Professor Aronax, "man can live under water, providing he carries with him a sufficient supply of breathable air. In submarine works, the workman, clad in an impervious dress, with his head in a metal helmet, receives air from above by means of forcing pumps and regulators".[41] Even if Jules Verne believed that the scaphander suit "imprisoned" the diver, and granted him only limited freedom of movement, its invention superseded far more unwieldy apparatuses such as the diving bell invented in the early 18th century by British astronomer Edmond Halley.[42]

Diving with some form of breathing device, along with the ability to stay down and move around at the bottom of the sea has been a subject of interest for various scholars over many years. However, while Leonardo da Vinci's designs from around 1500, or those of Borelli in 1680 demonstrate this interest, their ideas remained in the realm of theory without the possibility of practical implementation or widespread use. And while the lack of any practical development of the diving suit was perhaps attributable to limited technical options and financial investment in related research, the pace of scientific experimentation aimed at the conquest of the seafloor accelerated from the last decades of the 18th century onwards. In 1775. following the work of Halley and others who attempted to improve the heavy and cumbersome apparatus of the suit, Abbé Jean-Baptiste de la Chapelle published *Traité de la construction théorique et pratique du scaphandre ou du bateau de l'homme*, which included the first two designs of the "scaphandre".[43]

---

41   Jules Verne, *Twenty Thousand Leagues under the Sea*, Project Gutenberg, 1994. The Nautilus' crew used similar suits and apparatuses to explore the sea bottom, while, already in 1869, Jules Verne adopted the use of a metal tank filled with compressed air that is fitted on the diver's suit and allows him to move independently.

42   Although the invention is older and can probably be traced back to the 17th century, Halley found a way to renew the air in the apparatus while making it much more functional; see A. E. Boycott, G. C. C. Damant, J. S. Haldane, "Prévention de la maladie de décompression", Alain Foret (preface-translation), Montpellier 2008, pp. 16–19. For the description of how the apparatus made possible descents of up to 15 meters, see Sonrel, *Le Fond de la mer*, p. 188; Gustave Tallent, *Cloche à plongeur et scaphandre*, Melun 1899, pp. 4–6· Figuier, *Les merveilles de la science*, p. 620.

43   Jacques Lordat, "Essai sur l'iconologie médicale ou sur les rapports d'utilité qui existent entre l'art du dessin et l'étude de la médecine", Montpellier 1833, p. 190; Figuier, *Les merveilles de la science*, pp. 636.

In France as well as in the UK, forward-thinking scientists and engineers sought to combine the technological achievements of their day to construct practical and efficient diving apparatuses. In the new industrial era, with all its affordances and demands, these apparatuses could be deployed in numerous situations: in the construction of bridges and other underwater works, the exploitation of mines, the maintenance and cleaning of vessels, wreck removals and so on. In the medical field, "pressure chambers" were developed in the UK and have been in use since the 1660s, while their therapeutic applications multiplied in France beginning early in the 19th century. And elsewhere in Europe, the USA and Canada, pressure chambers were employed for medical purposes beginning in the 1860s.[44]

In the 1820s, John and Charles Deane invented a full-body suit, which was fire resistant and enabled firefighters to enter burning buildings. In the next few years, British and French manufacturers took an interest in the potential uses of the diving suit with scaphander and attempted to correct its defaults, and to improve on its impermeability. Among these manufacturers was Prussian-born Augustus Siebe who modified the suit in 1837 and improved the breathing system. He equipped it with a metal helmet and attached a special breastplate, thereby making it suitable for diving, and connected it to an air-pump that delivered compressed air to the diver.[45]

An improved version of the previous invention, the Cabirol "scaphandre", appeared in the 1860s. Its creator, Joseph Martin Cabirol, maintained that it could be used to great advantage in multiple applications as, for example, in scientific work, archaeological research, and mapping the sea bottom, as well as in sponge and coral harvesting. However, the suits were mainly intended for use by the French naval force and for the facilitation port works, as well as for tracking down and removing shipwrecks, making repairs, and maintaining the hulls of ships.[46]

In 1864, mining engineer Benoît Rouquayrol and Navy officer Auguste Denayrouze equipped the diving suit with a device placed on the diver's back to supply oxygen.[47] In 1867, Denayrouze published a manual in French that provides a detailed description of the breathing device, the scaphander diving suit and its parts,[48] as well as instructions and guidance on the assembly of the

44   Boycott et al., *Prévention de la maladie*, p. 12–15.
45   Sonrel, *Le Fond de la mer*, pp. 188–198; Kalafatas, *The Bellstone*, p. 13.
46   M. Cabirol, *Scaphandre, appareil de plongeur Cabirol*, Paris 1870, pp. 6–8.
47   Tallent, *Cloche à plongeur*, p. 8; Sonrel, *Le Fond de la mer*, p. 189; Figuier, *Les merveilles de la science*, pp. 649–658.
48   Auguste Denayrouze, *Manuel du matelot plongeur, et instructions sur l'appareil plongeur Rouquayrol-Denayrouze, basse pression*, Paris 1867.

suits; on how the suit should be put on and taken off; on the maintenance of all its components; and on handling technical issues and breakdowns.[49]

Because several versions of the diving suit were in existence at the same time, there is very little information on the exact types of diving suits that were introduced in the sponge fishery of the Dodecanese islands in the 19th century. We do, however, know that most of the suits in use at that time had seldom been tested in great depths. Moreover, although there were continuous improvements made to the diving suit as noted above, it was still a very recent invention in the 19th century and one that went rapidly from the laboratory into mass production and use.

2.3   *Skaphos Andros* or "Scaphander"[50]

In the 1860s, the industrial revolution took hold in the sponge-fishing areas of the southern Aegean Sea at full speed and large quantities of sponges were sought out. For the most part sponges supplied the industrial needs of the West, while fine soft sponges were marketed in London, Paris, Vienna, Saint Petersburg, and New York.

This growing demand called for the introduction of new technologies to improve the low productivity of pre-industrial sponge-harvesting methods. The scaphander, an undeniable symbol of the new sponge-fishing era, held the promise of enabling divers to work on the seafloor for prolonged periods, in pleasant tranquility, allowing for the careful selection of the most suitable sponges, free of time pressure.[51] Indeed, this 19th-century scientific and

---

49   Denayrouze, *Manuel du matelot plongeur*, pp. 24–33.

50   The word "σκάφανδρο" ("scaphandre" in French), is derived from σκάφος [*skáphos*, "hollowed"] + ἀνήρ [*anér*, "man"] in Greek (see Chapter 1 of the present volume, footnote 24, p. 14) and was reportedly first used in France to describe a sort of lifejacket made of cork. The original name of this diving apparatus was "*appareil plongeur*". According to Στέφανος Κουμανούδης, *Συναγωγή νέων λέξεων υπό των λογίων πλασθεισών από της Αλώσεως μέχρι των καθ' ημάς χρόνων* [Stefanos Koumanoudis, *Collection of New Words Introduced by Scholars from the Fall of Constantinople to the Present*], vol. 11, Athens 1900, p. 909, they started using the odd word "σκάφανδρο" in 1886 to signify the diver's suit. He also adds that Scarlatos Byzantios did not include the word's Greek spelling in his French-Greek dictionary, nevertheless, its use is much older on sponge-fishing islands while, as Dimosthenis Chaviaras notes in 1870, in the medical journal Ασκληπιός [*Asklipios*]: "we could consider that the word "σκάφανδρον" was formed in proportion to the word "σάκανδρος" ["*pudenda muliebria*"] which is found in Aristophanes (*Lysistrata* 824): "τον σάκανδρον εκφανείς""; see Χαβιαράς, "Τινά περί σπογγαλιείας" [Chaviaras, "On the Sponge Fishery"], p. 5.

51   Figuier, *Les merveilles de la science*, p. 627.

technological achievement brought about an impressive increase in the productivity of the Ottoman Empire's spongers. At the same time, however, the scaphander suit also introduced a series of dangers into divers' daily lives stemming from the use of a technological innovation with which they were unfamiliar, and the risks entailed in diving at great depths which were not yet widely known.

This first imported "technological innovation" brought about a series of changes in a professional sector which, up to that time, had known only traditional methods of diving and sponge fishing. The establishment of the "sponge-machine" or "machine", as they continue to call the diving suit with scaphander [σκάφανδρο] on the island of Kalymnos to this day, overshadowed not only divers' traditional expertise but also the effectiveness of sponge-fishing methods with hooking boats, or gagavas, and techniques that do not involve diving. The competition between natural ability and the skill of naked divers would soon shift in favour of the mechanical support of the diving suit with scaphander. The waterproof suit protecting the body of the diver, and the breathing system supplying him with oxygen on the seafloor made it possible to reach greater depths and to stay down longer on each dive,

IMAGE 2.3   Scaphander helmet and sponges, Hydra 2018, private collection
PHOTO: GELINA HARLAFTIS

IMAGE 2.4   The "machinist". Kalymnian diver with a scaphander diving suit, 1950
SOURCE: PHOTOGRAPH BY DIMITRIOS HARISIADIS, KALYMNOS 1950
© BENAKI MUSEUM/PHOTOGRAPHIC ARCHIVES

thereby increasing divers' productive capacity.[52] These technological advances also made it possible to extend the period in which divers' could work, from approximately four months for naked divers, to seven or even more for those

---

52   Méricourt tellingly explains that a diver in diving suit performs at least three times better than a naked diver; see Méricourt, "Considerations sur l'hygiène", p. 279. An anonymous journalist from Aθηναΐς [Athinais] estimated the value of the annual Greek sponge production before the use of diving suits at 20,000 francs, and at 2,000,000 francs in 1877. The difference being indeed considerable, we should take into consideration that the Greek sponge fishermen adopted the use of the diving suit without a significant previous yield in naked diving. See (Ανώνυμος), "Σπογγαλιεία", Aθηναΐς [(Anonymous), "Sponge Fishery", Athinais] 2/23 (1877), pp. 183–184.

wearing the suit and scaphander, which enabled them to dive in colder autumn or even winter waters. The islands that benefited the most from the use of the scaphander diving suit that began dominating the sponge fishery in the late 19th century were Kalymnos, Symi, Hydra and Aegina. What is more, these islands managed to join the sponge-trading sector proactively, and very rapidly secured a monopoly over the distribution of sponges in international markets.

The diver, now called a "machinist" [μηχανικός], wore the "machine's dress"; a heavy, watertight, full-body suit made of rubber, weighing roughly 25.6 kilograms, and metal shoes that weighed the same. On his back and chest, he carried lead plates weighing 19 kilograms, while on his shoulders the diver wore lead weights of 11.5 kilograms. On his head, he wore a 22-kilogram metal helmet, attached to a copper breastplate tightly fixed on his suit, hence the entire suit weighed 101 to 102 kilograms.[53] On the front of the helmet there was a glass window with a magnifying lens through which the diver looked, and a non-rotating exhaust valve, the "varvara", which the diver pressed with his temple in order to adjust the air pressure, which was then released in the form of bubbles. A flexible hose connected to the air pump on the vessel known as the "markoutso", was attached to the helmet and as soon as the diver jumped into the sea, he let the suit fill with air, checked for punctures, and then released the air through the helmet valve [the varvara] and descended at a steady rate. Two men constantly supplied the diver with oxygen from the air pump, the "roda" [the wheel], which was equipped with a gauge to measure the air pressure.

One of the men kept track of the duration of the dive, while the other, the "kolaouzieris", or diving supervisor held a rope – the "kolaouzos" [literally, "the one who shows the way"] – at all times which was tied around the diver's waist. The kolaouzos [rope] also served as a kind of telegraph between diver and supervisor, through which they communicated by means of tugs on the rope counted according to a specific code, thus permitting divers to signal what was happening below. A diver could signal if there were enough sponges to justify staying down, if the diver was in danger, if he wanted to resurface, and so on.[54]

---

53   Carabokyro, *Étude sur la pêche des éponges*, p. 9; Κριεζής, *Η σπογγαλιεία* [Kriezis, *The Sponge Fishery*], pp. 9–10.

54   Cabirol had already proposed some simple and intuitive signals for divers to communicate with their ships. See Cabirol, *Scaphandre*, p. 11. According to Kalymnian diver and rope tender Lefteris Mamouzelos: "one pull meant 'I am on the bottom', two meant 'send more air, I'm in trouble', two followed by many 'get ready to haul me up'. If the rope got stuck somewhere or if a dogfish appeared, three flat pulls meant 'haul me up slowly' and three hurried pulls or more consecutive ones meant 'haul me up as fast as you can'. I, on the other side, pulled once to let him know that 'your time is almost up', pulled twice and held the rope stretched meaning 'I'll haul you up in a bit', and at the third pull I started pulling him up. But sometimes the area was good, brimming with sponges and the mechanic didn't want to come up. I stretched the rope, but he would tug it on the

The air pump, or the "machine", was manually operated by two "*rodanitzides*", who had to ensure that the wheel of the pump [*roda*], revolved at a rate of 25 to 30 turns per minute for a smooth supply of oxygen to the diver. This constant supply of oxygen then extended the length of time the diver could spend at the bottom of the sea.[55]

Kalymnian author Giannis Zervos provided a vivid description of the vessel carrying the diving apparatus and its parts:

> The '*achtarmas*': a *trechandiri* [a kind of caique] is five to six meters in length, where there is no room left to set one's foot. The engine was back in the stern and on the deck, there were barrels of fuel and naphtha and equipment. In the middle was the hold, filled up with the diving machine. On the right side of the deck, a pile of coiled hoses. On the other gunwale, the one on the left, as if it were a human headless body, breastplate-arms-legs, the empty rubber machine suits hung like cold ghosts. The rest of the instruments could be found nearer the prow: the iron helmet, the iron breastplate, the iron shoes, the lead weights that they hung on the divers' chests and backs as they do with moribund people; a tragic ornament, the weight of which helps the diver to walk on the bottom of the sea, forty to forty-five fathoms deep, in rough seas. There was also the "*kolaouzos*", a thin rope like a string of gauze tied on his waist, so that the "*kolaouzieris*" on the prow can "fish" with him [casting him out and reeling him in]. And the "*skandali*", another rope tied from the prow that the diver can hold in his right hand while he jumps; by releasing it slowly he gets used to the weight of the liquid element, so that the blood won't go directly to his heart, thus avoiding strokes and paralyses.[56]

The vessels working with diving suits fell into three categories, "*richitika*" [shallow-water], "*mesarika*" [of average-sea depths] and "*vathytika*" [deepwater], depending on the depth at which divers worked. The duration of each

---

opposite direction and sometimes unfasten it. I then yelled 'take the rope out' and 'haul [him] up by the air hose'. Occasionally, if the air hoses were slack, he would tie them around a rock to prevent us from lifting him up. Even if we did manage to haul him, as the hoses went under his legs, we would haul him up head down." Testimony of *kolaouzieris* and captain Lefteris Mamouzelos published in the journal *Ελληνικό Πανόραμα* [*Elliniko Panorama*] (2007), p. 167. Informant Petros Marthas provides us with the same description, calling the rope [*kolaouzos*] the diver's "telephone". Testimony of *kolaouzieris* and captain Petros Marthas to E.O., 2/9/2004.

55   Carabokyro, *Étude sur la pêche des éponges*, p. 9. After the WWII the hand-cranked air pump was replaced by a mechanical pump that ran on diesel.

56   Γιάννης Ζερβός, *Μοιραίο σκάφανδρο και τ' ανάθεμα της μηχανής* [Giannis Zervos, *The Fatal Scaphander Diving Suit and the Anathema of the Machine*] Athens 1959, p. 70.

dive was inversely proportional to the depth, as was the number of divers employed on each vessel. At shallow depths of up to 25 to 30 meters, 4 to 5 divers who could carry out longer and more frequent dives each day were employed. Deep-water ships could hire more than 10 divers because their stay in waters of 40 or even 70 meters deep was brief. These vessels employed the most proficient divers, who gathered the largest quantities of sponges, earned the most, and were exposed to the greatest dangers.[57] They would usually dive three times per day, diving approximately every three hours.[58]

The depth, duration, and total number of dives per day were three interdependent parameters that determined the performance of divers and, consequently, their remuneration. Although concern for the precise calculation of depth and time is evident in the testimonies and popular writing of that period, the records do not demonstrate a concern with technique and duration.

So approximately how long did a dive last? Opinions are particularly contradictory on this point. Some of the oldest available sources are the observations of Alphonse Gal, a doctor who traveled in the Dodecanese in the late 1860s, while working on his doctoral thesis. Referring to cases of patients suffering from divers' disease, Gal recorded instances of dives that lasted from a half hour to one hour, at 35 to 40 meters. Neurologist and professor of medicine Michail Katsaras later conducted similar scientific research and collected patient narratives in order to study various symptoms of divers' disease. From this research it appears that, in the last three decades of the 19th century, most of the divers with whom Katsaras spoke stayed down 10 to 15 minutes at a depth of 25 to 30 fathoms, while they performed 3 to 6 dives per day. Some of them, however, dove more often, or remained under for 30 or 35 minutes at the same depth.[59] Therefore, in 1886 observer Miltiadis Carabokyros must had been exaggerating when he wrote that divers descended to a depth of 35 meters and remained there for 4 to 5 hours.[60] Nevertheless, more recent testimonies make it clear that the time spent at 60 meters was approximately 10 minutes, while it did not exceed 2 to 3 minutes in greater depths. This was

57   Ζώτος, Ἔκθεσις [Zotos, *Report*], p. 5. The production of the deep-water vessels was about twice that of the rest. Nevertheless, the average annual yield with diving suits and scaphander is calculated at 1,500–2,000 kilograms of sponges. See Χρίστος Σερμπέτης, "Η αλιευτική επιχείρησις εις την Ελλάδα", *Τεχνικά Χρονικά* [Christos Serbetis, "The Sponge-Fishing Industry in Greece", *Technika Chronika*] 24/ 279 (1947), pp. 31–32.
58   Testimony of *kolaouzieris* Vassilis Kampourakis to E.O., 1/9/2004.
59   M. Catsaras, "Recherches cliniques et expérimentales sur les accidents survenant par l'emploie des scaphandres", *Archives de Neurologie* 17/49–51 (1889), pp. 392–437.
60   Carabokyro, *Étude sur la pêche des éponges*, p. 9.

also dependent on the diver's abilities and the time needed to harvest 4 to 5 sponges, if he found a good spot.[61]

In their search for the location of sponge-bearing beds, sponge fishermen used the *"bara"*, a fine rope with a weight that was used for seeking out for the sponge bearing areas, known by spongers as the *"panghi"*, *"karines"*, *"louria"* [terms for sponge-bearing areas, meaning "banks", "keel", "straps"] of the sea bottom. Another method involved a small boat with a two-member crew who went out in search of adequate sponge-bearing areas. At any rate, the discovery of sponge-rich areas depended on exploratory dives, performed by the most experienced divers.[62] It was essential that they be followed by an assisting vessel, or *"depozito"*.[63]

The last *depozito* vessel, equipped with diving suit and scaphander, departed from the port of Kalymnos in 1975.

2.4 The "Pilot" *Kolaouzieris*: Supervising the Dive

> Our mother is the machine
> Our sister is the *roda*
> Our life depends on the *kolaouzieris*

The job of the *kolaouzieris* or diving supervisor was extremely important and crucial to the organization of sponge fishing. He was trusted by the captain and was usually an older seaman or diver.[64] Testimonies indicate that the supervisor participated in the selection of crew members, and sometimes sought to recruit divers and crews from neighbouring islands. The diving manager [*kolaouzieris*] was also the organizer on a technical level and arranged the diving process.

By observing the sea currents, weather changes, and the direction and intensity of the winds, the diving manager chose diving locations and tracked

---

61   Testimony of diver Giannis Loulourgas to E.O., 23/8/2004; testimony of diving manager and captain Petros Marthas to E.O., 2/9/2004.

62   See also the testimony of sponger Michail Stefadouros to Faneromeni Chalkidiou-Skylla, Ἡ σφουγγάρι ἡ τομάρι [*Either Sponge or Corpse*], p. 173. Πιζάνιας, "Ἡ ὀργάνωσις τῆς σπογγα-λιευτικῆς ἐπιχειρήσεως" [Pizanias, "The Organization of the Sponge-Fishing Enterprise"], pp. 3–32.

63   According to entries in the logbook of Kalymnos' Port Authority, as well as other sources in 1978, with a nine-member crew in direction to Lambedusa; see Φανερωμένη Χαλκιδιού-Σκυλλά, Ἡ σφουγγάρι ἡ τομάρι [Faneromeni Chalkidiou-Skylla, *Either Sponge or Corpse*], p. 46.

64   Ζώτος, Ἔκθεσις [Zotos, *Report*], p. 6.

the time that divers spent on the seafloor, as well as their movements.[65] The length of submerged knotted rope indicated fluctuations in the depth of each dive; this method of measuring depth was supplanted by the depth-sounder after WWII. However, with old manual methods, knots were measured by means of an hourglass, or the *"mantzaroli"*. According to testimonies, divers were mistrustful of the diving manager and preferred to have this part of the operation handled by another diver.[66] Every turn of the hourglass was roughly equivalent to half a minute; so at 30 fathoms they counted 15 turns of the hourglass, or around six and a half minutes.[67] As soon as the time elapsed, the diving manager pulled the thin rope, thereby letting the diver know that he should surface. The diver would then resurface immediately, given that spongers were not yet familiar with the rules for decompression. Divers who could stay down for long periods of time without being affected by the machine [scaphander] were dubbed *"mantzarolas"*.[68] One of the techniques that divers used for resurfacing on their own, was to shut the air valve [*varvara*], thus filling the suit with air so that the diver surfaced at great speed, often being even ejected dramatically by the force.[69]

The scarcity of mechanical clocks, however, does not entirely justify the use of the hourglass in an otherwise modernized activity, for which precise time-keeping was of paramount importance.[70] Indeed, most of the informants for this study noted that clocks came into use only after 1946 and that, even then, many spongers continued to trust the hourglass. This then, is a reminder that premodern and modern elements and practices continued to coexist in the industry for several decades, and that what ultimately mattered was performance and the supply of necessary raw materials and commodities to markets to satisfy new needs, and not the safety of those practicing the professions involved.

---

65 For the difficulties that divers working in great depths encountered due to sea currents, see Manuscript 1838/1973, *Ευαγγελία Λαμπαδαρίου* [*Evangelia Lampadariou*], p. 171, CFS. See also the testimony of Petros Marthas to E.O., 2/9/2004.

66 Testimony of Lefteris Mamouzelos to E.O., 3/9/2004.

67 See the testimony of machinist Nikolaos Sdregas to E.O., 30/8/2004. Other sources report that each turn of the hourglass was equal to one and a half minutes. For an illustration of the process, see Russell, "Η σπογγαλιεία της Καλύμνου" ["The Sponge Fishery of Kalymnos"], pp. 5–9.

68 Testimony of captain Lefteris Mamouzelos to E.O., 3/9/2004; Manuscript 2729/1976, Αγγελική Γεωργιάδου [Angeliki Georgiadou], p. 57, CFS.

69 Εστία [*Estia*], 14/4/1903, p. 1.

70 For the rational planning of productive time and the importance of the clock, see Ε. Π. Τόμσον, *Χρόνος, εργασιακή πειθαρχία και βιομηχανικός καπιταλισμός*, Βασ. Τομανάς (μετάφρ.) [E. P. Thompson, *Time, Work-Discipline and Industrial Capitalism*. Translation, V. Tomanas], Athens 1983; Thierry Paquot, *Η τέχνη της σιέστας*, Μαρία Παγουλάτου (μετάφρ.) [*The Art of the Siesta*. Translation, M. Pagoulatou], Athens 2009, pp. 32–43.

2.5   The Introduction of the Scaphander

Until the mid-19th century there were no diving suits with scaphanders in the Ottoman Empire, and opinions vary as to the year in which they were introduced on the island of Kalymnos. Kalymnian lawyer Miltiadis Carabokyros, who served as a delegate of the community to Constantinople, reported that the sponge-fishing populations of the Ottoman territories used diving suits for the first time in 1866,[71] and this date is confirmed by the reports and memoranda of the Elders [*Demogerontia*].[72] Carl Flegel expressed the same opinion, noting that the diving suit and scaphander were introduced into the southern Sporades by French merchant Aublé in the mid-1860s.[73]

As a matter of fact, Aublé, a representative on Rhodes of the newly formed "Société pour la pêche des éponges, au moyen des appareils plongeurs Rouquayrol et Denayrouze", drafted a particularly interesting text, most likely in 1868.[74] We do not know if the manuscript was published in a French newspaper or journal of that period, but it was, in any event, not an independent publication. However, Aublé's compatriots, who also wrote of the scientific achievements of their time, and of the diving suit between 1868 and 1870, also had knowledge of the Rouquayrol and Denayrouze suit. Aublé suggested that the first diving suit was introduced in Syria by M. A. Coulombel, co-founder of the Parisian house "Coulombel frères et Devismes".[75] This merchant house, which appears shortly afterwards to have supplied diving suits to the Dodecanesian importers as well, was also involved in the sponge trade and fishery in Tunisia.[76]

---

71 Carabokyro, *Étude sur la pêche des éponges*, p. 3.

72 This information comes up in a number of texts, decisions, and letters of the Demogerontia of Kalymnos. See, for instance, Doc. 1, 4/1/1894, Correspondence 1894–1895, MAK. However, in another letter to the Metropolitan of Tripoli, the Demogerontia traces their introduction to 1867. See Doc. 343, 5/2/1920, Minutes of Administrative Board 1892–1893, MAK.

73 See Κάρολος Φλέγελ, "Τα Δωδεκάνησα ή Νότιες Σποράδες από ένα υπόμνημα των αρχών του αιώνα", Κυριάκος Κων. Χατζηδάκης (μετάφραση-σχόλια), *Καλυμνιακά Χρονικά* [Carl Flegel, "The Dodecanese, or the Southern Sporades from Memo of the Beginning of this Century". Translation and annotation, Kyriakos K. Chatzidakis, *Kalymniaka Chronika*] 12 (1997), p. 63, and Χατζηδάκης, "Η σπογγαλιεία στις Νότιες Σποράδες" [Chatzidakis, "Sponge Fishing in the Southern Sporades"], p. 237. In another of his studies he refers specifically to 1866, Φλέγελ, "Το σπογγαλιευτικό ζήτημα" [Flegel, "The Sponge-Fishery Issue"], p. 212.

74 *Dictionnaire Encyclopédique des sciences médicales*, vol. 7, Paris 1870, p. 219.

75 Méricourt, "Considérations sur l'hygiène", p. 278; Figuier, *Les merveilles de la science*, p. 678.

76 *Colonies françaises et pays de protectorat à l'Exposition universelle de 1889*. Guide publié par la Société des études coloniales et maritimes, Paris 1889, p. 178.

When Coulombel arrived in Syria in the early 1850s, he was accompanied by a diver from Toulon, who was to teach spongers how to use the diving apparatus. They toured together through various areas demonstrating the diving suit's capabilities. However, while doing a demonstration, the French diver suffered from an accident and, after he insistently tugged on the rope, they hauled him to the surface while in terrible pain and he died a few hours later. Although rumors circulated that the diver had been poisoned, this incident apparently disheartened Coulombel and scared away prospective clients, hence no one spoke of the incident or attempted a new test dive.

According to Aublé, ten years elapsed before anyone else was willing to give the diving suit and scaphander a try; this time it was a Symiot diver, Fotis Mastoridis. Dimosthenis Chaviaras, Theodoros Kriezis and Sotirios Agapitidis also concur on this point, and their accounts differ only on the year: according to Aublé, the next attempt took place in 1860, whereas the others placed the event in 1863, 1865 and 1866 respectively. It seems, though, that Mastoridis had worked with English companies on port development works and wreck removal in India, where he descended to depths of up to 50 meters. Mastoridis reportedly returned to his birthplace, bringing with him a diving suit and accessories, which was a gift from his superiors, and he is credited with being the first to use it to harvest sponges.[77] The French merchant reported that until 1865, Mastoridis was the only one to use the diving suit with great success. However, according to Greek authors who have further fleshed out the narrative, the first trial took place at the port of Symi, and was undertaken by Mastoridis' pregnant wife Evgenia who wanted to persuade her compatriots that the apparatus was completely safe.[78] Here it is not entirely clear where historical truth parts company with legend, given that the most important and

---

77 See Κυριάκος Κ. Χατζηδάκης, "Ο αγώνας για την κατάργηση των σκαφάντρων και ο Κάρολος Φλέγελ", *Καλυμνιακά Χρονικά* [Kyriakos Kon. Chatzidakis, "The Fight to Abolish the Scaphander Diving Suits and Carl Flegel", *Kalymniaka Chronika*] 3 (1982), p. 38; Bernard Russell, "Kalymnian Sponge Diving", *Human Biology* 39/2 (1967), p. 113 and Αγαπητίδης, "Η οικονομική οργάνωση" [Agapitidis, "The Financial Organization"], p. 185; Χαβιαράς, *Περί σπόγγων και σπογγαλιείας* [Chaviaras, *On Sponges and Sponge Fishing*], p. 49; Χαβιαράς, "Τινά περί σπογγαλιείας" [Chaviaras, "On the Sponge Fishery"], p. 5; Θεόδωρος Κριεζής, "Η σπογγαλιεία", *Οικονομικός Ταχυδρόμος*, [Theodoros Kriezis, "Sponge Fishing", *Oikonomikos Tachydromos*] 14/8/1932, p. 1; Kalafatas, *The Bellstone*, p. 13. Symiot sponge merchant G. Georgas holds the opinion that the use of the diving suit was launched on Symi in 1863; see Γεώργιος Ελευθ. Γεωργάς, *Μελέτη περί σπογγαλιείας, σπόγγων και σπογγεμπορίου από των αρχαιοτάτων χρόνων μέχρι σήμερον* [Georgios Elefth. Georgas, *Study of the Sponge Fishery, Sponges, and the Sponge Trade from Ancient Times to the Present*], Piraeus 1937, pp. 27–28.

78 Kalafatas, *The Bellstone*, p. 13.

enduring issues were the performance and safety that the diving suit offered its users.

French doctor Alphonse Gal, who observed diving practices in the southeastern Aegean Sea, and who participated in diving as part of the research for his doctoral thesis in the early years that the suit and scaphander were in use, likewise provides us with valuable factual evidence.[79] According to Gal, in 1867 there were 24 divers using the first 12 British-made diving suits, in depths of up to 45 meters. They resurfaced in a very few minutes, and every diver engaged in several descents per day.[80] In 1868, there were at least 10 diving suits with scaphanders on Kalymnos, used by 30 divers. By 1869 there were more than 15 diving suits on Kalymnos used by 45 divers.[81] The discrepancy in the dates found in contemporary and subsequent texts follows a trajectory typical of technological innovations; the introduction, the failed trials, and people's reactions, in this case, after the suit was put into use.

Nevertheless, Aublé's testimony that Kalymnians were front runners in 1865, when they briefly used a diving suit with scaphander from a French merchant house in Constantinople, appears to be accurate. Both Aublé and Alfred Le Roy de Méricourt, a professor of naval medicine, did not hesitate to publicly decry the fierce reactions of local residents who destroyed the machine and attacked those who had used it. This apparently explains some of the written statements found in the records of Kalymnos, such as one from May 1866 by diver Ioannis Maillis in which he pledged, before the Elders of Kalymnos, not to work "with the underwater sponge-fishing machine under any circumstances. I therefore take responsibility for compliance with the abolishment resolutions issued by the community of Kalymnos".[82] In similar individual or collective statements of divers dating from the following year, it seems that they already knew the consequences of using the diving suit and scaphander, given that they stated that "the homeland has the right to send us into exile but, if we suffer from anything else, we do not retain any right to demand the slightest compensation".[83] Nevertheless, in 1866 seven diving suits with scaphanders were in use on Rhodes, Symi and Kalymnos, thereby stimulating the introduction of this new technology.

---

79   The title of his doctoral thesis was "Des dangers du travail dans l'air comprimé et des moyens de les prévenir", Montpellier 1872.
80   Paul Bert, *La pression barométrique. Recherches de physiologie expérimentale*, Paris 1879, p. 412.
81   Bert, *La pression barométrique*, p. 423.
82   Doc. 87, 20/5/1866, MC Minutes 1863–1884, MAK.
83   Doc. 109 and 110, 17/3/1867, MC Minutes 1863–1884, MAK.

2.5.1 *Procurement of Scaphander Diving Suits*

Although orders for equipment were most commonly placed directly with suppliers abroad, a few diving machines were occasionally purchased from intermediaries conducting business in various areas, such as Rhodes, Smyrna, Alexandria, Syros, and Piraeus.[84] Indirect allusions and references to prices suggest that the cost of equipment was particularly high, at least until the interwar period [i.e. following WWI]. If, for instance, the maximum annual production for each vessel amounted to about 1 ton in 1877 [i.e. a value of 30,000 French francs], then a scaphander diving suit that cost 5,400 francs was not a negligible investment for the ship's captain.[85]

The usual suppliers to Dodecanesian sponge fishermen were French and British manufacturers, although there was a clear preference for the British merchant houses, at least during the period for which any scant surviving evidence is available. In more recent years, oral testimonies and other accounts suggest that French machines [i.e., scaphander diving suits] were considered superior. We do know, however, that approximately 100 diving apparatuses were imported in 1878.[86]

The dealers were local merchants, usually sponge merchants, engaged in diverse business activities. One of them, Michail Olympitis, was a Kalymnian merchant and investor in sponge-fishing groups who ran a sponge merchant house jointly with his son in Paris. Olympitis procured scaphander diving suits and parts from Paris and London, and supplied them to the sponge-fishing markets of the Dodecanese, as well as to Samos and Çeşme in the late 19th and early 20th centuries.[87] Olympitis dealt with intermediary buyers and did not deal directly with captains,[88] and the foreign commercial houses with which he did business sent large numbers of suits and samples in order to test the quality and address clients' complaints. It appears, moreover, that there were indeed complaints, as a one community decision illustrates. In 1893, a relative of Ioannis Olympitis imported suits to Kalymnos which were judged inadequate for sponge fishing:

---

84   See, for instance, Doc. 308, 17/8/1896, MC Minutes 1896–1897, MAK.

85   [Ανώνυμος], "Σπογγαλιεία", Ἀθηναῖς [(Anonymous), "Sponge Fishery", *Athinais*] 2/23 (1877), pp. 183–184.

86   P. L. Simmonds, *The Commercial Products of the Sea or, Marine Contributions to Food, Industry and Art*. London, 1878, p. 183.

87   Archive of Michail Olympitis, Catalogue 1, Letter 9/21 March 1901, p. 21, Greek Literary and Historical Archive [*Elliniko Logotechniko kai Istoriko Archeio*, hereafter ELIA] – Cultural Foundation of the National Bank [*Morfotiko Idryma Ethnikis Trapezis*, hereafter MIET].

88   Archive of Michail Olympitis, Catalogue 1, Letter 13 March 1901, p. 21, ELIA/MIET.

We certify that, from the 17 sponge-fishing machine dresses [suits] sent last June to Ioannis Em. Olympitis from Munich, Bayern (by Mr N. Vouvalis, headquartered in London, and who purchased them from Metzeler et Co.), three were sold to local captains of sponge-fishing machines. Nevertheless, when the captains tested them on the job, and discovered that the suits were not completely impermeable and therefore useless [also not, usable in sponge fishery], and they complained to the Elders. Once it was established that they were indeed useless, the suits were returned to the seller Io. Em. Olympitis based on the Elder's decision and, in witness thereof, we provide this certification of monies owing him.[89]

Although used apparatuses and scaphander suits from Europe were not normally imported, used parts were indeed sold in the sponge-fishing markets of the Dodecanese. For instance, Michail Olympitis made an exception and accommodated a client from Vathy on Samos, providing him with a used scaphander diving suit in September 1901. In his letters, he describes its parts and the price: it consisted of the "trunk", a box containing the device, the air pump, two wheels, a helmet, two breastplates and a pair of bronze shoes, for a total value of 30 gold coins of 20 francs. The suits and hoses were calculated separately.[90] According to a subsequent letter, the order was completed with the addition of the rest of the parts: a scaphander diving suit, three 14-meter spools of tubing, two lead bars, and two handles with which the worker cranked the device. It was also specified that the device was suitable to a depth of 30 fathoms.

Parts, such as screws and washers, could be acquired at factories on Samos,[91] whereas additional works or minor repairs, such as the adjustment of the hose on the scaphander helmet, could be made at the smithies on Kalymnos. Local machine shops also continued to do repairs, while local craftsmen gradually obtained the machinery and technical expertise needed to construct an entire air pump, as well as the molded parts of the apparatus, the metal parts of the suit, and the diver's helmet.[92] The diesel engines that powered the ships after

---

89   The text in parentheses was written in the margin of the record. See Doc. 379, 16/12/1893, MC Minutes 1892–1893, MAK.

90   Archive of Michail Olympitis, Catalogue 1, Letter 9/22 November 1901, p. 43, and Letter 27/9 November 1901, p. 39, ELIA/MIET.

91   Archive of Michail Olympitis, Catalogue 1, Letter 9/22 November 1901, p. 42, and Letter 16/29 November 1901, p. 44, ELIA/MIET.

92   Testimony of machinist Nikolaos Sdregas to E.O., 30/8/2004; Testimony of captain Petros Marthas to E.O., 2/9/2004; Russell, "Η σπογγαλιεία της Καλύμνου" ["The Sponge Fishery of Kalymnos"], pp. 14–15.

1928, were imported but they were repaired in the same local, Kalymnian machine shops in the winter. Based on more recent testimonies, there were few machine shops before WWII:

> There was a craftsman from Symi, Nikitas Kougios, a Turkish craftsman who lived here and had been baptized, Manolis, Giorgos Lagopoulos, who was a mechanic-lathe turner – his father was a broker and had worked in Syros for many years – and others [...]. Machine shops repaired and adjusted diving machines every year, made helmets, mended the casings and the ship engines. Foundries built some of their parts here. The air pumps came from Syros' machine shops (from Barbetas machine works). In the past, the machines here were French, just like the Fernez. They say that a man from Koulouri brought the Fernez to Kalymnos. He was a caique captain. He was clever with finances.[93]

2.6   The Fernez Diving Apparatus

After WWI, sponge fishery in the Dodecanese saw the arrival of the Fernez diving apparatus, which was invented in 1912 and used in shell harvesting in the Red Sea.[94] In 1919, demonstrations of the new apparatus were given in the river Seine in France, in the presence of French and Greek interested parties, doctors, and the then Prime Minister of Greece, Eleftherios Venizelos.[95] In the same year, exploratory dives were carried out on Rhodes and Symi, in Piraeus, and shortly thereafter on Kalymnos.[96] In 1920, Daniil Pikramenos, Mayor of Kalymnos, drew up a certificate attesting that the three divers participating in these demonstrations,

> resurfaced as lively as if they had been on land. When the device was removed from their mouths, they started laughing and complaining because they were not allowed to stay longer at the bottom of the sea. After a medical examination, these divers were found to be in a most healthy condition, as confirmed by the doctors' report included herein.[97]

---

93   Testimony of Lefteris Mamouzelos to E.O., 3/9/2004.

94   Γεωργάς, *Μελέτη περί σπογγαλιείας* [Georgas, *Study of the Sponge Fishery*], p. 29. See also Κώστας Δαμιανίδης, "Μέθοδοι σπογγαλιείας", Αφιέρωμα: Η Ελληνική σπογγαλιεία, *Η Καθημερινή, Επτά Ημέρες*, [Damianidis, K. "Sponge-Fishing Methods in the Greek Sponge Fishery", *I Kathimerini*: Feature Section *Epta Imeres*] , 13/9/1998, pp. 13–15.

95   Γεωργάς, *Μελέτη περί σπογγαλιείας* [Georgas, *Study of the Sponge Fishery*], p. 50.

96   Ibid., p. 53.

97   Ibid., p. 54.

With this system, divers descended without a suit, wearing a mask with a fitted air hose.[98] The hose provided oxygen with an air compressor (initially hand-cranked and later mechanically driven), like that of the scaphander diving suit. Divers usually wore long black tunics sewn by the women of the island.[99]

The crews of vessels sponge fishing with the Fernez were made up of 18 to 22 men, of whom 8 to 10 were divers.[100] Proponents of the Fernez tried to compare it to naked diving and viewed it as an improved version of the earlier practice. They argued in favour of divers' improved performance, and how they were able to move freely on the seafloor while breathing natural air. For these same reasons, other captains and divers argued in their testimonies that the Fernez was more dangerous, precisely because divers were not wearing the heavy diving suit and were therefore more mobile, and could move more quickly between depths, or prolong the time spent under water. In addition, without the scaphander suit, divers were affected by the cold and could not last long in great depths in spring or autumn waters or participate in winter expeditions.[101]

The first apparatuses on Kalymnos were purchased in 1922 for 50 French francs by Symiot merchant G. Georgas, who also acted as a representative of their French manufacturer, Maurice Fernez.[102] Although it was already widely used, and particularly in the 1930s in periods of intense sponge fishing,[103] the Fernez apparatus was not as popular, nor did it enjoy the same longevity as the scaphander diving suit. In fact, it is reported that protests against the use of the Fernez took place on Symi in the 1930s, which resulted in the discontinuation of this diving method.[104] Moreover, based on calculations carried out in the early years following WWII, the average annual yield using the Fernez failed to match, and by far, the annual yield using the scaphander suit.[105]

The 1970s was the decade of the *"naryiles"* [hookah] method. Its name derives from the fact that the diver put the air tube directly into his mouth as

---

98   Αγαπητίδης, "Η οικονομική οργάνωση" [Agapitidis, "The Financial Organization"], p. 186.

99   Testimony of machinist Nikolaos Sdregas to E.O., 30/8/2004.

100   Πιζάνιας, "Η οργάνωσις της σπογγαλιευτικής επιχειρήσεως" [Pizanias, "The Organization of the Sponge-Fishing Enterprise"], pp. 30–31.

101   See also the testimony of captain Lefteris Mamouzelos, 3/9/2004.

102   58th Meeting, 30/4/1922, MC Minutes 1917–1922, MAK.

103   Roberto Pronzato, Renata Manconi, "Mediterranean Commercial Sponges: Over 5000 Years of Natural History and Cultural Heritage", *Marine Ecology* 29 (2008), p. 149.

104   Πιζάνιας, "Η οργάνωσις της σπογγαλιευτικής επιχειρήσεως" [Pizanias, "The Organization of the Sponge-Fishing Enterprise"], p. 28. The last Fernez apparatus was used by Kalymnian divers in 1980, based on information from the Port Authority of Kalymnos.

105   Δωδεκάνησος. Τετράτομος μελέτη του Υπουργείου Ανοικοδομήσεως [*Dodecanese. Study in Four Volumes by the Ministry for Reconstruction*], p. 141.

TABLE 2.2   Annual yield of different sponge-fishing methods after WWII (in kgs)

Fishery location	Scaphander			Fernez	Gagava	Hook	Naked divers
	Shallow-water	Medium-water	Deep-water				
Tripoli area	1,200	1,800	3,000	600–1,300	500	200–250	300–350
Cyrenaica	–					180–220	
Tunisia	1,950	2,200	2,800				

SOURCE: ΔΩΔΕΚΑΝΗΣΟΣ. ΤΕΤΡΑΤΟΜΟΣ ΜΕΛΕΤΗ ΤΟΥ ΥΠΟΥΡΓΕΙΟΥ ΑΝΟΙΚΟΔΟΜΗΣΕΩΣ [*DODECANESE. STUDY IN FOUR VOLUMES BY THE MINISTRY FOR RECONSTRUCTION*], P. 141

a sort of variation of the Fernez apparatus; the difference being that, in this case, the mask covers the diver's entire face and a mechanical air compressor, with a 100 to 300 meter long air hose, enables the diver to move about freely.[106] These devices are basically technical improvements on the unwieldy diving suit, given that they followed the same logic: they provided natural air to the diver via an air pump, initially hand-cranked and later machine driven. The naked divers' *skandalopetra* [or stone rudder], and other implements of divers working with the Fernez were replaced by metal weights tied around the diver's waist. Despite the improved and perhaps more efficient versions of these diving apparatuses which appeared in the first half of the 20th century,[107] Kalymnian divers continued to use the earlier types until the first decades after the WW II.

Today, ships are equipped with a special electronic echo-sounder system that locates sponge-bearing areas. Divers wear a special watertight suit and fins on their feet and are equipped with a compass and a depth sounder. Divers are also aware of diving rules and dangers that may arise from the violation

---

106   See Jacques Momot, "L'histoire des techniques et la plongée en scaphandre autonome", *Revue d'histoire des sciences et de leurs applications* 17 (1964), p. 252; Αγαπητίδης, "Η οικονομική οργάνωση" [Agapitidis, "The Financial Organization"], p. 186; Roberto Pronzato, "Sponge-fishing, Disease and Farming in the Mediterranean Sea", *Aquatic Conservation: Marine and Freshwater Ecosystems* 9 (1999), p. 486; E. Voultsiadou, T. Dailianis, C. Antoniadou, D. Vafidis, C. Dounas και C. Chintiroglou, "Aegean Bath Sponges: Historical Data and Current Status", *Reviews in Fisheries Science* 19 (2011), p. 38.

107   Some improved versions of the diving suit are presented in a newspaper article published in *Αθηναϊκά Νέα*, [*Athinaika Nea*], 24/10/1932, p. 2.

of these rules. Those who have collected, or who are still collecting sponges using this method, claim that they can stay in the sea for many hours (around 6 to 7, sometimes up to 10 hours) at various depths, resurfacing multiple times to empty their bag or to rest.[108]

2.7   Business Factors

Taken together, investors, sponge merchants, captains, divers, auxiliary crews, and workers in sponge processing constituted a major workforce, all involved in the sponge-fishing activities of Kalymnos. The majority were local inhabitants, but there were also foreigners engaged in the robust but unstable sponge industry. They usually came from other sponge-fishing areas; some provided the necessary capital; others contributed their knowledge or the work experience that this difficult and dangerous profession demanded. Archival evidence, moreover, shows how investments as well as people migrated from one place to another, and migration from different states was not uncommon. Although some lacked relevant experience, sponge fishing offered a temporary means of survival as a supplementary activity that also held out the promise of quick returns for some.

Sponge fishing was a seasonal activity divided into four distinct phases: preparation for the voyage, the fishing itself, the artisanal processing of the product, and finally, marketing the sponges. Where quantities were limited, the same people might be involved throughout the entire process, from harvesting the sponges to promoting them for sale. It was, however, more common to form short-term, business collaborations for sponge fishing, with partners who had more distinct roles, especially when large investments, such as those needed for the scaphander suit, the Fernez and *naryiles* [breathing device], were involved.

The partners who handled the business end were responsible for the vessels and their equipment, while the labor force organized and carried out the journey and dealt with the processing of the merchandise. The next steps were undertaken by merchant houses, which were headquartered in sponge-fishing areas or abroad, and which collected and introduced sponges into the international market. These merchant houses, which might involve local merchants, were also known to purchase the sponge production in advance and, on

---

108   Testimony of diver and captain Nikolas Kampourakis to E.O., 28/8/2002.

occasion, to lend shipowners the necessary capital to organize sponge-fishing expeditions, thereby reserving, *ex ante*, the catch.

When quantities of sponges harvested by each diver were more or less equal, and expedition costs were limited, as with naked diving for sponges, work could be organized on a cooperative basis by distributing costs and profits equally, and by taking joint decisions concerning fishing locations, travel, and the recruitment of divers and auxiliary staff.[109] Typically, most of the partners and workers on these vessels were related, and muster-roll documents also indicate that relatives – usually the sons of the divers – were sometimes on board as apprentices.[110]

What had formerly been limited financial investment in sponge-fishing or hooking boats on which two or three naked divers worked – one of whom was generally the captain – was replaced by a wide circle of financial transactions and creditors. Sponge-fishing groups working with scaphander suits or the Fernez required what amounted to significant investments at that time, in the form of start-up capital (equipment for the vessel, provisions, down payments, and remuneration of the crew). Although the overall costs and the size of the activity did not result in significant structural changes and permitted room for the small-scale character of the business, it became more difficult for large numbers of inhabitants to take on the job of sponger as a supplement to their family income. Therefore, those who possessed the required capital, or who were able to borrow it, now held the means of production. That said however, sponge fishing did not always yield the profits needed for most captains to finance themselves in the undertaking on the one hand, and on the other, for divers to ensure their own and their families' survival.

2.7.1   *The Investors: Sponge Merchants*

The systematic development of the sponge fishery from approximately the second half of the 19th century onwards brought gradual changes in the sponge trade, as for example, the *de facto* export business activities that led to the establishment of dynamic Greek businesses and merchant houses abroad. At that time, local sponge merchants were still headquartered on Kalymnos and they traded their merchandise in Greece, Smyrna, and Constantinople, as well as in various European countries.[111] One of the most frequent destinations was Venice, and numerous sources concur that, even as late as the 20th century,

---

109   See, for example, Doc. 1, 21/9/1884, MC Minutes 1881–1884, MAK.
110   See scattered references in MC Minutes 1881–1884, MAK.
111   Doc. 1, 4/1/1894, Correspondence 1894–1895, MAK.

IMAGE 2.5   Sponge merchant, 1950
SOURCE: PHOTOGRAPH BY DIMITRIOS HARISIADIS, KALYMNOS 1950
© BENAKI MUSEUM/PHOTOGRAPHIC ARCHIVES

bulky sponges were known as, "*éponges de Venise*".[112] The Drakos brothers are said to be the first to have sent sponges to Venice in 1840, while in the same period the Symeon brothers engaged in business activities in London.[113]

---

112   Michael D. Volonakis, *The Island of Roses and Her Eleven Sisters: Or, the Dodecanese from the Earliest Times to the Present Day*, London 1922, p. 61; Ιωάννης Σκεύου Ορφανός, "Η νήσος Κάλυμνος", *Καλυμνιακά Χρονικά* [Ioannis Skevou Orfanos, "The Island of Kalymnos", *Kalymniaka Chronika*] 17 (2007), p. 95.

113   See Μιλτιάδης Λογοθέτης, "Το εμπόριο στις Νότιες Σποράδες (Δωδεκάνησα) κατά τα τελευταία χρόνια της Τουρκοκρατίας", *Δωδεκανησιακά Χρονικά* [Miltiadis Logothetis, "Commerce

Prior to the widespread use of scaphander suits and the coastal shipping connection of Kalymnos, Symi and Chalki with Smyrna, sponge production was centered in Rhodes, the most important commercial transit center of the Southeastern Aegean Sea. From there, sponges were shipped to Smyrna or other European ports, mainly Trieste, on board Lloyd company steamboats.[114]

In the absence of other archival evidence, only a few reports and narratives from that period are available for consultation. From 1847 to 1849, sponges valued at 22,190 pounds sterling were exported from Rhodes to Constantinople, Smyrna, Trieste and Marseilles, while a small quantity was sent to Tuscany.[115] From 1854 to 1858, 554.3 tons of sponges were sold for 350,000 pounds sterling.[116] According to British archaeologist Charles T. Newton, the annual production on Kalymnos in 1854 and 1855 was generated by roughly 200 sponge-fishing vessels. The net value of the production amounted to 16,949 pounds sterling, and Smyrna consumed almost half of the overall sponges, while the rest was sent to Syros, Trieste, and Marseilles.[117]

Even though the timeline of the sponge trade put forward by Carl Flegel is not entirely accurate, it does show changes that occurred as a result of increased production, attributable to the prevalence of scaphander suits. He wrote that,

at first, the merchants of Kalymnos brought their sponges to the market of Nafplio until 1839, and afterwards to Smyrna and Trieste up until 1860. Since that specific year, many merchants have travelled with their goods

---

in the southern Sporades (Dodecanese) in the Final Years of Turkish Rule", *Dodekanisiaka Chronika*] 9 (1983), p. 143.

114   Newton, *Travels and Discoveries*, p. 292; Χατζηδάκης, "Η σπογγαλιεία στις Νότιες Σποράδες" [Chatzidakis, "Sponge Fishing in the Southern Sporades"], pp. 229–237; Ἔκθεσις περί γεωργίας, βιομηχανίας, ναυτιλίας της προξενικής περιφερείας Ρόδου ιδία διά το έτος 1910, Δελτίον του επί των Εξωτερικών Β. Υπουργείου, [*Report on Agriculture, Industry, Maritime Affairs of the Consular Precinct of Rhodes for the Year 1910, Bulletin of the Ministry for Foreign Affairs*], vol. 1, Athens 1911, pp. 30–31.

115   Χατζηδάκης, "Η σπογγαλιεία στις Νότιες Σποράδες" [Chatzidakis, "Sponge Fishing in the Southern Sporades"], p. 230.

116   Ibid., p. 234.

117   Newton, *Travels and Discoveries*, p. 295. See also Μιλτιάδης Λογοθέτης, "Το εμπόριο στις Νότιες Σποράδες (Δωδεκάνησα) κατά τα τελευταία χρόνια της Τουρκοκρατίας", Δωδεκανησιακά Χρονικά [Miltiadis Logothetis, "Commerce in the Southern Sporades (Dodecanese) in the Final Years of Turkish Rule", *Dodekanisiaka Chronika*] 9 (1983), p. 144. According to Collas, sponges were Rhodes' most important product for export of in 1850, while the value of the sponges exported from Kalymnos in 1860 is estimated at 625,000 francs. Collas, *La Turquie en 1861*, p. 224.

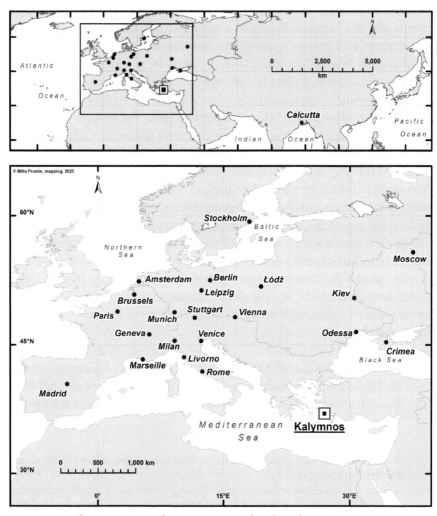

MAP 2.2   Kalymian sponge trade European network, 19th–20th centuries

to European and American countries, mostly to Russia, where more than
three hundred Kalymnians resided.[118]

---

118   For more on Carl Flegel, see Chapter 4 of the present volume, pp. 216–223. Φλέγελ, *H*
       νῆσος Κάλυμνος [Flegel, *The Island of Kalymnos*], p. 37. The same author in another of his
       works mentions 400 Kalymnians who live dispersed in Odessa and Saint Petersburg (see
       Φλέγελ, "Η Α.Θ. Παναγιότης ο Οικουμενικός Πατριάρχης Άνθιμος" [Flegel, "His Holiness the
       Ecumenical Patriarch Anthimos"], p. 10).

The merchant communities of Kalymnians established in various cities of Tsarist Russia were not exclusively engaged in the sponge trade although, according to many testimonies, they kept an eye on its fluctuations on the market.[119] Along with exporting and promoting the island's citrus fruits, Kalymnians of the Russian diaspora ran commercial shops and small factories, producing mostly slippers.[120]

If Kalymnian sponge merchants were still peddlers or needed intermediaries to promote their merchandise in the early 19th century, from the last decades of that same century, the development of the sponge trade continued to give rise to changes in the structure of the industry that would take the sponge trade itself to new, wider dimensions.[121] Sailing from Trieste, Odessa, Kiev, and Saint Petersburg, Kalymnian sponge merchants were able to create their own commercial networks and expand to Livorno, Vienna, Brussels, Amsterdam, Leipzig, Frankfurt, Madrid, Munich, Moscow, and Piraeus.

Many would later choose to establish headquarters in London, the world's largest sponge market.[122] In 1882 in London, Kalymnian Nikolaos Vouvalis established his sponge merchant house, which remained in operation until 1985. At the same time, the mobility necessitated by commerce and sponge fishing led to the creation of diasporic sponge-fishing merchant communities, such as those in Sfax, Tunis[123] and Tarpon Springs in Florida, USA, settled by Dodecanesian spongers and merchants in the early 20th century. In such cases, the creation of commercial businesses was a result of the settlement of spongers working with scaphander suits in the seas of Tunisia and in the Gulf of Mexico.[124]

---

119   For more on Kalymnians in Russia, and Kalymnians engaged in child labour in Russia at this time, see Chapter 4 of the present volume, pp. 264–268.

120   See Chapter 4 of th present volumve p. 266. See also, Λογοθέτης, "Το εμπόριο στις Νότιες Σποράδες" [Logothetis, "Commerce in the Southern Sporades"], pp. 142–145.

121   Despite the expansion of the sponge merchants' network, peddlers did not cease to exist. For instance, small-scale merchants continued to sell sponges in the commercial streets of Athens until quite recently. See Αθηναϊκά Νέα [Athinaika Nea], 25/2/1938, p. 3 and 24/11/1940, p. 3. In fact, "spongers" reportedly gathered at the entrance of the central post office in Athens.

122   Γεωργάς, Μελέτη περί σπογγαλιείας [Georgas, Study of the Sponge Fishery], p. 67. Georgas notes that, beginning in the last decades of the 19th century, they had established a sponge merchant trade union in London that controlled the international market.

123   For the commercial activities of Kalymnians in Sfax, see Doc. 141, 7/6/1907, MC Minutes 1906–1908, MAK.

124   Αντώνης Μαΐλης, "Στο Τάρπον Σπρινκς", Κάλυμνος, Η Καθημερινή, Επτά Ημέρες, [Antonis Mailis, "At Tarpon Springs", Kalymnos, I Kathimerini, Epta Imeres], vol. XIII, Δωδεκάνησα [Dodekanissa] Athens 1996, pp. 37–38.

The commercial activity, as it evolved late in the 19th century – when scientific and technological developments imposed the scaphander suit and the industrial market of the West absorbed production – was conducted by financial circles with networks and capital at their disposal, thus facilitating lucrative investments in a productive sector, with considerably high business risks. Indeed, we should not forget that investing in sponge fishing was somewhat unorthodox, as the activity itself relies on human skill and brings with it an element of chance, and therefore all the exposure to risk that this entails. Everyone involved in sponge fishing was, in effect, vulnerable and exposed to a series of unforeseeable considerations and circumstances, such as the exhaustion of sponge-bearing beds, frequent market crises, competition, and accidents. Given that the necessary sums were considerable, and that captains usually did not have the means to finance the undertaking themselves, they resorted to loans from one or more capital investors, the "*malsapides*" [from the Turkish "*malsahibi*": owner, financier], and the "*ksekinites*" [ξεκινητές: initiators], who demanded high interest rates and guarantees.[125]

These multitasking local financiers engaged in multifarious activities. They were financially robust figures in the local community, usually merchants or sponge merchants, who appear to have possessed significant capital, given that they could finance more than one sponge-fishing group. Antonios Kouremetis, for example, financed 10 vessels in 1894.[126] Apostolos Tyllianakis likewise provided the financing for numerous sponge-fishing vessels,[127] and expanded his activities by opening a flour shop on Kalymnos early in the 20th century that received supplies from various merchants from Smyrna.[128]

---

125   An example of two investors financing a sponge-fishing vessel can be found in: Doc. not numbered, 3/16 May 1923, Sponge-Fishing Issues 1922–1925, MAK, or of four or five investors in: Doc. not numbered, 1/5/1925, Doc. not numbered, 20/4/1925, Sponge-Fishing Issues 1922–1924, MAK.

126   Doc. 88, 20/4/1894, Correspondence 1894–1895, MAK.

127   Apostolos Tyllianakis had been, on several occasions, a member of the Elders council or its committees as well as a salaried municipal doctor, at least since 1881. Pursuant to the official contract cosigned with the community on 10 March 1881. Doc. 15, 6/4/1883, MC Minutes 1882–1883, MAK. See also in the same register, Doc. 6, 8/2/1883, Doc. 10, 20/3/1883, Doc. 34, 14/6/1883 and Doc. not numbered, 27/3/1885, MC Minutes 1885, MAK.

128   The largest quantity of imported flour was sold when vessels were preparing for their departure. It is at this time of year that retail commerce appears to have been revitalized, as crews received down payments and captains stocked up with the necessary provisions for the voyage. These small businesses must have been particularly profitable, given that many of the lenders were also grocers or wine sellers, according to more recent testimonies. Archive of Michail Olympitis, cat. 1, Letter 29 January 1901, p. 85, ELIA/MIET.

IMAGE 2.6   Trimming the sponges under the surveillance of the sponge merchant
SOURCE: PHOTOGRAPH BY DIMITRIOS HARISIADIS, KALYMNOS 1950
© BENAKI MUSEUM/PHOTOGRAPHIC ARCHIVES

Although loans were private, the majority were drawn up officially before the local authorities in the presence of witnesses or guarantors.[129] Credit extended for sponge fishing was short-term and loans had to be repaid at the end of the sponge-fishing season, that is, in a period of six to eight months. It would appear however, that this was practically impossible, when high interest rates are factored in that varied from 12% in 1884,[130] or 20% at the beginning of the 20th century, to as much as 25% in the first post-war years. Interest rates were usually calculated on April 1,[131] and sometimes they were even calculated *ex ante* and deducted from the capital.[132] If we also factor in the consideration that the divers' advance payments were interest-bearing loans with applicable interest rates, it is obvious that for half the year, the local community lived

---

129   See the relevant agreements for 1928–1929 in the register of sponge fishery. See also Σακελλάρης Τρικοίλης, *Νεότερη ιστορία της Καλύμνου, κοινωνική διαστρωμάτωση* [Sakellaris N. Trikoilis, *Modern History of Kalymnos. Social Stratification*], Athens 2007, pp. 264–267.

130   Doc. 190, 1/4/1884 and Doc. 192, 4/5/1884, MC Minutes 1863–1884, MAK.

131   This interest rate was fixed for the sponge-fishing regions of the Aegean Sea over several decades. See Παχουντάκης, *Η σπογγαλιεία εν Αιγύπτω* [Pachountakis, *Sponge Fishery in Egypt*], pp. 13–14. See, also Doc. not numbered, 7/5/1923 and the following document. "Sponge-Fishing Issues", 1922–1925, MAK.

132   Ζώτος, *Έκθεσις* [Zotos, *Report*], Athens 1904, p. 6.

on credit. In addition, a large portion of the local population was excessively indebted to a small number of people who accumulated capital through loans, through usurious practices, and the sponge trade. Furthermore, when they fished with scaphander suits or the Fernez, interest rates were high because of the longer sponge-fishing season, compounded by the multiple risks that each dive posed.[133] Those in charge of vessels, or groups of naked divers, or those who used other methods, also resorted to borrowing capital when crews were numerous and voyages long, although the sums borrowed were much smaller in these cases.[134]

In 1908, Carl Flegel reported that departure costs totaled 30,000 French francs for vessels fishing with scaphander suits off the coasts of northern Africa for a period of 6 to 8 months; 3,000 French francs for naked divers' vessels; 2,000 French francs for hooking boats; and 1,500 French francs for gagavas.[135] Although these amounts are estimated averages, since the total sum of each loan depended on multiple factors not mentioned in the archival records, we note here that, in the 1928 and 1929 agreements, loans granted for scaphander suits ranged from 2,000 to 6,000 pounds sterling, from about 450 to 2,500 pounds for the Fernez, whereas loans for naked divers did not exceed 150 pounds.[136] At that time however, neither the Italian authorities in the Dodecanese, nor the Bank of Rome, appear to have provided facilities or extended credit to investors in sponge-fishing expeditions.[137]

The guarantee to investors usually involved putting up properties, vessels, or even the sponge production itself, as collateral.[138] Ioannis Koukouvas and his sons borrowed 188 pounds sterling in 1921 from Ioannis Emmanouil Olympitis and Sakellarios M. Pantelis, which they had to repay at an interest rate of 20%, with "the entire catch of this year's expedition" as guarantee.[139] On other occasions, the interest rate was calculated on the date that the bill of exchange was

---

133   See also Αγαπητίδης, "Η οικονομική οργάνωση των σπογγαλιευτικών συγκροτημάτων" [Agapitidis, "The Financial Organization of the Sponge-Fishing Groups"], p. 194.

134   Doc. 6, 23/3/1928, Sponge-Fishing Issues 1928–1929, MAK.

135   Flegel, "The Abuse of the Scaphander", p. 518.

136   See also Doc. 11, 21/4/1928, Doc. 17, 17/5/1928, Sponge-Fishing Issues 1928 1929, MAK. For the costs of post-war departures see Πιζάνιας, "Η οργάνωσις της σπογγαλιευτικής επιχειρήσεως (τεχνικώς-οικονομικώς)" [Pizanias, "The Organization of the Sponge-Fishing Enterprise (on a Technical-Financial Level)"], pp. 29–36.

137   Letter of the Vice Consul in Tripoli to the Consul in Tunis (6/6/1914), Embassy in Tripoli-Libya, Folder 19 (1914), Subfolder 5, IAYE.

138   See, for example, Doc. 83, 30/4/1921, Sponge-Fishermen Recruitments 1921, MAK; Doc. unnumbered, 2/15 December 1923, Sponge-Fishing Issues 1922–1925, MAK.

139   The interest rate was calculated beginning 1 April, 1921. Doc. 83, 30/4/1921, Sponge-Fishermen Recruitments 1921, MAK. All departures for that year were funded at an interest

issued.[140] Nevertheless, it was also possible to obtain an interest-free loan for a specified period of time, usually a semester, if the borrower committed to paying it off within this timeframe.[141] However, when Georgios Korfias resorted to borrowing, his wife Kalliope offered her dowry as guarantee to the lender.[142]

The provisions concerning guarantees and mortgages are clearer in 20th century agreements and, more specifically, in those drawn up during Italian rule. Vessels, their diesel engines and equipment, divers' shares, the catch, as well as various other properties, were put up as collateral by captains in order to acquire the necessary funding.[143] During the interwar period, the existence of a few "ship owners" – both individuals and merchant houses – led to the formation of a specific group of local lenders who were able to invest in the expeditions of numerous groups equipped with scaphander suits.

In general, investors and lenders who financed these endeavours, were also the buyers of the sponge catch. This added yet another peculiar facet to sponge-fishing dynamics, given that production could not be freely distributed to the market. In such cases, the investor often demanded lower prices.[144] After selling the sponge product, it was not the captain who paid for the shares, but the sponge merchant who bought the catch, after deducting from the total value the tariffs and remunerations he was obligated to pay.[145] Importantly, crews' salaries, as our archival evidence demonstrates, were "preferential over any other claim",[146] although disagreements and disputes were not uncommon.[147]

There was ample room for speculation, however, and not only on financial loans. Various testimonies reveal that several investors in the expedition provisioned the vessels with a variety of materials, gear and foodstuffs or promoted the merchandise of specific people, thus resulting in the creation of

---

rate of 20%. It should also be noted that, in that year, the same investor also financed other sponge-fishing groups.

140   Doc. 124, 6/5/1921, Sponge-Fishermen Recruitments 1921, MAK.

141   Doc. 130, 6/5/1921 and Doc. 144, 7/5/1921, Sponge-Fishermen Recruitments 1921, MAK.

142   Doc. 99, 4/5/1921, Sponge-Fishermen Recruitments 1921, MAK.

143   See, for example, Doc. 2, 9/3/1928, doc. 3, 17/3/1928, etc., Sponge-Fishing Issues 1928–1929, MAK.

144   Πιζάνιας, "Η οργάνωσις της σπογγαλιευτικής επιχειρήσεως" [Pizanias, "The Organization of the Sponge-Fishing Enterprise"], p. 39.

145   As stated by the Elders [Demogerontia]: "We certify that the sponge-fishery industry custom applied in this place – and included in the Marine Sponge-Fishery Regulations – as per Legal Privileges, is that the person receiving the sponge product from the sponge-fishing crew shall pay the Legal Privileges, i.e. the 'imiri', the free shares of sponge fishermen and the salaries of the rowers, because these are paid from the sponge production". Doc. 556, 3/5/1884, MC Minutes-Correspondence 1884–1885, MAK.

146   Doc. 150, 7/10/1906, Land Disputes 1906–1908, MAK.

147   See, for example, Doc. 138, 13/5/1897, MC Minutes 1896–1897, MAK.

a multifaceted network of dependence.[148] Although the exact terms of such transactions remain unclear, it is often stipulated that captains obtain necessary provisions from specific people and shops indicated by the investor.[149] At the same time, not all investors were sponge merchants; local wealthy merchants invested their money in this activity as well. Those who owned commercial shops forced borrowers to shop from them, and the borrowers in turn forced their crews to do the same. Hence, merchandise was frequently sold at exorbitant prices, while poor quality food was also sold, and the catch resold to sponge-merchant houses abroad.[150] Whatever the case may be, captains claimed that there was an informal collaboration between merchants and sponge merchants so that they could "put pressure" on prices.

2.7.1.1 The Sponge Trade

There are few available sources on the trade, and even the earliest mentions of it found in the Municipal Archive of Kalymnos are scarce. One of these refers to the settlement of an old dispute over the sale of sponges in Smyrna in 1820, when the debtor's heirs were asked to pay off an old debt.[151] In a report drawn up on 16 June 1851, Niven Kerr, British Consul in Rhodes, wrote to Stratford Canning, British Ambassador to Constantinople, that Kalymnos' largest quantities of sponges were mainly exported to the England, and that Kalymnians themselves had engaged in trading their production.[152] "The entire commercial activity of the island consists of trivial retail commerce and the trade of sponges. It is this island that supplies Europe with the largest quantities of that product. [...] Spongers often load their merchandise, on their own account, bound for the UK, France, and Trieste".[153]

As archival evidence from the final decades of the 19th century attests, ship captains and divers frequently sold their sponge catch directly to sponge merchants in other locations – usually on Syros or in Piraeus – even in cases where they had binding agreements with local sponge merchants and investors.[154]

---

148 Ζώτος, Ἔκθεσις [Zotos, *Report*], p. 6.
149 Αγαπητίδης, "Η οικονομική οργάνωση" [Agapitidis, "The Financial Organization"], p. 189.
150 Testimony of Giannis Tsoulfas to E.O., 5/3/2002.
151 Doc. 49, 2/4/1864, MC Minutes 1863–1884, MAK.
152 Χατζηδάκης, "Η σπογγαλιεία στις Νότιες Σποράδες" [Chatzidakis, "Sponge Fishing in the Southern Sporades"], p. 233.
153 Κυριάκος Χατζηδάκης, "Κάλυμνος, 1851", Καλυμνιακά Χρονικά [Kyriakos Chatzidakis, "Kalymnos, 1851", *Kalymniaka Chronika*] 12 (1997), pp. 38–44. See also, by the same author, "Η σπογγαλιεία στις Νότιες Σποράδες" ["Sponge Fishing in the Southern Sporades"], p. 236.
154 Doc. 429, 20/3/1884, MC Minutes-Correspondence 1884–1885, MAK.

It was also common for investors and captains, with their crews' consent, to seek the highest offer for the catch from local and foreign merchants.[155] Sponges were delivered in sacks to local merchants, sorted by quality, and dispatched to representatives and shops in various European cities.[156] Profit margins were considerable, given that retail prices were several times higher than prices paid to fishermen.

Alexandros Lemonidis gives an account of various ways in which sponges were traded:

> Since antiquity, Smyrna has served as the warehouse for the sponge trade in the eastern coastal areas of the Ottoman state. The largest portion of this production was channeled into this city, either by the fishermen themselves, or by speculators who concluded advance deals with the spongers of those areas, for sizeable quantities. The sponges were then transported to Smyrna, where they were sold wholesale to merchants, who would then export the sponges or sell them to retail vendors who supplied them for internal [and local] consumption. Often, however, merchants – mostly Greek and some European – went to the sponge-fishing areas and obtained large quantities of sponges of all quality categories at current prices, and then transported them to Smyrna and Constantinople where they sold them independently. As well as the above, a great number of all types of sponges was gradually introduced in Smyrna and Constantinople throughout the year by the fishermen themselves, who sold them hurriedly to those well-versed in the workings of this sector of trade. By amassing small quantities of sponges, they eventually accumulated large amounts of every quality category, to cater to a variety of purposes in the different areas where they were bound to be used. Moreover, many agreements are concluded each year in anticipation of sponge deliveries in both Constantinople and Smyrna, or the fishing areas because, as far as their export to Europe or their distribution within the country are concerned, both constitute a significant trade in this product of the sea that takes place throughout the year.

---

155   Doc. 436, [23]/3/1884, Minutes and Correspondence 1884–1885, MAK.
156   Alexandras Dagkas, *Le mouvement social dans le Sud-Est européen pendant le XXᵉ siècle: Questions de classe, questions de culture*. Thessaloniki 2008, p. 134.

He goes on to discuss the differences in pricing for each fishing method, pointing out that sponges caught with a hook are worth less than those collected by divers.[157]

Carl Flegel describes the people and the locations of the sponge trade in the late 19th century in detail:

> The most important sponge-trading houses abroad were: Themelis Diamantis and Georgios Kouremetis in Vienna, the Zervos brothers in Brussels, the Symeon brothers in London, the Touloumaris brothers in Livorno, Antonios Mangos in Leipzig, Dimitrios Alexiadis in Madrid, Themelis Zervos in Munich, Georgios Skoumvourdis in Moscow, Georgios Pelekanos in Piraeus, Theodoridis and Tsapos in Stockholm, Theofilos Koutroulis in Trieste, the Iliadis brothers in Frankfurt am Main, and others elsewhere.[158] [In another list, he adds] Nikiforos Kokkinos in Amsterdam, Michail Pelekanos in Calcutta, Nikolaos Vouvalis in London, Georgios Boulafentis in London, the Patellis brothers in Odessa, Ioannis Pougounias and Ioannis Tiliakos in Saint Petersburg, Tsapos and Theodoridis in Stockholm, and Nikolaos Kolettis in Stuttgart. To these more recent references are added the most prominent Kalymnian sponge merchants residing on Kalymnos: Anagnostis Alexiadis, Iordanis Alexiadis, Nikolaos Drakos, Michail Kokkinos, Antonios Kouremetis, Aristidis Kouremetis, Nomikos Kountouris, Michail Lazarou, Michail Maglis, Ioannis E. Olympitis, Ioannis Th. Olympitis, Michail Th. Olympitis and Emmanouil N. Olympitis.[159]

While there are omissions in the above lists, as well as a number of other evident issues, we cite them because they provide at least a partial picture of the distribution of sponge-merchant houses at that time.

A certificate issued by the Elders of Kalymnos in 1919, records 775 boxes containing sponges that another sponge merchant, Michail Sapounakis, exported from Kalymnos to Piraeus, and from there, to London. In the document it is noted that "these sponges are of Greek production, and the enemies of the

---

157   Λεμονίδης, *Τὸ ἐμπόριον τῆς Τουρκίας* [Lemonidis, *The Commerce of Turkey*], pp. 158–159. Georgas presents similar details, *Μελέτη περὶ σπογγαλιείας* [*Study of the Sponge Fishery*], pp. 65–66.

158   Φλέγελ, *Ἡ νῆσος Κάλυμνος* [Flegel, *The Island of Kalymnos*], p. 37.

159   Φλέγελ, "Ἡ Α.Θ. Παναγιότης ὁ Οἰκουμενικός Πατριάρχης Ἄνθιμος" [Flegel, "His Holiness the Ecumenical Patriarch Anthimos"], pp. 27–28.

Entente shall have no benefit from them",[160] whereas it also mentions unprocessed sponges exported, this time to London by Alfred Hadji Theodorou.[161]

Because of the size of the industry, Kalymnos was established as the most important sponge-fishing island in the southeastern Aegean Sea, were transactions connected with sponge production also took place.[162] Local and foreign commercial and sponge-fishing vessels carried sponges from the coasts of northern Africa to be sold on Kalymnos, and then transferred to Europe by local buyers and their representatives. Sponge merchants also sent assessors on occasion, to check the quantity and quality of the sponges on sale.[163] Moreover, the Elders appointed a supervisor, whose task consisted of keeping records of all sponge-related transactions, in order to insure that the "local Sponge Fee" was paid.[164] It was also possible to bring large quantities of sponges onto the island that various sponge merchants had purchased elsewhere, to be processed before shipping abroad.[165] Nonetheless, a considerable number of Dodecanesian sponge merchants were also sponge buyers, who sold sponges to the foreign houses with which they had done business, or which they represented.[166]

The business culture of Dodecanesian sponge merchants seems consistent with the culture of their contemporary industrialists and shipowners. Many sponge-fishing businesses were family owned: brothers became associates, and sons and nephews were involved in other branches of the undertaking, so that various responsibilities in the business conducted between the islands of the Dodecanese and abroad were distributed among them. On Symi, brothers Agapitos and Sotirios Agapitidis established a cooperative commercial society in 1868. From the late 19th century onwards, Agapitos' sons specialized in sponge-fishing activities: they funded expeditions for sponge-fishing groups,

---

160   Doc. 6, 11/7/1919, Correspondence 1919–1920, MAK.

161   Doc. 56, 7/9/1919, Correspondence 1919–1920, MAK.

162   Doc. 101, 26/8/1883, MC Minutes 1882–1883, MAK.

163   Doc. 512 and 513, 20/4/1884, MC Minutes-Correspondence 1884–1885, MAK.

164   Doc. 595, 22/5/1884, MC Minutes-Correspondence 1884–1885, MAK.

165   Doc. 29, 3/7/1919, Correspondence 1918–1920, MAK; "Around 1930, the sponge trade reached about 100 tons per year in both Great Britain and Germany (Arndt 1937). 30 tons were exported to Italy, Holland, and France". Roberto Pronzato and Renata Manconi, "Mediterranean Commercial Sponges: Over 5000 Years of Natural History and Cultural Heritage", *Marine Ecology* 29 (2008), p. 150.

166   For example, in 1885 Symiot sponge merchant G. Georgas began collaborating with French sponge merchant and shop Coulombel-Devismes established in Paris in 1814. From 1900 to 1932 he also collaborated with sponge merchant Henri Duboscq (former Duboscq-Deffes), established in Paris in 1884; see Γεωργάς, *Μελέτη περί σπογγαλιείας* [Georgas, *Study of the Sponge Fishery*], p. 35.

imported scaphander diving suits, and traded in sponges.[167] The Municipal Archive of Kalymnos holds two surviving copies of agreements – "partner contracts" – for the establishment of a sponge fishing-business in 1911, head-quartered in Saint Petersburg. Of the brothers Themelis N. Hadji (Themelis and Lazaros N. Hadji), Themelis decided to partner with their cousins, Emmanouil and Ioannis Michail Koullias, also brothers. They each contributed equal sums for a total capital of 20,000 rubles and established the trade name "Themelis Hadji Themelis and Co". Profits and losses were to be equally distributed, while in their extensive contract they attempted to provide for any detail and or issue that might arise in their partnership.[168] Sources do not permit us to follow the activities and progress of the undertaking in subsequent years, however, in a document also submitted to the Municipality in 1921, the details of trans-porting 300 "bails" of Greek and American sponges in 1917, valued at 3,000 rubles are specified.[169] The sponges were purchased on Kalymnos by Nikolaos Vouvalis to be shipped to Saint Petersburg.[170]

Despite the increased demand for sponges and the upward trend in the sponge trade, neither international nor local circumstances were always favorable to smooth operation. Furthermore, the restrictions imposed by state governments where fishing took place, and [financial] charges imposed by the Italian administration on its Dodecanesian citizens are also among the factors that led to the gradual scaling down of the activity. The Italian credit institu-tions established in the Dodecanese beginning in 1918 focused on agricultural credit, the construction of irrigation facilities, and wetland drainage, as well as on encouraging Italians to immigrate and settle, while boosting Italian entrepreneurship. Their lack of interest in sponge fishing left the activity in the hands of Greek investors and merchants, as had previously been the case.[171]

---

167   Μιλτιάδης Ι. Λογοθέτης, *Οι πρωτοπόροι του δωδεκανησιακού εμπορίου, Οικονομική Βιβλιοθήκη Εμπορικού και Βιομηχανικού Επιμελητηρίου Ρόδου* [Miltiadis I. Logothetis, *The Pioneers of the Dodecanesian Trade,* Economic Library of the Chamber Of Commerce And Industry Of Rhodes], Athens 1968, pp. 23–24. Similarly, the "Aggelidis and Kypraios" company was established in 1898 and was replaced in 1938 by "Aggelidis and Theodorou". Ibid., pp. 35–36.

168   Doc. 190, 12/5/1911, Sponge-Fishermen Recruitments 1921, MAK. The documents are recorded in the 1921 register, because in that year the sons of the Koullia brothers submit-ted the copies to the Elders.

169   Bails: sacks of compressed sponges.

170   Doc. 191, 22/4/1917, Sponge-Fishermen Recruitments 1921, MAK.

171   *Δωδεκάνησος. Τετράτομος μελέτη του Υπουργείου Ανοικοδομήσεως* [*Dodecanese. Study in Four Volumes by the Ministry for Reconstruction*], pp. 231–236.

2.7.1.2   The Captains

While wealthy "initiators" generally handled the funding for sponge-fishing groups, it was technically the captains who ran sponge-fishing expeditions.[172] With greater or lesser investments of their own capital, a self-owned or rented vessel, and the necessary diving gear and technical apparatus, a captains' duties were specific: organizing the activity, managing human resources, preparing the vessels and the necessary provisions, promptly selecting an appropriate crew, attracting skilled divers, and supervising them for a period of about seven months, in the narrow, confining spaces of a ship.[173]

For captains, as intermediary links between financiers or "initiators" and crews, sponge fishing could be lucrative. It required a variety of abilities and skills that captains themselves customarily distill as "astute", "frugal", "hard-working", or "lucky". However, because of their financial dependence on businessmen-investors, and because the risk that their investment is exposed to entails human work, as well as the overexploitation of the labour force for potential profits, captains oppressed crews and especially the divers. Ultimately, the crew and divers amounted the captains' own capital.

But who were the captains of sponge-fishing vessels? How great was their ability to attract investment? What was the extent of their business acumen? Sources are not always clear: some captains appear to have been esteemed members of Kalymnian society, or to have held municipal offices, although few of them belonged to the wealthier or scholarly social class. For example, at least three captains of sponge-fishing vessels took part in the twelve-member Elders' council in 1884.[174] There were, nevertheless, also instances of captains who had already been divers and who dispensed small sums or gave the little they had – the family savings – in order to borrow and participate in this lucrative business, and the captains of sponge-fishing boats were not necessarily owners of the diving apparatus for sponge fishing. In the first case [i.e. captains who owned boats], the necessary working capital was less significant and loans were limited. However, the costs entailed in launching expeditions with

---

172   The Greek word εκκινητές or ξεκινητές is difficult to translate and means, initiator, entrepreneur or financier.

173   In the 20th century, captains were also occasionally responsible for insuring their sponge catch against "maritime dangers". Doc. 135, 7/5/1921, Sponge-Fishermen Recruitments 1921, MAK.

174   See for example the case of the Elder Theodosios M. Theodosiou, who had to temporarily abandon his office to join his ship's voyage. Doc. 425, 20/3/1884, MC Minutes-Correspondence 1884–1885, MAK, or the case of Nikitas Perivolarias (Doc. 536, 1/5/1884, MC Minutes-Correspondence 1884–1885, MAK) and of Sakellarios Diamantis (Doc. 537, 2/5/1884, MC Minutes-Correspondence 1884–1885, MAK) or of Konstantinos Hadji Themelis in 1885 (Doc. 48, 2/3/1885, MC Minutes 1885, MAK).

large crews, fishing with diving apparatuses created a need to borrow considerable amounts of money from individual lenders or the ATE, in the post-war period.[175] Owing to shortfalls and time gaps in archival evidence, it is generally impossible to trace the full development of sponge-fishing related cases in the archive's various registers.

There are several exceptions, however, and we chose the case of one captain, because it appears to typify Kalymnian business behaviour in the sponge fishery. In a written agreement between Sakellarios N. Chalipilias, captain of an underwater sponge-diving machine, and captain Drosos I. Machinis, it was stipulated that the latter would rent his five-ton bratsera [boat] *Evangelistria*, "in good condition and ready to sail", as a "depozito" [auxiliary boat] for the sponge-fishing crew on its 1884 expedition. The terms of the agreement were set down as follows:

> Drosos I. Machinis shall also take on board his brother, Theofilis, and all the food provisions and baggage that Sakell. N. Chalipilias approves and wishes. He will follow the sponge-fishing crew in the labour of the fishery from now until the end of October of the current year, 1884. The captain and manager of the sponge-fishing underwater machine [with scaphander] pledges – and is required – to pay for the rental of this vessel used as a storage facility, and for the salary of its captain Drosos Machinis and the sailor Theof. Machinis, a total of one hundred and ninety (190) *medjidie*[176] to the captain. The balance will be paid, after the sale of the sponges, by the buyer. Food for the aforementioned Drosos Machinis and Theof. Machinis is provided at the expense of the sponge-diving machine's crew.

At the close of the agreement, they arrive at an interest rate of 20% per year beginning April 1st.[177]

From 22 June to the end of November 1884, Sakellarios Chalipilias also rented a sponge-fishing machine [and scaphander] with breastplate and helmet.[178] It appears, however, that his departure was delayed due to insufficient

---

175   Γεωργάς, *Μελέτη περί σπογγαλιείας* [Georgas, *Study of the Sponge Fishery*], Piraeus 1937, p. 37. The funds required for the organization of a sponge-fishing undertaking depended on the method and the locale of fishing. For the costs of each departure in the early 1950s, see Πιζάνιας, "Η οργάνωσις της σπογγαλιευτικής επιχειρήσεως" [Pizanias, "The Organization of the Sponge-Fishing Enterprise"], pp. 29–36.

176   A Turkish coin formerly rated at 20 piasters, and after 1880 at 19.

177   Doc. 202, 24/5/1884, MC Minutes 1863–1884, MAK.

178   Doc. 224, 22/6/1884, MC Minutes 1863–1884, MAK.

funds and he borrowed 15,400 *kuruş* from Georgios Michaloudis, free of interest until the close of October 1884,[179] at which time he was required to deliver
his sponges to the lender, who would then sell them where and how he chose.

So, with a substantial delay, reduced means, and very little of his own funds,
as well as a series of loans and obligations, Sakellarios Chalipilias finally set
sail on his 1884 sponge-fishing voyage. The very next day, he hired his brother
Ioannis as a diver, who likewise had sponge-fishing debts owing to Antonios
Notaras, a merchant captain at Ermioni.[180] It seems, however, that Ioannis
Chalipilias was in arrears to his brother Sakellarios from a previous year, and
that he treated the Elders with contempt when he was summoned to settle his
debts.[181] Somewhat remarkably, another document in the same register further indicates that Sakellarios Chalipilias also owed his brother-in-law Nikitas
Kouros an unspecified sum. In other words, the contemptuous Chalipilias
was liable to two financiers: Michaloudis, who would be the first to collect the
money owed, and to N. Kouros, who would receive the remaining profit, if any.[182]

On the other hand, the same merchant ship captain from Ermioni conducted various commercial activities on Kalymnos and had at least two
vessels in his possession. Thus, Christodoulos Galanos, Ioannis Koutellas and
Theodoros Tiliakos, captains and owners of sponge-fishing machines, jointly
chartered a *goleta* [boat] owned by the same merchant captain, in order to
work in Benghazi from 15 April to 15 September 1884. They boarded the vessel
at Ermioni and returned it at the port of Hydra, for a charter fee of 240 French
gold liras.[183]

This example is perhaps illustrative of the best possible way that employment relations and interactions between the people involved in the
sponge-fishing network could operate. That is, as a function of binding kinship
networks, a constant shortage of capital, collaborations and co-operations,
and exorbitant loans and obligations that did not always correspond to the
expected profits. The high advance payments to divers left captains vulnerable to financiers; exponentially increased the amount of required funding; and
opened a door to particularly lucrative usurious activities. Everything points to

---

179   Doc. 227, 25/6/1884, MC Minutes 1863–1884, MAK.
180   Doc. 228, 26/6/1884, MC Minutes 1863–1884, MAK. Merchant ship captain A. Notaras, who
       stayed only temporarily on Kalymnos, appointed Drosos Karpathios as a proxy for him
       to sell the 70 bags of hardtack in his possession to sponge-fishing vessels, see Doc. 230,
       27/6/1884, MC Minutes 1863–1884, MAK.
181   Doc. 419, 19/3/1884, MC Minutes – Correspondence 1884–1885, MAK.
182   Doc. 231, 28/6/1884, MC Minutes 1863–1884, MAK.
183   Doc. 206, 26/5/1884, MC Minutes 1863–1884, MAK.

multiple networks of dependence in a high-risk activity which could produce unexpected profits but also heavy losses.

Captains in this configuration – as members of a medial group who were supposedly equipped with organizational abilities and therefore managed part of the means of production – were obviously better off than the divers. Captains also had the advantage of experience, as well as savings or property, and therefore possessed some of the necessary capital to take over responsibility for the undertaking. It would appear, however, that technical expertise was not sufficient in the case of sponge fishing with the scaphander diving suit or the Fernez because the capital invested was necessarily substantial, hence lending was always conducted at high interest rates. There were, moreover, a variety of other pressures from various sides, and uncertainty made every projection of future yields difficult to calculate.

Captains did not always take part in the voyage and could choose whether to participate based on the trustworthiness of the crew members who would replace them. The role of captain in such cases was usually assumed by the manager of the pump [*kolaouzieris*], who could also serve as captain, or some other substitute might be found. The role of deputy captain was, in fact, enviable because it was well-paid. When crews did leave the island, however, the usual practice was to appoint proxies charged with selling the unsold sponge product from the previous year, and paying or settling accounts with previous investors who withheld their debtors' sponges in their warehouses. However, if sponges remained unsold; if captains had borrowed considerable amounts of money at high interest rates to be able to work; if captains put up their vessel or home as collateral; then how could captains comply with the Marine Sponge Fishery Regulations, which stipulated that, before setting sail, prior debts must be settled?

There was a chance that a captain might be able obtain permission to sail if the Elders determined that he held no prior preferential obligations, i.e. prior debts.[184] Indeed the Elder's decision concerning captain Michail Nom. Lisgaris specified that he was "blocked" by his investor Ioannis Em. Giannikouris, who argued that his product remained unsold, and demanded that the captain be denied permission to sail. The problem may have been that the sponges could not be sold, or that it took too long to sell them and thus to see a return on the initial investment, but it may equally be the case that it was to Giannikouris' advantage that the catch remained in his warehouses until prices dropped.

But how would all these debts be paid off, especially if the captain remained unemployed on Kalymnos for an entire year? These pressures from both sides,

---

184   Doc. 42, 10/2/1900, MC Minutes 1899–1900, MAK.

which were usually passed on to ships' crews and the divers, are typical of
the organization of the industry at that time. In the end, Lisgaris obtained
the coveted permission, thus deepening his dependence on his old investor:
he borrowed a sum for the "platika" [in partial payment of the original debt]
from him [Giannikouris],[185] put up the two shares to which he was entitled
as collateral and borrowed from another lender to cover the expenses of the
expedition.[186]

At the close of the sponge-fishing session, captains undertook to sell the
catch, which had been offered as a guarantee of good faith to lenders, assuring
them of their preferential status as first in line to be repaid for their short-term
loans. After expenses were deducted, the net profits were distributed to bene-
ficiaries based on the agreement already concluded between the captain, the
divers, and the auxiliary staff. Nevertheless, the time that might elapse from
the return of the sponge fishermen to the sale of the sponge catch was left
undetermined, which also meant that it was not possible to pinpoint when
crews would be remunerated.[187] Since captains could mortgage the entire
catch, divers could then not be paid in full for their work – they received rather,
what was called a "resta" [i.e. the remainder, the rest] – if the loan had not yet
been repaid. On the other hand, if merchants put pressure on captains to let
them purchase the merchandise at lower prices and cause delays, they ran the
risk that part of or the entire catch would not be sold, thus creating further
debt for all parties concerned, captain and crew alike.

Even if most recruitment contracts were drawn up in the presence of the
Elders, the settlement of advance payments, earned wages and shares before
and after the expedition was not always carried out in an official fashion.
Hence, those involved questioned each other's word, while complaints from

185   Where the etymology of the word "platika" – advance payment made to divers – is con-
       cerned, there have been various suggestions. It may derive from the word "πλοιάτικα"
       ["*pliatika*" meaning "advance payment"], or even from the Italian word "*pratica*", that is
       "practice". See more in Μιχάλης Ευστ. Σκανδαλίδης, "Κοινά διαλεκτικά Καλύμνου – Κω (Β)",
       Καλυμνιακά Χρονικά [Michalis Efst. Skandalidis, "Common Dialectics of Kalymnos – Kos
       (B)", *Kalymniaka Chronika*] 17 (2007), p. 344.
186   Doc. 56, 14/3/1911, MC Minutes 1910–1912, MAK.
187   The emergency law 560/1937 of the Greek state sets out that payments should be completed
       in a period of two months. There was, however, no such provision for the Dodecanese
       islands. See Κωνσταντίνος Γουργιώτης, "Όροι εργασίας εις την σπογγαλιείαν", *Α' Πανελλήνιον
       Σπογγαλιευτικόν Συνέδριον* (Ρόδος 24–27 Φεβρουάριου 1949). Εισηγήσεις και Πρακτικά, Γενική
       Διοίκησις Δωδεκανήσου [Konstantinos Gourgiotis, "Working Conditions in the Sponge
       Fishery", 1st Colloquium on the Sponge Fishery (Rhodes 24–27 February 1949). Papers and
       Minutes, General Administration of the Dodecanese], Rhodes 1951, p. 75.

both sides about stolen sponges were neither uncommon nor easily proven.[188] On rare occasions in sponge-fishing disputes, it was also possible for a captain's committee to issue an opinion. For example, the Elders convened a committee composed of the three "best" captains in a case concerning a diver who fell ill during an expedition and stopped working. The committee was charged with deciding whether the diver was entitled to part or the entirety of his share, even though he had obtained a certificate from a doctor in Port Said.[189]

As noted above, captains did not always own diving gear and often rented it at rather high prices.[190] For example, Themelis Olympitis, rented the following to three captains, until the end of October 1884:

> A sponge-fishing underwater machine with all its accessories, boxes, two breastplates, one [scaphander] helmet, two pairs of shoes, leads, and two used hoses, on the condition that the renters buy the new parts with which to compliment the machine, that consists of two suits, one hose and shoes. These new items as well as the old parts must remain with the machine after the end of the sponge-fishing expedition.

To rent the used machine, the captains had to guarantee Themelis Olympitis a share of their haul. In addition, after selling the sponges, they had to pay Olympitis 4,250 *kuruş* because he was, evidently, the one who bought the missing parts after all. Finally, they were required to hand the entire sponge catch over to him and to consult him concerning its sale.[191]

Because their sponge-fishing expeditions were self-financed, captains may not have reaped exorbitant profits. They could, however, secure a comfortable life for their family, buy a property after a few years, and send their children off to study, or give them dowries.[192]

> They [captains] earned a lot of money. When the houses here at the port cost 4,000 and 5,000 [drachmas] in 1955, I made up to 80,000. I could buy them all. We were borrowing from the ATE. Back then, a captain could not find so much money without loans. Many captains spent all that money gambling. Captains stole sponges from the divers, because it was a lot of money and, even though there was a lot of money, they still

---

188   See, for instance, Doc. 444, 24/3/1884, Minutes and Correspondence 1884–1885, MAK.

189   Doc. 209, 19/11/1907, MC Minutes 1906–1908, MAK.

190   Doc. 195, 29/4/1894, Book 78, Sponge-Fishermen Recruitments 1894–1896, MAK.

191   Doc. 222, 21/6/1884, MC Minutes 1863–1884, MAK. See also doc. 140, 7/5/1921, Sponge-Fishermen Recruitments 1921, MAK.

192   Testimony of Giannis Tsoulfas to E.O., 5/3/2002.

couldn't get by. And they resorted to stealing sponges from the weaker to give them to those with plenty of money but no sponges. To balance things out because he had paid many "platika", so the poor didn't get the remaining wages. It was a big crime. Work was hard. Those earning much money could establish businesses, build houses. If they had spent half of that money, if they had saved it, they would have been rich. But they didn't manage to become rich or to build savings from a well-paid job. And the captains spent it. They were ruined.[193]

The same accusation – that captains stole sponges from those who had received lower advance payments and paid them to the ones with a higher rate of "platika" to balance their books – is found in almost all of the available testimonies of divers and crews.

Disputes between captains and crew members were particularly common, and they will be discussed again below. At the root of all disputes was the settlement of earned wages, divers' debts, and the terms of recruitment. Moreover, when weighing and selling the sponges divers were supposed to be present; however, this rule was not applied.[194] Disagreements could also arise from the distribution of the expenses incurred on the voyage. According to a 1919 municipal decision "concerning some items cited in general expenses and charged to the crew: crews should not be burdened with these expenses because, as it has always been the case, they belong exclusively to the machine and therefore they are [supplied] at the expense of the captain". In this document, these items are expenditures for the purchase and repair of gear parts, but also for the provision of bread to the crew.[195]

The events of WWI, the financial instability and the exchange rate crises that followed, ruined many of the Dodecanesian captains who were already indebted, dragging their lenders into bankruptcy along with them.[196] After the union of the Dodecanese islands with Greece however, the funding system improved, as the ATE assumed the role of granting sponge-fishing loans that covered a substantial share of the expenses or long-term credits for the supply of sponge-diving equipment.[197] Yet the number of captains continued to

193   Testimony of Lefteris Mamouzelos to E.O., 3/9/2004.
194   Γουργιώτης, "Ὅροι εργασίας εις την σπογγαλιείαν" [Gourgiotis, "Working Conditions in the Sponge Fishery"], p. 79.
195   Doc. 50, 5/10/1919, MC Minutes 1919–1922, MAK.
196   Γεωργάς, Μελέτη περί σπογγαλιείας [Georgas, Study of the Sponge Fishery], pp. 38–39.
197   The ATE took on the financing of sponge-fishing groups under favorable conditions (8%) and limited collateral requirements. Regarding Symi, see Αγαπητίδης, "Η οικονομική οργά-νωση" [Agapitidis, "The Financial Organization"], p. 195.

decrease: few people were now involved in organizing more groups. And while the total number of divers increased to 30–35 men, after 1947 the ATE established a minimum number of divers for each ship, depending on the depths at which they worked, as well as their remuneration. This measure might be considered as beneficial to divers, given that it reduced the time spent on the sea bottom, and the number of daily descents. Reportedly, however, it was common practice for the captains to hire as many as they needed, and then to round out the required total with divers who barely worked and were paid very little.[198]

The Captains' Association was founded in 1952 and the first cooperatives for the provisioning of expeditions were established. By 1966, 80–90% of captains owned sponge-fishing vessels and self-financed their expeditions.[199] Although the ATE also offered financing at tempting interest rates, their loans often obliged captains to make higher advance payments to their divers, this being one of the reasons why captains resorted to additional borrowing from local investors.[200] However, as Lefteris Mamouzelos recounts, "[t]he money required for the operation of a machine was considerable. We needed a lot of money, and the bank only gave us about half of it".[201] Furthermore, while the ATE did not force captains to sell their merchandise to specific buyers, as was the case in the past, its loan premiums were high.[202]

2.8   The Expenses

The most important revenue for sponge-fishing communities in the southern Aegean was generated by sponge-fishing activities, hence the necessary authorizations for vessel departures and crews, as well as the taxes imposed on imported and transiting fishery products. The local Greek community acted as a customs office that farmed out the collection of revenue to local collectors who paid the Elders' council the agreed upon sums. The Ottoman administration's attempt to collect part of this revenue by installing a customs

---

198   Testimony of a small boat owner [*trechandiri*] and captain Petros Marthas to E.O., 2/9/2004.

199   Emile Y. Kolodny, *La population des îles de la Grèce. Essai de géographie insulaire en Méditerranée orientale*, vol. 1, Aix-en-Provence 1974, p. 315; Roxane Caftanzoglou, "Kalymnos: Contribution à la connaissance d'une société" Mémoire de maîtrise en ethnologie spécialisée (unpublished thesis), Paris 1978, p. 8.

200   Testimony of Giannis Tsoulfas to E.O., 6/3/2002.

201   Testimony of Lefteris Mamouzelos to E.O., 3/9/2004.

202   Testimony of Giannis Tsoulfas to E.O., 5/3/2002.

office on the islands in 1874 met with concerted opposition from the islands' citizens. As the representatives of the sponge-fishing islands of the southern Sporades argued, sponge fishery was their sole productive resource. In their memoranda and reports, they protested that the lump tax [*maktu*] paid to the Empire's Treasury originated from income generated by sponge fishing, and that sponge tariffs provided them with the money necessary to meet the community's needs. It was the sponge fishery that covered the "local welfare fee" that provided the funding required for the maintenance of the community's educational institutions and public health care units, as well as the construction of public facilities and so on. The levy of additional customs tariffs on imported and exported products would damage the Ottoman state, it was claimed, because many sponge merchants bought sponges from Greece and then moved their business headquarters elsewhere. Taking into consideration the arguments presented by the communities, the State Council handed the customs rights back to each island's Elders in 1875.[203]

The Elders of Kalymnos do not appear to have directly interfered in the pricing or fixing of sponge prices (in contrast with how the situation evolved on Symi in the final decades of the 19th century),[204] and they regularly published currency exchange rate lists to facilitate trading. However, the Elders did intervene in the resolution of sponge-fishing disputes[205] with a mediation committee, in which some captains participated either as members or "experts".[206]

2.8.1   *Licenses*

Fishery in Ottoman or other seas presupposed special permits granted every year for a specific sum of money, hence sponge-fishing vessels paid 10 liras to the Treasury of the Ottoman administration in the late 19th century.[207] There

---

203   A translation from Turkish into Greek of the 1875 decision issued by the State Council's Department of Internal Affairs; Αλέξανδρος Καρανικόλας, "Νότιες Σποράδες. Σελίδες από την ιστορία των προνομίων τους", *Παρνασσός* [Alexandros Karanikolas, "The Southern Sporades. Pages from the History of Their Privileges", *Parnassos*] 13 (1971), pp. 25–27 (offprint).

204   See also Λογοθέτης, "Το εμπόριο στις Νότιες Σποράδες" [Logothetis, "Commerce in the Southern Sporades"], p. 145.

205   MC Minutes, Correspondence Various 1884–1885, pp. 108–109 (1/4/1884).

206   See also MC Minutes, Correspondence Various 1884–1885, p. 104 (31/3/1884) and in the same, p. 182 (15/5/1884). Money, as well as material (ropes, barrels etc.) was stolen.

207   For example, in the 1860s, Kalymnian vessels paid 3,000 liras to the Ottoman administration, whereas in the early 1890s, after the introduction of the scaphander diving suits, this fee was reduced to 1,300 liras. Doc. 1, 4/1/1894, Correspondence 1894–1895, MAK.

were, nonetheless, people who violated this rule, and went fishing without paying for a permit.[208]

At the beginning of each year, especially in February, the Elders settled outstanding sponge-fishing issues, and fees owing the Elders were paid. After settling these debts, the Elders issued a license entitling the holder to engage in sponge fishery and passports for the crews, a habit that appears to have persisted into the 20th century.[209]

In March of each year, the Elders issued the licenses, and the prerequisite for the timely departure of ships was efficient organization where procuring these documents was concerned. This was particularly true where vessels used for the first time in the sponge fishery were involved, as ownership certificates first had to be issued and a delay in this process would also mean a delay in the ship's departure.[210]

The sum to be paid at the public debt office had to be settled prior to the departure of the vessels and this practice created resentment against the Elders, and even motivated some vessels to leave without official permission.[211] At the same time however, payment due dates were not always fixed, and sources are not entirely clear on this matter. For example, a community decision of 1897 stipulated that "as the customs of sponge fishing in our land dictate, the royal permit fee for sponge fishing is paid from the sponge product", which means that the buyer is responsible for the payment.[212] Or, according to another source: "The person receiving the sponge catch of any sponge-fishing vessel, is liable to pay for the sponge-fishing license [*koçan*] in full".[213]

The smooth running of the sponge fishery was often hindered by the Ottoman administration's typically arbitrary decisions which could, for example, delay the issuance of permits. What is more, the Ottoman administration ignored established procedure and local custom, and demanded more control over and share in the activity's profits. There were where instances of the Ottoman military sub-administration issuing sponge-fishing permits for Kalymnian or "Greek ships" at a lower price with the result that the local

---

208   A rather common phenomenon for the European ships fishing sponges off the coasts of Tunisia. P. A. Hennique, *Les Caboteurs et pêcheurs de la côte de la Tunisie: Pêche des éponges*, Paris 1888, p. 74.

209   The permit was called a "*kotsani*" from the Turkish "*koçan*", meaning "stub". By extension the term was applied to the stub of the Fishing Permit. See Doc. 37, 25/2/1897, Correspondence 1896–1898, MAK·Doc. 70, 30/12/1919, MC Minutes 1919–1922, MAK.

210   Doc. 292, 28/4/1922, Correspondence 1922, MAK.

211   Doc. 453, 27/3/1884, Minutes and Correspondence 1884–1885, MAK.

212   Doc. 245, 2/9/1897, MC Minutes 1896–1897, MAK.

213   Doc. 51, 3/4/1897, Correspondence 1896–1898, MAK; Doc. 84, 13/3/1919, Correspondence 1918–1920, MAK.

community lost part of its income.[214] Problems such as these were both constant and repeated every year, while competition between Greek and Ottoman administrations for control over the system and revenue collection was also constant. It is perhaps not surprising then that documents in Elders' registers indicate that many captains skipped legal procedures.

A letter dated 1 March 1894, to the *Kaymakam* of Kalymnos, Elder Mehmet Tefik Bey, registers the following complaint:

> At this time of year, our sponge-fishing ships come to the office of indirect taxation to obtain their sponge fishing *koçan* [permit], so that the community can collect its fees from sponge fishermen, which it uses chiefly to pay the Empire's annual lump-sum tax for our island, and to cover the rest of our welfare needs; the tax also covers sponge-fishery related affairs between sponge fishermen, and facilitates their speedy departure, and there has always been a system in place which the esteemed *Kaymakamia* [the office of the Elders] continues to recognize. In the absence of this system, neither our community nor the sponge-fishing industry of our land could be sustained. According to this system, the Office for Indirect Taxation does not issue the permit [*koçan*] for sponge fishing for any ship without the Elders' prior permission, as it has always been the custom, every year.

The letter concludes by entreating the *Kaymakam* to respect the established practice and asks that no ship be granted a sponge-fishing permit without the required sum having been previously settled with the community.[215]

In 1857–1858, the tax on sea products was set at 20%, which was then revised and decreased to 75 francs per vessel when sponge fishermen protested. For those who undertook to cheat the system, fines on clandestine sponge fishing were considerable, and to avoid paying the fines spongers had to travel to distant areas such as the coasts of Northern Africa, where spongers clearly

---

214 MC Minutes, Correspondence Various 1884–1885, pp. 120–121 (14/4/1884) and pp. 125–126 (17/4/1884), MAK. The document is published by Σακελλάρης Τρικοίλης, *Νεότερη ιστορία της Καλύμνου, κοινωνική διαστρωμάτωση* [Sakellaris N. Trikoilis, *Modern History of Kalymnos. Social Stratification*], Athens 2007, pp. 287–288. On the same topic, see Doc. 170, 15/4/1885, MC Minutes 1885, MAK and doc. 71, 28/3/1896, Correspondence 1895–1896, MAK.

215 Doc. 52, 1/3/1894, Correspondence 1894–1895, MAK.

went to avoid taxes,[216] given that many fished illegally in that area.[217] Indeed in August of 1883, a merchant ship arriving from Benghazi was captured and the cargo confiscated, which reportedly contained "money and sponges belonging to sponge fishermen and merchants".[218]

In 1878, however, the "Sponge Fishing Permit" was introduced, and was an amount paid to the Port Services of the states where sponge fishery was conducted.[219] In a letter of 1879 to the Empire's Treasury, Kalymnos' notables protested against the levies on permits for sponge fishing, pointing out that the expenses sometimes exceeded the total value of the catch, while they also noted that the number of vessels, which had formerly numbered 300, had been reduced by half. They stated that, in combination with the problems caused by diving suits, they ran the risk of having to give up on sponging to seek other means of survival.[220]

Crete was a regular stopover for the sponge-fishing vessels[221] that remained stationed in its seas for a few of days at the end of the sponge-fishing season to harvest sponges. Fishing in those waters required a permit from the General Administration and the violation of this requirement would lead to the captain's arrest, the seizure of passports, and the levy of fines.[222] Hence, in a report issued in 1884, many captains of vessels fishing for sponges in Cretan waters complained that they paid 5 liras to the Treasury of the Cretan Administration for the permit, while the Ottoman Administration of Kalymnos demanded another 10 liras.[223]

It appears that captains faced similar problems in the Egyptian seas, where local authorities demanded additional taxes for the issuance of Sponge Fishing Permits, as in one case from 1886.[224] Marsa Matruh, or "Madruha" as the Greek

216   Ali Fuat Oreng, Yakindonem Tarihimizde Rodos ve Oniki Ada, Istanbul 2006, p. 510. In accordance with the law, they seized the illegal spongers' ship. Following Greece's reaction, however, they imposed a fine, which was heavier for ships with engines. Ibid., p. 512.

217   "Ἀντίγραφον υπομνήματος τῆς Υ. Πύλης" ["Memo Copy by the Sublime Porte"], 15/9/1875, Tripoli-Libya Embassy, Folder 4 (1875–1897), Subfolder 4, IAYE.

218   Doc. 101, 26/8/1883, MC Minutes 1882–1883, MAK.

219   Π. Πιζάνιας, "Η σπογγαλιεία τῆς Δωδεκανήσου", Ἐλευθερία [P. Pizanias, "The Sponge Fishery of the Dodecanese", Eleftheria], 1/7/1945, p. 3.

220   Doc. 39, 17/2/1879, MC Minutes 1879–1884, MAK.

221   In a report to the Greek Ministry of Foreign Affairs in October 1885, Kalymnian captain Mich. S. Diamantis reported that 36 Kalymnian sponge-fishing vessels with 300 men arrived from Africa at Ierapetra.

222   Doc. of 25/10/1885, Folder 1885, Γ 51/1, Fishery-Sponge Fishery, IAYE.

223   Doc. 396, 12/3/1884, MC Minutes-Correspondence 1884–1885, pp. 59–60, MAK.

224   Letters from the community of Symi to the Greek Consulate of Rhodes, 30/7/1886, Folder 1886, 51/1, IAYE.

sponge fishermen called it, was a natural harbor on Egypt's western coast, 138 nautical miles from Alexandria. The shallow shoals and safe anchorage, in combination with the rich sponge-bearing beds of the area, made Madruha a preferred destination for vessels working with scaphander diving suits as well as with naked divers. In the early 20th century, permits for fishing in Egyptian seas were issued in Marsa Matruh by the coast guard, and covered a period of one year. As an indication of the extent of this practice, although diving suits were banned from the Egyptian coasts, in 1904, there were 297 requests for fishing permits and in 1905, 280 fishing permits were requested in the area.[225] The price of the permit was based on the size of the vessel for which it was requested, hence the permit for a "*skaphe*" [boat] cost 8 British pounds while "*yiales*"-type sailing ships required a 4 pound permit. For vessels fishing in those waters at that time, these sums would have been considerable and difficult to afford.[226]

Permits were issued by the Port Authority both during and after Italian rule (1912–1947), and captains paid a sum for each vessel which varied according to the fishing method practiced. When vessels returned, their sponge catch was weighed, and a tax was paid to the customs office based on quantity and method of production. In 1922, 15 sponge-fishing permits were requested for the Fernez apparatus through a representative in Alexandria, Egypt,[227] while in that same year the community of Symi purchased all the permits [*koçan*] for Egypt. Therefore, in a letter, the Elders of Kalymnos requested that the remaining permits be allotted to Kalymnos and not to Greece.[228] When the issue remained unresolved, the local administration appealed to the Italian governor of Kalymnos and asked him to intercede on their behalf before the Italian Consul in Egypt and the Egyptian authorities, in order to obtain permits at a reduced customs duty fee, specifying that each boat working with Fernez had a 15-member crew, as was necessary in the use of these apparatuses.[229]

Along with these taxes and permit fees, Dodecanesian sponge fishermen also encountered occasional problems when fishing in both foreign and Greek seas. Minister of Marine Affairs, G. Tombazis, attempted to lift any obstacles, arguing that,

---

225   Παχουντάκης, *Η σπογγαλιεία εν Αιγύπτω* [Pachountakis, *Sponge Fishing in Egypt*], p. 5.

226   Ibid., pp. 12–13.

227   Doc. 253, 25/3/1922 and Doc. 258, 28/3/1922, Correspondence 1922, MAK.

228   Doc. 263, 5/4/1922, and the thank-you Letter to G. Georgas, doc. 270, 11/4/1922, Correspondence 1922, MAK.

229   Doc. 296 and 297, 2/5/1922, Correspondence 1922, MAK.

Greek seafarers too have always engaged in all kinds of fishery, and especially sponge fishery, off the Turkish coasts without any hindrance, enjoying equal rights with the locals. And today it is from sponge fishery alone that our merchant shipping earns important profits. [...] If the Greek government denies our demand to allow reciprocity in fishery, it is only natural that the Turkish government will ban ships sailing under the Greek flag from fishing off Turkish coasts.[230]

These permits lasted for one year and came into force on 1 March, the first day of the fiscal year in Turkey. In 1900, fees also varied according to the method of fishing, hence sponge-fishing "machines" [i.e., scaphander diving suits and apparatus] paid 32 Ottoman liras, vessels with skin divers paid 10, and boats with hooks paid 4, whereas gagavas paid 3 Ottoman liras for up to 5 tons capacity, and 6 liras for boats with a capacity of over 5 tons.[231]

Everyone fishing off the northern coasts of Africa paid a percentage of the sponge product as a fee, either to the local government or to local leaseholders, as was common practice in Sfax.[232] Permits issued for fishing off the coasts of northern Africa were limited; as noted above, their number was not fixed for various reasons. Moreover, the number of annual permits for scaphander diving suits and gagavas fluctuated, while occasional bans of a few months, or the entire sponge-fishing season, were not uncommon. Although like the islands of the Dodecanese, Libya was also an Italian colony, Dodecanesian spongers had to purchase sponge-fishing permits issued by the Port Authorities in Tripoli or Benghazi that were valid for specific areas only. Disputes between captains and Italian port authorities were frequent, with both sides seeming to break the rules. Often the sponge catch was the source of the problem, given that a percentage was deducted by either the Customs Offices or the Italian Sponge-Fishery Trade Union of Libya.[233]

The Italian Trade Union for Fishing and Trading in Sponges in Lybia [*Sindacato Italiano per la pesca ed il commercio delle spugne in Libia*] was founded in 1913. The "special regulation on the relations between the trade union and sponge-fishing captains" stipulated that those fishing in Libyan

---

230   Folder 1883, Γ/51-1 Fishery-Sponge Fishery, IAYE.

231   Report of the captain of the troopship *Crete* 28/5/1900, Embassy in Tripoli-Libya, Folder 6, Subfolder 9, (1890–1900), IAYE.

232   Consular correspondence, private letters, captain's report 19/10/1884, 18/12/1884, 20/1/1885, 25/1/1885, 29/1/1885 etc., Folder 1885, Γ 51/1 Fishery-Sponge Fishery, IAYE.

233   On the one hand, captains claimed that the sponges were harvested in another state, usually in Tunisia, whereas, on the other hand, customs authorities were trying to prove that the catch came from the zones under their control.

waters had to acquire a special permit, which was granted on an annual basis, and limited to a specified fishing zone. The number of permits issued was also limited, and only 20 scaphander diving suits could work in any given area each year, with the further caveat that those who had worked in a given area in one year, had priority standing in that area the following year as well. Directly after its creation, the Trade Union imposed an obligatory deposit of the sponge product in its warehouses, and captains were required to pay 5% of the catch's estimated value to cover costs for security, warehousing, transportation, and so on. In addition, the distribution of their merchandise was directed, and captains were forced to sell their sponges exclusively in the markets of Tripoli, Benghazi, and Derna.

Article 27 of the special regulation on relations between the Trade Union and sponge-fishing captains, made provision for the concession of sea zones to companies, individuals or trade unions for the creation of sponge farms.[234] However, it was not long before the regulation was amended following intense protests, and the number of permits increased by 5%, while the fee deducted fell to 4%, and the Trade Union's pre-emptive rights concerning the sale of sponges were revoked.[235] Eventually, the decree of 16 February 1923, adopted by the Italian government, abolished the Trade Union. Unofficially, however, the Trade Union did not cease its operations, and enjoyed the silent consent of the local administration, which received 15% of the Union's gross revenue, until the beginning of September 1923, when it was definitively abolished.[236]

The maritime borders were another source of conflict, namely the area under each state's control and within which the state demanded that sponge-fishing vessels pay a fee. Given the belief that "sea bottoms are underwater mines, the exploitation of which belongs to the state that possesses them", Italy, France, Turkey, as well as the UK in the Bahamas, did not accept the delimitation of maritime borders at three miles, exerting control over all the maritime areas where spongers fished.[237] Beginning in the late 19th century, however, the Greek government has insisted that "no one shall pay taxes for fishing beyond the three-mile distance from the shore, that is beyond 5,557 meters, which constitutes the borders of maritime control accepted by all states". However, in

234   Letters and reports 1/1/1913, 29/5/1913, 23/10/1913, 29/10/1913, 25/11/1913 etc., Folder 28, Subfolder 7, Archive of Vice Consulate of Benghazi, IAYE.
235   Report of the Minister of Finances L. Koromilas to the Minister of Foreign Affairs G. Streit, 23/6 May 1914, Embassy of Tripoli-Libya, Folder 19 (1914), Subfolder 5, IAYE.
236   Report 20/12/1924, Embassy of Tripoli-Libya, Folder 29 (1923–1924), Subfolder 17, IAYE.
237   On this subject see the "Report of the Minister of Finances L. Koromilas to the Minister of Foreign Affairs G. Streit", 23/6 May 1914, Embassy of Tripoli-Libya, Folder 19 (1914), Subfolder 5, IAYE.

order to be permitted to approach the shores, and "on account of other facilities", sponge fishermen were, in fact, compelled to pay to the local authorities the required levies.[238] In any event, there are indeed records of seizures of vessels and arrests of captains and sponge fishermen in the waters of foreign countries, the reasons for which are usually not specified in our sources.[239]

2.8.2 *Taxes and Custom Duties*

Until 1897, the Elders had assumed the role of Port Authority in collecting the "local fees" on imported goods and sponges sold.[240] That year, there was an attempt to impose an Ottoman harbour master on Kalymnos, who, as noted in Carl Flegel's manuscripts, rented a two-story residence on the wharf near the administrative center and took up power "without ever performing any official act; he was a statue, a ghost. Nevertheless, Kalymnians were very much afraid of this statue, because all of a sudden he could start running his office at the great expense of the freedoms of the island, which depends entirely on the sea".[241] Even though reports were submitted over the course of many months, and in spite of the systematic actions of the local community, this issue remained pending until the adoption of an imperial decree in the summer of 1899, which resulted in the Ottoman Harbour Master's departure from Kalymnos.[242]

The community's most important regular revenue derived largely from the "local Skala Fee" [Aegean Port Fee] and the respective "Local Sponge Fee", in other words the tax "on imported goods" or "School Tax", as noted in archival documents. In reality, these were duties on imported and exported merchandise. The community used these fees to pay taxes levied by the authorities to maintain schools, ports and churches, and to carry out public works.[243] Sponge

---

238 Letter of the Minister of Foreign Affairs Deliyiannis to the Vice Consul in Tunis 18/4/1891, Embassy in Tripoli-Libya, Folder 4 (1875–1897), Subfolder 4, IAYE.

239 Doc. 313, 27/5/1922, Correspondence 1922, MAK.

240 Every captain also paid a specific sum "as port fee" for the repair and maintenance of port facilities. Doc. 88, 20/4/1894, Correspondence 1894–1895, MAK.

241 From the manuscripts of Carl Flegel. The extract is also published by K. Chatzidakis who studied the topic in depth; Κυριάκος Κων. Χατζηδάκης, "Από τον αγώνα για την προάσπιση των προνομίων στις Νότιες Σποράδες. Το λιμεναρχικό ζήτημα στην Κάλυμνο (1897–1899)", *Καλυμνιακά Χρονικά* [Kyriakos Kon. Chatzidakis, "From the Fight for the Defence of the Privileges of the Southern Sporades. The Port Authorities Issue on Kalymnos" (1897–1899), *Kalymniaka Chronika*] 17 (2007), pp. 103–104.

242 Χατζηδάκης, "Από τον αγώνα για την προάσπιση των προνομίων" [Chatzidakis, "From the Fight for the Defence of the Privileges"], p. 99–172.

243 Doc. 21, 18/2/1864, MC Minutes 1863–1884, MAK; Doc. 390, 10/3/1884, MC Minutes-Correspondence 1884–1885, MAK.

merchants and sponge fishermen who sold sponges paid the "local fee on sponges" to the person who leased the right to collect the "fee". The community put this right – which was in effect from March 1, or, more rarely, from May 1, to April 30 of the following year – up for auction every year against an agreed upon sum, which the person holding the lease on collecting the fee paid in monthly installments to the Elders.[244] It was imperative to assign a financially trustworthy citizen to each of the highest bidders who won the contracts to collect the fee, and who would share the responsibility for paying off the required sum to the community. Lease holders, therefore, also had to own enough property to serve as guarantor.[245]

From 1902 to 1904, revenues from the local Skala and Sponge Fees ensured the functioning of Elder's Commission for Financial Affairs the income from which was used to provide medicines to the community, and to settle the community's debts.[246] In 1906, the collection of the local "Skala Fee" and "Sponge Fee", the so-called "Welfare Fee", was assigned to a special three-member commission that worked *pro bono* to manage the provision of medicines and the payroll of healthcare and teaching staff, as well as the island's general revenue.[247]

The Commission for Financial Affairs of the Elders produced various detailed documents in 1902, concerning vessel type – sail or steamship – and the right to collect the local sponge fee from ships arriving at the port of Kalymnos in April and May. Apparently, to address issues arising from related disputes between interested parties, the Commission specified that the former lease holder reserved the right to collect the fee up until the end of April, and that this right was passed on to the new lease holder at the beginning of May. Neither the lease holder nor the guarantor, however, could make any claim against the discontinuation of the use of the scaphander diving suits, in cases of outbreaks of epidemics or political developments which could potentially

---

244   Doc. not numbered, p. 215, 1/3/1870 and Doc. not numbered, p. 240, 25/2/1873, Minutes 1863–1884, MAK; Doc. 39, 17/2/1879 and Doc. not numbered p. 73, 14/3/1880, MC Minutes 1879–1884, MAK. Also Doc. not numbered p. 77–78, 29/4/1880, Doc. 265, 24/11/1883, Doc. 278, 2/12/1883, MC Minutes 1879–1884, MAK; Doc. 374, 6/3/1884, MC Minutes-Correspondence 1884–1885, MAK; Doc. 119, 30/4/1907, Minutes 1906–1908, MAK; Doc. 132, 22/5/1913, MC Minutes 1913–1914, MAK; Doc. 3, 9/2/1885, Minutes and Resolutions 1922–1948, MAK. This register contains copies of older resolutions and decisions.

245   Doc. 318, 4/5/1908, MC Minutes 1908–1909, MAK; Doc. 568, 3/2/1911, Correspondence of the Administrative Board 1910–1913, MAK; Doc. 90, 4/7/1915, MC Minutes 1915–1916, MAK.

246   Doc. 7, 10/10/1902, Minutes-Correspondence Financial Committee 1902–1904, MAK.

247   Doc. 13, 18/12/1906, MC Minutes 1894–1906, MAK. The decision was ratified by a new resolution adopted on 18/2/1907, MC Minutes 1894–1906, MAK.

affect the sponge fishing industry.[248] This phrasing from the early 20th century was amended in 1914–1915 as follows:

> The lease-holder of this local fee as well as his guarantor have no right to make any claim in the event of political circumstances, or epidemics, or the discontinuation of the use of the diving suit, nor put forward any claim as a consequence of the duration of the present state of war, an outbreak of a new small or big war, a new occupation of our island by any force, a new change of regime and, in general, of any present or future circumstances, and not even in case of a greater world conflict.[249]

Had this clause been applied to the letter, it would have proven catastrophic for those who held leases to collect the fee. As we shall see, even if the practice of holding leases fell into desuetude, those who held them could still demand monthly payments, in which case of course, the community would not receive its associated revenues. In this same year, however, adverse conditions forced the community to borrow 30,000 gold francs from sponge merchant Nikolaos Vouvalis, thus giving him the right to collect the revenue from the imported sponges.[250]

This form of revenue was not, however, always profitable. Especially in periods of slowdown in the activity, or in political crises, the proceeds declined, or no one sought to collect them. The Elders would then assign employees to collect the tax on the community's behalf.[251]

The oldest tax regime to which we have access is dated 1864. In this set of regulations, tariffs on imported and exported merchandise were jointly calculated with the tax on sponges. Based on comprehensive clauses, the differentiation in the tax applied was a result of whether the importer or exporter was a fellow Kalymnian, or a foreigner. Thus, local importers paid 2% while the rest paid 3%, whereas the tax for exported products was fixed at 2%. In the case of sponges, the tax was payable as soon as the vessel docked, even if sponges were not sold on Kalymnos. If sponges were sold from aboard one ship to another, the tax decreased by half, i.e., to 1.5%,[252] whereas no merchandise could be unloaded from the ship before the Customs Office had registered it.[253]

---

248 Doc. 3, 3/6/1902, Minutes-Correspondence Financial Committee 1902–1904, MAK.
249 Doc. 90, 4/7/1915, MC Minutes 1915–1916, MAK.
250 Doc. 150, 4/11/1915, MC Minutes 1915–1916, MAK.
251 Doc. 131, 5/5/1897, MC Minutes 1896–1897, MAK; Doc. 49, 9/7/1912, MC Minutes 1912–1913, MAK. On tax reduction see Doc. 17, 26/10/1903, Minutes and Resolutions 1922–1948, MAK.
252 Doc. 18, 16/2/1864 and Doc. 19, 17/2/1864, MC Minutes 1863–1884, MAK.
253 Doc. 21, 18/2/1864, MC Minutes 1863–1884, MAK.

In any case, every year the Elders appointed a supervisor (chosen by a council majority), to record sponge-related transactions with locals and foreigners on the island of Kalymnos. In accordance with the clauses on the "Local Sponge Fee", from the total quantity of sponges sold on Kalymnos, the community received 2% or 2.5%. This sum was borne by the seller captain and the buyer merchant who paid 1% or 1.5% and the remaining 1% respectively. It appears that many captains preferred to sell their sponges before their return to Kalymnos.[254] However, even when sponges were not sold on the island, the seller had to pay 2% of the total sum of their sale to the community.

Foreigners who brought sponges to Kalymnos for processing, but did not sell them on-site, were required to pay 1% of the estimated value of the sponges processed.[255] The community also levied taxes on the imported provisions necessary for sponge fishing, such as hardtacks, ropes, apparatuses, and so on.[256]

A decision of the Elders in 1897 determined that sponges exported to Europe were subject to a custom duty of 1 *kuruş* per crate and 2 *kuruş* per sack. When the customs office of Kalymnos caused delays or attempted to increase this sum, sponge traders threatened to buy sponges from Greece.[257]

On 25 April 1908, a resolution signed by 753 residents of Kalymnos raised the "Local Sponge Fee" from 2.5% to 3%. Half of this sum was to be paid by the sellers and the rest by sponge buyers.[258] From this tax, 2.5% would cover the Elders' needs, and the remaining 0.5% would be invested in the creation of a harbour fund, as well as the construction of the harbour.[259] It appears that, in the period that followed, percentages often fluctuated,[260] whereas in 1915–1916 they stabilized at 4%.[261] In 1920, the Italian government levied a tariff of 15% on sponges harvested in Cyrenaica, sparking the protests of fishermen.[262] In 1921, sponge merchants again requested that the tax to be reduced to 2.5%

---

254 Interestingly, enough one charter agreement includes a condition that the crew must sell their sponges in Piraeus itself. MC Minutes, Correspondence Various 1884–1885, pp. 76–77 (20/3/1884) and pp. 81, 84 (22/3/1884), MAK.

255 Doc. 44, 2/25/1879, MC Minutes 1879–1884, MAK; Doc. 58, 2/25/1893, MC Minutes 1892–1893, MAK; Doc. 12, 3/6/1902, Minutes-Correspondence Commission for Financial Affairs 1902–1904, MAK; Doc. 202, 12/2/1902, Correspondence 1902–1905, MAK; Doc. 133, 5/28/1907, MC Minutes 1906–1908, MAK; Doc. 132, 22/5/1913, MC Minutes 1913–1914, MAK.

256 MC Minutes, Correspondence Various 1884–1885, p. 44 (1884), MAK.

257 Doc. 18, 29/1/1897, Correspondence 1896–1898, MAK.

258 Doc. 318, 4/5/1908, MC Minutes 1908–1909, MAK.

259 Doc. 579, 25/2/1911, Correspondence 1910–1913, MAK, Resolution 28/2/1912, MC Minutes 1909–1913, MAK.

260 Doc. 42, 22/6/1911, MC Minutes 1912–1913, MAK.

261 Doc. 90, 4/7/1915, MC Minutes 1915–1916, MAK.

262 Doc. 265, 8/4/1922, Correspondence 1922, MAK.

given sponge-fishing activity's distress during and immediately after the war.[263] Although the issue seems to have remained pending, it appears that many captains continued to sell their catch before their return to Kalymnos, therefore maintaining an old practice. Once more, however, the Municipality tried to impose a tariff of 2% to preserve its income from sponge fishing.[264]

In the early 20th century, the tax was paid after the sponge-fishing vessels' return and following the sale of the catch. The Italian administration demanded that the applicable tax be paid in advance, a measure which investors and captains apparently could not meet in times of slowdown in sponge fishing, and increased amounts paid to captains of machines or boats, divers, skin-diving sponge fishermen, and rowers.[265] In the same period, and in 1906 in particular, a decision of the Elders established a Port Tax that was levied per vessel on sponge-fishing ships, hooking vessels and gagavas, whereas for vessels fishing with machines (scaphander diving suits and apparatus), the crew paid an additional tax on top of the tax on the vessel.[266]

2.8.3 *Sponge-Fishing Debts*

When the sponge fishermen returned to Kalymnos, their sponge product came, in a sense, under the investor's control. Investors in fishermen could push for the prompt sale of the merchandise to secure a return on their initial outlay. In cases where the investor was the buyer, he would try to set lower prices as loans came due, hence such interests put more pressure on captains, as well as on share prices, while the salaries of divers and crews were still outstanding.

After the product was sold, investors were the first to be repaid given that captains' debts to investors were defined as "preferential". On 16 September 1885, the Elders of Kalymnos attested that merchant and landowner Themelis Th. Olympitis "is the sole shipowner of, and investor in, the two sponge-fishing ships and crews of Ioannis N. Peronis". The ships were *Evangelistria*, a boat with a capacity of 4 tons, and *Agios Georgios* a lateen-rigged ship, also with a capacity of 4 tons. The terms of financing were clear: Ioannis Peronis, "the sponge fishing manager", was to be the temporary captain of both ships. At the end of the voyage, he and the ships' crews had to reimburse the shipowner's expenditures for the "departure and equipment of the ships"; both the capital and interests accruing to the voyage. Ioannis Peronis' debt to Themelis

---

263   16th Meeting, 2/7/1921, MC Minutes 1917–1922, MAK.

264   33d Meeting, 20/11/1921, MC Minutes 1917–1922, MAK.

265   Doc. 74, 1/3/1919 and Doc. 85, 2/4/1919, Correspondence 1918–1920, MAK; Doc. 70, 30/12/1919, MC Minutes 1919–1922, MAK.

266   Doc. 79, 6/3/1907, Land Disputes 1906–1908, MAK.

Olympitis was considered "preferential" and was subject to "the local customs of the sponge-fishery industry in force".[267]

Nevertheless, if profits did not suffice to cover the debt, if production did not compensate for the debt because of the divers' advance payment [*platika*], these obligations were carried over to the following year, creating problems even for the departure of ships. It is notable that, even though sponge-fishing expeditions were seasonal and short-term, outstanding debts of old crews were transferred to the next year, or even to the next few years. We can thus understand how frequent disagreements, or "sponge-fishing disputes" might have occurred, even when transactions were officially documented in the presence of witnesses and local authorities. In case of dispute, Elders specifically designated to deal with such matters assumed an intermediary role between involved parties, while interested parties often designated special mediators.[268]

If captains could not pay back the money that they owed, they were listed as "blocked" in Elders' registers, which prevented them from obtaining a Sponge-fishing Permit, and from setting sail on the next voyage. This was the case with captain Skevofylakas papa Ioannou Tsimouris who, in 1885, still owed his previous investors – brothers Christodoulos and Dimitrios Christodoulakis – 1,187 *kuruş* plus interest, based on records from the 1 April of the previous year.[269] In the same year, captain Georgios Droullos gathered 3.5 sacks of sponges with which he should have reimbursed his five investors and paid his crew.[270] The same captain, in 1893, chose to flee to the East, leaving outstanding debts to both his investor Ioannis Em. Magklis, and his crew.[271]

It would appear, moreover, that financiers could intervene in recruitment, when debts were carried over into the following year. Hence, in 1897, after having previously signed a promissory note to his investor Antonios Magkos, thereby handing over a 50% share of his ship to pay off previous debts, captain Nomikos Korfias had to keep Magkos informed about the crew he would hire and the advance payment [*platika*] he would give each crew member, if any.[272]

Captains were liable to repay investors from the current year, as well as previous investors, with part or all of their profits.[273] Therefore, in cases where a captain produced his recent debt balance for the Elders and yet claimed the

---

267   Doc. 411, Sponge-Fishermen Recruitments 1896, MAK.
268   Doc. 381, 5/9/1896, Doc. 82, 3/5/1897, MC Minutes 1896–1897, MAK; Doc. 468, 31/3/1884,
        Doc. 482 και 483, 4/4/1884, Minutes and Correspondence 1884–1885, MAK.
269   Doc. 257, 17/5/1885, MC Minutes 1885, MAK.
270   Doc. 318, 2/7/1885, MC Minutes 1885, MAK.
271   Doc. 31, 4/2/1893, MC Minutes 1892–1893, MAK.
272   Doc. 67, 26/2/1897, MC Minutes 1896–1897, MAK.
273   Doc. 187, 18/8/1884, MC Minutes 1863–1884, MAK.

rest of the money as profit, a former investor who had not yet been reimbursed could make a claim for the remainder.[274] For example, in 1915 debtor Nikolaos Tyllianakis and his investor were forced to use one third of the ship and machine's share to repay the captain's previous financier. One of the investors to whom Nikolaos Tyllianakis was indebted was his brother Apostolos. In this case, however, the rules were more favourable, despite the fact that the timely settlement of debts was still a prerequisite for carrying on with the activity.[275] Provided that captains and crews were in a position to do so – and after having settled prior outstanding debts – they had to repay interest-bearing loans granted by investors in their most recent voyage.[276] However, it appears that funds were not always sufficient for the entire duration of the voyage, and captains were occasionally compelled to borrow additional funds during the expedition while working off the coasts of Africa, in order to provide for their crews, and to avoid a forced return to Kalymnos.[277] Many captains were, however, not in a position to clear the debts in full, or simply refused to pay. In such cases, debts multiplied, and the outstanding amounts incurred interest, thus generating further difficulties for the captains. Nevertheless, the Elders set out an applicable institutional framework: "[…] withholding money belonging to a third party contravenes sponge-fishery regulations and customs; moreover, this illegal withholding of funds implies malice and deceit".[278]

Captains also commonly experienced difficulty in paying the taxes and necessary sums for sponge-fishing permits to the Elders.[279] If debtors did not go to the Elders, or if they failed to pay the required sums to the Municipal Treasury, the Elders sought the recourse of the District Governor [*Kaymakam*] to enforce its decisions.[280] Moreover, it perhaps goes without saying that debts were passed from father to son. Hence, captain Michail Soulounias' debts to Alfredo Hadji Theodorou were borne by his son Konstantinos M. Soulounias, given that the father could not join the expedition due to "suffering eyes".[281] There are also cases of a captain being forced to pay off the debts of one of his divers who had passed away.[282]

274   See, for instance, Doc. 156, 22/4/1893, MC Minutes 1892–1893, MAK.
275   Doc. 58, 15/5/1915, MC Minutes 1915–1916, MAK.
276   Doc. not numbered και doc. 1, 17/2/1915, Minutes 1915–1919, MAK.
277   Doc. 78, 2/10/1920, Correspondence 1919–1920, MAK.
278   Doc. 2, 6/10/1915, Minutes 1915–1919, MAK.
279   See, for example, the case of captain Nikolaos Kountouris: Doc. 604, 24/5/1884, MC Minutes-Correspondence 1884–1885, MAK.
280   There are numerous similar cases. See, for instance, Doc. 471–474, 31/3/1884, Minutes and Correspondence 1884–1885, MAK.
281   Doc. 573, 11/5/1884, MC Minutes-Correspondence 1884–1885, MAK.
282   Doc. 151, 21/4/1893, MC Minutes 1892–1893, MAK.

The accumulation of debt resulted in the adoption of numerous decisions of the Elders or of the Municipality of Kalymnos concerning the seizure of money, property and vessels due to outstanding debts.[283] Furthermore, as stipulated in the Elders' regulations, notables had the right to confiscate money originating from sponge-fishing debts on the interested party's request. Upon notification of the confiscation, the debtor was required to raise the necessary sum, and the creditor to present proof of his claims, within 8 days.[284] In its decisions, the Elders emphasized that,

> all sponge-fishing transactional disputes are not subject to appeal or annulment, because they are not part of the sphere of political and commercial litigation and, therefore, judgments and sentences are enforceable. Were this not the case, the industry would be destroyed, all transactions paralyzed, credit would be suspended, the area would face ruin, commerce would die out and the sponge-fishing industry would face the risk of discontinuation.[285]

In spite of this, sponges continued to be hoarded, given that it was also possible to pawn them. And, although sponges were constantly present and in abundance in the local market, they still held considerable value.

2.9   Framework and Institutional Organization of the Sponge Fishery

2.9.1   *Marine Sponge-Fishery Regulation*
Where the activities of so-called traditional societies are concerned, employment relations were dictated by "custom" and local usage, as well as by the more specific conditions associated with each professional specialization. In the present case, the sense of "custom", or "the sponge-fishing habit of our land", as it is commonly referred to in various archival documents, describes a complex system of financing and organizing work on sponge-fishing vessels. The most important factors that shaped this professional landscape over time are the singularity of the activity (the uncertain yield), diverse fishing methods, and the hierarchy of skills. In addition, the evolution of the industry as a result of the introduction of the scaphander diving suit gave rise to a strict, hierarchical, and competitive system which excluded many people, while it

---

283   See, for example, Doc. 51, 7/2/1897, Doc. 140, 14/5/1897, MC Minutes 1896–1897, MAK.
284   Doc. 1, 20/12/1894, Minutes and Resolutions 1922–1948, MAK.
285   Doc. 534, 30/4/1884, MC Minutes-Correspondence 1884–1885, MAK.

transformed sponge-fishing from an occasional or supplementary occupation
to a "profession". Given all this, central actors in the sponge fishery began to
feel the need for the institutional organization of employment relations and
transactions throughout the industry.

On 9 February 1884, the Elders of Kalymnos set up a six-member committee to conduct research on and draw up marine sponge-fishing regulations.[286]
Indeed, the resulting "Marine Sponge-Fishery Regulation", which included the
"Regulation on Sponge-Fishing Diving Machines", was adopted on 1 March of
the same year by the 485 members of the island's public assembly.[287] In its
43 articles, the regulation systematized the organization of sponge fishing, set
out rules guiding the participation of parties involved, including productive
relations, rights, obligations and remuneration, while at the same time, it also
organized the sponge trade. Furthermore, this written framework stipulated
the responsibilities of all parties towards the community, which in its turn
guaranteed its observance and enforcement.

Research into the records of the Elders reveals that this regulation was apparently not the first. In a decision of 1883, the Elders announced that "the articles
on crew recruitment included in the Marine Sponge-Fishery Regulation" were
in force.[288] Importantly, the dates indicate that the Sponge-Fishery Regulation
of 1884 was drawn up 20 years after the introduction of the scaphander diving
suit into Kalymnos' sponge fishery. It was an extensive text that incorporated
older customary law, "sponge fishing usage", "common practice", and "the local
custom concerning sponge fishermen", to which the island's notables constantly alluded. That said, the document was largely devoted to describing
the new working relations that arose from the modernization of the activity.
It was compiled during a period when the number of the people employed
on sponge-fishing vessels was gradually rising and when a new social stratum,
almost exclusively involved in sponge fishing, was being formed.

On the one hand, the regulation was an attempt to safeguard the captains of
sponge-fishing vessels from their crews, and on the other, the investors against

---

286   Doc. 321–322, 9/2/1884, MC Minutes and Correspondence 1884–1885, MAK.
287   The Marine Sponge-Fishery Regulation is published in Καλυμνιακά Χρονικά [Kalymniaka
      Chronika] 5 (1985), pp. 178–195. See also commentary on this topic by Διονύσης
      Μαυρόγιαννης, "Το συμμετοχικό σπογγαλιευτικό σύστημα της Καλύμνου: θεσμικό πλαί-
      σιο, οικονομικοί μηχανισμοί, κοινωνικός μετασχηματισμός", Καλυμνιακά Χρονικά [Dionysios
      Mavrogiannis, "The Participatory Sponge-Fishing System on Kalymnos: Institutional
      Framework, Financial Mechanisms, Social Transformation", Kalymniaka Chronika] 13
      (1999), pp. 241–248.
288   Doc. 155, 6/10/1883, MC Minutes 1882–1883, MAK.

borrower-captains.[289] The regulation contains a set of provisions largely pertaining to the capital invested in sponge fishing, and the thorny issue of sponge-fishing debts. At the same time, it also sought to regulate more specific issues related to employment relations in case of debts arising because of the high down payments involved in the modernization of the activity, as well as issues related to captains' financial obligations to investors. The regulation addressed, for the first time, the serious problem of victims of divers' disease without, however, conferring explicit rights on the victims and their families. There was little detail on what was already in force; the focus was to address new, growing problems. Moreover, as was stated early in the 20th century in a decision of the Commission for Financial Affairs: "for every case not provided for by this regulation, customary practice takes precedence".[290]

The basic principle applied in recruitment contracts, as stipulated in Article 13 of the regulation, was that "neither shall a captain abandon his mate, nor shall a mate desert his captain before the end of September", whereas in Article 7 it was stipulated that: "captains employing crew members not registered on the muster roll, without the consent of the captain or financier to whom the crew member belongs, and without drawing up the required official document, shall be subject to the interest-bearing payment of that crew member's debts". They thus established the compulsory recruitment of the indebted sponger either by the captain to whom he owed money from the previous year, or by another captain, according to the wish of his captain or, at least, with his consent. Between voyages and, "after the end of one sponge-fishing voyage, the captain was required to supply the indebted crew member with dry food for a period of one month before the next voyage began. Once this month expires, the crew member shall be recruited again". It is a peculiar kind of indentured labour that mostly affected divers, who, if indebted, were not only bound to pay their debts back by harvesting sponges, they were also not free to choose the terms of their employment. At the same time, captains were not permitted to dismiss incompetent or disobedient divers while their contract was valid.

This regulation also governed the means of distribution of the sponge product, as an attempt to safeguard the interests of the divers. Hence, in accordance with Article 29, captains had to obtain the crew's consent for the sale of the sponges and give the respective shares to each of the crew members. Article 2

---

289   Faith Warm argues that the Regulation standardized the existing practices, while intensifying the exploitation of spongers. See Faith Warm, *Bitter Sea: The Real Story of Greek Sponge Diving*, London 2000, p. 47.

290   Doc. 3, 3/6/1902, Minutes-Correspondence Commission for Financial Affairs 1902–1904, MAK.

specified that "all captains bear the obligation to issue a written bill within 5 days of having sold the crew's sponges to each crew member". It did not however, specify the time frame for the remuneration. Therefore, the longer the delay in selling the product, the longer the employees remained unpaid. The regulation attempted, to a certain degree, to ensure that the activity ran smoothly and to pre-empt employment and social conflicts, yet without incorporating any social welfare framework. To a certain degree, one may attribute the absence of social care, organized workers' associations, or collective protests to the singularities of the sponge fishery, and to the large profits it could mean for the workers.

Perhaps, the most crucial issue was the fate of those suffering from divers' disease, including their families' survival. It appears that the parties involved were, of course, aware of the existence if divers' disease without naming it and apparently the number of victims was so great that the Regulation included provisions for the sufferers; deceased and paralyzed. If, for example, the diver became ill at work, the arrangement to which he had agreed with the captain remained in force, but the regulation did not provide for any aid from the community or other source. However, the sponge-fishing undertaking bore additional responsibility for the treatment for any crew member falling ill after the ship's departure, as well as for the payment in full of his share, because he had been in the ship's employ. Under Article 24, the undertaking was also responsible for expenses connected with food, medical treatment, and burial in case of death. Finally, the heirs of the deceased were entitled to the entire share of the crew member who had passed away during the sponge-fishing voyage.[291]

Although recruitments carried out in late 1884 for the sponge-fishing expeditions of 1885 were conducted "by virtue of the Marine Sponge-Fishery Regulation",[292] in the introductory section of the recruitment register of 1884 it is explicitly stated that: "captains who declare their recruits here [i.e. Kalymnos] promise and have the obligation to comply with the terms included in the Marine Sponge-Fishery Regulation, on the basis of which recruitment for sponge fishing is conducted".[293] Notwithstanding the existence of the Regulation, it seems that many deals continued to be arranged orally or were not ratified by the Elders, even though the Elders constantly cited the

291   See also Μαυρόγιαννης, "Το συμμετοχικό σπογγαλιευτικό σύστημα της Καλύμνου" [Mavrogiannis, "The Participatory Sponge-Fishing System on Kalymnos"], pp. 244–245.
292   See MC Minutes 1881–1884.
293   Doc. 1, 219/1883, MC Minutes 1881–1884, MAK.

Regulation and the universal obligation to draw up official recruitment documents. In addition, the Elders often repeated that various articles were to be in force.[294]

Despite increased popular consent, and even though local authorities and those appealing to them on the grounds of continuous violations frequently invoked the Marine Sponge-Fishery Regulation, the Regulation seemed powerless, especially in the case of sponge-fishing debts. Reports are continuous and the cases with which the Elders had to deal each year were numerous, even at the very moment that vessels were almost ready to set sail. The issue of sponge-fishing debts was obviously particularly pressing, while violations of the relevant article of the Regulation occurred daily. Occasionally, the Elders, and later the Municipality, reminded concerned parties of the validity of the article as, for example, in a decision of 1915 that notes that "sponge-fishing restrictions shall be valid throughout the year. Any captain who conceals a crew member or rower and does not declare him in his permit, will be responsible for all the preferential debts of this person".[295]

In 1893, a number of recommendations and complaints were submitted to the Elders concerning the Regulation's shortcomings, and they proposed that it be revised. We have no further information on this matter,[296] and by all accounts the Regulation was not revised. However, several years later in 1906, a new decision complementing, or rather reinforcing the 1884 Regulation provisions, was adopted:

> Contrary to this long-established Sponge-Fishery Regulation, which states explicitly in Article 12 that, once captain and crew member enter into a written agreement, neither of them can abandon the other under any pretext; if another captain takes in a crew member who has deserted his captain and sets sail with him, then Article 7 of the Regulation shall apply, sentencing this captain to a reparation of forty Ottoman liras. Given that, when they appeared before the Elders, sponge-fishing captains reported that, in violation of the Regulation, irregularities concerning the recruitment took place daily; this is to say that many crew members, despite being officially recruited once by a captain in the presence of the Elders, are recruited again by another captain. Thus, if this practice persists, the industry and sponge-fishing crews will be completely brought to a halt. Therefore, in order to prevent this harm, the captains convening today

---

294   Doc. 158, 7/8/1907, MC Minutes 1906–1908, MAK.
295   Doc. 33, 4/4/1915, MC Minutes 1915–1916, MAK.
296   Doc. 89, 16/3/1893, MC Minutes 1892–1893, MAK.

unanimously decided the following: Any sponge-fishing captain who takes in a crew member recruited by another captain or registered in Elders' book as recruited, shall be required to pay a reparation of twenty Ottoman liras, without objection, to the captain under whom the crew member was registered. If a captain helps a crew member under another captain to escape, he shall take on that crew member's preferential debts. In this case, the investor is also liable. The above proceedings approved and signed by captains and investors were ratified by the Elders and were thus validated and came into force.[297]

The Italian administration of the Dodecanese issued Regulation for the Sponge Fishery [*Regolamento per la pesca delle spugne*] decrees in 1921, 1927 and 1937. These reflected the existing customary law in the Dodecanese islands to that time and covered all sponge-fishing methods.[298] A mandatory permit granted by the Port Authority upon payment of the fishery fee was necessary to resume the undertaking. Although all fishing methods were permitted, the number of scaphander diving suits was to be determined every year on the basis of the condition of the Dodecanese sponge-bearing beds; for depths of more than 60 meters gagavas were prescribed, whereas naked divers could not exceed a depth of 50 meters.[299] Contrary to the Greek law (5525/1932) that established shares (a system known as "*kopelli*") as an unique means of remuneration for divers using diving suits, the Italian Organization for Sponge Fisheries of 17 October 1927, recognized all existing customary employment relations. Remuneration could be provided monthly during the sponge-fishing season in shares (i.e. profit sharing), or in percentages of sponges harvested, without any minimum limit.[300]

On 1 December 1921, the Italian administration founded an insurance fund for the sponge fishermen of the Dodecanese islands, which began its

---

297   The title of the document is: "Supplementary Report to the Sponge-Fishery Regulation" Doc. 136, 23/10/1906 and is found in the register of Land Disputes 1906–1908, MAK.

298   See Θεόδωρος Κριεζής, "Η σπογγαλεία. Β' Νομοθεσία ελληνικού κράτους", *Οικονομικός Ταχυδρόμος* [Theodoros Kriezis, "The Sponge Fishery. The Second Legislation of the Greek State", *Oikonomikos Tachydromos*], 21/8/1932, p. 3 and Σωτήριος Ι. Αγαπητίδης, *Η εργασία εις την σπογγαλιείαν* [Sotirios I. Agapitidis, *Working in Sponge Fishery*], Athens 1938, p. 7.

299   Θεόδωρος Κριεζής, "Η σπογγαλιεία. Β' Νομοθεσία ελληνικού κράτους", *Οικονομικός Ταχυδρόμος* [Theodoros Kriezis, "The Sponge Fishery. The Second Legislation of the Greek State", *Oikonomikos Tachydromos*], 21/8/1932, pp. 3–4.

300   Ibid., p. 3.

operations in March 1922, and counted 2,000 members.[301] Based on the latest decree, the Port Authority of Rhodes issued a guideline on first aid for divers in 1931, and a welfare fund for sponge fishermen was established in 1932 in order to collect compulsory contributions from crew members and captains. Concurrently, sponge-fishing permits became mandatory, financial indemnity for accidents was introduced, and the sums involved varied depending on the gravity of the condition, or if the death occurred on the job.[302] The Royal Decree of 12 April 1937 regulated the modes of payment for sponge fishermen, making provision for either a monthly salary or percentages of harvested sponges. In addition, the decree stipulated that advance payments were to be made in installments, the largest of which would be given to families during the crews' absence.[303]

In the Greek state, employment relations were governed by customary law until 1910, when the first law on sponge fishing was adopted (law ΓΧΙΖ).[304] This law, together with its executive orders (of 13 January and 25 February 1912), was in force until 1937, when it was replaced by the emergency law 560.[305] This legislation was, in fact, based on the existing customary organization of the industry. It sought, however, to improve working conditions by imposing attendance at diving schools, and the assurance of competency certificates. The diving school's program, according to testimonies, was completed in 40 days and most divers – many of whom were already experienced – confessed that they were forced to attend diving school when authorities "pushed them into a corner".[306]

This first law of 1910 was the result of a sustained period of consultations and discussions at the Greek Parliament, as well as heated protests, mainly conducted through the press, about the working conditions of sponge fishermen, and the victims of the divers' disease. The obvious conflicts of interest of the people involved in the activity, and the thorny issue of the discontinuation

---

301   Γεωργάς, *Μελέτη περί σπογγαλιείας* [Georgas, *Study of the Sponge Fishery*], p. 34; Δωδεκάνησος. Τετράτομος μελέτη του Υπουργείου Ανοικοδομήσεως [*Dodecanese. Study in Four Volumes by the Ministry for Reconstruction*], p. 276.

302   Doc. 216, 3/5/1894 etc., Sponge-Fishermen Recruitments 1894–1896, ΜΑΚ. For legislation under Italian rule, see Κριεζής, *Η σπογγαλιεία* [Kriezis, *The Sponge Fishery*], pp. 16–17.

303   Δωδεκάνησος. *Τετράτομος μελέτη του Υπουργείου Ανοικοδομήσεως* [*Dodecanese. Study in Four Volumes by the Ministry for Reconstruction*], p. 276.

304   This is a Greek system of using the alphabet for numbering. We supply the original here for the purposes of research.

305   Also, *Αθηναϊκά Νέα* [*Athinaika Nea*], 9/4/1937, p. 4. See Αγαπητίδης, *Η εργασία εις την σπογγαλιείαν* [Agapitidis, *Working in Sponge Fishery*], p. 3.

306   Testimony of Nikolas Kampourakis to Ε.Ο., 25/8/2002.

of scaphander diving suits was sometimes introduced into the political sphere and divided early 20th-century Greek governments. Some of the measures implemented by successive Greek governments included tasking a military ship to oversee the sponge fishery, publishing directives for divers, and drawing up bills. Until 1910 they thus avoided adopting legislation for the entire industry. Recruited divers were subject to a health assessment beginning only in 1954, in accordance with a decision of the Minister of the Mercantile Marine and the Royal Decree "on the health assessment of divers to be recruited".[307] In any event, sponge-fishing contracts drawn up on Kalymnos continued to cite the 1884 Sponge-Fishery Regulation, which was still in force until the early post-war years.

2.9.2   *The Role of the Community*

The community played an important institutional role in the organization of the sponge fishery. Apart from its interest in collecting the "local sponge fee", the community was also responsible for the validation of agreements between captains and crews. Consequently, recruitment contracts were considered a type of notarial document. "The industry of this land requires that the administrators of public life be aware of all dealings of the sponge fishery so as to prevent any complications, confusion, and resulting disputes and altercations, that may lead to a standstill of the industry upon which life on this land depends". Hence, every agreement was to be made in writing, at the office of the Elders, where the relevant fee would be paid, and the original document kept. Any other document was considered "void, valueless and unenforceable".[308] Therefore, in the presence of the representatives of the Elders – of the Municipality, or of a notary and the Port Authority from 1927 onwards[309] – the necessary documents specifying employment relations and the financial terms in place between the employee and the captain were drawn up and signed by the two parties, the Elder (Mayor or Harbour Master), and two witnesses. Along with the aforementioned resolution, the Elders repeatedly issued decisions with which it stipulated that all sponge-fishing recruitment

---

307   *Οικονομικός Ταχυδρόμος* [*Oikonomikos Tachydromos*], 16/12/1954, p. 13.

308   "Resolution of the People of Kalymnos" Doc. 115, [6/9/1883] and Doc. 117, 9/6/1883, MC Minutes 1882–1883, MAK.

309   See, for example, Doc. 132, 21/9/1883 and Doc. 155, 10/6/1883, MC Minutes 1882–1883, MAK. Until 1927; thereafter, a decree by the Italian government ordered that contracts be concluded at the Port Authority. The Port Authority of Kalymnos does not possess any surviving recruitment documents for 1927–1943. The recruitment contracts found in the Archive of the Municipality are dated 1926. In the Greek state, agreements were drawn up before the Port Authorities beginning in 1937, in accordance with emergency law 560/1937. See Γουργιώτης, "Όροι εργασίας εις την σπογγαλιείαν" [Gourgiotis, "Working Conditions in the Sponge Fishery"], p. 74.

contracts had to be drawn up officially in the presence of representatives; otherwise, contracts were not considered valid.[310]

Contracts "opened" (as informants call it) in March or April,[311] and in the post-war years divers had to obtain health certificates attesting that they were healthy and able to engage in sponge fishing. The Municipal Council had a mediating and decision-making role, settling sponge-fishing disputes, and imposing fines and sanctions. By invoking the existing regime, community officials tried to settle arguments, disputes and even violent confrontations between the parties involved.[312] Although in some cases of financial dispute, private arbitration was not excluded, the Elders would intervene when the situation reached a deadlock,[313] whereby the Elders were called upon to interpret the sponge-fishing Regulation and to honour the "custom". The community also issued sponge-fishing permits and collected the applicable sums for each vessel and its crew members. As noted above, some captains attempted to avoid paying, concluded private agreements with their crews, and set off in secret. The community would then lodge a complaint and demand the monies due from both captains and their investors.[314]

All employment relations in the traditional or pre-industrial world, or even the world of unstable, rapid mechanization presented their own typical frameworks. These frameworks were determined by local practices and customary law, whether the custom was expressed orally, or captured in community and trade union documents. Oral and written agreements set the pace and the discipline governing the organization of all forms of work, based on familiar and commonly accepted rules by which all stakeholders had to abide. Even the breaches, evasions, and omissions of this system[315] seem to present their very own regularities. Every written representation of the customary framework, such as that of 1884, depicts a particular density in this professional domain, and the obvious monetization of the activity, which might, after all, encompass dynamics of change or the overturning a traditional system.

---

310   Doc. 132, 9/21/1883, MC Minutes 1882–1883, MAK; Doc. 41, 2/10/1900, MC Minutes 1899–1900, MAK; Doc. 134, 19/10/1906, Land Disputes 19061908, MAK.

311   Testimony of Nikolas Kampourakis to E.O., 25/8/2002.

312   See also the case of three captains and investors who turn to the Demogerontia to resolve their sponge-fishing dispute. The incident ends in a violent altercation and damages to the furniture, windows etc. of the Demogerontia's building. Doc. 74, 26/4/1902, Correspondence 1902, MAK.

313   Doc. 34, 5/2/1900, MC Minutes 1899–1900, MAK.

314   Doc. 131, 3/10/1911, MC Minutes 1910–1912, MAK.

315   For many reasons, they seem to be limited in our case, and they mostly pertain to female or child labour and to a more limited degree, male labour.

CHAPTER 3

"Hunters at the Bottom of the Sea"

3.1   The Sponge-Fishing Fleet

For the long period of interest to us here, statistical surveys on sponge-fishing activities were only conducted on an occasional basis. The absence of systematic records of intense or slow periods of activity, requires that such information be indirectly inferred from various kinds of documents. That said however, throughout this study we cite figures on employees and vessels from Kalymnos, as well as the quantities of sponges harvested and sold.

In this chapter, we will attempt to aggregate the scattered quantitative data that we have been able to retrieve concerning quantities, and particularly data on the sponge-fishing labour force on the island of Kalymnos, in order to assemble a more exhaustive – albeit incomplete – picture, rather than a comprehensive account. Here again, testimonies and archival evidence cover a long period of time, and various registers have been lost or are unclear; all of this raises obvious challenges for any attempt to compile comprehensive evaluations. Likewise, the data on the places of origin of workers in the sponge fishery are not consistent, yet sporadic and incomplete archival evidence suggests that those seeking employment on the sponge-fishing vessels of Kalymnos came from the surrounding islands and other sponge-fishing areas of the Dodecanese and the Greek state. A careful examination of records also reveals some – rare indeed – references to divers from Evia [*Euboea*] or the Peloponnese.

That said, all the sponge-fishery permits and vessel registration documents of which we have knowledge – at least to the mid-19th century when the records become comprehensive – when taken together, do reveal a fairly clear picture of the number of people employed. In a report to which we have previously referred, written before 1854 by the British Consul to Rhodes, Robert Campbell, we read that the sponge-fishing vessels of Kalymnos numbered 120, manned by 840 sponge fishermen, whereas in 1858 the number of vessels had increased to 254, and the number of sponge fishermen to 2,000.[1] If the

---

1   The title for this chapter referes to the name divers were given in the press. See also, *Ελευθερία* [*Eleftheria*], 12/2/1967, p. 3. The report is dated 24 February 1859, and addressed to Stratford Canning, British Ambassador to Constantinople; Κυριάκος Χατζηδάκης, "Η σπογγαλιεία στις Νότιες Σποράδες στα μέσα του 19ου αιώνα", *Καλυμνιακά Χρονικά* [Kyriakos Kon. Chatzidakis,

islanders of that period actually numbered 9,500, or as many as 7,600 inhabitants, then those involved in sponge fishery made up a significant portion of the island's male population.[2] European and Ottoman sources accord fully with these figures, and add that Symi had 190 sponge-fishing vessels that year (1858), Leros 30, Kassos 2, and Astypalaia 12. Moreover, Halki counted another 65 sponge-fishing vessels, Kastellorizo 40, and Telos 7. Out of a comprehensive total of 600 vessels, 70 were engaged in harvesting sponges off the coasts of Rhodes, 150 off the coasts of Crete, 180 in the area of Syria and 200 in northern Africa.[3] If the figures to which we have previously referred are indeed accurate, it appears that, in the mid-19th century, about ten years before the introduction of the scaphander diving suit, the sponge-fishing fleet of the eastern Aegean witnessed a rapid expansion. Even more spectacular was the increase in size described by Hippocrates Tavlarios in 1862: 450 Kalymnian sponge-fishing vessels, with crews of 5 to 10 men each.[4] This figure is probably somewhat exaggerated, even though Tavlarios had considerable knowledge of the Kalymnian sponge fishery. However, if this were indeed the case, the sponge-fishing population would have ranged from 2,250 to 4,500 persons. That said, the data from the Elders' Council does not to concur and, in 1865, when sponge fishing conducted by naked divers was still prevalent, there were 352 sponge-fishing vessels, with that number increasing to 355 in 1866.[5] Another source indicates that Kalymnos had 254 sponge-fishing vessels employing 1,600 men in 1870,

---

"Sponge Fishing in the Southern Sporades in the Mid-19th Century", *Kalymniaka Chronika*] 13 (1999), pp. 229–240.

2 Information concerning the population of 9,500 inhabitants is contained in the report of British Consul to Rhodes, Niven Kerr, drawn up in June 1851; Κυριάκος Κων. Χατζηδάκης, "Κάλυμνος, 1851", *Καλυμνιακά Χρονικά* [Kyriakos Kon. Chatzidakis, "Kalymnos, 1851", *Kalymniaka Chronika*] 12 (1997), pp. 38–44. Other researchers estimate the population at 7,600. See Σωτήριος Αγαπητίδης, "Ο πληθυσμός της Δωδεκανήσου", *Δωδεκανησιακή Επιθεώρησις* [Sotirios Agapitidis, "The Population of Dodecanese", *Dodekanisiaki Epitheorisis*] 2–4 (1948), p. 88 and Γεώργιος Μ. Σακελλαρίδης, "Η εξέλιξη και διαμόρφωση του πληθυσμού της Καλύμνου", *Καλυμνιακά Χρονικά* [Georgios M. Sakellaridis, "The Development and Configuration of the Population of Kalymnos", *Kalymniaka Chronika*] 9 (1990), p. 395.

3 Ali Fuat Oreng, Yakindonem Tarihimizde Rodos ve Oniki Ada, Istanbul 2006, p. 510.

4 Ιπποκράτης Ταυλάριος, "Περί της νήσου Καλύμνου", *Πανδώρα* [Hippocrates Tavlarios, "About the Island of Kalymnos", *Pandora*] 12 (1861–1862), pp. 518–522. The text is republished in Δανιήλ Ζερβός, "Μια περιγραφή της Καλύμνου του 1862 και ένα πολιτικό κείμενο του 1908", *Καλυμνιακά Χρονικά* [Daniil Zervos, "A Description of Kalymnos in 1862 and a Political Text from 1908", *Kalymniaka Chronika*] 18 (2009), pp. 100–125. Θέμελης Κινδύνης [Themeli Kindynis] shares a similar report in *Η νήσος Κάλυμνος* [*The Island of Kalymnos*], Athens 1879, pp. 24–26.

5 Ledger 29/1881–7/8/1884, Archive of Kalymnos' Elder Council, ΜΑΚ. See more information in Ευδοκία Ολυμπίτου, "Η εισαγωγή του καταδυτικού σκαφάνδρου στη σπογγαλιεία της Καλύμνου", *Τα Ιστορικά* [Evdokia Olympitou, "The Introduction of the Sponge-Fishing Scaphander Diving Suit in the Sponge Fishery of Kalymnos", *Ta Istorika*] 38 (2003), pp. 163–186.

while the net worth of the sponge catch was valued at around 2,500 pounds sterling.[6]

In 1884, the year in which the "Marine Sponge Fishery Regulation" was drawn up, 178 sponge-fishing permits for departures from the island of Kalymnos taking place from 19 March to 2 July were issued.[7] All permits stated the amount of tax (12, 20 or 25 *kuruş*) paid to the Municipal Treasury by each crew member (see Table 3.1).[8]

TABLE 3.1   Sponge-fishing vessels and crews, Kalymnos (1884)

Crew members per ship	Sponge-fishing vessels	Total number of employees
3	3	9
4	12	48
5	16	80
6	3	18
7	15	105
8	71	568
9	36	324
10	4	40
11	1	11
12	2	24
13	4	52
14	4	56
15	2	30
16	2	32
25	1	25
33	1	33
Average 8.2	177	1,455

SOURCE: MC MINUTES 1881–1884

---

6   P. L. Simmonds, *The Commercial Products of the Sea or, Marine Contributions to Food, Industry and Art.* London 1878, pp. 185–186.
7   In two cases of permit entries more than one serial number appears, yet it is not clear if these numbers indicate a corresponding number of vessels.
8   MC Minutes 1881–1884, p. 9, and the following, MAK.

TABLE 3.2   The sponge-fishing fleet of Kalymnos, 1884–1894

Year	Sponge-fishing machines	Sponge-fishing vessels with divers	Sponge-fishing boats	State revenue from permits*	Sponge catch value of the island of Kalymnos*
1884	26	140	30	2,352	48,500
1885	16	130	32	1,940	45,100
1886	22	112	26	1,928	40,300
1887	25	98	29	1,896	38,450
1888	26	90	25	1,832	36,750
1889	28	78	23	1,768	34,200
1890	25	67	40	1,630	30,500
1891	27	58	36	1,598	28,600
1892	26	55	40	1,510	25,700
1893	26	36	40	1,352	22,000
1894	29	19	50	1,126	-------

*   in Turkish lira
SOURCE: PROCESSED DATA FROM MC MINUTES 1881–1884 AND THE FOLLOWING, MAK

From the number of groups shown in this register, we can calculate the number of men employed on every fishing vessel in a specific year. Given that this number ranges from 3 to 33 crew members, it logically takes all fishing and diving methods into account (i.e. naked diving, with scaphander diving suit, with gagavas and hook). Therefore, 1884 the labour force involved in sponge fishing amounted to a total of 1,455 men (see Table 3.1).

All subsequent totals of the registration of vessels and employees were drawn up, as we shall see elsewhere in this study, to make a case against the disastrous effects of scaphander diving suits, and to argue for decreasing the number of crews involved in sponge fishing on Kalymnos. The number of vessels appears thus to decrease year by year, shrinking from 358 vessels in 1870 to 28 in 1900, whereas, according to Flegel's estimates, those employed in sponge fishing numbered 1,300 in the late 19th century.[9] Another source for the following decade, which presents similar fluctuations, is the "Statistics on the sponge fishery of Kalymnos island dating from the year 1884 to 1894,

9   Κάρολος Φλέγελ, Η νήσος Κάλυμνος [Carl Flegel, The Island of Kalymnos], Istanbul 1896, p. 28.

extracted from the official crew lists of the Elders' Council of Kalymnos, as well as from the receipts that the esteemed Imperial Government collected from sponge-fishing permits granted to vessels on Kalymnos, and from this land's sponge produce from the aforementioned years" (See Table 6).[10]

From the sponge-fishing permits issued in 1928, 1929 and 1930, we may trace the outlines of a representative picture of the sponge-fishing industry during the period of Italian rule on Kalymnos.[11] Each entry in the register corresponds to a single vessel and includes the kind of sponge fishing practiced. Records also contain each vessel's captain and crew member's names; scaphander and Fernez diving suits are listed as divers and rowers, and as sailors for the remaining cases. Each person's contributions are likewise listed as well as, in some instances, the areas where sponge fishing was conducted. It should also be noted that, beginning in 1926, some machines were petrol-powered.[12]

In the last pre-war decade (1929–1939), workers in the sponge fishery numbered 1,350 to 1,700, a figure which we may assume is the equivalent of 60–70% of the island's population.[13] Up until 1960, there were around 60 sponge-fishing groups, large and small, employing 850 divers and 700 sailors.[14] Crews usually consisted of five men: the engineer who was responsible for the petrol-powered engine, the air pump and the rest of the machinery; the steersman; the diving manager [kolaouzieris]; and one sailor. On each vessel, there were 5 to 12 divers. In the two-year period from 1963 to 1965, the average number of divers per vessel was slightly less than seven.[15] In the first years following the dictatorship which ended in 1974, (known as the political changeover or metapolitefsi in Greece), many Egyptian divers worked on Kalymnian sponge-fishing ships.[16]

---

10   Doc. 220, 25/8/1894, Correspondence 1894–1895, ΜΑΚ; Φλέγελ, *Η νήσος Κάλυμνος* [Flegel, *The Island of Kalymnos*], p. 28. The same table is published in Milt. Carabokyro, *Étude sur la pêche des éponges. Les pays spongifères de l'Empire et le scaphandre*, Istanbul 1886, p. 15.
11   The processed data of the registers for this three-year timespan – 1928, 1929, 1930 – are presented in Appendix I.
12   The first person to bring a petrol-powered engine to Kalymnos was reportedly Giorgis Galopoulos. See Νίκη Γρ. Μπιλλήρη, *Σφουγγαράδες από την Κάλυμνο*, [Niki Gr. Billiri, *Sponge Fishermen from Kalymnos*] Athens 1995, p. 75.
13   Αντ. Παπακωνσταντίνου, "Σπογγαλιευτική και αλιευτική δραστηριότητα (Από τη σκοπιά της Αγροτικής Τράπεζας)", *Καλυμνιακά Χρονικά* [Ant. Papakonstantinou, "Sponge Fishing and Fishing Activity (From the Perspective of the ΑΤΕ)", *Kalymniaka Chronika*], 2 (1981), p. 165.
14   Ριζοσπάστης [Rizospastis], 15/5/1976, p. 11.
15   Bernard Russell, "Η σπογγαλιεία της Καλύμνου", *Σπουδαί* ["The Sponge Fishery of Kalymnos", *Spoudai*] 1 (1970), p. 4.
16   Παπακωνσταντίνου, "Σπογγαλιευτική και αλιευτική δραστηριότητα" [Ant. Papakonstantinou, "Sponge Fishing and Fishing Activity"], p. 165.

3.1.1   The Crews

From the mid-19th to the mid-20th century, dozens of vessels were involved in the Kalymnian sponge fishery and numbered several hundred men aboard, despite various fluctuations, working every year. Along with local crews, the high figures indicate the casual employment of foreigners in the sponge fishery on Kalymnos. The supply of labour, better remunerated there than elsewhere, attracted divers from neighboring islands – even from the sponge-fishing areas of the Greek state – seeking career opportunities, employment on a casual basis, or even a get-rich scheme. The reverse was also the case: Kalymnian seamen and divers were recruited on vessels from Symi, Hydra, Aegina and Ermioni. The local labor force was usually familiar with the peculiarities of the profession, and when the activity experienced spectacular growth, the necessary labor force was supplemented with agricultural labourers from neighboring islands. Without experience in long-distance sea voyages and diving, these men generally amounted to a cheaper workforce seeking casual and supplementary employment.[17] These casual workers typically believed that anyone could do the job of a diver without any particular specialization or prior experience.

The size of this labor force was not always stable and, although there was an upward trend, until at least 1912, its numbers were influenced by various factors. For example, in the second half of the 19th century, the major problem for the Kalymnian community was integrating changes brought about by new diving technology; namely, the scaphander diving suit. Moreover, as previously noted, the professional environment of the sponge fishery underwent other crises as well which, however severe they may have been, were mostly exogenous. The root cause of these crises was the administrative restructuring that took place in the Dodecanese Island complex and, by the 20th century, the events of the war that afflicted the Eastern Mediterranean further impacted the sponge fishery. Hence, on the eve of WWII, when demand from the Western industrial market for natural sponges had decreased noticeably, the Dodecanese sponge fishery had already sustained several severe blows.

In "traditional" sponge fishing, naked divers were usually partners of the captain – himself a diver – and they were all uniformly remunerated in kind, and with the same sums of money, plus a share of the vessel. With the adoption of the scaphander diving suit there was a deterioration in the co-operative organization of work, even on naked divers' vessels, while their remuneration was no longer equal. The high fishing costs led to a reshuffling of the circle

---

17   Π. Ζώτος, Ἔκθεσις περί τῆς ἀνά τας αφρικανικάς ακτάς διά σκαφάνδρου σπογγαλιείας [Zotos, *Report on Sponge Fishing by Diving Suit along the African Coasts*], Athens 1904, p. 7.

of investors, while it excluded many people from the opportunity to finance long voyages and large crews. The structure of the undertaking and employment relations were modified, whereas the activity's expansion in every aspect limited opportunities to practice a lucrative seasonal job. The observation that the scaphander diving suit "distinguished capital from work right from the outset" was perhaps apt.[18] On the other hand, work on vessels equipped with scaphander diving suits prolonged working time, while the remuneration offered could, in theory, sustain crews throughout the entire year. These developments were instrumental in the consolidation of the spongers' social stratum, inside which, as we shall see, significant differentiations existed. Work aboard sponge-fishing vessels, especially on those using scaphander diving suits and the Fernez, was now characterized by a division of labor and a specialization. The divers who descended to the bottom of the sea wearing the "machine" were distinct from those monitoring the air pump on the vessel, while the rest of the men were employed in various auxiliary tasks. Hence, the captain was no longer a "mate" diver but rather became the "manager" of the undertaking. A diverse system of labour relations with distinct roles, and significant discrepancies in earnings was thus established.

Aboard "naked diving" vessels there were divers and sailors, the latter being referred to as rowers [κωπηλάτες or κουπάδες] in more recent testimonies. They were not only the small sponge-fishing ships' rowers, and the same term was also used for sailors performing various auxiliary tasks, even the cleaning of sponges. They were paid a fixed sum or, more rarely, one half of a share.[19]

For the crews working with the scaphander diving suit or Fernez methods, the number of divers ranged from 3 to 20, depending on the investor's means, or the destination. The rest of the crew amounted from 20 to as many as 50 men.[20] Younger workers were employed in these positions as apprentices.

The deck crew included the "motoristas" [μοτορίστας], that is the person responsible for the diesel-powered engine of the vessel (when they became motorized), and the daily maintenance of the air pump, hand-cranked or later mechanical. The crew also included a "trechadinieris" [τρεχαντηνιέρης],

18   This phrase is found in a brief geography of Kalymnos by Io. Orfanos, published by Ioannis Patellis, dating back to 1926. Ιωάννης Σκεύου Ορφανός, "Η νήσος Κάλυμνος", *Καλυμνιακά Χρονικά* [Ioannis Skevou Orfanos, "The Island of Kalymnos", *Kalymniaka Chronika*] 17 (2007), p. 96.

19   Κάρολος Φλέγελ, "Το σπογγαλιευτικό ζήτημα της Μεσογείου (Χανιά 1903)", *Καλυμνιακά Χρονικά* [Carl Flegel, "The Sponge-Fishing Issue of the Mediterranean Sea (Chania, 1903)", *Kalymniaka Chronika*] 5 (1985), p. 209.

20   See also more recent information in Russell, "Η σπογγαλιεία της Καλύμνου" ["The Sponge Fishery of Kalymnos"], p. 4.

the man at steering the wheel who followed the diver's moves while on the seafloor and moved the vessel slowly.[21] There was also the *"markoutseris"* [μαρ-κουτσέρης] who manned the air hoses. All of the above crew members were responsible for the preparation and monitoring of the diving, but the combined responsibility fell on the *"kolaouzieris"*, who communicated with the diver (i.e., in problem situations) while tracking the duration of the dive. The crew also included a cook and the *"balaristis"* [μπαλαριστής] or *"sortiristis"* [σορτιριστής], that is the men who sorted the sponges into types and sizes, took charge of their cleaning, and packed them into sacks on board an auxiliary vessel, or "depozito" [ντεπόζιτο].[22] More recent written and oral testimonies indicate that the majority of men began as apprentice auxiliary crew members and later became familiar with one of the above tasks; or they might switch to a different specialization, pursuing the better-paying jobs of *kolaouzieris*, or deputy captain, when the captain was not on board.

3.2 Crew Employment Relations

Family and kinship ties appear to have played an important role in the formation of work teams, as well as in other forms of collaboration and co-operation, while contributing to a more flexible way of dealing with debts. This is related to historical archival evidence and more recent testimony, which suggests the frequent presence of relatives on board sponging expeditions, especially on vessels with naked divers and divers with reveras. Given this, professional succession was a near inevitability for the members of a sponging family, hence in the professional and industrial milieu of the sponge fishery, the involvement of boys and young men was considered the sole means of survival on Kalymnos. Indeed, in their testimonies, young spongers explain that "Everybody here spoke of sponges. What else could one do?" and, as a young boy tells his mother in one modern fairytale ("The Tailor Boy," 1908),[23] "[my father] was a diver, and

---

21   Testimony of *trechandinieris* and captain Petros Marthas to E.O., 2/9/2004.

22   Auxiliary vessels accompanying the sponge-fishing groups in their long expeditions. They were larger watercrafts and were used to store provisions, to accommodate the crews, and to dry, process – to a rudimentary degree – and pack the sponge product. It is difficult to determine their overall number because a *deposito* could accompany a single sponge-fishing vessel, when they worked individually, or two and even three sponge-fishing vessels which could be sharing it.

23   From the story "Το ραφτόπουλο" ("The Tailor Boy") documented on Kalymnos by Karl Dieterich, *Sprache und Volksüberlieferung der südlichen Sporaden im Vergleich mit denen der übrigen Inseln des Ägäischen Meeres*, Vienna 1908, pp. 481–487.

so will I be",[24] thus affirming family succession as self-evident. And this kind of familial succession occurred even in professions where no workshop or equipment was inherited; rather expertise and experience were the legacy.

Employment relations were organized in accordance with "the Sponge-Fishing Custom of the land", and the Sponge Fishery Regulation, to which the parties involved always referred. It should be noted, however, that a similar organization of employment relations was common to all sponge-fishing areas. Recruitments, shares, *platika* (more on this directly below) or those who worked as *kolaouzieris, markoutseris, motoristas, trechadinieris* and so on, were remunerated with sums that could be supplemented with a percentage of the profit.[25] On the other hand, there were also fluctuating forms of remuneration (percentages or shares) on net profit that were paid to divers, with important pre-agreed gradations, based on the diving method and depth.[26] The main difference in recruitment contracts was concerned with whether the work was conducted from a "sponge-fishing boat", a "sponge-fishing ship", or with a "sponge-fishing machine". The first two terms describe divers working by means of apnea (i.e., naked divers with no breathing apparatus), while the second group consisted of those using scaphander diving suits and Fernez. The absence of co-operatives, or of groupings or collective claims until the 1950s may probably be attributed to this singular customized employment regime.

The "platika", the "regalo" and the share were all forms of remuneration paid to the men working on sponge-fishing vessels, and the sums were determined individually for every crewmember. The "mechanic's" payment was different from that earned by the diver working with the "machine" (scaphander diving suit), and this in turn was different from how divers working with the

---

24   "Σαν ήτο, μάνα μου, βουτηχτής, τσ᾽ εγώ βουτηχτής θα γενώ."
25   It would be interesting to compare the employment relations of workers on Kalymnian sponge-fishing vessels to those working on Symiot sponge-fishing vessels. See Σωτήριος Αγαπητίδης, "Η οικονομική οργάνωση των σπογγαλιευτικών συγκροτημάτων – ειδικότερα στη Σύμη", *Τα Συμαϊκά* [Sotirios Agapitidis, "The Economic Organization of Sponge-Fishing Groups – Particularly on Symi", *Ta Symaika*] 3 (1977), pp. 187–191.
26   Νικόλαος Σ. Πιζάνιας, "Η οργάνωσις της σπογγαλιευτικής επιχειρήσεως (τεχνικώς-οικονομικώς)", Α᾽ Πανελλήνιον Σπογγαλιευτικόν Συνέδριον (Ρόδος 2427 Φεβρουαρίου 1949). Εισηγήσεις και Πρακτικά, Γενική Διοίκησις Δωδεκανήσου [Nikolaos R. Pizanias, "The Organization of the Sponge-Fishing Enterprise (on a Technical-Financial Level)", The First Colloquium on the Sponge Fishery, Rhodes 24–27 February 1949, *Papers and Minutes*, General Administration of the Dodecanese], Rhodes 1951, p. 36. The case of fishery, with its fluctuating profit margins is, perhaps, relatable. For the remuneration of fishermen with percentages of the total catch of the vessel, see J. Acheson, "Anthropology of Fishing", *Annual Review of Anthropology* 10 (1981), p. 278. Cf. also John J. Poggie, Jr., "Deferred Gratification as an Adaptive Characteristic for Small-scale Fishermen", *Ethos* 6/2 (1978), pp. 114–123.

"machinery" (Fernez) or "sponge-fishing divers" (naked divers) were paid. And finally, remuneration for the rest of the men working as part of the deck crew was much lower than the rates just noted. This is, therefore, a multifaceted system of employment relations with considerable elasticity in remuneration practices, which not only differed in amount but also in kind, since crew members were paid, as already noted, a fixed sum. In contrast, divers mostly received diversified percentages. In this way, most people, and mostly the divers, shared in any profits or losses arising from the sponge-fishing activity.

Crew members received part of their remuneration in advance (the *platika*), or the full remuneration for their services at the beginning, or at the end of the sponge-fishing season, or as a monthly salary. Divers were paid after the sale of the sponges, either with shares commensurate with their participation in the undertaking's profits, or with a percentage of their individual production (the *kopelli*), ranging from 25% to 45% and, in exceptional cases, as much as 50%.[27] The amount also fluctuated in proportion to the depths in which the diver worked, as well as to his competence.[28] In the 1910s, the divers' shares amounted to approximately 30% to 35% of the value of premium and standard quality sponges, whereas the *platika* was paid in one or two instalments.[29] In addition, captains assumed the costs for the crew's keeping, as well as a part of the expenses for the issuance of the sponge-fishing permit.

Divers' agreements set out the terms of employment, which were based on loans at particularly high interest rates, and on potentially usurious relations, masked behind down-payments higher than the diver's productive capacity. Despite the shares and divers' specialized participation in the undertaking's subsequent profits, these relationships were not founded on cooperation. Agreements commonly set out conditions for employment that implied "unflagging work" and "obedience to the captain's orders until the end of the voyage without question". The constant reiteration of such formulations in

---

27 Πιζάνιας, "Η οργάνωσις της σπογγαλιευτικής επιχειρήσεως" [Pizanias, "The Organization of the Sponge Fishery",], p. 38; Κωνσταντίνος Γουργιώτης, "Όροι εργασίας εις την σπογγαλιείαν", Α' Πανελλήνιον Σπογγαλιευτικόν Συνέδριον (Ρόδος 24–27 Φεβρουάριου 1949). Εισηγήσεις και Πρακτικά, Γενική Διοίκησις Δωδεκανήσου [Konstantinos Gourgiotis, "Working Conditions in the Sponge Fishery", 1st Colloquium on the Sponge Fishery (Rhodes 24–27 February 1949). *Papers and Minutes*, General Administration of the Dodecanese], Rhodes 1951, p. 76.

28 In Greece, pursuant to law 560/1937, and in the Dodecanese complex in the post-war years, two depth categories were established, while it was suggested that they be increased to three: a). up to 18 fathoms, b). from 18 to 25 fathoms, and c). starting from 25 fathoms for deep-water caiques; Γουργιώτης, "Όροι εργασίας" [Gourgiotis, "Working Conditions"], p. 76.

29 Tripoli-Libya Embassy, Folder 28, Subfolder 4, Benghazi Vice Consulate Archive, IAYE, where many employment contracts drawn up by the consular authorities in Libya survive.

every recruitment document would seem to indicate that this was customary practice. In reality, such formulations conceal other binding terms descriptive of a work environment wherein "fleeing" and "deserting" were not uncommon. Moreover, divers were enmeshed in a particularly coercive structure of dependency, given that they were already indebted to their captains and had to clear their debts by the end of the year. They were also vulnerable and exposed to a series of imponderable factors and circumstances, such as the exhaustion of sponge-bearing beds in various areas, frequent real or artificial market crises, competition, dangers, unfortunate circumstances, and accidents.

In the documents it drew up, the Elders' Council of Kalymnos did not often refer to accidents. Although one of the more prominent arguments in Elders' fight for the abolition of scaphander diving suits is indeed the dangers involved in sponge fishing, the archive does not contain annual accident reports. One might conclude, therefore, that the Elders did keep records of accident frequency, but that they were lost or are kept elsewhere.

Documents on victim claims from sponge fishermen are scarcer. In this case the community played a decisive role, as it was called upon to apply the Sponge Fishery Regulation and, above of all, to interpret the custom. For instance, in an 1894 community decision, it is specified that even if the diver had worked for only one day before his accident, he was entitled to the full amount of his salary or share.[30]

3.3   Pay Grades: Divers

As previously noted, the expected or possible remuneration for "mechanics" (the divers working with the "machine" or the scaphander diving suit), was contracted on an individual basis and different from that of naked divers.[31] These variations were explained by the conditions and specifications that were set out *ex ante* in the recruitment agreements [*tsourmarismata* – "the crewing"], beginning in the two final decades of the 19th century: the diver's skill and experience, the diving method, the depth to which the diver agreed to work, or beyond which he would not commit to descend (of course, this last stipulation was almost never applied), as well as the duration of the sponge-fishing voyage.

---

30   Doc. 8, 10/1/1894, Correspondence 1894–1895, MAK.

31   The nature of sponge fishing required a spirit of cooperation, mutual trust and solidarity among the people working and living on board. At the same time, however, it nurtured individualism and rivalries, due to the system of employment relations, especially in those cases where remuneration was calculated based on individual productivity.

The diver's value was thus not only proportionate to his physical stamina, but also depended on his ability to discern and harvest plenty of sponges – and good quality sponges. Experienced divers could swim against strong currents and spot sponges hidden in the lush marine vegetation,[32] hence on Kalymnos it is said that "good divers went up for auction and whoever offered the best price got them".[33] In fact, the best or most capable "mechanical" divers ["*maghiori*"] could demand advance payments – as much as six times more than the rest of the crew, or half of the sponges they harvested. These were the "mechanical divers" whom captains strove to sign up at the beginning of the winter, by luring them with high down payments. Given this, it is interesting to note that various sources and testimonies from the late 19th and 20th centuries offer positive reports of competition and fair play among divers while making clear, however, that the yardstick for the terms of recruitment was their reputation. Whatever the case may be, high-yielding men and cooperative men saw their recruitment agreements renewed for the coming year.

It goes without saying that there was yet another important parameter to such agreements not explicitly mentioned in the archival evidence, namely, the age of the diver. Age influenced the amount of money divers received and forced them to retire from the profession prematurely. Child labour in the sponge fishery, as in light or heavy industry, was cloaked in the practice of apprenticeship and was not only commonplace, but custom dictated that it take the form of a trial period aboard a vessel. It was suggested that the apprenticeship period for boys could begin at a very early age, as boys grew familiar with the sea bottom while diving off local coasts. From the age of 10 or 12, boys were hired as auxiliary staff on vessels, while from the age of 14 or 15 they worked as "novices" [Turkish "*ajamides*"] for a reduced wage.[34] However, complaints of underage children being hired as sailors, and then being forced into diving, were not uncommon.[35] Generally speaking, with the help and guidance of experienced senior naked divers, adolescent boys became fully-fledged

---

32   Ζώτος, Ἔκθεσις [Zotos, *Report*], p. 7.

33   This occurred in other sponge-fishing areas as well. See Ζώτος, Ἔκθεσις [Zotos, *Report*], p. 8.

34   In some cases, apprentices were even younger; around 1912, Apostolos Kardoulias worked with naked divers for the first time on a sponge-fishing vessel at the age of 8. See Liberty Kovacs, *Liberty's Quest*, Bandon 2008, p. 50. See also the testimony of Symiot diver Manolis Tabakakis, who started working as naked diver at 14–15 years old. Ροδούλα Λουλουδάκη, "Η Σύμη ήταν το κέντρο των σφουγγαράδων", *Σαμιακός* [Rodoula Louloudaki, "Symi Was the Center for Sponge Fishermen", *Samiakos*], Folder 213 (2008), p. 5.

35   The report of lieutenant Aggelis, captain of the troopship *Crete* supervising the Libyan maritime area in 1906, mentioned two cases involving ten-year-olds. Ἐμπρός [*Empros*], 25/6/1906, p. 3.

spongers at about 20 years of age, while the retirement age for divers was roughly 40 to 45 years.[36] We are not aware if documents were drawn up in such cases or if, among the recruitment agreements, there are contracts for minors.[37]

Novices and minors alike were paid low wages. For example, one typical recruitment contract of 1883, states that the son of a diver is hired as ship-boy, and that "if he continues to swim regularly during the entire sponge-fishing voyage, he will be paid his share of food and ropes accordingly, minus one tenth; if he doesn't swim at all or swims only occasionally, he will receive no payment".[38] A similar provision appears in a subsequent contract, where again, the ship-boy was the son of a diver and his expenses were paid in proportion on how frequently he swam.[39] This kind of vague language appears often and in several contracts in 1883, and is perhaps better clarified in another document from the same year, which fixed the value of the catch required for the young ship-boy, to be exempted from paying for the costs of his maintenance.[40] The Elders, nonetheless, did not appear to intervene in such cases, with the exception of one instance discovered in the records, when two minors signed recruitment agreements without the consent of their legal guardians.[41]

Existing documents do not indicate the sum of shares of the catch, presumably because this sum was taken as a given or as common knowledge.[42] Nevertheless, the share was not always paid "in full" and there are instances in which a diver was contracted to receive a ⅔ or ¾ share.[43] P. Zotos, lieutenant commander of the troopship *Crete* which supervised Greek sponge fishermen

---

36   The information in this section, offered in many testimonies, is also corroborated by relevant publications. See Faith Warm, *Bitter Sea: The Real Story of Greek Sponge Diving*, London 2000, pp. 54 and 68. Bernard Russell writes of extremely rare occasions when some working divers exceeded the age of 50. Russell, "Η σπογγαλιεία της Καλύμνου" ["The Sponge Fishery of Kalymnos"], pp. 20–21. See also Doc. 85, 10/8/1921, Correspondence 1920–1922, MAK. Document 85 was a certificate issued for divers who had worked for 25 years on vessels equipped with scaphander diving suits before quitting the profession, while also participating in the construction of Kalymnos' breakwater.

37   At any rate, official recruitment documents were drawn up beginning in the 1950s, which included a written consent by guardians when hiring minors.

38   Doc. 3, 24/9/1883, MC Minutes 1881–1884, MAK.

39   Doc. 4, 26/9/1883, MC Minutes 1881–1884, MAK.

40   Doc. 27, 21/10/1883, MC Minutes 1881–1884, MAK.

41   Doc. 181, 10/9/1907, MC Minutes 1906–1908, MAK.

42   In the first decades of the 20th century, the "*kopelli*" ranged from 20–30% of the divers' individual production. See Γιάννης Αντ. Χειλάς, *Το έπος των σφουγγαράδων της Καλύμνου* [Giannis Ant. Cheilas, *The Epic Saga of Kalymnos' Sponge Fishermen*], Athens 2000, p. 38. According to oral testimonies, the share – from the 1940s onwards – ranged from 35% to 60% on rare occasions. It usually fluctuated about 40%.

43   See, for example, Doc. 9, Sponge-Fishermen Recruitments 1904–1905, MAK.

off the coasts of North Africa in 1903, describes the share as "belonging to the realm of fantasy, to say the least". In his opinion, this was because many people died on the job, whereas the rest, being illiterate, could either be deceived by the captains or forced to lower the amount of their claims.[44]

As previously noted, naked divers, of which there were, as a rule, 2 to 6 aboard one vessel, received equal remuneration, *platika*, and shares.[45] There are cases, however, in which important wage differentiations may be observed, based clearly on skill and experience.[46] On vessels working with naked divers, rowers were paid lower wages, and these were also subject to slight differentiations. Nevertheless, rowers received a *platika* and, in some cases, a percentage of the share.[47] From the first decade after the war, although shares were still used as a form of remuneration for naked divers, a percentage system prevailed for other divers, with percentages inferior to full shares.

As the key players in the industry, divers constituted a distinct professional workforce, evaluated on the basis of experience and dexterity, yet their position in the local market was precarious, given that it was redefined after each expedition, in a highly competitive environment. To achieve success, to ensure re-employment, to make high wages, and the repay their debts, divers had to intensify their work output. Intensification in sponge fishing is measured by the number of dives performed, the depth of the dive and how long divers remain on the seabed.

3.4   The *Platika*

Advance payments that crew members received after signing recruitment agreements, and until the moment they set sail for the "sponge-fishing voyage" were called *platika*. These sums were intended for the upkeep of divers and their families. Ultimately this meant that divers lived through the entire winter on an expanding loan with high interest rates – credit extended on anticipated future yields – which had to be repaid by the end of the autumn of the following year, after the sale of the sponge product. Moreover, rather than using the term "*platika*", some contracts describe the agreed upon sum as being released in the form of "a winter convenience", sometimes as a lump sum

---

44   Ζώτος, Ἔκθεσις [Zotos, *Report*], p. 8.
45   See Doc. 76, 78, 30/4/1921, Sponge-Fishermen Recruitments 1921, MAK.
46   See, for instance, Doc. 3, 2/10/1906, Sponge-Fishermen Recruitments 1905–1907, MAK; Doc. 79, 30/4/1921 and doc. 92, 95, 3/5/1921, Sponge-Fishermen Recruitments 1921, MAK.
47   See Ledger 113, doc. 76, 86, 30/4/1921, MAK.

and sometimes in two or more instalments, the last one being given before the ship's departure.[48]

The following is taken from a contract for a mechanical diver, drawn up in 1897:

> It is declared before the Elders' Council of Kalymnos that Nomikos N. Tsagkaris, captain of a sponge-fishing machine, hires Nomikos Kardoulis as a member of the machine crew of his sponge-fishing vessel, in the capacity of mechanical diver, for the forthcoming sponge-fishing voyage in the summer months of the year 1897, that is until the end of October 1897, under the following terms:
>
> a. The aforesaid captain pledges to grant, in installments, a *platika* of 12,000 *kuruş* at Kalymnos' market value, to the here-named mechanic, at an interest rate of 20% per year, beginning on the first day of the up-coming month of April. For this purpose, he pledges to issue an interest-bearing promissory note in accordance with Sponge-Fishing Custom.
>
> b. The captain pledges to pay the mechanical diver a *regalo* of 4,500 *kuruş* in addition to his share, in accordance with Sponge-Fishing Custom.
>
> Having agreed to the above, the aforesaid mechanical diver, Nomikos Kardoulis, pledges to work tirelessly throughout the entire sponge-fishing voyage and to obey his captain's orders. Kalymnos, 9 January, 1897[49]

Frequently however, initial agreements were concluded orally and the *platika* was paid before signing the contracts at the Municipality or the Port Authority. Once the crew was recruited, a comprehensive list was filed with the Port Authority, following which contracts were drawn up, just days before setting sail.[50] As noted above, the *platika* also varied based on expected productivity, which was conditional on the diver's or rower's experience and skill, according to their prior assessment by the local labor market, whereas the down payments and wages for novices were, of course, low.

The 46 documents concerning individual or collective crew recruitment for the summer sponge-fishing voyage of 1897, present a considerable range of fluctuation in the remuneration of divers. For mechanical divers, the *platika* ranged from 2,500 to 14,000 *kuruş*, (usually amounting to 6,000 to 10,000 *kuruş*, except for novice divers to whom sums of 2,000 to 3,500 *kuruş* were

---

48   See, for example, Doc. 2, 21/9/1883 and Doc. 43, 12/3/1884, MC Minutes 1881–1884, MAK.
49   Doc. 544, Sponge-Fishermen Recruitments 1897, MAK.
50   Testimony of Nikolas Kampourakis to E.O., 25/8/2002.

paid) and the *regalo* from 800 to 4,000 *kuruş*. For naked sponge divers, payment did not exceed 1,200 to 1,500 *kuruş*, while the regalo and percentages did not apply. This should, perhaps, come as no surprise, given that the sponge catch was limited and the necessary start-up capital and the profits from the voyage were less sizable for the "captain of sponge-fishing boat" than for the "sponge-fishing machine captain".

Work was seasonal, and each year crews were recruited by the same or different captains for a set period. For those working on the deck, the *platika* usually accounted for their entire remuneration, which they received either in its entirety in advance, or in installments before the voyage as soon as the contract was signed. The "mechanical diver", unlike the rest of the crew, received a *platika* in the form of an interest-bearing loan, the amount of which corresponded to his estimated performance, rather than part of a previously agreed-upon, fixed wage. For the period spanning from mid-January to late March – the period in which most recruitment took place, and during which relevant documents were drawn up – prepaid remuneration was interest-free. Beginning on the 1st of April, however – as shown in almost all the documents studied – the *platika* bore an interest rate of 20%.[51] The divers' aim was to collect as many sponges as they could, so that they could use their share together with the *regalo* to repay their *platika*, and keep the "surplus", if any.[52]

The "*kopellia*" [those who received a *kopelli*] were a particular category of divers who were paid in shares. They kept their sponges apart from the rest of the catch, and the divers were paid based on the selling price, after the vessel's share ("of the machine") was deducted.[53] In other words, the divers in this category received a share of the total profits at a predetermined percentage, after the advance payments (*platika*) made by the captain were deducted. This system applied to the most proficient divers from the beginning of the 20th century, but in the post-WWI years its scope was expanded to encompass almost all divers, especially those on deep-sea caiques.[54] It would appear, however, that the terms of such contracts were not always entirely favorable. For

---

51 This practice survived in the post-war years, as well.

52 Quoted terms and expressions are commonplace in recruitment documents.

53 This turn of phrase is common in late 19th-century documents and especially in 20th-century documents, as this system apparently includes a larger number of divers. See, for instance, Doc. 180, Book 83, Sponge-Fishermen Recruitments 10 April 1904–11 April 1905, MAK.

54 Γουργιώτης, "Όροι εργασίας" [Gourgiotis, "Working Conditions"], p. 75. The same occurred on Symi, as well. See Αγαπητίδης, "Η οικονομική οργάνωση" [Agapitidis, "The Economic Organization"], pp. 199–200. See also E. Papataxiarchis, "A Hypothesis on the 1965–1977 Transition in the Socio-economic Structure of the Sponge-Fishing Industry in Kalymnos", (doctoral diss.), Department of Social Anthropology, London School of Economics, p. 8.

example, on 6 May 1921, Antonios Magkos, captain of a sponge-fishing machine, recruited machine diver Athanasios Lyberis as *kopelli*, who agreed to receive 25% of his sponge catch and *platika* of 2,000 francs.[55]

Some documents that make no mention of a *platika*, such as a recruitment contract dated 29 April 1896, make mention of a "*hartziliki, sermagia, refenedes*" rather than a *platika*. For example, in another recruitment contract dated 22 April 1896, we read that "a credit receipt [for a sum of money] bearing the customary annual interest rate of twenty percent (20%)" was issued by a recruited diver.[56] This diver and shareholder was also required to hand over any surplus generated from his work, as well as "the corresponding shares". In another similar document, the wording becomes more precise in the first section: "[he] shall provide the sponge fisherman the *refenedes* [share in common crew materials] of ropes and food, and a *sermagia* [collective advance capital] on their departure for the sponge-fishing voyage, for which he shall be reimbursed from shares, along with the customary sponge-fishing interest".[57] Similarly, elsewhere the annotation of "all surpluses accruing to the diver's share, after the deduction of the sum already paid plus taxes of 20%"[58] occurs, and in other documents the interest rate is again defined as the "customary sponge-fishing interest".[59] Other recruitment documents state that the *platika* included the winter advance payment, the "*hartziliki*" [allowance] and the "*refenedes*" [share in common crew materials].[60] In a recruitment contract concluded on Kalymnos for a Symiot mechanical sponge diver on board a vessel from Hydra, it is stated that this diver will receive three and a half shares from the sponge product, and that his *platika* is interest-free and will be deducted from his shares after the sale of the sponges.[61]

In addition to the above payment forms – *platika, hartziliki, refenedes* – one might also receive a *regalo*, the amount of which appears likewise to be

55   Doc. 120, 6/5/1921, Sponge-Fishermen Recruitments 1921, MAK.
56   Doc. 526, Sponge-Fishermen Recruitments 1896, MAK. Many similar agreements can be found in the recruitments for the years 1883 and 1884 (MC Minutes 1881–1884). In fact, many agreements specify that the "*hartziliki*" is destined for divers' families.
57   Doc. 41, 19/10/1883, MC Minutes 1881–1884, MAK.
58   Doc. 529, 24 April 1896, Archive of Kalymnos' Elder Council, Sponge-Fishermen Recruitments 1896, MAK.
59   Doc. 535, 16 May 1896, Archive of Kalymnos' Elder Council, Sponge-Fishermen Recruitments 1896, MAK.
60   A crew recruitment contract signed in October of 1896, in view of the 1897 sponge-fishing voyage. See also Doc. 538, 5 October 1896 Archive of Kalymnos' Elder Council, Sponge-Fishermen Recruitments 1896, MAK.
61   Doc. 535, 30/8/1896, Archive of Kalymnos' Elder Council, Sponge-Fishermen Recruitments 1896, MAK.

dictated by Sponge-Fishing Custom. Another type of contract stipulated that the *regalo* of one crewman was to be paid by the rest of the divers and the captain,[62] or even that it be subtracted from the ship's share and awarded to the most competent diver, as per a signed agreement.[63] The phrasing of a 1884 recruitment contract describes the *regalo* as "a token of competency in sponge fishing".[64] Notably as well, men working on gagavas, such as the gagava operator, or the "gagavaris", could also be paid in both *platika* and shares.[65]

Occasionally, nonetheless, agreements were not honored and, despite having recruited the divers, and captains did not pay them the agreed upon *platika*.[66] It seems also likely that crew members – especially divers – would illegally receive various sums as *platika* from people other than their captains, without declaring these sums in their recruitment agreements.[67] Moreover, an agreement could be modified during the voyage. Hence, captain Andreas Dounias pledged to pay his divers a full share instead of the agreed upon $3/4$, if during the voyage they went to work at Port Said.[68]

Be that as it may, the recruitment of skillful divers was essential to a successful undertaking. By offering enticing advance payments, captains and investors attempted to attract the best divers, even if divers had already signed employment contracts with other captains.[69] Captains employed other means to recruit divers as well, such as pressuring crews in various ways, or by force under various pretexts, and by preventing foreign divers from seeking employment on another island.[70] Therefore, friction between captains and crews concerning the final settlement of shares was frequent.

The sponge-fishing season for vessel crews began after Christmas, when men were looking for work and contracts "opened", such as recruitment agreements for the "big summer voyage" of 5 to 7 months. The duration of contracts depended on the diving method and the area in which they were going to harvest the sponges. On vessels carrying naked divers, crews were teamed up by late March, whereas all necessary preparations were made in April.[71] During

---

62   Doc. 162, 26/4/1893, MC Minutes 1892–1893, MAK.
63   Doc. 3, 24/9/1883, MC Minutes 1881–1884, MAK.
64   Doc. 4, 26/9/1883, MC Minutes 1881–1884, MAK.
65   Doc. 208, 30/4/1894, Book 78, Sponge-Fishermen Recruitments 1894–1896, MAK.
66   Doc. 56, 24/2/1893, MC Minutes 1892–1893, MAK.
67   Doc. 158, 7/8/1907, MC Minutes 1906–1908, MAK.
68   Doc. 207, 16/11/1907, MC Minutes 1906–1908, MAK.
69   This mostly occurred with investors from other islands who sought crews on Kalymnos. See, for example, Doc. 41, 8/3/1902, Correspondence 1902, MAK.
70   Doc. 32, 21/2/1902, Correspondence 1902, MAK.
71   See, for example, studies that discuss the period from 1863 to 1868, such as Alfred Leroy de Méricourt's " Considérations sur l'hygiène des pêcheurs d'éponge ", *Annales d' hygiène*

the recruitment period, in accordance with the Sponge Fishing Regulation, crews were required to settle their previous debts, which would have to be cleared prior to departure.[72]

The employment agreements consulted here, do not allow us to investigate how the recruitment of divers took place. However, according to relevant documents on Kalymnos, we do know that novice divers were not permitted to switch job functions if they proved to be incompetent. In contrast, in a report published in 1903 in the Athens press, we read that:

> No man is hired for the position of diver against his will, but rather in response to his request. An official contract drawn up with the captain clearly explains that the worker is recruited as a diver under an explicit agreement. If the diver is experienced, he is then aware of all the risks of the job and is free to choose not to be recruited. If a diver is recruited for the first time as an apprentice, a strictly respected clause of the contract stipulates that if, during the voyage he is not able to work as a diver, he is free to opt for the job of sailor and therefore receives an advance payment of only 800–1,000 drachmas. Indeed, many apprentice divers who prove not to be suited to the job resign and work as sailors. It is not in the captain's interest to waste time while the diver is on probation [the "*atzamis*"] learns the job. Therefore, the popular notion that sailors are forced to become divers is a lie.[73]

The recruitment of divers for brief winter voyages – cited as "*cheimonika*" [of winter] in the documents, or "*hysterotaxida*" [late or final voyages] in oral testimonies – were far more rare, as only those working "with the machine's dress" could work in winter as well.[74] Nevertheless, many vessels sponge fishing with scaphander diving suits worked for shorter periods until April, and before setting sail for their long summer voyage.[75] Although it would appear that the majority of vessels reached Tripoli and Benghazi in late March to early May, several stayed in that area for winter voyages, beginning in October, and

---

publique et de médecine légale 31 (1869), p. 276; Louis Figuier, *Les merveilles de la science, ou Description populaire des inventions modernes*, Paris 1870, p. 624.

72   Doc. 446, 26/3/1884, Minutes and Correspondence 1884–1885, MAK.

73   Δ. Α. Πανάγος, "Οι σπογγαλιείς μας. Τα κακουργήματά των μύθοι. Μία απάντησις εις την Εστίαν", *Εμπρός* [D. A. Panagos, "Our Sponge Fishermen. The Legends of their Crimes. An Answer to Estia", *Empros*], 15/4/1903, p. 3.

74   Doc. 798, 16/9/1884 and Doc. 822, 3/12/1884, MC Minutes-Correspondence 1884–1885, MAK.

75   Doc. 14, 16/1/1893, MC Minutes 1892–1893, MAK.

renewing their crews either partially or entirely. A number of winter voyage agreements were drawn up by the Consular Authorities or Port Authorities of Libya, when vessels stayed on and continued their fishing activity there. For example, in the 1922–1923 winter season, 7 scaphander diving suits remained in Libya, one of which came from Kalymnos. Their crews comprised a total of 117 men, 54 of whom were divers.[76]

Winter fishing along the coasts of Northern Africa was apparently particularly lucrative. As we read in a report from the Greek Consul in Tripoli to the Directorate of Merchant Shipping of the Ministry of National Economy, six Greek vessels and one Italian (from the Dodecanese islands) worked in Tripoli from October 1922 to April 1923. Their overall yield amounted to 7,920 kilograms.[77] More specifically, these vessels harvested 440 kilograms of sponges in October, 2,973 kg. in November, 2,326 kg. in February and 2,181 kg. in March 1923.[78] From this report we may conclude that the Greek vessels declared a total of 36,756 tons of sponges valued at 2,309,523 Italian lira in this period. Therefore, on average each vessel would have earned 384,920.5 Italian lira during this period.[79]

3.4.1   *The Debtor Mechanical Diver*

Even though the undertaking could be lucrative for divers, debts owing to their captains were commonplace and not easy to settle, as an investigation into recruitment documents reveals. After the sale of the sponge product and the final settlement with the captain, the divers had no "*resta*" [the remaining money] to collect. Either they owed "preferential sponge-fishing debts" from previous years, or they were paid in shares, which were often not sufficient to cover that year's advance payments or prior debts. Hence, divers found themselves "hostages" to one or more captains. Where more than one captain was involved, the "first entitled", or the oldest employer took precedence, followed by the rest of the captains to whom money was owing.[80] Therefore, those presenting and substantiating their "preferential sponge-fishing claims" before the local authorities, were also the ones who chose the vessel on which the

---

76   See Embassy of Tripoli-Libya, Folder 28 (1920–1923), Subfolder 2, Benghazi Vice Consulate archive and Folder 29 (1923–1924), Subfolder 17, IAYE.

77   Due to the phrasing in the Greek Consul's presentation of the figures, it is not entirely clear whether these figures correspond to the six Greek vessels or to the total of seven vessels. The first scenario is the most likely.

78   Embassy of Tripoli-Libya, Folder 29 (1923–1924), Subfolder 17, IAYE.

79   Report 20/12/1924, Embassy of Tripoli-Libya, Folder 29 (1923–1924), Subfolder 17, IAYE.

80   See the decision of Elders' Council, in which the Council attempts to interpret the Sponge-Fishing Custom in Doc. 231, 6/5/1885, MC Minutes 1885, MAK.

diver would work the following year, as well as the conditions of employment, and drew up the relevant documents. One such document reads:

> It is officially declared, before the Elders' Council of Kalymnos, that Evangelos Ninis grants his man Sakellarios Apokoumastos or Mamouzellos to be recruited by captain Nikitas I. Tsakirgiou or Pervolargia, provided that the captain shall pay him forthwith three hundred *kuruş*. After the end of the voyage, the aforesaid man shall entirely belong to Evangelos Ninis, to whom Nikitas I. Pervolargias shall lay no claim.[81]

On other occasions, the official consent of the captain to whom the divers owed money sufficed for them to be able to work again, with a specific investor, or on any other vessel.[82] If the captain to whom the diver was indebted agreed, the captain could "grant his man" to another captain on the condition that he would be considered first privileged, and that he would pay the amount still owing the "mechanic" [i.e. diver with scaphander] from his share plus the "usual sponge-fishing interest of 20%". Disputes between captains concerning who would be the first to collect the divers' debts were frequent, and captains customarily appeared before the local authorities to claim this privilege.[83] In any case, the diver could not be recruited and work in the following year without the permission of his "privileged" creditor.[84]

To overcome such pending matters, or "sponge-fishing hindrances", captains employed various means. Sometimes the captain would withhold a part of the debtor's *platika* to cover his debt right from the beginning of the diver's contract.[85] On occasion indebted divers were forced to hand over their entire *platika* in repayment of debts owing to a previous captain.[86] A new captain was also required to pay the diver's debt to the previous captain in the form of an advance payment as part of the diver's future salary. At the end of the voyage however, the "aforesaid man belonged entirely" to the investor or captain to whom he still owed money.[87] On other occasions, a new captain might

81   Doc. 191, 29/4/1894, Sponge-Fishermen Recruitments 1894–1896, MAK.

82   See, for instance, Doc. 216, 3/5/1894 and so on, Sponge-Fishermen Recruitments 1894–1896, MAK.

83   See Doc. 118, 9/4/1893, MC Minutes 1892–1893, MAK, or the decision of the Municipality of Kalymnos Doc. 62, 22/5/1915, MC Minutes 1915–1916, MAK.

84   Doc. 231, 7/5/1885, MC Minutes 1885, MAK; Doc. 395, 4/12/1896, MC Minutes 1896–1897, MAK; Doc. 144, 2/7/1913, MC Minutes 1913–1914, MAK.

85   See Doc. 518, 18/4/1896, Sponge-Fishermen Recruitments 1896, MAK.

86   See Doc. 201, 29/4/1894, Sponge-Fishermen Recruitments 1894–1896, MAK; Doc. 520, 19/4/1896, Sponge-Fishermen Recruitments 1896, MAK.

87   Doc. 191, 192, 201, 202, 29/4/1894, Sponge-Fishermen Recruitments 1894–1896, MAK; Doc. 133, 18/10/1906 and so on, Land Disputes 1906–1908, MAK.

have to prepay all of the outstanding debts for the divers he recruited from the previous captain.[88] That said, however, since early in the 20th century, divers customarily reimburse debts in interest-free installments or at intervals [εκ διαλειμμάτων], as is frequently noted in archival evidence. Thus, the diver Ioannis M. Nistazos (or Lisgaris), was required to pay 720 *kuruş* owed to captain Theodosios Papa Germanos in three equal, annual, interest-free instalments. The captain who then recruited him in 1907 was required to pay the first instalment to Papa Germanos.[89]

Articles 21 and 22 of the 1884 "Marine Sponge Fishery Regulation" clearly stipulate that "every sponge fisherman, diver or rower, shall engage in sponge fishing in order to repay his debt to his investor. With his work he will reimburse the debt which he took on voluntarily, in the hope of future work". This practice was dictated by special terms, since debtors do not appear to have been able to exercise control over the conditions of their new recruitment, their remuneration, the captain and the crew with which they would work, and the destination or duration of the next voyage. In such cases, recruitment agreements were referred to as "sponge-diver concessions", the "consignment of divers" or, less frequently, "diver rental".[90] The wording used here is very precise: "the debtor belongs to and is a man of the captain ...",[91] or "the debtor shall be the man of the investor and the captain until fully clearing his debt to them, both capital and interest"[92] or,

> given that captain Skevofylax Koufos must collect sponge-fishing preferential money from diver Antonios Papantonakis, he allows the diver to be recruited by captain Nikolaos Myris. [...] At the end of the voyage and following the sale of the product, any surplus remaining of the aforesaid diver's share will belong to the "privileged" Skevof. Koufos; in case of deficit, on the other hand, captain Nikolaos Myris shall hold first "privilege" until he collects his money in full, with interest.[93]

---

88   Doc. 120, 10/4/1893, MC Minutes 1892–1893, MAK.

89   Doc. 104, 11/4/1907 και έγγρ. 110, 16/4/1907, MC Minutes 1906–1908, MAK.

90   See, for instance, doc. 104 and 108, 4/5/1921, doc. 133, 6/5/1921 etc, Sponge-Fishermen Recruitments 1921, MAK.

91   Doc. 41, 29/4/1883, MC Minutes 1882–1883, MAK.

92   E.g. Doc. 164, entitled "Conditional Consignment of Diver", 1/4/1905, Sponge-Fishermen Recruitments 1904–1905, MAK.

93   In a note to a document, yet another beneficiary is added to whom the diver was indebted, named Nikolaos Petridis, sponge-fishing machine investor, on Symi. See doc. 65, 13/1/1905, Sponge-Fishermen Recruitments 1904–1905, MAK.

Furthermore, contracts also stipulate that, having collected the money owed by the debtor diver, the captain hands over any monies remaining to his investor, as well as "to the man after the completion of the sponge-fishing voyage".[94] The examination of archival evidence and references in the decisions of local authorities suggest that many divers found themselves in this situation of indebtedness for long periods, if not "indefinitely".[95]

Notably, even divers who found themselves compelled to seek employment in other countries needed the permission of the captain to whom they were still indebted. In one document we read that, "said captain Skevofylax N. Tsagkaris – grants his aforesaid man Ilias Psaromatis his full permission to leave for Hydra, etc".[96] In such cases, the indebted diver could usually benefit from a clause provided for in article 15 of the "Marine Sponge Fishery Regulation", which made it possible to pay off debts in instalments.[97] Captains were not allowed to recruit someone else's "man" – as they used to say at the time – that is, any person indebted to a former captain.[98]

Following the sale of the sponges, indebted divers often reimbursed not only the advance payments to their lenders, but also had to clear their debts with one, or even up to three successive captains.[99] Since this was not easily done, divers gave in to forced recruitments for several consecutive years,[100] however disagreements between captains and divers concerning the amounts of money owed were numerous. Even though most recruitments were officially concluded before the Elders' Council, many eluded formal procedures in

---

94   Doc. 17, 15/10/1883, MC Minutes 1881–1884, MAK.

95   Doc. 140, 17/4/1893, MC Minutes 1892–1893, MAK.

96   Doc. 35, 25/2/1900, Sponge-Fishermen Recruitments 13/5/1899–31/4/1900, MAK.

97   This article stipulates that "[...] divers who have concluded explicit and written agreements, setting out the amount of money provided for the launch of the voyage, are not entitled to request more than the sums agreed upon. If, however, the existence of a proven and reasonable need is established, they may receive up to five hundred kuruş in installments." See the publication of the "Marine Sponge Fishery Regulation" in *Kalymniaka Chronika* 5 (1985), p. 182.

98   See for example the following phrasing: "Antonios Karafyllakis, captain of sponge-fishing crew, recruits Skevofylax N. Koufos, man of Apostolos Tyllianakis and Antonios Kouremetis, in the role of diver for the upcoming sponge-fishing voyage, with the consent of the latter [...]. After said captain collects from said diver the amount of *platika* and *refenes* plus their sponge-fishing interest. He will deliver the remaining amount to the Elders' Council, which will then turn it over to the people to whom it belongs". Doc. 62, 1/1900, Sponge-Fishermen Recruitments 1899–1900, MAK.

99   We refer to Doc. 132, 10/10/1906, Land Disputes 1906–1908, MAK, in which the debts of diver Nikolaos Papantonakis to three "privileged" captains, as well as the priority of reimbursement, are calculated.

100   See also the case of diver Emmanouil Nom. Kardoulias who was thus recruited for three consecutive years, without being able to repay his debts, in Doc. 118, 9/4/1893, MC Minutes 1892–1893, MAK.

order to avoid paying taxes,[101] or recruited debtor divers without bringing the recruitment to their investors' attention.[102] At the same time, payments made before and after the voyage were not formally transacted, hence the parties involved questioned each other's word and honesty, while complaints from both sides about stolen sponges were neither uncommon nor easily proven.[103] In instances where divers were truly entrapped, they entered into agreements that disregarded both the law and custom. They worked on various vessels without being declared as members of the crew, without obligation to tax or customs authorities, or later to the community, or the Port Authority – but also without rights, especially in case of an accident.[104]

In general, any outstanding matters were to have been resolved by the time that insurance for sponge-fishing permits was purchased, either through the clearance of debts or a settlement agreed to before the Elders' Council.[105] However, along with the common practice of seeking recruitment on board other Kalymnian ships in order to steer clear of debts, it would appear that divers also fled on many occasions.[106] Some divers from other islands changed their names to avoid repaying their debts,[107] while still others left under the pretext of setting off in the direction of Chios, Smyrna or other neighboring areas.[108] The majority, however, sought recruitment on vessels from other sponge-fishing islands,[109] whereas they very often left for Hydra, where they tried their luck in a new life.[110]

---

101   Doc. 24, 25/2/1885, MC Minutes 1885, MAK.

102   See, for example, Doc. 346, 16/10/1896, Doc. 189 and 190, 21/6/1897, MC Minutes 1896–1897, MAK.

103   See, for example, Doc. 131, 13/4/1893, MC Minutes 1892–1893, MAK; Doc. 444, 24/3/1884, Minutes and Correspondence 1884–1885, MAK.

104   See for instance, Doc. 102, 25/7/1915, MC Minutes 1915–1916, MAK.

105   Doc. 333, 13/6/1908, MC Minutes 1908–1909, MAK.

106   There were numerous similar cases. See, for instance, Doc. 16, 20/1/1893, MC Minutes 1892–1893, MAK; Doc. 156, 16/8/1913, MC Minutes 1913–1914, MAK.

107   Doc. 268, 14/6/1896, MC Minutes 1896–1897, MAK.

108   Doc. 118, 11/5/1894, Correspondence 1894–1895, MAK. See also the description of this phenomenon in a novel entitled Νίκη Μπιλλήρη, Σφουγγαράδες από την Κάλυμνο [Niki Billiri, The Sponge Fishermen from Kalymnos], pp. 16–24.

109   There is a great number of cases, see Doc. 558, 5/5/1884, MC Minutes-Correspondence 1884–1885, MAK; Doc. 121, 10/4/1893, MC Minutes 1892–1893, MAK; Doc. 50, 24/3/1895, Correspondence 1894–1895, MAK; Doc. 49, 31/3/1897, Correspondence 1896–1898, MAK; Doc. 470, 20/3/1911, Correspondence 1910–1913, MAK; Doc. 594, 20/4/1911, Correspondence 1910–1913, MAK.

110   See for instance, Doc. 531, 28/4/1884 and doc. 761, 16/10/1884, MC Minutes-Correspondence 1884–1885, MAK; Doc. 61, 14/3/1896, Correspondence 1895–1896,, MAK; Doc. 47, 9/4/1904, Correspondence 1902–1905, MAK.

Through recurrent decisions, and letters to the Elders' Councils of neighbouring sponge-fishing islands, the community of Kalymnos sought to prohibit divers from being recruited in other areas until they had settled their debts,[111] whereas the debtors' names, those who had been "blocked" as noted above, were flagged in the Elders' Council registers.[112] In other cases, captains from neighbouring islands were accused of helping indebted Kalymnian divers escape their obligations, in order to have them work on their vessels.[113] Such was the case of Sakellarios Kampouris, who fled to Symi in 1884, while still owing his investor Emmanouil I. Olympitis more than 20,000 *kuruş*; a sizable amount of money at that time.[114] Unsurprisingly, the reverse also happened, with divers from Symi or Chalki, and even from Chios seeking recruitment on Kalymnos to escape their debts.[115]

The captains of sponge-fishing boats or vessels with sponge-fishing machines – i.e., scaphander diving suits – also drew up official declarations pledging that, after the sale of the sponges, they would repay debts owing to their former investors. Moreover, the Elders' Council of Kalymnos kept a special record of those "blocked" or "thwarted from taking other employment by their captains".[116] At the same time, the Elders proclaimed that,

> any captain taking on sponge-fishing divers or mechanical divers after having obtained written permission from their captains or investors or the Elders' Council, and who departs from here, or any individual found to have directly or indirectly helped sponge-fishing divers or mechanical divers escape, these captains or individuals are forthwith considered liable for the runaways' debts to their investors or captains.[117]

---

111   Doc. 21, 7/8/1879, Correspondence 1879–1881, MAK.

112   Doc. 293, 4/4/1908, MC Minutes 1908–1909, MAK.

113   See, for example, Doc. 80, 5/6/1897, Correspondence 1896–1898, MAK; Doc. 116, 24/4/1897, MC Minutes 1896–1897, MAK.

114   Doc. 421, 19/3/1884, MC Minutes-Correspondence 1884–1885, MAK.

115   Doc. 14, 22/1/1902, Correspondence 1902, MAK; Doc. 155, 13/8/1902 and doc. 157, 21/8/1902, Correspondence 1902, MAK.

116   Although indirect reports of the existence of these registers and local authorities' allusions to them are constant, no evidence thereof was found in the Archive. See, for instance, Doc. 201, 25/5/1893, MC Minutes 1892–1893, MAK or Doc. 70, 8/6/1915, MC Minutes 1915–1916, MAK; Doc. 145, 2/7/1913, MC Minutes 1913–1914, MAK. Apart from the payment of municipal contributions, captains were bound to provide the Elders' Council with their crew lists to be examined for "sponge-fishing hindrances". See Doc. 73, 10/1/1915, MC Minutes 1915–1916, MAK.

117   Doc. 358, 1/3/1884, MC Minutes-Correspondence 1884–1885, MAK.

Any participants were considered as sharing the responsibility before the local authorities and, together with the indebted divers or rowers, they were held to account for clearing the debts.[118] There are many documents that testify to recruitment under such conditions. When Dimitrakis Karalis from Ermioni recruited debtor diver Antonis Th. Kalitsis, and tried to help him run away from Kalymnos, he was called to account by the Elders' Council and, after confessing to the facts, he was forced to pay the diver's debts himself.[119]

Research into the Elders' Council archives reveals how frequently divers found themselves heavily indebted. For example, the Elders' Council of Kalymnos adopted a decree on 1 March 1884 that prohibited captains from taking on indebted sponge fishermen without the permission of the divers' captains, investors, or the Elders' Council. The runaways' debts would otherwise burden the people who had helped them.[120] It seems that this measure was prompted by one vessel that was spotted in a secluded area of the island,[121] while a few days later another ship was discovered with the same intentions [i.e., taking on illegal divers] off the island's coasts.[122]

In a letter addressed to local *Kaymakam* Reouf Bey, the Elders' Council stressed the notion that many sponge fishermen fled to Greece to engage in this activity, thus negatively affecting local trade, and leaving behind debts owed to individuals and the municipal treasury. Bey called, therefore, for measures preventing divers' escape on board foreign vessels that anchored around the island, which moreover, did not comply with sanitary regulations.[123] The contents of the letter are revealing:

> Given that many sponge fishermen flee this place [i.e. Kalymnos] and head to Greece without paying off either their debts to local captains and investors, or their obligations to the Municipal Treasury; and given that, as a result of the above, the island is depopulated, captains face ruin, merchants lose their money, trade shrinks and relocates elsewhere; and given that we are not able to pay taxes, we ask you to make provision in order to prevent the destruction of this land, and to take all necessary measures to deter fleeing on board foreign ships, which violate sanitary regulations. As a matter of fact, we are informed that, at this very moment, a foreign

---

118 Doc. 171, 4/6/1897, MC Minutes 1896–1897, MAK; Doc. 102, 22/7/1915 and Doc. 118, 19/8/1915, MC Minutes 1915–1916, MAK.

119 Doc. 513, 21/4/1884, MC Minutes-Correspondence 1884–1885, MAK.

120 MC Minutes, Correspondence Various 1884–1885, p. 32, MAK.

121 MC Minutes, Correspondence Various 1884–1885, p. 41 (6/3/1884), MAK.

122 MC Minutes, Correspondence Various 1884–1885, p. 65 (15/3/1884), MAK.

123 MC Minutes, Correspondence Various 1884–1885, pp. 34–35, MAK.

ship is moored somewhere around the island and has helped men flee and will help many more run away.[124]

On 3 March 1884, the Elders' Council issued a new decree ruling that the families of the runaways would be deprived of access to health care and education for their children. It set a fine of one Ottoman lira for every runaway and reminds divers that the burden of their debts will be passed on to the people who hired them.[125]

> It was unanimously approved and decided, in a general meeting, that any sponge fisherman, diver, mechanical diver, or rower fleeing this land without previously settling his debts with his captain or investor, and without being granted permission by the Elders' Council, in order to pay off any money owing to the community, shall be deprived of any municipal benefit and his family will be deprived of access to doctors, medicines and public schools. On his return, he shall also pay a tax of one Ottoman lira. The person who hires the runaway will be liable forthwith for any amount owing to the community and to the debtor's captains or investors.[126]

On 6 March, an announcement regarding this matter was published,[127] wherein it was demanded once again that the Ottoman Governor General intervene because "in order to have many sponge fishermen on board and help them escape, a foreign ship is sailing along the coasts of our island and is currently in an area called 'Karavostasi', in violation of sanitary regulations".[128] A letter sent to the Elders' Council of Symi a few days later, denounced a specific Symiot captain for having taken on an indebted diver from Kalymnos, and reminded the Elders of Symi that his debts were now transferred to the Symiot captain.[129]

Although in some cases old debts were used by divers as a means of extortion, "*ta piso*" or the arrears as old Kalymnian sponge fishermen call them,

---

124 Doc. 361, 2/3/1884, MC Minutes and Correspondence 1884–1884, MAK.
125 MC Minutes, Correspondence Various 1884–1885, p. 36, MAK.
126 Doc. 363, 3/3/1884, MC Minutes-Correspondence 1884–1885, MAK. Three days later, the decision was again put in writing, Doc. 369, 6/3/1884, MC Minutes-Correspondence 1884–1885, MAK.
127 MC Minutes, Correspondence Various 1884–1885, p. 40 (6/3/1884), MAK.
128 Doc. 371, 6/3/1884, MC Minutes-Correspondence 1884–1885, MAK. The letter is sent again a couple of days later, see Doc. 406, 15/3/1884, MC Minutes – Correspondence 1884–1885, MAK.
129 MC Minutes, Correspondence Various 1884–1885, p. 73 (19/3/1884), MAK.

debts continued to worry divers until the first post-war decades when a debt-relief policy was put in place. Regardless of whether debts existed or not, this common practice on the part of divers carried on. Since many divers spent their advance payments or *platika* before even setting sail, they pressured their captains until the last possible moment in order to get a *"kapaki"* [advance payment], according to many testimonies.[130]

Nevertheless, in December 1919 and February 1921, during a period of noticeable decline in the sponge fishery, local authorities, along with captains and investors, decided to grant divers' a discount on their previous debts to enable them to resume work in hopes of future profits. Hence, it was stipulated that diver mechanics would repay 20% of debts owing to captains, whereas naked divers would pay 10%, provided that the sums owed exceeded 100 and 200 francs respectively.[131] In 1922, the situation had apparently become more dire, given that it was decided that anyone would be able to set sail without old debts being taken into consideration and that, on return, all would be freed from debt incurred during the voyage of 1922.[132]

At the same time, mothers and wives were forced to put up their estate property as collateral which, in case of their mens' desertion, would pay for damages sustained by the captains.[133] Although testimonies, which are repeatedly found in various forms in the archives do not permit us to present any specific quantitative information, they do set a particular tone and depict the most important problem of the practice of the sponge fishery: high returns at great risk, in a precarious workplace that could leave many people heavily indebted.

Significantly more numerous are 20th-century testimonies. By way of illustration, I allude to the 1927 "revolt" in Libya, when 32 sailors and divers working on 16 sponge-fishing vessels of the Italian Alessandro Pacchiani refused to keep on working and were arrested.[134] The "mutineers" or "deserter sea workers", as sources call them, were arrested, brought to trial and punished, not only for having broken their contracts, but mostly for owing the advance sums paid to

---

130   See also the testimony of diver Nikolaos Monokandylos Φανερωμένη Χαλκιδιού-Σκυλλά, *Ἡ σφουγγάρι ἤ τομάρι. Η ζωή των σφουγγαράδων της Καλύμνου μέσα από αληθινές μαρτυρίες* [Faneromeni Chalkidiou-Skylla, *Either Sponge or Corpse. The Life of the Sponge Fishermen of Kalymnos through Real Testimonies*], Kalymnos 2009, p. 171.

131   Doc. 69, 16/12/1919, MC Minutes 1919–1922, MAK; Doc. 118, 5/2/1921, Correspondence 1920–1922, MAK.

132   57th meeting, 25/4/1922, MC Minutes 1917–1922, MAK.

133   Doc. 20, 22/2/1885 and Doc. 21, 23/2/1885, MC Minutes 1885.

134   See relevant reports and letters: Embassy of Tripoli-Libya, Folder 33 (1926–1927), Subfolder 10 and Folder 34 (1927–1929), Subfolder 1, IAYE.

them upon recruitment. Some archival evidence offers yet more vivid accounts this matter, including one report concerning a diver from a sponge-fishing vessel captain that reads,

> I declared him [the diver] a deserter in accordance with the law because he abandoned the ship without cause. Having abandoned his work and having inflicted damage on the enterprise [...] he did not work as he ought to, inventing various pretexts and attempting in every way possible to instigate others to give up their work. He is an anarchist, a rebel, etc. Under no circumstances will I accept him aboard as he is very dangerous and harmful.[135]

According to another report, in 1947, a scaphander suit diver "showed signs of unwillingness to work from the very first [...]; since the very beginning, he dove only once instead of three times per day, under the pretext that he was indisposed. He continued to work thus, inciting the other divers of the aforementioned ship to not perform the agreed number of dives, i.e., three descents per day". After describing a number of disputes, he writes about another diver who "is a member of the communist party, he is one of the commanders of the Organization for the Protection of the People's Struggle [Οργάνωση Περιφρούρησης Λαϊκού Αγώνα – ΟΠΛΑ] (i.e. the squad that slaughtered, etc.) and the captain has already reported him to the police in Piraeus [...]".[136] Another captain's letter of the same year, addressed to the Consul in Benghazi, reports the case of a diver who refused to work but led a "promiscuous life, getting drunk day and night after midnight".[137] Captains' complaints report gratuitous hospital visits, alleged treatments, pretexts to leave the ship and return to Kalymnos, and so on.

In some cases, however, when captains' claims were excessive, the Elders' Council interpreted the Regulation and Sponge-Fishing Custom in favour of the divers. Hence, when Spyridon Ant. Maillis forbade his debtor diver Michail S. Mavros to work on any sponge-fishing vessel in 1885, while refusing to provide the necessary resources for the diver and his family's sustenance, the appointed Elders granted the diver permission to work under a different captain, provided that he keep half of his advance payment and give the rest to Sp. Maillis for the money owed.[138]

135　Embassy of Tripoli-Libya, Folder 45 (1947–1948), Subfolder 3, letter 17/8/1947, IAYE.
136　Embassy of Tripoli-Libya, Folder 45 (1947–1948), Subfolder 3, letter 29/8/1947, IAYE.
137　Embassy of Tripoli-Libya, Folder 45 (1947–1948), Subfolder 3, letter 12/9/1947, IAYE.
138　Doc. 288, 3/6/1885, MC Minutes 1885, MAK.

On some occasions, divers without the burden of debts from previous years attempted to deceive their captains and, following the payment of their *platika* did not join the voyage. In cases where crew members feigned illness, local authorities would request a medical opinion from the municipal doctors in order to ascertain the veracity of their ailments.[139] Indeed, after having collected their *platika* from Kalymnian captains, two divers from Leros set off to seek employment on Hydra,[140] while another diver from Leros, under the pretext that he wanted to bid his priestmonk uncle goodbye, hid out on the island to escape the voyage. His fleeing impeded the departure of the vessels because, as reported, it was impossible to replace him at the last moment with another equally competent diver.[141] As surviving archival evidence in the Kalymnian records reveals, these incidents were quite common, especially in the months of February and March.

Divers also fled occasionally during the voyage. For example, while owing more than 12,000 *kuruş*, diver Anagnostis Tsoukalas, "stubbornly refused to go to work in 1893; in the summer of 1894, he feigned remorse, received a considerable *platika* and followed the voyage to Madruh. There, he worked for a couple of days, only to run away on the 5th of June, not to be seen again since that moment ...".[142] In 1907 however, Pantelis Magklis whose nickname was "Panagia" [Holy Mary], was recruited on a sponge-fishing gagava, and "ran away from [...] the boat and from his work, having only worked for four to five days". His captain, Nikolaos Th. Pizanias, factored in the former's debts and all expenses incurred "from the soldiers he hired to find the man".[143] Fleeing was also reported to the Greek consular authorities, especially in the case of Kalymnian divers working on Greek vessels. The opinion circulated and prevailed in the consular correspondence of that period that, if runaways and insurrectionists were not arrested, others would follow their lead.[144]

---

139   Doc. 133, 6/5/1897, MC Minutes 1896–1897, MAK.
140   Doc. 46, 18/3/1895, Correspondence 1894–1895, MAK.
141   Doc. 52 and 53, 22/3/1902, Correspondence 1902, MAK.
142   Doc. 30, 28/2/1895, Correspondence 1894–1895, MAK. See also one document on the fleeing of a rower (Doc. 20, 4/7/1913, Correspondence 1910–1913, MAK) or of a diver (Doc. 342, 18/8/1908, MC Minutes 1908–1909, MAK) or of yet another diver who worked for only a week before running away (Doc. 37, 20/6/1912, MC Minutes 1912–1913, MAK). See also the case of a captain asking his investor to send him a diver to replace the one who had run away in early September off the coasts of Africa. Doc. 173, 6/9/1907, MC Minutes 1906–1908, MAK.
143   Doc. 1,134, 25/4/1907, MC Minutes 1906–1908, MAK.
144   Consular correspondence 14/1/1894, 26/4/1894, Embassy of Tripoli-Libya, Folder 6, Subfolder 9, 1890–1900, IAYE. See also "Ἔκθεσις εν σχέσει με την διεξαγωγήν της σπογγαλιείας εις τα παράλια της Λιβύης κατά την θερινή περίοδον 1952" ["Report on the Undertaking

Where those suspected of having the intention of fleeing was concerned, the Elders' Council intervened demanding the repayment of their debts; if this did not transpire, the Kaymakam was asked to arrest and detain them until departure.[145] Many were forced to board the sponging vessels as prisoners,[146] whereas those who refused to pay their debts were arrested and held in custody until they settled accounts.[147]

For reasons that are not clear in the archival evidence, some divers, despite having signed agreements, refused to follow the rest of the crew at the last minute. In these cases, their captain would lodge a complaint and the Elders' Council would once more intervene.[148] It appears, however, that this phenomenon persisted, leading to a new decision of the Elders' Council:

> Because it has been observed that, due to the unreasonable demands and the bad faith that mechanical divers, sponge fishermen, rowers and the rest of the workers in the sponge fishery show in recruitment contracts, the trust of investors has been shaken of late; and given that the sponge fishery of our land has not only deteriorated, but is also threatened with complete paralysis, we declare that all aforesaid sponge mechanics, sponge fishermen, rowers and sponge fishery workers respect their contracts. In addition, none of the above has the right to demand more *platika* than that already agreed upon, or to put up resistance at the moment of setting off sponge fishing. They must bear in mind that in such cases the Elders' Council, jointly with the local Esteemed Imperial Authorities, will set in motion all legal coercive measures and with all due rigor, and that runaways shall be prosecuted everywhere and by all legal means.[149]

According to testimonies and articles published in the early 20th-century Greek press, when public opinion was divided on the sponge-fishery issue, divers would exploit it, using any means in to get more money from captains. "They are paid 3,000 to 6,000 drachmas in advance" wrote the editor of *Empros*

---

of Sponge Fishery off the Coasts of Libya in the Summer Season of 1952"], Lieutenant Commander Em. A. Koutsikopoulos, sponge fishing supervisor, Tripoli 28/11/1952, Embassy of Tripoli-Libya, Folder 46 (1952), Subfolder 4, IAYE.

145   There are again many cases of this phenomenon. See, for instance, Doc. 441, 23/3/1884 or Doc. 532, 30/4/1884, MC Minutes-Correspondence 1884–1885, MAK; Doc. 73, 24/5/1897, Correspondence 1896–1898, MAK; Doc. 40, 12/3/1904, Correspondence 1902–1905, MAK.

146   See Doc. 78, 22/4/1895, Correspondence 1894–1895, MAK; Doc. 46, 14/3/1902, Correspondence 1902, MAK.

147   Doc. 72, 22/4/1902, Correspondence 1902, MAK.

148   See, for example, Doc. 137, 28/5/1894, Correspondence 1894–1895, MAK.

149   Doc. 77, 9/3/1893, MC Minutes 1892–1893, MAK.

newspaper, "and yet at the moment of setting sail from Hydra, they create obstacles and cause trouble for captains for 2 or 3 days while the ship sails outside the port, with the entire crew already on board waiting for the diver, who very often demands and receives an additional 500 or even 2,000 drachmas on top of the amount agreed upon, the famous '*palamariatika*' [*platika*]".[150]

However, it was not always divers who owed money to their captains. The reverse also occurred with captains often not making good on earned wages, and the crew's legal profits. It was reported that captains swindled their crews in the calculation of their sustenance costs for the crew during the voyage.[151] The Elders' Council, or later the Municipality, intervened in these cases as well, often requesting the help of the Ottoman administration in order to enforce the payment of the wages owed.[152] Moreover, in situations where the mechanical diver was considered inexperienced or a novice, things became more complicated. In such cases, "after being tested" – as stated in written agreements – or "if he was deemed capable", or "if he proves to be successful in his craft" he received his *platika*; "if, however, he proves to be incompetent, he shall pay back any *platika* he may have been paid by the captains up to that time".

It was necessary, nevertheless, to have previously issued a promissory note bearing an interest rate of 20% per year "in accordance with Sponge-Fishing Custom",[153] and the same seems to have applied to foreigners recruited by the sponge-fishing groups of Kalymnos. Therefore, it was only after proving their competence to Kalymnian captains that divers from Karpathos, Kos, Astypalaia, Leros, and so on could insist on safer conditions and higher wages on future voyages. It was also not uncommon for men hired as rowers, "*koupades*", to eventually work as divers,[154] while captains often deceived divers and redistributed the sponge catch based on the advance payments they had given.[155] As captains themselves confess, this would happen at the expense of those given smaller sums of *platika* and shares. This was a way for captains to compensate for advance payments to highly remunerated divers who had

---

150   Δ. Α. Πανάγος, "Οι σπογγαλιείς μας. Τα κακουργήματά των μύθοι. Μία απάντησις εις την Εστίαν", *Εμπρός* [D. A. Panagos, "Our Sponge Fishermen. The Legends of their Crimes. An answer to Estia", *Empros*], 15/4/1903, p. 3; Νίκη Μπιλλήρη, *Σφουγγαράδες από την Κάλυμνο* [Niki Billiri, *Sponge Fishermen from Kalymnos*], p. 17.

151   Testimony of *kolaouzieris* Vassilis Kampourakis to E.O., 1/9/2004.

152   Doc. 20, 22/1/1896, Correspondence 1895–1896, MAK.

153   Doc. 556, 20/1/1897, doc. 558, 22/1/1897, Sponge-Fishing Issues 1896–1898, MAK.

154   Doc. 125, 12/4/1893, MC Minutes 1892–1893, MAK.

155   Testimony of Giannis Tsoulfis to E.O., 6/3/2002; Roxane Caftanzoglou, "Kalymnos: Contribution à la connaissance d'une société". Mémoire de maîtrise d'ethnologie spécialisée (unpublished thesis), Paris 1978, p. 9.

not turned out to be competent enough, and who would become permanently indebted to the captains.

3.4.2 The Remuneration of the Rest of the Crew

The *kolaouzieris*, or diving manager, usually received a lump sum, which was lower than that of the diver (usually ¼), with no right to percentages or bonuses. Like the rest of the crew, he could receive part of his remuneration in advance, as a *platika*.[156] The same arrangement also applied to the owner of the vessel [*trenchandieris*], who was paid a wage.[157] As for those who rowed and assisted the divers, as well as the rest of the auxiliary staff, the recruitment system varied depending on the captain, the diving method, the voyage's estimated profits, and the time period. Most men were remunerated with a lump sum. Some of them, however, were paid a portion of the share from the sale of sponges.[158] Hence, Theodoros Choullis, captain of a sponge-fishing boat, hired two rowers on 1 May 1921 for an expedition that would last until late September of the same year. Both of them would be remunerated with ¾ of the share, and part of that money was paid in advance.[159] On that same day, the same captain also hired three divers who would receive full shares, but only two of them got an advance payment.[160] More rarely, agreements included a quantity of tobacco provided to the crew by the captain.[161] Given that productivity or the share's percentage was sometimes conditioned on "working proactively and diligently" or "working until the end of September with all due energy, keenness and obedience", we may assume that problems and disagreements arose.[162]

Debtors did not necessarily remain in a position of permanent indebtedness thanks to state intervention and the introduction in the Dodecanese complex of the institutional framework already in force in Greece. This included the establishment of a Bank [ATE] on Kalymnos,[163] the registration of sponge

---

156   Doc. 555 "Ναυτολόγησις κολαουζέρη", 16/1/1897, Σπογγαλιευτικά 1896–1898, ΜΑΚ.

157   Doc. 195, 13/5/1921 Sponge-Fishermen Recruitments 1921, ΜΑΚ.

158   Doc. 73, 76, 77, 78 στο Βιβλίο 110, "Sponge-Fishermen Recruitments" 30/3/1925–21/4/1926, ΜΑΚ. See also Κάρολος Φλέγελ, "Η Α.Θ. Παναγιότης ο Οικουμενικός Πατριάρχης Άνθιμος ο Ζ' εν Καλύμνω" [Carl Flegel, "His Holiness the Ecumenical Patriarch Anthimos"], Samos 1896, p. 14.

159   Doc. 86, 1/5/1921, Sponge-Fishermen Recruitments 1921, ΜΑΚ.

160   Doc. 87, 1/5/1921, Sponge-Fishermen Recruitments 1921, ΜΑΚ. The same case is repeated elsewhere. See Doc. 89, 1/5/1921, Sponge-Fishermen Recruitments 1921, ΜΑΚ.

161   Doc. 32, 30/10/1883, MC Minutes 1881–1884, ΜΑΚ.

162   Doc. 19, 15/10/1883 and Doc. 34, 27/3/1884, MC Minutes 1881–1884, ΜΑΚ.

163   The ATE took on financing sponge-fishing groups under favourable conditions (8%) and limited collateral requirements. Concerning Symi, see Αγαπητίδης, "Η οικονομική

fishermen with the Seamen's Pension Fund [Ναυτικό Απομαχικό Ταμείο – ΝΑΤ] and the inauguration of the Greek Port Authority in 1948, which was now in charge of crew recruitment. In this regard, the testimony of one Kalymnian sponger is telling:

> All this began in 1947–1948, and especially after 1950. First, we made contracts with the divers in the winter. They had to be examined by a cardiologist and have a general check-up in order to be recruited. We submitted their medical reports to the Port Authority and only then did we enter into contracts, after the Port Authority had made sure that the men were in good health, because unexpected incidents often occurred in the sponge fishery. Everyone on Kalymnos knew the divers – knew who was good and who was average. We started in January, when we set off on the winter voyage. There was permanent staff on the caique, the men that we knew we paid well and took them along with us. If a good sponger was not yet hired, we paid a good deal of money to take him on board. We recruited 14 men on the ship. We had to have 5–6 good ones and the rest were of second and third level so that we made enough dives.[164]

In sum, we could say that the 20th century brought gradual improvements to the employment relations of crews by means of various regulations such as the shared costs [refenes and syrmayia], "the monthly wages of the colleagues," a sum withheld from the platika and given to the families of crews[165] and, from the 1920s until 1948, the extra share ["koufo"] split among all the divers, or given to "those who worked well", or granted to the man "who caught the largest number of sponges".[166] For example, in 1924, Ioannis Glynatsis assumed the roles of both captain and diver of a sponge-fishing machine financed by

---

οργάνωση" [Agapitidis, "The Economic Organization"], p. 195. The first financial aid to the sponge fishery granted by the ΑΤΕ was for the launch of the 1947 summer voyage. The sponge-fishing fleet of Kalymnos of that year was comprised of 51 vessels equipped with scaphander diving suits, and 42 with Fernez. Seventy-eight percent of the vessels and 89% of crews worked off the coasts of Cyrenaica. Out of a total of 1,441 divers and crew members, 4 deadly accidents occurred, while another 5 divers suffered from complete paralysis. See, Georgios M. Sakellaridis' "Η Ελληνική Επαρχία. Η σπογγαλιεία εις την Κάλυμνον", Καλυμνιακά Χρονικά [Georgios M. Sakellaridis, "Greek Provinces. Sponge Fishery on Kalymnos", Kalymniaka Chronika] 6 (1986), pp. 207–208.

164   Testimony of Lefteris Mamouzelos, 3/9/2004.
165   Χειλάς, Τὸ ἔπος των σφουγγαράδων [Cheilas, The Epic Saga of Kalymnos' Sponge Fishermen], p. 31.
166   Πιζάνιας, "Η οργάνωσις της σπογγαλιευτικής επιχειρήσεως" [Pizanias, "The Organization of the Sponge-Fishing"], p. 36. See also Χειλάς, Τὸ ἔπος των σφουγγαράδων [Cheilas, The Epic

Georgios Nystazos. His remuneration would consist of one mechanical diver's share, one of the four shares of the sponge-fishing machine and an extra share, the "*koufo*", deducted from the investor's profit.[167]

The most important change, which was gradually imposed on the sponge fishery during the post-war years, was the transition from shares to percentages, and there was a continuous drop in the number of auxiliary staff as opposed to the number of divers. In the case of vessels fishing with *revera*, and shallow water vessels with *naryiles*, co-operations and collaborations between friends and relatives prevailed. They owned the vessels, and the necessary capital was ¼ to ½ of that required for fishing with the scaphander diving suit. To cover their expenses, they relied more on family savings than on private or bank loans. Hierarchy thus waned, everyone could dive, and the roles assigned on board the vessel alternated, even that of diving supervisor [*kolaouzieris*]. The use of auxiliary staff decreased as it was not cost-effective. Expenses and profits could be equally distributed among the team, except perhaps for the vessel's owner, who got an extra share.[168]

As the study in this chapter reveals, cases of divers accumulating the necessary capital to transition from diver to captain – the manager of production means and crews – were few when compared with the other cases of divers examined here. According to recent testimonies, this transition was very difficult, "given that captains came from specific families". And finally, even if the yield was high in one year, unforeseeable events in the following year could quickly turn the table.

Saga of Kalymnos' Sponge Fishermen], p. 37, which refers to four specific documents from 1946. Testimony of captain Giannis Tsoulfas to E.O., 6/3/2002.

167   Doc. undated, 19/12/1924, Sponge-Fishing Issues 1922–1925, MAK.

168   Papataxiarchis, "A Hypothesis on the 1965–1977 Transition in the Socioeconomic Structure of the Sponge-Fishing Industry in Kalymnos", Department of Social Anthropology, London School of Economics, pp. 6–7.

"When the Scaphander Diving Suit Took Down the Skandalopetra ..."

4.1   "The Sponge-Fishery Issue"

The introduction of the scaphander diving suit into sponge fishing transformed the industry into a modern, professional activity characterized by imposed intensification of work; required specialization and distribution of labour; increased investments and earnings; a transition from a family or co-operative organization to a business structure. The prevalence of sponge-fishing groups working with scaphander diving suits led to a significant drop in the naked divers' numbers and remuneration. These work-related changes, and the development of a new socio-economic organization gave rise to various social shocks in sponge-fishing populations in the final decades of the 19th century. The high rate of productivity made possible by the scaphander diving suit side-lined the financial importance of "traditional" sponge-fishing methods, pushing out competition in long-established sponge-fishing areas, which did not adopt the new fishing method.

On islands such as Patmos, Leros, and Astypalaia, where they formerly practiced free-diving sponge fishery [with the apnea method], the activity was abandoned for good. The coast was thus basically open to those who had adopted the scaphander diving suit and were able to adapt to the financial and social structuring exacted by the new fishing method. From the islands of the Dodecanese, Kalymnos, and Symi led the way in terms of vessels and worker numbers, and monopolized international sponge markets, followed by Chalki and Kastellorizo. Nevertheless, these sponge-fishing populations spearheaded the protests and battles for the abolition of the scaphander diving suit, and the reversion to "familiar" fishing methods.

From the 1860s, and for more than 40 years, despite the scaphander diving suit's widespread use in Greek sponge fishing, the pursuit of its ban was ceaseless and systematic. This was the core of the (in)famous "sponge-fishery issue", which frustrated Aegean sponge-fishing populations and rallied opponents of the new technology of the scaphander diving suit on the basis of four principal arguments: a) the scaphander diving suit threatened sponge-bearing areas with extinction, b) it caused financial damage to the population, c) it decreased the number of divers, and d) above all, it endangered the life and health of its users.

This "sponge-fishery issue" is our main point of interest in what follows here below. The term dates to the 19th century and is attributed to Lithuanian Charles Flegel, who dedicated himself to denouncing the scaphander diving suit, bringing this matter to the attention of the public, and fighting for its abolition. However, because all surviving texts are strategically biased, the sources at our disposal allow for only a partial view of the actual proportions of the issue. Indeed, it appears that the other side of the discussion is missing, namely the arguments put forward by people who understood the need for modernization and its resultant benefits, or even the reaction of those struggling to adapt to the new state of affairs. Indeed, protests apparently spoke louder than the silence of those who immersed themselves in their ledgers, calculating their earnings and expanding their businesses abroad. We choose, however, to focus on this debate for yet another reason: the line of argumentation put forward by the authors of the documents, their protests, and the tension and conflicts implied in these documents. Together, all of the above is concerned with a well-known issue in other industrial sectors, namely the introduction of new technology into areas where pre-industrial techniques of production are in use.

We know of various reactions on Kalymnos and Symi in the final decades of the 19th century; their most insistent and vocal demand, however, was the abolition of the "machine", or the scaphander diving suit. They claimed that banning the machine would save them from the danger of shark attacks and the "sponge worm" that inflicted serious wounds, eczema, and purulent abscesses on the diver's naked body, but many more new and unknown dangers awaited in the great depths of the sea.

Violent protests and upheavals occasionally took place,[1] and scattered reports of these events survive in various sources along with references to public reactions, as well as scores of institutional interventions and protests. Announcements by the Elders' Council, documents setting up special

---

1 Michael Grigoropoulos notes that Kalymnos faced serious incidents caused by local sponge fishermen who destroyed many diving machines belonging to Frenchmen. For this reason, a French warship arrived in the area to protect the interests of French citizens who had invested in the fishery. See Michael Grigoropoulos, *Η νήσος Σύμη, πραγματεία υπό γεωγραφικήν, ιστορικήν και στατιστικήν έποψιν* [*The Island Symi, Treatise from a Geographical, Historical and Statistical Perspective*], Athens 1877, p. 57. Various sources also report that the first protests took place on Astypalaia in 1868, on Kalymnos in 1875 and on Symi in 1880. See more in Michael N. Kalafatas, *The Bellstone: The Greek Sponge Divers of the Aegean. One American's Journey Home*, Brandeis University Press, Hannover 2003, p. 34.

committees for the examination of the issue, continuous correspondence with Elders' Councils from other sponge-fishing islands of the Ottoman Empire, letters to Metropolitans and to the Patriarch of Constantinople, successive memoranda to the Ottoman authorities and the Sultan, emissaries dispatched to Constantinople; these are only some of the actions taken and found in the Municipal Archive. An examination of these texts leads to the logical conclusion that, in the last decades of the 19th century and the first years of the 20th century, the community of Kalymnos – as well as the communities of the other sponge-fishing islands – was unsettled due to the "sponge-fishery issue".

Some claim that the backlash against the diving suit began almost directly after its introduction by Kalymnian and Symiot divers at the close of the 1860s.[2] More specifically, according to M. P. Aublé, a commercial representative of Rouquayrol-Denayrouze on Rhodes, the unrest was sparked on Kalymnos in 1865.[3] According to the authors of available archival sources, it was ignorance, the spongers' "blindness", and investors' financial concerns that led the local population to destroy the first diving apparatus – which belonged to a French merchant house in Constantinople – and then to come after those who had used it. By that time the atmosphere had already become tense and, in the following year, 11 vessels that set sail from Symi, Kalymnos and Rhodes to harvest sponges were manned and equipped with scaphander diving suits.

Aublé described the islanders' reaction as a "revolution", which term is probably a fair depiction of the reality, given that ensuing developments show how the situation remained explosive. According to various reports, during the absence of the sponging vessels, people threatened to destroy the diving machines, and to punish or ostracize those using them, as "traitors to the homeland". When the vessels returned, Kalymnians and Symiots destroyed the scaphander diving suits that arrived with them, and it was also reported that groups of ten-year-old children grabbed the keys to the owners' warehouses by force and destroyed the machinery. According to Aublé's testimony, Europeans did not know how to deal with "such a population", as it infringed on every notion of law and order. In the end, local authorities agreed to pay a part of the reparations for the damages inflicted.[4] In an attempt to interpret the intensity of the riots, the Europeans attributed the uprisings to the "backwardness" and

---

2 Alfred Leroy de Méricourt, "Considérations sur l'hygiène des pêcheurs d'éponge", *Annales d'hygiène publique et de médecine légale* 31 (1869), pp. 274–286; M. Caravokyro. *Les pays spongifères de l'Empire et le scaphandre*, Constantinople 1886, p. 3.

3 *Dictionnaire Encyclopédique des sciences médicales*, vol. 7, Paris 1870, p. 219; Méricourt, "Considérations sur l'hygiène", p. 278.

4 Excerpts from Aublé's handwritten text are published in Louis Figuier, *Les merveilles de la science, ou Description populaire des inventions modernes*, Paris 1870, p. 678.

"tumultuous spirit" of the Archipelago islanders, as well as to the uprising in Crete that had created an opportunity for the southeastern Aegean populations to spark violent protests against the Ottomans.[5]

The coordinated efforts of the French and Ottoman governments put an end to the incidents in 1867. Testimonies concurrent with the events, suggest that the French government's intervention took place because French citizen Zourounias was a partner in one of the businesses affected by the uprisings on Kalymnos.[6] Thanks to the intervention of the French Navy with their vessel *Le Forban*, and the help of a Turkish frigate, the extensive damages came to a halt. Use of scaphander suits could now continue freely under the supervision of the Ottoman authorities, and hefty fines were levied on the communities of Kalymnos and Symi for their interruption of the activity and the financial losses incurred.[7]

According to proponents of the scaphander diving suit, the turnover made possible by its use seemed to argue in favour of this outfitting: all 11 vessels working with scaphander diving suits generated 161,000 francs in 1866, that is, 14,600 francs per machine, and at least three times more than the earnings of vessels with naked divers. Overall production had already doubled, and the mean annual exports of sponges during the 1869–1873 period were valued at 148,700 pounds sterling for the islands of the South Sporades, as opposed to the 70,000 pounds generated by annual sales during the 1854–1858 period, based on the reports of British Consul on Rhodes.[8] Hence, in 1867 the number diving suits in use in the South Sporades grew to 15 or 18.[9]

The first records of systematic protests in the Kalymnos archives concern both the ban on diving suits, and impediments to the industry's expansion.[10] The literature of the Dodecanese complex cites a decision taken by the

5   This is how the events are described in Figuier, *Les merveilles de la science*, p. 678.

6   Carl Flegel, "Το σπογγαλιευτικό ζήτημα της Μεσογείου (Χανιά, 1903)", *Καλυμνιακά Χρονικά* ["The Sponge-Fishery Issue in the Mediterranean (Chania 1903)", *Kalymniaka Chronika*] 5 (1985), p. 213; Γεώργιος Ελευθ. Γεωργάς, *Μελέτη περί σπογγαλιείας, σπόγγων και σπογγεμπορίου από των αρχαιοτάτων χρόνων μέχρι σήμερον* [Georgios Elefth. Georgas, *Study of the Sponge Fishery: Sponges and Sponge Trade from Ancient Times until Today*], Piraeus 1937, p. 30.

7   Méricourt, "Considérations sur l'hygiène", p. 279.

8   Reports of British Consul Robert Campbell and Vice Consul C. Billioti. See Κυριάκος Κων. Χατζηδάκης, "Η σπογγαλιεία στις Νότιες Σποράδες στα μέσα του 19ου αιώνα", *Καλυμνιακά Χρονικά* [Kyriakos Kon. Chatzidakis, "Sponge Fishing in the Southern Sporades in the Mid-19th Century", *Kalymniaka Chroinika*] 13 (1999), pp. 234, 239.

9   Figuier, *Les merveilles de la science*, p. 679.

10   See Doc. 5, 20/3/1880, Correspondence 1879–1881, MAK; Doc. 30, n.d., Correspondence 1879–1881, MAK.

Ottoman government in 1881 for a widespread ban on scaphander diving suits all over the Empire's seas. However, although the Elders' Councils of the Dodecanese was notified of this decision, it was not fully implemented.[11] In a letter of 1882, the Elders of Kalymnos noted an announcement made by the Governor to some of the citizens of Kalymnos, that sponge-fishing machines were to be banned beginning in March of the same year. Given that the Elders were obviously cut off from developments in the industry on Kalymnos, as well as from the circles of the local Ottoman administration, the Elders questioned the validity of the announcement and requested an official briefing by the Governor-General of the Archipelago.[12]

Until new evidence is uncovered that sheds light on the gaps in our historical documentation, we must assume that there had already been a pertinent decision on scaphander diving suits, or that a new decree was indeed issued and remained in force, although not implemented, over the next few years. As early as July of 1882, the Greek Embassy in Constantinople informed the Ministry of Foreign Affairs that "sponge fishing using diving suits and other machinery was banned across the seas of the Ottoman state, pursuant to a decision of the Council of State, and was implemented on the 28th of June of the year 1881. They were also informed that the ban is still in force and will be actively applied, yet the foreign embassies were not notified [...]".[13] A few days later, the Greek Ministry of Foreign Affairs requested confirmation of the ban on sponge fishing off the Turkish coasts, as well as information concerning the ban.[14]

On the[15] 12th/24th of June 1882, the Greek Consul in Tunis stopped granting sponge-fishing permits for scaphander diving suits on the grounds of a law introduced by the Sublime Porte on 2 February 1882. At that time news of the law had already been published in the press, and communicated to all foreign

---

11   Δημοσθένης Χαβιαράς, *Περί σπόγγων και σπογγαλιείας από των αρχαιοτάτων χρόνων μέχρι των καθ' ημάς* [Dimosthenis Chaviaras, *On Sponges and Sponge Fishing from Ancient Times until Today*], Athens 1916, p. 50; of the same author "Τινά περί σπογγαλιείας", *Συμιακός* ["On the Sponge Fishery", *Symiakos*] 5 (2010), p. 5 (republished in Κωνσταντίνος Σκόκος, *Εθνικόν ημερολόγιον, χρονογραφικόν, φιλολογικόν και γελοιογραφικόν* [Konstantinos Skokos, *National Journal: Chronological, Philological and Satyrical*] vol. XII, 1903, pp. 411–415). Georgas shares this opinion in *Μελέτη περί σπογγαλιείας* [*Study of the Sponge Fishery*], p. 30. See also Ιπποκράτης Φραγκόπουλος, *Ιστορία της Καλύμνου* [Hippocrates Fragkopoulos, *History of Kalymnos*], Athens 1995, pp. 104–106.

12   Doc. 44, 16/8/1881, doc. 51, 9/10/1881, Correspondence 1879–1881, MAK.

13   *Πέραν* [*Peran*] 22/7/1882, Folder 1882, 51/1, ΙΑΥΕ.

14   Folder 1882, 51/1 26/7/1882, ΙΑΥΕ.

15   Editors' note: The Gregorian calendar was established officially in Greece on February 1924. Until then two dates of the Julian and Gregorian calendars were used.

embassies, however, the Greek Consul was unsure of whether the law applied to foreign citizens as well. At any rate, all those fishing with diving suits had relocated to the coasts near Tunis for that year.[16] It is also reported that, in 1883, the spongers of Kalymnos raised objections to the upcoming removal of the scaphander diving suit ban, with the prefect [*vali*] of the province of the Aegean, known as the Eyalet of the White Sea. The prefect answered that he would consider the matter. However, many used scaphander diving suits illegally, although they were not sanctioned by the administration.[17]

Meanwhile, an increasing number of voices was raised in protest against the scaphander diving suit, apparently striking a chord with the press at that time.[18] In the first months of 1884, correspondence between the local Elders' Council and its supervisory Ottoman authorities was regular, which would indicate that the issue remained unresolved. In a reply to the Archipelago administration concerning whether the sponge-fishing diving machines were harmful, the Elders' Council of Kalymnos produced arguments that, in the following years, would be consolidated and systematically developed. The Council cited the destruction of the seafloor, the decrease in vessels and crews, the emigration of divers in search of employment, and a decline in the sponge trade, which also meant a decrease in the Ottoman state's revenues.[19] The Elders protested once again against the failure to implement the Imperial Edict [*"irade"*] banning scaphander diving suits across all the seas of the Empire.[20]

Also in 1884, the Elders' Council of Symi sent Dimosthenis Chaviaras to Constantinople to take all necessary action for the implementation of the ban. This development is noted in a letter addressed to the Elders' Council of Kalymnos, in which Chaviaras requested a similar mandate to represent Kalymnians as well at the Sublime Porte.[21] In the power of attorney which was immediately drawn up and intended for Dimosthenis Chaviaras and Agapitos Zagoras, Kalymnian notables argued that illegal sponge fishing continued unhampered, while the machines "continued to fish even in close proximity

16   Letter of the Greek Consul in Tripolis to the Greek Minister of Foreign Affairs, 12/24 June 1882, Folder 1882, 51/1, ΙΑΥΕ.

17   Ali Fuat Oreng, *Yakindonem Tarihimizde Rodos ve Oniki Ada*, Istanbul 2006, p. 510, note 2,262. Here one wants to ask however, how these vessels could be illegal, when official agreements for "mechanical" divers and loans for the starting funds of the scaphander diving suits were signed before the Elders' Council.

18   Carabokyro, *Étude sur la pêche des éponges*, p. 3.

19   Doc. 455, 27/3/1884, Minutes and Correspondence 1884–1885, ΜΑΚ.

20   Doc. 485, 27/3/1884, Minutes and Correspondence 1884–1885, ΜΑΚ.

21   Doc. 432, 21/3/1884 and Doc. 452, 27/3/1884, Minutes and Correspondence 1884–1885, ΜΑΚ.

to the islands".[22] In the same month, April 1884, violent incidents broke out on Symi; G. Georgas, sub-secretary of the community of Symi at the time described throngs of people who invaded the port, broke into the shipowners' warehouses and destroyed 45 scaphander diving suits.[23]

The information available in similar archival evidence of the Greek state's competent services helped in cross-checking the lacking documentation, and better understanding certain aspects of the issue. Administrative and dip-lomatic correspondence suggests that the issue was still pending in the first months of 1884, and reveals that it was impossible to issue sponge-fishing per-mits for Greek citizens working with scaphander diving suits in Austrian seas, and in the maritime area of Trieste.[24] Along with a lack of evidence, at least in the Greek archives, a pronounced obscurity surrounds this matter. We could perhaps assume that the Ottoman administration issued decrees without rig-orously enforcing their implementation unilaterally, or that its local delegates were not promptly informed. Nevertheless, occasional incidents did occur, such as the case of the confiscation of two sponge-fishing vessels from Trikeri, together with their diving gear and their cargo, while fishing in the seas sur-rounding Mount Athos in August 1885. Similarly, Prime Minister Theodoros Deligiannis' administration was unaware of whether or not sponge fishing with scaphander diving suits had been banned, or if their use was subject to restric-tive conditions, thus demonstrating that it was difficult to apply the decrees, and violations were rampant.[25] It appears, however, that this was also a finan-cial matter, because in the same month the ban was lifted, sponge-fishing permits were issued for 32 Ottoman liras.[26]

It was expected that the same fluid situation would persist into the next sponge-fishing season. In November of 1885, following a question raised by Members of the Parliament, the Greek Ambassador to Constantinople informed Th. Deligiannis that he had no information whatsoever concerning a new ban on sponge-fishing machines in the seas of the Ottoman Empire.[27]

---

22   Doc. 485, 27/3/1884, Minutes and Correspondence 1884–1885, MAK.

23   Γεωργάς, Μελέτη περί σπογγαλιείας [Georgas, Study of the Sponge Fishery], pp. 31–32.

24   Letters of the prefect of Aegina 15/2/1884, 27/3/1884 and of the Greek Ambassador in Trieste to the Ministry of Foreign Affairs of Greece 16/3/1884, Folder 51/1 Fishery: Sponge Fishery, IAYE.

25   Letter from the Consul in Thessaloniki to the Ministry of Foreign Affairs, 9/10/1885, rel-evant publication of Ακρόπολης [Acropolis], parliamentary session 25/10/1885, telegrams and documents of the Ministry of Foreign Affairs 27 and 30/8/1885 etc., Folder Γ 51/1 Fishery: Sponge Fishery, IAYE.

26   Letter from the Greek Consul in Rhodes to the Greek Ministry of Foreign Affairs 13/8/1885, telegram 8/7/1885, Folder 1885, Γ 51/1 Fishery-Sponge Fishery, IAYE.

27   1/11/1885, Folder 1885, Γ 51/1 Fishery: Sponge Fishery, IAYE.

Contradictory interests, disobeyed orders and illegal fishing were, in one way or another, commonplace in this professional sector. Moreover, "friends of the scaphander" diving suit ["φιλοσκάφανδροι"], must have been particularly importunate, guaranteeing higher custom earnings to the Ottoman administration.[28] Mitrophanis Kalafatas described them in his poetic narrative of 1902:

> Our people destroyed
> by its ways,
> honor and pride are lost,
> self-interest glories in their place.
> There are no ethics, arrogance rules,
> pouring out of those Helmets.
> The diving bosses are the cause
> of this barbaric shamelessness.
> My own eyes saw a merchant
> frequent these villains, sit with them
> at dominoes and cards,
> blacken his honor and his name
> to gain advantage for his gear,
> till frequency turned to arrogance
> and arrogance became habit.[29]

Although the prohibition was ratified in 1884, and renewed in 1887,[30] it was only put into effect for a limited period of time, and the issue was still pending, dividing the sponge-fishing populations of the southeastern Aegean. In an interview conducted in 1902, Emmanouil Repoulis, Member of Parliament for the Ermionida constituency, noted two bans on scaphander diving suits: the first ban, in 1885, was put into effect for a brief period, and the second ban, in 1891, was never implemented.[31]

The correspondence exchanged between Dodecanesians reveals their discomfiture where this issue was concerned. In 1893, the Elders' Council of

---

28   Georgas, Μελέτη περί σπογγαλιείας [*Study of the Sponge Fishery*], p. 30.

29   Μητροφάνης Καλαφατάς, "Χειμερινός Όνειρος" [Mitrophanis Kalafatas, "Winter Dream"] in Michael N. Kalafatas, *The Bellstone: The Greek Sponge Divers of the Aegean. One American's Journey Home*. Hannover: Brandeis University Press, 2003, pp. 230–231., p. 267.

30   According to Carabokyro, the ban on scaphander diving suits was achieved in 1887. See Carabokyro, *Étude sur la pêche des éponges*, p. 3.

31   *Εμπρός* [*Empros*], 4/3/1902, p. 1, 14/3/1902, p. 4. On the same topic see *Εμπρός* [*Empros*], 31/3/1902, p. 1, 5/5/1902, p. 2.

Kalymnos sent letters to the Elders' Councils of Symi, Kastellorizo, Astypalaia, Tilos, Leros, and Alikarnassos [Bodrum], seeking their opinions on this matter. Declaring itself against the scaphander diving suit, it proposed that they join forces to tackle the issue.[32] It appears, however, that only the Elders' Council of Astypalaia and Alikarnassos replied and sided with the views of the Elders of Kalymnos. Kalymnians thus decided to send two envoys to Symi to "feel out" the intentions of local authorities there.[33] Thinking that the reason for their silence lay possibly in their unwillingness to support any scheme financially, they sent a new letter to the Elder's Council of Leros. In this letter they it made clear that they were asking for moral support only and not material contributions, as they knew that the people of Leros no longer engaged in sponge fishing due to the widespread use of the scaphander diving suit.[34] Immediately following this letter, the Elders of Kalymnos sent a similar letter to the Elders' Council of Patmos,[35] as well as another letter to the Metropolitan in Tripoli, Libya.[36] In the last two months of 1893, they managed to obtain the consent of the remaining Elders' Councils and lead the procedure.[37]

Along with institutional actions taken, public protests increased in frequency and, with two resolutions, on 2 November and 14 December 1893, the population of Kalymnos insisted on the "abolition" of the scaphander diving machines. After setting up a twenty-member committee to study the matter and coordinate with the other sponge-fishing areas, and after forming a five-member committee tasked with exploring a course of action and the means that would enable the abolition of the scaphander diving suit, it was finally decided that a three-member committee should be created to deal exclusively with this issue. Moreover, the public assembly decided to levy an extraordinary tax on all sponge-fishing vessels, the island's merchants, and every household on the island, so that the community could meet the necessary expenses. Additionally, it appointed two representatives who would travel to Symi and collaborate with local authorities in order to pursue their purpose in concert.[38]

---

32   Doc. 300, 10/07/1893, MC Minutes 1892–1893, MAK.

33   Doc. 309, 21/10/1893 and Doc. 333, 11/02/1893, MC Minutes 1892–1893, MAK.

34   Doc. 311, 23/10/1893, MC Minutes 1892–1893, MAK.

35   Doc. 313, 23/10/1893, MC Minutes 1892–1893, MAK.

36   Doc. 343, 10/11/1893, 1892–1893 1892–1893, MAK.

37   Carabokyro, *Étude sur la pêche des éponges*, p. 12. Although his text appears to have been published in 1886, it includes a second section (with continuous numbering) for 1886–1895.

38   Doc. 345, 11/11/1893 and doc. 373, 15/12/1893, MC Minutes 1892 1893, MAK; Doc. 3, 2/11/1893, Minutes and Resolutions 1893–1907, MAK. See also Φραγκόπουλος, Ιστορία της Καλύμνου [Fragkopoulos, *History of Kalymnos*], p. 104.

Beginning in January 1894, the Elders' Council, headed by Michael Magklis, actively sought to tackle this issue, by constantly lodging complaints with the appropriate Ottoman officials.[39] The new Elders' Council sent a memorandum to the Sultan, Patriarch Neophyte IV, the General Governor of the Aegean Sea, and the local governor [*mutasarrıf*] of Chios, on behalf of other islands as well. Each time the Elders' Council presented a claim to the Ottoman authorities, it also sought the support of the Church to improve their chances of success, and particularly where the critical issue of the ban on the sponge-fishing machines was concerned.[40]

In a document dated 5 May 1894, we read that "the people of the island of Kalymnos are fully aware that the damage inflicted by sponge-fishing machines on the sponge fishery – the only source of livelihood of this island – has reached its highest point, making it thus impossible for the residents of the island to survive unless the aforesaid machines are rapidly abolished".

The existing committees were then dismissed and the task of handling the issue was once again handed over to the Elders' Council, who drew up a memorandum to the Sultan, and appointed representatives to transfer the request of the island's inhabitants to Constantinople.[41] This was, in fact, a repetition of the earlier decision of 1893,[42] and on 5 May, through a new resolution, the people of Kalymnos appointed Kalymnian lawyer Miltiadis Carabokyros, residing in Constantinople, as their representative and made him responsible for taking the necessary steps at the Sublime Porte.[43]

In the summer of the following year, after months had passed and their efforts continued to bear no fruit, the Elders' Council appointed school principal Nikolaos Kalavros to go to Constantinople to assist Carabokyros in his efforts to have the machines banned. Both agents, distinguished men on the

---

39   Flegel attributes this activity to the passionate support that Magklis himself showed for the "sponge fishery issue". See Flegel *Η νήσος Κάλυμνος*, [*The Island of Kalymnos*], p. 42.

40   See the letter to the Metropolitan of Leros-Kalymnos Chrysanthos, Doc. 110, 5/5/1894, Correspondence 1894–1895, MAK.

41   Doc. 11, 5/5/1894, Minutes and Resolutions 1922–1948, MAK.

42   Doc. 7, 2/11/1893, Minutes and Resolutions 1922–1948, MAK.

43   It appears that later the stance of Elder Leonidas Carabokyros, brother of Miltiadis, was ambiguous: he was "until yesterday a rover and nomad and homeless; a person who deceived voters by promising them that, thanks to his brother's actions in Constantinople, the sponge-fishing machines would be banned; a person whom the entire population and the body of the Elders' Council disowned, but maintained his position with the authority and with the support of the Governor, for whom he acts as an obedient instrument and spy". Letter from Kalymnos consular agent, N. Symeon to Ioannis Kaloutsis, Consul in Rhodes, 1/9/1896, Consulate in Rhodes, Folder 44 (1911), Subfolder 2, IAYE.

island, were to act on behalf of Kalymnos, Patmos, Leros, Astypalaia, Symi, Kastellorizo, and Alikarnassos [Bodrum]. Material support for the case was supplied entirely by the community of Kalymnos, which allocated 100 liras to cover travel and accommodation expenses for agents representing them in Constantinople. Moreover, in the event that the use of the scaphander diving suits was discontinued, the community of Kalymnos pledged to grant their representatives another 300 Turkish liras.[44] Notably, the newly elected Patriarch of Constantinople, Anthimos VII, also supported the Elders' Council.[45]

According to Carabokyros, in May of 1894, the Ottoman administration, in consultation with the appointed economic advisors, came to a decision to prohibit sponge fishery by means of scaphander diving suits for ten years.[46] The Elders' Council sent a letter of thanks to the Sultan, while the public enthusiastically participated in a doxology held at the Metropolitan Church of Christ in Pothia.[47] However, because no imperial edict was issued, the decision was never enforced.

Efforts to abolish the scaphander diving suit intensified in 1895 and 1896. For example, in early 1895, it the Ottoman administration promised to ban "the machine" for three years, hence in a piece published in the Constantinople *Neologos* that worried the Kalymnian population, we read that:

> It has been decided that sponge fishery will be prevented entirely in March, April, and May and that sponge fishing will be halted for a period of three years at those sites where the sponge fishery has declined due to the use of the machine. The first measure will come into effect immediately, whereas an examination of sites where the sponge fishery is headed

---

44   Doc. 183 and 184, 12/7/1894, Correspondence 1894–1895, MAK; Resolution 5/5/1894, Minutes and Resolutions 1893–1907, MAK.

45   This was also noted by Carl Flegel, who published a part of the memorandum drawn up in 1894. See Flegel, *Η νήσος Κάλυμνος* [*The Island of Kalymnos*], pp. 31–33 and Carl Flegel, "Η Α.Θ. Παναγιότης ο Οικουμενικός Πατριάρχης Άνθιμος ο Ζ' εν Καλύμνω" ["His All-Holiness Ecumenical Patriarch Anthimos VII from Kalymnos"], Samos 1896, pp. 19–21. See also Κυριάκος Κ. Χατζηδάκης, "Ο αγώνας για την κατάργηση των σκαφάντρων και ο Κάρολος Φλεγέλ", *Καλυμνιακά Χρονικά* [Kyriakos K. Chatzidakis, "The Struggle for the Abolition of the Scaphander Diving Suit and Carl Flegel", *Kalymniaka Chronika*] 3 (1982), p. 34. See also Doc. 19, 1/15/1894, Correspondence 1894–1895, MAK. M. Carabokyros and Hipp. Tavlarios also represented the community in Constantinople on the matter of the Port Authority. See Doc. 269, 29/10/1897, MC Minutes 1896–1897, MAK.

46   Carabokyro, *Étude sur la pêche des éponges*, pp. 12–13.

47   Ibid., p. 14.

for complete disaster will be conducted prior to the implementation of the second measure.[48]

In a letter to Miltiadis Carabokyros written ten days after the publication of this piece, the Elders' representative in Constantinople questioned its accuracy. They also described growing agitation in the population given that this blanket ban applied equally to those not using scaphander diving suits. And while the three-year ban on scaphander diving suits was considered inadequate, the Elders also argued that the swimmers' vessels would not be able to make up their losses in a period of only three years.[49] They furthermore claimed that small sponges need to grow for at least three years in order to reach a size worth harvesting, and that the investments needed for the construction of new ships and for assembling crews would neither generate profit, or attract capital, if the measure were only to be implemented for a period of three years. The Elders' council then proposed a ten-year halt to sponge fishing.[50]

However, the ban never came into effect because, according to the Elders in January of 1896, "this decision was not ratified by an Imperial Edict, which would be needed in order for it to be put into practice".[51] In a renewed attempt to negotiate, the Elders authorized Miltiadis Carabokyros to formally request a ten-year ban of scaphander diving suits in Benghazi, Marsa Matrouh and Crete, so that these areas could be made available to naked divers.[52]

In 1897, when the Ottoman administration sought to impose a three-month ban (March, April, and May) on sponge fishing, Greek local authorities protested, arguing that the measure was both inadequate, and detrimental to the sponge fishery. They wrote that the measure would not contribute to the improvement of sponge-bearing beds.[53] The local authorities also pointed out that the scaphander diving suits departed in early March and that by the middle or, at the latest, the end of the month the machines would have reached their place of work. When the weather was mild, most of the fishing was conducted before the end of June. When the etesian winds [*meltemia*] begin to blow, the

---

48   Νεολόγος [*Neologos*], Folder 7644, 6/2/1895, p. 1.
49   Doc. 17, 16/2/1895, Correspondence 1894–1895, MAK.
50   Doc. 126 and 127, 20/6/1895, Correspondence 1895–1896, MAK.
51   Doc. 2, 3/1/1896, Correspondence 1895–1896, MAK.
52   Doc. 4 and 5, 3/1/1896, Correspondence 1895–1896, MAK. C. Flegel notes that this proposal was made by the lead Elder Leonidas Carabokyros. See more in Flegel, "Η Α.Θ. Παναγιότης ο Οικουμενικός Πατριάρχης Άνθιμος" ["His All-Holiness Ecumenical Patriarch Anthimos VII from Kalymnos"], p. 46.
53   N. Vouvalis is of the same opinion; Flegel, "Η Α.Θ Παναγιότης ο Οικουμενικός Πατριάρχης Άνθιμος" ["His All-Holiness Ecumenical Patriarch Anthimos VII from Kalymnos"], annex n.n., pp. 53–56.

work became much more difficult and, in September, the sea becomes colder. Therefore, the ban hindered work without improving the situation.

Furthermore, local authorities also argued that crews were formed and advance payments had already been made, and that investors had already put up their money for that year's departures.[54] In a subsequent letter to the local Governor [*Kaymakam*], the Elders decried the situation and protested that "the people are hungry and in a state of utmost despair, because they have lost their work now that the only industry in this land is banned. Likewise, investors who make advance payments for the sustenance of the sponge fishermen, place their trust in future work and profits". Following a meeting of the notables it was decided "to feed the people during that week by means of a contribution".[55] However, despite such persistent efforts, it appears that nothing changed and, as may be deduced from archival evidence, sponge-fishing vessels departed from Kalymnos in late May of 1897. The people of the Dodecanese islands also appealed to the Principality of Samos and, also in 1897, the assembly of the Samian people voted for the abolition of scaphander diving suits; a decision that was ratified by the Prince of the island on 5 February 1898.[56] According to reports, scaphander diving suits were banned on Cyprus, in Egypt, and partially in Tunis in 1897,[57] and that same year they were also banned off the coasts of Florida.[58] In 1899, the scaphander diving suit was also banned on Crete.[59]

This issue was still pending at the close of the 19th century and, despite public backlash, the constant protests of the Elders to Ottoman civil and military authorities, as well as the support of ecclesiastic officials and the Patriarch of Constantinople, the bans were either only partially enforced; their implementation was short-lived; or they were unenforceable in practice. Indeed,

---

54   Letter to the local Governor [*Mutasarrif*] of Chios (Doc. 20, 1/2/1897) and the Elders' Council of Symi (Doc. 21, 3/2/1897), the Metropolitan of Rhodes (Doc. 36, 21/2/1897), Correspondence 1896–1898, MAK. Beginning in 1836, Kalymnos formed a separate administrative division under the administrative district [*mutasarrifate*] of Chios. It continued, however, to depend on Rhodes financially given that the sum of the lump tax was destined for charitable organizations on Rhodes, in accordance with a decision made by the Sultan. See Γιώργος Κουκούλης, "Δύο έγγραφα της Δημογεροντίας Καλύμνου προς τη Δημογεροντία Σύμης", *Καλυμνιακά Χρονικά* [Giorgis Koukoulis, "Two Documents from the Elders' Council of Kalymnos to the Elders' Council of Symi", *Kalymniaka Chronika*], 6 (1986), p. 46.

55   Doc. 48, 30/3/1897, Correspondence 1896–1898, MAK.

56   Doc. 116, 6/6/1902, Correspondence 1902, MAK. The contribution of Carl Flegel to reaching this decision was reportedly decisive. See Chatzidakis, *Ο αγώνας για την κατάργηση των σκαφάντρων* [*The Fight to Abolish the Scaphander Diving Suit*], p. 37.

57   Georgas, *Μελέτη περί σπογγαλιείας* [*Study of the Sponge Fishery*], p. 33.

58   Jules Toutain, La *Tunisie au début du xxième siècle*, Paris 1904, p. 166.

59   Flegel, *Το σπογγαλιευτικό ζήτημα* [*The Sponge-Fishery Issue*], pp. 216–217.

the archive of the Kalymnian Elders' Council contains a substantial number of reports, as well as accounts and letters (1894–1902) addressed to local representatives of the Ottoman administration, the Metropolitan of Leros-Kalymnos, the Sultan, and the Patriarch, that all touch on the same topic: the abolition of scaphander diving suits.

4.1.1   The "Anathema" of the Machines

In a letter dated 29 May 1895, the Elders of Kalymnos called upon the local Governor [*Kaymakam*] of Kalymnos, Hilmi Bey, to take the necessary measures in to protect inhabitants, since – as they argued – he was well-aware of the perpetrators of destructive incidents.

> Yesterday, on Sunday, a handful of people, of whose identity the local administrative police and the Esteemed *Kaymakam* are well aware, went to Chora and tolled the bells of the Metropolitan Church of Virgin Mary, where they assembled some of the local residents, deceived them and greatly provoked them with various lies and calumnies; namely that the Elders' Council supposedly does not wish to abolish the sponge-fishing machines and refuses to take appropriate action for the successful resolution of this issue, and many more lies and calumnies. On the contrary, however, the Elders' Council can, at any time, prove by the most official means possible, that the Council takes every necessary step to successfully satisfy the inhabitants' desire, and with all due avidity. Th crowd then set out with women and children towards Pothea. They piled rocks along the road from Chora to Pothea as a sign of their complete distain [*anathema*] for us who are supposedly the great enemies of this land. All the while they hurled vile insults and threats and entered Pothea holding rocks in their hands. Without the Elders' Council and the Esteemed *Kaymakam* having any prior knowledge, they gathered in the Church of Christ, and when they rang the church bells, more people assembled while the organizers shouted out their calumnies against us, and continued to insult and threaten us until the protestors reached the administrative centre. Because your Excellency did not accept them – many as they were – we were informed that they sent a delegation, and when they left the administrative centre, they went back to the town where they continued to foment, insult, and threaten us.[60]

---

60   Doc. 117, 29/5/1895, Correspondence 1895–1895, MAK. The text in its entirety is published in Kyriakos K. Chatzidakis, "Η Κάλυμνος στα τέλη της Τουρκοκρατίας", *Καλυμνιακά Χρονικά* ["Kalymnos in the Late Years of Turkish Rule", *Kalymniaka Chronika*] 8 (1989), pp. 86–87. The incidents repeatedly took place in the following years with protests and

Similar incidents seem to have been provoked on Symi in April 1884. There, the inhabitants attacked a sponge shop and destroyed many of the island's diving apparatuses. Order was restored by a contingent of the Turkish army that landed on the island, arrested 40 divers, and transferred them to a prison on Chios.[61] A few years later in Boston, Symiot school teacher Mitrophanis Kalafatas published a poem entitled "Winter Dream", in which he recounted the anger of the people of Symi when they attacked the machines:

> The people meant no crime.
> They only meant to break the gear
> and pay for it, but not buy more.[62]

4.1.2   *"Great Issues Call for Great Patience"*[63]

In 1868, namely when the abominable scaphander diving suits were first introduced into the sponge fishery, at which time sponges were not even valued at one quarter of their current price, and because sponges [...] had always been bountiful and inexhaustible across the Ottoman coasts of the Mediterranean Sea and in those shallow waters, our island generated a significant income with minimal sponge-fishing costs, and almost without any risk to either the life or the health of sponge fishermen. The land thrived because its entire labour force, from the age of fifteen to seventy, worked advantageously, comfortably, and risk-free in the sponge fishery, and on our island's sponge-fishing ships. The population increased and, in a nutshell, sponge fishing was a source of prosperity and progress for our island and the other fellow sponge-fishing areas of the Ottoman state as a resource of sizable, ever-increasing, direct, and indirect benefits to the administration's treasury.[64]

The account is taken from a long report signed by the Elders' Council of Kalymnos on 1 May 1901, and addressed to Mahir Bey, the island's Local Governor [*Kaymakam*]. The text was a part of the "General statistics on the

---

violent demonstrations, especially in 1900, 1901 and 1902. See Doc. 195, 3/11/1902, Doc. 198, 21/11/1902, Correspondence 1902–1905, MAK.

61   Chaviaras, Περί σπόγγων και σπογγαλιείας [*On Sponges and Sponge Fishing*], p. 51.

62   Μητροφάνης Καλαφατάς, "Χειμερινός Όνειρος" [Mitrofanis Kalafatas, "Winter Dream"] in Michael N. Kalafatas, *The Bellstone: The Greek Sponge Divers of the Aegean. One American's Journey Home*. Hannover: Brandeis University Press, 2003, p. 233.

63   Typical phrasing used by the Elders of Kalymnos in a letter to Hippocrates Tavlarios; Doc. 99, 10/5/1901, p. 29, Archives of Kalymnos Elders' Council, MAK.

64   Doc. 88, 1/5/1901, p. 4, Archives of Kalymnos Elders' Council, MAK.

status of our island's sponge-fishing industry" which was drawn up at the behest of Georgios Kaplanoglou, Inspector of the General Directorate of the Ottoman Public Debt in the Aegean Sea. As the Elders wrote:

> Your Excellency has asked us to provide general statistics and a report on the condition of our island's sponge-fishing industry, which is – as it is well-known – the sole means of survival for the inhabitants of this rocky and barren land. This was the situation before the use of the scaphander diving suit, as well as the actual situation; on these grounds, despite the fact that a year ago, and on later occasions, our Elders' Council, either directly or through Hippocrates Tavlarios, our island's esteemed representative in Constantinople, has on numerous occasions respectfully presented the high Imperial Government with long and detailed official explanations on this issue, namely the issue concerning the abolition of these horrible scaphander diving suits, on which our land's existence depends entirely.[65]

In response, local authorities expounded on the dire consequences that they argued arose from the use of the scaphander diving suit, and which they characterized as a "horrible", "abominable", "deadly", and "worse than the plague". In their efforts to persuade the Ottoman administration, their arguments pivoted on two keystones: the island's welfare and the state's tax revenue. In both cases, the major argument addressed the devastating consequences of the use of the scaphander diving suit for divers' health, and more generally, for their lives.[66]

In a memorandum of 1894, it was noted that every year fatal accidents amounted to 10% of all divers, whereas paralyses affected 15% of all divers. In addition, difficult conditions took their toll and divers were unable to pursue this profession for more than 4 or 5 years.[67] A few years earlier, Miltiadis Carabokyros pointed out that the large number of victims resulted in multiple problems in sponge-fishing communities, which were subsequently unable to care for and sustain their many affected families. Wealth and general prosperity then declined, and the community's resources were insufficient for commissioning new public works. Young widows, orphans, paralyzed men, and beggars only served to exacerbate social problems.[68] Carl Flegel advanced similar arguments on the subject of the "sponge-fishery issue" in his works published after 1894. The premature and sudden deaths of divers, the paralyses

---

65   Doc. 88, 1/5/1901, p. 4, Archives of Kalymnos Elders' Council, MAK.
66   Doc. 1, 4/1/1894, Correspondence 1894–1895, MAK.
67   Doc. 1, 4/1/1894, Correspondence 1894–1895, MAK.
68   Carabokyro, *Étude sur la pêche des éponges*, p. 11.

of young men, the significant number of widows and orphans, the shortage of men, and the poverty inflicted on sponge-fishing populations were all recurring topics in his writings.[69]

This central argument was directly connected with the one that followed it, which is to say that, besides "man-killing", scaphander diving suits were also "sponge-damaging". Overfishing led to the exhaustion of sponges found in shallow depths and forced sponge fishermen to dive even deeper to find them.

> Sponge fishermen working with scaphander diving suits are mercilessly killed by this abominable tool or become completely paralyzed and therefore unnecessary burdens on this earth; [...] the mortality and paralysis of machine divers dramatically increases on an average of fifteen percent per year, and from one year to the next. Although the scientific regulation of the scaphander diving suit does not allow divers to descend to a depth greater than thirty-five French meters, as a result of the exhaustion of sponges in medium depths, machine divers are already forced to work in depths of sixty, and up to seventy meters on a systematic basis and thus the sponge fishery is threatened with complete ruin throughout the Ottoman state.[70]

The destruction of seabeds caused by fishing with scaphander diving suits, and the destruction of the sponge-bearing beds of the Mediterranean, are recurrent arguments in all the texts studied here. The ability to stay on the seafloor for longer periods of time, the descent to great depths, as well as the magnifying glass with which the scaphander diving suit was equipped, tempted divers to collect more sponges and led to the destruction of sea beds.[71] Although sponges were found in abundance, and although there was enough work for everyone – divers, rowers, spongers of all ages – following the introduction of the scaphander diving suit, unemployment hit sponge-fishing populations. Naked divers were the first to be pushed to the side-lines, along with those fishing with hooks or gagavas. New diving methods, they argued, negatively affected the composition of sponge-fishing populations. It was also argued that only the populations of the Ottoman Empire engaged in what was called "swimming sponge fishery", whereas the practice of sponge fishing with the scaphander diving suit had spread over various areas of the Greek state. In

---

69   Flegel, Τὸ σπογγαλιευτικό ζήτημα [The Sponge-Fishery Issue], p. 205.

70   Doc. 88, 1/5/1901, pp. 7–8, Archives of Kalymnos Elders' Council, MAK. See also doc. 1, 4/1/1894, Correspondence 1894–1895, MAK.

71   Doc. 1, 4/1/1894, Correspondence 1894–1895, MAK. The same argument seems to be reiterated in other Mediterranean areas, as well. See also L. Lortet, La Syrie d'aujourd'hui, Le tour du monde, Paris, (1875), p. 174.

addition, Greek vessels went sponge fishing illegally in the eastern Aegean, where sponge-bearing beds were more plentiful, hence the fishery and trade were developing in Greece more rapidly and to a greater degree.[72]

For opponents of the scaphander diving suit, it was the root cause of a "crazed extravagance and profligacy" that possessed the divers.[73] In more recent texts moreover, authors also estimate that every year divers using scaphander diving suits destroyed 8 to 10 million small sponges of limited or no commercial value.[74] This picture of destruction took on an even more vivid tint when combined with the decrease in the number of sponge-fishing vessels. It is reported that the vessels in Syria, which totalled more than 800 in the late 19th century, had dropped to only 40 vessels fishing with scaphander diving suits, while spongers left for America and Greece in search of other means of survival. Kalymnos, with 370 sponge-fishing ships at its disposal, only had 26 vessels that were equipped with diving suits by the 19th century, with 36 vessels devoted to naked diving. Moreover, only 1/10 of the inhabitants of Kalymnos worked on these ships. The same applied to the other sponge-fishing islands of the Greek state, with more than 1,000 sponge-fishing boats equipped with harpoons, as well as approximately 300 gagavas.[75] In other sources it is noted that the "swimmers' vessels" of the Dodecanese populations totalled 700, whereas Symi had an additional 250 gagavas.[76]

Some also argued that the significant number of accidents, the strained financial circumstances of the spongers, and the poverty of their families were some of the factors that resulted in the "social disintegration" of sponge-fishing areas, and drove workers to abandon the activity, and to emigrate to United States, Russia, and Argentina.[77] Flegel vividly described the prosperity that existed before the arrival of the scaphander diving suit, which he attributed not only to the financial prosperity of sponge-fishing populations, but also to social cohesion, religiosity and respect for tradition. On the other hand, "the man working with the scaphander diving suit attempts to forget his horrible position by indulging himself in frivolous entertainments", because he fears abandoning his family in utter poverty, or that he will become paralyzed and

---

72   Doc. 1, 4/1/1894, Correspondence 1894–1895, MAK.

73   Ibid., p. 38.

74   Georgas, Μελέτη περί σπογγαλιείας [Study of the Sponge Fishery], p. 36.

75   Doc. 1, 4/1/1894, Correspondence 1894–1895, MAK. See also Flegel, "Η Α.Θ. Παναγιότης ο Οικουμενικός Πατριάρχης Άνθιμος" ["His All-Holiness Ecumenical Patriarch Anthimos VII from Kalymnos"], p. 21; Georgas, Μελέτη περί σπογγαλιείας [Study of the Sponge Fishery], p. 37.

76   Ibid.

77   Carabokyro, Étude sur la pêche des éponges, pp. 11–12; Doc. 2, 2/1/1894, Correspondence 1894–1895, MAK; Flegel, Το σπογγαλιευτικό ζήτημα [The Sponge-Fishery Issue], pp. 205, 212.

end up a beggar.[78] Flegel often revisited this topic in his work, and attributed the excessive financial requirements associated with the industry, along with the money wasted on lavish feasts, gambling, entertainments, and vain ostentation to divers' fear of death and paralysis.[79] That said, however, proponents of the scaphander diving suit, of course, simply argued that the machines were "wealth-generating".

4.1.3 "The Drop in State Revenues"[80]

Various documents also note a decline in the activity and an economic slump, which threatened the sponge-fishing islands of the Aegean.

> Due to the sad and desperate situation of the sponge fishery, only one fifth of the labouring population finds work, which is underpaid in this industry. Left with no work at all for some years now as our island is rocky and barren, and there is no other available employment than sponge fishing, necessity drives the those who remain to emigrate to countries abroad to seek their livelihood. Gradually, more than three thousand Kalymnians have now emigrated to various locations abroad, especially Russia, and if this situation carries on [...] our island will soon be emptied of residents. If anything, as a result of the abolition of the scaphander diving suits, whether it be a blanket ban all over the Ottoman seas, or a partial ban enforced in a reasonable number of Ottoman maritime areas, which we have indicated in detail and respectfully to the Superior Imperial Government, sponges will gradually proliferate and grow in size in those areas within a maximum of two to three years, and they will always be abundant and inexhaustible as long as sponge fishery by natural means is practiced.[81]

Our focus will now shift to the content as well as to the underlying beliefs that pervade the archival evidence of the Elders' Council of Kalymnos. The source for the aforementioned report is data extracted from the Elders' Council official annual muster rolls; these are corroborated by the respective logbooks held by the Health Office and the Office of the Governor [*Kaymakam*], which collected the tax directly from the annual permits of sponge-fishing vessels until 1887. From 1888 onwards – at least until 1901, when the report was drawn

---

78   Flegel, *Τὸ σπογγαλιευτικὸ ζήτημα* [*The Sponge-Fishery Issue*], p. 207.

79   Carl Flegel, *La question des pêcheurs d'éponges de la Méditerranée*, Cairo 1902, p. 6; by the same author, *Τὸ σπογγαλιευτικὸ ζήτημα* [*The Sponge-Fishery Issue*], p. 210.

80   Doc. 2, 2/1/1894, Correspondence 1894–1895, MAK.

81   Doc. 88, 1/5/1901, pp. 8–9, Archives of Kalymnos Elders' Council, MAK.

up – this tax was collected by the Public Debt Office, which was headquartered on Kalymnos. In the table attached to the report, the first recorded year is 1865, in which 352 sponge-fishing permits for naked diving vessels were issued. Until 1869, when the scaphander diving suit was launched in the Kalymnos sponge fishery, perhaps a couple of years after its introduction in Symi,[82] there is a slight upward trend in the number of naked diving vessels (368 vessels in 1868). And while there were three vessels with scaphander diving suits in 1869, that number grew to 18 in the following year, whereas the number of naked diving vessels fell to 340.

TABLE 4.1A   Statistics for the sponge fishery on the island of Kalymnos extracted from the muster rolls held by the Elders' Council of Kalymnos[a]

Years	Sponge-fishing ships Class A sponge-fishing with naked divers.	Sponge-fishing permit annual tax of 10 Ottoman liras per ship	Scaphander diving suits	Sponge-fishing permit annual tax of 32 Ottoman liras per ship	Hooking boats	Sponge-fishing permit annual tax of 4 Ottoman liras per ship	Total number of sponge-fishing ships	Sponge-fishing annual tax permit of 3 Ottoman liras per ship	Total number of sponge-fishing ships	Total amount of the annual sponge-fishing permits tax, imposed on all sponge-fishing vessels working in the Ottoman seas
1865	352	3520							352	3520
1866	357								357	3570
1867	360								360	3600
1868	368								368	3680
1869	356		3	96					359	3656
1870	340		18						358	3976
1871	314		26						340	3972
1872	280		32						312	3824
1873	243		28						281	3646

a   The table discussed here shows minor differences when compared with the tables included in the letter of the Elders' Council to its representative in Constantinople, Hippocrates Tavlarios (Doc. 99, 10/5/1901, Archives of Kalymnos Elders' Council, MAK). The second group of tables was compiled by the Public Debt Office headquartered on Rhodes; it covers the period from 1888 to 1900 and lists vessels from Kalymnos, vessels from other Ottoman areas, and vessels from Greek areas (Hydra, Aegina, etc.) separately. These, however, obtained a sponge-fishing permit from Kalymnos. The small discrepancies between the table under examination and the other group of tables, as well as the letters attempting to explain these discrepancies, require special deliberation, which is beyond the scope of the present study.

82   For more on the year that the scaphander diving suit was introduced on the island of Symi, see Chapter 2.

TABLE 4.1A Statistics for the sponge fishery on the island of Kalymnos (*cont.*)

Years	Sponge-fishing ships Class A sponge-fishing with naked divers.	Sponge-fishing permit annual tax of 10 Ottoman liras per ship	Scaphander diving suits	Sponge-fishing permit annual tax of 32 Ottoman liras per ship	Hooking boats	Sponge-fishing permit annual tax of 4 Ottoman liras per ship	Total number of sponge-fishing ships	Sponge-fishing annual tax permit of 3 Ottoman liras per ship	Total number of sponge-fishing ships	Total amount of the annual sponge-fishing permits tax, imposed on all sponge-fishing vessels working in the Ottoman seas
1874	226		42						268	3604
1875	204		44						248	3448
1876	180		49						229	3368
1877	170		55						225	3460
1878	158		62						220	3564
1879	152		56						208	3312
1880	148		52						200	3144
1881	143		45						188	2870
1882	136		42						178	2704
1883	132		40						172	2600
1884	129		38						167	2506
1885	165		32		30				227	2794
1886	100		20		28				148	1752
1887	92		22		26				140	1728

"A) From 1865 to the end of 1887, at which time the tax on the annual sponge-fishing permits was directly collected by its Highness the Imperial Government."

The parallel trajectories of the two fishing methods clearly indicate that naked diving entered a slow but steady decline, which led to the granting of only eight permits in 1900.[83] In contrast, the number of permits for vessels using the scaphander diving suit increased, despite important fluctuations that followed, and which one might assume were linked to the backlash.

---

83   The Elders' Council attributed the halt in the decline of naked diving vessel issuance permits in 1885 to another unexpected parameter: "It was the year 1885, at a time much sponge-fishing activity was supposedly discovered in Zoara (off the coasts of Tripoli, Barbary), to which a great number of new sponge-fishing vessels flocked, but it turned out to be a fiction". Doc. No 88, 1/5/1901, Archives of Kalymnos Elders' Council, MAK.

TABLE 4.1B   Statistics for the sponge fishery on the island of Kalymnos (*cont.*)

Years	Class A sponge-fishing ships with naked divers.	Sponge-fishing permit annual tax of 10 Ottoman liras per ship	Scaphander diving suits	Sponge-fishing permit annual tax of 32 Ottoman liras per ship	Hooking boats	Sponge-fishing permit annual tax of 4 Ottoman liras per ship	Gagavas	Sponge-fishing permit annual tax of 3 Ottoman liras per ship	Total number of sponge fishing ships (all four techniques)	Proceeds of the local Public Debt Office from sponge. vessels of all techniques, which all worked in the Ottoman seas
1888	88	810	26	852	28	112			135	1754
1889	77		32		24				133	1890
1890	66		28		42				136	1724
1891	57		30		37		13	39	137	1717
1892	53		30		52		1		136	1701
1893	44		40		47				131	1908
1894	19		34		60		5		118	1533
1895	19		30		57		11		117	1411
1896	13		38		70		18		139	1680
1897	6		38		53		8		105	1512
1898	8		41		93		8		150	1788
1899	7		32		78		6		123	1424
1900	8		20		70		9		107	1027

"B) From 1888 to the end of 1900, at which time the tax on the annual sponge fishing permits was collected by the General Directorate for the Public Ottoman Debt."

The fluctuations are ostensibly the result of temporary restrictions and bans, as well as general circumstances, which either facilitated or restricted the smooth functioning of sponge fishing in the area. Some fluctuation may also be attributable to the export of sponges which was not always possible, and the absorption of the annual production in other countries.

Despite fluctuation, the average number of vessels with scaphander diving suits that were granted a permit over a period of thirty years (1871–1900) remained high, namely at around 37 vessels per year. The years in which a large number of permits was issued – 62 in 1878, and 56 in 1879 – are very few; equally few are the years with a limited number of permits granted – i.e. 20

permits in 1886 and 1900.[84] In the years in which a decrease in the number of vessels fishing with scaphander diving suits was recorded, there was not an equivalent rise in the number of permits issued for other fishing methods.

Nevertheless, the table includes neither the total number of people involved in the sponge fishery, nor the number of those participating in each type of fishing, separately. However, by studying the comprehensive 1884 crew register, which we chose because it is concurrent with the compilation of the "Marine Sponge Fishery Regulation", we the know that the number of people working on sponge-fishing vessels in that year was 6,201.[85] This register contained extensive notes on 178 sponge-fishing permits for departure from the island of Kalymnos.[86] It offered a detailed record of each vessel's crew; first the name of the captain, followed by the names of the entire crew, without any particular mention of each person's specialty.

Having a general picture of the number of crew members that usually participated in the two different diving practices, one might observe that vessels with crews of ten or more members amount to 21, and the total number of men is 303. Even if we assume that vessels with smaller crews used the scaphander diving suit, the number of people employed in this type of fishing is notably inferior to that of people working with the traditional methods.[87] For example, although it is not known exactly when people began using hooking boats in sponge fishing, the first mentions of it appear in the records of 1885 and it would appear that, from 1885 to 1900, this method was employed by an average of approximately fifty vessels per year, with a notable rise from 1894 and onwards. One might hypothesize that this increase is correlative with the concomitant abandoning of naked diving.

The same applies to the gagava. Vessels using this method appeared for the first time in 1891, though in characteristically small numbers. The total number of sponge-fishing vessels in the thirty-five-year period presented in Table 7, was on a steady decline, only to conclude with fewer than 150 vessels in the final decade of the 19th century. This may explain the argument presented by the

---

84   Another report compiled in 1884 by the Elders' Council stated that the number of vessels with scaphander diving suits amounted to a total of 250; out of these, 150 were Greek and only 100 came from sponge-fishing areas of the Ottoman Empire. Doc. 1, 4/1/1894, Correspondence 1894–1895, MAK.

85   Logbook 29/1881–7/8/1884, Archives of Kalymnos Elders' Council, MAK.

86   There were 178 permits registered in the 1884 muster roll. The 167 permits recorded in "Statistics" were perhaps those issued after the repayment of the monies due.

87   The register included 36 vessels with nine-member crews. We speculate that some of them are vessels with scaphander diving suits while others are naked-diving vessels.

Elders' Council regarding the drop in the number of people employed in the sponge fishery, especially if its other argument concerning the gradual disappearance of sponges in shallower waters where naked divers were able to fish is taken into account.

In early February of 1900, the Elders' Council of Kalymnos, following a public assembly resolution, appointed Hippocrates Tavlarios[88] as its representative in Constantinople, in order to take action at the Sublime Porte with regard to issues related to the sponge fishery.[89] In the letter sent to him by the Elders on 10 May 1901,[90] another argument was put forward: Samos, Crete and Cyprus had already banned the use of the scaphander diving suit and, as a result, many sponge-fishing vessels with naked divers from other islands went fishing in their seas.[91] It was estimated that Crete and Cyprus, in particular, whose coasts, as noted in the document, stretched over more than 360 miles, and were rich in sponges, and would absorb the largest share of the sponge-fishing activity in the Aegean. As they argued,

> Why should Kalymnian sponge fishermen sit on those dry rocks and starve to death, and not emigrate to the coasts of Crete or Cyprus, where they will be able to catch sponges in abundance and without any expenses? [...] Already since last year, many families of our island's sponge fishermen were planning to emigrate and settle on the coasts of Crete. The only thing that prevented them from leaving was the Imperial Government's repeated reassurance, conveyed by your Excellency and

---

88   He was a legal practitioner, who served as a senior official of the Ottoman state, according to Flegel. Flegel, *Η νήσος Κάλυμνος* [*The Island of Kalymnos*], p. 44. Upon his death, the Elders' Council decided to hold a state funeral recognizing him as a benefactor of his homeland. Doc. 27, 15/11/1918, MC Minutes 1915–1919, MAK. For more biographical details, see Giannis Kl. Zervos, *Ιστορικά σημειώματα* [*Historical Notes*], Athens 1961, pp. 183–184. See also Sakellaris Trikoilis, *Νεότερη ιστορία της Καλύμνου. Κοινωνική διαστρωμάτωση* [*Modern History of Kalymnos: Social Stratification*], Athens 2007, pp. 254–255.

89   Doc. 28, 29, 2/2/1900, MC Minutes 1899–1900, MAK. However, the first time he was appointed representative of the community was in 1873, for issues regarding privileges (Documents not numbered p. 287 and 289, 15/10/1876, MC Minutes 1863–1884, MAK).

90   In this letter, they inform him that the inspector of the General Directorate of the Ottoman Public Debt in the Aegean Sea visited Kalymnos, Leros and Symi: "This gentleman is Greek, and his name is Georgios Kaplanoglous. He arrived recently. He is very polite and nice and well educated". Document 99, 10/5/1901, Archives of Kalymnos Elders' Council, MAK.

91   Carl Flegel estimated that the positive effects from the abolition of the scaphander diving suit were immediate, particularly with regards to the increase in revenue from the taxed sponge-fishing vessels. See Flegel, *La question des pêcheurs d'éponges*, p. 21.

our Esteemed *Kaymakam*, concerning its paternal interest, and that it would shortly resolve this issue, as everyone wished.[92]

A few months later, in January of 1902, the Elders of Kalymnos announced the ban of the scaphander diving suit in the maritime area of Egypt and, at the same time, expressed their gratitude to the Sultan.[93] Their stocktaking capitalized on the same arguments listed above, which are constant throughout their battle for the abolition of the diving devices. On this account, among others, they deemed that they were no longer in need of a representative in Constantinople, and they relieved Hippocrates Tavlarios of his duties.[94] However, some were too hasty to conclude that the ban was finalized, such as Symiot Mitrophanis Kalafatas:

The diving gear is old and soon will cease,
the divers will again be strong,
the time has come, the end is near,
the diving stone will rule once more.
The diving gear has weakened,
the naked dive will bloom again,
our forefathers' art will flower.[95]

---

92   On children immigrating in 1900 from Kalymnos to Odessa, Kiev, Saint Petersburg, and Warsaw, to work in various manufactures and industries, see Giannis D. Gerakis, *Σφουγγαράδικες ιστορίες από την Κάλυμνο του* [*Sponge Stories from Kalymnos in the 1900s*], Athens 1999. The first migration of Kalymnians to Tarpon Springs, Florida, took place in 1905. Antonis Mailis "Στο Τάρπον Σπρινκς" ["In Tarpons Springs"], *I Kathimerini, Epta Imeres*, vol. XIII, Dodecanese, Athens 1996, pp. 37–38.

93   Doc. 10, 11/1/1902, and thank-you letter to the Sultan Doc. 119, 6/6/1902, Correspondence 1902, MAK.

94   Doc. 29, 21/2/1902, Correspondence 1902, MAK. A month earlier, in a resolution of 22 January 1902, the people of Kalymnos decided to dismiss Hippocrates Tavlarios. The displeasure of the community was evident, as the text notes the following: "neither did he take any clear and specific action, nor were any letters of reply from him found in the archives which would enlighten the public on this matter, nor is there any hope left for a happy ending; on the contrary, the esteemed Mr. Carl Flegel, without any moral mandate, without any material benefit, but impelled by his kind and charitable intentions, is a grand and effective example in his actions in favour of the people of Kalymnos, and of all neighbouring sponge fishing populations. [These include] the complete abolition of sponge-fishing diving machines on Samos, Crete, Cyprus and lately in Egypt", Doc. 2, 22/1/1902, MC Minutes 1894–1906, MAK. Flegel, who apparently did not hold Hippocrates Tavlarios in very high esteem, intuited that there were a variety of selfish motives behind Tavlarios' actions.

95   Μητροφάνης Καλαφατάς, "Χειμερινός Όνειρος" [Mitrofanis Kalafatas, "Winter Dream"] in Michael N. Kalafatas, *The Bellstone: The Greek Sponge Divers of the Aegean. One American's*

And yet, on 5 May 1902, the Elders' Council sent a telegram to the Department of Public Debt in Constantinople, asking to be informed whether a blanket ban against scaphander diving suits was in place across the seas of the Ottoman Empire.[96]

It appears, however, that nothing was certain and that the issue caused dissension in the local community and, more importantly, just before the departure of sponge-fishing vessels. When employment contracts had already been signed, crews readied, and significant sums paid out for organizing the sponge-fishing expedition, and divers' advance payments had been made, uncertainty still gave rise to contradictory reactions in the sponge-fishing community. Controversies that were perhaps internal between current and former notables, very often investors and sponge merchants, resulted in heated conflicts and complaints. In recurrent letters and grievances to the Ottoman administration, the Elders' Council reported that former representative Hippocrates Tavlarios sent a telegram from Constantinople to former Elder Aristidis Kouremetis, informing him that scaphander diving suits had been abolished. In his turn, the former Elder invited the people to a general assembly by tolling the bells.[97] The Elders wrote: "the blame for such movements of an anarchist nature, your Excellency, falls on the shoulders those conducting them, given the existence here of an administration and the Elders' Council serving this administration, which represent the people in such matters".[98] Nevertheless, they complained that the Governor's [*Kaymakam*] Office did not intervene, and did not fail to denounce the instigators of these episodes for speculation and financial abuses as a result of how the matter was handled.[99]

It is perhaps not our task here to try to understand the stance of these men. Furthermore, the material at our disposal does not bring out the different views and practices concerning this controversial topic. Here, as well as in various pieces of archival evidence, there are indeed hints that opposing political groups existed, and that the issue was capitalized on by those involved

---

Journey Home. Hannover: Brandeis University Press, 2003, p. 265.

96   Doc. 81, 5/5/1902, Correspondence 1902, MAK.

97   Doc. 84, 7/5/1902, doc. 86, 9/5/1902, Correspondence 1902, MAK.

98   Doc. 86, 9/5/1902, Correspondence 1902, MAK.

99   It seems, however, that there were suspicions concerning the Elders' role in the abolition of the scaphander diving suits, which were not very clear in the official documents under investigation. Thus, in another letter to the *Kaymakam* of Kalymnos, the Elders claimed that the instigators of the episodes were defaming them by spreading the rumour in the town coffee shops that Elders' Council did not want the diving machines to be abolished. Doc. 169, 9/9/1902, Correspondence 1902, MAK.

in public life. According to Carl Flegel, Michael Magklis,[100] who succeeded Aristidis Kouremetis in the Elders' Council in 1902, gave prominence to the issue of the abolition of the scaphander diving suit in his electoral program.[101] Here again, one might focus on our main topic of interest: the process of evolution of the Kalymnian sponge fishery from "traditional" to "modern", and Table 7 demonstrates that the transformation was continuous. Even though for more than thirty years both options coexisted, the traditional method was in decline, while the use of the scaphander diving suit is continuous.

Meanwhile, on 29 August 1902, the abolition of sponge-diving machines was officially announced,[102] causing new incidents and assaults against investors and scaphander diving suit owners.[103] By means of a new resolution, however, the Elders reinstated Tavlarios and denounced the stance of the preceding Elders' Council.[104]

Where the ban of 1902 is concerned, Dimosthenis Chaviaras, who experienced the events wrote: "[...] the fight against the sponge-fishing machines took place again lately. It is uncertain which opinions will prevail in the future among the many and various that keep opposing the interested parties".[105]

In 1902 the use of scaphander diving suits was completely banned along the Turkish coasts, throughout the Aegean Sea and off the coasts of Africa. It would nevertheless appear that this ban never became law. In his manuscripts Carl Flegel wrote that, "[u]nfortunately, in 1902 Turkey replayed the game of 1881, that is, abruptly abolishing the scaphander diving suits in its then large maritime territory, so that its clerks collected money".[106] It appears, however, that the situation was more complicated than this. In this same period, when indeed the Turkish Government decided to abolish the scaphander diving suit in the areas under its control (northern Africa, European and Asian coasts

---

100   Carl Flegel notes that Michael Magklis was a legal practitioner, who had studied in Paris, as well as a sponge merchant and representative of the Ottoman Bank. He owned considerable property in the area of Alikarnassos [Bodrum], and he had served twice, in 1899 and 1902, as leading Elder. See his manuscript "Οι ευεργέται της Καλύμνου" ["The Benefactors of Kalymnos"].

101   As noted in "Οι ευεργέται της Καλύμνου" ["The Benefactors of Kalymnos"], which is kept in Kalymnos' reading room, and in Flegel, "Παναγιότης ο Οικουμενικός Πατριάρχης Άνθιμος" ["His All-Holiness Ecumenical Patriarch Anthimos VII from Kalymnos"], p. 19.

102   Doc. 175, 20/9/1902, Correspondence 1902, MAK. See also relevant letters and thank-you telegrams to the Sultan. Doc. 165 and 166, 1st and 2/9/1902, Correspondence 1902, MAK.

103   Doc. 175 and 176, 20/9/1902, Correspondence 1902, MAK.

104   Doc. 20, not dated, Minutes and Resolutions 1922–1948, MAK.

105   Chaviaras, "Τινά περί σπογγαλιείας", ["On the Sponge Fishery"], p. 5.

106   The excerpt is from Chatzidakis, *Ο αγώνας για την κατάργηση των σκαφάντρων* [*The Struggle for the Abolition of the Scaphander Diving Suits*], p. 38.

of Turkey), the sponge-fishing lands of the Greek state were in turmoil. The Government under Zaimis and King George was placed under intense pressure from sponge merchants, ship owners and those who had invested in the sponge fishery in 1902. These people claimed that they were threatened with ruination because all Greek sponge-fishing vessels worked with scaphander diving suits. The Members of Parliament from the constituencies of Argolida and the Argosaronic islands, as well as the Mayors of Aegina, Hydra and Spetses, turned to the Prime Minister, and asked him to intervene with the Sublime Porte, and to authorize Mavrokordatos to lead the negotiations.

The issue took on wider political implications on the front pages of the contemporary press, with the German ambassador's intervention in Constantinople, in favour of the Greek Government's policy,[107] while the Sultan's decision was interpreted as being provocatively hostile against the Greek state. Simultaneously, in April of 1902, Egypt issued a decree, with which it demanded a special permit for those harvesting sponges on its coasts, while making it clear that sponge fishing by means of the scaphander diving suit was prohibited, and that the boats and the sponges of violators would be seized. In May of that same year, the opposition took advantage of the issue by deeming the Government under Zaimis incapable of handling the problem, while on Aegina, Hydra and Spetses, demonstrations and protests were organized.

Once the prohibition was in force, fishermen of the Greek state were obliged to do their sponge fishing in the open sea. Representatives of sponge-fishing areas – Hydra, Spetses, Aegina and Ermionida – asked the Zaimis government for permission to deploy a Greek ship off the coasts of northern Africa, to protect Greek fishermen. In mid-May of 1902, following an undefined period during which sponge fishermen either dove unobstructed at a 5-mile distance from the shore, or were hampered by local authorities, the Egyptian government decided to allow Greek sponge fishermen to work for a period 4 months. The issue was still present in the Parliament[108] and remained pending until at least mid-1903.[109] The topic of scaphander diving suits also troubled public opinion and divided the press at the time. Countering the arguments of

107   It was thought that a substantial part of the revenues would be directed to paying the loan of 120,000,000 francs that the Greek Government had obtained; Εμπρός [Empros], 25/5/1902, p. 2.

108   Εμπρός [Empros], 11/2/1903, p. 1.

109   Press articles are almost a daily phenomenon; see Εμπρός [Empros], 13/3/1902, pp. 3–4, 14/3/1902, p. 1, 16/3/1902, p. 3, 23/3/1902, p. 3, 28/3/1902, p. 4, 31/3/1902, p. 1, 18/4/1902, p. 2, 20/4/1902, p. 3, 26/4/1902, p. 3, 2/5/1902, p. 3, 3/5/1902, p. 2, 4/5/1902, p. 4, 5/5/1902, p. 1 and 3, 7/5/1902, p. 3, 10/5/1902, p. 2, 11/5/1902, p. 2, 12/5/1902, p. 2, 13/5/1902, p. 3, 21/5/1902, p. 2, 22/8/1902, p. 4,11/2/1903, p. 1.

the opponents of the scaphander diving suit, and those reporting cases of diver mistreatment, *Empros* newspaper was openly in favour of the use of the machine, and considered it the only realistic and efficient means of fishing for sponges.[110]

On 8 January 1903, the Elders' Council of Kalymnos decided to increase the municipal tax levied on sponge-fishing crews, because "due to the abolition of sponge machines, the local sponge tax will be reduced, leading to a reduction in the community budget".[111] At any rate, however, some people violated the ban on the scaphander diving suit. The Elders' Council, which was able to check the violations only when they occurred in Kalymnos' surrounding area, turned to the Turkish administration, and asked that measures be undertaken.[112]

However, sponge fishing permits for scaphander diving suits were apparently granted when applicants stated that they were to be employed in seas other than those of the Ottoman Empire. Therefore, in 1903, a total of 40 ships from Kalymnos, Symi and Chalke worked off African coasts, where there were also other Greek sponge-fishing vessels equipped with scaphander diving suits.[113] In 1904 a new ban came into force,[114] and remained in force until 1907, and specifically concerned the scaphander diving suit. These decisions often seemed to take the Elders by surprise.[115] The governments of the Ottoman Empire, Cyprus, Samos, Egypt, and Tunis had banned the scaphander diving suit, yet the same did not apply in the case of the Greek government. Even at this time, sponge fishermen worked around the official bans by different means, such as bribery and illegal fishery.[116] Indeed, in 1907, when Ioannis Emm. Olympitis complained to the Elders' Council that "it subordinated his rights and did not protect his interests", because it allowed "his blocked mechanical divers to set off to work", local authorities replied that "since sponge-fishing machines are completely banned on imperial orders, we are unable to obstruct these people

110   D. A. Panagos, "Οι σπογγαλιείς μας. Τα κακουργήματά των μύθοι. Μία απάντησις εις την Εστίαν", *Εμπρός* ["Our Sponge Fishermen. Legends of their Crimes. An Answer to the Newspaper *Estia*", *Empros*], 15/4/1903, p. 3.

111   Book 23, Doc. 16, Archives of the Elders' Council of Kalymnos, MAK.

112   Doc. 130, 21/12/1904, Correspondence 1902–1905, MAK.

113   Doc. 15, n.d. [1904], and Doc. 74, 9/3/1905, Correspondence 1902–1905, MAK. See also Adamantios E. Pachountakis, *Η σπογγαλιεία εν Αιγύπτω* [*Sponge Fishing in Egypt*], Alexandria 1905, pp. 8–9.

114   Doc. 11, 24/1/1904, Correspondence 1902–1905, MAK.

115   Έκθεσις περί γεωργίας, βιομηχανίας, ναυτιλίας της προξενικής περιφερείας Ρόδου ιδία διά το έτος 1910, Δελτίον του επί των Εξωτερικών Β. Υπουργείου, [*Report on Agriculture, Industry, Maritime Affairs of the Consular Precinct of Rhodes for the Year 1910*, Bulletin *of the Ministry for Foreign Affairs*], Athens 1911, p. 31.

116   Pachountakis, *Η σπογγαλιεία εν Αιγύπτω* [*Sponge Fishing in Egypt*], p. 9.

and to stop them from doing their work".[117] It is not clear, however, if this referred to working with scaphander diving suits beyond the borders of the Ottoman Empire or if it referred to recruitments on vessels with naked divers.

Nevertheless, in February of 1904, despite prohibitions, the Elders' Council of Kalymnos sent a letter to the Commissioner in Cyprus, seeking to be informed whether fishing by scaphander diving suit was allowed there. The maritime area of Cyprus was indeed one of Kalymnian vessels' fishing areas, either throughout the entire summer, or in August and September, when vessels were on their way back from the coasts of Africa. As the notables of the island wrote:

> According to a rumour circulating here, government of Cyprus has granted the exclusive rights to work with scaphander diving suits in the island's waters, in order to export sponges. This unexpected and horrible piece of news caused so much sadness and disquiet to our island's poor sponge fishermen that they immediately found themselves in despair, not knowing what to do; and, while exceptionally this year many ships were ready to depart for Cyprus, as they knew that about three years ago scaphander diving suits were not permitted, they have already halted and anxiously await positive and clear information. We cannot believe that the Government of Cyprus took such a measure, given that we are aware that three years ago, as an act of charity and relief for the hapless sponge fishermen, the man-killing scaphander diving suits were banned, for which thousands of people were grateful and prayed for the prosperity and progress of charitable and mighty England.[118]

Quite obviously the information was correct, and in a subsequent letter the Elders attempted to persuade the Cypriot authorities that it would be in their best interest to have no scaphander diving suits in use, and a greater number of naked sponge divers employed. At the same time, they urged the Elders' Council of Symi to join them in their struggle.[119]

In 1906 the issue resurfaced, as the ban in force was not applied. In a new resolution that gathered 337 signatures, the people of Kalymnos requested that the Elders' Council present itself in full to the local Sub-administration, and send a delegation to Rhodes, consisting of one Elder and captains, who would

---

117   Doc. 124, 7/5/1907, MC Minutes 1906–1908, MAK.

118   Doc. 20, no date, Correspondence 1902–1905, MAK.

119   Doc. 49, 12/4/1904, Doc. 50, 17/4/1904 and Doc. 61, 18/5/1904, Correspondence 1902–1905, MAK.

demand that the law be enforced.[120] In 1908 the problem persisted. Following a letter from the Elders' Council of Symi to that of Kalymnos, and with the consent of 13 Kalymnian captains, it was decided that they would address the issue in concert, and hunt down those fishing illegally with scaphander diving suits.[121] However, in January of 1909, sponge fishing with scaphander diving suits was once again permitted in the seas of the Ottoman Empire.[122] Yet, in 1910, the use of scaphander diving suits was once more prohibited by order of the Council of Ministers. Given that sponge-fishing vessels had already acquired their permits and were already in the fishing areas, the decision was deemed "detrimental, and certain to deal a heavy blow to the sponge fishery", whereas sponge investors and sponge merchants protested vehemently against the prohibition.[123] In 1912, the Italian Administration prohibited sponge fishing off the coasts of Tripoli and Cyrenaica because of the Italo-Ottoman war, which prohibition was lifted in the following year.[124] By 1917, the sponge fishery was in absolute decline.[125]

The absence of official statistics, the international reach of the issue, the dispersion of sponge-fishing population, and their inability to defend their interests in an effective manner, were among the reasons for the perpetuation the problem. The main reason, however, was those profiting from the abuse of the scaphander diving suit. "People filled with an insatiable thirst for gain", as Flegel passionately described them, asserting with great clarity that they were not foreign merchants but rather local "avaricious" businessmen who saw the sponge fishery as a "gambling game". These individuals succeeded in deceiving the press, and influencing public opinion and governments that it was a national industry and national source of wealth that ought to be supported.[126] In 1903, P. Zotos wrote the following in his analysis of the investment and advance payment system: "Sponge fishing by scaphander diving suit is a financial enterprise in which speculation has stifled the idea of honest work".[127] In 1937, G. Georgas wrote that as soon as the government decides to study the issue of the abolition of the scaphander diving suit,

---

120   Doc. 18, 24/9/1906, Minutes and Resolutions 1922–1948, MAK.
121   Doc. 276, 8/3/1908, MC Minutes 1908–1909, MAK.
122   Doc. 380, 16/1/1909, MC Minutes 1908–1909, MAK.
123   Letter of Consul N. Souidas to the Ministry of Foreign Affairs, 30/5/1910, Consulate in Rhodes, Folder 44 (1911), Subfolder 2, IAYE.
124   Doc. 2, 5/1/1913, Correspondence 1910–1913, MAK.
125   Doc. 48, [1917], Minutes 1915–1919, MAK.
126   Flegel, Carl. La question des pêcheurs d'éponges, p. 7; also by Flegel, Τὸ σπογγαλιευτικό ζήτημα [The Sponge-Fishery Issue], pp. 206–207.
127   P. Zotos, Ἔκθεσις περί τῆς ἀνά τας ἀφρικανικάς ακτάς διά σκαφάνδρου σπογγαλιείας [Report on Scaphander Diving-Suit Sponge Fishery across the African Coasts], Athens 1904, p. 11.

those in favour of the scaphander diving suit, and some new ship and scaphander diving suit owners, in their ill-conceived interest, will oppose its abolition, tenaciously putting forward, as it has happened in the past, absurd questions such as what will become of the diver mechanics' families, what will happen to the few bits of scrap metal from the scaphander diving suits, and the few rubber dresses and pipes? These questions, in our opinion, deserve only the slightest attention because regular diver mechanics are now scarce (other mechanics come from the lowest strata of society), whereas their families will of course be saved from being widowed and orphaned. As for the scrap metal parts, they will be sold as such.[128]

4.1.4   Lithuanian "Philanthropist" Carl Flegel

The battle for the abolition of the scaphander diving suit was taken up by Carl Flegel (Carl Vasilievich Flegel 1850–1928), a Lithuanian Professor of Ancient Languages at the University of Vilna, who visited Leros in 1890. From Leros, Flegel travelled to Kalymnos and Patmos, and in 1892 he relocated to Kalymnos, motivated by his interest in the ancient Greek world, and hoping at the same time to distance himself from personal issues.[129]

In his writings, Flegel offers a personal account of his first encounter with the world of sponge fishermen and the scaphander diving suit:

On a beautiful day in June of 1892, I went on an excursion to Emporion to visit the significant fortress, as I was fascinated by the words of simple people, shepherds, and fishermen. I set off on foot from Chora, where I was lodged in the Metropolitan Bishopric of Bishop Chrysanthos, who was abroad; I reached the small island Telendos and from there I hired a boat to get to Emporion. The boat's skipper was a 40-year-old man, Nikolaos Stambas, accompanied by his 12-year-old son, Sakellarios. Having noticed that the boatman's legs were paralysed, I asked him about his condition, and he revealed how it happened to me, simply and in great detail, when he was working as a sponge fisherman with a scaphander diving suit. He told me of the disaster that the machine brought to sponge fishermen not

---

128   Georgas, Μελέτη περί σπογγαλιείας [Study of the Sponge Fishery], p. 74.

129   In his writings Flegel mentions the death of his 34-year-old brother, Edward, who was an explorer living in Africa, and who was killed on the banks of the Niger river in 1886, under circumstances that remain obscure. He described his settlement on Kalymnos and his activity in Flegel, La question des pêcheurs d'éponges, pp. 12–20. For Carl Flegel see Kalymniaka Chronika 3 (1982), pp. 25–54. On the same topic see also Faith Warm, Bitter Sea: The Real Story of Greek Sponge Diving, London 2000, p. 46.

only on Kalymnos, but also in all sponge-fishing lands. The simple narrative of the afflicted sponge fisherman was enough for me to immediately form the opinion that this situation could not carry on much longer, and to decide that I should dedicate myself entirely to the fight against this newly discovered evil. I took notice, however, of the existence of a share of the population that favours scaphander diving suits, yet I was certain that soon enough of a consensus on this matter would be achieved and I waited, preparing all the while the immaterial weapons for the fight. And the time for the fight came promptly.[130]

Indeed, Flegel soon embarked on a dynamic crusade by means of reports, memoranda, and articles published in the international press and various other publications, in his efforts to persuade the governments of the Mediterranean countries to take the "sponge-fishery issue" seriously. He exhausted all means of communication with civil and religious authorities, the Sublime Porte, the Patriarch, the Consul of Russia in Rhodes, the court of the Tsar, as well as distinguished figures of the Greek and Italian political sphere. He expounded his views in associations, at expositions and conferences, as well as in the press in sponge-producing areas.[131] By 1893, Flegel had prepared a brief treatise entitled "The Island Kalymnos", dedicated to the Ecumenical Patriarch Anthimos VII, which was published in 1896 at the patriarchal printing office in Constantinople. In this treatise, he likened Kalymnos to "a rose devoured by worm. An Andromeda under the threat of a monster, waiting for Perseus".

In the same year on the island of Samos, Flegel published a new study entitled "His All-Holiness Ecumenical Patriarch Anthimos VII of Kalymnos", which he dedicated to the ruler of Samos. Both texts contain rich, factual material on Kalymnos, its residential and social organisation, as well as the residents' economic condition. Nevertheless, denouncing the scaphander diving suit remained Flegel's central concern. His activist writings were polemical and focused on the cause to which he had entirely dedicated himself, namely foregrounding and raising awareness of the issue in the eyes of the international public, while pressuring governments to find a solution.

The foreword to the second text noted above ("His All-Holiness") is particularly explicit:

---

130   He described his settlement on Kalymnos and his activity in Flegel, *La question des pêcheurs d'éponges*, pp. 12–20, and in a manuscript kept in the Reading Room of Kalymnos.

131   Flegel, *Τὸ σπογγαλιευτικό ζήτημα* [*The Sponge-Fishery Issue*], p. 214.

With these writings of mine, I am trying to make the horrible consequences of the scaphander diving suit's abuse in sponge fishery known
to a wider public. The machine has made many victims, some of whom
are deceased while others are paralyzed. Moreover, the extermination of
sponge species leads, on the one hand, to the desolation and contraction
of the Aegean sponge-fishing areas that once boomed, counting a total
population of 100,000 souls and, on the other hand, it does significant
damage to the Imperial Treasury. I ardently hope that this philanthropic
and charitable cause is addressed and taken care of before long.[132]

On 2 March 1896, the Elders' Council of Kalymnos sent Flegel a letter thank-
ing him for his zealous endeavours to promote "an issue of the most vital
importance for the island and for the rest of the sponge-fishing islands of the
Sporades, namely the abolition of the sponge-fishing machines",[133] while the
following year the Council offered 325 *kuruş* for the purchase of 100 copies of
his study.[134]

In 1902, Mitrophanis Kalafatas of Symi, recounted some of Flegel's actions
in verse:

> That, as his angel, sent a man
> guileless and full of spirit,
> Flegel by name and Russian-born,
> in whom I recognized a kind,
> masterful benefactor.
> Blessed more than once he reached our shores,
> studied and learned our torments,
> and was so moved by the machine's
> criminal miserable results,
> he undertook himself the task
> to practice good and undo harm.
> He gave it all his power,
> spent without mercy his own funds,
> coming and going first to France
> and Italy in tandem,

132 Flegel, "Η Α.Θ. Παναγιότης ο Οικουμενικός Πατριάρχης Άνθιμος" ["His All-Holiness
      Ecumenical Patriarch Anthimos"], pp. 5–6.
133 Ibid., p. 51. See the *Kalymniaka Chronika*, 3 (1982), p. 25, as referenced above.
134 Doc. 181, 13/6/1897, MC Minutes 1896–1897, MAK.

and then to Crete to meet success
and leave again for Cyprus,
where he found England willingly
coming to our defense.
From there to Egypt without rest
where he delayed Mandroucha.
He wastes no time in laziness,
from there he sails to Samos,
who also swore to ban the gear,
hating its very sight.[135]

In August 1896, Flegel presented his arguments to Stefanos Mousouros, the ruler of Samos, and lodged a petition to abolish the scaphander diving suit. While in Samos, Flegel printed his third study on the sponge-fishery issue in the Mediterranean and submitted it to the General Assembly of Samos in November of 1897, while reiterating his plea. In that study, Flegel described the warm welcome that he received from the people of Samos, and their unanimous decision to abolish the scaphander diving suit, which was ratified by the ruler in February of 1898.[136]

In the autumn of 1899, Flegel travelled to Crete for what was probably for his first time. His arguments were like those already known to us from his memos to the Elders' Council.[137]

Since the concurrent introduction of the scaphander diving suit in 1863 in the Dodecanese islands and in Greece, many unfortunate circumstances have begun to afflict otherwise happy sponge-fishing populations: premature and sudden deaths, young lads and men suffering from chronic diseases, a corresponding and great number of widows and orphans without bread and butter. Daughters who will never marry because of a shortage of men, and many are met with difficulties in finding their daily bread because the sponge-fishing beds are gradually perishing due to the scaphander diving suits. These circumstances, and the poverty they have created, have resulted in begging, and in imposed emigration,

---

135 Μητροφάνης Καλαφατάς, "Χειμερινός Όνειρος" [Mitrofanis Kalafatas, "Winter Dream"] in Michael N. Kalafatas, *The Bellstone: The Greek Sponge Divers of the Aegean. One American's Journey Home.* Hannover: Brandeis University Press, 2003, pp. 237–238.

136 Flegel, "Το σπογγαλιευτικό ζήτημα" ["The Sponge-Fishery Issue"], p. 215.

137 See Flegel, *Η νήσος Κάλυμνος* [*The Island of Kalymnos*], p. 32.

especially to Russia and America. In short, [the scaphander diving suit] is
the reason for social decay in the vilest of forms. [...] This is the deplorable situation in which I encountered the sponge fishermen of Kalymnos
and the Mediterranean Sea in 1892.[138]

In 1899, through interventions and memoranda, the Cretan State banned the
use of the scaphander diving suit in Cretan waters and imposed a fine on violators. In a law drafted 6 November 1899, it was specified that sponge fishing, by
means of naked diving or other methods from vessels, was allowed.[139]

Following his work in Crete, Flegel presented the case of the Kalymnian
sponge divers against the scaphander diving suit at the International
Exposition of Athens in 1900. Directly thereafter he travelled to Cyprus with
the same mission, and in March of 1901, a law prohibiting scaphander diving
suits was adopted in Cyprus.[140] Several Symiots were involved in this concerted
endeavour, such as Dimosthenis Chaviaras, and sponge merchant G. Georgas,
who became allies.[141]

Also in 1901, the Elders' Council and the inhabitants of the island bestowed
accolades on those who contributed in various ways to the fight against the
scaphander diving suit. Their gratitude for Carl Flegel took the form of a public resolution to honour his disinterested contribution to the struggle.[142] The
people of Kalymnos also honoured Flegel with another resolution that made
him an "honorary citizen" of the island in gratitude for his publications. His
honorary citizenship was also granted in thanks for his work "in pushing for
an order to ban the man-killing and sponge-destroying scaphander diving suit,
and for the successful resolution of the sponge-fishery issue, which is of vital
importance for the island, as well as for the rest of the sponge-fishing lands of
the Mediterranean".[143]

---

138   An excerpt from Carl Flegel's manuscripts, published in Χατζηδάκης, "Η Κάλυμνος στα τέλη
      της Τουρκοκρατίας", Καλυμνιακά Χρονικά [Chatzidakis, "Kalymnos at the End of Turkish
      rule", Kalymniaka Chronika] 8 (1989), p. 85.
139   It is the second time that the use of diving machines was prohibited throughout the
      Cretan maritime area. See Εμπρός [Empros], 15/11/1899, p. 1; Flegel, Το σπογγαλιευτικό
      ζήτημα [The Sponge-Fishery Issue], pp. 216–217 and Χατζιδάκης, Ο αγώνας για την κατάργηση
      των σκαφάντρων [Chatzidakis, The Struggle for the Abolition of the Scaphander Diving
      Suit], p. 37.
140   Flegel, Το σπογγαλιευτικό ζήτημα [The Sponge-Fishery Issue], p. 219.
141   Georgas, Μελέτη περί σπογγαλιείας [Study of the Sponge Fishery], p. 17.
142   Doc. 2, 22/1/1902, MC Minutes 1894–1906, MAK.
143   The document bore 185 signatures. Doc. 3, 17/6/1902, MC Minutes 1894–1906, MAK.

In 1905, Flegel advocated for the foundation of insurance funds for mechanical divers and the creation of a care unit for their treatment. Queen Olga of Greece, who held this great humanitarian in particularly high esteem, persuaded the Greek government to send a military ship to provide care for the victims of the scaphander diving suit for several years, and to maintain – for an extended period of time – a hospital in Tripoli, present-day Libya, for the severely afflicted.

In 1908, following a recommendation from Flegel, Crete provided for the compensation of mechanical divers, which we read in his handwritten notes:

> In 1908, due to clandestine sponge fishing by means of foreign scaphander diving suits in Cretan waters, the enlightened Government of the heroic Megalonissos substituted the life-saving law of 1899 with another equally important one, which limited the number of scaphander diving suits to ten, with compensation for the inevitable victims. A few years later, Italy and Greece also followed the example of this law.

Indeed, in 1913 the same measures were introduced in Greece and the Ottoman Empire, once again following a recommendation made by Flegel.[144] In his later years Flegel wrote:

> I introduced the righteous case of the sponge fishermen to the following international congresses: Saint Petersburg in 1902, Vienna in 1905, Washington and Frankfurt am Main in 1908, Rome in 1903 and 1911, Brussels, Ostend and Vienna in 1913; and at the following international expositions: Athens in 1900, Saint Petersburg in 1902, Milan in 1906, Bordeaux in 1907 and San Francisco in 1915. I received distinguished awards, and I was even decorated in Egypt in 1902, in Greece in 1909 and in motherland Russia in 1910. I was declared an honorary citizen of Kalymnos in June 1902, precisely ten years after I first moved to this charming island. What adventures! A real novel. And I owe all this to dear Kalymnos, and no one knows how many wonderful surprises it has to offer![145]

---

144   Chatzidakis, "Ο αγώνας για την κατάργηση των σκαφάντρων" ["The Fight for the Abolition of the Scaphander Diving Suit"], pp. 39–40.
145   Chatzidakis, "Ο αγώνας για την κατάργηση των σκαφάντρων" ["The Fight to Abolish the Scaphander Diving Suit"], p. 39.

In March 1911, Flegel undertook an initiative to found an international charitable Society for the Defence of Sponge Fishermen, headquartered in Chania,
Crete, under the protection of Queen Olga of Greece and Prince Albert of
Monaco.[146] The Society made their case known through publications and pleas
to the philanthropists around the world in order to attract the necessary funding. At the same time, they actively recruited more members, while organizing
various charity events to help the victims. Donations, such as the one publicized in *Kritikos Asteras* (1911), were heart-warming: "To add to the necessary
funding, Royal Navy doctor Mr Evangelos Evangelidis (Aggelos Tanagras) contributed the earnings from the translation of his highly publicized novel *The
Sponge Fishermen of the Aegean Sea*, while Mr. Hornstein offered the revenues
from his own theatrical drama, *The Mysteries of the Waves*".

The Society appointed Carl Flegel as the supervisor of the sponge fishery
and the Society's representative in various international conferences and
expositions on the fishery. In a request made by Flegel in his capacity in as the
Society's representative in 1914 to the King of Italy, he asked for "a royal favour
for the crews of six sponge-fishing boats, namely that the sponges, which were
seized in the aftermath of a conviction in Tobruk, be returned to the crew
which was accomplished to their great joy. Five of the boats had Kalymnian
crews, whereas the sixth consisted of Symiots".[147]

While remaining documentation on the activity of the Society is scant, it
appears that its activity was intense given that, by 1915 when its operations
ceased due to the events of WWI, the Society had circulated more than 2,500
documents. Flegel continued to pursue his activism and complied studies on
the sponge fishery until the final days of his life. In 1927, the Municipality of
Kalymnos decided to support the publication of Flegel's writings "as a moral
satisfaction" for his contribution of many years to the sponge-fishing issue.[148]

---

146   Georgas, Μελέτη περί σπογγαλιείας [*Study of the Sponge Fishery*], p. 33; Theodoros A. Kriezis,
        "Η σπογγαλιεία", *Οικονομικός Ταχυδρόμος* ["Sponge Fishing", *Oikonomikos Tachydromos*]
        14/8/1932, p. 3; by the same author, *H σπογγαλιεία* [*The Sponge Fishery*], Athens 1937, p. 14.
147   From his handwritten notes. See also Chatzidakis, "Ο αγώνας για την κατάργηση των σκα-
        φάντρων" ["The Fight to Abolish the Scaphander Diving Suit"], p. 40.
148   Doc. 9, 31/12/1927, Decisions of Royal Commissioner and Mayors of Kalymnos, 1927–
        1934, MAK.

4.2   The "Black Book" of the Sponge Fishery[149]

The dangers with which sponge divers were confronted were numerous; on their descent and stay in great depths, and especially on their steep ascent to the surface. Naked divers were exposed to attacks by sea creatures such as sharks and dogfish, and risked sudden fainting fits, bleeding, and heart problems, as well as drowning by suffocation. What is more, they all suffered from deafness and rheumatism. Yet the greatest and most frequent risks stemmed from "divers' disease" – the culprit here being not water but the air they inhaled – and all these ailments and afflictions were a threat to those diving with the scaphander diving suit and the Fernez.

4.2.1   *The Cetaceans of the Sea*
The most widely known, yet not particularly common, danger to the naked divers were sharks and predatory dogfish – "the man-eating cetaceans who dwell in Poseidon's vast domain" – that caused deadly accidents and serious injuries.[150] Oral and written accounts record legendary incidents of attacks by mysterious fish, giant octopodes, and massive creatures living at the bottom of the sea. Fierce struggles with these "pirates of the seas" were also cited and indeed, it is said that as soon as divers signaled sudden danger to the pilot [*kolaouzieris*] of the boat, the crew would throw out some form of human or animal figure to distract the shark.[151] Moreover, divers apparently took special care to tan their skin, because they believed that tanning would prevent attacks.[152] Nevertheless, divers wearing the rubber suit with the scaphander also spoke of shark attacks, and while they may not have been in grave danger of being attacked by sea creatures, they were vulnerable to delays or jerky movements on the sea bottom.

---

149   I borrow this title from *Εστία* [*Estia*], 9/4/1903, p. 1.

150   Θεμέλης Κινδύνης, *Η νήσος Κάλυμνος* [Themelis Kindynis, *The Island of Kalymnos*], Athens 1879, p. 29. On shark attacks see also Newton's account, written in 1854; C. T. Newton, M.A. *Travels and Discoveries in the Levant*, vol. 1, London 1865, p. 292.

151   *Αθηναϊκά Νέα* [*Athinaika Nea*], 22/4/1938, p. 5.

152   Τάσος Ζάπας, "Στον κάβο με τους γυμνούς σφουγγαράδες", *Αθηναϊκά Νέα* [Tassos Zappas, "At the Headland with the Naked Sponge Fishermen", *Athinaika Nea*], 23/9/1937, p. 3.

There were also some, albeit few, victims of attacks among those diving with the Fernez.[153] Needless to say, however, there were also accounts of unexpected miracles.[154] In one testimony by Giannis Gerakis, we read that,

> [i]t is rare for a diver to encounter dogfish in the Barbary waters, and even rarer for a fish to eat a man, because sponge beds are found in waters that are bright and soft; an endless sandy bottom with seaweed beds, "traganes", "louria", "karines" [types of sandy sea bottom], shallow areas with sponge vegetation of good quality – the sponges that were the most valuable were the well-formed or shapely [*formada*, φορμάδα], "fine pores" [*psiloroúthouna* ψιλορούθουνα], and "thin cloth" [*psilópana* ψιλόπανα]. The dogfish have nowhere to nest, nowhere to hide. Hence, in the entire history of our sponge fishermen, there was only one man eaten by a dogfish: Giannis the "Demeli".[155]

Carl Flegel wrote that I. Peronis, this same "Demeli", "fell prey to a shark on the Barbary coast near Tripoli in June 1893". He added that "such accidents were so rare that sponge fishermen did not even take them into consideration. This summer [1903], two highly uncommon accidental events took place, the victims being Manolis Galanomatis (the "Volari") and Matsos. These accidents occurred in the sea around Crete".[156]

The members of sponge-fishing communities in the Southern Aegean still recount well-known incidents of "fish-eaten" sponge fishermen to this day, such as one incident involving an anonymous victim from Hydra or, in some

---

153 Testimony of Maria Filippou Soulounia to Faneromeni Chalkidiou-Skylla, *Ἡ σφουγγάρι ἡ τομάρι. Ἡ ζωή των σφουγγαράδων της Καλύμνου μέσα από αληθινές μαρτυρίες* [*Either Sponge or Corpse. The Life of the Sponge Fishermen of Kalymnos through Real Testimonies*], Kalymnos 2009, p. 252.

154 See Figuier, *Les merveilles de la science*, p. 626; Nikitas Chaviaras, "Συμαίων γυμνών σπογγαλιέων φρικτά επεισόδια", *Τα Συμαϊκά* ["Horrible Accidents Suffered by Symiot Naked Sponge Divers", *Ta Symaika*] 3 (1977), pp. 285–289; Giannis Ant. Cheilas, *Τὸ ἔπος των σφουγγαράδων της Καλύμνου* [*The Epic Saga of Kalymnos' Sponge Fishermen*], Athens 2000, p. 217; Ioannis Ant. Cheilas, "Που να σε φάει το ψάρι", *Καλυμνιακά Χρονικά* ["May the Fish Eat You", *Kalymniaka Chronika*], 18 (2009), pp. 275–287.

155 Gerakis, *Σφουγγαράδικες ιστορίες* [*Sponge-Fishing Stories*], pp. 112–113.

156 Carl Flegel, *Η νήσος Κάλυμνος* [*The Island of Kalymnos*], p. 29. On the same incident, see Gerakis, *Σφουγγαράδικες ιστορίες* [*Sponge-Fishing Stories*], pp. 99–103. Two more fatal accidents occurred in 1904 off the coasts of Crete. The victims were naked divers Theofilis Mazoros and Nikitas Splagounias, see Faneromeni Chalkidiou-Skylla, *Ἡ σφουγγάρι ἡ τομάρι*, [*Either Sponge or Corpse*], pp. 276–277.

versions, another victim, Giannis Triantafyllos, known as "Latari".[157] In the case of naked diver Triantafyllos's, the accident reportedly happened in the summer of 1888 or 1889 near Tripoli, present-day Libya. Descending quickly to the bottom of the sea with his skandalopetra [bellstone], Triantaphyllos "plunged directly into the fish's insides". As the story goes, the heavy stone became lodged in the great fish's esophagus, forcing it to spit Triantafyllos out immediately, with its sharp teeth cutting deep into the diver's upper body. Following his rescue, the "new Jonah" abandoned the sea until his death in 1945.[158]

In 1897, just as he was resurfacing, diver Manolis Ellinas was also attacked by a dogfish, which left the diver with severe injuries to his back. Ellinas survived, but he was no longer able to work.[159] According to Carl Flegel, there were two more fatal accidents in Crete in 1902, prompting the Cretan Parliament's decision to create a 500-drachma subsidy for the hunt of dangerous sharks.[160] A similar piece of news was published in 1906 in Ταχυδρόμος [Tachydromos], an Alexandria newspaper:

---

157   The frequent use of nicknames is typical of the professional and social group of sponge fishermen; especially those sobriquets that derived from their behaviour and work performance. Even in recruitment agreements in the community's official archival evidence, crew members were registered with their given name, family name, and nickname. "Taraxias" [Troublemaker], "Panagia" [Saint Mary], "Dynamitis" [Dynamite], "Xeparalymenos" [someone who was paralyzed, and rehabilitated], "Zoumi" [Juice], "Mavrostomos" [Black Mouthed], "Koufos" [Deaf], "Koufalis" [variation of Deaf] are only a few of the nicknames that we recovered from recruitment deeds of the 1880s and 1890s. More limited in number and rare in written evidence are nicknames for captains, although sobriquets for particular captains, such as "Psyllos" [Flea], or cruel captains, such as "Korea" [i.e. with reference to soldiers who died in the war], or "Nekrofora" [Hearse] survive in oral culture. We found no nicknames for investors in sponge-fishing expeditions and sponge merchants. If nicknames formed yet another mechanism for social control and societal integration, it could be said that they are also a mechanism for societal segregation and marginalization. See also Bernard Russell's view on this topic, "Paratsoukli: Institutionalized Nicknaming in Rural Greece", Ethnologia Europaea 11–111 (1968–1969), pp. 65–74.

158   Similar stories occur repeatedly in testimonies and fictional narratives. See Angelos Tanagras, Σπογγαλιείς του Αιγαίου [Sponge Fishermen of the Aegean Sea], Empros, 18/6/1903, p. 2; Gerakis, Σφουγγαράδικες ιστορίες [Sponge Stories], pp. 112–114; Niki Billiri, Η Κάλυμνός μας [Our Kalymnos], p. 28; Niki Billiri, Σφουγγαράδες από την Κάλυμνο [Sponge Fishermen of Kalymnos], p. 11; Kalafatas, The Bellstone, p. 12. On the same topic, see the account of Ioannis Triantafyllou, grandson of the "Psarofagomenos" [Fish-Eaten] to Faneromeni Chalkidiou-Skylla, Ή σφουγγάρι ή τομάρι [Either Sponge or Corpse], pp. 40–42 and 200–201.

159   Gerakis, Σφουγγαράδικες ιστορίες [Sponge Stories], p. 114.

160   Flegel, Το σπογγαλιευτικό ζήτημα [The Sponge-Fishery Issue], p. 211.

One expatriate sponge fisherman from Symi, Michael Karakatsanis, was transferred to Marsa Matruh to be hospitalized following an injury caused by a shark while the man was working at the bottom of the sea. The victim recounts how he fought with the dreadful beast. Each time that the shark attacked with its jaws open wide, the diver held out his skandalope-tra [bellstone] against the beast's terrifying teeth. Thus, he escaped with only bodily injuries, mostly on his arms, where the beast bit him.[161]

Oral testimonies have been added to the few cases recorded in written sources, such as one that concerns: "some Kalymnians and Symiots who were eaten in 1903 and, in 1936, a 72-kilogram shark devoured a Kalymnian man. They ended up catching the fish, though".[162]

Even if we were to rely on the trustworthiness of local reminiscences, accidents of this nature were still very few, and sources concur that, until the use of the scaphander diving suit became widespread, the number of naked diving victims was less than 2%.[163] This percentage should be probably attributed to the composite of dangers and unforeseen incidents that apnea divers faced, which were not limited to dogfish and shark attacks.[164] Symiot sponge merchant G. Georgas came to a similar conclusion and claimed that, "throughout the entire period [1866–1915], there was only a total of 8–10 naked sponge diver victims; half of them were injured by sharks and the rest lost their hands due to the "skandali" [the rope tied to the naked sponge diver's wrist]".[165]

It should, however, be taken into account that such testimonies were usually part of targeted texts that cited the benefits of the old methods, as opposed to the "man-eating" scaphander diving suit.[166] The accounts of victims, as well as the stories of men who fought against the wild "fishes", as sponge divers called them, exalted in the skills of naked sponge divers who cleaved to a fishing method now considered outdated, and indeed, almost archaic. Unlike "machine" divers, protected by impenetrable diving suits, the less efficient

---

161 *Ταχυδρόμος* [*Tachydromos*], 9/12/1906, p. 1 and Cheilas, *Που να σε φάει το ψάρι* [*May the Fish Eat You*], p. 279.

162 Testimony of captain Giannis Tsoulfas to E.O., 5/3/2002.

163 Carabokyro, *Étude sur la pêche des éponges*, p. 6.

164 In free diving, hypoxia may occur, that is, fainting due to lack of oxygen. When the diver surfaces, he has already consumed a considerable amount of oxygen due to the effort made up to that point. The lungs' volume, therefore, increases, but the oxygen is not enough to oxygenate body and brain. Most frequent symptoms of hypoxia are nausea, twitching, loss of motor control, black out and, ultimately, drowning.

165 Georgas, *Μελέτη περί σπογγαλιείας* [*Study of the Sponge Fishery*], p. 40.

166 Carl Flegel wrote compellingly about this in *The Sponge-Fishery Issue* [*Το σπογγαλιευτικό ζήτημα*], pp. 208–209.

"free swimmers" assuaged their injured pride by vaunting their diving skills and their bravery in the face of unforeseeable dangers.[167] Moreover, in the world of divers, competition involved more than productivity alone, which naked divers took for granted. Experience, boldness, resourcefulness, physical stamina, and *"filotimo"* [sense of honour], determined everyone's place in the labour market, as well as in collective public opinion. *"Levendia"* [valiance] and *"palikaria"* [intrepidness] were, therefore, the key traits that formed the masculine identity of Kalymnian sponge fishermen.

4.2.2   Naked Sponge Divers' Disease

The disease of the naked sponge divers, also known as "Skevos Zervos disease", was described for the first time by the Kalymnian Professor of Medicine and politician, Skevos Georges Zervos (1875–1966), at the 2nd Panhellenic Medical Conference, held in Athens in May 1903.[168] This illness affected the skin of those diving without a suit, or "in their Adam suit". It was caused by a venomous worm belonging to the Phylum of Coelenterata, the "actinion", as Zervos named it, which lives near the root, or on the surface of sponges, or the "bubble". In a manuscript wherein M. Aublé recorded the testimonies of sponge fishermen from 1863–1866 he also described this phenomenon.[169] At points where the sponges contact divers' bodies, the actinion worm inflicts deep wounds or caused abscesses, itchiness, and a burning sensation along with a high fever. Despite the difficult and rather lengthy healing process – prolonged due to the lack of appropriate medication – the disease of the "sponge worm" was indeed curable, yet it plagued many naked divers for much too long and left deep scars on the skin.[170]

Zervos noted that naked divers were aware of the "worm", as they called it, and brought dried actinions back from their voyages, which they cut into small

---

167   On Kalymnian naked sponge divers see also Zappas, "Στον κάβο με τους γυμνούς σφουγγαράδες" [Tassos Zappas, "At the Cavo with the Naked Sponge Fishermen", *Athinaika Nea*], p. 3.

168   Skevos Zervos, "Η νόσος των γυμνών σπογγαλιέων" ["The Disease of Naked Sponge Fishermen"], paper presented at the *2nd Panhellenic Medical Conference*, Athens 1903. See also Giannis Th. Patellis, "Επιστημονική δράση" ["Scientific Action"], in "Αφιέρωμα στον Σκεύο Ζερβό", Καλυμνιακά Χρονικά ["Tribute to Skevos Zervos", *Kalymniaka Chronika*] 9 (1990), p. 25. In 1934, the Paris Academy of Medicine [*Académie de médecine de Paris*] named this condition "Skevos Zervos disease".

169   Figuier, *Les merveilles de la science, p. 626.*

170   The actinion was also later became known to Fernez divers, hence following WWII, they began wearing protective clothing. See Faneromeni Chalkidiou-Skylla, Ή σφουγγάρι ή τομάρι [*Either Sponge or Corpse*], p. 271.

pieces and used as poison for household pests.[171] Naked divers were also aware of the consequences of contact with actinions, especially in August, when they were at their most venomous, but the divers had no choice but to continue fishing.[172]

> Of all the damage there is one
> that causes great misfortune,
> they call it Filth. It has its root
> sunk deep under some sponges.
> If it's uprooted whole, intact,
> it's harmless but if crushed
> and touched or badly handled,
> not even linseed oil and flax
> will offer an easy cure.[173]

Skevos Zervos included another marine organism in the same category as the actinion, namely a sea anemone that lives on rocky sea bottoms. On contacting the naked diver's body, the *"agriomaloupa"* [algae], as they call it on Kalymnos, causes symptoms like those caused by the actinion, the most frequent being a burning sensation, skin redness and, more rarely, chills, and nausea. These symptoms, despite the discomfort they caused the divers for a few days, would go away without medication.[174]

These afflictions from marine organisms aside, all divers, as well as all of those cleaning the catch aboard the vessels, suffered from the milky substance inside the sponges. Always working with their bare hands, they developed blisters, and their hands became swollen and painful; these blisters were referred to as "blacks", and made the men's work more difficult.[175]

---

171   Zervos, "Η νόσος των γυμνών σπογγαλιέων" ["The Naked Divers' Disease"], pp. 1–6; Zervos, "Η νόσος των γυμνών σπογγαλιέων ή 'νόσος Σκεύου Γ. Ζερβού'", *Καλυμνιακά Χρονικά* ["The Sponge Divers' Disease or 'Skevos Zervos Disease'", *Kalymniaka Chronika*] 18 (2009), pp. 241–247.

172   Although we do not have specific data on the number of affected divers at our disposal, dozens of men were reportedly affected. See Zervos, *Η νόσος των γυμνών σπογγαλιέων* [*The Naked Divers Disease*], p. 3; Zervos, "Η νόσος των γυμνών σπογγαλιέων ή 'νόσος Σκεύου Γ. Ζερβού'" ["The Sponge Divers' Disease or 'Skevos Zervos Disease'"], p. 247.

173   Μητροφάνης Καλαφατάς, "Χειμερινός Όνειρος" [Mitrophanis Kalafatas, "Winter Dream"] in Michael N. Kalafatas, *The Bellstone: The Greek Sponge Divers of the Aegean. One American's Journey Home.* Hannover: Brandeis University Press, 2003, pp. 249–250.

174   Skevos Zervos, *Les anemones de la mer dans la pathologie de l'homme, L'Hellenopolype,* Paris 1937.

175   Testimony of diver Thrasyvo(u)los Politis to E.O., 18/8/2004.

4.2.3   *Decompression Sickness or Diver's Disease: the Bends*

The use of the scaphander diving suit resulted in a great many accidents. Some accidents were due to the bad condition of the equipment and the failure to maintain it properly. Air pumps were especially susceptible to breakdowns, or leakages in the hose supplying the diver with oxygen. Numerous accidents were a result of "unfortunate coincidences", negligence and human error, mostly that of the divers or the pilot [*kolaouzieris*] who was responsible for the "machine" and the divers.[176] Moreover, it was particularly dangerous when divers from different vessels were fishing for sponges in the same location but at different depths, as the divers risked tangling their air hoses.[177] The root cause of the majority of accidents, however, was a new disease, unknown until then, the "hit" [χτύπος, *"khtípos"*], as older sponge divers call it, referring to the "hit of the machine", that is, the scaphander diving suit.[178]

Under normal conditions, nitrogen in the air is inhaled and exhaled without negative consequences for the human body. During the descent, due to increased pressure,[179] all bodily tissues absorb nitrogen through the bloodstream. However, bodily tissues rich in lipids such as the tissue of the nervous system, retain nitrogen, and their capacity to do so is increased under pressure while the temperature of the water and the amount of time spent in the depths also play a role.

During the ascent, with the decrease in pressure, nitrogen follows the reverse path and circulates from the tissues into the bloodstream and is then exhaled. When a decrease in pressure takes place gradually and unhurriedly, the nitrogen dissolved in the bloodstream is converted into a gas and has the time to move to the lungs to be exhaled. However, if the ascent is abrupt, nitrogen is not only released into the lungs, but also into the entire circulatory system and the tissues through which it is absorbed and, as a result, the excess nitrogen expands and bubbles.

The type and gravity of the disease depend on the areas in the body where the bubbles form, as well as on their size and number. The symptoms of

---

176   Accidents due to the misplacement of machine parts during the daily check have also been reported. Testimony of *"balaristis"* Michalis Lampos to E.O., 29/7/2005. Testimony of machinist/engineer Nikolaos Sdregas to E.O., 30/8/2004.

177   Kalafatas, *The Bellstone*, p. 71.

178   According to testimonies, in the case of naked sponge divers, there was also a small number of accidents caused by the disease when they descended to greater depths. See also Chaviaras, "Συμαίων γυμνών σπογγαλιέων φρικτά επεισόδια" ["Horrible Accidents Suffered by Symiot Naked Sponge Divers"], pp. 285–293.

179   The pressure on the diver during descent is equal to the atmospheric pressure at sea level, i.e., one atmosphere (atm) plus the water pressure calculated as one atm per ten meters. For instance, in a depth of 30 meters, the diver sustains a total pressure of 4 atm.

diver's disease include fatigue, numbness, weakness and pain in the extremities, rashes, or oedemas (swelling) in the body, vertigo and nausea, difficult breathing, hallucinations, loss of consciousness, and so on. If the bubbles accumulate in the heart, the diver suffers thrombosis and dies almost instantly. Neurological symptoms result from bubbles forming in the brain or the spinal cord, and divers may suffer deadly brain embolisms, as well as partial or total limb paralysis that may be temporary or permanent.[180]

Cabirol, one of the first scaphander diving suit manufacturers, did not anticipate the fatal consequences of the suits' unrestricted use in great depths. In a publication in 1870, Cabirol pointed out that the diver should be in good physical condition, calm, sober, and fasted. Although he recommended a slow descent to the sea bottom to protect the diver's ears, he noted that the ascent could be performed swiftly, as long as the diver was not held back by physical obstructions. Divers needed only to close the oxygen control valve and let the suit inflate. Thus, Cabirol contended that diving was safe up to a depth of 50 meters.[181]

However, as noted in a Chapter 2, Auguste Denayrouze who, together with Benoit Rouqayrol, developed an improved version of the scaphander diving suit in 1864, entertained a different opinion. In his well-known manual, published in 1867, Denayrouze wrote that, in case of a malfunction in the air hose "a quantity of air, allowing the diver to breathe for 2–3 minutes, that is, the time he needs to resurface" remained.[182] This observation, nevertheless, referred to diving in relatively shallow depths. For those descending to depths of 30–50 meters, the manufacturer's instructions were clear: "By ascending very slowly, one avoids an abrupt transition to ambient pressure. Decompression runs smoothly with several stops along the way to the surface. If the diver disregards this precaution, he exposes himself to the danger of very serious

---

180   See Οστική νέκρωση της βραχιονίου κεφαλής εκ της νόσου των δυτών ή υπερβαρική οστεονέκρωση [*Avascular Necrosis of Humeral Head due to Diver's Disease, or Dysbaric Osteonecrosis*], an unpublished study by Konstantinos Nomikarios. See also Faith Warm, *Bitter Sea*, pp. 40–42; Kalafatas, *The Bellstone*, p. 14.

181   M. Cabirol, *Scaphandre, appareil de plongeur Cabirol*, Paris 1870, p. 9. Gustave Tallent referred to the use of scaphander diving suits in the construction of the Brooklyn Bridge, *Cloche à plongeur et scaphandre*, Melun 1899, p. 12. David McCullough offered a very vivid description of the symptoms of the disease from which the divers working there suffered in his book *The Great Bridge. The Epic Story of the Building of the Brooklyn Bridge*, New York 1972. Washington Roebling, engineer of the bridge, also suffered from the disease, which left him paralyzed until the end of his life in 1926.

182   Auguste Denayrouze, *Manuel du matelot plongeur, et instructions sur l'appareil plongeur Rouquayrol-Denayrouze, basse pression*, Paris 1867, p. 40. See also section "Diving apparatuses: Scaphander diving suit, Fernez, narghiles".

accidents, on which his life may depend". Denayrouze advised divers to resurface at a rate of 1–2 meters per minute, estimating the total ascent duration at 20–40 minutes for a depth of 20 to 40 meters.[183] And while the manual was supposedly translated into Greek in 1870, we were unable to confirm the existence of the Greek version. However, one might imagine that its distribution must have been extremely limited – if it reached the Dodecanese – and that the divers themselves had no knowledge whatsoever of its contents.

Still other problems accompanied the rapid developments and direct exploitation of the scaphander diving suit, right from its introduction. Despite the excessive enthusiasm of British and French scientists for the conquest of the bottom of the seas and the practical implementation of diving apparatuses, it soon became obvious that, along with the advantages of their material achievements, they would have to face their adverse effects. Without questioning the validity of science and technology, British and French scientists admitted that greater depths and compressed air caused detriment to the human body. Be that as it may, they did make a point of expressing their own biases, which included decrying the divers' ignorance, mistrust, and lack of discipline; Greek doctors' complete or partial lack of knowledge; the overall inferiority of the Archipelago populations that used the scaphander diving suits in the sponge fishery. While not taking entire responsibility for the accidents, the authors of several texts written after the publication Denayrouze's – just as scaphander diving suits were being introduced into sponge-fishing populations – expressed their alarm about paralysis in divers' lower extremities and their deaths.[184]

In 1868, Alfred Le Roy de Méricourt, Professor of Naval Medicine, published a study in which he linked diver's serious, peculiar accidents to compressed air at 5 or 6 atm, where divers worked in depths of 45–65 meters. Méricourt, as well as all those interested in this topic at the time, relied on a hand-written report by M. Aublé, the commercial agent on Rhodes for the Rouqayrol-Denayrouze scaphander diving suits.[185] Aublé's observations, albeit casting the company he represented in a favourable light, are extremely interesting. Writing in 1867, Aublé claimed that, with a slow ascent, divers using the Rouqayrol-Denayrouze apparatus could work safely in depths of up to 35 meters, for approximately two and a half hours per day. In that same year however, of 24 divers working with 12 English-made scaphander diving suits, 10 died, reportedly because they

183   Denayrouze, *Manuel du matelot plongeur*, pp. 42–43.
184   See also the literature of the period from 1881–19 on diver's disease in *The Great Greek Encyclopedia* [Μεγάλη Ελληνική Εγκυκλοπαίδεια], entry "Αεραιμία", vol. A, p. 671.
185   Méricourt, *Considérations sur l'hygiène*, p. 275 et seq.

descended to depths of 45–54 meters.[186] Despite reservations concerning the English scaphander diving suits' quality and, in Aublé opinion, the locals' inability to provide sufficient information, he did indeed point out that diver's disease was quite a serious issue. Three of divers in the group just noted died instantly, while the remaining seven were paralysed from the waist down and survived only one to three months.

Assuming that paraplegia and death were caused by internal bleeding, Méricourt concluded that the bleeding originated from the inhalation of compressed air, and the dissolution of highly pressurized gas in the diver's body, due to an unstable oxygen supply or to an abrupt ascent to the surface. However, according to Méricourt himself, naked divers were not at risk because they descended in apnea and stayed down for a very short period only.[187] In his publication, Méricourt also made various suggestions concerning the age, the health, and the diet of the divers. He insisted, however, that divers should strictly observe the time restrictions of their stay at the bottom of the sea that corresponded to the depth of the dive: two hours in 30 meters, with time being decreased as the depth increases. Decompression should last one minute per meter.[188]

This unusual disease and its clinical symptoms were unknown until they were addressed in a publication by French physician, biologist and physiologist Paul Bert in *La Pression barométrique* (1879).[189] In this famous study, Bert documented the impact of changes in atmospheric pressure on various living organisms and he was the first to conceptualize decompression. Based on the observations of young physician Alphonse Gal, who traveled throughout the Aegean in 1868, and catalogued symptoms of afflicted divers for his doctoral thesis,[190] Bert identified problems caused by inhaling pressurized nitrogen in humans. According to Bert, the root of the problem lay in the diver's abrupt ascension, which led to excessive nitrogen concentration which formed bubbles that could damage the nervous system and obstruct the circulation of blood. To avoid these symptoms, he proposed that divers ascend slowly to the

---

186   Méricourt, *Considérations sur l'hygiène*, p. 280.
187   Ibid., pp. 282–284.
188   Ibid., pp. 285–286.
189   Paul Bert, *La pression barométrique. Recherches de Physiologie Expérimentale*, Paris 1879 [*Barometric Pressure: Research in Experimental Physiology*, 1943] and Leon Sonrel, *Le fond de la mer*. Paris, 1880 : pp. 193–194. Sonrel considered that for a diver to safely ascend to the surface, he must cover two meters per minute.
190   Alphonse Gal, "Des dangers du travail dans l'air comprimé et des moyens de les prévenir", Montpellier 1872 (doctoral thesis).

surface and, in cases where symptoms had already manifested, Bert recommended the diver's "decompression" in a special chamber.[191]

European scientists had been familiar with the disease since 1879, and Greek physicians were not far behind in describing it, particularly since they had also observed the achievements of their European colleagues and had, more importantly, direct contact with the field under observation. Thus, in 1871, physician N. Lampadarios published a study of four cases of diver paraplegia cured by means of electrotherapy in scientific journal *Asclepius* [*Ασκληπιός*]. In 1881, moreover, I. Tetsis published a study in Paris under the title, *The Island of Hydra and Divers Diseases*, in which he presented manifestations of the disease in four progressive stages: transitory cerebrovascular events, paraplegia, bleeding that may lead to death, or a comatose state, which always results in death.[192]

N. Katsaras, Symiot Professor of Neurology at the University of Athens, also pointed out the dangers of diving, beginning in the late 19th century.[193] Having studied 62 patient cases on Symi, he described various forms of the disease, and recommended measures that divers could take to avoid it; among these measures he recommended limiting time spent at the bottom of the sea in proportion to depth, and slow, gradual ascension.[194]

In 1901, Anakreon Stamatiadis, physician and Senior Medical Officer of Samos, likewise described the causes and symptoms of diver's disease: "oxygen poisoning, high pressure, rushed decompression that causes deafness and loss of balance due to bleeding in the brain, spasms, paraplegia, and multiple bleedings. These are some of the symptoms caused by the abuse of the scaphander diving suit".[195] The work of the above-mentioned physicians was, however, of a descriptive nature and they do not seem to have been aware of the embolism that nitrogen causes. Had they been aware of it, these physicians may well have been able to propose treatments.

Although there were many knowledge gaps in work on the disease in the past, it is perfectly clear that it was a known problem. Indeed, in a report from

191   Bert, *La pression barométrique*, pp. 408–426. Faith Warm also refers to his study, *Bitter Sea*, pp. 40–41.

192   *L'Île d'Hydra et les maladies des plongeurs*, cited in The *Great Greek Encyclopedia* [*Μεγάλη Ελληνική Εγκυκλοπαίδεια*], vol. A, Athens 1926, pp. 671–672, entry "*αεραιμία*".

193   See M. Catsaras, *Les hematomyelies des pêcheurs d'éponges de l'Archipel*, Paris 1888; by the same author, "Recherches cliniques et expérimentales sur les accidents survenant par l'emploie des scaphandres", *Archives de Neurologie* 17/49–51 (1889), pp. 392–437. See also Flegel, *Η νήσος Κάλυμνος* [*The Island of Kalymnos*], p. 31; Kriezis, *Η σπογγαλιεία* [*The Sponge Fishery*], pp. 11–12.

194   Carl Flegel, "The Abuse of the Scaphander in the Sponge Fisheries", *Bulletin of the Bureau of Fisheries* 28 (1908), Washington 1910, p. 521.

195   Published in Flegel, *La question des pêcheurs d'éponges*, p. 10.

1900, the captain of the troopship *Crete*, a vessel supervising Greek sponge fishermen along the coasts of Northern Africa,[196] had already begun calling it a "special disease", and "divers' paralysis".[197] In 1903, The Greek Ministry of Marine Affairs published clear instructions for those working in the sponge fishery with scaphander diving suits, and sponge fishermen were required to comply with specified working hours. They were also required to follow a particular diet, observe a maximum depth limit of no more than 42 meters, with a maximum stay of 10 minutes on the sea bottom, and guidance for hauling divers to the surface at a steady, rhythmic pace was also imposed.[198] Furthermore, in 1908, John Scott Haldane, Arthur Boycott and Guybon Damant published the first diving tables, which indicated the amount of time that divers needed to recuperate, depending on the depth and the duration of the dive.[199]

Unfortunately, there is little archival documentation in which the views of non-specialists, who lived in the environment and witnessed the consequences of the "machine," are expressed. Neither do we have at our disposal late 19th- and early 20th-century records of popular beliefs about the disease, its causes, and symptoms. The voices recorded in available documentation vaguely blame the "guillotine machine" for all their tribulations, including, among other things, the great number of deceased and paralysed divers. However, various pieces of information and descriptions have survived in texts written by Carl Flegel, the most vocal polemical scholar of the period. In 1896 Flegel wrote that:

> In depths greater than 16, or up to 30 or 40 fathoms, where [the diver] is currently forced to descend for sponges, the air pumped to the diver by the scaphander machine, is compressed to compensate for water pressure, [which is heavier than atmospheric pressure at the surface]. The water pressure hermetically tightens the rubber garment against the flesh

---

196   In the early 20th century, it appears that sponge fishing off the coasts of Africa had evolved into an organized form, at least for the sponge-fishing populations of the Greek state, and accidents had taken a dramatic upward turn. Following a recommendation by the Consul in Tripoli, the Greek troopship *Crete* cruised the coasts of the area, to inform the divers about the diving guidelines and to assist sponge-fishing crews in every possible way. The vessel had a hospital on-board and was accompanied by two physicians. See *Εμπρός [Empros]*, 26/2/1900, p. 3; 21/3/1900, p. 3; 21/2/1901, p. 3; 25/3/1901, p. 3; 6/4/1901, p. 3; 12/5/1901, p. 2.

197   Report 28/5/1900, Embassy of Tripoli-Libya, Folder 6, Subfolder 9, 1890–1900, ΙΑΥΕ.

198   Zotos, *Report*, pp. 10–11.

199   A. E. Boycott, G. C. C. Damant, J. S. Haldane, "The Prevention of Compressed-air Illness", *The Journal of Hygiene* 8 (1908), pp. 343–443.

of the diver's lower extremities, constantly driving the blood towards the upper parts, the heart, and the head.

Flegel then writes that the diver experiences the symptoms of the disease only when he has resurfaced, and is back on the deck of the vessel, where "he is hit by a more or less severe, or even fatal, paralysis [...] due to the violent burst of the highly compressed air circulating in the veins".[200]

In a study published in 1886, Kalymnian lawyer Miltiadis Carabokyros, representative of the community of Kalymnos in Constantinople, attributed the divers' deaths and paralysis to the descent into great depths, where it was difficult or impossible to breathe, claiming that deaths amounted annually to 15% and paralysis to 18%.[201] Similar views are found in 19th- and early 20th-century literature, wherein great depths were considered, in vague terms, to be responsible for manifestations of the disease.[202]

The systematic observations of Alphonse Gal offer a clearer picture of diver's disease in the first years of the use of the scaphander diving suit, as well as interesting information on the remedies used by Kalymnian physicians. According to Gal, in 1867, 24 divers used the first 12 English-made scaphander diving suits bought in the Southern Aegean, in depths of up to 45 meters. They resurfaced in a very few minutes, and every diver was engaged in several dives per day. Ten of them suffered from a new, previously unknown sickness; three died instantly, and the remaining seven survived as paraplegics for a period of 1–3 months.[203] In 1868, scaphander diving suits multiplied; there were at least 10 of them on Kalymnos, manned by 30 divers. Two deaths and two paralyses occurred. In 1869, Kalymnos counted more than 15 scaphander diving suits and 45 divers working with them. Three deaths and three cases of paraplegia occurred.[204]

By way of illustration, the following is a description of one accident included in Gal's doctoral thesis:

200   C. Flegel, "Ἡ Α.Θ. Παναγιότης ὁ Οἰκουμενικός Πατριάρχης Ἄνθιμος" ["His All-Holiness Ecumenical Patriarch Anthimos"], p. 16 and Flegel, *Ἡ νήσος Κάλυμνος* [*The Island of Kalymnos*], pp. 30–31. By the same author, *The Abuse of the Scaphander*, pp. 518–519; also by the same author, *Τὸ σπογγαλιευτικό ζήτημα* [*The Sponge-Fishery Issue*], p. 210.

201   Carabokyro, *Étude sur la pêche des éponges*, pp. 9–10.

202   See also Léon Arnou, *Manuel de l'épicier. Produits alimentaires et conservés, denrées coloniales, boissons et spiritueux ... etc.*, Paris 1904, p. 437.

203   Bert, *La pression barométrique*, p. 412.

204   Ibid., p. 423.

On the 1st of July 1869, off the coast of Rhodes, Nikolaos Roditis, who had already been using a scaphander diving suit for 3 months, descended to a depth of 35 to 40 meters. Approximately one-half hour after his ascension, Roditis experienced extreme abdominal pain and was unable to move his legs. He was transferred to Rhodes, where they initially turned to a healer (a "charlatan"). The healer put the diver into a furnace to no avail. The pain in the abdomen was not alleviated, his body was covered in lesions, and he suffered from a complete paralysis of his lower extremities. He had been in agony for three days, when they called an Italian physician, who attempted by, means of medication and liniments, to treat the diver's paraplegia. He did not know, however, which was the most appropriate method of treatment. One month later, Roditis returned to Kalymnos, and was taken on as a patient by physician Antonios Pelekanos. This physician gave him sirop of lactic acid, quinine, old Cypriot wine, and light food. He cleaned the wounds with chamomile, and a bitter alcoholic beverage and flavoured wine. At intervals, he gave the patient a laxative with oil or powder from a plant, without achieving any improvement. The wounds kept spreading, while every afternoon he ran a fever. One month later, the pain and fever symptoms were eased, but the diver's paralysis saw no improvement.[205]

It seems, however, that concerns put forward by scientists – either in the form of clinical observations on work that was in its experimental stages at the time, or in the form of their first guidelines on diver's disease – did not reach those managing or working with diving apparatuses, or it fell on deaf ears. Until at least the end of the 1950s, divers continued to surface in a very few minutes from depths of over 50 or even 60 meters, using precisely the same equipment that had been in use for decades. Recalling the period from 1949 to 1955, Giannis Loulourgas recounted his experience working as a diver:

> We, the divers, knew that we shouldn't come back up so fast because the blood didn't have enough time to get to the legs. It took us two and a half to three minutes for 30 fathoms, and we believed that this was enough. Our patience ran thin, and we wanted to get back up to the surface.[206]

---

205   Gal also described symptoms of many cases during the period from 1869 to 1871. See also Bert, *La pression barométrique*, p. 421.
206   Testimony of diver Giannis Loulourgas to E.O., 23/8/2004.

On the other hand, many divers repeated the same rhyming couplet – Twelve fathoms and a handspan, and the machine gets you – thus reinforcing the knowledge that in such depths, for then-unknown reasons, the probability of being struck by the disease was far greater.

4.2.3.1   The Number of Victims

As noted above, there is no comprehensive data at our disposal concerning the number of Dodecanesian victims who suffered from diver's disease in the 19th, and the first half of the 20th centuries. "More than 15 men perished during summer due to the machines", wrote Themelis Kindynis in 1879.[207] A fierce opponent of sponge fishing with scaphander diving suit, Flegel noted that the victims of the scaphander diving suit amounted, in the 30 years of its use in Kalymnos sponge fishery, to at least 800 deceased and 200 suffering from severe paralysis, while almost all divers experienced light paralysis.[208] In contrast, the number of naked diving victims was equal to one out of 2,000 divers.[209] In a later study, Flegel emphasized that, from 1866 to 1915, 10,000 deaths and 20,000 paralyses occurred in cases where the scaphander diving suit was in use on the sponge-fishing islands of the Dodecanese, when in the same period naked diving accounted for only 10 victims.[210] In Flegel's well-known paper on the Mediterranean sponge-fishing issue, he wrote that annual mortality rates were as high as 20% and that, from 1866 to 1902, victims numbered 5,000 deceased and 2,000 paralysed.[211] According to other sources however, in the first years following the introduction of the scaphander diving suit, the annual number of deceased amounted to 100 for all of the Dodecanese sponge-fishing islands.[212] Whether these numbers were controversial, true or exaggerated,

---

207   Kindynis, *Η νήσος Κάλυμνος* [*The Island of Kalymnos*], pp. 24–26.
208   Flegel, C. "Η Α.Θ. Παναγιότης ο Οικουμενικός Πατριάρχης Άνθιμος" ["His All-Holiness Ecumenical Patriarch Anthimos"], p. 17. In another document he noted that the deaths amounted annually to 10%, and the victims suffering from permanent paralysis to 15%, whereas the rest of the divers were rendered "feeble"; Flegel, C. *Η νήσος Κάλυμνος* [*The Island of Kalymnos*], p. 32.
209   Flegel, C. "Η Α.Θ. Παναγιότης ο Οικουμενικός Πατριάρχης Άνθιμος" ["His All-Holiness Ecumenical Patriarch Anthimos"], pp. 19–20.
210   Flegel, C. "Η Α.Θ. Παναγιότης ο Οικουμενικός Πατριάρχης Άνθιμος" ["His All-Holiness Ecumenical Patriarch Anthimos"], p. 17 and Chatzidakis, "Ο αγώνας για την κατάργηση των σκαφάντρων" ["The Fight to Abolish the Scaphander Diving Suit"], p. 32. G. Georgas replicated these figures in his own study. See Georgas, *Μελέτη περί σπογγαλιείας* [*Study of the Sponge Fishery*], pp. 39–40.
211   Flegel, C. *Το σπογγαλιευτικό ζήτημα* [*The Sponge-Fishing Issue*], p. 211.
212   Billiri, N. *Σφουγγαράδες από την Κάλυμνο* [*Sponge Fishermen from Kalymnos*], p. 12.

contemporary and subsequent sources reproduced the figures of victims delivered largely by Flegel, due to the lack of any further relevant sources.[213]

The fact that sponge fishermen embraced the occupational hazards; the absence of social welfare in any form; the solidarity among captains; as well as the divers' fear that they would not be recruited again, reduced complaints and grievances to zero, even in more recent years. Archival evidence is typically unclear or silent on this issue; the information that can be deduced from documents on living conditions aboard vessels, diseases and accidents is minimal. The wording of the scant Kalymnian archival evidence from the 19th and 20th centuries does not permit us to infer whether the "sickness" or "malaise" of crew members was related to divers' disease in each case. It was certain, however, that after divers had recuperated from a "malaise" they were required to work again; otherwise, they would have to return the advance payment [*plakia*] received.[214]

The causes of death also remained vague, as may be deduced from archival evidence. In one declaration, captain P. Paraskevas stated that, "on 28 May [1930], Wednesday, at 3.30 PM, diver Athanasios Limnios passed away on the bank of Lampedusa, having worked at a depth of 25 fathoms for 4 minutes. Forty minutes after having resurfaced, he had some sort of blackout and died on the spot, without experiencing symptoms or pain".[215]

The official documents of community authorities do not make specific mention of diver injuries or deaths, unless there were pending personal items to return, or claims made on behalf of the families, in accordance with the Sponge-Fishing Regulation. Such was the case of machine-diver Georgios Sperlas of Hydra, who died during a winter trip in 1896, while working on a Kalymnian vessel. The report of the Elders' Council is limited to a mere log entry concerning the diver's very few personal items, namely a ring and some used clothing.[216] Two years earlier, in October of 1894, Kalymnian diver Georgios Oikonomidis (or Oikonomou), was recruited for a period of four months aboard the vessel of Filippos Mastrogiannis of Hydra. The agreement was

---

213   The fragmentary nature of relevant archival evidence is also typical. Various public and government services and consulates, as well as the press, drew up or published accounts and reports of victims of the disease at the beginning of the 20th century, focusing on either the areas under their jurisdiction, or only on the citizens of the states they represented. The cases of Dodecanesian divers were logged only when the captain called at the Greek consular authorities, or if the divers worked on vessels flying the Greek flag.

214   Doc. 169, 25/10/1910, AC Proceedings 1910, MAK; Doc. 132, 6/10/1911, AC Proceedings 1910–1912, MAK.

215   Declaration, 19/6/1930, Embassy of Tripoli-Libya, Folder 36 (1930), Subfolder 6, IAYE.

216   Doc. 30, 21/1/1897, AC Proceedings 1896–1897, MAK.

official and was concluded in writing before the consular authorities in Tripoli, Libya. In his report of an afflicted diver to the Greek Vice-Consul D. Foros, the captain wrote that,

> unfortunately, as soon as he got to work, the sponge-machine made him sick. Given that it was impossible to treat him aboard the vessel, I was forced to accommodate him at a hotel owned by the Kostalas Bros and take all necessary measures in terms of physicians and appropriate medication; his four-month care and treatment cost me 635.90 francs.

In the spring of 1895, when the diver had recovered, he resumed work with the same captain because, in addition to the sum of money mentioned above, he owed the *platika* of 838.55 francs that he received on signing the agreement. In the end, the diver appears to have hidden on a French steamship and fled to Sfax, Tunisia.[217] More importantly however, the surviving details from this report provide an explicit description of the employment regime, rights, obligations, and some predominant practices in the sponge-fishing business sector.

At the beginning of the Italian occupation, when things had apparently changed, the Mayor of Kalymnos had not yet been informed as to the new administrative regime's intentions. Hence in 1913, he wrote to the Mayor of Tripoli, Libya, explaining that he had received a letter in which he was informed of the death of,

> our fellow citizen Nikolaos Tsikouris, who passed away, as we believe, and as you may be informed, because of the awful contraption of the scaphander diving suit. Being certain that the law provides for these unfortunate victims, and since the deceased left behind a young wife without any means of survival, we implore, your Excellency, to kindly inform us whether the diver's spouse will be able to obtain any legitimate compensation.[218]

However, it was left to the front pages of the early 20th-century Greek press to raise awareness of the issue and battle it out, as journalists deployed arguments and testimonies in favour of, or against, the scaphander diving suit.

---

217   Report of Filippos Mastrogiannis to Vice-Consul D. Foros, 17/3/1895, Embassy of Tripoli-Libya, Folder 6 (1890–1900), Subfolder 9, IAYE.

218   Doc. 30, 25/7/1913, Correspondence 1910–1913, MAK. Given that even these documents are rare, are we to assume that earned wages were paid in an orderly fashion, and that any disputes were settled orally with no further mutual accusations?

Journalists took up the cause of many parties concerned about the political tension surrounding the Turkish government's ban on the suit in 1902, along with that of one political sector that wanted to resume the use of the machine.[219] Opponents of the scaphander diving suit insisted that there 200–300 victims created annually among divers off the coasts of Africa. More specifically, in 1902, there were 150 deaths among divers on vessels from Hydra, and 40 deaths on vessels from Aegina.[220] In 1905, there were only 8 deaths, however the fact that fatalities occurring on sponge-fishing vessels working outside the area under the supervision of troopship *Crete* were not recorded, accounts for the low number.[221] In 1906, there were 6 deceased divers holding Greek citizenship in the maritime area of Libya, and 4 who suffered paralysis, according to a report written by lieutenant commander Aggelis', captain of troopship *Crete*.[222] At the same time however, others argued that there were hazards involved in every means of earning a "livelihood",[223] or that "no more than 35–40 out of a total of 500–700 divers passed away, and that the reasons for their deaths could gradually be eliminated through governmental intervention and care".[224] Accidents could moreover, be attributed to various causes and the editor of *Empros* newspaper suggested that,

> the recruitment of apprentice divers is completely unsupervised, and no supervision whatsoever is possible as long as there are no relevant provisions or laws. Each year, approximately 100 new apprentice (novice) divers are recruited, many of whom are culled from those who haunt the dives of Piraeus, or life's castaways, suffering from various diseases, in the worst possible condition and physically incapable of coping with the risks of the job. Hence, captains avoid these novices and prefer those who come from rural areas, who can easily adjust and endure sever conditions;

---

219 *Εμπρός* [*Empros*], 30/3/1903, p. 4. The government under Zaimis was favourable to the free use of the scaphander diving suit; its prohibition was a result of mishandled operations of the government under Deligiannis. On the other hand, in a Parliamentary speech Prime Minister D. Rallis announced that "we cannot let our fellow citizens suffer horrible deaths on the bottom of the sea", *Εμπρός* [*Empros*], 3/7/1903, p. 2.

220 *Εστία* [*Estia*], 8/4/1903, p. 1. The losses of Dodecanesian divers did not figure in the Greek press of at that time.

221 *Εμπρός* [*Empros*], 20/10/1905, p. 2.

222 *Εμπρός* [*Empros*], 25/6/1906, p. 3.

223 *Άστυ* [*Asty*], 16/4/1903, p. 1.

224 D. A. Panagos, "Οι σπογγαλιείς μας. Τα κακουργήματά των μύθοι. Μία απάντησις εις την Εστίαν" ["Our Sponge Fishermen. Legends of their Crimes. An Answer to the Newspaper *Estia*"], *Εμπρός* [*Empros*], 15/4/1903, p. 3.

thus, they are much sought-after and are able to secure higher advance payments.[225]

Lieutenant commander P. Zotos, captain of troopship *Crete*, which supervised the sponge-fishing activity off the African coasts on behalf of the Greek government in 1903, insisted that there were 100 deaths annually, and that almost all divers suffered from some form of paralysis to the lower extremities at the end of the sponge-fishing season.[226]

Other articles in the popular press attempted to polish the scaphander's tarnished image, by reminding readers that the number of fatalities and injuries was low when compared with the number of men employed aboard the vessels. In fact, it was argued, in a group of 117 divers working from 1922–1923, only two fatal accidents and three mild instances of paralysis were reported and, in 1923–1925, five deaths of sponge divers were reported in the area around Libya. Disputes as to whether some divers' deaths were the result of other diseases with similar symptoms, and not from the diver's disease, were also not uncommon.[227] In 1927, there were another five deaths reported in the same maritime area, despite the insistence of those who wrote the reports that local authorities were not informed of a large number of deaths because sponge fishing was conducted far from the shore.[228] In 1929, physician and president of the community of Hydra, A. Lignos pointed out that "the accidents among divers working from Hydra's engine-driven caiques are ten times fewer than accidents related to the use of compressed air for work in the Seine, and fewer by ⅓ than accidents that occur at Le Havre, France".[229]

In the 1930s, the number of victims among the total number of sponge divers who were Greek citizens did not exceed 3%.[230] More systematic data are available for the maritime area of Libya thanks to reports drawn up by the Greek consular authorities. Specifically, in 1949, of a total of 518 active divers,

---

225 D. A. Panagos, "Our Sponge Fishermen. Legends of their Crimes. An Answer to the News-paper *Estia*", *Empros*, 15/4/1903, p. 3

226 Zotos, *Report*, pp. 10–11. "It is obvious that part of the political sphere accused the captain of troopship *Crete* of biases in favour of the divers, and of arbitrarily prohibiting the use of scaphander diving suits in the area under his supervision". *Εμπρός* [*Empros*] 3/7/1903, p. 3.

227 Embassy of Tripoli-Libya, Folder 29 (1923–1924), Subfolder 17 and Folder 32 (1925–1928), Subfolder 1, ΙΑΥΕ.

228 Embassy of Tripoli-Libya, Folder 33 (1926–1927), Subfolder 10, Folder 34 (1927–1929), Subfolder 1, ΙΑΥΕ.

229 Document of A. Lignos, dated 22/12/1929, in reply to a circular of the Ministry for National Economy of 23/10/1929. See Theodoros A. Kriezis, "Η σπογγαλιεία", *Οικονομικός Ταχυδρόμος* ["Sponge Fishing", *Oikonomikos Tachydromos*], 14/8/1932, p. 3.

230 *Οικονομικός Ταχυδρόμος* [*Oikonomikos Tachydromos*], 31/5/1937, p. 1.

12 were afflicted with the disease, and another 9 died, and all of those who died were Kalymnian. In 1950, of a total of 777 divers, there were 6 deaths, and 4 cases of paralyses. In 1951, of a total of 554 divers there were 6 deaths, and 15 reported cases of paralyses and, in 1952, of 220 divers, there were 2 deaths and 5 cases of diver's disease.[231]

In the period from 1957 to 1965, the annual accident rate for Kalymnian divers ranged from 4% to 7%.[232] In 1947, there were 4 deaths and 5 cases total paralysis,[233] while in 1949 there were 18 deaths reported among Dodecanesian sponge fishermen.[234] Even from that time, however, logs are wanting: on the one hand, many divers did not have "maritime booklets", and were not entitled to compensation; on the other hand, reporting every accident meant the captain's automatic prosecution. It should also be noted that the existing figures were far lower than those set forth in the testimonies of old sponge fishermen who claimed that almost everyone "had been caught" in one dive or another, some experiencing a milder form of the disease, others more severe. One fisherman claimed that "every sponge was equal to one life, one young lad".[235] Another lamented that "accidents were not logged for many reasons. They didn't keep any books. The Port Authority should be the one to write them down, though. I remember about 30 deaths in the 20-year period from 1950 to 1970. From 1970 and onwards, we didn't have any deaths".[236]

Table 4.2, compiled from the logs of the Port Authority of Kalymnos showing the period from 1950 to 1970 is cited here, given that this the only period for which complete data are available. From 1970 to 1987, the number of divers was not recorded, while in 1983 the total number of victims of diver's disease is 6, plus one deceased.[237]

---

231 Embassy of Tripoli-Libya, Folder 45 (1947–1948), Subfolder 3 and Folder 46 (1952), Subfolder 4, IAYE.

232 Bernard Russell, "Η σπογγαλιεία της Καλύμνου", Σπουδαί ["The Sponge Fishery of Kalymnos", Spoudai] 1 (1970), pp. 3 and 23–24.

233 The data are taken from an article published in The National Herald of New York, 21/10/1948, p. 3; Georgios M. Sakellaridis, "Η Ελληνική Επαρχία. Η σπογγαλιεία εις την Κάλυμνον", Καλυμνιακά Χρονικά ["Rural Greece: Sponge Fishery on Kalymnos", Kalymniaka Chronika] 6 (1986), pp. 207–208.

234 N. S. Pizanias, "Διά την ανασυγκρότησιν της σπογγαλιείας της Δωδεκανήσου" ["For the Reconstruction of the Dodecanese Sponge Fishery"], Rhodes 1950, p. 7.

235 Manuscript 2729/1976, Angeliki Georgiadou, p. 54, CFS.

236 Testimony of Lefteris Maouzelos to E.O., 3/9/2004.

237 The numbers provided in various sources from that time do not completely concur with one another. See tables published in Russell, "The Sponge Fishery of Kalymnos", pp. 3 and 23–24, which refer to the period from 1957 to 1965. See also Roxane Caftanzoglou, "Kalymnos: "Contribution à la connaissance d'une société", Mémoire de Maîtrise d'Ethnologie Spécialisée" (unpublished MA thesis), Paris 1978, p. 11; Dimitrios Geroukalis,

TABLE 4.2   The Kalymnian sponge fishery and diver's disease, 1950–1970

Year	Number of Divers	Victims of divers' disease	Deaths
1950	513	15	0*
1951	429	12	3
1952	409	12	8
1953	305	7	1
1954	386	9	2**
1955	409	10	2
1956	342	10	1
1957	386	11	6***
1958	384	12	2
1959	351	8	0
1960	279	11	1
1961	247	7	1
1962	240	7	1
1963	257	7	3
1964	235	8	1
1965	197	9	6
1966	94	3	0
1967	229	6	1
1968	199	7	1
1969	250	3	1
1970	–	–	–

Observations

*   In contrast, an anonymous journalist for newspaper *I Machi* [*Η Μάχη*] estimated that there were 12 deaths in 1950. See Dodecanisios, "Η σπογγαλιεία έχει εγκαταλειφθεί" ["The Sponge Fishery Has Been Abandoned"], *I Machi*, 25/3/1950, p. 6.

**   In 1954, a total of 11 accidents were attributed to the entire population of Greek sponge fishermen (*Οικονομικός Ταχυδρόμος* [*Oikonomikos Tachydromos*], 6/1/1955, p. 12), while the data in our table show that there were only 11 accidents in the sponge fishery of Kalymnos.

***   According to data retrieved from the Association of Captains of Sponge Fishermen of Kalymnos, in 1957 there were 7 deaths and 15 cases of paralysis.

SOURCE: LOGS OF THE PORT AUTHORITY OF KALYMNOS

"Φαινομενολογία, προφίλ προσωπικότητας των δυτών και κλινική εικόνα της νόσου των δυτών υπό το πρίσμα της θεωρίας των καταστροφών", *Καλυμνιακά Χρονικά* ["Phenomenology: Divers' Personality Profiles and Clinical Picture of the Divers' Disease in the scope of Catastrophe Theory", *Kalymniaka Chronika*] 9 (1990), pp. 392–393.

When compared with the respective data provided by the Association of Captains of Sponge Fishermen of Kalymnos for the period from 1957 to 1965, we discover substantial discrepancies in the table above. Rather than the 80 deaths and 21 paralyses recorded by the Port Authority, captains logged 28 deaths and 96 paralyses, for a total divergence of more than 38%.[238]

A comparison of the data in the Table 4.2 with data pertaining to the Greek sponge fishery in its entirety in Table 4.3, albeit interesting, cannot be used in a comprehensive manner because the data in this case is fragmentary, and from the popular press rather than official sources. The information gathered from these sources is included in the following table.

TABLE 4.3   The Greek sponge fishery and diver's disease, 1950–1970

Year	Number of divers	Victims of the divers' disease	Deaths
1950		3	8[a]
1951			
1952		6	2[b]
1953			
1954	885	25	5[c]
1955	814	10	3[d]

Sources – Observations

a   *Αθηναϊκά Νέα* [*Athinaika Nea*], 30/12/1950, p. 6.

b   These figures concern only the Tripoli area. See lieutenant commander Em. A. Koutsikopoulos, sponge fishery supervisor, "Έκθεσις εν σχέσει με την διεξαγωγήν της σπογγαλιείας εις τα παράλια της Λιβύης κατά την θερινή περίοδον 1952" ["Report on the Undertaking of Sponge Fishery off the Coasts of Libya in the Summer Period of 1952"], 28/11/1952, Embassy of Tripoli-Libya, Folder 46 (1952), Subfolder 4. IATE.

c   *Οικονομικός Ταχυδρόμος* [*Oikonomikos Tachydromos*], 30/12/1954, p. 6. In other sources, the fatal cases numbered 7. See Ibid., 8/11/1956, p. 10.

d   Ibid., 8/11/1956., p. 10.

238   Roxane Caftanzoglou, "Kalymnos", p. 11. There are, however, discrepancies between our data and those presented by Émile Kolodny, which are based on records kept by B. Russell and the Port Authority. More specifically, Kolodny notes 24 deaths and 106 cases of paralysis from 1950 to 1959, and 14 deaths and 65 cases of paralysis from 1960 to 1968. Émile Y. Kolodny, *La population des îles de la Grèce. Essai de géographie insulaire en Méditerranée orientale*, vol. 1, Aix-en-Provence 1974, p. 318.

TABLE 4.3   The Greek sponge fishery and diver's disease, 1950–1970 (*cont.*)

Year	Number of divers	Victims of the divers' disease	Deaths
1956	586	9	$-^e$
1957			
1958		–	$-^f$
1959			
1960			
1961			
1962	457		4^g
1963			
1964			
1965			
1966			
1967			
1968			
1969			1
1970			–

e   Ibid., 8/11/1956., p. 10.
f   Ibid., 18/09/1958., p. 10.
g   Ibid., 30/1/1964, p. 7.

4.2.3.2   Accidents Recorded in Regulations and Legislative Documents

Notwithstanding social pressure and the local authorities' constant allusions to the high number of victims of the sponge fishery, communal decrees on preventing and tackling accidents in the sponge-fishing Dodecanese islands, until their annexation by Greece, did not exist or have not survived. In any event, it is important to keep in mind that the number of afflicted men was particularly high given that, in its provisions, the Marine Sponge Fishery Regulation of 1884 included special stipulations on those affected (i.e., the deceased and paralyzed). According to article 23, deceased divers' heirs were entitled to all their shares, as well as to their earned profits. The heirs of the "mechanical diver" also received his regalo (Part B, article 1). The provisions for divers falling gravely ill were similar.

Moreover, the increased likelihood of accident resulted in the imposition of the following provision of the Sponge-Fishing Regulation, which attempted to limit the recruitment of "machine-divers" for winter voyages:

Diving machine captains recruiting an external mechanic for the winter sponge-fishing season without consulting the mechanic's captain or
investor [*"malsapis"*], become jointly responsible with his investor for
the repayment of the mechanical diver's debt to the latter's captain or
investor, if the concerned mechanic perishes, or falls ill in a manner that
renders him incapable to work. (Part B, Article 3)[239]

When the working conditions and accidents aboard sponge-fishing vessels
were made public and commented on in the early 20th-century Greek press,
local actors and politicians from Hydra, Aegina and Ermioni repeatedly
brought the topic to the Greek Parliament. To champion the use of scaphander
diving suits, most of them proposed that governments draw up an institutional framework for the industry. In the summer of 1902, under the pressure
of various circumstances, the government of Alexandros Zaimis dispatched
troopship *Crete* off the coasts of Northern Africa for a fourth year, in order to
supervise Greek sponge-fishing vessels, and provide rudimentary health care
for the diseased.[240]

In 1910, the government under Eleftherios Venizelos passed the first law
on sponge fishing with scaphander diving suits. The law's provisions indicate
that diver's disease was a major issue for Greek society at that time. The law
provided for the creation of diving schools on Hydra and Aegina and established a mandatory medical consultation prior to the recruitment of divers,
and the immediate declaration of accidents either to the captain of the naval
vessel supervising sponge-fishing vessels throughout the entire sponge-fishing
season, or to the closest consular authority. The authorities just noted were
responsible for the collection of the patient, who was to be hospitalized either
aboard the naval vessel, or in a local hospital. The law was intended as a general rationalization of the system by introducing sponge-fishing permits and
prerequisites for granting them. Other important issues were the provisions
determining the minimum number of divers that a vessel with scaphander
diving suits should have, based on the depths in which they worked. This regulation was directly linked to the disease because it was intended to protect

---

239   See also the reference to this article in similar decisions of the Elders' Council, Doc. 155,
      10/10/1911, MC Minutes 1910–1912, MAK.
240   In the following years, vessels "Paralos" and "Salamina" undertook similar missions. See
      Alexandras Dagkas, *Le mouvement social dans le Sud-Est européen pendant le XXième siècle:
      Questions de classe, questions de culture*, Thessaloniki 2008, p. 140.

divers working on deep-sea vessels [*vathytika*], by prescribing fewer dives and more resting time during the day (Article 10).[241]

The international legislation's provisions on occupational accidents were limited and imperfect during the inter-war period. The employee insurance or compensation for the diseased fell to businesses. Even though the issue is wider and extends far beyond our subject-matter here, the discussion seemed to focus on the concept of labour accidents, and concerned mainly the industry.[242] Greek sponge-fishing shipowners' obligation (to the authorities of Greece as well as to the authorities of the countries where the vessels were working), to guarantee double compensation to divers in the case of accident, led shipowners to petition the International Labour Organization and the Geneva Convention, requesting the elimination of this double guarantee. They advanced the argument that emigration was temporary, and that the families of sponge fishermen remained in Greece, hence Greek shipowners demanded that they pay the guarantee to the Greek state only.[243]

The provisions of Greek Law No 5525 of 1932[244] delt with divers' accidents in a similar way, however, foreign divers were exempted from the mandatory requirement to hold a certificate attesting to their competence (Article 3).[245] Moreover, the law forbade sponge fishing in depths of greater than 60 meters, abrupt ascents to the surface, and more than three dives per day. For the compensations envisaged in case of accident or death, compliance with the provisions of the law was a prerequisite (Articles 48 and 49).[246]

In 1937, the Greek 4th of August regime issued Emergency Law no. 560 on the sponge fishery.[247] It incorporated several points from previous laws, while offering more clarity on issues concerning accidents and victim compensation. It set the maximum diving depth at 35 fathoms (Article 24), while specifying the time spent on the sea bottom, and the duration of the ascent to the surface (Articles 21 and 24). It rectified Greek law No. 5525/1932, by granting

---

241   Law 3617/1910 on fishing with scaphander diving suits, *Government Gazette* (1910) vol. A. See also Theodoros Kriezis, "Η σπογγαλεία Β' Νομοθεσία ελληνικού κράτους", *Οικονομικός Ταχυδρόμος* ["The Sponge Fishery. The Second Legislation of the Greek State", *Oikonomikos Tachydromos*], 21/8/1932, p. 4.

242   See *Οικονομικός Ταχυδρόμος* [*Oikonomikos Tachydromos*], 14/8/1932, p. 1.

243   See *Οικονομικός Ταχυδρόμος* [*Oikonomikos Tachydromos*], 18/1/1926, p. 1.

244   The law was not applied, and this is acknowledged in the text of Emergency Law no. 60/1937.

245   Translator's note: Here, "foreign" probably refers mainly to Ottoman Greeks.

246   Law 5525/1932, *Government Gazette* (1932), vol. 1, nr. 187.

247   Emergency Law no. 560/1937 on sponge fishing, *Government Gazette* 26 March 1937, vol. A. See also *Αθηναϊκά Νέα* [*Athinaika Nea*], 9/4/1937, p. 4.

"those belonging to the Greek nation" and those who came from areas outside the limits of the Greek state the same sponge-fishing labour rights as Greek citizens. Considered "sea workers", divers were registered with the Seamen's Pension Fund [NAT] and were entitled to compensation in case of accidents that occurred during the dive. The amount of compensation depended on the contracted remuneration, the duration of work, and the severity of the accident (Articles 43–46). Lastly, captains and diving managers [*kolaouzieris*] who infringed on the regulations, either deliberately or because of negligence, were to be held legally accountable (Articles 48–50).

In areas under Italian occupation, the relevant legislation was clearer. The "Italian Union for Fishing and Selling Sponges in Libya" [*Sindacato Italiano per la pesca ed il commercio delle spugne in Libia*], founded in 1913, imposed medical checks aboard vessels, performed by physicians from local health offices, given that it was forbidden for paralyzed divers to work. Those divers able to present health certificates were exempted from local health services' examinations. This particular provision was withdrawn in the year that followed. Nevertheless, even while this provision was still in place, many captains reported to the authorities that some of the divers' they used had been previously paralyzed.[248] Later however, the Italian government's regulation did stipulate that captains were responsible for paying compensation for accidents suffered by divers who were recruited to work with scaphander diving suits.[249] Individual responsibility was deemed preferable to state responsibility, because it was thought that state intervention would "encourage captains' negligence, which could lead to a possible rise in accidents". Captains or investors deposited monies for compensation with the Port Authorities, who would then hand the money over to local authorities, to proceed with the compensation of families of afflicted divers. According to the special regulation, the Port Authority bore the responsibility for all sponge fishing-related issues, whereas the age limit for divers dropped from 50 to 45 years.[250]

Under Italian rule in 1922, a Sponge Fishermen Insurance Fund was founded in the Dodecanese that provided for the payment of compensation to divers in case of work-related accidents. The fund, which was governed by the Harbour Master of Rhodes, managed the capital that originated from the contributions of its 2,000 sponge fishermen who were members, as well as from fines on

---

248   Embassy of Tripoli-Libya, Folder 28, Subfolder 2, Benghazi Vice Consulate Archive, IAYE.
249   Report of Vice Consul in Tripoli to the Greek Ministry of Foreign Affairs (18/4/1914), Embassy of Tripoli-Libya, Folder 19 (1914), Subfolder 5, IAYE.
250   Report of Vice Consul in Tripoli I. Lampridis to L. Koromilas, Greek Ambassador in Rome (30/4/1914), Embassy of Tripoli-Libya, Folder 19 (1914), Subfolder 5, IAYE.

violations of sponge-fishery and sponge-trade practice. Beginning in 1923, as soon as they acquired a fishing permit in the Dodecanese and the rest of the Italian possessions, captains, shipowners, or investors in scaphander diving suits were required to pay to the Port Authority issuing their permit a one-year lump sum of 12,000 Italian liras for the entire crew, 4,000 of which was given as compensation to the family of every deceased diver. If no accident occurred, the sum was returned in full to the depositor. The decision included facilities for the payment of the sum, as well as guarantees and arrangements to supplement that sum should it prove insufficient. However, the sums were not fixed because, towards the end of Italian rule, compensation amounted to 2,000 liras in case of partial disability; 4,000 liras in case of total disability; and 1,000 liras was to be paid to the family of the victim in case of death. Captains had to pay similar compensations for the divers' medical and hospitalization expenses.[251]

More specifically, a legislative decree issued by the Italian government in 1923, which was sent by the Greek Vice-Consul in Libya, A. Avgerinos to his homologue in Sfax, determined the conditions with which one had to comply, should one wish to be granted a permit for sponge-fishing with the scaphander diving suit in Libyan waters:

> 1) to submit a crew list with detailed recruitment conditions to the Port Authority 2) to send the divers to the Health Service for a medical examination of their physical capacity; unfit divers will be rejected 3) to bring the diving machine and the rest of the gear to a competent public engineer for inspection 4) to be equipped with a first aid kit that shall always contain the medication and instruments specified for providing first aid aboard the ship 5) to procure a diary, where every incident or accident taking place in open sea is logged – even in Greek.

The same decree determined captains' responsibilities in case of accident, as follows:

> Should a diver fall ill, captains must bring him to the closest port and deliver him to a physician. If the physical damage inflicted on the victim is considered incurable, captains are subject to pay to the Port Authority

---

251   See Embassy of Tripoli-Libya, Folder 32 (1925–1928), Subfolder 1, ΙΑΥΕ. See also Δωδεκάνησος. Τετράτομος μελέτη του Υπουργείου Ανοικοδομήσεως και συνεργατών του υπό την διεύθυνσιν του κ. Κ. Α. Δοξιάδη Σειρά Εκδόσεων του Υπουργείου Ανοικοδομήσεως [Dodecanese. Study in four Volumes by the Ministry for Reconstruction Under Mr K. A. Doxiadis, Publication Series of Ministry for Reconstruction], Athens 1947, pp. 276–277.

the amount of 8,000 liras for the diver's compensation. If the diver dies, his family shall receive 4,000 liras. All this is executed in detail and, if need be, sponges shall be confiscated.

As Vice-Consul A. Avgerinos noted, "due to these measures, a drop in the number of victims equal to 80% was noted", and he concluded that this "suggests that nowhere else can afflicted divers find greater protection in their favour".[252]

One might perhaps agree with the author of the document just cited, had the author taken into consideration a series of affidavits from various sponge-fishing crew members who attempted to attest to the fact that their captains were not negligent or were not responsible for accidents. By way of illustration, two passages from numerous similar affidavits are cited below. These are statements made by divers, co-workers of victims, attesting that the key conditions of sponge-fishing labour – the number of dives, depth, duration of stay at the sea bottom – were complied with. In the first of these statements, diver Dimitrios Tarasis explained that:

> On the 17th of August [1926], on which day we were harvesting sponges off the coasts of Tripoli, deceased diver Sotirios Giannoulis performed the three standard dives at the standard depth of 24 fathoms, as was usual. On his third dive, however, at approximately a quarter to five o'clock in the afternoon, after spending only 16 minutes at the sea bottom, he was "hit"; they hauled him up on the deck, and he said, "I'm not feeling well". They then dropped him immediately into the sea to reoxygenate him; after bringing him back on deck, they started rubbing him. But he was too "hit", and he succumbed. The deceased was a good diver, in good health and with stamina, and we were all saddened by his death.[253]

A statement made by Kalymnian diver, Emmanouil Kleanthis Magklis, is similar:

> Deceased diver Sotirios Giannoulis was one of the best divers. I never heard him complain about his health, and he was always eager to work. On the 17th of August, on which day we were 3 miles from the coast of Tripoli, said diver performed his three regular dives. On his first two dives

---

252   Letter of A. Avgerinos, Vice-Consul in Libya to Greek Vice-Consulate B. in Sfax, 14/1/1924, Embassy of Tripoli-Libya, Folder 32 (1925–1928), Subfolder 1, IAYE.

253   An accident that took place aboard the vessel "Vassiliki" from Hydra in August 1926. See Embassy of Tripoli-Libya, Folder 33 (1926–1927), Subfolder 10, IAYE.

he didn't feel anything; on the third dive though, which took place at around 4:30 PM at a standard depth, namely 24 fathoms, and even though he didn't stay down longer than 16 minutes, he met his death. I saw the deceased diver before he went for his third dive, and he was very well, in a good mood and eager to work; therefore, the entire crew are wondering how he got sick and passed away, because he was a diver of great stamina and experienced in this job. I saw that, when they hauled him back up, they took care of him, and rubbed him following standard procedures, but he was too "hit" and he didn't make it.[254]

Given that these witnesses agreed that everything went by the book and followed standard procedure, and given that they offer virtually identical descriptions of the circumstances of the accident, the authorities concluded that these deaths were caused "by the labour involved in diving alone".[255] The report containing these findings thus came to the conclusion that the captain was not guilty of negligence and bore no responsibility, which meant that he only had to pay 14,000 liras to the family of the deceased. Although disputes, in other similar cases, on causes of divers' deaths were not uncommon,[256] crews did not make a practice of lodging complaints against captains and diving managers [*kolaouzierides*]. Was it fear, pressure, and threats, or did accidents indeed happen randomly? Despite the paucity of accident testimonies, it is perhaps worth noting that, in September of 1926, a few days after Sotirios Giannoulis' death, 8 divers and 8 sailors of the vessel "Vassiliki" refused to continue to work; as sources describe it, they "mutinied", and were sent to jail.[257]

Therefore, in spite of the intentions of the authors of these rules and regulations to create a framework of social welfare, the decrees remained vague and impracticable. When burdens were split between public organizations and investors in the undertakings, and when both were held accountable and supposedly brought to justice for any omissions or the dereliction of responsibility, very few of the victims had access to the fund, and were unable to claim any compensation, as is noted in several subsequent testimonies.

The spirit informing the Italian legislation appears to underpin the 1946 decisions of the Elders' Council of Kalymnos, concerning the "afflicted sponge

---

254   Embassy of Tripoli-Libya, Folder 33 (1926–1927), Subfolder 10, ΙΑΥΕ.
255   See the series of these statements; Embassy of Tripoli-Libya, Folder 33 (1926–1927), Subfolder 10, ΙΑΥΕ.
256   Embassy of Tripoli-Libya, Folder 32 (1925–1928), Subfolder 1, ΙΑΥΕ.
257   Embassy of Tripoli-Libya, Folder 33 (1926–1927), Subfolder 10, ΙΑΥΕ.

fishermen" of the summer and winter sponge-fishing period of that same year (i.e., 1946).

> 1) In the case of a diver's death while on duty, the employer must attribute to and pay the diver's heirs the equivalent of two rower's shares, plus one more rower's share as a means of compensation: a total of three rower's shares. 2) In cases of the entire paralysis of a diver's lower extremities, rendering him incapable to work, along with the two rower's shares to be paid to him, said diver shall also receive compensation equaling another two rowers' shares. 3) In case of partial paralysis, divers shall receive the two rowers' shares owing to him, plus one rower's share as compensation.[258]

The text continues, making specific mention of whether the victim is a *kopelli* [a diver who receives a bonus based on performance], a diver, or a member of auxiliary staff, without, however, examining the causes or holding anyone accountable.

Articles published in the press after wwii, by parties interested in the prospects of sponge-fishing, attributed the accidents to ill-informed crews, outdated equipment, unfit devices and air-pumps, inexperience, and so on. However, many accidents did take place, as our informants recalled, at the small island Nera, off the coast of Kalymnos, where the first trials concerning the scaphander suit were conducted immediately following the vessels' departure. Experienced divers, and novice divers [*atzamides*] especially, had much to relate concerning the incidents that caused them permanent disabilities.[259] Albeit not a cure-all, lawmakers and competent officials considered the establishment of specialized schools as a means of curbing ignorance and, therefore, accidents. It was only in 1956, however, that a school for divers was founded on Kalymnos to help familiarize those seeking work as divers or diving managers [*kolaouzieris*] with diving, and with using breathing devices.

---

258   See the logbook Sponge-fishing Permits 1932. Sponge-fishing Regulations 1946, Doc. n.n., 20/2/1946, MAK.

259   Testimony of captain Lefteris Mamouzelos to E.O., 3/9/2004. Testimony of *kolaouzieris*-captain Petros Marthas to E.O., 2/9/2004. Inexperience was considered one of the main factors leading to accidents. To decrease the number of accidents, attempts were made to exclude apprentice divers from sponge-fishing undertakings in the years following wwii. See proposals in Konstantinos Gourgiotis, "Όροι εργασίας εις την σπογγαλιείαν" ["Working Conditions in the Sponge Fishery"], *1st Panhellenic Sponge-Fishing Conference*, Rhodes, 24–27, February 1949. See also *Papers and Minutes*, General Administration of the Dodecanese, Rhodes 1951, pp. 80–81.

4.2.3.3   Empirical Means of Treating Disease

From the beginning of the 20th century, when divers surfaced, they would immediately remove the scaphander helmet while sitting on the deck and light a cigarette. This was a means of verifying if and how the diver's body was functioning: if the diver felt nauseous or dizzy, if his hand was shaking while holding the cigarette, or if the smell of the smoke he exhaled was strange, he was likely in the "grips of the machine".[260]

According to old sponge fishermen, along with the cigarette test the "machine's hit" could also be spotted instantly from bites, itchiness and rashes that appeared on the skin. If the diver had swollen patches, "black lumps", or blotches on his body, the sailors rubbed him with oil or onions until the marks disappeared.[261] In serious cases, when the diver's face turned black, they used a razor to make cuts on the skin and release the "killed" blood.[262] If the vessel was close to the shore, they sometimes transferred the diver to the beach and covered his whole body with hot sand. A crew member would then stay with him, under the blazing sun, until the suffering diver showed signs of improvement, or expired.[263] In the cases described by Professor of Neurology, Michael Katsaras, it seems that the only method for treating the disease on board at the end of the 19th century was to make the diver who had been "hit" drink oil in order to induce vomiting.[264]

---

260   On the "deathly" smell of cigarette smoke exhaled by divers who were "caught" or "hit by the machine", see also Faith Warm, *Bitter Sea*, p. 55; Faneromeni Chalkidiou-Skylla, Ἡ σφουγγάρι ἡ τομάρι [*Either Sponge or Corpse*], pp. 79–83. On the same topic, see the testimony of Spyros Kappos or Aeginitis, published in Εστία [*Estia*], 18/4/1903, pp. 1–2, as well as the testimony of an anonymous diver in Βήμα [*Vima*], 29/4/1962, p. 11, who remarked that "the cigarette was the diver's health thermometer. [...] If we accepted it and smoked it with pleasure, it meant that all was well. But if it made us sick, if we became dizzy, and if red dots appeared on our face or arms, it meant that we had been 'hit'". See also the testimony of diver Thrasyvoulos Politis to E.O., 18/8/2004.

261   Testimony of Nikolas Kampourakis, 23/7/2005, Michael Lampos, 29/7/2005, and of Dimitris Peros to E.O., 24/8/2004; Testimony of diver Thrasyvoulos Politis to E.O., 18/8/2004; Testimony of *kolaouzieris* captain Petros Marthas to E.O., 2/9/2004; Cheilas, Τὸ ἔπος των σφουγγαράδων [*The Epic Saga of Kalymnos' Sponge Fishermen*], pp. 210–211; Manuscript 1838/1973, Ευαγγελία Λαμπαδαρίου [*Evangelia Lampadariou*], p. 66, CFS. As orthopedic specialist K. Nomikarios explained, this was caused by the accumulation of nitrogen in adipose tissue. Testimony of Konstantinos Nomikarios to E.O., 31/8/2004.

262   This is what they called the accumulated blood that left marks on the skin, such as oedemas and bruises. See also the testimony of motorist Giorgos Kamarakis to Faneromeni Chalkidiou-Skylla, Ἡ σφουγγάρι ἡ τομάρι [*Either Sponge or Corpse*], p. 179.

263   Εστία [*Estia*], 20/4/1903, p. 2; Faith Warm, *Bitter Sea*, p. 56; Testimony of Dimitris Peros to E.O., 24/8/2004; Testimony of diver Giannis Magklis-Kavouras to Faneromeni Chalkidiou-Skylla, Ἡ σφουγγάρι ἡ τομάρι [*Either Sponge or Corpse*], p. 209.

264   Catsaras, "Recherches cliniques et expérimentales", pp. 392–432.

In his report, P. Zotos, commander of troopship *Crete* who was charged with providing medical care for the crews of sponge-fishing vessels, wrote that many of the divers suffering from mild paralyses thought that they "had a cold". They wore many clothes under the blazing sun and asked for ointments to treat their "cold" symptoms. Zotos added that the mildly paralyzed were so numerous that dragging one's leg was considered a sign of bravery or knowledge of the profession.[265]

From the beginning of the 20th century, it was observed that those who demonstrated a milder form of the disease, and who carried on diving, could indeed improve their physical condition.[266] At least since the 1920s, those "'caught' were doing oxygen", that is, using a practical method of decompression. This meant that affected divers had to wear the scaphander diving suit again, dive back in at once, and stay down on the sea bottom for a sufficient period of time. They began at a shallow depth, or descended to approximately the depth at which they felt ill, either alone or accompanied by another diver if they were unable move easily in the water.[267] Others insisted that they had to "have the oxygen" at 13 fathoms for a duration of 3 hours, thinking that greater depths would worsen the "hit".[268] This practical decompression method could be repeated, and could go on for about 14 hours in order to be successful, as suggested in more recent testimonies.[269] It has also been said that while using this method of decompression the diver could continue to fish, and therefore did not waste precious working time.[270] For those naked diving, or diving with the Fernez, it was difficult to remain on the sea bottom under these conditions.[271]

---

265   Zotos, *Report*, p. 19.
266   Zotos, *Report*, p. 19; Flegel, *The Abuse of the Scaphander*, p. 519.
267   The second diver was obviously connected to the air pump of a partner or nearby vessel.
268   They claimed that Italian divers taught them this technique, according to the testimony of captain Petros Marthas to E.O., 2/9/2004.
269   More on this in Russell, *Η σπογγαλιεία της Καλύμνου* [*The Sponge Fishery of Kalymnos*], pp. 26–27. The first person to put this method into practice by chance was diver Giannis Valis, according to Niki Billiri. Μπιλλήρη, *Η Κάλυμνός μας* [*Our Kalymnos*], pp. 29–30; Cheilas, Το έπος των σφουγγαράδων [*The Epic Saga of Kalymnos' Sponge Fishermen*], pp. 192–196; Kalafatas, *The Bellstone*, p. 17; Testimony of diver Giannis Koutouzis to E.O., 25/8/2003; Testimony of diver Dimitris Peros to E.O., 24/8/2004; Testimony of diver Giannis Loulourgas to E.O., 23/8/2004; Testimony of motorist Nikolaos Gourlas to Faneromeni Chalkidiou-Skylla, *Η σφουγγάρι ή τομάρι* [*Either Sponge or Corpse*], p. 176; Testimony of motorist Giorgos Kamarakis ibid., p. 180; Testimony of boat owner [*trechantinieris*], Ilias Mastoros, ibid. p. 236.
270   Testimony of orthopedic specialist Konstantinos Nomikarios to E.O., 31/8/2004.
271   Testimony of diving manager [*kolaouzieris*] Skevos Makris to Faneromeni Chalkidiou-Skylla, *Η σφουγγάρι ή τομάρι* [*Either Sponge or Corpse*], p. 183; Testimony of boat owner [*trechantinieris*], Ilias Mastoros, ibid., p. 236.

Moreover, if we take into consideration that each decompression using this method engaged the sole air pump of the vessel, it is not difficult to imagine the circumstances and conditions under which it was, or was not, carried out.

Lefteris Mamouzelos, who worked as a diving manager [*kolaouzieris*], recounted his experience, providing illuminating and important insights:

> Our caique was a deep-sea vessel; I worked at 40 fathoms and did a few *matzarolia* [turns of the hourglass], which meant that I had to dive more times. In the first week we let the divers do only a few *matzarolia* to see how they did. I never used a clock. One minute was equal to two *matzarolia*. If the diver went against the current of the sea, you had to reduce the *matzarolia*, because he risked getting "hit". We kept a close eye on the bubbles coming to the surface. Some divers used to move a lot and got tired against the sea current. Many times, those were the ones "hit". They were pig-headed, that's why. Some of them were not careful, tried to get more sponges, and untied the *kolaouzos* rope. On many occasions, the ones to blame were the diving managers [*kolaouzierides*].
>
> I knew the sea bottom like I knew my home, and I guided them from the deck. Many were clumsy; it's not like we were not to blame, but they weren't careful enough either. A diver could stay at the sea bottom for a single sponge. Other captains and diving managers [*kolaouzierides*] loved the *matzarolia*: they used to ease up on the *matzarolia*, they were man-eaters. As long as the diver asked for it, they would give him more time on the sea bottom. They shouldn't have let the divers do what they wanted, though; they should cut down the *matzarolia*, and only grant them to half of them, to keep the divers in good health. This was the most important goal when running divers: to make sure that the diver wouldn't get "caught" or, at least, wouldn't get gravely "caught". I have seen so many "hits" since I was 13 years old …
>
> When the diver resurfaced, the procedure was as follows: the man sat calmly on a stool to get undressed. He smoked a cigarette, and if it made him feel ill, he had been badly hit by the machine; that's how he saw if he was "caught". If the machine had gotten to him, when he took off his shirt, someone would look at his back, which should be white, and not directly under the sun for us to be able to see. If he had spots, he was "caught". At first, they would resuscitate the diver with water; they threw sea water on him, he got cold and then felt better. In mild cases we rubbed him too. We used to cut a big onion and rub it on the diver's back with oil. The onion absorbed the burning sensation. That's how they fished with the divers all day long. The divers were careful that any bruises or blotches on their

body wouldn't be seen because that was a sign that they were "hit". There were some divers who didn't inspect their bodies because they were too tired. The next time, however, they might not get away with it. When the diver understood that the rubbing didn't work, he had to do oxygen. Then, we dressed him immediately, and threw him into the sea. He would let the air blow the diving suit up, and then come to the surface like a bubble. One man would then jump into the sea, hug the affected diver and see how he was doing. If the pain and dizziness were gone, he yelled, and we hauled him back up. We called for help from other caiques, too.

If you saw that an afflicted diver received oxygen 3–4 times for two hours each time, and wasn't getting any better, that meant that you could give up on him. If the pain was severe both in front and at the back, and wouldn't go away, that meant that the diver wouldn't make it. If he was hit hard, he died when the sun set or rose; those were the hours that elapsed before morning. We did the oxygen at 20–25 fathoms, that's what we knew at the time. We're talking about the interwar years. We stopped at the depth at which the diver informed us that the pain went away. We used to leave him there for about an hour. And then he started a slow ascension, which lasted many hours. At 15 fathoms he did another oxygen. If he resurfaced and was still dizzy, we threw him back in.[272]

All these practical methods for treating divers "hit by the machine" demonstrate that, even if divers, diving managers [*kolaouzierides*] and their captains did not know or ignored the cause of the disease, they could treat or at least relieve its symptoms, based on common practices undertaken with the means at their disposal. That said however, improvements in the divers' health were, of course, also occasionally attributed to saintly miracles, especially if incidents coincided with any of the religious festivals that take place in the summer.[273]

Divers were also subject to a mandatory day-long fast which, according to oral reports, sometimes even included water[274] despite high temperatures, and this was yet another empirical means of treating the consequences of nitrogen accumulation in the body. Smoking, inspecting the skin, keeping the divers

---

272   Testimony of captain Lefteris Mamouzelos to E.O., 3/9/2004.
273   See also the testimony of *balaristis* Michalis Lampos to E.O., 29/7/2005.
274   Carl Flegel wrote that those suffering from the disease should not drink a single drop of water, even if they suffered from raging thirst. Flegel, "Η Α.Θ. Παναγιότης ο Οικουμενικός Πατριάρχης Άνθιμος" ["His All-Holiness Ecumenical Patriarch Anthimos"], p. 17. More recent testimonies concur that the "caught" should not drink even a single sip of water or coffee. See the testimony of diver Giannis Koutouzis to E.O., 25/8/2003.

warm, and most often immediately returning to the seafloor as a practical method of decompression could help with the diagnosis or limit the disease to its milder forms. These techniques, however, could not save those men whose spinal marrow or brains were affected, or those who died within a few minutes or hours. A long-standing familiarity with accidents evidently created an empirical tradition, whose practitioners however, continued to ignore, deliberately or through a lack of knowledge, the most important, albeit extremely injurious business, means of protection; namely, a gradual, slow ascent from great depths.

The health risks from lengthy dives at great depths – paralyses and sudden death – may well have been attributable to a lack of knowledge of decompression procedures, although these procedures do indeed appear to have been followed as required. Risk taking was, however, the only way to repay debts, and to generate profits for investors in the sponge fishery, as well as for those practicing it. Moreover, the time required for decompression, which necessitated a gradual, prolonged ascent to surface, would have been an impossible luxury for sponge-fishing vessels equipped with just one breathing device, one scaphander helmet, and two suits at most.[275]

Stories of these darkest moments in the history sponge fishing tell of the just and the unjust, the innocent and the guilty alike. The literature on sponge fishing recounts labour and social conflict, while dramatically demarcating the "old" from the "new" era, and fingering ostensible culprits in vague, past-tense accounts. Captains' narratives include supposedly typical expressions such as, "that was his fate", "watch, listen, and don't speak", or "old captains used to say, 'That's the job, what can you do about it?'". One also hears accounts that begin with "back then, when ships carried crews of 15, two out of five of the divers got 'caught', whether mildly or severely. Most accidents were due to the diving manager [*kolaouzieris*] messing around; they ought to be very careful, especially with the currents."[276] Such stories and notions are very common in the testimonies of spongers.

---

275   In 1905, Scottish physician and physiologist John Scott Haldane complemented Bert's observations and published the first decompression tables, based on which the diver must ascend 3 feet per minute.

276   Testimony of *kolaouzieris* Vassilis Kampouris to E.O., 1/9/2004, testimony of wooden ship builder Manolis Cheilas to E.O., 25/8/2002.

4.2.3.4   So Many Wounds and Traumas

The divers themselves credited their own "sacrifice to the Minotaur of the sponge fishery" – as the scaphander diving suit is called in old and new testimonies[277] – to ignorance, which apparently prevailed after WWII. Particularly in the early years after the war, financial circumstances forced many from neighbouring islands to seek work on Kalymnos with scaphander diving suits and Fernez, with no little or no knowledge of the sea or diving. Hence, reduced financial circumstances and lack of experience may be at least two of the root causes of the toll that sponging took on divers. In 1952, The Supervisor of the Sponge Fishery in Libya wrote that "[t]he victims were neither aware of, nor did they ever comply with the speed of surfacing as set out in the Regulation; almost all divers do the same". He therefore concluded that most of the accidents were caused by the speed at which divers surfaced.[278]

The testimony of Michalis Lampos who, although he came from a family of spongers, chose to work on vessels as a sorter [*sortiristis*] and cleaner [*balaristis*][279] from 1947 to 1970, is particularly revealing: "Screw your ships and your money and the job. I prefer to have the sweat running through my trousers, and my legs strong, because the machine can 'hit' you hard. And if you kick the bucket straight away, all the better. The worst part is when the machine breaks your back and makes you drag yourself for the rest of your life".[280]

As previously explained, the parties involved, as well as witnesses, declared in reports and official statements that the accidents were random events, and

---

277   See also Georgas, *Μελέτη περί σπογγαλιείας* [*Study of the Sponge Fishery*], p. 44. And Γιάννης Θεοφ. Πατέλλης, "Ο αγνοημένος", *Καλυμνιακά Χρονικά* [Giannis Theof. Patellis, "The Missing One", *Kalymniaka Chronika*] 3 (1982), pp. 27–29; Kalafatas, "Χειμερινός Όνειρος" ["Winter Dream"] in Kalafatas, M. *The Bellstone*, p. 268. Present editors: In *The Bellstone*, M. Kalafatas discusses this topic at length and attributes the accidents to a combination of factors: "poor equipment, ignorance of proper deep-diving technique, the greed of the merchants and captains, the greed of the divers themselves, the *platika* system, 'the poetics of manhood' in Greece – and the incontrovertible truth that the inhabitants of these beautiful but rock-strewn islands had only the sea to turn to" (*Bellstone* p. 31). Michael Herzfeld coined the term "poetics of manhood" which he describes as a social phenomenon connected with "performative excellence"; the ability "to foreground manhood by means of deeds that strikingly speak for themselves" (*Bellstone*, p. 81).

278   "Έκθεσις εν σχέσει με την διεξαγωγήν της σπογγαλιείας εις τα παράλια της Λιβύης κατά την θερινή περίοδον 1952" ["Report on Sponge Fishing off the Coasts of Libya in the Summer Season of 1952"], Lieutenant Commander Em. Α. Koutsikopoulos, Sponge Fishery Overseer, Tripoli 28/11/1952, Embassy of Tripoli-Libya, Folder 46 (1952), Subfolder 4, IAYE.

279   The person who has the job of sorting the sponge catch by quality and size (i.e., the *sortiristis*), and cleaning them aboard the vessel (i.e. the *balaristis*).

280   Testimony of sponge cleaner [*balaristis*], Michalis Lampos to E.O., 29/7/2005.

that there were no indications of negligence, pressure, or regulation violations. Although these official documents leave no room to question the "randomness" of the accidents, other sources – dating back to the beginning of the 20th century – cited "ignorance or illiteracy", "greed", "bad habits", and "intentions" as the most common causes of the misuse of the scaphander diving suit, along with the "unfair and barbaric human sacrifice" of sponge fishermen.[281] While everybody seems to have believed that there were numerous unforeseen incidents that could arise, they also blamed the accidents on greed, disobedience, and the recklessness of the divers themselves, who would prolong their stay at the bottom of the sea when there were plenty of sponges. Divers using breathing devices or free-diving (i.e., by means of apnea) spoke of "the intoxication of the deep", when they espied rich sponge-bearing areas.[282] "You get giddy, dizzy, when there are many sponges in one spot down there. You want to catch them all, and you might not catch a single one", confessed a diver from Leros working on Kalymnian vessels.[283] Turning a deaf ear to the warning tugs of the diving manager [kolaouzieris], they kept harvesting sponges for much longer than the prescribed time; some of them even untied the rope in order to fish as much as possible.[284] Spongers were also familiar with the expression "kolaouzos is out" [φόρα κολαούζο], which the diving manager shouted out for the entire crew to hear. The expression meant that the diver had released his hand from the rope, so that whatever happened to him next was his responsibility.

Other unforeseen unfortunate incidents, such as shark attacks, did however occur and, while such incidents may not have posed a threat for those wearing the scaphander diving suit, they did slow divers down on the sea bottom.[285]

---

281 Zotos, *Report*, p. 13.
282 See the testimony of diver Georgios Trikoilis-Nassos to Faneromeni Chalkidiou-Skylla, Ἡ σφουγγάρι ἤ τομάρι [*Either Sponge or Corpse*], p. 243.
283 Testimony of diver Dimitris Peros to E.O., 24/8/2004.
284 "Εκθεσις εν σχέσει με την διεξαγωγήν της σπογγαλιείας εις τα παράλια της Λιβύης κατά την θερινή περίοδον 1952" ["Report on Sponge Fishing off the Coasts of Libya in the Summer Season of 1952"], Lieutenant Commander Em. A. Koutsikopoulos, Sponge Fishery Overseer, Tripoli 28/11/1952, Embassy of Tripoli-Libya, Folder 46 (1952), Subfolder 4, IAYE; Testimony of diver Giannis Koutouzis to E.O., 25/8/2003; Testimony of diver Giannis Loulourgas to E.O., 23/8/2004; Testimony of *kolaouzieris*-captain Petros Marthas to E.O., 2/9/2004. See also Faneromeni Chalkidiou-Skylla, Ἡ σφουγγάρι ἤ τομάρι [*Either Sponge or Corpse*], pp. 78–79.
285 There are several surviving testimonies, written and oral, on this topic. See *Εμπρός* [*Empros*], 18/6/1903, p. 2. This report concerns the case of diver Dimitris Peros from Leros, who fell ill from the disease and his lower extremities were paralysed. The accident occurred during his third dive at a depth of about 40 fathoms. According to the diver, he was forced to prolong his stay on the bottom because a very large shark was prowling

Still others believed, and continue to believe, that the reason for divers' decision to make an abrupt ascent, achieved by closing the helmet valve and filling the suit with air, was a "misconception of bravery".[286]

Nevertheless, many also speak of the cruelty of captains, who pressured or deceived the divers. Others claimed that captains cared little for the lives of divers, especially when the catch was already enough to cover for their advance payments [i.e., their *platika*].[287] In their testimonies, older divers repeatedly mention a captain who set sail with 17 divers in 1952, to return from the voyage with only 3 of them alive. They also speak of another captain who hired 12 divers in mid-summer, because he had already had 6 casualties. Not surprisingly then, the expression "either sponge or corpse" [ή σφουγγάρι ή τομάρι] recurs in all sponging narratives.

Captains, on the other hand, complain of the ignorance and financial pressure they were subject to, as well as the multiple consequences and delays that every accident entailed for them. Lefteris Mamouzelos confessed: "When you have borrowed a lot of money from the bank and you have mortgaged your house, you must earn it back without losing much time. This means that the divers have to get back up very quickly".[288] Captain Giannis Tsoulfas wondered: "How many tens or hundreds of hours must there be in a day in order for me to do my job, make money that is not mine, pay back the bank, and pay the men?".[289] In this regard it is telling that, when the Supervisor of Sponge Fishery in Libya suggested reducing the duration of the ascent, which was provided for in Law 560/37, he argued that,

> the speed of 2 fathoms per minute is extremely slow and would entail, if it were complied with, a substantial delay in the course of work. For instance, a sponge-fishing vessel working at a depth of 25 fathoms with 10 divers, each of whom will dive three times per day, would spend more than 6 hours waiting for the divers to surface.[290]

---

around him. When the shark swam away, the diver was so afraid that he resurfaced in "the blink of an eye". Testimony of Dimitris Peros to E.O., 24/8/2004. The story of the 1928 fernez accident of Theofilis Lampos, as told by his son Michalis Lampos, is similar. Testimony of sponge cleaner [*balaristis*] Michalis Lampos to E.O., 29/7/2002, and testimony of Nikolas Kampourakis to E.O., 25/8/2002.

286   Theodoros A. Kriezis, "Η σπογγαλιεία", Οικονομικός Ταχυδρόμος, ["Sponge Fishing", *Oikonomikos Tachydromos*], 14/8/1932, p. 3.

287   G. Georgas recounts a similar incident. See Georgas, *Μελέτη περί σπογγαλιείας* [*Study of the Sponge Fishery*], p. 40.

288   Testimony of Lefteris Mamouzelos to E.O., 3/9/2004.

289   Testimony of captain Giannis Tsoulfas to E.O., 6/3/2002.

290   "Έκθεσις εν σχέσει με την διεξαγωγήν της σπογγαλιείας εις τα παράλια της Λιβύης κατά την θερινή περίοδον 1952" ["Report on Sponge Fishing off the Coasts of Libya in the Summer

Many testimonies lay the blame for the accidents at the feet of diving manager [*kolaouzierides*], whom captains pressured to maximize the divers' yield and performance, and to alternate from one dive to the next quickly, while concealing the real depth and duration of dives.[291] Carl Flegel called diving managers "the executioners of their mates", believing that they were either deliberately, or due to ignorance, responsible to a great extent for the large number of the victims of the disease.[292] However, the *markoutserides* [person who manned the air hose] might also have concealed the real depth. Manolis Saroukos confessed that,

> some divers told me not to call out 30 fathoms, but 25 [...], because, instead of staying half an hour on the bottom, the diver would stay one hour; the shallower the depth, the longer the diver stayed, whereas the deeper he went, the less time he was allowed to stay. That's how that divers were tricked into it, and they either suffocated or were left crippled.[293]

The incidents were recorded, in principle, in the ship's logbook; however, captains themselves admitted that they could not be precise in their logging given the legal consequences.[294] If, for example, a diver had concluded a contract for 25 fathoms, but discovered sponges at greater depths, he would obviously fish there. If, however, an accident occurred in such cases, the actual depth would not be declared. Likewise, who would keep records of, or count the temporary "hits" or mild paralyses that did not prevent divers from continuing to work, yet later compromised their health?[295] "And, when the caique worked at 100–150 miles off the coast, would the captain take you to a hospital? He wouldn't, because it was not to his advantage".[296] Even when the shore was in

---

Season of 1952"], Lieutenant Commander Em. A. Koutsikopoulos, Sponge Fishery Overseer, Tripoli 28/11/1952, Embassy of Tripoli-Libya, Folder 46 (1952), Subfolder 4, ΙΑΥΕ.

291   Testimony of diving manager Skevos Makris to Faneromeni Chalkidiou-Skylla, Ἡ σφουγγάρι ἤ τομάρι [*Either Sponge or Corpse*], p. 184.

292   Flegel, "Η Α.Θ. Παναγιότης ὁ Οἰκουμενικός Πατριάρχης Ἄνθιμος" ["His All-Holiness Ecumenical Patriarch Anthimos"], pp. 16–17.

293   Testimony of *markoutseris* Manolis Saroukos to Faneromeni Chalkidiou-Skylla, Ἡ σφουγγάρι ἤ τομάρι [*Either Sponge or Corpse*], p. 225. Poor maintenance of equipment was yet another reason cited in the sources. Flegel, Τὸ σπογγαλιευτικό ζήτημα [*The Sponge-Fishery Issue*], p. 211.

294   Testimony of captain Giannis Tsoulfas to Ε.Ο., 5/3/2002.

295   All "caught" divers agreed that their symptoms got much worse as the years passed.

296   Testimony of Michalis Lampos to Ε.Ο., 29/7/2005, and testimony of Giannis Koutouzis to Ε.Ο., 25/8/2003. Nevertheless, in the years following WWII, the most serious cases were transferred to hospitals in Egypt or Libya, whenever possible. Testimony of Dimitris Peros to Ε.Ο., 24/8/2004.

closer proximity, "not more than three miles away, they waited until the job was done, so that they wouldn't waste any time; by then, though, we were finished".[297] Moreover, as many claimed, nobody was punished. "They came to the Port Authority; they were given food to eat and left unscathed. All these years, I didn't see a single person end up in jail",[298] or "the victim would never get justice, neither would the deceased diver's family".[299]

The early 20th-century press published accusations made by divers against captains who burnt the legs of the divers who had been "caught" to make sure that they were telling the truth.[300] Many testimonies also questioned the captains' Christian feelings, praising the help that some local Muslims offered the victims. One of the most tragic moments repeatedly found in oral testimonies, as well as in older written accounts, was the forced decapitation of deceased divers, in order to release the helmet of the scaphander diving suit, so that the next diver was able to use the suit straight away.[301] As Michalis Lampos recalled, "Using a hacksaw, the motorist cut the deceased diver's neck, so that the next one could put on the helmet, and the diving sequence would resume smoothly. There was thick black blood all over the place. They rinsed it slightly in the sea, and the next diver in line placed it on his head, having already put on the suit".[302] Some believed that the swollen head was the result of a very severe "hit from the machine", whereas in older testimonies it appears to be attributed to a damaged air pump.[303] Whatever the cause may be, this was a very common phenomenon due to the cerebral oedema caused by severe forms of the disease.[304]

Reports of dead divers buried at the sea, and emotionally charged accounts of tragic events such as moribund and deceased divers abandoned off the coasts of Africa and on desert islands fed the press at that time with highly

---

297   Testimony of diver Georgios Maillis to Faneromeni Chalkidiou-Skylla, Ἡ σφουγγάρι ἡ τομάρι [*Either Sponge or Corpse*], p. 205.

298   Testimony of diving manager Skevos Makris, ibid. p. 185.

299   Testimony of diver Georgios Maillis, ibid. p. 206.

300   Εστία [*Estia*], 18/4/1903, pp. 1–2.

301   Εστία [*Estia*], 14/4/1903, p. 1; 20/4/1903, p. 1 and 21/4/1903, p. 1–2; Flegel, "Η Α.Θ. Παναγιότης ο Οικουμενικός Πατριάρχης Άνθιμος" ["His All-Holiness Ecumenical Patriarch Anthimos"], p. 17; Flegel, *Το σπογγαλιευτικό ζήτημα* [*The Sponge-Fishing Issue*], p. 211; Flegel, *The Abuse of the Scaphander*, p. 519; Georgas, *Μελέτη περί σπογγαλιείας* [*Study of the Sponge Fishery*], p. 40; Testimony of Michalis Lampos to E.O., 29/7/2005.

302   Testimony of Michalis Lampos to E.O., 29/7/2005.

303   Flegel, "Η Α.Θ. Παναγιότης ο Οικουμενικός Πατριάρχης Άνθιμος" ["His All-Holiness Ecumenical Patriarch Anthimos"], p. 17.

304   Testimony of orthopedic specialist Konstantinos Nomikarios to E.O., 31/8/2004.

charged stories of spongers.[305] And of course, captains who refused to waste precious working time under any circumstance were considered inhumane. The infamous Aspronissi [White Island], off the coast of Benghazi; Poulionissi [meaning "inhabited only by birds"] a little further away; the Tzortzu islet in the sea of the famous Madruh of Kalymnian sponge fishermen; the Karavelonisi in Bombah; the isolated Lampedusa island between Tunisia and Malta; Glaronisi [Seagull Island] off the coast of Heraklion, are all mentioned in various testimonies as depositories for deceased divers.[306] Particularly Karavelonisi, the "island of death heads" as spongers called it, was reportedly covered in skulls. According to legend, captains abandoned not only divers whose death was imminent on the island, but also their fellow divers to avoid sharing profits.[307]

The substantial number of accidents, along with the suffocating framework of interconnected variables and actors in which sponge fishing is conducted, with its high advance payments, unpaid debts, and the expectation of considerable profits, shaped an idiosyncratic diving culture. The instability and uncertainty that divers experienced were not only financial or professional; both were largely attributable to the agony of survival. Indeed, even as late as the 1970s, divers requested their total remuneration in advance, arguing that they might not come back alive from the expedition.[308]

In all sponging narratives – both written and oral – the names of "guilty" parties are prevalent, although the burden responsibility was passed on from one person to the next: from captains to divers, from diving managers to divers and captains, from divers to everyone else involved. Nevertheless, given that guiding and supervising the man at the bottom of the sea was everyone's job, a web of silence or complicity seems to have shrouded this critical and tragic topic.

---

305   "Πολλών όμως τα πτώματα πέτραι ξηραί καλύπτουν / Και μερικούς στην θάλασσαν μη θέλοντες τους ρίπτουν" ["So many corpses piled with rocks, some thrown to sea unwilling"], Μητροφάνης Καλαφατάς, "Χειμερινός Όνειρος" [Mitrophanis Kalafatas, "Winter Dream"] in Michael N. Kalafatas, *The Bellstone: The Greek Sponge Divers of the Aegean. One American's Journey Home*. Hannover: Brandeis University Press, 2003, p. 245. *Εστία [Estia]*, 8/4/1903, p. 1 and 11/4/1903, p. 1; Flegel, *The Abuse of the Scaphander*, p. 519.

306   See also Cheilas, *Το έπος των σφουγγαράδων [The Epic Saga of Kalymnos' Sponge Fishermen]*, pp. 219–220; Faith Warm, *Bitter Sea*, p. 56; Kalafatas, *The Bellstone*, pp. 26–28; Testimony of diver Dimitris Giannis Koutouzis to E.O., 25/8/2003; Testimony of diver Dimitris Peros to E.O., 24/8/2004; Testimony of diver Thrasyvoulos Politis to E.O., 18/8/2004; Testimony of motorist Nikolaos Gourlas to Faneromeni Chalkidiou-Skylla, *Ή σφουγγάρι ή τομάρι [Either Sponge or Corpse]*, p. 177; Testimony of captain Chara Lampos Vavlas, ibid., p. 188; Testimony of diver Giannis Magklis-Kavouras, ibid., p. 210; Testimony of *trechantinieris* Ilias Mastoros, ibid, p. 237.

307   Tassos Zappas, "Ξεκίνημα των σφουγγαράδων για τα αφρικανικά παράλια", *Αθηναϊκά Νέα* ["Sponge Fishermen Setting Sail for the African Coasts", *Athinaika Nea*], 4/5/1938, p. 3.

308   Roxane Caftanzoglou, "Kalymnos", p. 8.

Moreover, despite scientific papers, decrees, legal provisions, protests and public complaints, accident and illness in the sponge fishery remained a vague and
questionable topic, at least since the introduction of the scaphander diving
suit, and until the decline of the activity. The obligations and consequences
that go with the acceptance of responsibility shaped a precarious workplace,
vulnerable to a variety of coercive behaviours.

Unfortunately, even after the installation of a decompression chamber in
the hospital of Kalymnos in 1970, sick divers would often misrepresent the
depths to which they had descended, the time they had spent there, and the
duration of their ascent to the medical staff charged with their care. This data
would have contributed greatly to the acceptance and practice of successful
gradual, mechanical decompression. There is, moreover, a general consensus
that the reasoning behind such behaviour was divers' fear of being excluded
from the professional network. As diver Michalis Lampos explained, "If you go
into this kind of garden, this is the cabbage you get. They all knew, but there
was no other way. If you stood up to a captain in broad daylight, they didn't hire
you again. There were only a few who dared to".[309] In spite of such problems
however, the decompression chamber did substantially improve the health of
several patients, at a time when sponge fishery on Kalymnos was still an ongoing activity.

4.2.4   The Emigration of Kalymnians
Local published writings attributed the great crisis that impacted the
Kalymnian sponge fishery in the final decades of the 19th century and the first
decades of the 20th century, to the widespread use of the scaphander diving
suit. Their authors described the devastating consequences of the scaphander
diving suit for those conducting the activity by traditional means, as well as the
"machine's" decisive role in the depletion of the Mediterranean sponge beds.
This protracted crisis is seen as the reason for the seasonal employment of children in small-scale industries owned by Kalymnians in Russia, as well as the
expatriation of the island's male population to Tarpon Springs, USA, and Sfax,
Tunisia.[310]

The first colonies of Dodecanesian merchants in Odessa were reportedly
established at the end of the 18th century;[311] around 1900, it is estimated that

---

309   Testimony of Michalis Lampos to E.O., 29/7/2005.
310   Georgas, Μελέτη περί σπογγαλιείας [Study of the Sponge Fishery], p. 29.
311   Miltiadis I. Logothetis, "Οι πρωτοπόροι του δωδεκανησιακού εμπορίου" ["The Pioneers of
       Dodecanesian Trade"], Economic Library of the Chamber of Commerce and Industry of
       Rhodes, Athens 1968, p. 10.

there were approximately 1,000 to 1,500 Kalymnians residing in various Russian cities.[312] This suggests that the first Kalymnians in Russia may have been itinerant sponge-merchants. Likewise, to avoid recruitment into the precarious and perilous labour conducted on sponge-fishing ships, many Kalymnian families were reduced to sending their children to work in factories and sponge merchant houses of fellow Kalymnians in Russia.[313] References in local sources are very few, but collective memory has safeguarded a number of testimonies concerning this kind of emigration. The same is true of mementos of those who lived there which survive to this day, from household utensils and various items found in Kalymnian houses,[314] to the *Kozakios*, the Cossack dance that the Roussakia [little Russians][315] used to dance when they returned to Kalymnos from Russia. As Giannis Gerakis wrote in his diary:

> Year 1900, February 29th, Monday. Two ships of the Smyrna-Antalya regular line docked at the port of our island. The ship Roumeli of the P. Pantaleon Company and the ship Olympia of the Hadji Daud company, with the late Arist. Kouremetis as the first company's agent, and the late Nikolaos Svynos as the second company's agent, competed to see to which ship the largest number of passengers would be transferred.
>
> It was that time of year when our little Russians departed for Russia. They began being brought to Kalymnos in October-November: some came to shop for a bit of sponge, some came to see their families, their relatives, or some, the single ones, came to find a bride. But there were some others who, along with all of those above, recruited a bunch of kids aged twelve to fifteen or sixteen years old. Those were mostly the

---

312   Gerakis, Σφουγγαράδιχες ιστορίες [*Sponge Stories*], p. 34.

313   Ioannis Skevou Orfanos, "Η νήσος Κάλυμνος", *Καλυμνιακά Χρονικά* ["The Island of Kalymnos", *Kalymniaka Chronika*], 17 (2007), p. 96; Manuscript 2729/1976, Angeliki Georgiadou, p. 122, CFS; Niki Gr. Billiri, *Της θάλασσας και της στεριάς* [*Of Sea and Land*], Athens 1986, p. 263–264.

314   In the period under examination, social stratification is evident on the island. There were houses of financially and socially affluent people that contained a large number and variety of items and pieces of furniture brought from Western Europe and Russia, as well as small buildings in Pothia and Chora – the *katzies*, with rudimentary built-in wooden constructions and a minimum of mobile pieces of furniture. Themelina Kapella, *Λαογραφικές Σελίδες Καλύμνου* [*Folklore Pages of Kalymnos*], Athens 1997, p. 19; Manuscript 778/1968–1969, Maria Koutouzi, pp. 1–2, CFS.

315   Maria Zairi argued that the *Kozakikos* dance could perhaps be introduced into the local repertoire, given that it is reminiscent of Kalymnos of old; Maria Zairi, "Ρωσίας ενθυμήματα", *Καλυμνιακά Χρονικά* ["Mementos from Russia", *Kalymniaka Chronika*] 15 (2003), pp. 266–267.

slipper makers [*Pantouflatzides*], that is, those who possessed the famous *Masterskayas* [slipper manufactures], which were thriving at that time in almost all the largest cities of Russia. Most of them were in Odessa, Warsaw, Lodz (Poland) which belonged to Russia at the time; then followed Moscow, Kiev, Kharkof, Crimea and Caucasus, whereas in Saint Petersburg there were fewer of them: there were one or two, and these a few years before the revolution.

At this time, around 1900, the recruitment of children had reached its peak, and had almost evolved into a kind of forced recruitment of children [παιδομάζωμα, *paidomazoma*].

On this day, February the 29th, which was also the big Lent, most of our little Russians left; they had organized everything in such a way that they celebrated all the winter festivities, the Carnival, the Cheese Week [known as Τυρινή Εβδομάδα, *Tiriní Evdomáda*] before the beginning of Lent, and Ash [or Clean] Monday [the first day of Lent] and, according to our island's strict custom, they received the Holy Communion on Saturday of the first week after exhaustive and strict fasting, and they departed on the second week. That's why, on that day, we were about 150 passengers on those two ships, of which 118 were children, as we said, of twelve to fifteen years of age, destined to staff the *Masterskayas*.[316]

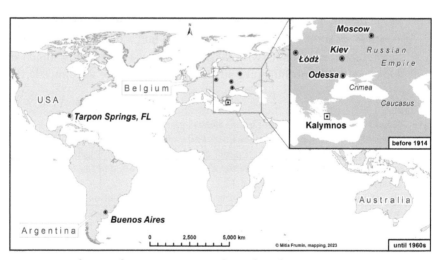

MAP 4.1   Kalymnian diaspora communities, late 19th–20th centuries

---

316   Gerakis, Σφουγγαράδικες ιστορίες [*Sponge Stories*], pp. 27–29, Ibid., pp. 32–33. The contracts were usually for a 3 to 4-year period with very low wages.

Yet another testimony about the emigration of children survives in the archives of Kalymnos. In 1882, Nomikos Emm. Stavris took Emmanouil Kassiotis, the underage son of Georgios Em. Kassiotis, to Russia to work in his shop on a three-year contract, under obligation to pay for the child's transport, as well as 1,500 *kuruş* to the child's father. However, Stavris did not honour this written agreement and abandoned the minor because, as he claimed, he was not able to pay the wages owing. Following a complaint lodged by the father, the merchant was forced to cover for the expenses for the child's return to Kalymnos.[317]

On the other hand, many Dodecanesians set out on a quest for better luck in the rich sponge-bearing areas of far-off Florida, USA. Tarpon Springs was created at the beginning of the 19th century as a holiday resort on the shores of the Gulf of Mexico, which targeted well-off visitors from the northern United States. The city's physiognomy shifted in the 1890s, when the local population discovered that its sea was rich in sponge-bearing beds. The first Greeks to settle in Tarpon Springs, on the eastern side of the Gulf of Mexico, were the brothers Kokoris from Leonidio. It was supposedly the Kokoris brothers who discovered the rich sponge-bearing beds of the area, equipped the first vessel with a scaphander diving suit, and prompted their compatriot sponge fishermen to try their luck in that part of Florida.[318] By 1905, there were twenty sponge-fishing vessels in Tarpon Springs, with 20 divers and 50 rowers, and the value of the daily catch amounted to 200 dollars. The editor of *Empros* newspaper noted that this amount could increase exponentially were the number of divers working on each vessel to increase. However, the editor also criticized the Greek sponge fishermen because they taught the art of sponge fishery to the locals, who had already started undertaking the activity.[319] By the end of the first decade of the 20th century, more than 800 sponge fishermen from Symi, Halki, Kalymnos, Hydra and Aegina had established themselves at the Gulf of Mexico and, on 30 January 1922, Prime Minister Eleftherios Venizelos visited Tarpon Springs.[320]

The flow of immigration to Tarpon Springs, had multiple impacts on Kalymnian society and its economy: first, remittances contributed to the upkeep of the families of sponge fishermen; the thinning of the population decreased pressure on those engaging in the sponge fishery; new sponge trade

---

317   Doc. 266, 23/5/1885, MC Minutes 1885, MAK.

318   Michail Iord. Kindynis, "Τάρπον Σπρινγκς Φλώριδα", *Καλυμνιακά Χρονικά* ["Tarpon Springs, Florida", *Kalymniaka Chronika*], 3 (1982), pp. 162–164.

319   *Εμπρός* [*Empros*], 26/11/1905, p. 4.

320   Antonis Mailis, *Στο Τάρπον Σπρινγκς* [*In Tarpon Springs*], pp. 37–38.

markets were opened; and finally, a sponge-fishing colony on the other side of the Atlantic Ocean, "Little Kalymnos", as is called even today, was created.

The Greek community in Sfax was formed at the end of the 19th century, and was consolidated on the eve of WWI, largely by sponge fishermen and merchants, as well as by a few craftsmen, scientists, and businessmen. They came from various areas, which were already actively involved in the sector, mainly from Kalymnos and Hydra. Many knew the area from their stay during the sponge-fishing season; others had already tried their luck in other northern African areas.[321] It was reported that, beginning in the 1870s, the Greeks introduced new fishing methods such as the gagava and the scaphander diving suit to local sponge fishermen who, until then, were naked diving. As is usually the case, the majority of the first settlers worked in the area for some time, before they decided to settle with their families in Tunisia. In 1911, there were 752 Greeks in Sfax of a total of 20,000 inhabitants.[322] In 1926, the Greek community consisted of 343 people, which dropped to 274 in 1936, whereas about ⅓ of them had already obtained French citizenship.[323] In WWII, during their brief stay in the city, Germans reportedly collaborated with some high-profile personalities of the colony, and entered into commercial transactions with them, mostly for the sale of sponges.[324] The independence of Tunisia in the 1950s, and the crisis that hit sponge markets in the 1960s, as well as commercial competition with locals, presented the Greek community with problems, and many of its members were forced to leave for France or continental Greece.

The first decade following WWII was probably the most difficult for the people of Kalymnos. The volatility of the sponge-fishing market, the lack of capital, and the restrictions placed on sponge-fishing beds forced many Kalymnians

---

321 H. Kazdaghli noted that there were about 390 Greek and Sicilian sponge fishermen in 1888, while in 1914 the Greeks amounted to approximately 400 people; Habib Kazdaghli, "Les Grecs de Sfax à l'heure des choix", unpublished paper for *Παραδοσιαχές καλλιέργειες και προϊόντα στο Αιγαίο και τη Μεσόγειο* [*Traditional Crops and Products in the Aegean and Mediterranean Seas*] held July 11–12, 2003 at the Institute for Neohellenic Research of the National Hellenic Research Foundation (INE/EIE) and the Faculté des Lettres, Université de Manouba. Tunisia, as part of the "Σεμινάρια της Ερμούπολης" ["Seminars of Hermoupolis"].

322 Alexandras Dagkas, *Le mouvement social*, p. 133.

323 Habib Kazdaghli, Les Grecs de Sfax. See also Habib Kazdaghli, "Communautés méditerranéennes de Tunisie. Les Grecs du Millet-i-rum a l'assimilation française au XVIIᵉ–XXᵉ siècles", *Revue des mondes musulmans et de la Méditerranée* 95–98 (2002), pp. 449–476.

324 Habib Kazdaghli, *Les Grecs de Sfax*.

to seek employment abroad. In 1953 – when the 1952 sponge production had not been yet sold and the ATE was no longer granting loans but rather seizing vessels – many moved to Australia[325] to work as divers in coral harvesting, while others headed to Belgium to work in Belgian coal mines.[326]

---

325 Giannis Marinos, "Πώς άρχισε η μετανάστευση από την Κάλυμνο στην Αυστραλία", *Καλυμνιακά Χρονικά* ["How Emigration from Kalymnos to Australia Started", *Kalymniaka Chronika*], 15 (2003), pp. 429–433.

326 On emigration to Belgium after WWII, see Lina Ventoura, *Έλληνες μετανάστες στο Βέλγιο* [*Greek Immigrants in Belgium*], Athens 1999.

CHAPTER 5

The Protagonists' View of Daily Life

Poor Kalymnos, your mountains turned black.
Away go your young lads and your valiant at heart.[1]

• • •

It's May again, summer is here,
And off we go to Barbary again this year.[2]

∴

5.1 The Voyage

There is no mention made in the official archival evidence of sponge-fishing voyages themselves; nor is what happened aboard vessels contained in written testimonies. The conditions during the voyage, the terms of employment, interpersonal relationships, the settling of disputes, and accidents are not recorded. Here, the authorities had no say, and written regulations and provisions granted no rights to workers; it was the local population that absorbed the constraints and losses endemic to the profession. There are, however, some very few indirect, albeit rare, references – complaints made solely by captains – cases of fleeing, accident, and death. Indeed, the traditional oral lore and emotionally charged accounts given by those who worked on sponge-fishing vessels, and those who remained on the island and safeguarded the conditions for the daily life, contain legends and emotions, most of which come from the years following WWII. At the same time, popular and journalistic accounts, as well as fictional texts of the later 19th and 20th centuries, focus on the most tragic or heroic moments of the job of sponge fishermen. This poem, from a diary kept at an all-girls residence on Kalymnos, is an excellent example:

---

1 Manuscript 2728/1976, Maria Sevastopoulou, p. 57, CFS.
2 Niki Gr. Billiri, *Η Κάλυμνός μας* [*Our Kalymnos*], Athens 1982, p. 18.

"A Wish for Our Sponge Fishermen"
Farewell to your prow, and may your summer be good
May fair winds blow your way, and may fair winds blow you back
May be the waves be light, and sway you gently
And may the summer breeze sweetly cool you
Who bravely fight a wild struggle
On the boat of "*yiali*", with the stone, the *skandali*
In the machine's dress with its helmet
In *kolaouzos*, the Fernez, o valiant youth
Bold captains and worthy, brave divers
Pride glory and honour of Kalymnos. And soldiers!
May divine strength give you courage
And epiphany to the captains, and guide you
May you with health and joy and good work
Have a good return, honoured lads[3]

As noted in previous chapters, after arranging crews and signing agreements, preparations began in earnest. Crews took on ship maintenance and tested diving apparatuses. A six or seven-month long sponge-fishing voyage necessitated stocks of important provisions of food and potable water for the crews' upkeep, while ensuring that there was enough storage space left for sponges.

When sponge fishing was conducted in faraway places, vessels working with naked divers formed sponge-fishing groups consisting of sponge-fishing boats and an auxiliary vessel, the *depozito*, as is called on Kalymnos. This ship was used to transport small sponge-fishing boats from the point of departure to the destination, as well as to store food, potable water, and fuel for the voyage. The necessary cleaning, drying, and storing of sponges also took place on board the *depozito*, where part of the crew slept, and meals were prepared.[4] The *depozito* is also where the air pump, the suits and all the tools and parts were kept.[5]

---

3 *Michailion House of Loving Care, All-girls Housing of Kalymnos*, 1973. Diary, no page numbers.
4 In the 1960s, each sponge-fishing group usually consisted of three vessels; two of them were sponge-fishing ships, measuring approximately 10 meters in length, 3.5 in height and 1.2 in width. The third vessel, the *depozito*, which was the largest one, had a length of 15 meters. Bernard Russell, "Η σπογγαλιεία της Καλύμνου", *Σπουδαί* ["The Sponge Fishery of Kalymnos" *Spoudai*], 1 (1970), p. 4.
5 Every sponge-fishing vessel was equipped with one air pump, but it could possibly have more suits. According to L. Mamouzelos, who spoke of roughly the period from 1950–1960, every caique had four breastplates and two helmets. Testimony of captain Lefteris Mamouzelos to E.O., 3/9/2004.

However, the transfer of small *"trechandiria"*[6] to greater distances also required a larger vessel known as a *brazzera*;[7] for which the *depozito* served as the ship's warehouse.[8] This vessel, 25–30 meters long, transported the parts of the "machine" as well as other sundry equipment.[9] Aboard this vessel – the *brazzera* – food was also prepared and the final cleaning and permanent storage of the sponge catch was also carried out there, and divers often spent their nights on the *brazzera*,[10] although some even slept on the *"achtarmas"* ships.[11] In this regard, a certificate issued by the Municipality of Kalymnos in 1915 is revealing:

> The sailing ship berthed at the port of Kalymnos, of the *trechandiri brazzera* type and weighing 45 tons, named "Evangelistria", under the command of captain Mr Dimitrios N. Galopoulos, resident of Kalymnos, loaded up sponge-fishing crews, food provisions, tools, and supplies, in order to transfer them to the coasts of Africa and to Lampedusa for the needs of the sponge-fishing undertaking. It also carries two Fusil Gras system guns bearing the numbers 1875 and 1877. Said sailing ship is accompanied by two other small sailing boats [*achtarmas*], on which sponge-fishing machinery is placed during the working period. They are also carrying two guns on board, one Mauser system gun No 49163, and one Fusil Gras system gun No 53737.[12]

---

6   Archival evidence and various testimonies show that the sailing or motorized vessels (from the late 1920s onwards), which were used to fish sponges with scaphander diving suits or Fernez, were *"trechandiria"* which were longer. Testimony of machinist Nikolaos Sdregas to E.O., 30/8/2004. To be precise, it was a variation of the *"trechandiri"*, that was known as an *"achtarmas"* on Kalymnos. Kostas Damianidis, *Museum of Maritime Tradition and Sponge-Fishing of Nea Koutali*, Limnos 2006, p. 11.

7   The agreement between the owner of the *brazzera* and the captains of sponge-fishing vessels was written as well. Surviving pieces of evidence from the Archive of the Elders' Council of Kalymnos inform us that its owner was also paid with shares. He usually received one diver's share from each captain. In such an agreement in 1921, the *brazzera* would transport seven boats to the coasts of Cyrenaica "on and below the deck" along with their crews. See, for instance, register book 113, doc. 73, 29/4/1921, MAK.

8   Or "mana" [mother], as they called it in Hydra. See Gian. A. Karamitsos, *Hydra, An Entirely Dryopian Island,* Hydra, 1998, p. 13.

9   All European sponge-fishing groups harvesting sponges in the maritime area of Tunisia in the second half of the 19th century were organized in the same manner; P. A. Hennique, *Les Caboteurs et pêcheurs de la côte de Tunisie: pêche des éponges*, Paris 1888, p. 44.

10   P. Zotos. Ἔκθεσις περί τῆς ἀνά τας ἀφρικανικάς ἀκτάς διά σκαφάνδρου σπογγαλιείας [*Report on Sponge Fishing by Diving Suit along the African Coasts*], Athens 1904, pp. 4–5.

11   They were called *"achtarmatzides"*. Testimony of diver Giannis Koutouzis to E.O., 25/8/2003.

12   Doc. 48, 30/4/1915, MC Minutes 1915–1916, MAK.

Another kind of vessel, known to locals called as a "*paggeto*", "*baketo*" or "*paket-tho*", all of which meaning package (i.e., they were mules that carried packages back and forth), also served the sponge-fishing industry without being part of the sponge-fishing groups. It was a free-trade vessel, servicing sponge fishermen on an occasional basis, as S. Agapitidis observed. It carried letters and food sent to sponge fishermen by their families, and supplied them with various goods; if needed, the vessel also brought new crew members or divers. According to others, the vessel usually arrived in fishing areas after the first half of the sponging season, or beginning in July, when supplies had dwindled, and crews craved news.[13] It then returned to the island bringing news from those on the expedition.[14]

The sponge-fishing season began quite early, and sponge-fishing expeditions lasted many months. Depending on the destination and means of fishing, the usual duration of a sponging voyage varied from 150 to 220 days.[15] Most informants argued that it is very difficult to understand what the co-habitation of approximately fifteen men on a vessel that measured just a few meters over the course of several months would have been like. Certainly working and living conditions on board were especially difficult, and many confessed that sponge fishermen used to refer to these voyages as "tyranny". Indeed, for seven months, crews worked non-stop "between sky and sea", under the scorching sun, while dealing with constant humidity,[16] "in places where the sun bakes the bread".[17] The harsh conditions of these lengthy stays at the sea do, however, survive in oral testimonies:

> Whether you want to or not, you stay on the boat. Where else would you go? The space is limited, there's sea all around you. Six months without any water to wash your face, only sea water. They forbade us to use any potable water because it was only for drinking and cooking. We washed our clothes with sea water. In the day they were stiff, and in the night,

---

13   Zotos, *Report*, p. 5; Sotirios Agapitidis, "Η οικονομική οργάνωση των σπογγαλιευτικών συγκροτημάτων – ειδικότερα στη Σύμη" ["The Economic organization of Sponge-Fishing Groups – Particularly on Symi"], 3 (1977), p. 188.

14   Niki Billiri, *Σφουγγαράδες από την Κάλυμνο* [*Sponge Fishermen from Kalymnos*], Athens 1995, p. 203.

15   See the table published in Russell, "Η σπογγαλιεία της Καλύμνου" ["The Sponge Fishery of Kalymnos"], p. 11.

16   Testimony of diver Giannis Koutouzis to E.O., 25/8/2003; testimony of diver Thrasyvoulos Politis to E.O., 18/8/2004.

17   Since vessels carried food and tobacco, they often had confrontations with the customs authorities of Tripoli, who asked them to prove that they were not smuggling, as the sponge fishermen of Hydra said. See *Αθηναϊκά Νέα* [*Athinaika Nea*], 20/7/1937, p. 3.

they were wet with the humidity. That was our life. You get dirty, you get lice; and in the night, bedbugs sucked our blood. Six months without being able to have a haircut or a shave. These years are best forgotten.[18]

Caiques rarely approached land if at all, either because sponge-bearing beds were often located far off shore, or because there were periods of time when approaching the land was forbidden due to the fact that sponge fishermen were suspected of smuggling.[19] Moreover, approaching land was also impossible if the appropriate permit had not been obtained due to constant bans on fishing with scaphander diving suits, or the many dangers noted in various sources consulted in this study.[20] Perhaps unsurprisingly moreover, there are also accounts of pirates and bandits attacking sponge-fishing vessels.[21]

Conflicts between sponge fishermen and locals were not uncommon, either. One of the oldest known references is the testimony of Greek Vice-Consul D. Foros, who reported confrontations and bloody incidents between sponge fishermen and local Arab populations in 1888.[22] Foros revisited this issue one year later: "In previous years, many unpleasant incidents took place between local Arabs and Ottoman soldiers. These people not only greatly harmed the interests of sponge fishermen, but also inspired horror and terror, and forcibly prevented them from nearing lands that abound in sponges of premium quality [...]." Foros went on to emphasize how "the shoreline of Tripoli was a bandits' nest full of murderous Arabs". Thanks to the efficient intervention of Governor General Ahmet Rasim Pasha, however, they were finally able to work safely and, what is more, when they approached land to get food and water, soldiers hurried to help them.[23]

Although they avoided land for practical purposes, as well as for security reasons, replenishing supplies was sometimes imperative. When crews needed supplies, or when breakdowns and unforeseeable incidents occurred, the *depozito* ship would go ashore and acquire the necessary supplies. It was captains most often who took care of procuring food supplies, water, and fuel from

---

18   Testimony of diver Dimitris Peros to E.O., 24/8/2004.

19   There is a reference in a testimony of 1929 concerning Derna; see Niki Gr. Billiri, Τῆς θάλασσας καὶ τῆς στεριάς [*Of Sea and Land*], Athens 1986, pp. 66–67.

20   Louis Figuier, *Les merveilles de la science, ou Description populaire des inventions modernes*, vol. 4, Paris 1870, p. 624.

21   Doc. 112, 22/7/1897, Correspondence 1896–1898, MAK; Doc. 642, 23/9/1911, Doc. 645, 29/9/1911, Doc. 646, 7/10/1911, Correspondence 1910–1913, MAK.

22   Report 17/9/1888, Embassy of Tripoli-Libya, Folder 4 (1875–1897), Subfolder 4, IAYE.

23   Letter from Vice Consul D. Foros to the Greek Embassy in Constantinople, 16/6/1889, Embassy in Tripoli-Libya, Folder 4 (1875–1897), Subfolder 4, IAYE.

the locals, as well as from businesses that traded with sponge-fishing ships. In the years following WWII, some companies undertook the brokerage of ships, supplying vessels with essential commodities on a regular basis, for a fixed price. There were, however, complaints that these companies charged excessively inflated prices for the goods they sold sponge fishermen.[24]

5.1.1   *Life on Board*

Having prepared exactly so,
and ready now to venture,
they wake at dawn, their bedding store
along the ship's sharp corners,
and wash their face and cross themselves,
call God their only helper,
who instantly heals the open wound,
protects from any danger.
After this call they sit at stern,
dipping their bread in coffee.
Then they set out to tack their sails,
coursing toward their work.
Finding a rock ledge, they decide
to drop the iron anchor.[25]

The work of sponge fishing began at dawn, when the divers on the *depozito* boarded the fishing vessels and traveled to the areas to be fished, which were often as far as one or two-hours away. As Petros Marthas explained, "we got up in the morning at 4 AM, and we got back after 10 PM, when the working areas were far. There was hardly any time left to eat and rest".[26] On other occasions, they traveled to new fishing areas in the night, so that the divers would be ready to work very early in the morning. The intensification of labour, the prolonged work stretching daily from dawn to sunset, was inevitable, considering the expected yield of a sponge-fishing expedition; also inevitable were

---

24   "Έκθεσις εν σχέσει με την διεξαγωγήν της σπογγαλιείας εις τα παράλια της Λιβύης κατά την θερινή περίοδον 1952" ["Report on Sponge Fishing off the Coasts of Libya in the Summer Season of 1952"], Lieutenant Commander Em. A. Koutsikopoulos, Sponge Fishery Overseer, Tripoli 28/11/1952, Embassy of Tripoli-Libya, Folder 46 (1952), Subfolder 4, IAYE.

25   Μητροφάνης Καλαφατάς, "Χειμερινός Όνειρος" [Mitrophanis Kalafatas, "Winter Dream"] in Michael N. Kalafatas, The *Bellstone:* The Greek Sponge Divers of the Aegean. One American's Journey Home. Hannover: Brandeis University Press, 2003, p. 248.

26   Testimony of captain Petros Marthas to E.O., 2/9/2004.

the constraints and time restrictions that nature itself imposed on sponge fishermen. The working crew laboured intensely; it was a job without any fixed schedule.[27] There were no public holidays, and Sundays were usually considered work days.[28] It is reported, however, that divers did not work on three important holidays: 29 June [St. Peter and St. Paul], 15 August [the Repose Virgin Mary] and 14 September [The Elevation of the Holy Cross];[29] according to other sources, they suspended their work for the feasts of Agia Marina [Saint Marina, 17 July], Agios Panteleimon [Saint Pantaleon, 27 July], Panagia [Virgin Mary, 15 August], Cross [Elevation of the Holy Cross, 14 September] and Agios Nikitas [Saint Nicetas, 21 June].[30]

Bad weather was one important and imponderable factor, both during the voyage to destination areas as well as throughout the entire working season. Mechanical failures, or even shipwrecks, were not uncommon. In bad weather conditions, work did not pause, given that divers with scaphander suits were able to work even in choppy seas.[31] "Caiques were small, but wide and deep. Winds of 9 or 10 on the Beaufort scale were a walk in the park for us".[32]

The harsh living conditions on board remain etched in everyone's memory – the poor food and small quantities thereof, the lack of potable water, and the maggoty hardtack:[33] "Our everyday food was beans, pasta with kavurma meat, some pilaf (rice), and even a bit of potato, if there was any. We had pulses four times per week, and the other things three times a week. As for fruit, we got that only if we came across a captain with a conscience, then we might get it; otherwise, they gave it to us while carping about it or under threat".[34] In an attempt to support this manner of sustenance, it was reported in one sailor's statement of 1926 that, "as on any other vessel, they give us meat three

27   Testimony of captain Giannis Tsoulfas to E.O., 5/3/2002.

28   Even though, already in 1926, international legislation provided for the existence of a specific work schedule for those working on sponge-fishing vessels, the particularities of the activity did not permit the improvement of the conditions for those working in underwater fishery, and more specifically in sponge, coral, and pearl fishery. See *Les Marins et le Bureau International du Travail*, Paris 1930, pp. 15–16.

29   Zotos, *Report*, pp. 4 and 14; Russell, "Η σπογγαλιεία της Καλύμνου" ["The Sponge Fishery of Kalymnos"], p. 11.

30   See also the testimony of sponger Michail Stefadouros to Faneromeni Chalkidiou-Skylla, *Ή σφουγγάρι ή τομάρι. Η ζωή των σφουγγαράδων της Καλύμνου μέσα από αληθινές μαρτυρίες* [*Either Sponge or Corpse. The Life of the Sponge Fishermen of Kalymnos through Real Testimonies*], Kalymnos 2009, p. 175.

31   Testimony of diver Thrasyvoulos Politis to E.O., 18/8/2004.

32   Testimony of Lefteris Mamouzelos to E.O., 3/9/2004.

33   Faith Warm, *Bitter Sea: The Real Story of Greek Sponge Diving*, London 2000, pp. 54–55.

34   Manuscript 1838/1973, Evangelia Lampadariou, testimony of diver Micke Mastrokoukkos, pp. 71–72, CFS.

times per week, and the rest of the week pasta and beans".[35] The poor diet of
the crews and their daily food is a recurring element in most testimonies. The
poor quality and small portions of food, the lack of fresh produce, but mostly
the spoiled food. Despite recommendations for the improvement and establishment of a single diet regime,[36] conditions do not appear to have changed
as time went by. "We were starving! If God could call what we ate food. We
baked the hardtack so that we didn't eat the worms alive. We used to get water
from Africa, fruit, and some tomatoes once a month. The coasts near where we
fished were uninhabited".[37]

Divers did not eat during the day, neither did they drink coffee or water; they
were only allowed to moisten their lips. The rest of the crew ate olives with a
piece of hardtack or some cured sardines. They all waited until the evening for
the food that the group's cook prepared,[38] given that crews had only one meal
per day, early in the evening at the end of the working day.[39] Two to five people
ate from the same plate, sitting cross-legged on the deck of *depozito*. Only in a
storm did they all get their own plate, so that they could hold it between their
knees to avoid spillage. The same foods were served on a fixed rotation: beans,
pasta with sauce, with or without meat, meat stew and rice. Their meat was
kavurma, or cured beef chopped into small pieces, which was stored in large
tin cans filled with grease.[40] The meal was accompanied by some sort of hardtack baked by the women and the bakeries of the island, that was made to be
preserved a long time.[41]

> Three times per week we cooked the kavurma meat with pasta or pota-
> toes, if we had any, and the entire caique smelled nice. There was too

---

35   Statement of Petros Tsakos, sailor on the vessel "Vassiliki" from Hydra; Doc. 20/9/1926,
        Greek Embassy Tripoli-Libya, Folder 33 (1926–1927), Subfolder 10, ΙΑΥΕ.

36   See Konstantinos Gourgiotis, "Όροι εργασίας εις την σπογγαλιείαν" ["Working Conditions in
        the Sponge Fishery"], *1st Panhellenic Sponge-Fishing Conference*, Rhodes, 24–27 February
        1949. *Papers and Minutes*, General Administration of the Dodecanese, Rhodes 1951, pp.
        78–79.

37   Testimony of diving manager Vassilis Kampouris to Ε.Ο., 1/9/2004. It is reported that
        there were not many fruits in Libya, "but even if you could find any, you had to go to
        the seashore, and we couldn't leave the areas where we worked". Testimony of captain
        Giannis Tsoulfas to Ε.Ο., 5/3/2002.

38   Testimony of sponge cleaner [*balaristis*] Michalis Lampos to Ε.Ο., 29/7/2005.

39   Zotos, *Report*, p. 14.

40   Testimony of *trechandiri* owner and captain Petros Marthas to Ε.Ο., 2/9/2004.

41   Newton referred to the hardtack that the women made in the mid-19th century to meet
        the sponge fishermen's needs; C. T. Newton, *Travels and Discoveries in the Levant*, vol. 1,
        London 1865, p. 298.

little meat, and the mechanical divers used to eat the best bits to regain their strength. If we ran out of kavurma, we used to get sheep from nomad camps on the coasts of Africa [*haimes*]. We ate more meat on the ship than on the island. If the departure was massive, with three or four *achtarmas* ships and a *brazzera depozito* of one hundred tons, it even had a coop [*agoumas*] with roosters. Let alone the fishes; you only had to throw in a fishhook, and you got two fishes.[42]

During the dives, it was strictly forbidden to fish for octopi, fish, or lobster, "even if they were right in front of you", as most attested. "That wasn't our job", divers reported. In the hours spent waiting between one dive and the next, divers used to fish from the vessel. Since the catch was rich, most of the fish were dried under the sun and preserved for their return to Kalymnos; or, on occasion they sold their catch when they reached the shore.[43]

Water was stored in metal oil barrels, in which a piece of sponge was placed to absorb any other substances. Water shortage was perhaps the greatest problem of all:

> We were doing okay in terms of food, but we were always short of water. We kept it in oil barrels [*baizanoi*] that were lined with cement on the inside to prevent the water from smelling, and whitewashed on the outside to protect them from the sun. Two, or three hundred kilograms each. Every ship needed up to ten barrels per month, only for drinking. We washed with sea water. At the very beginning of the voyage, the water was good, but then went bad; it tasted of rust. But what could you do? The ship was boiling under the blazing sun. Whether you liked it or not, you drank it. If we ran out of water, we sent a water-carrying caique [*respettho*], which drew water from the wells of the Arabs. We knew where each one of the wells were. Their water was dirty and brackish, hard to drink. But if we went fishing on the upper areas [of the Greek islands] we took as much fresh water as we wanted; we washed ourselves regularly and our bodies sweetened with the pleasure. For sponge fishermen all water was holy.[44]

---

42 Testimony of Lefteris Mamouzelos published in Ελληνικό Πανόραμα [*Elliniko Panorama*] 57 (2007), p. 167.

43 Testimony of diver Thrasyvoulos Politis to E.O., 18/8/2004. Gaston Deschamps mentioned that Kalymnian divers sold lobsters on Amorgos. See Gaston Deschamps, *La Grèce d'aujourd'hui*, Paris 1894, p. 211.

44 Testimony of Lefteris Mamouzelos published in the journal Ελληνικό Πανόραμα [*Elliniko Panorama*] 57 (2007), p. 167.

It was only on the rare approaches to land that vessels obtained fresh water, fruits, and vegetables.[45] The following testimony provides a typical description of the food on board:

> We didn't have what younger people have now. In our time, the hardtack was maggoty, the sardines were really picarel, which they prepared and grilled here, and that made them completely stiff. They served you 5–6 of them. And we waited until the evening, till 10 or 11 PM, for the cooked food to come from the big ship. They gave you 5 olives. This was our lunch. As for the water, when the barrel containing the oil for the engine was left empty, we washed it twice with sea water, shook it once or twice, and flipped it; then we got out on the sand and dug until sea water came out, to drink water. That's how we got water in these Arab lands. Because we couldn't bring water from here [i.e., the island]. We only carried two or three barrels of water for the trip to our destination. What mattered the most was loading more barrels with fuel. Because the fuel we got from the island had to get us back home, too. There, we emptied oil barrels and turned them into water barrels, as I said. We were too far from any port. Along with the fact that the water was covered by a layer of oil three to four fingers thick, and that it was on the deck of the ship, exposed to the African sun ... You drank it and you thought that it was nice and cool ... As if your stomach was a machine oiled with diesel. And if you left the barrel open overnight, in the morning you would find a drowned rat, big like that, inside. They were years of pain, you had to go through a lot of pain to earn a day's wage. You were sick, you were this close to dying, and he would tell you "it's a lie". The captain didn't believe you. For two months, I didn't have a bed. It took me two months to open my mattress and lie on it. How did I sleep? I got into the piles of the thick, round ropes, and I just wanted to rest my bones until the sun came out. I slept like that because there wasn't any space. We had to wait one or two months for wood to burn, or a barrel or sack of hardtack or food supplies to empty, so that there was some more space to sleep. Since the 1950s, the situation has gradually improved. By that time, even deck hand and rowers were demanding a better life on board.[46]

Beginning in the 1960s, every February a group of sponge-fishing fleet captains cooperated by issuing a call for the most economically advantageous

45   Russell, "Η σπογγαλιεία της Καλύμνου" ["The Sponge Fishery of Kalymnos"], pp. 5–9.
46   Testimony of Michalis Lampos to E.O., 29/7/2005.

contender for the provision of necessary supplies, to meet the needs of the
sponge-fishing fleet. According to the tables and data published by Russell,
it appears that, in 1965, 600 grams of cured beef corresponded to the weekly
consumption of one person. Almost all the foods contained tomato concen-
trate; they included sugar in the preparation of many dishes as a source of
energy; and olives accompanied every meal. Many divers had small reserves
of dried fruits, dried nuts, vegetables, and fruit compotes. The consumption
of alcoholic beverages was strictly forbidden. They did consume them, however, during the last month of the voyage, when production had declined, and
divers were eager to get back home. The living conditions aboard the vessels
caused, on some occasions, heated protests, or even "work stoppages" by the
crew. Many complained that they had been deceived as to the working conditions involved in the industry, that the vessels were in a terrible state, and that
they did not even have a compass.[47]

Friction and disputes between captains and crews were not uncommon.
Although there is little surviving archival material on this topic, the municipal
and public authorities held the right of arbitration, while the press published
stories of crew mutinies and recalcitrance, which "harm the future of the
sponge fishery".[48] According to oral testimonies, having accumulated a catch
large enough to pay back their *platika* and make a profit (the "*resta*", as they
called it), many divers refused to continue to dive. Although captains insisted
that divers were under obligation to work until the end of the expedition, many
divers apparently refused to continue diving, or pretended to look for sponges
while avoiding a descent to great depths.[49]

P. Zotos described brutal scenes on board sponge-fishing caiques in 1903.
Discussing an inspection that he carried out himself, and quoting diver affidavits, he refers mainly to ailing divers who received no care or treatment from
their captains. In contrast, if they were able to move, divers were dragged by
force into the sea to get sponges. If their condition was very grave, divers were
left helpless to die; then, when the vessels were able to approach land, the
deceased were buried in the sand of deserted islands or on the coasts in the
night. In other cases, divers were put in sacks with stones and buried at sea.[50]

---

47   Embassy of Tripoli-Libya, Folder 34 (1927–1929), Subfolder 1, ΙΑΥΕ.
48   *Αυγή Δωδεκανησιακή* [*Avgi Dodekanisiaki*], 15/2/1926, p. 4; Ion Dragoumis, "Οι σφουγγα-
      ράδες", *Εκλεκτά Μυθιστορήματα* ["The Sponge Fishermen", *Eklekta Mythistorimata*] 12
      (1935), p. 11.
49   See also the testimony of sponge cleaner [*balaristis*] Michalis Lampos to Ε.Ο., 29/7/2005.
50   The tragic fate of divers struck a chord in literature, as well. In "The Sponge Fishermen",
      Ion Dragoumis writes: "They tied a stone on his body and they put him back into the sea in
      the night; the weight went down and disappeared in the black waters. Old Nikolas crossed

"We didn't know what we were doing. Those were despicable, wicked years. We were in great need", confessed Giannis Koutouzis – a diver from Leros who worked on Kalymnian sponge-fishing vessels from 1945 to 1950.[51] His compatriot, Giannis Loulourgas, compared sponge fishery (1949–1955) to labouring in the Belgian mines, where he began working in 1956. He wondered if working in a mine is not, "the same thing as being on a boat with another 25 to 30 people, descending alone into the murky, dark depths; living between the sky and sea for seven months and then coming home" And, he continued: "These two things cannot be compared. They're worlds apart. I didn't feel fear in the mines. And what exactly were our rights on the sponge-fishing vessels?"[52]

Cooperation, camaraderie, and solidarity among divers was a prerequisite for their survival, however, in such a competitive environment many turned their back on these values. The following testimony is typical of the working experience of sponging crews: "Many people cheated at the work; they were not interested in harvesting sponges. There were conspiracies, foul play, and brawls. Despite their being paid with shares, there were some who didn't give their families a dime. They asked for a doctor, they rebelled".[53] It is evident then, that prolonged co-habitation of so many people in such a limited space was not easy, while the work itself fostered tension, friction, and competition.

5.1.2   The Fear and Allure of the Bottom of the Sea

Constant confrontation with the elements, the vastness of the sea, sudden changes in the weather, severe storms, the dangers of navigation, as well as unusual, unpredictable phenomena such as the tides; these factors combined were a source of insecurity and anxiety. Even when crew members had deep knowledge of the movements of the sea, and when know-how had reduced the risks of long voyages, the sea continued to be a threatening space, far removed from the stability of land. It was, therefore, a personal feat, and an adventure for those who dared to travel, fish, or dive into the watery depths.

In popular culture moreover, the sea was a mysterious space where demonic creatures and terrifying beasts resided,[54] and many of the island populations

---

himself, and they dropped the anchor a little bit farther", Dragoumis, "Οι Σφουγγαράδες" ["The Sponge Fishermen"], p. 11. In the years following WWII, the deceased were transferred to hospitals and buried in Christian cemeteries.

51   Testimony of diver Giannis Koutouzis to E.O., 25/8/2003.

52   Testimony of diver Giannis Loulourgas to E.O., 23/8/2004.

53   Testimony of diving manager [kolaouzieris] Vassilis Kampouris to E.O., 1/9/2004.

54   Michel Mollat, "Les attitudes des gens de mer devant le danger et devant la mort", Ethnologie française 9 (1979), p. 191; James M. Acheson, "Anthropology of Fishing",

had only a limited knowledge of the sea. If untamed nature was regarded as threatening, at sea uncertainty was much greater as various dangers, both natural and supernatural lay in wait, lurking at the bottom of the sea. Indeed, some thought magic or a consultation with the Divine was necessary to ensure a safe expedition and a good catch, or a successful dive. This is interesting in light of Malinowski's work on the Trobriand islands in which he showed that, when fishing in enclosed lagoons, the inhabitants of the islands he studied did not think it necessary to use magic, yet when they ventured into the open seas, the natives always performed magic rituals before departing. The magic was intended to protect the crew on the trip, and to secure a good catch,[55] while other magical incantations or religious rituals were supposed to propitiate bad weather and offer protection to those traveling great distances.

Similarly, the sponge fishermen of Kalymnos brought their Easter candles on the voyage; when the sea was rough, they would light the candles and extinguish them by plunging them into the sea in the hopes that their act would calm the waters. Similarly, myrrh taken from the procession of the Epitaph was dropped into the sea,[56] in keeping with the widely held belief that icons can travel on water, and indicate places where temples must be built in honour of the saint depicted on them.[57] The invocations to Saint Nicolas [Agios Nikolaos] to protect ships in bad weather conditions and on rough seas, prayers and ovations to the island saint just before departure, and the custom of the "saint's dive" appears in various sources. In sum, unforeseen events and dangers were regarded as insurmountable without divine intervention.

> Then in the spot they call the works,
> they hazard a few dives
> until they come up with a sponge.
> First sponge in hand, they make a cross
> upon the ship, this custom
> they call Crossing.
> Then raise a flag atop the mast,

Annual Review of Anthropology 10 (1981), pp. 276, 288; Jean Rieucau, "Océan et continent, deux éspaces vécus en mutation chez les gens de mer", *Annales de Géographie* 98/549 (1989), p. 516.

55 Bronislaw Malinowski, *Magic, Science, Religion and other Essays*, New York 1954, pp. 30–31.

56 Themelina Kapella, "Ποκινήματα, αγιασμός, αναχώρηση" ["Preparation, Sanctification, Departure"]; *Αφιέρωμα: Η Ελληνική σπογγαλιεία, Η Καθημερινή, Επτά Ημέρες* [*Greek Sponge Fishery – I Kathimerini: Feature Section Epta Imeres*], 13/9/1998, pp. 28–30.

57 Charles Stewart, "Hegemony or Rationality? The Position of the Supernatural in Modern Greece", *Journal of Modern Greek Studies* 7/1 (1989), p. 77.

reach for some food and drink,
and bless the work to start.[58]

It was also customary for the divers to offer the catch from the final dive of the season to the saints to whom they had promised it. On the crew's return, the promised sponges were given to the administrators of the churches, and their sale paid for repairs to the churches of Kalymnos and their general maintenance, as well as icon painting, and strings of sponges were hung in front of the saint's icon.[59] At the same time, however, an indication of the sponge fishermen's contradictory feelings about the object of their toil is retained in the Kalymnian saying that sponges have been cursed ever since a thirsty Jesus Christ on the cross asked for water, only to be given a sponge soaked in bile and vinegar to drink. "Since that moment, God sent sponges into the depths of the sea, so that people will go out of their way to find them".

The record of another religious custom survives in the archives of Kalymnos. In a response from the governor's office in 1896 claiming that sponge-fishing vessels were supposedly flying foreign flags, the Elders explained that,

> for a very long time now, in the last one or two hundred years, our churches are poor, and they cannot afford their maintenance costs. According to tradition, in the days preceding the sponge-fishing vessels' departure, every church gives each vessel sail-cloth icons of Christ, the Virgin Mary, Saint Nicolas, and others. Out of religious respect, each of the sponge-fishing vessels sails for one day for the church that gave the vessels their icons. Sponges caught on that specific day are given to the corresponding church. Serving as a blessing, and out of respect of a purely and exclusively religious nature, they hoist these icons up on the ships' masts, to have, so to speak, the saints' help in this dangerous professional activity, namely, the sponge fishery. And thus, wherever they wanted to go – to all corners of the Ottoman state, to Rhodes or Chios, or Benghazi – or wherever they went to work in the Ottoman state, crews hoisted these icons. As said above, no one, in the last two hundred years has admonished spongers on behalf of any Imperial Authority, because

---

58 Μητροφάνης Καλαφατάς, "Χειμερινός Όνειρος" [Mitrophanis Kalafatas, "Winter Dream"] in Michael N. Kalafatas, *The Bellstone: The Greek Sponge Divers of the Aegean*. One American's Journey Home. Hannover: Brandeis University Press, 2003, p. 250.

59 See Figuier, *Les merveilles de la science*, p. 624; Themelina Kapella, "Ποκινήματα, αγιασμός, αναχώρηση" ["Preparation, Sanctification, Departure"], pp. 28–30.

as noted above, it is evident that these are not flags but icons of a purely religious nature.[60]

For those exploring the sea's dark depths, the terror inspired by the uncertainty and danger of navigating unpredictable seas, cannot be overstated.[61] Various pieces of archival evidence from the late 19th century refer to sponge fishing as the "most dangerous" of occupations, and note that sponge fishermen fed "their poor families by fighting the terrible elements of nature: sea, wind, excessive heat, and even the great fish [cetaceans] of the sea".[62] Thus, the Kalymnian curse "may the sea eat you" may come as no surprise.[63] In the island's coffee shops, divers are said to recount shark attacks and encounters with enormous cetaceans, as well as tales of strange shadows and unknown beings slithering through the great depths.[64]

Allusions to the fear of sea – diving in the dark, uncharted depths – as well as both the acceptance and denial of that fear, is common in written and oral testimonies. On 3 October 1911, when local authorities summoned mechanical diver Ioannis Kefalianos or Anatolitis to explain why he did not set sail with Ioannis Gialafos's vessel, the diver replied "because I was afraid".[65] Another diver made a solemn statement requesting the termination of his employment "not due to any pathological illness or any other cause, but due to fear, as this year I feel my body is too physically weakened to dive".[66] Citing fear, whether genuine or a feigned excuse, could not possibly have been considered a valid

---

60   Doc. 87, 27/4/1895, Correspondence 1894–1895, MAK; Doc. 116, 17/5/1896, Correspondence 1895–1896, MAK. Moreover, as stipulated in the "local sponge fee": "sponges dedicated to local churches and sold by the committees of said churches are not subject to any local fee". Doc. 90, 4/7/1915, MC Minutes 1915–1916, MAK.

61   Cleveland Moffett considered diving to be one of the most dangerous professions, *Careers of Danger and Daring*, New York 1901, pp. 40–86.

62   The excerpt featured above is taken from a letter of the Elders' Council of Kalymnos addressed to the Elders' Council of Symi, dated 1 August 1885, and has been publshed in Giorgis Koukoulis, "Δύο έγγραφα της Δημογεροντίας Καλύμνου προς τη Δημογεροντία Σύμης", *Καλυμνιακά Χρονικά* ["Two Documents of the Elders' Council of Kalymnos to the Elders' Council of Symi", *Kalymniaka Chronika*] 6 (1986), pp. 53–55.

63   Eirini Marinou, "Η λειτουργία των μοτίβων στα παραμύθια και στις παραδόσεις της Καλύμνου", *Καλυμνιακά Χρονικά* ["The Function of Patterns in Tales and Traditions of Kalymnos", *Kalymniaka Chronika*], 13 (1999), p. 82.

64   Michael N. Kalafatas, *The Bellstone: The Greek Sponge Divers of the Aegean. One American's Journey Home*, Brandeis University Press, Hannover 2003, p. 75.

65   Doc. 127, 3/10/1911, MC Minutes 1910–1912, MAK.

66   Solemn Statement [1948] Embassy of Tripoli-Libya, Folder 45 (1947–1948), Subfolder 3, IAYE.

justification for work relief in this demanding labour context, where financial obligations and advance payments existed.

Logically, moreover, novice divers were more vulnerable to fear, as the Sponge Fishery Supervisor in Libya noted in 1952, in a report in which he mentions the following concerning divers in the Dodecanese:

> Those wishing to take up diving as a profession enter into a contract with an investor in a sponge-fishing vessel in the capacity of novice and, after receiving an advance payment, they are recruited. Said novices, having absolutely no knowledge of the regulations, are taught how to handle the oxygen control valve poorly and, without delay, they are forced to dive far deeper than what their inexperience would permit. If fear grips them, which is quite probable (given that it is not a rare phenomenon to recruit novices who have had no prior contact with the sea whatsoever), and if they express their wish to terminate their contract, they will fall out with the investor or the captain, because work will suffer a setback on one hand and, on the other hand, they will not be in a position to return the advance payment, which they spend, in most cases, as soon as they get it.[67]

Giannis Loulourgas also described the fear that could grip divers, recalling "I crossed myself a thousand times, when it was my turn to go down to 60 or 70 meters, alone in the dark sea. It was only at 10 meters from the sea bottom you could see and fish".[68] As Dimitris Peros also lamented:

> You were forced to go drown yourself for nothing. When I first started working with sponges, I was very scared. It was too deep and dark; you couldn't see a thing. You reach a point where blood comes out of your ears and your nostrils. Your mouth goes dry. You cross yourself before you dive because the job is dangerous. The diving manager [*kolaouzieris*] crosses himself, too. If you come back, you come back.

---

67   "Έκθεσις εν σχέσει με την διεξαγωγήν της σπογγαλιείας εις τα παράλια της Λιβύης κατά την θερινή περίοδον 1952" ["Report on Sponge Fishing off the Coasts of Libya in the Summer Season of 1952"], Lieutenant Commander Em. A. Koutsikopoulos, Sponge Fishery Overseer, Tripoli 28/11/1952, Embassy of Tripoli-Libya, Folder 46 (1952), Subfolder 4, IAYE.

68   Testimony of Giannis Loulourgas to E.O., 23/8/2004.

Diver Peros, however, also explained that even though his lower extremities were paralyzed from diver's disease, the beauty of the sea bottom was unparalleled. "The sea down there is beautiful. You marvel at it. It has lush vegetation, mountains, and lovely caves. Does the land have all these beauties? No, it does not".[69]

Popular beliefs and practices – or whatever term we might choose to describe beliefs and practices that are common – concerned with securing the safe return of sponge fishermen, were assimilated into various aspects of the lives of divers and their families, as well as those of the entire population. Before departing, for example, ships would fall into formation in the sign of a cross while still in port, and only then leave. There are, moreover, a great number of couplets and songs – the "Kalimerismata"[70] in particular – that were sung on the island at the departure and on the return of the sponge fishermen. Women, daughters, and mothers expressed their anger, appeased the sea, and begged the saints to protect their loved ones, and help bring them back with many sponges.

Saint Nicolas of Pothia, protector of our island
Watch over our sponge fishermen, who are our life
Give them, Blessed Mary, many years to live
As many as the branches of the lemon trees
May Blessed Mary give you safe travels,
Give them Blessed Mary, Give them
Fine sponges at their feet
May you find many sponges and come back fit
I will cover the machine's suit with gold and silver
Your little body to hold, that thus I might save it
My dear azure sea, keep an eye on my child in thee[71]

---

69   Testimony of Dimitris Peros to E.O., 24/8/2004. The sea bottom's beguiling appeal made it possible for many divers to shrug off the fear, at least in hindsight. They also appear to have been able to confront their role in the industry more rationally. "I was never scared of my job. It was as if I was going to a fair. I really liked it. I built a large fortune thanks to it." Testimony of Antonis Kampourakis to E.O., 25/8/2002.

70   With these, they wished their loved ones the best of luck and a safe return. See Carl Flegel, *Η νήσος Κάλυμνος* [*The Island of Kalymnos*], Constantinople 1896, p. 36; and by the same author, "Η Α.Θ. Παναγιότης ο Οικουμενικός Πατριάρχης Άνθιμος ο Ζ' εν Καλύμνω" ["His All-Holiness Ecumenical Patriarch Anthimos VII"], Samos 1896, p. 22.

71   Manuscript 778/1968–1969, Maria Koutouzi, p. 34, CFS.

5.2   Sponge Processing

To avoid rot, sponges must be carefully cleaned, and the initial processing took place during the voyage on the deck of the largest auxiliary vessel. When extracted from the sea, sponges are black, covered with a thin protective membrane, and have a slimy, viscous surface.[72] While all sponges are initially black, the first step in the process is separating the "tame" sponges from the "wild" sponges that cannot be processed and softened, and are therefore, useless, and valueless. Wild sponges harvested due to inexperience or by mistake were thrown back into the sea, and the rest of the catch was logged by the captain and the divers together, so that each knew the quantity harvested.

The crew then began the arduous task of thoroughly squeezing the sponges to break up the membrane covering, during which part of the process the sponges secrete a white, milky liquid. This task required careful attention to avoid destroying the sponges in the slow process of breaking down the membrane covering.[73] This they did with their feet or with a beating tool [*kopanos*] made from the trunks of various plants and trees, most often date palms and palm trees, which had a smooth, wide surface. After cleaning the sponges, the crew trimmed perturbances and irregularities and, with a special sponge-needle, threaded them onto a fine rope, and left them submerged in sea water over night. On the following day, any unwanted debris was cleaned from the surface of the sponges. The sponges were then washed again, squeezed, and hung under the sun – in what spongers called "*armathiasma*" – that is, hanging in bunches – from the vessel's masts to dry for approximately three days. When an experienced crew was available, a rough trimming [*kapetanistiko*] could be done on the vessel, prior to sorting the sponges into categories [*sortirisma*], that is, by quality from "first" and "second", to "sixth" and "seventh", which were worthless [*skarta*]. The sponges were then piled and compressed by workers who trod on the sponges to reduce their volume [*balarisma*].[74]

---

72   It is reported that, during the 1860s, sponges were placed in large wooden crates soaked in sea water, and then transported "almost alive" from the coasts of Syria to Marseilles; J. Toutain, *La Tunisie au debut du xxième siècle*, Paris 1904, p. 155.

73   Testimony of sponge cleaner [*balaristis*] Michalis Lampos to E.O., 29/7/2005; Testimony of diver Thrasyvo(u)los Politis to E.O., 18/8/2004; Toutain, *La Tunisie*, p. 167.

74   Pachountakis, Η σπογγαλιεία εν Αιγύπτω [*Sponge Fishing in Egypt*], pp. 9–10; Leon Arnou, *Manuel de l'épicier. Produits alimentaires et conservés, denrées coloniales, boissons et spiritueux ... etc.*, Paris 1904, p. 438; Roxane Caftanzoglou, "Kalymnos: Contribution à la connaissance d'une société", Mémoire de maîtrise d'ethnologie spécialisée (unpublished MA thesis), Paris 1978, pp. 20–21.

IMAGE 5.1   Washing the sponges, 1950
SOURCE: PHOTOGRAPH BY DIMITRIOS HARISIADIS, KALYMNOS 1950
© BENAKI MUSEUM/PHOTOGRAPHIC ARCHIVES

The compressed sponges were then placed in numbered sacks by quality and, for those working for shares, sponges were stored in sacks on which
the name of each diver was written. When large quantities of sponges were
accumulated, they were weighed and sent back on the "*paketo*" or by steamship. "As time went by and numbers increased, the *sortirisma*, the sorting, got
messier", confessed M. Lampos, by which he meant that sponges of inferior
quality ended up in sacks of first and second quality sponges.[75] As Alexandros
Lemonidis explained in greater detail,

75   Testimony of Michalis Lampos to E.O., 29/7/2005.

IMAGE 5.2 *Sortirisma* or Sorting the Sponges into Categories
SOURCE: PHOTOGRAPH BY DIMITRIOS HARISIADIS, KALYMNOS 1950
© BENAKI MUSEUM/PHOTOGRAPHIC ARCHIVES

When sponges were taken from the sea, the finest of them were mostly dark-coloured, and did not contain any sand. To bleach them, sponge fishermen washed them on the shore, scrubbing them with fine sea sand. To make them heavier, they introduced some kind of sand into their pores which is very difficult to remove. As is customary, the buyer weighed the sponges only after airing the agreed upon quantities for 4 and 5 days in a row, and then beating or shaking them. Only after this double procedure [was the purchase finalized]. But it was always almost impossible to completely remove the foreign substances inside the sponges. They estimated the waste from these sponges at 20, 30, 40, up to 50 per cent. In general,

IMAGE 5.3   Sponges put in numbered sacks, 1950
SOURCE: PHOTOGRAPH BY DIMITRIOS HARISIADIS, KALYMNOS 1950
© BENAKI MUSEUM/PHOTOGRAPHIC ARCHIVES

the body of sponge is a blackish flexible mass, twiggy and with holes on all over its surface, composed of a compact substance, which is an irritant or hard, and is removed by washing.[76]

In one report written by Newton in 1854, as well as in another written in 1873 by Billioti, Vice Consul of England in Rhodes, we again read that sponge fishermen

---

76   Alexandros Lemonidis, *Το εμπόριον της Τουρκίας* [*Turkey's Trade*], Constantinople 1849, pp. 159–160.

put fine sand in sponges to increase their weight. In response merchants began buying sponges by the piece.[77]

There is an estimated total of 5,000 species and varieties of sponges in the world's various seas, of which approximately 400 are considered marketable.[78] Their scientific names were, and remain, unknown to the sponge fishermen of the Mediterranean, who simply make a distinction between "tame" and "wild" sponges because wild sponges are difficult to uproot, as well as being easily destroyed, and non-processable. Given that different kinds of sponges look alike, divers must be familiar with different species in order to tell them apart.

"Tame" sponges, the marketable species, are classified by various categories based on their texture, size, and hardness from fine to bulky, from first to sixth or most common. The varieties of sponges are referred to as thick or "*tsimoucha*" [also known as leather sponge, or *Spongia zimoca*], mainly used in the manufacture of porcelain; "*kapadiko* or main sponge" [honey comb, or *Hippospongia communis*]; "*matapas*" [*Spongia adriatica*]; the irregularly shaped "*lagofyto*" [elephant ear, or *Spongia lamella*]; and "*fino*" or "*melat(th)io*" or "*levantiniko*" [*Spongia mollissima*], which are very soft and absorbent.[79] Each category was priced differently on the market.[80] The best, the biggest, and those with a soft texture and a particular shape could be sold by the piece, and the remainder was sold by the oka (1.282 kilograms).[81]

Sponge fishermen considered sponges from Libya to be the best, followed by those from Crete, whereas the Aegean sponges were of inferior quality, and sold at lower prices. However, according to Alexandros Lemonidis,

77   Newton, *Travels and Discoveries*, p. 293; Kyriakos Kon. Chatzidakis, "Η σπογγαλιεία στις Νότιες Σποράδες στα μέσα του 19ου αιώνα", *Καλυμνιακά Χρονικά* ["Sponge Fishery in the Southern Sporades in the Mid-19th Century", *Kalymniaka Chronika*], 13 (1999), p. 233.

78   Roberto Pronzato, "Sponge-Fishing, Disease and Farming in the Mediterranean Sea", *Aquatic Conservation: Marine and Freshwater Ecosystems* 9 (1999), p. 485; Alain Gilli, Patrick Maillard, *Plongée dans le monde de spongiaires: Guide des éponges de la Méditerranée*, Marseilles 2000, p. 30. For the different species and their characteristics, see Edward Potts, *Fresh Water Sponges: A Monograph*, Academy of Natural Sciences, Philadelphia 1887; H. V. Wilson, *The Sponges*, Cambridge, USA, 1904.

79   For marketable species, see also Ernest J. J. Cresswell, *Sponges: Their Nature, History, Modes of Fishing, Varieties, Cultivation, etc*, London 1921, pp. 22–28.

80   Themelis Kindynis, *Η νήσος Κάλυμνος* [*The Island of Kalymnos*], Athens 1879, pp. 24–26; Tutain, *La Tunisie*, pp. 153–154; Sotirios Agapitidis, "Η οικονομική οργάνωση των σπογγαλιευ- τικών συγκροτημάτων – ειδικότερα στη Σύμη", *Τα Συμαίικα* ["The Economic Organization of Sponge-Fishing Groups – Particularly on Symi", *Ta Symaiika*], 3 (1977), pp. 200–201.

81   Testimony of Nikolas Kampourakis to E.O., 28/7/2005.

The fine quality sponges from Kalymnos, Ikaria, the islands of Greece and Syria rank higher than sponges of all other qualities from other areas. They are divided into three classes according to use: fine white sponges, fine hard yellow sponges, and common thick ones – the first category was used in toiletries, the second was used for household applications, military and surgical purposes, and the final category was used for cleaning houses, stables, vehicles of all kinds, and so on.[82]

According to reports, various species were found in different areas.[83] However, in terms of quality, the *"tsimouches"* of Cyrenaica and Egypt sponges are high quality, along with the *"lagofyta"* of Lampedusa and Pantelleria, and the *"fina"* of Egypt and Syria.[84]

When fishing vessels arrived at the island, they laid out the sponges, the "lots" [*partides*], at the port on public display to attract sponge merchants. After the necessary negotiations, the merchandise was sold as a single load, excepting a very few cases where the sponge merchant selected the sponges he wanted to buy. The crew members who were entitled to a share from the catch took part in the negotiations and the final deal.[85] Everyone, including the divers, was present in the sale.[86]

Once sold, the next step in the processing of the sponges began in the sponge merchants' warehouses[87] in which many of the inhabitants of the

---

82   Lemonidis, *Το εμπόριον της Τουρκίας* [*Turkey's Trade*], pp. 156–157.

83   Dimosthenis Chaviaras, *Περί σπόγγων και σπογγαλιείας από των αρχαιοτάτων χρόνων μέχρι των καθ' ημάς* [*On Sponges and Sponge Fishing from Ancient Times to the Present Day*], Athens 1916, pp. 26, 43–44. On the same topic see P. L. Simmonds, *The Commercial Products of the Sea or, Marine Contributions to Food, Industry and Art*, London 1878, pp. 164–170; *Δωδεκάνησος. Τετράτομος μελέτη του Υπουργείου Ανοικοδομήσεως και συνεργατών του υπό την διεύθυνσιν του κ. Κ. Α. Δοξιάδη", Σειρά Εκδόσεων του Υπουργείου Ανοικοδομήσεως* [*Dodecanese. Study in Four Volumes by the Ministry for Reconstruction Under Mr K. A. Doxiadis, Publication Series of Ministry for Reconstruction*], Athens 1947, pp. 131–133.

84   Ant. Papakonstantinou, "Σπογγαλιευτική και αλιευτική δραστηριότητα (Από τη σκοπιά της Αγροτικής Τράπεζας)", *Καλυμνιακά Χρονικά* ["Sponge-Fishing and Fishing Activity (From the Point of View of the Agricultural Bank)", *Kalymniaka Chronika*] 2 (1981), p. 165.

85   Nikos Papazoglou, "Επεξεργασία και εμπόριο", *Αφιέρωμα: Η Ελληνική σπογγαλιεία* ["Processing and Trade", *Greek Sponge Fishery, I Kathmerini: Feature Section Epta Imeres*, 13/9/1998, pp. 9–12.]

86   Faith Warm, *Bitter Sea*, pp. 60–61.

87   M. Zairi wrote that "the big warehouses of Vouvalis, Olympitis, Alfred, Tavlarios, Tsagaris, Sapounakis and others, processed up to 100 tons of sponges". She added that, at that time, the people, whose families traditionally processed sponges, imported and sold them in Greece and abroad. Maria Zairi "Οι αποθήκες των σφουγγαριών", *Καλυμνιακά Χρονικά* ["Sponge Warehouses", *Kalymniaka Chronika*] 15 (2003), pp. 417–419.

islands worked. Since 1948, sponges have been stored in special warehouses under the supervision of the ATE [Agricultural Bank of Greece], provided that the ATE had granted the sponge-fishing loan for the expedition on which the sponges were harvested. In such cases, both a manager acting on behalf of the ATE and the captain kept a key to the warehouse in their possession. This phase included another systematic cleaning, washing, drying, trimming, and sorting of the sponges into different categories – based on their size and quality and, finally, packing the sponges into wooden crates. After the sale, further processing took place in the merchant's warehouses. The sponges were then unpacked and rewashed with sea water by hand, and cleaned for any remaining stones, sand, or other foreign substances. The sponges were then carefully sorted into categories and qualities and trimmed to improve their shape. The largest leftover pieces, the "clippings" [*psalidies*], were also marketed for a variety of more specialized purposes, such as shoemaking.

In more recent years, sponges are placed in a hydrochloric acid solution for several hours to remove any solid components in their interior cavities. They are then immersed in sea-water tanks to be rinsed and cleaned. To fully neutralize the hydrochloric acid, which makes the sponges darker and harder, sponges are dipped in a solution of caustic potash or caustic soda for a few minutes, thus softening them and improving their elasticity. Sponges undergo a more intense bleaching by immersion into permanganic acid, followed by a wash with a sulphuric acid solution to soften them. Having been thoroughly cleaned by means of continuous washings, sponges were again dipped into a diluted solution of caustic soda to insure a soft texture and elasticity. The sponges were then immersed in sea water tanks again to remove all chemical substances. This process was repeated two or three times, until the sponges are thoroughly cleaned and bleached.[88]

Along with the other methods of sponge processing described above, the next step was to dry the sponges and compress them with a manual press. Sponges were then sorted into qualities and sizes and, to facilitate their transport they were pressed again, either by stomping on them or with large manual presses. Finally, sponges were packed in sacks on which the quantity and type was written.

The records show that, in the period between the two world wars, approximately 700 people were employed in sponge merchants' warehouses, and large sponge trading houses, such as the one belonging to N. Vouvalis, which employed about 100 workers, both male and female. In the 1950s, men and women would apparently beg for temporary employment, which meant

---

88   Roxane Caftanzoglou, *Kalymnos*, p. 23.

working from dawn to sunset for a small wage, which was often nothing more than a bit of food.[89] "At least 350 people worked at trimming", claimed Michalis Lampos. "As soon as I returned from the voyage, I would go to the warehouse. In the evening, I finished work at 11 or 12 o'clock. This went on until Easter. Then it was time to set sail again."[90]

In the 1970s, there were approximately 100 employees, and all of them worked on a seasonal basis. Active or retired sponge fishermen, as well as various other people, worked in sponge processing to supplement their income. The sponge trade house of Koutouzis, which had relocated its headquarters in Bordeaux late in the 19th century, had warehouses on Kalymnos, but the final chemical processing was carried out in Bordeaux.[91] At the same time, the 1970s saw the emergence and increase of synthetic sponge manufacturing, and the use of synthetic sponges would change consumer habits, and have a significant impact on the trade in natural sponges.[92]

5.3   Labour and Social Conflicts

Informants depict sponge fishing as a powerful web of competing interests between involved parties: crews, captains, investors, and sponge merchants. Collective memory is still in pursuit of victimizers and victims, manipulators and guilty parties, speculators, and breadwinners, with each group blaming the other for problems related to the industry, and particularly divers' disease.

Various contradictory points of view are all legitimated by the past, and by the "small" and the "big" people who formed the Kalymnian community. They tell of unrest and confrontations about the rights of the working classes, universal suffrage, the organization of education, and the system of taxation.[93] Testimonies describe a pre-existing, established social stratification that continued to inhere, as well as the island's important families whose members exploited workers in the sponge fishery – both captains and crews. Adding

---

89   Faith Warm, *Bitter Sea*, p. 62.
90   Testimony of Michalis Lampos to E.O., 29/7/2005.
91   Roxane Caftanzoglou, *Kalymnos*, p. 21.
92   Synthetic sponge manufactures are mentioned beginning in 1976; ibid., p. 23.
93   See Ludwig Ross, "Νησιωτικά ταξείδια (*Inselreisen*) Κάλυμνος-Τέλενδος. Κατά μετάφρασιν υπό Μ. Μιχαηλίδου Νουάρου", *Δωδεκανησιακή Επιθεωρία* ["Island Travels: Kalymnos – Telendos". Translation, M. Michailidou Nouarou, *Dodekanisiaki Epitheorisi*] 8 (1947), p. 335. See also Theofilos M. Tsoukalas, "Αναφορά στον Λέρνης Ιερεμία Πατελλάκη (1819–1844)", *Καλυμνιακά Χρονικά* ["Report to Ieremias Patellakis of Lerne (1819–1844)", *Kalymniaka Chronika*], 13 (1999), pp. 147–158.

further to the discussion, the literacy of the rich and the illiteracy of sponge fishermen acted as a social shibboleth and further reinforced how status shaped the terms of social distinctions. According to sources and more recent testimonies, the largest number of sponge fishermen continued to reside in Chora, whereas the wealthiest resided in Pothia: "There were both poor and rich people on the island. I've told you; captains were the rich ones. They had big houses, they ate wheat bread, and instead of sending their children to work with sponges, they sent them to Athens to study".[94]

Archival material safeguards the scattered records of this kind, while the general observation that Kalymnos has experienced social conflict since at least the beginning of the 19th century still holds. Moreover, the social group that enjoyed power seems to have been represented by those holding communal offices, although the characteristics of this class, in the absence of detailed sources, are not readily discernable. Further adding to the difficulty of examining the structure of social groups on the island, the underlying social stratification of Kalymnos was not based exclusively on land assets, given that arable areas were limited in size and divided into small parcels.

Until 1922, except for a very small number of families who maintained sizable farmlands on the coasts of Asia Minor opposite Kalymnos, the rest of the population was more or less forced to secure its survival by means of a variety of activities and non-agricultural occupations. Indeed, even prior to its "modernization" and "mechanization", Kalymnian sponge production had been significant. Figures, where available, suggest that a considerable sector of the population was engaged in the harvesting of sizable quantities of sponges, and the export of the sponges to international markets by various means. According to Miltiadis Carabokyros, while Kalymnians might have spent 4 or 5 months each year "living like amphibians", the sponge fishery allowed them to survive on their barren island. Moreover, they created a booming industry, which in Carabokyros' opinion, made almost unbelievable progress possible. Carabokyros cites the foundation of cities adorned with large private and public buildings, the foundation of schools for boys and girls, the admirable organization of social benefits for all citizens, the merchant houses that thrived in European cities, and the education of Kalymnians abroad.[95]

The number of Kalymnian artists, scientists and prelates who studied in Greece and abroad was substantial and, beginning in the final decades of the 19th century, Kalymnos also serviced the neighbouring island areas with

---

94   Manuscript 2729/1976, Angeliki Georgiadou, p. 121, CFS.

95   Milt. Carabokyro, *Étude sur la pêche des éponges. Les pays spongifères de l'Empire et le scaphandre*, Constantinople 1886, p. 7.

teachers and physicians.[96] Scions of well-off families, who studied in Athens and abroad, moved between Kalymnos, London, Paris, Trieste, and Odessa, and came together with their fellow Kalymnians, forming a group with their fellow Kalymnians', forming a Kalymnian diaspora. As Th. Kindynis noted,

> Kalymnians sent their sons to Athens to benefit from the best education; from 1867 to 1878, Kalymnos counted more than 15 scientists trained in Athens and in Europe among its natives. Currently, there are approximately 30 students in Athens, of which only a few are studying at the university; the rest are high school students, who are distinguished thanks to their intelligence and diligence among all other high school students.[97]

Compatriots and relatives of sponge merchants sought a means of livelihood in their businesses, as well as ways to escape from the island environment where the most common way out was working on vessels.[98] It was among these literate, cosmopolitan groups that the ideas of liberation from colonial rule and of annexation to Greece were formed. National self-determination and social advancement in Greece were linked to education, and the wealthy sought to educate their children to university level and contributed in various ways to their birthplace. They built schools, funded their operation, and granted scholarships to underprivileged young men to study in Athens or abroad.[99]

The island's labour and social scene changed in the final decades of the 19th century, given that a significant number of those involved were unable to keep up with the new developments and terms under which work on board sponging vessels was organized, and the trade of the catch conducted abroad was reshaped. Even though the old business group was supplemented with new faces, even though developments made some of them obsolete, they nevertheless kept fishing and trading small quantities of sponges. This context made it possible for many Kalymnians to adjust to new conditions, including conducting international commercial activities, and the possibility of quick

---

96   Relevant references are scattered in the archive. See, for example, Georgios M. Sakellaridis, "Η εξέλιξη και διαμόρφωση του πληθυσμού της Καλύμνου", *Καλυμνιακά Χρονικά* ["The evolution and formation of the population of Kalymnos", *Kalymniaka Chronika*], 9 (1990), p. 399.

97   Kindynis, *Η νήσος Κάλυμνος* [*The Island of Kalymnos*], p. 26.

98   See, for example, Giannis Th. Kindynis, "Ιωάννης Σκεύου Ορφανός", *Καλυμνιακά Χρονικά* ["Ioannis Skevou Orfanos", *Kalymniaka Chronika*] 17 (2007), pp. 85–92.

99   See also David Sutton, "Re-Scripting Women's Collective Action: Nationalist Writing and the Politics of Gendered Memory", *Identities* 5/4 (1999), p. 474.

enrichment. The precarious conditions under which the sponge fishery and sponge trade were carried out, as well as the significant capital required for the organization of fishery using scaphander diving suits, with its multi-member crews and prolonged voyages to the coasts of North Africa, has previously been pointed out.[100]

The activity's peak period is the focus of our interest here, yet the favourable circumstances in which it occurred lasted for less than a century. The sponge fishery constituted social capital that shaped the choices, strategies, and the culture of Kalymnian society, perhaps not uniformly, but through much interaction and many common features. At the same time, however, social diversification and stratification was also maintained through the deep memory of social fabric – the warp and weave of class structure – including all the subsequent modifications to that fabric. Were one to seek analogies with other lands and environments, one might say that Kalymnian "aristocracy" maintained its self-references to the past, while continuing to hold a prominent position in local society, as well as in its diaspora communities. And while the local population did indeed make a distinction between former sponge merchants and former sponge fishermen, or sponge-fishing vessels' captains, this distinction was not made on the basis of material criteria, which have now possibly changed. In other words, in the post-peak period, social class might have been determined on the basis of other factors such as scientific distinction, artistic virtuoso, public office, or running one of the commercial businesses that replaced the sponge trading houses.

Here it is worth citing Ludwig Ross' account, in which he refers to the events of August 1841, at some length:

> The island's population had gathered for an assembly in front of the church of Panagia at that time, and the meeting was quite turbulent. The island, according to university students and their relatives, was facing internal worries. To achieve its ascension, the rising and struggling middle class wants good schools. The middle class consists mostly of well-off seafarers and small-scale merchants, including all of the Greeks, that is, approximately one hundred householders who hold Greek citizenship, or who reside here with Greek passports. The members of the middle class have gathered a nominal capital of 100,000 kuruş, so that the interest rate paid for each share (10,000 kuruş) is invested in the maintenance of such an educational institution, as well as in its teachers. Local notables, however, took a stand against this initiative; the Kalymnian-born Bishop of

---

100   See chapters 4 and 5 of the present volume.

Leros spearheaded the opposition and asked: "What do we need all this education for? This is what damages us; we get lost with it. Let us deal with the sponge, just like our fathers did".

Apart from these grievances, there were other, material reasons for discord, such as various old debts with which people continued to be officially burdened. Last fall, discord exploded in the most intense fashion. After being threatened by the inhabitants, officials came upon the idea of winning over those dependent on them such as day-laborers and the poor, to whom they offered bread and promises. Hence, the bed of a wider stream flowing from the mountains split the city into two enemy camps. On the one bank stood the liberals, who by a paradoxical reversal of their convictions, called themselves "Spartans", and on the other bank stood their aristocratic rivals and their supporters, who had taken the party name of "Athenians".

In November and December, and almost daily for forty days, the two opposing parties would come down to the flat bed on either side of the stream and shoot one another. Fortunately, however, outcomes were less bloody than those of the battles fought in the first ten years of the siege of Ilion [Troy], and a total of five or six people were killed and approximately twenty people were injured over the course of the war. Since that time, a truce prevails, except for the Easter period when a deplorable mob killed one of the officials by beating him with clubs and then shooting him.

In the meantime, they have turned to the Pasha of Rhodes and to an Agha who has given his commanding capacity [*Soubashi*, or commander of the town], along with an Ottoman policeman [*kavass*]. But the fire is still burning beneath the ashes, and all the inhabitants believe that when the sponge fishermen return in fall, the fight will resume much more intensely than before. If the poor Agha, together with his policeman, dares to intervene between the fighting parties, then it is very likely that he will be on the receiving end of the first bullet. Everyone has grown tired of this situation and wishes for better administration. "If only we had just ten policemen here, these things wouldn't happen", they complained. I asked them why they wouldn't bury the hatchet, given that they wanted to find peace, and they replied: "our suffering has reached its peak, and without violence no one will be first to take a step back".

If one were to remove the inhabitants' modern attire, the Ottoman Agha, and the riffles, would it not be just as if I were recounting infighting among small (city-) states in ancient times? Apart from the present-day low level of education with which we are provided by the autonomous Greek municipal authorities under Ottoman rule, this is a faithful reproduction of the state of affairs in ancient Greek democracies or in the free communities of medieval cities. To this is worth adding the expression of one ingenious author, who quite astutely called the island of Hydra a "Turkish free state city", just slightly before the [Greek] Revolution.[101]

However, twenty years later, Hippocrates Tavlarios also wrote an article about the civil war that broke out in 1840 in the journal *Pandora* [Πανδώρα], in which he blamed the war on the "greed and profiteering of the notables".[102]

A similar internal conflict appears to have taken place in 1880, when some attempted to divide the integrated community into the Municipality of Beach-Port [*Paralia-Limin*] and the Municipality of Chora, or to transfer its administrative seat from Chora to Pothia.[103] Although archival evidence is not particularly enlightening on this point, one cannot help but wonder who these Kalymnians were, "the ones who were known for their social stature", who reportedly collaborated with the local Elders [*Kaymakam*], and divided the island's population. At that time, was it perhaps a segment of the local elite, with their own conflicting interests, that arose within the leading social group as new social conditions were taking shape due to capital invested in sponge fishery, and the profits generated by the booming international sponge trade?

5.3.1 *The Scaphander Diving Suit and the Restructuring of the Social Fabric*

As discussed in detail in Chapter 4, the technical tools for sponge fishery were very few and, most importantly, rudimentary, until around the mid-19th century. The introduction of the scaphander diving suit in the 1860s upset the activity's traditional structures, and greatly impacted on the physiognomy of the sponge-fishing islands of the Dodecanese. "Naked diving" and fishing

---

101 Γεώργιος Χρ. Χαραμαντάς (επιμ.), "Λουδοβίκος Ρος (Ludwig Ross), "Νησιωτικά ταξίδια. Κάλυμνος-Τέλενδος. Εικοστή πρώτη επιστολή"", *Καλυμνιακά Σύμμεικτα* [Georgios Chr. Charamandas (ed.), "Ludwig Ross, 'Island Travels: Kalymnos-Telendos. Twenty-First Letter'", *Kalymniaka Symmeikta*] 1 (1993), pp. 71–74. See also the writings of Σακελλάρης Ν. Τρικοίλης, "Κοινωνική διαστρωμάτωση στην Κάλυμνο του 18ου και 19ου αιώνα", *Καλυμνιακά Χρονικά* [Sakellaris N. Trikoilis, "Social Stratification on Kalymnos in the 18th and 19th centuries", *Kalymniaka Chronika*] 17 (2007), pp. 60–61.

102 Hippocrates Tavlarios, "Περί της νήσου Καλύμνου", *Πανδώρα* ["About the Island of Kalymnos", *Pandora*] 12 (1861–1862), pp. 518–522. The text is republished in Δανιήλ Ζερβός, "Μια περιγραφή της Καλύμνου του 1862 και ένα πολιτικό κείμενο του 1908", *Καλυμνιακά Χρονικά* [Daniil Zervos, "A 1862 Description of Kalymnos and a Political Text of 1908", *Kalymniaka Chronika*] 18 (2009), pp. 85–125.

103 See Kyriakos K. Chatzidakis, "Η Κάλυμνος στα τέλη της Τουρκοκρατίας", *Καλυμνιακά Χρονικά* ["Kalymnos at the End of the Turkish Rule", *Kalymniaka Chronika*], 8 (1989), pp. 66–67.

from on board a vessel using a hook could no longer compete with the productive capacities of the new method, any more than spongers could meet
the increased demand for sponges from the industries of the West. Improved
performance, however, was dependent on high investments, given that crews
of 30–50 men, and their equipment, required significant capital investment in
the 19th century.

The "mechanization" of the sole productive activity on the island of
Kalymnos set a number of internal processes in motion and restructured the
social fabric. Mid-19th-century Kalymnian society may be characterized by
several factors, among which are changes in the composition of population,
the emergence of a local elite and of a labour force with its own distinct internal hierarchy. Carl Flegel's account of the sartorial habits of Kalymnian men is
perhaps revealing in this regard:

> The attire of men is rather diverse, as is to be expected, since the island
> features men ranging from the most conservative shepherd to the bold
> navigator and diver, and the elegant, high-profile merchant of the capitals
> of Hesperia [Western Europe] [...] The popular, until then, red fez with
> its black or cyan [sky blue] tassel has already become rare. We often see
> the straw hats of Florence, sometimes we also see the Russian caps, worn
> by those going to Russia, who are commonly called "*Róssioi*" [*Ρώσιοι*].[104]

Therefore, at the end of the 19th century, a new set of social correlations takes
form which, as elsewhere, is the result of some being able to take advantage
of a favourable economic situation; this does not however, create conditions
that insure stability and durability. In the sponge fishery moreover, insecurity
and uncertainty are more intense given that this is a productive sector with a
high business risk factor, which is reflected in the structure of investment that
supported it. Indeed, launching sponge-fishing groups was a peculiar investment in human skill as well as in chance, with all the risks that the enterprise
entailed. All parties involved in the sponge fishery were, in effect, vulnerable
and exposed to a series of unforseeable factors and unpredictable events, such
as the exhaustion of sponge-bearing beds in various areas, frequent real or artificial market crises, competition, and accidents.

Along with the above, new conditions in sponge production and international sponge trade organization changed the structure of exports, and

---

104   Flegel, *Η νήσος Κάλυμνος* [*The island of Kalymnos*], pp. 40–41. For more on the topic of
        Kalymnians who left the island to work in Russia, see Chapter 4 of the present volume,
        pp. 264–267.

resulted in the foundation of robust Kalymnian businesses, headquartered in the most important European trade centres. On the one hand, the operation of commercial shops abroad put Kalymnians in touch with the culture of the Greek diaspora and, on the other, led to a more efficient organization of their activities in their homeland. At the same time, port development, and the improvement of maritime transport and urban infrastructure were essential components of the proper functioning of a sponge-fishing business. Lenders, investors, captains, and sponge merchants formed a dynamic social group that expanded the limits of its activities, while materially improving lives and adopting "modernizing" behaviours, attitudes, and consumer standards.

A lack of sources makes it difficult to form a clear picture of the population's composition, and the number of those engaging directly or indirectly in sponge fishing. In 1884, a decision of the Elders' Council of Kalymnos cited "citizens of all classes", who paid municipal taxes ("local fees") for the maintenance of schools, medical practices, and pharmacies on the island. They were "intermediary merchants, captains of sponge-fishing ships, captains of underwater sponge-fishing machines, sponge fishermen, mechanics, coffee sellers, shoemakers, carpenters, farmers, gardeners, porters, and immigrant foreigners".[105] Of these, merchants and captains were considered to be the most esteemed residents, given that the municipal council consulted them on critical issues.[106] Employment relations and professional competitive behaviours made for a highly confrontational environment for all of those involved in the professional sponge industrial network. The classification for the remuneration of divers, the conditions and obligations laid out in their recruitment contracts, the high frequency of deadly or serious accidents, the meagre social welfare for victims, the harsh working conditions, as well as a complete lack of unionization, gave rise, already at the close of the 19th century, to a framework within which the sponge fishery was denounced, and identified with "slavery" or "trafficking in human beings".

Victimizers and victims – captains and divers: these were two professional groups with conflicting interests and different profiles in a society that had become highly stratified due to the sponge fishery. Members of these two groups were commonly together for the duration of the fishing expedition, and many captains were also divers. And while some mechanical divers managed to become captains, this was not an easy feat, "given that captains came from specific clans". On occasion however, "the prudent ones made it"; reportedly because they did not waste their money in the island's coffee shops and taverns.

---

105   MC Minutes, Correspondence Various 1884–1885, p. 15 (22/2/1884), MAK.
106   MC Minutes, Correspondence Various 1884–1885, p. 39 (5/3/1884), MAK.

Many, both old and young, attribute problems in the system, as well as controversies between involved parties, to the advance payment regime. In December 1903, P. Zotos wrote that "the advance payment renders captains petty tyrants, and divers rapacious".[107] Indeed informants maintain that exorbitant investments in the sponge fishery were not necessary for equipping vessels and the upkeep of crews, but went rather to pay the exorbitant *platika* that some divers demanded. P. Zotos went on to explain that,

> beginning on the day when the sum of harvested sponges compensates the captains' debt, a divers' life has little value for the captains; by the end of the fishing season, their lives are of no value at all. If the divers suffer from paralysis, they are obliged to work. If they die, captains will benefit from the deceased divers' share of the profits.[108]

Some fifty years later, the supervisor of sponge fishery in Libya expressed a similar opinion:

> The extortionate advance payments deal the greatest blow to the sponge fishery. This payment practice foments discord between investors, captains and divers, and prompts the often cruel behaviour of captains toward divers whom they believe to be feigning illness when they are actually sick or worn-out, and this in turn instigates desertion, mutiny and disinterest in the work, especially from those bad divers (and there are quite a few of them), who, having spent their advance payment in a prodigal manner, dedicate themselves to avoiding their obligation by various means.[109]

In 1903, an editor of the *Empros* [Εμπρός] newspaper defended captains, and offered an answer to an article that was published in the *Estia* [Εστία] newspaper:

> Captains, who, having borrowed 25–40 thousand drachmas for their work, without putting up any collateral or guarantee, go above and

---

107   Zotos, *Report*, p. 9.

108   Ibid., p. 12.

109   "Έκθεσις εν σχέσει με την διεξαγωγήν της σπογγαλιείας εις τα παράλια της Λιβύης κατά την θερινή περίοδον 1952" ["Report on Sponge Fishing off the Coasts of Libya in the Summer Season of 1952"], Lieutenant Commander Em. A. Koutsikopoulos, Sponge Fishery Overseer, Tripoli 28/11/1952, Embassy of Tripoli-Libya, Folder 46 (1952), Subfolder 4, ΙΑΥΕ.

beyond in their work, putting their lives at risk yet they are portrayed in the darkest of colours [by the author of the *Estia* article]; and while nothing stops them from appropriating the harvested treasure, they pay back the capital and profit to investors, without reaping profit from their work, or they pocket only the amount of money necessary to provide for their upkeep, because very few captains make a fortune. [...] Therefore, captains, and not divers, are the ones struggling in this profession; in reality, it is primarily divers who earn from this work.[110]

Reportedly, captains responsible for keeping records of the catch for each diver working on shares – especially in the case of deep-sea scaphander diving suits – often deceived novice divers. When the amount of the *platika* was covered, captains put the extra production of novices under the name of other experienced divers with higher *platikas*, in order to even up the sums and lower their future remuneration.[111] The manipulation of sponge production logs, and the transfer of catches from one diver to another, may have been the main accusation that captains faced, but it was not the only one. The crews' mistrust of the people managing the catch and its sale to sponge merchants – which also meant that they managed the final remuneration of the divers – pervaded. Captains were suspected of carrying out secret negotiations and agreements that were much more beneficial to them.

A singular employment regime was formed between employer and employees, in which the employer was either the intermediary between investors and crews or was burdened with loans and debts. Understanding this system means not only understanding employment relations, which were personalized and characterized by significant variations – it also means understanding the other manifold dependences, submission, discipline, disobedience, and desertion. Maggoty hardtack, water shortage, decapitation of victims to reuse the scaphander diving suit's helmet, and deceased left unburied were only some of the strong symbols that local memory raised in lamenting the harsh, inhumane labour conditions, and the relations between the involved parties. Who was to blame for all of this? Who earned the most when these things

---

110 Δ. Α. Πανάγος, "Οι σπογγαλιείς μας. Τα κακουργήματά των μύθοι. Μία απάντησις εις την Εστίαν", Εμπρός [D. A. Panagos, "Our Sponge Fishermen. Legends of their Crimes. An Answer to *Estia* Newspaper"], *Empros*, 15/4/1903, p. 3.

111 Russell, "Η σπογγαλιεία της Καλύμνου" ["Kalymnos' Sponge Fishery"], p. 30. See also the testimony of *kolaouzieris*-captain Petros Marthas to E.O., 2/9/2004.

[accidents and mortality] occurred? The archive of collective memory also contains controversies.

> Old captains took advantage of their crews. They had the craftsmen, those who sold fabric, and the grocers. You shop from one man, or another, they said. And the captain made arrangements with specific shops. To be recruited as a crew member, your wife had to go to the captain's house and serve as a maid ... The captain was boss back then. But they all went to hell. Their offspring was not good, neither did they have good deaths.[112]

In this configuration, the diving managers [*kolaouzierides*], captains' right hand, were thought to be responsible for many of the woes of the voyage – the accidents in particular. Some of the diving managers replaced captains who did not board the vessels, or those who spent prolonged periods in the cities of Africa.[113] Many of our diver informants dubbed them "captains' rats", reproaching them with deceiving divers as to the depth and the duration of their stay on the sea bottom. "They were cheating on the *matzarolia* [hour-glass timekeeping] they said. It is also alleged that some were bribed by the divers to make precise measurements of the air pump's pressure gauge, the time, and later the depth sounder. Which one of us made so much money? Who was able to go to London, Paris, or Berlin? Who measured gold in carats?", former captain Giannis Tsoulfas asked rhetorically, implicitly alluding to sponge merchants, the "notable aristocrats of Kalymnos", as he called them.[114]

   In a highly competitive working environment, rivalries between divers should also not be underestimated. At stake was not only the total symbolic capital of their skill set, but also a question of unequal distribution of material earnings, determined by each diver's productive capacity. Were the fraud that went on in the counting and categorizing of sponge catches which both sides admitted to, and the respective settlement actually factored in, one might be able to clearly discern the nature of confrontational relationships on board. As discussed previously, such aspects of the sponge fishery combined resulted in crew members and divers frequently fleeing, as well as in violent episodes on the vessels, as various sources testify.[115]

---

112   Testimony of Manolis Cheilas to EO, 25/8/2002.
113   Zotos, *Report*, p. 18.
114   Testimony of Giannis Tsoulfas to E.O., 6/3/2002.
115   Zotos, *Report*, p. 9.

More recently, captains have asserted that there were no rivalries and competitive spirit, at least in the final years:

> This bloody job had its misfortunes, too. We take care of people now. In the past, captains were not nice people, they were very harsh. They didn't take care of their people, neither in the job nor with the food. As of 1960 we are all new captains. When someone "takes good care of his business" and works hard he can build up a large fortune. And the divers that were healthy and prudent – they also made money.[116]

The rationalization of the advance payment system, the loans granted by the ATE, the decrease in the number of divers' disease victims, and the improvement of living conditions on board the sponging vessels, also improved relations between crews and captains, at a time when the sponge fishery suffered heavy external blows.

---

116   Testimony of Nikolas Kampourakis to E.O., 25/8/2002.

CHAPTER 6

Social Composition and Representation

6.1 The Women

The women had to keep everything on an even keel.[1]

Pieces of written archival evidence and oral testimonies attribute an important role to family, and family ties in the environment under study here. Blood relatives or in-laws organized social and professional life. Cooperatives, recruitment on board family vessels, hiring, and a more flexible attitude towards debt where brothers or fathers and sons, sons-in-law or other relatives were concerned, all suggest the importance of networks of relatives in the professional sponge-fishing network. In this field, dominated by men, women occupied marginalized and secondary roles by default. The prolonged seasonal emigration of sponge fishermen,[2] however, accorded mandatory "privileges", additional charges, and forward behaviours on the part of women. Where women's role is concerned, a text written by Kalymnian university student Themelis Kindynis sheds light on the system of values in his era, and contains impressions of his homeland:

> During the long sponge-fishing season, Kalymnos is almost deserted by men, except for the elders and some practicing the trade profession; their wives are left alone there, managing household matters with the utmost prudence. These women are distinguished for their decency, industriousness, and devotion to their husbands.[3]

---

1 From the testimony of captain Lefteris Mamouzelos to E.O., 3/9/2004.

2 In fact, the sponge fishery imposed a form of collective seasonal emigration, which impacted the organization of social life in the land of origin. The brief testimony of French merchant M. P. Aublé, compiled in 1868, is characteristic: "By mid-May, all ships are already far away, and the islands' population consists of women, young children, elderly and some sick people. It is a terrifying loneliness, a horrible sight in this bone-dry landscape". Louis Figuier, *Les merveilles de la science, ou Description populaire des inventions modernes*, vol. 4, Paris 1870, p. 624.

3 Themelis Kindynis, *Η νήσος Κάλυμνος* [*The Island of Kalymnos*], Athens 1879, pp. 24–26. Gerasimos Drakidis repeated the same account 34 years later, describing Kalymnian women as "decent and industrious to an extreme degree"; Gerasimos D. Drakidis, *Λεύκωμα των Δωδεκανήσων* [*Album of the Dodecanese*], Athens 1913, p. 68.

Descriptions like this one from 1879, recur in local literature and local memory, shaping a variety of representations that reproduce the same narrative pattern in various ways, albeit in a stereotypical fashion.

Throughout this chapter therefore, two topics will be explored: the conditions under which the women of the island lived and, in particular, the wives of sponge fishermen; and the nexus of values through which local society viewed these women at different points in time. Even if men occupied the major roles, the contributions made by women in their daily lives were a necessary supplement to this dramatic life and circumstances. Shared, collective narratives, that are part of popular culture, give prominence to the exceptional working conditions on board vessels and the seasonal emigration of the male population. However, woven through these stories are indications of the traits, behaviours, and dynamic forbearance of women, along with their necessary toughness and imposed independence.

6.1.1 *Responsibilities: Housework and Paid Employment*
In maritime and fishing communities, the distribution of daily activities is more evident than anywhere else. When men's work is no longer tied to the domestic surroundings, and when that work requires the prolonged absence of the male population, women are required to shoulder domestic obligations, as well as those activities and responsibilities that relate to farming and urban life, and this for at least the period of time in which they are alone.[4] In addition, the particularities of the profession of the diver, the increased risks, and the social and emotional tension caused by the high rate of fatal accidents, put women in a special position, and created a gender-based field of relations with both complementary and contrasting features.[5]

Testimonies of various types document women shouldering family responsibilities, while examples of the women's desperate attempts to sustain their

---

4 C.f. Joao de Pina Cabral, "'Matriarcat' et rôles conjugaux dans le Nord-Ouest du Portugal", *Recherches en anthropologie au Portugal* 4 (1992), p. 40. Similar consequences for those working on fishing vessels and for their families are reported in James Acheson, "Anthropology of Fishing", *Annual Review of Anthropology* 10 (1981), p. 277.

5 Female and male traits and corresponding roles are perceived as being different. This contrasts with most ethnographic studies carried out in the Greek space, in which it is believed that female and male traits and roles accord with cultural values. See John Campbell, *Honour, Family and Patronage: A Study of Institutions and Moral Values in a Greek Mountain Community*, Oxford 1964; Marie-Elisabeth Handman, Βία και πονηριά, Άντρες και γυναίκες σ' ένα ελληνικό χωριό [*Violence and Wiles, Men and Women in a Greek Village*], Athens 1987; Jill Dubisch, "Greek Women: Sacred or Profane", *Journal of Modern Greek Studies* 1/1 (1983), pp. 185–202.

under-age children have been preserved in the oral tradition.[6] Along with daily domestic chores, it appears that all of the women on the island took on a variety of agricultural activities for which they were almost exclusively responsible;[7] they were involved in viticulture, arboriculture, harvesting, threshing, and beekeeping, as well as in the gathering of tree branches from the surrounding mountains for kitchens, bread making and washing[8] – and these were constant duties. The family, moreover, formed a productive unit that organized its survival by means of a variety of work activities in which all family members were engaged, including children and the elderly. Jobs in agriculture, working at home, women's occasional salaried employment, and child labour supplemented the unstable income of sponge fishermen.

Even when men were on the island, however, the burdens did not seem to be equally distributed or carried out on an equal basis. Here, an anonymous narrative in verse entitled "The Complaints of the Women of Kalymnos", published by Karl Dieterich in 1908, is particularly interesting. Its 70, 4-line stanzas offer a realistic depiction and a harsh critique of the living conditions of Kalymnian women. The daily agricultural and household chores depicted in the poem, the burdensome responsibilities carried for many months, the men's indifference, even on return from their voyages, add up to a much crueler image of the peculiar world of sponge fishermen than that of seafarers.

> In what other place in the world
> do men like *Aghas*[9]
> spend weeks in coffee shops
> playing cards

---

6   See Eleni Kypraiou, "Η γυναίκα της Καλύμνου", *Καλυμνιακά Χρονικά* ["The Woman of Kalymnos", *Kalymniaka Chronika*], 18 (2009), pp. 371–372. The matter has been studied in the case of the wives of fishermen. See Dona Lee Davis, Jane Nadel-Klein, "Gender, Culture and the Sea: Contemporary Theoretical Approaches" in Carolyn E. Sachs (ed.) *Women Working in the Environment*, Washington 1997, pp. 49–61. For the duties and responsibilities of women see pp. 52–55.

7   Women's recent testimonies typically address agricultural jobs as a responsibility that belonged exclusively to them, claiming that all wives and daughters of sponge fishermen did the same thing. Manuscript 2174/1974, Maria Kapella, pp. 65–89, CFS; and Manuscript 2728/1976, Maria Sevastopoulou, p. 24, CFS.

8   Carl Flegel, *Η νήσος Κάλυμνος* [*The Island of Kalymnos*], Constantinople 1896, p. 38; by the same author, "Η Α.Θ. Παναγιότης ο Οικουμενικός Πατριάρχης Άνθιμος ο Ζ' εν Καλύμνω" ["His All-Holiness Ecumenical Patriarch Anthimos VII of Kalymnos"], Samos 1896, p. 23; Roxane Caftanzoglou, "*Kalymnos: Contribution a la connaissance d'une société*", Mémoire de maîtrise d'ethnologie specialisée (unpublished), Paris 1978, p. 29.

9   Translator's note: An *Agha* is a well-to-do Ottoman official.

And they send their wives
to mountains and ravines
To fetch wood and branches
Needed for their ovens[10]

It appears, however, that one of these taxing jobs – namely gathering faggots – was not undertaken by women exclusively for household needs; many women sold the branches they gathered to the island's well-to-do families. The figure of *"klaofora"* [woman carrying branches] – and, more specifically, the sponge fisherman's widow – present throughout written and oral accounts, is a deep memory of what ultimately amounted to the cruel enslavement of the women of Kalymnos.[11]

Research in the 19th-century archival evidence reveals how often the Elders' Council appealed to the Ottoman administration to respect the population, and especially the female population, given that women were almost the sole inhabitants of the island in the months when the sponge fishermen were absent.[12] With the male population gone, household and agricultural activities, as well as other family obligations, forced women to make their way to secluded areas of the island. The violent incidences and rape that occurred as a result caused concern in the local population, the members of which were striving to maintain order with the assistance of the Elders' Council.[13] On the other hand, Flegel also attributed the "companies" [*syntrofies*] that were formed by women for the group execution of various agricultural tasks, to the long periods of the men's absence from the island necessitated by the sponge

---

10   Karl Dieterich, *Sprache und Volksüberlieferungen der südlichen Sporaden im Vergleich mit denen der übrigen Inseln des ägäischen Meeres*, Vienna 1908, pp. 328–336; Themelina Kapella, "Τα παράπονα των γυναικών της Καλύμνου (από την καταγραφή του Καρόλου Ντίτεριχ)", *Καλυμνιακά Χρονικά* ["The Complaints of the Women of Kalymnos (Taken from the account of Karl Dieterich)", *Kalymniaka Chronika*], 4 (1984), pp. 43–47. By the same author, *Λαογραφικές Σελίδες Καλύμνου* [*Folklore Pages of Kalymnos*], Athens 1997, pp. 122–135.

11   K. Giannatou argues that a statue of the *"klaofora"* should be erected on Kalymnos, in honour of the mothers whose willpower and sacrifices made it possible for ther sons to study so that they would not be forced to turn to the sponge fishery for their livelihood. See Katerina Giannatou, "Η μάνα Καλυμνιά", *Καλυμνιακά Χρονικά* ["The Kalymnian Mother", *Kalymniaka Chronika*], 17 (2007), pp. 392–394.

12   See also a letter of the Elders' Council of Kalymnos to the Patriarch in Constantinople, Anthimos VII, Doc. 98, 10/5/1895, Correspondence 1895–1896, MAK.

13   Doc. 162, 12/9/1895, Doc. 168, 17/9/1895, Doc. 171, 19/9/1895, Correspondence 1895–1896, MAK.

fishery.[14] Indeed, even in recent years women's cooperative labour has become habitual, particularly in periods of men's absence.[15]

The types of paid employment that the women of the island took up were few and defined the social group from which they came. Indeed, even in the late 1970s, young women stayed mostly in the home and were occupied principally with domestic or agricultural chores, and only rarely did girls from the sponge-fishing milieu learn a craft and seek work outside the home.[16] There were exceptions however, and in the late 19th century and the beginning of the 20th century a small number of well-known literate women did study to become teachers or pursue another course of study. From the inter-war period to the 1960s women were also employed on an occasional basis, and paid day wages to sort and trim the sponges. Women also worked in tobacco processing warehouses that had been created after the close of the Ottoman administration. Given the above, it is moreover, also evident that in periods of intensified sponge-fishing or manufacturing activity, the shortfall in the male labour force was bridged by female labour, which had the added advantage of being cheaper.

It appears as well that other, much more inconspicuous forms of female and child labour also occurred. For example, wives and children of sponge fishermen were reportedly compelled to serve at the residences of captains throughout the winter, to ensure that their men would to be able to find work.[17] And while many women worked as maids in the homes of wealthy Kalymnians and sponge merchants on Kalymnos, they also worked in Asia Minor and abroad.[18]

A variety of testimonies, and especially those of women, on the organization of daily family life survives. Most of the testimonies describe women's skills in managing domestic responsibilities with the very limited available means at their disposal – few supplies and food, and the remainder of the advance

---

14   Flegel, *Η νήσος Κάλυμνος* [*The Island of Kalymnos*], p. 38.
15   Manuscript 2174/1974, Maria Kapella, p. 91, CFS, and Manuscript 1628/1971, Emmanouil Sarikas, pp. 153–154, CFS; Marina Petronoti, "Συμβολή στη μελέτη της οικονομικής αυτονομίας των γυναικών στα νησιά Κάλυμνο, Σάμο και Κάρπαθο", *Καρπαθιακαί Μελέται* ["Contribution to the Study of Financial Autonomy of Women on the Islands of Kalymnos, Samos and Karpathos", *Karpathiakai Meletai*], 1 (1984), p. 249.
16   Roxane Caftanzoglou, *Kalymnos*, p. 29.
17   Manuscript 2729/1976 Angeliki Georgiadou, p. 121, CFS.
18   Doc. 632, 12/6/1884, MC Minutes-Correspondence 1884–1885, MAK. See also Flegel, "Η Α.Θ. Παναγιότης ο Οικουμενικός Πατριάρχης Άνθιμος" ["His All-Holiness Ecumenical Patriarch Anthimos"], p. 26; Niki Gr. Billiri, *Της θάλασσας και της στεριάς* [*Of Sea and Land*], Athens 1986, p. 145; Faith Warm, *Bitter Sea: The Real Story of Greek Sponge Diving*, London 2000, p. 67.

payments left to them by the sponge fishermen. Carl Flegel, an astute observer of Kalymnian society, pointed out that,

> the daughters and women of Kalymnos also have the advantage of con-
> fecting delicious and nutritive barley rusks, which they send together
> with other items to the divers fishing off the coasts of Africa, to show
> them that they think of them and love them; they send these treats by
> special ships, that maintain the communication between divers and their
> homeland.[19]

In the years following WWII, when life on the island of Kalymnos included moving the family nearer to the sea in the summer, it was women who organized the entire operation, including the construction and maintenance of makeshift accommodations made of wood, stones, sacks, and various other fabrics.[20]

6.1.2   *Public Presence*

It was uncommon for women to manage family or personal property assets themselves. Their fathers, husbands, or custodians acted "on their instructions", without women's names appearing on official legal documents. Yet, when these women were left alone, either on a temporary or permanent basis, circumstances or necessity brought them to the public space more often.[21] The women represented the family in the community,[22] while they frequently petitioned the Elders' Council for their sons' recruitment, or their husband's, or attempted to block it. A letter on this topic has survived in the archives, in which the mother of a diver appeared before local officials and "protested tearfully against the actions of captain Michail Kampourakis and requested that he be prevented from taking her son on as a 'mechanical diver'". After obtaining the captain's reassurance, she left. A few days later, however, she appeared again before the Elders' Council, declaring that her son had set sail

---

19   Flegel, *Η νήσος Κάλυμνος* [*The Island of Kalymnos*], p. 36.
20   The testimony of Maria Filippou Soulounia referred to the area of Agios Antonios [Saint Antony], in the location of Sykomeria. There they rigged up their summer cabins. See Faneromeni Chalkidiou-Skylla, *Ή σφουγγάρι ή τομάρι. Η ζωή των σφουγγαράδων της Καλύμνου μέσα από αληθινές μαρτυρίες* [*Either Sponge or Corpse. The Life of the Sponge Fishermen of Kalymnos through Real Testimonies*], Kalymnos 2009, pp. 252–253.
21   M. Kalafatas called them "business widows"; Michael N. Kalafatas, *The Bellstone: The Greek Sponge Divers of the Aegean. One American's Journey Home*, Brandeis University Press, Hannover 2003, pp. 66–67.
22   Marina Petronoti, "Συμβολή στη μελέτη της οικονομικής αυτονομίας των γυναικών" ["Contribution to the Study of the Financial Autonomy of Women"], p. 245.

with said captain, and that he "had been hit by the machine and he was already unable to move". A similar complaint was made on the same day by the wife of another diver recruited on the same vessel. Unfortunately, available factual material does not record the circumstances under which these incidents occurred. In this case, however, the Elders' Council did step in, and requested the mediation of the Ottoman *Kaymakam* in order to transport the men who had been "hit" from the small island of Levitha to Kalymnos, where they would receive medical care.[23]

If we rely on available historical information, we also discover that some captains' wives carried on the activity of their deceased husbands, such as arranging sponge-fishing groups, usually through a proxy.[24] Others found themselves forced to put up their dowry agreement, or real estate that was part of their dowry, as collateral for their captain husbands' sponge-fishing loans.[25] In addition, many widows managed their estates, had debts, called for the repayment of compensations and debts, bought and sold vessels,[26] and had transactions with individuals and communal authorities. By way of illustration, one might note the case of Maria, widow of Georgios Mavros, who demanded that, according to sponge-fishing custom, divers who owed her husband money from previous voyages pay it back to her. Therefore, she recruited the debtors via her custodian.[27] The widows or mothers of deceased divers likewise commonly attempted to settle sponge-fishing debts, and to claim the wages of their deceased relatives working on vessels from Kalymnos, Symi, Chalki or Hydra.[28] Indeed, in order to make ends meet, women even tried to sell the sponges harvested by their deceased husbands or sons themselves.[29] Moreover, the widows of captains also claimed "preferential" debts, denounced debtor divers to the local authorities, and settled the pending sponge-fishing business

---

23   Doc. 122, 18/5/1894, Correspondence 1894–1895, MAK.

24   Doc. n.n., 3/16 May 1923; Doc. n.n., 16/29 May 1923; Doc. n.n., 3/5/1924, Sponge-Fishing Affairs 1922–1925, MAK.

25   Doc. n.n., 12/5 January 1924, Sponge-Fishing Affairs 1922–1925, MAK.

26   Cat. 113, Doc. 71, 29/4/1921, MAK. Similar cases survive in other documents in the archive, as well. See, for instance, Doc. 8, 10/1/1896, doc. 46, 22/2/1896, Correspondence 1895–1896, MAK.

27   Doc. 205, 30/4/1894, Recruitments 1894–1896, MAK.

28   See, for instance, Doc. 190, 27/10/1895, doc. 196, 7/11/1895, doc. 8, 10/1/1896, doc. 46, 22/2/1896, Correspondence 1895–1895, MAK; Doc. 25, 11/2/1897, Correspondence 1896–1898, MAK. See also Report, 23/11/1895, Embassy of Tripoli-Libya, Folder 6 (1890–1900), Subfolder 9, IAYE.

29   Doc. 116, 7/4/1893, MC Minutes 1892–1893, MAK; Doc. 66, 19/3/1896, Correspondence 1895–1896, MAK.

of their deceased spouses.[30] Along with the other difficulties involved in settling their deceased husbands' accounts it should also be taken into consideration that, since the beginning of the 20th century,[31] the men died as a rule, far away from the island in Greek or African seas, or even in Tarpon Springs, USA, and that their bodies never made it back to Kalymnos.

As is to be expected, the vast majority of these women were not literate. In 1865, Newton wrote: "The women of Kalymnos, from always remaining on the island, are very much less civilized than the men. Their dialect is very barbarous and difficult to understand; but since the establishment of schools, [their language] is gradually improving".[32] In 1896, when the Ottoman administration ordered the Elders' Council to replace the oka (1.282 kilograms) with kilograms as a unit of measure, the Council expressed strong opposition, arguing that the female population would not be able to adapt to the new metric system. In a letter, the Elders explained that,

> the implementation of the new system is a most onerous task, and will be extremely damaging to our land, especially for its sponge-fishing industry. Because of said industry, as is well-known, the common people are absent from our island for half of the year, that is, in the summer. In most cases, women remain alone during this period, and they alone buy the necessary provisions for their families. These women are a long way from understanding this different new system; as a result, they don't want to fall victim to local shopkeepers and foreign merchants who bring a variety of merchandise here by ship and sell it in retail.[33]

Although this situation is representative of the overwhelming majority of the female population, attempts were indeed made to provide for women's education. The foundation of an all-girls school was decided on September 1864;[34] and it also would appear that an all-girls school had been in operation in Pothia

---

30 Doc. 198, 5/7/1897, MC Minutes 1896–1897, MAK; Doc. 141 and 142, 14/6/1913, MC Minutes 1913–1914, MAK.

31 See, for example, Doc. 24, 19/3/1915, MC Minutes 1915–1916, MAK.

32 C. T. Newton, *Travels and Discoveries in the Levant*, vol. 1, London 1865, p. 298.

33 Doc. 51, 26/2/1896, Correspondence 1895–1896, MAK. Similar decisions were issued several years later, once again due to the "ignorance of women" in relation to the exchange rates for the different currencies available in the market of Kalymnos. Doc. 40, 17/4/1915, MC Minutes 1915–1916, MAK.

34 Doc. 132, 15/9/1864, Doc. 166, 13/11/1864, MC Minutes 1863–1884, MAK.

since the late 1870s,[35] under the direction of a female teacher, Kalliopi Nom. Kalavrou, who came from a family of educators and had studied at the Arsakeio school for teachers.[36] Kalymnian women, "practicing the profession of teaching", taught the little girls in the schools of Pothia and Chora.[37] Furthermore, there were families that supported their daughters' studies. Such is the case of a poor family that requested, through the Elders' Council, the Patriarch's assistance in order to have their daughter admitted to the all-girls school in Constantinople to study midwifery;[38] or, the case of Sevasti Kallisperi, who applied for admittance to the University of Athens in 1884.[39] In 1893, "in the interest of improving the education of our female population", it was decided to hire a graduate teacher from abroad (i.e. Athens) for the all-girls' school in Pothia.[40] And, in his valuable observations on Kalymnos, Flegel added that local women were sent to the Arsakeio School to be trained as teachers, in order to replace those women who came from other areas.[41]

---

35   Kindynis, *Η νήσος Κάλυμνος* [*The Island of Kalymnos*], p. 27. The school was located near Ammoudara, at the residence of Michail Th. Pelekanos' wife. Doc. 90, 20/8/1883, MC Minutes 1882–1883, MAK.

36   It is most likely, however, that Kalliopi Kalavrou (1855–1922) taught in Pothia from the beginning of the 1880s. See Doc. 41, 20/6/1883, Doc. 50, 25/7/1883, Doc. 108, 08/08/1883, MC Minutes 1882–1883, MAK. See also Flegel, *The Island of Kalymnos* [*Η νήσος Κάλυμνος*], p. 27. For more biographical details, see Themelina Kapella, "Καλλιόπη Νομ. Καλαβρού", *Καλυμνιακά Χρονικά* ["Kalliopi Nom. Kalavrou", *Kalymniaka Chronika*], 6 (1986), pp. 305–306. It is also reported that illiterate Kalymnian Kastrovakina Skoni, aunt of archimandrite Nikiforos Zervos, donated part of her land in a will of 1872, and a donation document dated 1891, to the Metropolis, with which to build schools; Daniil A. Zervos, "Για την Καστροβακίνα Μ. Σκόνη μια σχεδόν άγνωστη ευεργέτισσα της Καλύμνου του 19ου αιώνα", *Η Αργώ της Καλύμνου* ["About Kastrovakina M. Skoni, an Almost Unknown Benefactor of the Kalymnos of the 19th Century", *I Argo tis Kalymnou*] 234 (2009), p. 2.

37   See also the documents for the appointments of various female teachers in the following registers: Doc. n.n., p. 302, 31/10/1877 and p. 312, 2/10/1878, MC Minutes 1863–1884, MAK; Doc. 67, 8/8/1883, Doc. 69, 10/8/1883, Correspondence 1882–1883, MAK.

38   Doc. 132, 28/6/1895, Correspondence 1895–1896, MAK.

39   Despite the favourable decision of the ten-member committee of inquiry, the General Director of the Ministry of Education did not validate the minutes, and the woman in question was not able to attend the Greek University. She later pursued her studies at the Sorbonne; Georgios N. Pizanias, "Η συμβολή της Καλυμνιάς Σεβαστής Καλλισπέρη στην ελληνική παιδεία", *Καλυμνιακά Χρονικά* ["The Contribution of Kalymnian Sevasti Kallisperi to Greek Education", *Kalymniaka Chronika*] 4 (1984), pp. 64–68; Kostas Minettos, "Νικόλαος Καλλισπέρης, ο αγωνιστής και πολιτικός", *Καλυμνιακά Χρονικά* ["Nikolaos Kallisperis, the Fighter and Politician", *Kalymniaka Chronika*] 13 (1999), pp. 179–184.

40   Doc. 235, n.d. [7/1893], MC Minutes 1892–1893, MAK.

41   In Flegel's manuscript "Οι ευεργέται της Καλύμνου" ["The Benefactors of Kalymnos"], which is stored in the reading room of Kalymnos. See also the names of the women

At the beginning of the 20th century, there were five elementary schools in Pothia, of which two were all-boys' schools and counted 700 male pupils, and one was an all-girls school with 600 female pupils. The two respective schools in Chora had 400 male pupils and approximately 350 female pupils.[42] In January of 1912, the Vouvaleio All-Girls School was inaugurated, the building for which had been constructed with funding granted by Kalymnian sponge merchant Nikolaos Vouvalis.[43] Shortly before the arrival of the Italians, two all-girls schools with 6 teachers and 400 pupils operated on Kalymnos.[44] In 1921, Pothia had a junior secondary all-girls school, and 7 female pupils attended the Nikiforeio Secondary School. Nevertheless, the Municipality invoked moral grounds to prohibit secondary school attendance for girls. Its decision sparked the protest of 191 men, who gathered signatures in favor of high school educa-tion for women. It appears that they accomplished their mission, because local authorities backed down, and the girls were admitted to the school until 1930, when the Greek Secondary School system was discontinued.[45]

6.1.3   *Special Women, "Tough Like Men"*
Among the "anonymous" women of the island, some stand out for their unique personality and their virtuosity in literature and the arts. For example, Kalymnians think of Aikaterini Vouvali, widow of Nikolaos Vouvalis, the most powerful sponge merchant on the island, as an exceptional case and a shrewd woman with outstanding business acumen. From the 1920s through the 1950s, "The Vouvalina" or "The Lady" as Kalymnians called Aikaterini Vouvali, took over the direction of the business enterprises she inherited from her husband. In various accounts she is described as harsh, strict, intelligent and a skilled economic manager,[46] and prolific humanitarian acts have been attributed to

educated abroad in Flegel, "Ἡ Α.Θ. Παναγιότης ὁ Οἰκουμενικός Πατριάρχης Ἄνθιμος" ["His All-Holiness Ecumenical Patriarch Anthimos"], p. 29.

42   Dionysios N. Reisis, Περιγραφή τῆς νήσου Καλύμνου [*Description of the Island of Kalymnos*], Athens 1913, pp. 14, 20.

43   Niki Reisi-Glynatsi, "Βουβάλειο Παρθεναγωγείο Κοιτίδα πνευματικῆς ζωῆς στὴν Κάλυμνο", *Καλυμνιακά Χρονικά* ["Vouvaleio All-Girls' School, Cradle of Kalymnos Intellectual Life", *Kalymniaka Chronika*] 15 (2003), pp. 406–414.

44   Dodecanese Statistics 1912, Rhodes Consulate, Folder 43 (1912), Subfolder 3, ΙΑΥΕ. Drakidis, however, reported that there were 11 female teachers. Drakidis, Λεύκωμα τῶν Δωδεκανήσων [*Album of the Dodecanese*], p. 66.

45   Maria Zairi, "Ἀπό τὴν ἱστορία τοῦ πρώτου ἡμιγυμνασίου θηλέων στὴν Πόθια (1921)", *Καλυμνιακά Χρονικά* ["From the History of the First Semi-Secondary School for Girls in Pothia (1921)", *Kalymniaka Chronika*] 13 (1999), pp. 165–178.

46   David Sutton, "Greeks of Kalymnos", in Carol Ember, Melvin Ember (eds.), *The Encyclopedia of Sex and Gender: Men and Women in the World's Cultures*, vol. 1, New York 2004, p. 420.

her. In addition, it is said that she managed the local shop of her late husband's commercial house, and that she supervised and worked in the processing of sponges.[47]

The deep religiosity of the female population of Kalymnos typified women everywhere in the Greek state. However, unlike women in other parts of Greece, Kalymnian women took on multiple church-related duties due to the prolonged absence of the men while on sponging expeditions.[48] The women of Kalymnos also participated in official ceremonies when these were related to religious matters, such as the official greeting of Patriarch Anthimos VII on Kalymnos, and the festivities organized in his honour by the Elders' Council in 1895.[49]

Although they did not engage actively in public affairs, women who were perhaps more agitated appear to have participated collectively in various protests and actions in which they took the law into their own hands;[50] it also appears that women committed offenses which were punishable by imprisonment.[51] Furthermore, local literature and collective memory attribute the most dynamic, spontaneous social protests in the island's history to women of all ages, namely the "smashing of the machines" or the "anathema" of 1895,[52] and the "Rock War" of 1935.[53] In each of these cases, the women's actions and

---

47   Maria A. Magkli, "Αικατερίνη Βουβάλη", *Καλυμνιακά Χρονικά* ["Aikaterini Vouvali", *Kalymniaka Chronika*] 5 (1985), p. 59; David E. Sutton, *Memories Cast in Stone: The Relevance of the Past in Everyday Life*, Oxford-New York 1998, pp. 94–95.

48   Bernard Russell, "Kalymnos: The Island of the Sponge Fishermen", *Annals of the New York Academy of Sciences* 268 (1976), p. 299; Sutton, "Greeks of Kalymnos", p. 420; Cf. Jill Dubisch, "Greek Women", pp. 185–202.

49   Flegel, "Η Α.Θ. Παναγιότης ο Οικουμενικός Πατριάρχης Άνθιμος" ["His All-Holiness Ecumenical Patriarch Anthimos"], pp. 31–37.

50   Doc. 142, 3/6/1894, Correspondence 1894–1895, ΜΑΚ.

51   There was a women's prison facility in the area of Agios Nikolaos (Saint Nicolas), where the female owner of the house was the guard. The Elders' Council paid the rent and her salary. See Doc. 143, 3/6/1894, Doc. 186, 13/7/1894, Correspondence 1894–1895, ΜΑΚ.

52   Where the machines are concerned, it is reported that the women had lodged an official protest with the Pasha.

53   It is also interesting to recall the participation of women in the 1935 "Rock War" as it was known to the local community. The entire population took part in this protest against the Italian administration which attempted to impose the state of autocephaly on the Dodecanese Church, disuniting it from the Patriarchate of Constantinople. The protest was sparked by the female population of the island when the unconstrained performance of their religious duties was threatened, but it soon evolved into a violent manifestation of resistance against the Italian administration. For the events of 1935, see Themelina Kapella, "Ο αγώνας των γυναικών στο 1935 και ο πετροπόλεμος", *Καλυμνιακά Χρονικά* ["The Fight of the Women in 1935 and the Rock War", *Kalymniaka Chronika*] 6 (1986), pp. 87–102; by

IMAGE 6.1   Kalymnian Women "Tough like Men", 1930s
PHOTOGRAPH BY ELLI PAPADIMITRIOU, KALYMNOS 1932–36
© BENAKI MUSEUM/PHOTOGRAPHIC ARCHIVES

IMAGE 6.2   Kalymnian Women, 1930s
PHOTOGRAPH BY ELLI PAPADIMITRIOU, KALYMNOS 1932–36
© BENAKI MUSEUM/PHOTOGRAPHIC ARCHIVES

crowds of women [*gynekomani*] who took to the island's streets are commemorated in collective memory in a special way.[54]

Local literature, as well as eyewitness accounts describing the three-day-long protest of 1935 do not include the names of the female instigators. They refer vaguely to "women" who were in the church, who went in "mob" formation to the port, and "unarmed phalanxes" who poured out into the street.[55] While many believe that Kalymnian women were brave, their participation in the events of April 1935 is almost entirely missing or simply underestimated in local historiography, and the forefront is occupied by priest [*papa*] Tsougranis, as the instigator of the resistance; shepherd Kazonis, as the fallen martyr; and those arrested shortly after the uprising.[56] At any rate, even if existing accounts record female initiative-taking, mentions thereof make it possible to reconstruct legendary narratives that give prominence to the women of Kalymnos, and their ability to take charge of both the household and public space, while taking on the active roles they were compelled to accept given their husbands' long absences while sponge fishing.[57]

If this is indeed how the situation evolved, it may be assumed that it was women who militated for the "rights" of the Dodecanesian people when they were compromised or threatened by arbitrary measures. As sources reveal, the decimation of the male population caused by the scaphander diving suit directly impacted Kalymnian women, as did the threat of being constrained

---

the same author, Ιστορικές μνήμες Καλύμνου [*Historical Memories of Kalymnos*], pp. 43–85; Zacharias N. Tsirpanlis, "Στην Κάλυμνο του 1935. Συλλήψεις και εκπατρισμοί", *Καλυμνιακά Χρονικά* ["On the Kalymnos of 1935: Arrests and Expatriations", *Kalymniaka Chronika*], 7 (1988), pp. 153–189; Niki Gr. Billiri, *Η Κάλυμνός μας* [*Our Kalymnos*], Athens 1982, pp. 25 and 75–102; Georgios Ch. Charamandas, Ένα γνήσιο λαϊκό ποίημα για τον ήρωα της Καλύμνου Μανόλη Καζώνη γραμμένο από τον Μανόλη Θεοδώρου Τρουμουλιάρη [*An Original Popular Poem for the Hero of Kalymnos, Manolis Kazonis, Written by Manolis Theodorou Troumouliaris*], Athens 2002; Sutton, *Memories Cast in Stone*, pp. 87–97; Kalafatas, *The Bellstone*, pp. 60–61; David Sutton, "Re-scripting Women's Collective Action: Nationalist Writing and the Politics of Gendered Memory", *Identities* 5/4 (1999), pp. 469–500; by the same author, "Greeks of Kalymnos", pp. 420–421. Press articles, however, made no mention of the contribution of women. See also *Αθηναϊκά Νέα* [*Athinaika Nea*] 25/1/1935, p. 5; 26/1/1935, p. 4; 27/1/1935, p. 4; 25/5/1935, p. 5; 19/9/1935, p. 5; 19/9/1936, p. 6.

54   The expression *gynekomani* [γυναικομάνι] is attributed to Themelina Kapella, "Ο αγώνας των γυναικών" ["The Fight of the Women"], p. 92.

55   See the testimonies published by Themelina Kapella, ibid.

56   Sutton, "Re-scripting Women's Collective Action", pp. 478–483.

57   Ibid., p. 487. It is worth noting that similar incidents had taken place previously, triggered by different causes, on Symi and Kastellorizo in 1934. Nicholas Doumanis, Nicholas G. Pappas, "Grand History in Small Places: Social Protest on Kastellorizo (1934)", *Journal of Modern Greek Studies* 15/1 (1997), pp. 103–123.

in the performance of religious duties. Interestingly enough, the Kalymnian women's behaviour might have been met with far greater tolerance than men's behavior would have been by the Ottoman or Italian administrations because of their gender.[58] Whatever the case may be, women remained actively involved in public affairs as custodians of tradition, even when that role became confrontational; safeguarding the Orthodox faith from the enforcement of Catholicism under Italian rule was a way for the female population to express "national, patriotic" feelings.[59] Seen differently however, some might understand the desire for social stability and the preservation of tradition as being essentially female. From this perspective women's protests against irresponsible behaviours and abuses of administrative power could be construed as gendered, and therefore, not necessarily political in nature.[60]

In a letter published in English in 1935, the women of Kalymnos addressed women all over the world, recalling the letters of Evanthia Kairi and Mando Mavrogenous, and their role in claiming national rights. These were defiant, heroic women, dressed entirely in black who lived a grueling life of self-denial. Like them, the women of Kalymnos belong to the registry of women who, like the women of Souli [*Souliotisses*], are distinguished for their collective self-sacrifice, and powerful women like Laskarina Bouboulina, who took on traditionally "masculine" roles when circumstances demanded.[61]

6.1.4 *The "Mechanissines": the Wives of the Mechanical Divers*
The men's stay on the island was treated like a period of rest; as a respite from hard labour. For those diving with scaphander diving suits, the period of their stay on land was far shorter than the time they spent at sea. Their absence compelled women to strengthen other kinship ties, and to strengthen their religious fervor. Moreover, as noted above, when the men departed, having irresponsibly spent their advance payments with little consideration for their families, the women were left to survive in forced austerity, and in debt to local

---

58 It is equally interesting that these historical episodes have been etched in collective memory, as shown in the entirety of the testimonies collected. See also Faith Warm, *Bitter Sea*, pp. 46–47. The same picture is reproduced in Kalafatas, *The Bellstone*, p. 53 and 59–66. Kalafatas referenced protests of the women of Symi and Kastellorizo against the Italian administration of the island in 1930 and 1934.

59 Despite the argument of the Italian administration of the Dodecanese, that the measures were aimed at rendering the Church of the Dodecanese independent from the Patriarchate, the population believed that these actions sought to place the Church of the Dodecanese under papal jurisdiction.

60 C.f. Jill Dubisch, "Greek Women", pp. 200–201.

61 See also Sutton, "Re-scripting Women's Collective Action", pp. 483–488.

merchants to whom their husbands were financially tied in their capacity as divers or captains.

Female virtue is then reduced to tolerance against this *sui generis* male behaviour: "I didn't answer to my wife, neither did she know how much I was paid. There was nothing more than the amount I gave to her".[62] The divers' disrespectful behaviour, which many testimonies reference and praise, appeared to provoke strong protests in local society, especially from the female population. It is reported that in 1963 the women of Kalymnos demanded that the Municipality shut down a brothel operating on island.[63] Until 1965, captains and diving managers [*kolaouzierides*] brought women from neighbouring islands and the coasts Asia Minor to the taverns and brothels of Kalymnos; this practice was discontinued as a result of rising social concern, which, once again, was spearheaded by the Kalymnian women.[64] They also attempted to limit divers' idiosyncratic, reckless and irresponsible behaviours such as burning banknotes to light cigarettes. From 1960 onwards, moreover, in response to pressure exerted by the women of Kalymnos a system was put in place whereby half of divers' advance payments were deposited at the bank, so that the money would be given to the divers' families.[65]

Given that they lived alone for the better part of the year, Kalymnian women found themselves restricted within a suffocating framework of social control mechanisms, which also supported the judgmental treatment of the women and validated a negative view of their public image and behaviour. In societal formations and groups with traditional habits such as the one under study here, acceptable and expected roles for women were both limited and explicitly defined. Hence, although the seasonal, prolonged absence of men made relative freedom possible for women, it did nothing to elevate their role, nor did it leave room for them to fully take on the roles of their husbands.[66] They were forced to accept supplementary domestic burdens and duties, while

---

62   Testimony of captain Petros Marthas to E.O., 2/9/2004.

63   Russell, "Kalymnos", pp. 304–305.

64   Testimony of *kolaouzieris* Vassilis Kampouris to E.O., 1/9/2004; Bernard Russell, "The Fisherman and His Wife", in William Mernard, Jane Schieber (eds.), *Oceans: Our Continuing Frontier*, California, 1976, p. 309.

65   Russell, "The Fisherman and His Wife", p. 309; Testimony of Giannis Koutouzis to E.O., 25/8/2003. This practice makes its appearance in individual recruitment documents beginning in the years of Italian occupation. See, for instance, Doc. 44, 21/9/1919, MC Minutes, 1919–1922, MAK.

66   See also Russell, "The Fisherman and His Wife", p. 306. For the traits of the female gender in anthropological studies conducted in the Greek space, see Jill Dubisch, "Greek Women", pp. 187–188.

they managed household affairs, yet they were not in a position to renounce gender-based bias and inequity, or to occupy a decisive role in the public sphere. Most importantly, women were not permitted to act "in the men's stead" or to act "like men".

Widowed, married, and single women were, moreover, vulnerable to all kinds of criticism and any possible deviation from prescribed female behaviour could render these women questionable in public opinion. In such cases, the sympathy of local society – compassion and tolerance – could easily and quickly become judgment.[67] Given various approaches to and interpretations of the position of Kalymnian women offered in a variety of anthropological studies, one may safely conclude that peculiarities of sponge fishing informed the dominant structure of daily life for these women. For example, where a father was absent from various social events during sponge-fishing season, the social framework for his unmarried daughters, which was already highly constraining, became even more suffocating. Their presence in public space was then more limited, in contrast with young women from other social or professional groups.[68]

The average age at which divers married ranged from 30 to 35,[69] while the marriageable age for women ranged from 18 to 22 years of age.[70] In the mid-19th century however, the marriageable age for women was significantly lower and, according to Newton; at that time young Kalymnian girls generally got married at 14 years of age, and occasionally even as young as 12 years of age.[71] These figures vary, of course, and are dependent on the time period and the social stratum of the women in question, and arranged marriages [*proksenia*] usually took place after girls' 16th birthday.[72]

Because men's protracted absences perhaps only seemed to afford women freedoms that they were not, in fact, able to enjoy, this study explores the social status of women in conjunction with the social status of their sponge fishermen husbands. Indeed, it is important to keep in mind that informants' opinions are contradictory on the role and behaviour of Kalymnian women when left on their own. For example, a society that cultivates a cherished image

---

67 The fictional rendering of the life of a young diver's widow is interesting as well, in Katerina Giannatou, "Η Ειρήνη η Τουμπλού", *Καλυμνιακά Χρονικά* ["Irene the Toumplou", *Kalymniaka Chronika*] 13 (1999), pp. 101–104.

68 Roxane Caftanzoglou, *Kalymnos*, p. 31.

69 Testimony of "*balaristis*" Michalis Lampos to E.O., 29/7/2005.

70 Roxane Caftanzoglou, *Kalymnos*, p. 32.

71 *Newton, Travels and Discoveries*, p. 297.

72 Manuscript 2729/1976, Angeliki Georgiadou, p. 94, CFS.

of "Kalymnian motherhood", questions mothers' behaviour as wives, hence while in local memory women are often portrayed as victims of sponge fisher-men's frivolous life style, the notion that women had clandestine affairs while their husbands were away fishing also circulates in local memory.[73] Moreover, women living alone without spousal surveillance suggests looseness in Greek society – an idea which is commonly held.[74]

Kalymnian women's attire was also far more conservative, and evolved at a much slower pace, than that of men. That said however, various aspects of Kalymnian women's attire did indeed gradually change, beginning with shoes, although it took some time for European fashion to be fully embraced.[75] At any rate, "the rich, the wives of captains [*kapetanisses*] wore short velvet waist-coats over their long coats [*kava(d)i*]",[76] and the kerchief [*tsemberi*] assumed an important role in the social perception of women independent of older sar-torial customs. While in the past women were required to cover their heads with a headscarf or kerchief, for Kalymnian women the kerchief was also sym-bolically linked with joy and grief, as well as with the departure and return of the sponge fishermen. Reports contain accounts of the fair at the Church of Virgin Mary Full of Grace in Chora every year on the last Sunday before the beginning of Lent ["Cheese Sunday"], at which the women wore white ker-chiefs because it was the last social event before the departure of the sponge fishermen.[77] Elderly and widowed women always wore a black kerchief, whereas young women wore a dark-coloured kerchief while their husbands were sponge fishing, and took it off on the ships' return.[78]

Memory, however, becomes conflated with local myth and frozen in time. It was impossible for sponge fishermen to accept the possibly that their women might "roam about dressed in silk", when they were gone for seven months,

---

73 Russell, "The Fisherman and His Wife", p. 305; Marina Petronoti, "Συμβολή στη μελέτη της οικονομικής αυτονομίας των γυναικών" ["Contribution to the Study of Financial Autonomy of Women"], pp. 252–253.

74 A press article on a murder committed by a sponge fisherman in Piraeus, wherein the victim was his unfaithful wife, conveys the concept of honour, as well as of all the extenu-ating circumstances that the article sites in siding with the murderer, "the miserable diver, who had to eat the sea bottom of Benghazi to sustain her". *Αθηναϊκά Νέα* [*Athinaika Nea*], 23/1/1935, p. 1.

75 Flegel, "Η α.Θ. Παναγιότης ο Οικουμενικός Πατριάρχης Άνθιμος" ["His All-Holiness Ecume-nical Patriarch Anthimos"], p. 25.

76 Manuscript 2729/1976, Angeliki Georgiadou, p. 14, CFS.

77 Eirini Marinou, "Η λειτουργία των μοτίβων στα παραμύθια και στις παραδόσεις της Καλύμνου", *Καλυμνιακά Χρονικά* [*The Function of Patterns in Tales and Traditions of Kalymnos*", *Kalymniaka Chronika*] 13 (1999), p. 78.

78 Ibid., pp. 81–82.

IMAGE 6.3 "For Kalymnian women the kerchief was symbolically linked with joy and grief, as well as with the departure and return of the sponge fishermen". Changing the white with the black kerchief.
PHOTOGRAPH BY DIMITRIOS HARISIADIS, KALYMNOS 1950
© BENAKI MUSEUM/PHOTOGRAPHIC ARCHIVES

working in harsh conditions, and facing many dangers.[79] Given that there were no telephones or other easy ways to communicate at that time, particular constructs and images preoccupied local society along with fact.

> Damn you Barbary, and you too, damned Madruh
> You turned children into orphans, and women into widows
> The waves of Barbary pass one by one

---

79   Testimony of captain Giannis Tsoulfas to E.O., 5/3/2002.

And my love is far away in foreign lands[80]

Or, as I heard it on Kalymnos:

> Damn you Barbary, and you too, damned Madruh
> You made Kalymnian women put on black clothes
> Your name has been erased in the book of the Port Authority
> And now it is registered in the book of the Grim Reaper

6.1.5   *Wedding Strategies*

> Daughter, love the shepherd, and not the sailor
> Because shepherd's love burns like charcoal
> What would I do with a shepherd from a clan
> Who enters the coffee shop and they yell to him "get out, you idiot. You
>   ox"?
> What would I do with a shepherd who would
> Put me on a mountain tending his goats?
> My dear shepherd, put your love in the basket [*zebili*]
> And hang it up high so that fleas won't eat it
> What would I do with the shepherd, to eat, to whistle?
> I will marry a sponger so that I can wish him good day
> I couldn't care less about your curds, I couldn't care less about your
>   cheeses
> Wherever it rains and it thunders, that's where I will [have to] shepherd
>   your lambs[81]

In the local marriage market, sponge fishermen were an inevitable evil, or even a hope for a comfortable life or, as in the epigram for this section suggests – at least more comfortable than the life one might lead with a shepherd. Maintaining and reinforcing professional relations, commitments, and dependencies were all connected to the choice of one's spouse. In some cases, marriages with non-native divers were arranged at a captian's behest, so that these foreign divers would remain on the island of Kalymnos.[82] However,

---

80   Manuscript 2729/1976 Angeliki Georgiadou, p. 36, CFS.

81   Manuscript 778/1968–1969, Maria Koutouzi, pp. 7–8; and a shorter version of this song in
      Manuscript 2728/1976, Maria Sevastopoulou, pp. 49–50, CFS; and in Manuscript 941/1969,
      Petroula Gialouzi, no page number, CFS.

82   See the relevant passages on Hydra in P. Zotos, Ἔκθεσις περί της ανά τας αφρικανικάς ακτάς
      διά σκαφάνδρου σπογγαλιείας [*Report on Sponge Fishing by Diving Suit along the African
      Coasts*], Athens 1904, p. 8.

money aside, the prolonged absences of sponge divers, their frivolous life-style while on land, and the risk of accidents, created feelings of ambivalence towards them in the female population and their families. Flegel insisted that "many young ladies did not get married due to a lack of men, and because marriages to divers working with scaphander diving suits augured an imminent widowhood or the upkeep of a sickly spouse".[83] Likewise, many additional sources from the late 19th century also note a shortage of men due to the number of accidents, the frequent fleeing of divers, and even due to the migratory waves caused by periodic crises in the sponge fishery.[84] The fictional rendering of women's feelings in this regard is revealing. Ion Dragoumis vividly depicted women's feelings as he imagined them in his juvenile novel *The Sponge Fishermen* (1898/1899), set in Aegina:

> She will never marry a diver. Never. To stay three or six months completely alone, not knowing if her husband is coming back? And then, what if he does come back and he gets drunk? To have him come home late at night and beat her? And what if he dies at sea and never comes back? Then she will wear black just like *kyra* Georgaina, the neighbourhood laundress.[85]

In accordance with local custom, the family home was given to daughters as a dowry, and to the first-born daughter in particular. And, to get married, young women had to have a house to offer as a dowry,[86] and sponge fishing was the

---

83   Carl Flegel, "Το σπογγαλιευτικό ζήτημα της Μεσογείου [Χανιά, 1903]", *Καλυμνιακά Χρονικά* ["The Sponge-Fishery Issue of the Mediterranean (Chania, 1903)", *Kalymniaka Chronika*] 5 (1985), p. 211.

84   Flegel, "Η Α.Θ. Παναγιότης ο Οικουμενικός Πατριάρχης Άνθιμος" ["His All-Holiness Ecumenical Patriarch Anthimos"], p. 17. Deadly accidents also increased the number of young widows. Their number is difficult to quantify, as we did not retrieve extensive census data for a lengthy period; by means of illustration, one might note the existence of 1,008 widows and 971 orphans out of 14,737 inhabitants in total, 7,972 of them being women, in 1946. In that very same year, 235 people were registered as unfit for work. *Δωδεκάνησος. Τετράτομος μελέτη του Υπουργείου Ανοικοδομήσεως και συνεργατών του υπό την διεύθυνσιν του κ. Κ. Α. Δοξιάδη* [*Dodecanese. Study in Four Volumes by the Ministry for Reconstruction and Affiliates under the Direction of Mr. K. A. Doxiadis*], Ministry for Reconstruction Publication Series, Athens 1947, p. 275.

85   Ίων Δραγούμης, "Οι σφουγγαράδες", [1898/1899], *Εκλεκτά Μυθιστορήματα* (Ion Dragoumis, "The Sponge Fishermen", [1898/1899], *Eklekta Mythistorimata*) 12 (1935), pp. 3–11.

86   Iakovos R. Ragavis, *Τα Ελληνικά ήτοι περιγραφή γεωγραφική, ιστορική, αρχαιολογική και στατιστική της αρχαίας και νέας Ελλάδος* [*Greek: Geographical, Historical, Archaeological and Statistical Description of Ancient and Modern Greece*], vol. 3, Athens 1854, p. 395; Sutton, *Memories Cast in Stone*, pp. 103–104; Faith Warm, *Bitter Sea*, p. 6; testimonies of Nikolas Kampourakis and Michalis Lampos to E.O., 25/8/2002.

only way to acquire the necessary funds. Importantly, according to customary law, the distribution and inheritance of property in the nuclear families of Kalymnos was either matrilineal or patrilineal, the "parental to the parental", as it was sometimes formulated in dowry agreements.[87] Parental property was transferred to the descendants as follows: daughters received maternal property, sons received paternal property. In the case of a childless marriage, and after the death of one of the spouses, the property was returned to the parents of the deceased. "If one of the spouses passes away, parental property will go to the parents",[88] which is to say that the surviving spouse did not inherit the property of the deceased spouse.[89] The custom of returning the property of the deceased spouse to its previous owners was observed at least until the mid-20th century, as is demonstrated by petitions drawn up and addressed to the Community, calling for intervention into and enforcement of the "law" in cases of disputes or tampering and appropriation of property.[90] The existence of this custom on Kalymnos is often attested to by claims for the return of dowries or other property assets, made on behalf of the families of deceased sponge fishermen against the widowed wife.[91] In case of marriages with offspring, custom dictated the following:

---

87   Themelina Kapella, *Λαογραφικές Σελίδες Καλύμνου* [*Folkore Pages of Kalymnos*], p. 19.

88   See the transcription of dowry agreement with the date 5/3/1856 that is contained in Manuscript 2729/1976, Angeliki Georgiadou, pp. 102–103, CFS.

89   See M. G. Michailidis-Nouaros, *Νομικά έθιμα της νήσου Καρπάθου της Δωδεκανήσου* [*Legal Customs of the Dodecanese Island of Karpathos*], Athens 1926, pp. 60 and 168–170. For the inheritance rights of the surviving husband see Io. and Pan. Zepos, *Jus Graecoromanorum*, vol. 8, Athens, 1931, pp. 484–486. On Paros, at least until 1755, the husband did not inherit anything from his deceased wife's dowry. See Iakovos T. Visvizis, "Το κληρονομικόν δικαίωμα των συζύγων επί ατέκνου γάμου εις την Πάρον κατά τον 18ον αιώνα", *Επετηρίς του Αρχείου της Ιστορίας του Ελληνικού Δικαίου* ["The Inheritance Right of Spouses in a Childless Marriage on Paros in the 18th Century", *Archive of the History of Greek Law Yearbook*] 8 (1958), p. 141. On Naxos, by contrast, the widow (but not the wife) had the right of usufruct on the deceased husband's dowry: I. T. Visvizis, "Ναξιακά νοταριακά έγγραφα των τελευταίων χρόνων του Δουκάτου του Αιγαίου (1538–1577)", Επετηρίς του Αρχείου της Ιστορίας του Ελληνικού Δικαίου ["Notarial Documents of Naxos from the Final Years of the Duchy of the Aegean (1538–1577)"], *Archive of the History of Greek Law Yearbook* 4 (1951), p. 141. The same applied on Venetian-ruled Crete, see Chrysa A. Maltezou, "Η παρουσία της γυναίκας στις νοταριακές πράξεις της περιόδου της Βενετοκρατίας", *Κρητολογία* ["The Presence of Women in Notarial Acts in the Period of Venetian Rule", *Cretologia*] 16–19 (1983–1984), p. 66. On the case of Samos in the mid-19th century, see Vassiliki Galani-Moutafi, "Προίκα και κοινωνική οργάνωση στη Σάμο στα μέσα του 19ου αιώνα", *Αντιπελάργηση. Τιμητικός τόμος για τον Νικόλαο Α. Δημητρίου* ["Dowry and Societal organization on Samos in the mid-19th Century", *Antipelargisi. Honorary Volume to Nikolaos A. Dimitriou*], Athens, 1992, pp. 72–73.

90   For instance: Doc. 329, 31/05/1908, MC Minutes 1908–1909, MAK.

91   See Doc. 14, 212 and 220, 17/5/1921, Sponge-Fishermen Recruitments 1921, MAK. These are the documents of a settlement between the Magkos and Touloumaris families, and the

Upon the death of a husband, his widow is entitled to allot her dowries to her offspring as she wishes; however, she has no right to dispense the property of her deceased husband without the consent of her offspring, both sons and daughters, or of their guardians, if they are underage. The same rules apply for a husband whose wife is deceased.[92]

Given that social life was organized around periods of sponge fishermen's presence and absence, the celebration of engagements and marriages, even the duration of an engagement, which could vary from just days to many months, was determined by the departure and return of the sponge fishermen.[93] Couples established themselves matrilocally, meaning that they settled in the residence provided by the bride – usually the family home if the bride was the first-born daughter.[94] Following the marriage, the parents changed their place of residence, while the father assumed the duty of providing a dowry for his other daughters. The bride's dowry, and especially that of the first-born daughter, was called a *stoivi* [στοιβή] and consisted of white linen, and various items and utensils largely for daily use, as well as some more valuable items which were stored in trunks or kept under the large bed to be used on special occasions, and which were destined for the dowry of the next daughter.[95]

Name-giving also adhered to local custom, which ensured family continuity and dictated that the first girl be named after her maternal grandmother, and the first boy after his paternal grandfather.[96] On Kalymnos, matronymics were

      return of the dowry residence of Emmanouil Magkos. The diver died near Derna while working on Antonios, Magkos, his father's, vessel.

92   Doc. 72, 02/28/1897, MC Minutes 1896–1897, MAK.

93   Themelina Kapella, Λαογραφικές Σελίδες Καλύμνου [*Folkore Pages of Kalymnos*], pp. 19–20; Manuscript 1628/1971, Emmanouil Sarikas, p. 168, CFS.

94   Marina Petronoti, "Συμβολή στη μελέτη της οικονομικής αυτονομίας των γυναικών" ["Contribution to the Study of the Financial Autonomy of Women"], p. 249; Sutton, "Greeks of Kalymnos", p. 419. It has been argued that matrilocality in the Dodecanese, as well as customary name-giving, suggest that the control exercised by women in the private sphere on Kalymnos is much stronger when compared with the control exercised by women in other areas in Greece or Crete. See Sutton, "Rescripting Women's Collective Action", p. 473.

95   Roxane Caftanzoglou, *Kalymnos*, p. 35; Eirini Marinou, "Η λειτουργία των μοτίβων" ["The Function of Patterns"], p. 79; Katerina Giannatou, "Η μάνα Καλυμνιά" ["The Kalymnian Mother"], p. 392.

96   Roxane Caftanzoglou, *Kalymnos*, p. 32; Sakellaris N. Trikoilis, "Καλύμνικα βαπτιστικά ονόματα", *Καλυμνιακά Χρονικά* ["Kalymnian baptismal names", *Kalymniaka Chronika*] 13 (1999), p. 25; David E. Sutton, "Local Names, Foreign Claims: Family Inheritance and National Heritage on a Greek Island", *American Ethnologist* 24/2 (1997), pp. 421–425.

also common, either due to the father's absence in Russia or the USA, or to the large number of widows.[97]

It has been argued that women held significantly more power in family affairs on the island of Kalymnos than anywhere else and enjoyed more financial power. This female autonomy, to which Marina Petronoti has also referred,[98] was delimited by clearly defined boundaries and circumscribed space, and was concerned with family life and domestic organization for the period during which the men were away fishing. On their return, men once again took up their dominant social roles. The question remains, therefore, as to whether the temporary increase in women's responsibilities during the sponging season had any impact on the place of women in Kalymnian society. While the women of Kalymnos may have retained some of their male-gendered responsibilities or duties after the return of the men, one must always take into consideration the strong male model of the sponge fisherman that pervaded society.[99]

Of equal importance is the role of the Kalymnian mother as hard worker and moral role model for children, that came into being as the local population was shaping its sponging traditions. This position, as well as the priority of female children in the matter of the dowry and matrilocality, added to a narrative of a "matriarchal past" in the island's popular culture.[100] According to Katerina Giannatou, the care of her children was a life goal for the Kalymnian mother: the preparation of the girls' dowries and her sons' education:

> I'll raise him, and he will be handsome and brave, if he takes after his father. I'll educate him, I'll send him away to study, I'll make him ... a doctor! Sure I will! A great doctor whom all of Kalymnos will admire! My child won't go to the sponges, no! He will become a man whom everyone will respect. And I'll be praying day in, day out, thanking God because I didn't go weak in the knees and managed to help all my children.[101]

---

97   Sakellaris Trikoilis, *Νεότερη ιστορία της Καλύμνου* [*Modern History of Kalymnos*], p. 383, note 482.

98   Marina Petronoti, "Συμβολή στη μελέτη της οικονομικής αυτονομίας των γυναικών" ["Contribution to the Study of the Financial Autonomy of Women"], p. 249.

99   Cf. also João de Pina-Cabral's criticism of anthropological theories that support the notion that fishing communities of the North-Western Iberian Peninsula exhibit a form of matriarchal organization: "Matriarcat", pp. 37–51.

100 This view also appears in Sutton, "Greeks of Kalymnos", p. 417.

101 Katerina Giannatou, "Η μάνα Καλυμνιά" ["The Kalymnian Mother"], p. 393.

Εἰκ. 319.

Πρόσφυγες ΚΑΛΥΜΝΙΑΙ εἰς τὰς ὁδοὺς τοῦ Πειραιῶς.

οὗτοι ὅλους τοὺς ἀνθρωπίνους νόμους
διενεργοῦσι πόλεμον μέχρι θανάτου   Εἰκ. 320.
κατὰ τῶν Φιλελευθέρων Ἐθνῶν.

IMAGE 6.4   Kalymnian Refugees in Piraeus after the Greco-Turkish War, 1920s
SOURCE: SKEVOS ZERVOS, *DODECANESE: THE HISTORY OF DODECANESE
THROUGH THE CENTURIES AND THEIR SERVICES TO HUMANITY AND THEIR
RIGHTS*. LONDON, 1919

Nevertheless, their melancholic, humble presence is condensed in women's own simple daily beliefs and behaviours. For example, Kalymnian women thought that it was "bad luck" [*grousouzia*] to set foot on the sponge-fishing caiques before their departure.[102] Similarly, to ward off bad luck, women would go down to the port dressed in black in anticipation of their men's possible death,[103] crying the name of the man they came to meet in anguish: "Michali, are you in there?"[104]

6.2   The Mechanical Diver

> We did it out of necessity, but it was a brave job.[105]
> The manliest and most dazzling job in the world![106]

Given the difficult circumstances that shaped the highly competitive professional landscape of sponging over the course of many decades, the mental and behavioural landscape of the island developed in analogous ways. In sponge-fishing areas, physical prowess and experience in diving were regarded as important assets that made good divers stand out, while what sources refer to as "old as time" and "proud", namely naked diving, became trivialized in the culture, given that its efficiency was limited. Even though it was believed that Kalymnos became known as the "island of sponge fishermen" thanks to the men who fished with natural breathing methods, those engaged in the sponge fishery with the scaphander diving suit enjoyed an elevated status in a variety of ways in the local community.[107] In the world of sponge fishermen, the professional divers were those who dove with the "dress of the machine"; they were the sponge fishermen *par excellence*. Although the wish "[may you catch] many sponges and in shallow waters", is preserved in local memory, the most proficient divers dared to fish in great depths: the "*vathytes*". These

---

102   Themelina Kapella, "Ποκινήματα, αγιασμός, αναχώρηση" ["Preparation, Sanctification, Departure"], Feature article: "Greek Sponge Fishery, I Kathimerini", *Epta Imeres*, 13/9/1998, p. 28; Faith Warm, *Bitter Sea*, p. 101.

103   Faith Warm, *Bitter Sea*, p. 57.

104   Testimony of Giannis Koutouzis to E.O., 25/8/2003.

105   Testimony of Dimitris Peros to E.O., 24/8/2004.

106   Expression retrieved from a press article in *Βήμα* [*Vima*], 7/5/1961, p. 6.

107   See Sakellaris N. Trikoilis, "'Το δελφίνι του Δάμου Καλυμνίων'. Ο διπλός συμβολισμός: Απόλλων-Θάλασσα", *Καλυμνιακά Χρονικά* ["The Dolphin of Damos Kalymnou' and its Double Symbolism: Apollo-Sea", *Kalymniaka Chronika*] 14 (2001), p. 13.

were the men who could "walk on the sea bottom", and harvest the greatest quantities and the largest sponges, and defied the "hit of the machine" with more bravado than the others. Among them the *matzarolades* were "singled out" as the men who "coped with the *matzarolia*", and "were not affected easily by the machine". The *"kopelia"*, the independent divers were distinguished as those "who managed affairs on their own", as they stored their catch separately and were paid based on a share for their catch. Some even earned the extra percentage awarded to the best diver based on a consensus among the crew members.[108] In a similar vein, the *"maggiora vathytika kaikia"* [largest deep-sea caiques] traveled the farthest and worked off the coasts of Northern Africa. In sum, the desire for greater profits entailed greater risk, and put an end to the methods of free apnea diving, hooking, and the use of the gagava as traditional, antiquated, unproductive means of fishing.

The scaphander diving suit ushered in many changes and completely restructured the organization of the sponge fishery, including the "responsibility" that came with the harsh working conditions it involved. The inhumane living conditions on board the vessels, the exploitation of divers by captains, and especially the increase in the number of the victims of divers' disease are retained in collective memory and provide the inspiration for popular creative works such as literary representations of the sponge fishery, often containing emotionally charged narratives. These texts all depict the conflicting desires of the parties involved, the harsh life and the valiance of divers, as well as their singularly flamboyant lifestyle when on land. Stories contain examples of boldness and bravery, as well as tales of tortures for which the scaphander diving suit was largely responsible. The scaphander diving suit is blamed for the "discord" and "hatred" among crews working on the vessels, and it is held accountable for "the segregation into classes of the people and their emotions across the entire island".[109]

Both more recent and older testimonies have impeached the "prodigality", and the "bacchanalian waste"[110] of the divers who earned large sums of money by means of the scaphander diving suit and squandered even more. The divers drank, bought rounds of drinks for their mates, gambled, and recklessly spent their advance payments and their earnings from the expedition – usually at

---

108   Testimony of Giannis Tsoulfas to E.O., 6/3/2002.

109   Kyriakos Chatzidakis, "Ο αγώνας για την κατάργηση των σκαφάντρων και ο Κάρολος Φλέγελ", *Καλυμνιακά Χρονικά* ["The Fight to Abolish the Scaphander Diving Suit and Carl Flegel", *Kalymniaka Chronika*] 3 (1982), p. 31.

110   Ibid.

the expense of their families.[111] The image of the diver-hero, which also shaped the collective identity of sponge-fishing lands, has two faces because bold-ness leads, with almost mathematical precision, to death or – the ultimate humiliation – paralysis. Written in 1902 about the events of 1883, Mitrophanis Kalafatas' narrative in verse paints just such a picture:

> Those who would dive inside the suits
> are labeled the Mechanics,
> and carry on with unheard of pride
> when first donning the helmet,
> as if it were an olive wreath.
> They put on airs, look down their nose –
> look closely: they piss their trousers.
> They come on two legs, leave on three,
> all strength weakened by water.[112]

The work and the divers themselves are central nodes of *sui generis* constructed social capital, which elevates divers, crediting them with the character of fear-less popular heroes, while rendering their "anti-social" behaviour tolerable if not laudable. The divers' harshness of character was attributed to the dif-ficulties of life on a barren island, and their idiosyncratic behavior was also understood as an element in the undertaking of other dangerous jobs such as bridge painting, in which Kalymnians engaged in the USA when the sponge fishery was in decline.[113]

Social prestige was founded on a disregard for death, which manifested itself in asocial behaviours. Although some might say that "the scaphander diving suit makes one a man", to paraphrase a popular song that is well-known on the island, those who took a stand against the use of the scaphander diving suit and courageously and persistently fought against it, also became popular, timeless heroes. Of these heroes, one was selfless foreigner Carl Flegel, and many think that an imposing statue should be erected in his honour.[114] However, not one single street on the island of Kalymnos has been named for the professor who

---

111   On the same topic see also Faith Warm, *Bitter Sea*, p. 68. After WWII, captains deposited the advance payments with the Port Authority and, during the divers' absence, these pay-ments were paid in monthly installments to the divers' families.
112   Μητροφάνης Καλαφατάς, "Χειμερινός Όνειρος" [Mitrophanis Kalafatas, "Winter Dream"] in Michael N. Kalafatas, *The Bellstone: The Greek Sponge Divers of the Aegean. One American's Journey Home.* Hannover: Brandeis University Press, 2003, pp. 243–244.
113   Kalafatas, *The Bellstone*, p. 78.
114   See Faith Warm, *Bitter Sea*, p. 46.

dedicated his life to the fight for the abolition of the scaphander diving suit; the "deus ex machina", as Michael Kalafatas dubbed him.[115] The only traces of Flegel's existence on the island are the name of a hotel on Kalymnos[116] and the nickname "*Flegeli*" which survives in popular memory.

6.2.1   *The Dance of the Mechanical Diver*

The limited employment opportunities for those who suffer from divers' disease, the poverty of the divers themselves and their families, as well as the exclusion of part of the active population from a variety of events, created an acute social problem in the small island communities discussed in this study. One might well imagine what a significant number of young men with mobility issues meant for the communities that lived from the sponge fishery.

The emotional and social tension generated by this incurable disease is manifested in the island's culture in various ways, such as in "The Dance of the Mechanical Diver". This dance is not traditional. It was created by Theofilos Klonaris, a Kalymnian graduate of the Department of Sports and Physical Education, who first presented the dance with the Dora Stratou ensemble in 1952.[117] As Themelina Kapella has written, the dance is suggestive of a mildly "caught" [*piasmenos*] mechanical diver, that is, a diver who descended to the bottom of the sea in a scaphander suit and was "hit" with the disease. He drunkenly attempts to join the festivities at an island tavern, and tries to take a few steps, dragging his legs while being supported by the other dancers.[118] Even if Klonaris drew his inspiration from real experiences and images, the fact that the dance was incorporated into local tradition, at a time when there were still many new victims of the disease, is interesting.

The principle dancer in "The Dance of the Mechanical Diver" mimics a "caught", semi-paralyzed sponger who leads the dance with his cane, while his legs tremble in his struggle to move; he falls down and gets up again several times. Towards the end of the dance, however, he is cured, throws away his cane, and joins in the lively movement with the other dancers. Given that dance requires flexibility, skillfulness, and physical well-being, and particularly

---

115   Kalafatas, *The Bellstone*, p. 42.

116   Ibid., p. 45.

117   Editor's note: Dora Stratou (1903–1988) was a patron of culture and particularly dance and folk culture. She helped establish a national folk ensemble in Greece and was the author of three books: *A Tradition, an Adventure, Greek Dances, a Living Link to Antiquity*, and *Traditional Greek Dances*. Stratou also made 50 recordings of folk music which is one of the largest collections of folk music in the world.

118   Themelina Kapella, "Ο χορός του 'μηχανικού'", ["The Dance of the 'Mechanic'"], Feature article: *Greek Sponge Fishery, I Kathmerini, Epta Imeres*, 13/9/1998, p. 30.

on the part of the leading dancer, this dance destigmatizes paralyses. In this way, the disease is not seen as a marginal problem and its victims are neither excluded nor ignored. On the contrary, the problem is embraced by the local community, whose members make wishes that the evil be exorcised. Moreover, as Sofia Giannatou astutely observed, "it is the only in the tradition of the navel of the Earth that one is permitted to get tears in his eyes without being considered weak."[119]

6.3   "An Easter Full of Gunpowder"

Another typical manifestation of the cultivation of daring, fearlessness and laughing in the face of danger might be the excessive use of dynamite in fishing; a logic of survival based on the overexploitation sea, and its customary abuse on Kalymnos during Easter.[120] Indeed, the use of dynamite is linked to sponge fishing along with references to the "boldness", "valiance", and "rebellious character" of Kalymnians:[121] dynamite was part of the "spoils", the remnants of war that were discovered by Kalymnian divers at the bottom of the sea. The consumption of dynamite also brings to mind another aspect of behaviours attributed to divers with regard to danger and death.[122] In spite of the use of dynamite being common practice for fishermen in various areas, its abuse by professional and amateur fishermen from Kalymnos appears to be more extensive than in any other place.[123] Some place the origins of this habit in the years of Italian occupation as another form of Kalymnians' dynamic resistance.[124] The Elders' Council of Kalymnos was actually aware of the practice beginning in the final decades of the 19th century, at which time it announced a

---

119   Sofia Giannatou, "Η Πόθια", *Καλυμνιακά Χρονικά* ["Pothia", *Kalymniaka Chronika*] 15 (2003), p. 258.

120   Sutton commented that such behaviour is mostly attributable to the "harshness" or the "craziness" with which Kalymnians used to self-identify. David E. Sutton, "'Tradition and Modernity': Kalymnian Constructions of Identity and Otherness", pp. 241, 248; by the same author, *Memories Cast in Stone*, pp. 60–65 and 74–76.

121   Niki Billiri, *Της θάλασσας και της στεριάς* [*Of Sea and Land*], p. 235.

122   Sutton, *Memories Cast in Stone*, p. 59.

123   See also Tassos Zappas' press publication "Ο εφιάλτης των ακτών μας. Στον κάβο με τους δυναμιτιστάς", *Αθηναϊκά Νέα* ["Our Coasts' Nightmare: At the Cavo with the Dynamite Throwers", *Athinaika Nea*], 29/9/1937, p. 3.

124   Niki Billiri, *Της θάλασσας και της στεριάς* [*Of Sea and Land*], p. 235; Sutton, *Memories Cast in Stone,* pp. 65–67; by the same author, "Re-scripting Women's Collective Action", pp. 491–492.

ban on fishing with dynamite, and encouraged the local governor's office [*Kaymakamia*] to assist in the enforcement of its decree.[125]

Local society and authorities seem to have participated in dynamite fishing, or to have adopted a somewhat tolerant stance towards the "custom". By way of illustration, I include the following:

> The dynamite explosions are an inextricable part of every Kalymnian's psyche. The ritual began in the old days, when sponge-fishing vessels set sail around this time of year, and it took sponge fishermen 6 to 8 months to see their loved ones again, while facing one thousand and two dangers![126]

Where boldness parts company with delinquent behaviour was not always clear; especially when behaviours deemed simply "manly" were involved, and manifested in a society that might be characterized as traditional and conservative on many levels.[127] Moreover, the use of dynamite at Easter legit-

---

125 See Evdokia Olympitou, "Ψαρεύοντας στο Αιγαίο τον 19ο αιώνα" ["Fishing in the Aegean in the 19th Century"], in Dimitris Dimitropoulos, Evdokia Oympitou (eds.), Ψαρεύοντας στις ελληνικές θάλασσες. Από τις μαρτυρίες του παρελθόντος στη σύγχρονη πραγματικότητα [*Fishing in the Greek Seas: From Testimonies of the Past to Modern Reality*], Research Notebooks 33, Athens 2010, pp. 143–144, where relevant archival references.

126 http://kalymnos-cosmos.blogspot.com/2010/03/blog-post_30.html. Cf. also the webpage of the vocational senior secondary school of Kalymnos: "They always threw dynamite on Kalymnos, and everybody knew how to make "*trigonakia*" (firecrackers in small triangle shape) and "*varelota*" (firecrackers in sticks); but the habit of throwing a large number of them, and from over the mountains, started after the political changeover in Greece. As a reaction to the Greek junta, in the year of its fall, many Kalymnians climbed the mountains and threw a lot of dynamite; it has continued ever since. Little by little, they started to exaggerate in the use of dynamite, reaching a point where firecrackers were thrown at the centre of the island around the Church of Christ. To avoid this, the Lyceum Club of Greek Women [*Lykeion Hellenidon*] held a dance at the [Church of] Christos, instead of the traditional dance that took place at the [Church of Resurrection] that was holding a celebration. Whoever visits Kalymnos in Easter will enjoy, among other things, the beautiful work of the Club of Greek Women [*Lykeion Hellenidon*] in combination with the sound and the flare of the dynamite detonated from high on the mountain". See also the website of the Holy Metropolis of Leros-Kalymnos and Astypalaia, where it is noted: "Of course, the island's custom of using dynamite and the dances of the *Lykeion Hellenidon* of Kalymnos, which brought a celebratory hue to the Resurrection feast on the island, should be also mentioned here".

127 C.f. Michael Herzfeld, *The Poetics of Manhood. Contest and Identity in a Cretan Mountain Village*, Princeton University Press 1985, p. 33. See also what David Sutton wrote in "'He's too cold': Children and the Limits of Culture on a Greek Island", *Anthropology and Humanism* 23 (1998), pp. 127–138.

imized Kalymnian singularity, and embodied the proud spirit of the island's inhabitants.

6.4   Festivities for the Departure of the Sponge Fishermen:
"The *AGAPE* Banquet"

One might expect that the population-wide participation in the ceremonies for the departure and return of the caiques mostly touched those who had loved ones on board on an emotional level. In reality, the entire local population came together at these moments of bidding farewell and welcoming back the island' s protagonists, the sponge fishermen. "Those moments had a certain glory, they were majestic", as many recalled. We do not know, however, if the stories committed to oral memory and literature from the postwar years took place in the more distant past, and if by that time the departure of the vessels had become more akin to a popular fair or funeral cortege. The ceremony for the departure might have remain unchanged, and fair and funeral might have happened together. Indeed, if many of the "mechanical" divers set sail taking their shrouds with them,[128] it is not difficult to imagine the prevailing mood at their departure.

The sanctification of the caiques with holy water[129] is recalled in variety of recent testimonies along with the litany of the icon of Saint Nicolas,[130] both of which were accompanied by mass festivities.[131] "We danced and sang with violins and lutes; we were throwing our money away, because we didn't know if we were going to come back alive".[132] "Sailors or cooks didn't spend their *platika*, but we, the divers, were well aware that the black water of Madruh might eat us up, so we threw the *platika* down the drain".[133] "Utter mayhem at

---

128   Flegel, "Το σπογγαλιευτικό ζήτημα" ["The Sponge Fishery Issue"], p. 212; Georgios Elefth. Georgas, *Μελέτη περί σπογγαλιείας, σπόγγων και σπογγεμπορίου από των αρχαιοτάτων χρόνων μέχρι σήμερον* [*Study of the Sponge Fishery, Sponges and Sponge Trade from Ancient Times to the Present*], Piraeus 1937, p. 41.

129   Manuscript 1838/1973, Evangelia Lambadariou, p. 69, CFS; Niki Billiri, *Η Κάλυμνός μας* [*Our Kalymnos*], p. 18.

130   Testimony of Emmanouil Karageorgios in Manuscript 1628/1971, Emmanouil Sarikas, p. 58, CFS. See also the testimony of sponger Michail Stefadouros to Faneromeni Chalkidiou-Skylla, *Η σφουγγάρι ή τομάρι* [*Either Sponge or Corpse*], p. 173.

131   The sponge fishermen from Leros mentioned that every year, before departing from their island, parties were thrown at every diver's house. Testimony of Giannis Koutouzis to E.O., 25/8/2003.

132   Manuscript 1838/1973, Evangelia Lambadariou, p. 69, CFS.

133   Manuscript 2729/1976 Angeliki Georgiadou, pp. 59–60, CFS.

IMAGE 6.5   Feast in Kalymnos, 1950
            SOURCE: PHOTOGRAPH BY DIMITRIOS HARISIADIS, KALYMNOS 1950
            © BENAKI MUSEUM/PHOTOGRAPHIC ARCHIVES

the port", Michail Lampos recalled. "Kids were running, priests were chanting, everyone was down there. Mayhem. It was a marvelous panorama!"[134] Many boarded the caiques drunk, by force, or crying. "It was a very scary and dreadful [*gouliasmeni*] day for our island. You saw women wearing black kerchiefs, children crying as they watched their mothers cry. And as if our grief wasn't enough, the bells were tolling a deathly tune, as if they were sending us off to die. I swore at them, telling them to go to hell".[135]

---

134   Testimony of Michalis Lampos to E.O., 29/7/2005.
135   Manuscript 2728/1976 Maria Sevastopoulou, p. 66, CFS.

Beginning in the early 1950s, prior to the departure of sponge-fishing vessels every April or May, the island honoured its sponge fishermen with a series of events, which gradually took on an official nature.[136] The Pothia seaside road was lined with flags, with banners hung in every corner, and representatives of the political leadership and government, foreign visitors, journalists and TV crews were in attendance at the ceremonies wishing the men a safe return.[137] The ceremony followed a standard procedure: doxology and blessing of the ships by the Metropolitan and the island's priests; fireworks and dynamite; the presence of the local authorities and the population of the island; a send-off; drunken "mechanical divers", "veteran" and "caught" sponge fishermen; bells tolling.[138]

Local bodies organized the customary Agape Banquet, or banquet of love, in which the city authorities and the vessel crews participated.[139] Originally, the Agape Banquet represented a halt to any controversies between crews, captains and sponge-fishing investors before the expedition. Such events organized in the 1960s, however, were aimed at the island's promotion of tourism. The municipality, as the organizer of the events, sought to highlight this singularity of Kalymnos – the Agape Banquet – for the Greek and international public, in an effort to attract visitors from around the globe.

Every year, press articles featured descriptions of the events, pointing out the unique "quaintness" of the departure of the sponge fishermen.[140] In 1962, the events included local dances and all-night parties with the "mechanical divers" of the island, and hotels offered discount prices for those wishing to attend the two-day celebrations.[141] Beginning in the 1970s, events also included excursions to various locations on the island, as well as shows about sponge-fishing and other local customs, and even theatrical plays for visitors.[142]

At the 1965 Agape Banquet, which was by then a well-established tradition, Ioannis Zigdis, the Minister for Industry, was provided with an opportunity to announce a number of measures in support of the sponge fishery.[143] Reportedly however, by 1965 there were very few participants. In spite of the

---

136   In 1952, the Minister for Industry, Ioannis Zigdis, had already attended the ceremony
       To Βήμα [*To Vima*], 8/5/1952, p. 4.
137   See also Russell, "The Fisherman and His Wife", p. 304.
138   *Τα Νέα* [*Ta Nea*], 25/4/1959, p. 3; *To Βήμα* [*To Vima*], 22/5/1960, p. 8; 3/5/1961, p. 2 and
       7/5/1961, p. 6.
139   *To Βήμα* [*To Vima*] 27/4/1969, p. 5; Niki Billiri, *Η Κάλυμνός μας* [*Our Kalymnos*], p. 18. See
       also Faith Warm, *Bitter Sea*, p. 66.
140   See also *To Βήμα* [*To Vima*], 29/4/1962, p. 11 and 6/5/1981, p. 11.
141   *To Βήμα* [*To Vima*], 8/4/1962, p. 11; *Ta Nea*, 18/4/1962, p. 12.
142   *To Βήμα* [*To Vima*], 29/4/1970, p. 5.
143   *To Βήμα* [*To Vima*], 28/4/1965, p. 8.

profits that sponges continued to generate for the island, the idiosyncratic lifestyle that came with sponging, and the divers' behaviour were no longer acceptable, at least outside of the island's working classes.[144] According to Russell, the social degradation of sponge fishermen and the depreciation of their profession in the collective local opinion also took hold at this time. His informants regularly stated that the sponge fishermen defamed the island with their rough manners and lifestyle. In 1974, an effort to maintain the Agape Banquet despite the industry's poor reputation, the organizers began incorporating the "folklore culture of the island" into the festivities. And while special invitations were required, very few sponge fishermen actually participated, and investors gradually turned to tourism.[145]

6.5   The Sponge Fishery in Literature: Representations of the Professional Life of Sponge Fishermen

> I never coveted the craft of the sponger, not once in my entire life! I loved the bays, the islands, the sea – its rages and its peace – but never its treasures, no! Since childhood I get sick to my stomach in front of a "machine". I don't know what impression it gave me; I don't remember what I used to compare it to. I never saw it as flotsam, as God's blessing and pride of the sea. To my eyes it appeared to be a disgusting thing, an artefact of the Devil. Every year, in the week of Thomas [the week after Easter], when our island wept with the sobbing and trepidation of mothers and "wives" [*stefanotikes*], or when it was buzzing with the divers' feasting, I only pictured Barbary as *Lamia* [a child-eating monster], making her crystal beds so that she could lay down, while those envious of her riches are never to wake up. And when everyone went to the cape to greet the sponge fishermen as they returned in the late autumn, I ran driven by a morbid curiosity to count those who returned paralyzed, their lives in tatters, and to see how many were left at the Aspronissi, to become the food and playthings of the vile Arabs.

This passage is taken from Andreas Karkavitsas' short story, "The Spongers", first published in the journal *Acropolis* [*Ακρόπολις*] on New Year's Day, 1899. This was one of the first literary texts that depicted the sponge fishery, and it was instrumental in exposing the topic to a wider public. The publication of

---

144   Russell, "Kalymnos", p. 305; of the same author, "The Fisherman and His Wife", p. 304.
145   *Τα Νέα* [*Ta Nea*], 9/5/1977, p. 5.

Karkavitsas' story also coincided with a period in which sponge-fishing islands' communities were in turmoil due to the "Sponge-Fishery Issue", that is, the fight to abolish the scaphander diving suit, which was introduced to the Greek sponge fishery in the late 1860s.

In this historical context, authors who drew material and inspiration from the sponge fishery and transformed it into literary narratives, would see their paths converge. Departing from different ideological points of view and approaches, authors like Andreas Karkavitsas, Kostas Paroritis, Aggelos Tanagras, Petros Pikros, Ion Dragoumis, as well as men of letters from sponge fishing lands – Giannis Magklis, Giannis Zervos[146] and others – wrote short stories and novels about the daily life of sponge fishermen, the dangers of diving, the divers' idiosyncratic lifestyle when on land, and the eerie close calculus with death that their job entailed. The heroes of these stories are dramatic characters, trapped by their fate on the island, or by their destiny as sponge fishermen, which invariably leads to paralysis or death. But the island is their cherished homeland and where they must reside, so they are left with no choice but to fish for sponges. This is the double bind in which the young sponge fishermen of Aegina find themselves in Ion Dragoumis' short story of 1898 or 1899, that he wrote at an early age.[147] Perhaps the only exception to this narrative trajectory is Giannis, the hero of Kostas Paroritis' novel, Στ' άλμπουρο [On the Mast], who hopes not only for a better life, but more broadly, for better working conditions in locations that were thriving, thanks to the sponge fishery.

In these sponging narratives, the mythical Aegean Sea – its bright light, white houses, and clear, luminous blue sea – which traditionally signifies Greekness,[148] is supplanted by a rocky, barren landscape in which the inhabitants, unable to sustain themselves, are forced to take tremendous risks in order to survive. In the preface to Kalymnian author Giannis Zervos' 1959 novel, *Fateful Scaphander and the Anathema of the Machine*, he writes:

---

146 G. Valetas placed him in the inter-War generation, see G. Valetas, *Επίτομη Ιστορία της Νεοελληνικής Λογοτεχνίας* [*Abridged History of Modern Greek Literature*], Athens 1966, p. 162.

147 Ion Dragoumis, "Οι σφουγγαράδες" ["The Sponge Fishermen"], pp. 3–11.

148 See also G. Seferis, *Δοκιμές* [*Essays*], vol. I, Athens 1981, pp. 167–168; Mario Vitti, *Η γενιά του Τριάντα, Ιδεολογία και μορφή* [*The Generation of the 30s, Ideology and Form*], Athens 1995, pp. 201–203; Eratosthenis Kapsomenos, "Η μυθολογία του Αιγαίου στη νεοελληνική λογοτεχνία", *Η Ελλάδα των νησιών από τη Φραγκοκρατία ως σήμερα* ["The Mythology of the Aegean Sea in Modern Greek Literature", *Greece of the Islands from the Frankish Rule to Today*], vol. I, Athens 2004, pp. 399–413.

Those who gaze at it from afar, from the sea, or sail close to the sponge-fishing island with its arid, wild mountains; if they had only lived there in the wintertime, if only for a day, [...] they would wonder how it is possible for human souls to survive there.

Accounts of life on the island in literary texts such as these concur with testimonies in archival documents on one specific point, namely the ultimatum with which life on this baren island presented its inhabitants: sponge fishing or emigration.

Given that literary writing on sponging is quite extensive, and given my own approach to this literature, which I treat as source for and testimony about sponge fishing, I will limit this discussion to a brief presentation of topics that come to the fore in a review of these texts. As part of the canon of modern Greek literature, these works tell the story of different generations and trends in the culture. Along with Karkavitsas's "The Sponge Fishermen" (1899), I will explore two novels: Kostas Paroritis' novel, *On the Mast* [Στ' άλμπουρο], (1910) and Giannis Zervos' *Fateful Scaphander and the Anathema of the Machine* [Μοιραίο σκάφανδρο και το ανάθεμα της μηχανής] (1959).

Andreas Karkavitsas (1865–1922) wrote "The Sponge Fishermen" while on Hydra, following two years of service as a doctor for steamship company *Panellinios Atmoploia* (1892–1894).[149] In this short story, later included in a collection entitled *Words of the Prow* [Λόγια της Πλώρη], Karkavitsas explores the world of the sea, a world which much resembles, perhaps, the traditional agricultural world on land. The sea attracted interest from the intelligentsia in the late 19th century, within the framework of an emergent genre of Greek national literature which aimed to familiarize citizens with their own country.[150] Folklore studies, which were developing at that time as well, also encouraged observing and recording the cultural wealth and the ethos of daily life in rural populations. This led to an appreciation of agricultural communities which, along with urban populations, came to be seen as making valuable contributions to arguments for the long-standing presence of Hellenism.[151]

---

149   See also Eri Stavropoulou, "Ανδρέας Καρκαβίτσας, Παρουσίαση – Ανθολόγηση", Η παλαιότερη πεζογραφία μας, 1880–1900 ["Andreas Karkavitsas, Presentation-Selection of Stories"], vol. VIII, Athens 1997, pp. 174–251.

150   Giannis Kordatos viewed it as the best story in the collection, see Giannis Kordatos, Ιστορία της νεοελληνικής λογοτεχνίας (από το 1453 ως το 1961) [*History of Modern Greek Literature (from 1453 to 1961)*], vol. I, Athens 1962, pp. 418–421.

151   In 1883, Εστία [*Estia*] launched a competition "for the writing of Greek short stories", which required a Greek "plot" and the "description of scenes from the life of

Influenced by the work of Nikolaos Politis, pioneer of folklore studies in Greece, Karkavitsas devoted his career to the portrayal of rural life and dedicated a significant portion of his work in prose to the sea and its people – the seamen, the fishermen, and the spongers. Writing between romanticism and realism, Karkavitsas conscientiously and imaginatively adapted insights and collected material made available by folklore studies. In "The Sponge Fishermen", he captures the traditional world threatened by technological progress and new working conditions.

Written in the first person, the narrative concerns two brothers – both sponge fishermen – recruited into different sponge-fishing crews. With only a limited catch, captains begin to oppress their crews, and the divers are forced to face off in a highly competitive contest. The author demonstrates a detailed and clear knowledge of the system of shares or percentages of harvested sponges, which was widely used in the sponge fishery at great depths, as a highly differentiated system of payment which depended on divers' skillfulness and performance. As previously discussed, high advance payments to the most proficient divers, which were usually spent recklessly before the expedition began, resulted in heightened professional competitiveness, hence the tragic ending of Karkavitsas's story. In an attempt to snatch a large sponge from another diver, one brother kills the other whom he has failed to recognize, clad in scaphander suit and helmet.

Kostas Paroritis (1878–1932) was among the first to support the cohesion and combined discourses of demoticism[152] and socialism, movements[153] that frequently came together around issues such as social injustice, exploitation,

---

the Greek people". Bulletin of *Εστία* [*Estia*] 333, 15 May 1883. On this topic see Epam. Baloumis, "Εθνικο-κοινωνικά στον Αν. Καρκαβίτσα", *Διαβάζω* ["Ethno-social Ellements in An. Karkavitsas", *Diavazo*] 306 (1993), pp. 46–54. See also Giannis Baskozos, "Ανδρέας Καρκαβίτσας: Από την ηθογραφία στο ρεαλισμό", *Διαβάζω* ["Andreas Karkavitsas: From Ethography to Realism", *Diavazo*] 306 (1993), pp. 57–60.

152   Editor's note: Demoticism was an intellectual movement that began in 1880s and prevailed in its influence on the Greek language in the 20th century. It arose from a perceived need to simplify the Greek language from elements of ancient forms found in *Katharevusa*, used as the official language. Demoticism became a social and national issue that was resolved in 1976 with the establishment of Demotiki as the official Greek language.

153   In the intellectual and ideological circle to which he belonged, realism was used as a medium of social analysis. Paroritis faced backlash from his contemporary and later peers, such as Angelos Terzakis or Alkis Thrylos, because he was thought to have promoted communist ideas in his novels. His work is also characterized by a lack of creative impetus and a stifling atmosphere of seedy dives. Mario Vitti, *Ιστορία της νεοελληνικής λογοτεχνίας* [*History of Modern Greek Literature*], Athens 1978, p. 330.

corruption and social deprivation.[154] As a school principal on Hydra from 1904 to 1917, he had the occasion to become well acquainted with the world of sponge fishermen,[155] which he describes in his first novel in 1910.[156]

Giannis, the main character of *On the Mast* [*Στ' άλμπουρο*] (1910), is a desperate man, who resorts to sponge diving following his father's death in a work-related accident. The story "unfolds on one of the islands of the Dodecanese", but the precise location of the setting is never revealed, perhaps because Paroritis wanted to suggest that his story might have taken place on any sponge-fishing island. Apart from this detail, the author announces his intentions vividly, along with his intention to decry the conditions under which sponge fishermen worked and lived. Paroritis describes the networks to which men fell victim and which bled them dry before sending them off to their death. The network consists of multiple agents from the person who recruits marginalized and unemployed young men in Piraeus as sponge fishermen and pays their traveling expenses to the island; to the loan-shark grocer who rents squalid rooms to the new recruits and sustains them by charging exorbitant prices in anticipation of their *platika*; to the rich merchant-investor in sponge-fishing groups and the policeman serving him.

When the recruiting season begins, future divers find themselves trapped between their debts and readily available employment on the sponging vessels. Any attempt to improve the terms of their contracts, or any attempt to flee as the hero of the story does, rapidly runs into the collaborative network of exploitation. "I used to say things about the factory. Everywhere is the same. These mighty people are all cut from the same cloth", Giannis muses at one point, thereby condensing, in a single phrase, what was perhaps Paroritis' own perspective. In the suffocating, dismal world of the text, what follows is almost unsurprising: Giannis' wife, who works as a maid in investor Dimitrakis' house,

---

154 Paroritis' texts belong to the genre of the social novel, the most consistent and prominent representative of that generation being Konstantinos Theotokis. His writings are militantly committed to socialist ideas. It should be noted that his novel *On the Mast* [*Στ' άλμπουρο*] was published in 1910, three years after *Our Social Issue* [*Κοινωνικόν μας ζήτημα*] of Skliros, which laid the foundations of socialism in Greece.

155 Quoted in G. Kordatos; see Kordatos, *Ιστορία της νεοελληνικής λογοτεχνίας* [*History of Modern Greek Literature*], p. 440. During this period, Paroritis used an address on Hydra for his correspondence with literary magazine *Νουμάς* [*Noumas*]. See Stelios Fokos, *Κώστας Παρορίτης, εισαγωγή στη ζωή και το έργο του* [*Kostas Paroritis: Introduction to His Life and Work*], Athens 1979, p. 21.

156 Prompted by K. Chatzopoulos, he abandoned the short story genre and turned to the novel; Alexis Ziras, "Κώστας Παρορίτης, Παρουσίαση-Ανθολόγηση", *Η Παλαιότερη πεζογραφία μας* ["Kostas Paroritis, Presentation of a Selection of Stories", *I palaioteri pezografia mas, 1900–1914*], vol. III, Sokoli, Athens 1997, pp. 366–421.

is raped by him and conceives an unwanted child. The baby is murdered, and Giannis' wife and her mother are imprisoned, following which the hero suffers a slow death from divers' disease.

The narrator of *On the Mast* explains the violent behaviour of captains on board the vessels as a transference of the pressure placed on them by investors. This is to say that the captains in charge of sponge-fishing groups owned or rented the mechanical equipment and the sponge-fishing vessel and were sometimes divers themselves. For these intermediary chain links between investors and the crews, the sponge-fishing undertaking was usually quite profitable, yet the business risk involved in an investment in human labour, combined with the potential profit from its overexploitation, motivated captains' own behaviour with crews, and particularly with the divers. Indeed, the divers were ostensibly part of the captains' own capital and in Paroritis' novel, the crew rises in revolt against the captain's harshness. As Giannis, the protagonist, explains, the captain forced them to dive to great depths, beat them, and tied them onto the mast when they failed to work efficiently. And when divers were "caught" by the machine, the captain threw them half-dead into the ship's hold or left them semi-paralyzed on a desert island.

The novel contains two narrative themes, namely the island and the expedition. One strand of Paroritis' narrative follows events that take place on the island in the sponge fishermen's absence. Here, the island is of interest because every aspect of daily life there revolves around the sponge fishery. Given that the sponge fishery evolved into a systematic occupation, and essentially the only professional specialization in the areas in which the novel is set, a detailed account thereof is also typical of the naturalist novel – the genre to which *On the Mast* belongs. The most dramatic moments in the narrative, however, are the sponge fishermen's expedition, recounted in the text from the perspective of the divers.

The scaphander diving suit is the topic of Giannis Zervos's *Fateful Scaphander and the Anathema of the Machine* [Μοιραίο σκάφανδρο και το ανάθεμα της μηχανής] (1959). In this novel, all the arguments made against the use of the scaphander that appear in 19th- and 20th-century documentation make an appearance. For example, the story opens with a violent protest scene wherein a raging crowd takes to the streets of Pothia, cursing the scaphander diving suit, throwing stones, and threatening the people who imposed it on the divers and led them to paralysis and death with curses. Even though we come across violent reactions of this kind in other sources as well, this particular Kalymnian protest is described in a letter previously noted in Chapter 4, from the Elders' Council to the Kaymakam of Kalymnos, Hilmi Bey, on 29 May 1895. While it is not known whether Zervos was aware of the documents referring to the incidents, it is likely that he would have had knowledge of oral accounts of the riots, which are known on Kalymnos to this day.

The changes brought to the organization of the sponge fishery with the arrival of the scaphander diving suit, as well as its "responsibility" for harsh working conditions and the inhumane living conditions on board the vessels, the exploitation of divers by captains, and the increase in the number of the victims of divers' disease, provided literary authors with dramatic material. The opposing desires of the parties involved in the industry and the resulting tensions likewise opened interesting plot lines. Importantly however, despite the many years separating some of these works from each other, they are all concerned with the profound impact of the scaphander diving suit and the consequences of its widespread use.

The literary representations of the sponge fishery discussed here, the social ills they recount – begging, prostitution, deprivation, alcoholism, violence, criminality – are not framed as being random, or simply the result of conjuncture. Indeed, the social pathogenesis of the sponge fishery is the result of structural elements inherent to the industry, and how the industry was organized while in a process of change – which change also imposed its stamp on working relationships. Hence in these narratives, the image of the diver as social hero is demystified. The diver is nothing more than a desperate, socially marginalized, poor islander; a man who struggles daily to make ends meet while trapped in a survival game that is lost in advance.

If the ethnography of that period often renders images from the reality of its time in idyllic tones, the literature of the sponge fishery is committed to realistic-naturalistic narration. It is tempting therefore, to read such literary portrayals of the world of sponge fishery as early, artistically expressed, ethnographic observation that depicts, records, and seeks to understand the characteristics of local societies that developed and sustained this skill for a long time. Moreover, sponge-fishing populations also provided a compelling and evocative subject for ethnographic readings as these communities developed unique identities, systems of social organization, and ways of conducting daily life.

Regardless of aesthetic or other qualitative criteria, which are not part of our approach, and regardless of possible reservations concerning any representation of this type, I believe that historical and anthropological research can leverage literary production in multiple ways. The realistic, naturalistic depictions of daily life offered in the literary texts discussed here aside, literature has the capacity to appropriate what we know from archival evidence and recast it in a (quasi) faithful way. The leveragability of literary production, however, is mostly attributable to its capacity to the capture mindsets, collective mentalities and practices extant at a given moment in time and professional space, which are reproduced and fed by collective memory in the sponge-fishing islands, just as they are today.

6.6   "Brave Kalymnos": Multiple Realities and Identities

Oh valiant and much-lauded Kalymnos,
Famous all over the world for your sponges[157]

Older as well as more recent sources and testimonies attribute characteristics to Kalymnians that have become stereotypical. For example, in 1862 Hippocrates Tavlarios wrote the following about the crews of the vessels with which Kalymnians engaged in the sponge fishery:

> And yet these incredible people, who fight against all the elements, do not hesitate to cross so many seas, but treat the seas and the winds as if they were child's play! This demonstrates a spirit of risk-taking, as well as the excellency of Greek seamen; the inhabitants of the island are clever, jolly, and witty, but of unstable character, and much more envious than the rest. We hope, however, that with time and perhaps imported culture these vices will be eradicated.[158]

Sponges, "gold from the bottom of the sea", forged a stable relationship between the sea and Kalymnians, substantiating claims of legendary swimmers and unparalleled divers. By and large, testimonies chronicle divers' impressive familiarity with the water, in ways very different from how fishermen working safely from land or on boats are described.

On occasion however, this swimming and diving prowess is not attributed to Kalymnian's special relationship with the sea, but to the stimuli the men received from an early age in the unique environment in which they lived, so that the sea "gets under their skin".[159] On this topic, Newton's impressions of

---

157   I borrow the expression from Manuscript 888/1969, Poseidon Zairis, p. 1, CFS.

158   Tavlarios, "Περί της νήσου Καλύμνου" ["About the Island of Kalymnos"], pp. 518–522. The text was republished by Daniil Zervos under the title of "Μια περιγραφή της Καλύμνου" ["A Description of Kalymnos"], p. 100.

159   The unique familiarity of Kalymnian children with the sea is also reflected in their individual or collective games in the sea. Most of them consisted of *makrovoutia* dives, [shallow, long-distance dives that skim along under the surface of the sea], speed races and makeshift spearguns that they used from a very young age. The game of "*hazies (hazides)*" is

young Kalymnians' skillful swimming,[160] as well as the testimony of Ludwig Ross are two of the oldest on record:

> Half a dozen of small-boned and sunburned boys, who lay naked on the beach, jumped into the sea – because we were on the famous island of the divers – and swam and dived like ducks around the yacht, even though we had anchored at a depth of 2 fathoms, bringing back up sand and small pebbles, which they threw at each other.[161]

Customary practices, such as the habit of mixing salt with the first bath water of newborn male infants in the hopes that they will be fond of the sea,[162] go hand in hand with stereotypical perceptions of Kalymnians and are part of the constant promotion of their singularity. "From the moment he is born, the Kalymnian male inherits the genetic code for becoming a proficient swimmer – a true dolphin".[163] Similarly, in a satirical essay dedicated to Kalymnian naked divers Tassos Zappas referred to them as "amphibians",[164] and divers themselves attribute their resilience in the face of the hardships of their work to their distinct "race", as a "race" of seamen, and even more so, as a "race" of divers.[165]

Furthermore, swimming and diving skills often counterbalanced what was lacking in crews' experience with long-distance navigation, hence diving know-how was also regarded as being more complex than navigation. Here it is interesting to note how Kalymnians admitted that they were incapable of leading their sponge-fishing vessels to Libya, by also claiming that they even resorted to hiring "foreign" captains from Leros, whom they did not consider

---

also notable: it was played according to sponge-fishing tradition in two teams, "dressed in their birthday suits". After a fight in the sea, the team that wins sinks the greatest number of opponents. See Theodoros Kavasilas, "Αξεθώριαστες εικόνες απ' τα παλιά ...", Καλυμνιακά Χρονικά ["Unfading Images from the Past ...", Kalymniaka Chronika] 6 (1986), p. 318 and Nikitas Sk. Karafyllakis, "Πηαίνετε α παίξετε", Καλυμνιακά Χρονικά ["Go play", Kalymniaka Chronika], 14 (2001), pp. 313–316.

160   Newton, Travels and Discoveries, p. 298.

161   Ludwig Ross, "Νησιωτικά ταξείδια (Inselreisen) Κάλυμνος-Τέλενδος" ["Island Travels Kalymnos-Telendos"], p. 335.

162   Eirini Marinou, "Η λειτουργία των μοτίβων" ["The Function of Patterns"], p. 79.

163   Trikoilis, "Το δελφίνι του Δάμου Καλυμνίων" ["The Dolphin of Damos of Kalymnians"], p. 13.

164   Tassos Zappas, "Στον κάβο με τους γυμνούς σφουγγαράδες", Αθηναϊκά Νέα ["At the Cavo with the Naked Sponge Fishermen", Athinaika Nea], 23/9/1937, p. 3.

165   For the world of the mainlanders and the world of sea people, collective perceptions, myths, and mentalities, see Aliette Geistdoerfer, "De l'origine des marins. La genèse mythique d'une spécialisation technique", Techniques et Culture 43–44 (2004), pp. 2–14.

as "maritime people" like themselves. As the president of the Association of Sponge Fishermen Captains of Kalymnos, Giannis Tsoulfas, confessed; "this is something that I do not tell everyone, because it does not honour Kalymnians".[166]

6.6.1   *"The Navel of the Earth"*

The residents of Kalymnos, or the native Kalymnians, have all most certainly heard that their island is the "the navel of the earth",[167] and they might well have come across and even adopted, a strong, albeit not unique, localism. Such localism is not however congruent with the natural environment, and the employment opportunities available on this island. Thus arose the belief that this rough island has pushed its inhabitants to take advantage of every opportunity, and to pit themselves against any adversity in order to survive and thrive. Therefore, if the "earth's navel" is not the centre of the world or the cradle of civilization, it is most certainly a unique example of social prosperity. As Sofia Giannatou wrote:

> If the Earth had a navel, its capital city would be Pothia. The navel is in the Aegean Sea, surrounded by islands of minor importance, which need not be named. They just exist there for ornamental purposes. They float about casually, and accumulate masses of visiting tourists, leaving the navel to be enjoyed in its starkly outlined singularity by inhabitants and insiders. The inhabitants are the island's indigenous; the former inhabitants who come back to the island at least once a year, craving their fix like addicts; the children of the former inhabitants, who also know in the blood and through education the desire to return. It is in their blood like a disease; the children of the children; and the spouses, daughters-in-law, parents-in-law, brothers-in-law, and uncles of all of them, they too feel joined to the umbilical cord by marriage.[168]

Kalymnian identity is shaped by "tradition", and informed by references to the "then" or to a time "in the past", hence a tendency to look to the past distinguishes Kalymnians from "others", and especially the "other neighbours".[169]

---

166   Testimony of Giannis Tsoulfas to E.O., 6/3/2002.
167   A term known to Sutton, as well; David Sutton, "'Tradition and Modernity': Kalymnian Constructions of Identity and Otherness", *Journal of Modern Greek Studies*, vol. 12, nr. 2 (1994), p. 245.
168   Sofia Giannatou, "Η Πόθια" ["Pothia"], p. 255.
169   C.f. Sutton, "'Tradition and Modernity': Revisited Existential Memory Work on a Greek Island", pp. 84–85. See also Herzfeld, *The Poetics of Manhood*, p. 34.

Indeed, there is a well-known competition between Kalymnos and Symi as to which first introduced the scaphander diving suit and, more generally, which island can claim to have started the sponge-fishing industry.[170] The rocky and barren morphology of Kalymnos' land and shores also set the island apart from its neighbouring islands, to which a different lot had fallen, and especially the agrarian island of Kos. Kalymnians treated those attached to the land as Koans,[171] as fearful, less intelligent, and soft, hence the characteristic Kalymnian saying "O! Land of Hippocrates, what are those donkeys that you produce now?"[172]

One further area in which Kalymnians distinguish themselves as adventurers of the sea is, as opposed to those who rely on the security of the land, the potential yield of the work. The limits of working the land are clear; whereas the sea that can only be conquered with boldness and skill, holds hidden treasures. "Would it be ever possible for Kos to attract as much foreign currency as Kalymnos did, before the war?" Kalymnians ask. "Don't judge by what's happening today: tourism and the construction of hotels. In the past, they used to starve on Kos. Women from Kefalos used to come and work in the shops of Kalymnos, and the tangerine production."[173] As Kalymnians all agree, "we didn't need anyone", "we didn't beg for tourists, like Koans or Rhodians did".

Yet, their familiarity with the sea and their sponge-fishing past are not the only traits thought to distinguish the people of Kalymnos from their Dodecanesian neighbours. Texts written by both locals and foreigners, Greeks, and Europeans, associate the life of the sponge fisherman with boldness, and an independent spirit that resists conquerors. They often allude to Kalymnians' patriotism, arguing that they stood up to the Italians, unlike their neighbours on Leros, who capitulated and accepted surviving by working for the Italian conquerors or providing services to them.[174] "The conquerors did not settle a single stone on our island", Kalymnians say.

---

170   For the relationship of Kalymnos with Symi, see B. Russell's comparison of their populations and economies; Russell, "Kalymnos", p. 302. See also Sutton, "'Tradition and Modernity': Kalymnian Constructions of Identity and Otherness", pp. 241, 244–245.

171   Or "Kotes" as they were also called. Translator's note: "*Κώτες*" is a homophone of the word "*κότες*", which means "chickens" in Greek.

172   See the characteristic examples from various islands of the Dodecanese reported by Niki Billiri, Niki Billiri, *Της θάλασσας και της στεριάς* [*Of Sea and Land*], pp. 223–234 and Sutton, *Memories Cast in Stone*, p. 44.

173   Testimony of "*balaristis*" Michalis Lampos to E.O., 27/8/2002; testimony of captain Antonis Kampourakis to E.O., 27/8/2002; testimony of captain Petros Marthas to E.O., 2/9/2004.

174   C. D. Booth, Isabelle B. Booth, *Italy's Aegean Possessions*, p. 176; Sutton, "'Tradition and Modernity': Kalymnian Constructions of Identity and Otherness", pp. 241, 245. Kalymnians

As partial and generalized as this catalogue of Kalymnian stereotypes may seem, some traces of it persist in discourse, as well as in space. By way of illustration, I cite the habit of alternating between white and blue-painted facades of certain houses in the semi-circular settlement of Pothia.[175] The locals explain that, during the Italian occupation, they chose this additional form of silent resistance, so that the houses at Marasia would form the Greek flag, visible to everyone arriving at the island's port.

Kalymnians insist that they more rigorously preserve elements of their tradition than other Dodecanesians,[176] and cite their religious ceremonies, holiday celebrations and fairs, dietary habits, and hospitality as evidence. In this practice of comparing and denigrating the neighbours, the most prominent objects were Kalymnians' sponge-fishing rivals. The Turks, therefore, were seen as "lazy", a "jinx", and incapable of taking advantage of the treasures of the sea, because "they tremble before water".[177]

It has been argued that the modern Kalymnian identity is no longer grounded in the sponge-fishing tradition,[178] given that life was particularly harsh for sponge fishermen. Moreover, it is no longer a professional prospect or expectation for the largest portion of male population as it was in the past. Yet even if this is the case, it is indeed on their sponge-fishing past that Kalymnians construct their collective identity, because it sustains the notion of their uniqueness, and informs the distinct local history.

References to Kalymnians' democratic past is also a component of their identity and the tradition that underpins it, just as Dodecanesians are characterized as having a democratic spirit in the nationalist literature written under the Italian rule.[179] Local literature also frequently makes mention of

---

consider the very few Italian administrative buildings on Pothia's dock, in comparison to those built on Kos, Rhodes and Leros, as a proof of their resistance against the Italians. "We didn't let the Italians build on our island", they often state. This widespread view is also discussed in Sutton, *Memories Cast in Stone*, pp. 29, 41.

175   The same observation is made by Roger E. Kasperson, *The Dodecanese: Diversity and Unity in Island Politics*, Chicago 1966, p. 91.

176   Myths and realities, or mythologized versions of a special historical course, accompany the locals' perceptions of their island. "Descendants of the Dorians", its defiant and unsubdued inhabitants are thought to be different than the other, mild Ionian Dodecanesians – mostly than their neighbours – because they were brought up in the sea, and managed to prosper, standing up to every conqueror.

177   See Niki Gr. Billiri, "Πώς άνοιξε η Ανατολή και έμαθαν οι Τούρκοι να βγάζουν σφουγγάρια", *Της θάλασσας και της στεριάς* ["How the Orient Opened up and the Turks Learned to Harvest Sponges", *Of Sea and Land*], pp. 98–105.

178   Sutton, "'Tradition and Modernity': Kalymnian Constructions of Identity and Otherness", pp. 241, 247.

179   Iakovos N. Kazavis, *Οι Δωδεκανήσιοι* [*The Dodecanesians*], New York 1950, pp. 24–25.

the exemplary form of self-government established in 19th-century Kalymnos, the local Elders' Council, which was elected by universal suffrage of the male population, and provided for free education, medical care and other forms of social welfare for all of the island's inhabitants. It has also been argued that the clear preference shown for centrist politics in the elections of the 1960s on Kalymnos, and on the other sponge-fishing islands of the Dodecanese, might be attributed to higher rates of literacy, and frequent communication with the outside world, as well as to Kalymnians' historic resistance to political oppression.[180] Their electoral behaviour in the elections that took place in the post-junta (after 1974), is seen in a similar light to this day.[181]

6.6.2 The Island of Sponge Fishermen

The special skills of the Kalymnian people, the heroism of divers, the deadly risks involved in the profession, and the controversies among involved parties – these are the basic elements of sponge-fishing culture.[182] One must also take into consideration the basic working conditions of a profession that did not change for more than 100 years while accidents persisted, and the powerful representations of sponge fishing evident in all facets of Kalymnian life, including the lives of those who were not directly involved in the sponge-fishing network. Formal and informal institutions, mores and folk customs, individual and collective practices and attitudes towards life, resistance and reconciliation, representations and symbols, a rich literature and social memory: these all shape the ideological and cultural context that acts as a frame for the singular locality of this island community, the characteristics of which we have attempted to describe in this research. We looked at various elements that incorporate and preserve symbols of the past, as well as the ways in which local memory manages its relationship to the sponge-fishing past. In Kalymnian culture there are pronounced singularities arising from the long-lasting intensive engagement in the sponge fishery on the part of a significant sector of the island's population. Within the Aegean space, and most likely in the Greek space as well, Kalymnos and its culture occupy a unique position.

It is perhaps well known that, in the socially stratified environment under study here, literacy coexisted with orality and its idiosyncratic characteristics.[183]

---

180   Kasperson, *The Dodecanese*, pp. 91–95.

181   See also David Sutton on the referendum of 1974, as well as the parliament elections of the 1980s and 1990s; Sutton, *Memories Cast in Stone*, p. 21.

182   See Michel Mollat's "Les attitudes des gens de mer devant le danger et devant la mort", *Ethnologie Française* 9 (1979), pp. 191–200.

183   On oral and literate cultures, see Walter Ong, *Orality and Literacy. The Technologizing of the Word*. Methuen, 1982.

This environment produced social mixtures, professional behaviours, tensions and conflicts that resulted in a diverse culture. However, when one looks more closely, these contradictions and complexities are more complementary than competitive on many points and appear as undifferentiated strata. These strata contain both rational and irrational biotheories, which transcend, in varying degrees, the social body in its entirety. The urbanization of mores probably affected only a few, while at the same time, the propagation and reproduction of cultural values created common traditions more universally or partially applicable.

Historical experiences are recast as living social memory, which reconstructs the past tense, and transforms it into a familiar, experienced, memory.[184] A testimony from 1976 that refers to incidents that occurred in the 1880s, is characteristic of the process just described:

> Listen to what happened. I remember this as if it was a dream because I was very young. When they first brought the dress to Kalymnos, many people were drowned. That's why, once, the women and mothers of the mechanical divers gathered and went to the (Church of the) Virgin Mary of Tsoukouno. They yelled at *papa* Ieremias to get out and made him anathematize the dress and those who brought it; then they went to Pothia, and they were bent on killing them.[185]

On the one hand, this rich, oral tradition is saved and recorded in local literary production, which also results in the selection of the modes of survival of local collective memory. On the other hand, literary production is typified by a preference for the dramatization of what it considers to be memorable, as well as a capacity to purge people and incidents from the past, and to erase ugly details. This purgative role assumed by local scholarship attempts to mitigate old controversies between involved parties, and, most of all, to develop a single and generally accepted sponge culture. Hence, the history of sponge fishing holds on to both tragic and heroic moments from the life of sponge fishermen and their families, as well as the selfless contributions to society made by those who rose to affluence by means of the sponge trade. The performance of Kalymnians in letters and in the arts does not stem from the choices made by

---

184   For the various versions of historical discussion of memory, see Rika Benveniste, "Μνήμη και ιστοριογραφία" ["Memory and Historiography"] in R. Benveniste, Th. Paradellis (eds.), *Διαδρομές και τόποι της μνήμης. Ιστορικές και ανθρωπολογικές προσεγγίσεις* [*Paths and Places of Memory: Historical and Anthropological Approaches*], Athens 1999, pp. 11–26.

185   Testimony of diver Nikolaos Choullis in 1976. See Manuscript 2729/1976, Angeliki Georgiadou, p. 57 and another of version in Manuscript 2728/1976, Maria Sevastopoulou, pp. 60–61, CFS.

a cosmopolitan and outward-looking social stratum, which took advantage of the island's workforce and imposed inhumane conditions of employment on board the vessels; it is an innate trait of an undifferentiated Kalymnian culture. In their accounts, the Kalymnian diaspora appears to arise, in any case, from the dynamism and skillfulness of the Kalymnian people; whether it was in accounts of the merchant houses that dominated the international sponge market, or stories of the competent sponge fishermen that made sponge fishery known to the people of Barbary and the poor fishermen of Tarpon Springs.

On the other hand, the workers of the sea, the illiterate women, the poor and oppressed, inspired the production of an "epic history", which selects what is worth remembering of the sponge-fishing past of the island: the heroism of the sponge fishermen, the deadly accidents, and the mass reaction against the scaphander diving suit. In this version of the story, it appears as though there were no conflicting interests within local society, and as though external factors and foreign rulers of the island were always to blame: the idleness of the Ottoman state and the cruel Italian occupation. These instances of passing over in silence are not easily detectable, not even in the written pieces of archival evidence of the late 19th century and the 20th centuries. Formal or informal, written, or oral, versions of the past are similar. Thus, Kalymnians' narratives converse with the material and ideological needs of contemporary society on the island, and forge an undifferentiated cultural identity, and a unified sponge culture.

> There are two classes of men on Kalymnos. The sponge fishermen and the scientists. The people of knowledge and the people of the heart. But both those worlds are firmly tied to each other, because both came from Kalymnos, a motherland of the poor, that offers shade to everyone and a heart that welcomes and accommodates the whole of Greece, which it so gloriously represents and honours.[186]

This view is reinforced by various testimonies, which argue that the financial support of sponge fishermen permitted Kalymnos to grow and develop. "It was the sponger's hard work that backed everything on Kalymnos. The Municipality, and the doctors, and the hospitals, and the schools. If it weren't for us, what else would exist?"[187] Niki Billiri's account seems to bring together several of the elements noted above:

---

186 Manuscript 888/1969, Poseidon Zairis, p. 2, CFS.
187 Testimony of Antonis Kampourakis to E.O., 27/8/2002. See also Pantelis Mich. Mavros, "Ο πατριωτισμός των Καλυμνίων και οι συντελεστές του Εθνικού φρονήματός των", *Καλυμνιακά*

I lived up there, at the Marasi of Agios Nikolaos, among sea people and poor housewives, and I felt the soul of the people, of the Kalymnian man and the Kalymnian woman, with all its advantages and disadvantages. I saw and experienced the fight of the Kalymnian woman, as a housewife and as a mother, to eke out a living with the meagre means of that period; and to raise a bunch of kids, strong and upright souls, decent people, with a strict devotion to religion, to the Mother land, and to their duties towards their families and fellow human beings; and I admired her, for her loyalty, her courage, her valiance, her resilience and her pride. I saw and experienced the courage of the Kalymnian sponge fisherman: he knows how to defy danger and struggles in the sea to bring home bread for his family; he knows how to work honestly, how to endure deprivations and adversities patiently; but he also knows how to have fun and spend his money open-handedly, when he has any.[188]

Looking for the historicity of this unifying cultural process, one may observe that its onset coincides with the declining trajectory of the sponge-fishing industry. The mitigation of the past becomes possible and necessary when confrontational elements have been eliminated; when the life cycle of those who worked on the vessels slightly before the war and in the first post-war decades closes; when the historical tense is detached from the experiential one; and when there is nothing more to contest than the handling of the remains of the past, and the construction of a myth unifying the present through the past.

It is not easy to search for the starting point in time in which Kalymnos was established as the "island of sponges" because the exercise of sponge fishery was continuous and systematic for more than a century; and because, in relation to Symi or Hydra, Kalymnos matched, or even outproduced them. The factor that differentiates the Kalymnian sponge fishery, however, is the fact that it remained active while all other areas gradually abandoned the activity. That is, perhaps, the reason why this singular physiognomy, or rather the identity that is of interest to us here, is attributed to Kalymnos in the final decades of the industry.

It appears that local communities that develop and maintain a skill, promote it as a local singularity, and elevate it to the status of an essential feature of their identity; in particular, when this skill is not only a fundamental resource for the sustenance of an important group of the population, but a way of life

---

Χρονικά ["The Patriotism of Kalymnians and the Factors of their National Beliefs", *Kalymniaka Chronika*] 3 (1982), p. 107.

188   Niki Billiri, *Η Κάλυμνός μας* [*Our Kalymnos*], p. 7.

as well, even for those not directly involved in the professional network. Thus, Kalymnos remains "the island of sponge fishermen", even to this day (perhaps mostly today) even though the activity has drastically dwindled.[189] While there are several sponge importing businesses, the processing and trade of sponges continues to operate on the island. To a large extent, Kalymnian businesses buy sponges from countries of the African and American continents, which they then supply to Greek and international markets. Local tradition, as well as the rise to prominence of Kalymnos as exclusively an island of sponge fishermen, have a beneficial effect even when production is very limited, and the raw material is no longer fished but mostly bought. Through this process, Kalymnian society attempts not only to manage its historical memory, but also to build strategies for future growth on it. The singularity of the sponge-fishing culture is complemented by other features and habits of the everyday life that Kalymnians try to enrich.

Having left behind a past, in which involvement in sponge fishery and seasonal or permanent emigration were a prerequisite for survival, Kalymnians reminisce about the "old days", restructuring the past and its negative features, while feeding the present with selective elements from the past, narratives, habits and practices – "mnemonic places of memory" which make up "local tradition".[190]

---

189   The practice of sponge fishery is limited to 15–17 caiques and 120 divers, most of whom dive using the "*narghiles*", and very few dive with "*revera*". In 2005, the Diving School operating on Kalymnos closed. *Ροδιακή* [*Rodiaki*], 7/4/2010, p. 1.

190   C.f. Sutton "'Tradition and Modernity': Revisited Existential Memory Work on a Greek Island", pp. 84–105.

Appendix 1

TABLE I   Sponge-fishing permits for the year 1928

S/N	Fishing type	Fishing location	Captains	Divers	Rowers	Sailors
1	Scaphander diving suit	Crete	1	4	10	
2	Scaphander diving suit	Madruh	2	18	31	
3	Boat	Greece	1			3
4	Boat	Greece	1			3
5	Boat	Greece	1			3
6	Boat	Greece	1			3
7	Boat	Greece	1			3
8	Boat	Greece	1			3
9	Boat	Greece	1			3
10	Scaphander diving suit	Benghazi	2	16	25	
11	Scaphander diving suit	Greece	1	3	15	
12	Scaphander diving suit	Madruh	1	9	15	
13	Scaphander diving suit	Greece	1	4	7	
14	Boat	Cyprus	1			3
15	Boat	Cyprus	1			3
16	Boat	Dodecanese	1			1
17	Boat	Dodecanese	1			1
18	Boat	Dodecanese	1			1
19	Boat	Dodecanese	1			1
20	Boat	Dodecanese	1			1
21	Petrol-fuelled scaphander diving suits		4[*]	30	51	
22	Scaphander diving suit	Greece	1	4	13	

*   Two of them are first officers.

© KONSTANTINOS EFTHYMIOU, 2025 | DOI:10.1163/9789004701946_009

TABLE I   Sponge-fishing permits for the year 1928 (*cont.*)

S/N	Fishing type	Fishing location	Captains	Divers	Rowers	Sailors
23	Scaphander diving suit	Greece	1	3	13	
24	Fernez		2	14	19	
25	Fernez		2	5	10	
26	Fernez		1	9	16	
27	Fernez		1	8	16	
28	Fernez		2	13	21	
29	Fernez		3	15	26	
30	Scaphander diving suit	Upper Lands	1	7	15	
31	Scaphander diving suit		1	4	12	
32	Fernez		1	6	8	
33	Fernez		1	6	10	
34	Fernez	Porto	1	14	27	
35	Fernez		1	16	38	
36	Fernez		1	5	11	
37	Boat		1			3
38	Boat		1			3
39	Fernez		1	12	24	
40	Scaphander diving suit	Greece	1	4	13	
41	Fernez		1	5	9	
42	Boat		1			3
43	Boat		1			3
44	Boat		1			3
45	Fernez		1	5	8	
46	Fernez		1	3	10	
47	Fernez	Tripolis	1	4	12	
48	Scaphander diving suit	Crete-Greece	1	4	13	

Total: 853 people

TABLE II   Sponge-fishing permits for the year 1929

S/N	Fishing type	Fishing location	Captains	Divers	Rowers	Sailors
1	Scaphander diving suit	Egypt	1	9	17	
2	Scaphander diving suit	Egypt	2	20	28	
3	Scaphander diving suit	Dodecanese – Cyclades	1	4	10	
4	Sponge-fishing boat	Cyprus	1			5
5	Sponge-fishing boat	Cyprus	1			4
6	Sponge-fishing boat	Cyprus	1			4
7	Scaphander diving suit	Crete	1	7	17	
8	Scaphander diving suit	Cyrenaica	2*	11	21	
9	Scaphander diving suit	Cyrenaica	2*	12	18	
10	Fernez	Tripolis	1	7	5	
11	Fernez	Tripolis	1	7	13	
12	Sponge-fishing boat		1			4
13	Fernez	Benghazi	1	6	9	
14	Fernez	Benghazi	1	4	10	
15	Sponge-fishing boat	Benghazi	1	6	9	
16	Sponge-fishing boat	Greece	1			3
17	Sponge-fishing boat	Greece	1			3
18	Sponge-fishing boat	Greece	1			4

---

* One of them was a first officer

TABLE II   Sponge-fishing permits for the year 1929 (*cont.*)

S/N	Fishing type	Fishing location	Captains	Divers	Rowers	Sailors
19	Scaphander diving suit	Benghazi	1	6	14	
20	Fernez	Tripolis	1	7	9	
21	Scaphander diving suits	Benghazi	2	9	19	
22	Fernez	Tripolis	1	7	10	
23	Fernez	Egypt	1	13	20	
24	Sponge-fishing boat	Greece	1			3
25	Sponge-fishing boat	Greece	1			3
26	Scaphander diving suit	Qars, Libya	1	7	17	
27	Fernez	Benghazi	1	5	9	
28	Sponge-fishing boat	Greece	1			3
29	Fernez		1	13	19	
30	Sponge-fishing boat	Islands	1			3
31	Sponge-fishing boat	Islands	1			3
32	Sponge-fishing boat	Islands	1			3
33	Sponge-fishing boat	Islands	1			3
33	Sponge-fishing boat	Islands	1			3
34	Scaphander diving suit	Islands	1	3	11	
35	Sponge-fishing boat	Islands	1			3
36	Scaphander diving suit		1	5	7	
37	Scaphander diving suit		1	6	12	

TABLE II   Sponge-fishing permits for the year 1929 (*cont.*)

S/N	Fishing type	Fishing location	Captains	Divers	Rowers	Sailors
38	Scaphander diving suit		1	6	10	
39	Scaphander diving suit		1	3	11	
40	Fernez		1	5	7	
41	Scaphander diving suit		1	4	11	

Total: 631 people

TABLE III   Sponge-fishing permits for the year 1930

S/N	Fishing type	Fishing location	Captains	Divers	Rowers	Sailors
1	Gagava		1			1
2	Gagava		1			2
3	Scaphander diving suit	Cyrenaica	1	15	10	
4	Scaphander diving suit	Cyrenaica	1	9	18	
5	Scaphander diving suit	Dodecanese	1	14	26	
6	Scaphander diving suit	Kastellorizo	1	7	15	
7	Scaphander diving suit	Cyrenaica	1	14	15	
8	Scaphander diving suit	Tripolis	1	9	16	
9	Scaphander diving suit	Kastellorizo	1	5	14	
10	Scaphander diving suit	Tripolis	1	12	19	
11	Sponge-fishing boat	Cyprus	1			3
12	Scaphander diving suit	Dodecanese	2	5	10	

TABLE III   Sponge-fishing permits for the year 1930 (*cont.*)

S/N	Fishing type	Fishing location	Captains	Divers	Rowers	Sailors
13	Scaphander diving suit	Tripolis	2	21	23	
14	Scaphander diving suit	Tripolis	2	12	34	
15	Scaphander diving suit	Dodecanese	1	6	12	
16	Scaphander diving suit	Egypt	1	6	11	
17	Scaphander diving suit	Dodecanese	1	5	12	
18	Fernez	Tripolis	1	6	11	
19	Fernez	Tripolis	1	7	14	
20	Scaphander diving suit	Egypt	1	17 in total		
21	Scaphander diving suit	Dodecanese	1	4	15	
22	Sponge-fishing boat	Greece	1			3
23	Sponge-fishing boat	Greece	1			3
24	Sponge-fishing boat	Greece	1			3
25	Sponge-fishing boat	Greece	1			3
26	Scaphander diving suit	Cyrenaica – Crete	1	12	24	
27	Sponge-fishing boat	Greece	1			3
28	Fernez	Cyrenaica	1	6	12	
29	Sponge-fishing boat	Egypt	1	6		
30	Sponge-fishing boat	Egypt	1	6		
31	Fernez	Cyrenaica	1	5	10	
32	Fernez	Egypt	1	4	9	
33	Fernez	Cyrenaica	1	11	21	

TABLE III Sponge-fishing permits for the year 1930 (*cont.*)

S/N	Fishing type	Fishing location	Captains	Divers	Rowers	Sailors
34	Sponge-fishing boat	Egypt	1	6		
35	Sponge-fishing boat	Egypt	1	6		
36	Scaphander diving suit	Tripolis	1	13	20	
37	Fernez	Crete	1	4	9	
38	Sponge-fishing boat	Egypt	1	6		
39	Sponge-fishing boat	Egypt	1	6		
40	Scaphander diving suit	Tripolis	1	7	9	
42	Scaphander diving suit	Egypt	1	6	10	
43	Scaphander diving suit	Cyrenaica	1	17	42	
44	Sponge-fishing boat	Egypt	1	6		
45	Sponge-fishing boat	Egypt	1	12		
46	Sponge-fishing boat	Greece	1	4		
47	Scaphander diving suit	Crete	1	4	9	
48	Scaphander diving suit	Cyrenaica	1	14	18	
49	Sponge-fishing boat	Cyrenaica	1	9		
50	Scaphander diving suit	Cyrenaica	1	5	10	
51	Scaphander diving suit	Kastellorizo	1	5	12	
52	Scaphander diving suit	Tripolis	1	7	12	

TABLE III   Sponge-fishing permits for the year 1930 (*cont.*)

S/N	Fishing type	Fishing location	Captains	Divers	Rowers	Sailors
53	Scaphander diving suit	Dodecanese	1	4	10	
54	Sponge-fishing boat	Greece	1	6		3
55	Sponge-fishing boat	Greece	1			4
56	Sponge-fishing boat	Greece	1			5

Total: 974 people

Appendix 2

Michael N. Kalafatas, *The Bellstone: The Greek Sponge Divers of the Aegean. One American's Journey Home*. Hannover: Brandeis University Press, 2003, pp. 109–110.

Πέτραν λευκήν υπόμακρον επί λεπτού σχοινίου
εφεύρον ίνα δένωσι προς χρήσιν εργαλείου
ταύτην "Καμπανελλόπετραν" την σήμερον καλούσι
δι' ης οι δύται δύνανται στα βύθη να βυθούσι
Πάνω σ' αυτήν θα κρεμασθή οπόταν να βουτήση
και πηδαλιουχούμενος φθάνει όπου θελήσει
[...] Κουμβά την πέτραν στο πλευρό με το ζερβόν του χέρι
και εσκυμμένος ψηλαφά σπόγγους διά να εύρη.
Αν εύρη μέρος κοπτερόν την πέτραν του θ' αφίση
θα ξεριζώσ' όσους μπορεί τον σάκκον να γεμίση
Φύλακες δύο στέκονται στην κουπαστήν του πλοίου
και διοικούν τον άνθρωπον διά μακρού σχοινίου.
Αφού σωθεί η εισπνοή, τραβάει το σχοινίον
και εννοούν οι άνθρωποι που στέκονται στο πλοίον
Αφού νοιώσουν το τράβηγμα πάνω τον ανεβάζουν
αυτούς τους δύο φύλακας Κουπάδες ονομάζουν
Εάν συμβή εις τον κουπάν ακούσιόν του λάθος
θα υποφέρ' ο άνθρωπος στο της θαλάσσης βάθος
Εάν όμως το λάθος του υπέρ το μέτρον γείνη
υγείαν και χαιρετισμούς ο άνθρωπος τ' αφίνη
Έχουσιν όμως πάντοτε τον νουν στην κεφαλήν των
όρθιοι στέκονται κ' οι δυο μ' όλην την προσοχή των".[1]

•••

Εχάθη η υπόληψις και η φιλοτιμία
και αντ' αυτών ερρίζωσεν η αφιλοτιμία
Εξέλειψεν η ηθική το αγέρωχον ακμάζει
όπερ από τας μηχανάς την σήμερον πηγάζει
Σ' όλην την βαρβαρότητα και την αναισχυντίαν
οι μηχανοξεκινηταί διέδωκαν αιτίαν

---

1 Μητροφάνης Καλαφατάς, "Χειμερινός Όνειρος", πρόλογος Μιχαήλ Καλαφατάς, *Καλυμνιακά Χρονικά* [Mitrophanis Kalafatas, "Winter Dream", preface by Michail Kalafatas, Kalymniaka Chronika] 13 (1999), pp. 283–284.

Έβλεπον οφθαλμοφανές ένα απ' τους εμπόρους
όστις συναινεστρέφετο τους κακοήθεις όλους
Τους έβλεπον κατάσκαλα εις το αυτό τραπέζι
την πρέφαν και το ντόμινον μαζύ των να συμπαίζη
Ημαύρωνε και την τιμήν και την υπόληψίν των
χάριν των συμφερόντων του διά την μηχανήν του
Ώστε το θάρρος το πολύ και η μεγάλη σχέσις
επέφερεν εγωϊσμόν και έκτοτ' έγιν' έξις[2]

• • •

Και του λαού το φρόνημα δεν ήτο εναντίον
ουδέ ανουσιούργημα ουδόλως και αχρείον
Απέβλεπεν μεν ο σκοπός τας μηχανάς να σπάσουν
να τας αναπληρώσωσιν, άλλας να μη γοράσουν.[3]

• • •

Αι μηχαναί παρήκμασαν και πρόκειται να παύσουν
Οι δύται πάλιν στο εξής πιστεύω θα ακμάσουν
η προθεσμία έληξε το τέλος πλησιάζει
και η καμπανελλόπετρα θ' αρχίση να ακμάζη
εξήνθησεν η μηχανή, το βούττος θα βλαστήση
κι η τέχνη των προγόνων μας θέλει τελεσφόρηση.[4]

• • •

Κι ως άγγελος παρά Θεού εφάνη εσταλμένος
Άνθρωπος καλοκάγαθος ανήρ εμψυχομένος
Φλέγελ ονομαζόμενος και Ρώσσος την πατρίδα
τούτον φιλευεργέτην μου και κύριόν μοι οίδα.
Ούτος ο τρισμακάριστος φθάσας στα χώματά μας
εξήτασε και έμαθε τα δυστυχήματά μας.
Μαθών δε και της μηχανής τα κακουργήματά της
τ' άθλια και ελεεινά αποτελέσματά της.
Συνεκινήθη κι έλαβεν ο ίδιος την ευθύνην

---

2 Μητροφάνης Καλαφατάς, "Χειμερινός Όνειρος", *Καλυμνιακά Χρονικά* [Mitrophanis Kalafatas, "Winter Dream", *Kalymniaka Chronika*] 13 (1999), p. 267.

3 Kalafatas, "Χειμερινός Όνειρος" ["Winter Dream"], p. 270.

4 Kalafatas, "Χειμερινός Όνειρος" ["Winter Dream"], p. 265.

να αποσύρη το κακόν να πράξη καλωσύνην.
Κατέβαλεν ο άνθρωπος όλα τα δυνατά του
διέφθειρεν ανηλεώς ως και τα χρήματα του.
Ένθεν κ' ακείθεν έτρεξε πρώτον εις την Γαλλίαν
συνάμα δε ενήργησε και εις την Ιταλίαν.
Αναχωρήσας απ' εκεί στην Κρήτην πρώτον ήλθε
των ζητημάτων έτυχεν άπρακτος δεν απήλθεν.
Ευθύς στην Κύπρον έτρεξε δι' αύτην την αιτίαν
πρόθυμον υπερασπιστήν εύρε και την Αγγλίαν.
Επέρασε στην Αίγυπτον χωρίς ν' αργοπορήση
και την Μανδρούχαν ίσχυσε να την καθυστέρηση.
Δεν αναβάλλει τον καιρόν ουδόλως να οκνεύση
εκείθεν απεφάσισε στην Σάμον ν' αποπλεύση.
Και αυτή συνεφώνησεν εις την κατάργησίν των
μη υποφέρουσα οράν ποσώς την ύπαρξίν των[5]

• • •

Μηχανικούς ωνόμασαν αυτούς που κατεβάζουν
και φαντασμόν ανήκουστον επάνω των βαστάζουν
Όταν πρωτοφορέσωσι την περικεφαλαίαν
νομίζουν πως τους έστεψαν κλάδον από ελαίαν
Μεγάλως δε φαντάζονται και υψηλοφρονούσι
αν εξετάσης ακριβώς πάνω των κατουρούσι
Με δύο πόδια έρχονται καλώς στανιαρισμένοι
με τρία όμως φεύγουσι νερά καλαρισμένοι[6]

• • •

Εκ τούτων όσα βλάπτουσιν, έχει έν είδος άλλο
και προξενεί στον άνθρωπον δυστύχημα μεγάλο.
Βρώμην την ονομάζουσι και είναι ριζωμένη
εις μερικά σπογγάρια, στους πάτους κολλημένη.
Εάν εκριζωθή γερή χωρίς ποσώς να σπάση
είναι ανυποψίαστος από του να τον βλάψη.
Αν δυστυχώς δε συντριβή κ' επάνω τον εγγίση
και με εγχείρησιν κακήν, αν την κακοφορμίση

---

5   Kalafatas, "Χειμερινός Όνειρος" ["Winter Dream"], p. 272.
6   Kalafatas, "Χειμερινός Όνειρος" ["Winter Dream"], p. 279.

Ξανθή και λιναρόσπορον ανάγκη να ζητήση
και θεραπείαν δύσκολον, πάλιν θα απαντήση.[7]

•••

Πολλών όμως τα πτώματα πέτραι ξηραί καλύπτουν
Και μερικούς στην θάλασσαν μη θέλοντες τους ρίπτουν[8]

•••

Αφού θα κάμουν ακριβώς την προετοιμασίαν
και είνε πλέον έτοιμοι διά την εργασίαν
Ξυπνώσιν από το πρωί και τας αυτών στρωσίας
αφού τοποθετήσωσι στου πλοίου τας γωνίας
Το πρόσωπόν των νύπτουσι και κάμνουν τον σταυρόν των
κι επικαλούνται τον θεόν τον μόνον βοηθόν των
Όστις τα πάθη των πληγών αμέσως θεραπεύει
και από πάντα κίνδυνον καθένα προστατεύει.
Μετά την επικάλεσιν στην πρύμνην θα καθίσουν
λίγον ψωμί εις τον καφέ θα βάλουν να μασήσουν
Κι έπειτα θα σαλπάρωσι να κάμουν τα πανιά των
διά να αρμενίσουσι να πάγουν στην δουλιά των
Μέρος πετρώδες θα ευρούν κι εκεί θ' αποφασίσουν
το σίδερον να ρίψωσι διά να κολυμβήσουν[9]

•••

Εις τον λεγόμενον "σεφτέν" βουτιαίς ολίγαις κάμνουν
έως ότου να εύρωσι σπόγγον να τον εκβάλουν
Τον σπόγγον τον πρωτοφανή στο χέρι του τον ποιάνει
και εις το πλοίον με αυτού Σταυρόν σημείον κάμνει
Είνε και τούτο έθιμον σταύρωμα ονομάζουν
και την σημαίαν στον ιστόν πάραυτα ανεβάζουν
Και έπειτα θ' αρπάξουσι να φάγουν και να πιούσι
και καλορίζικος σεφτές όλοι θα ευχηθούσι[10]

---

7   Kalafatas, Metrophanes. "Χειμερινός Όνειρος" ["Winter Dream"], pp. 284–286.
8   Kalafatas, "Χειμερινός Όνειρος" ["Winter Dream"], p. 280.
9   Mitrophanis Kalafatas, "Χειμερινός Όνειρος", *Καλυμνιακά Χρονικά* ["Winter Dream", *Kalymniaka Chronika*], 13 (1999), p. 283.
10   Mitrophanis Kalafatas, "Χειμερινός Όνειρος", *Καλυμνιακά Χρονικά* ["Winter Dream", *Kalymniaka Chronika*] 13 (1999), p. 285.

Lexicon of Greek and Other Foreign Words

(Double quotation marks indicate dialect or idiosyncratic words)

Achtarmas   A type of boat

Agha   Turkish chief of a community

"Ajamides"   Turkish. Young men who worked as "novices" for a reduced wage.

"Armathiasma"   Sponges strung on cord and hanging in bunches.

Aspronissi   White Island, so named because it served as a repository for the bones of divers killed at sea.

"Atzamides"   Novice divers

Baizanoi (baizáni)   Oil barrels lined with cement on the inside to prevent the water stored in them from smelling, and whitewashed on the outside to protect them from the sun.

"Baketo" [μπακέτο]   A ship for transporting packages /mule.

"Balaristis"   The person charged with the job of cleaning the sponges aboard the vessel.

"Bara"   A fine rope with a weight that was used for seeking out sponge bearing areas.

Bratsera, brazzera   A sponge-fishing vessel.

Demogerontia   Elder's Council

Demogerontes   Elders or administrators of the Ottoman empire who controlled such things as public order, the military, and central taxes.

"Deposito"   Auxiliary supply boat, equipped with diving suit.

Devshirme   The Ottoman practice of forcibly recruiting soldiers and bureaucrats from among the children of their Balkan Christian subjects.

Draga   A kind of trawl or boat used in sponge fishing.

"Fino"   A soft, absorbent type of sponge.

Gagava, Gagamo, Grypos   Trawl, i.e. drawn by a boat.

Gala [γάλα]   The "milk" of sea sponges

Gassa [γάσα]   A line tied to the apnea diver's arm and held by a crew member on the boat. The cord was also used to signal the need to resurface when a diver was out of breath.

Goleta   A kind of boat

"Gouliasmeni"   Frightening and dreadful

"Grousouzia"   Bad luck resulting from having set foot on sponge-fishing caiques before their departure.

"Gynekomani"   Crowds of women

Hartziliki   Allowance for crew members on sponge-fishing expeditions.

Ha(ta)ides [χα(τα)ήδες]   Sponges uprooted by means of the gagava that do not make it into the catch and are set adrift.

"Himonika"   Brief sponge fishing expeditions undertaken in the winter.

Hippospongia communis   Honeycomb sponge

Hondros [χονδρός]   One of the three most popular types of sponges fished for the market.

"Hysterotaxida", *"himonika"*   Late or final sponging expeditions

Irade   An imperial edict under Ottoman rule, i.e. against the use of the scaphander diving suit. See chapter 4, p. 190.

Kambanelli or kambanellopetra   Bellstone; a flattened stone, often from a smoothly ground block of marble, weighing roughly 12-14 kilograms or more, and tied to sponging vessels by a 30-meter-long rope. See also *skandalopetra*.

"Kapadiko"   Main sponge [Sponge most commonly fished].

"Kapaki"   Advance payment

"Kapetanisses"   Wives of captains

"Kapetanistiko"   A rough trimming of the sponges.

Kapuj-bash   Chief Chamberlain

"Karines"   Also *"keel"*; term for a particular kind of sponge-bearing seabed.

Kavass   An Ottoman policeman.

"Kava(d)I"   Short velvet waistcoats over long coats. A fashion worn by captains' wives.

Kavurma   A kind of meat eaten on sponging expeditions. Cured beef, chopped into small pieces, stored in large tin cans filled with grease.

Kaymakam   District Governor

Kaymakamia   The office of the Kaymakam.

Kaymakamlik   District

Kaza   Sub-district

"Klaofora"   Woman carrying branches. [i.e., women who collect and carry branches used for fuel].

Kopanos   A beating tool used in processing sponges.

"Kopellia"   Divers who received a *kopelli*, or payment paid based on the selling price, and received a share of the total profits at a predetermined percentage, after the advance payments (*platika*) made by the captain were deducted.

Koufo   An extra share [*"koufo"*] split among all the divers, or given to "those who worked well", or "who caught the most sponges".

"Kotsani"   From the Turkish "koçan", meaning "stub", such as the stub of a Fishing Permit.

"Kolaouzieris" (*kolaouzos*)   A diving supervisor who always held a rope and communicated with the diver in problem situations while tracking the duration of the dive. The *"kolaouzos"* [literally, "the one who shows the way"].

"Kopelli"   A percentage of a diver's individual production as remuneration.

Koupades   Rowers

Kozakikos   Traditional Greek folk dance

Kuruş   Ottoman unit of currency. Turkish lira equal to 100 *kuruş* as of the 2005 revaluation of the lira.

Ksekinites [*ξεκινητές*]   Initiator or investor

"Lagofyto" or *"lagoftio"*   Elephant ear, or *Spongia lamella*. A type of sponge.

"Levantiniko"   *Spongia mollissima*. A soft and absorbent type of sponge.

"Louria"   "Straps"; name for a particular kind of sponge-bearing area.

Markoutserides   The person who manned the *markoutso*

"Markoutso"   A flexible hose connected to the air pump on the vessel.

"Makrovoutia"   Shallow, long-distance dives that skim along just under the surface of the sea.

Madruh (Makruh)   Natural harbour on the West coast of Egypt

Malsapis (Malsapides)   Investor. From the Turkish *"malsahibi"*: owner, financier.

"Mantzaroli"   Hourglass

"Matapas"   *Spongia adriatica*. A type of sponge. *Spongia officinalis adiatica* (Linnaeus 1759).

"Mantzaroli"   Hourglass

"Matzarolia"   One turn of the hourglass: approximate duration of 30 seconds.

Maktu   Lump tax

Medjidie   A Turkish silver coin formerly valued at 20, but since 1880 at 19, piasters (about 83 cents).

"Melat(th)io"   A very soft and absorbent type of sponge.

Meltemia   Etesian winds

"Messarika"   Of average-sea depths. Vessels working with diving suits fell into three depth categories.

Moutasarrifate   Administrative district

Mudir, Mutasarrıf   Local Governor

Nahiye   Sub-district or commune.

"Naryiles"   Breathing device, [also; hookah].

Oka, okka, or oke   Ottoman measure of mass, equal to 400 dirhems or Ottoman drams. Its value varied, but it was standardized in the late empire as 1.2829 kilograms.

"Paggeto" [*παγκέτο*]   A type of ship.
also: *"Pakettho"* [*πακέτθο*]

Paidomazoma   The forced evacuation of children from communist-held parts of Greece in 1948-1949.

"Panghi"   "Banks", a term for a particular kind of sponge-bearing area.

Pantouflatzides   Slipper maker

Philoskaphandroi [*φιλοσκάφανδροι*]   Friends of the scaphander diving suit.

Piasmenoi   A lightly "caught" mechanical diver – i.e., a diver suffering from a mild case of decompression sickness.

"Psalidies"   Left over bits of sponge after they have been trimmed.

Psilos [ψιλός],   One of the main types of sponges prepared for the market and exported.

Platika   Advance payment for sponge divers.

(A)Pochi [(*α*)*πόχη*]   Fishnet

Proksenia   Arranged marriages

Refenes   A share crew materials as part of a crew members payment for a sponging expedition.

Regalo   A token of competency in sponge fishery. A bonus payment.

Revera   Apnea diving with wet suit, fins, and weights.

"Richitika"   A shallow-water vessel working with diving suits.

"Roda"   "Wheel" of the air pump that supplies compressed air to the diver in the scaphander diving suit.

"Rodanitzides"   The person responsible for manning the wheel of the air pump [*roda*].

"Rossioi" [*Ρώσιοι*], *also*   Sobriquet or nickname for Greek children who went to work in Russia.

"Roussakia"

"Sanjak"   District

"Sfefanotike"   Wife

Skandali, or skandalopetra   Trigger stone used by divers.

Skaphe [*Σκάφαι*]   Boat used in sponge fishing.

"Skarta"   A sponge rejected as valueless in the sorting process.

"Sortiristis"   The person charged with the job of sorting the sponge per quality and size.

Soubashi   Town commander.

"Sphoungaromakhaládes" [*σφουγγαρομαχαλάδες*]   Densely populated neighbour-hoods on the island of Kalymnos, inhabited largely by those involved in the sponge industry.

Sporidia [*σπορίδια*]   Small, infertile parcels of land.

"Stefanotikes"   Wives of sponge fishermen.

"Stoiví" [στοιβή]   Bride's dowry, and especially that of the first-born daughter, consisting of white linen, and various items and utensils largely for daily use, as well as some valuable items which were stored in trunks or kept under the large bed to be used on special occasions, and destined for the dowry of the next daughter.

"Syntrofies"   Companies formed by Kalymnian women for the group execution of various agricultural tasks.

Tanzimat   A period during which the Ottoman state carried out administrative reforms and institutional changes.

Ta piso   Arrears on sponge divers' debts.

Tiriní Evdomáda   Lent, also known as cheese week.

Trechantiri, trechandiri   A small lateen rigged boat or caique.

Trechantinieris   Person who mans the trechantriri boat.

"Trigonakia"   Festive firecrackers in small triangle shape.

"Tsemberí"   A kind of kerchief worn by captains' wives.

Tsimoucha   A type of thick sponge. *Spongia zimoca*, leather sponge.

"Tsourmarismata"   "The crewing". Drawing up and signing recruitment agreements.

Vali   A prefect of the Aegean Sea.

"Varelota"   Firecrackers in stick form for festive occasions.

"Varvara"   A rotating exhaust valve.

Vathytika   Deep-sea vessel working with diving suits.

"Vathytes"   Divers who braved great depths and could "walk on the sea bottom".

"Vilayet"   1867 "Law on Provinces"

Yialades   Men in charge of handling the *yiali*.

Yiales   A type sailing of ship

Yiali   A cylindrical tin bucket with a glass bottom, used to better view the seafloor.

"Zaptiyes"   Ottoman gendarmes

"Zebili"   Basket

"Zipkin" [ζηπκήν]   A kind of boat used in the sponge fishery.

Sources – Literature

Sources

Archives

Δημοτικό Αρχείο Καλύμνου [Municipal Archives of Kalymnos (MAK)], see Classification Chart pp. 395–402.

> Folders and Logbooks numbered, based on a classification undertaken by the author and a group of Ionian University students.

Ελληνικό Λογοτεχνικό Ιστορικό Αρχείο [Greek Literary and Historical Archive / Elliniko Logotechniko kai Istoriko Archeio – ELIA] / Μορφωτικό Ίδρυμα Εθνικής Τραπέζης [Cultural Foundation of the National Bank / Morfotiko Idryma Ethnikis Trapezis – MIET].

Ιστορικό Αρχείο Υπουργείου Εξωτερικώ [Historical Archive of the Greek Ministry of Foreign Affairs / Istoriko Archeio Ypourgeio Exoterikon – IAYE].

> Embassy of Tripoli-Libya, Folder 4 (1875–1897).
> Embassy of Tripoli-Libya, Folder 6 (1890–1900).
> Embassy of Tripoli-Libya, Folder 19 (1914).
> Embassy of Tripoli-Libya, Folder 28 (1920–1923).
> Embassy of Tripoli-Libya, Folder 28, Subfolder 4, Subfolder 7.
> Embassy of Tripoli-Libya, Folder 29 (1923–1924).
> Embassy of Tripoli-Libya, Folder 32 (1925–1928).
> Embassy of Tripoli-Libya, Folder 33 (1926–1927).
> Embassy of Tripoli-Libya, Folder 34 (1927–1929).
> Embassy of Tripoli-Libya, Folder 36 (1930).
> Embassy of Tripoli-Libya, Folder 45 (1947–1948).
> Greek Embassy Tripoli-Libya, Folder 46 (1952).
> Consulate in Rhodes, Folder 43 (1912).
> Consulate in Rhodes, Folder 44 (1911).
> (General Folders) Folder 1882, 51/ 1.
> (General Folders) Folder 1883, Γ/51–1 Fishery: Sponge Fishery.
> (General Folders) Folder 1884, 51–1 Fishery: Sponge Fishery.
> (General Folders) Folder 1885, Γ/51/1, Fishery: Sponge Fishery.
> (General Folders) Folder 1886, 51/ 1.

Σπουδαστήριο Λαογραφίας Πανεπιστημίου Αθηνών [**Center for Folklore Studies of the National and Kapodistrian University of Athens**].

> Manuscript 778/1968–1969, Μαρία Κουτούζη [Maria Koutouzi].

Manuscript 888/1969, Ποσειδών Ζαΐρης [Poseidon Zairis].

Manuscript 941/1969, Πετρούλα Γιαλουζή [Petroula Gialouzi].

Manuscript 1628/1971, Εμμανουήλ Σαρικάς [Emmanouil Sarikas].

Manuscript 1838/1973, Ευαγγελία Λαμπαδαρίου [Evangelia Lampadariou].

Manuscript 2174/1974, Μαρία Καπελλά [Maria Kapella].

Manuscript 2728/1976, Μαρία Σεβαστοπούλου [Maria Sevastopoulou].

Manuscript 2729/1976, Αγγελική Γεωργιάδου [Angeliki Georgiadou].

Port Authority of Kalymnos

Crew List Book of the Port Authority of Kalymnos (1975–2003).

Newspapers

Αθηναϊκά Νέα [*Athinaika Nea*]

Η Αργώ της Καλύμνου [*I Argo tis Kalymnou*]

Άστυ [*Asty*]

Το Βήμα [*To Vima*]

Ελευθερία [*Eleftheria*]

Ελεύθερον Βήμα [*Eleftheron Vima*]

Εμπρός [*Empros*]

Εστία [*Estia*]

Καιροί [*Kairoi*]

Η Κάλυμνος [*I Kalymnos*]

Η Μάχη [*I Machi*]

Νεολόγος [*Neologos*] [Constantinople]

Τα Νέα [*Ta Nea*]

Οικονομικός Ταχυδρόμος [*Oikonomikos Tachydromos*]

Ριζοσπάστης [*Rizospastis*]

Η Ροδιακή [*I Rodiaki*]

Συμιακός [*Symiakos*]

Σκριπ [*Skrip*]

Ταχυδρόμος [*Tachydromos*] [Alexandria]

Testimonies Recorded by Evdokia Olympitou

Glynatsi Argyro, 4/2/2011

Kampourakis Antonis (Diver-Captain), 25/8/2002 and 27/8/2002

Kampourakis Nikolas, 25/8/2002, 23/7/2005 and 28/7/2005

Kampouris Vassilis (*Kolaouzieris*), 1/9/2004

Koutouzis Giannis (Diver), 25/8/2003

Konstantaras Vassilis (Diver), 17/8/2004

Lampos Michael (*Balaristis*), 27/8/2002 and 29/7/2005

Loulourgas Giannis (Diver), 23/8/2004

Mamouzelos Lefteris (Captain), 3/9/2004

Marthas Petros (*Kolaouzieris*-Captain), 2/9/2004

Nomikarios Konstantinos (Orthopedist), 31/8/2004

Peros Dimitris (Diver), 24/8/2004

Politis Thrasyvoulos (Diver), 18/8/2004

Sdregas Nikolaos (Machinist), 30/8/2004

Tsoulfas Giannis, 5/3/2002 and 6/3/2002

Cheilas Manolis (Wooden Ship Builder), 25/8/2002

Municipal Archive of Kalymnos [MAK]

Classification List
Correspondence

1. Elders' Council Correspondence 22/2/1910–28/4/1912 and Municipal Office Correspondence 2/5/1912–21/8/1914.
2. Correspondence 8/2/1879–8/2/1881.
3. Correspondence and Decisions of the Municipal Council [MC] 1/12/1882–6/10/1883.
4. Elders' Council Correspondence 4/1/1894–9/5/1895.
5. Elders' Council Correspondence 10/7/1896–4/2/1898.
6. Elders' Council Correspondence 13/2/1898–8/12/1899.
7. Correspondence 3/1/1902–24/9/1902.
8. Elders' Council Correspondence 4/1/1903–26/12/1903.
9. Elders' Council Correspondence 4/1/1902–13/12/1902.
10. Elders' Council Correspondence with the Holy Metropolis of Kalymnos-Leros 4/1/1902–28/11/1902.
11. Elders' Council Correspondence 30/3/1905–12/7/1907.
12. Municipal Office Correspondence-Protocol 4/3/1915–5/6/1916.
13. Municipal Office Correspondence 21/2/1917–12/2/1918.
14. Municipal Office Correspondence 12/2/1918–16/3/1920.
15. Municipal Office Correspondence 10/1/1922–3/11/1922.
16. Municipal Office Correspondence 2/9/1925–20/1/1927.
17. Correspondence concerning the bequest of N. Vouvalis 28/5/1919–19/9/1919, Recruitments 22/4/1926–10/5/1926.
18. Notarial deeds, Minutes and Correspondence of the Municipal Office 28/8/1915–18/2/1917.
19. Elders' Council Correspondence 3/1/1900 and 4/1/1900, Recruitments other sponge fishing-related notarial documents 18/11/1902–4/4/1904.
20. Municipal Office Correspondence 3/5/1920–10/1/1922.

21. Certificates-Correspondence 3/6/1919–24/11/1920.
22. Elders' Council Correspondence 13/11/1898, 25/9/1902–20/3/1905.
23. Municipal Office Correspondence 28/2/1922–27/8/1925.

Notarial Documents

1. Notarial Deeds 13/1/1879–28/4/1884.
2. Real Estate Notarial Deeds 3/9/1884–14/1/1891.
3. Notarial Deeds 24/4/1890–8/10/1891.
4. Minutes and Notarial Deeds 1890–1893.
5. Notarial Deeds Of The Elders' Council 17/4/1893–20/2/1896
6. Notarial Deeds, Sponge-Fishing Activities, Leases, Bill of Sales Handling Disputes 20/2/1896–27/3/1898.
7. Real Estate Notarial Deeds 19/11/1897–27/4/1901.
8. Notarial Deeds 18/6/1899–7/1/1902.
9. Real Estate Notarial Deeds 4/5/1901–25/6/1903.
10. Notarial Deeds 7/1/1902–11/10/1903.
11. Real Estate Notarial Deeds 15/7/1903–17/12/1904.
12. Notarial Deeds 3/9/1904–11/12/1906.
13. Real Estate Notarial Deeds 2/1/1905–22/11/1905.
14. Real Estate Notarial Deeds 22/11/1905–31/3/1907.
15. Notarial Deeds 3/1/1906–11/4/1909.
16. Real Estate Notarial Deeds 31/3/1907–2/9/1910.
17. Investments [Εκκινήσεις] and Other Notarial Documents 1909–1912.
18. Bills of Sale, Mortgage Loans 13/9/1910–6/5/1913.
19. Power Of Attorney and Other Notarial Deeds 15/5/1912–30/10/1913.
20. Bills Of Sale and Mortgage Loans 9/5/1913–25/4/1915.
21. Notarial Deeds 3/12/1913–20/12/1914.
22. Bills Of Sale, Power Of Attorney and Other Notarial Deeds 8/1/1915–26/8/1916.
23. Bills Of Sale, Mortgage Loans and Other Notarial Documents 25/4/1915–18/4/1916.
24. Notarial Deeds 24/1/1920–4/3/1920, AC Minutes 1915–1917.
25. Notarial Deeds 5/2/1916–13/1/1927.
26. Mortgage Loans 28/3/1916–4/11/1920.
27. Bills Of Sale, Mortgage Loans and Conveyance Deeds for Land Property 18/4/1916–2/10/1920.
28. Notarial Deeds 30/8/1916–26/7/1917.
29. Notarial Deeds 1917–1919.
30. AC Minutes, Notarial Deeds, Recruitments, Deeds of Ship Transfer 26/2/1917–2/10/1919.
31. Notarial Deeds 25/8/1920–28/4/1921.

32. Bills Of Sale, Purchases, Mortgages, Loans and Other Notarial Deeds 6/9/1920–19/2/1926.
33. Power Of Attorney, Recruitments and Other Notarial Deeds, 19/5/1921–15/10/1921.
34. Contracts, Power of Attorney and Other Notarial Deeds, 5/1921–7/1921.
35. Notarial Deeds 19/7/1922–29/5/1923.
36. Power of Attorney and Other Notarial Deeds 1923–1924.
37. Notarial Deeds 3/5/1924–19/11/1925.
38. Notarial Documents: Contracts; Contract Awards; Amendments; Appointments; Decisions of the Administrative Council 11/4/1925–1/3/1932.
39. Notarial Deeds 16/11/1925–20/9/1926.
40. Mortgage Loans 10/3/1926–7/6/1948.
41. Notarial Deeds 20/9/1926–29/9/1927.
42. Notarial Deeds 30/9/1927–1/6/1928.
43. Power of Attorney and Other Notarial Deeds 1928–1930.
44. Consensus Documents and Other Notarial Deeds 1930–1935.
45. Real Estate Notarial Deeds 10/10/1943–15/6/1948.
46. Notarial Deeds Of Northern Dodecanese Court of First Instance [Kos, Kalymnos, Leros] 17/9/1945–7/12/1946.
47. Notarial Deeds Signed By Notary D. Gounaris In The Period 7/12/1946–22/4/1947.

Sponge Fishing-Related Documents

A.   *Sponge Fishermen Recruitment*
1. Sponge-fishing-related documents: Ναυτικά συμβόλαια, ναυτολογήσεις, εκκινήσεις, πωλήσεις πλοίων [*Marine Contracts, Recruitment Contracts, Departures, Vessel Sales*] 13/4/1888–24/4/1890.
2. Συμβολαιογραφικές πράξεις ναυτολογήσεων, συμβόλαια επίλυσης προνομιούχων και σχετικές αποφάσεις Δημογεροντίας [*Recruitment Deeds, Contracts on the Resolution of Preferential Conflicts and Relevant Decisions of the Elders' Council*] 13/10/1889–23/3/1892.
3. Ναυτολογήσεις και λοιπά έγγραφα [*Sponge Fishermen Recruitment and Other Documents*] 1892–1894.
4. Ποικίλα σπογγαλιευτικά [*Various Sponge-Fishing Issues*] 18/4/1896–14/3/1898.
5. Ναυτολογήσεις [*Sponge Fishermen Recruitment*] 13/5/1899–31/3/1900.
6. Ναυτολογήσεις [*Sponge Fishermen Recruitment*] 1901–1902.
7. Ναυτολογήσεις [*Sponge Fishermen Recruitment*] 12/4/1905–16/4/1907.

8. Ναυτολογήσεις και προνομιούχες εκκινήσεις [*Sponge Fishermen Recruitment and Preferential Departures*] 16/4/1907–8/1/1910.

9. Documents on Sponge-Fishing Issues: Ναυτολογήσεις [*Sponge Fishermen Recruitments*] 4/1/1922–18/12/1923.

10. Ναυτολογήσεις πληρωμάτων σπογγαλιευτικών σκαφών [*Sponge-Fishing Vessel Crew Recruitment*] 30/3/1925–21/4/1926.

B. *Preferential Departures*

1. Documents on Sponge-Fishing Issues: Έγγραφα προνομιούχων εκκινήσεων [*Preferential Departure Documents*] 16/2/1922–2/5/1925.

2. Documents on Sponge-Fishing Issues: Άδειες σπογγαλιευτικών [*Sponge-Fishing Permits*] 1928–1931.

3. Προνομιούχες εκκινήσεις σπογγαλιείας [*Sponge-Fishing Preferential Departures*] 20/2/1928–9/4/1929.

4. Προνομιούχα σπογγαλιευτικά χρέη [*Preferential Sponge-Fishing Debts*]

5. Αποθήκη Φαρμάκων Δημοτικών Φαρμακείων [*Drug Warehouse of Public Pharmacies*] 26/9/1938–30/11/1938. Λιμενικά Δικαιώματα [*Port Fees*] 1/8/1946–30/11/1948.

C. *Sponge-Fishing Notarial Documents*

1. Notarial Deeds: ενοικιαστήρια, πωλητήρια, σπογγαλιευτικά, δανεισμοί, εξοφλη-τικά και χρεωστικά έγγραφα [*Rental Agreements, Bills of Sale, Sponge-Fishing Agreements, Loans, Repayment and Debt Documents*] 4/11/1882–31/11/1883.

2. Έγγραφα ναυτικά και λοιπές συμβολαιογραφικές πράξεις [*Marine Documents and Other Notarial Deeds*] 20/11/1886–13/4/1888.

3. Συμβολαιογραφικές πράξεις [*Notarial Deeds*] 9/10/1891–19/4/1893.

4. Documents on Sponge-Fishing Issues: Ναυτολογήσεις, διακανονισμοί χρεών, ενοι-κιάσεις σκαφών [*Sponge Fishermen Recruitment, Debt Settlement, Vessel Rentals*] 29/4/1894–18/4/1896.

5. Εκκινήσεις και λοιπές συμβολαιογραφικές πράξεις [*Departures and Other Notarial Deeds*] 3/1898–6/1899.

6. Notarial Documents: Ναυτολογήσεις, προνομιούχα χρέη, ενοικιαστήρια, πωλητήρια, κλπ. [*Sponge Fishermen Recruitment, Preferential Debts, Rental Agreements, Sale Agreements, etc.*] 17/4/1893–20/2/1896.

7. Ισολογισμός εσόδων και εξόδων Ι. Ν. Ιωάννου Θεολόγου [*Revenue and Expenditure Account of the Church of Ioannis Theologos*] [19/5/18894/3/1890 and 24/6/1890–12/5/1891], Ναυτολογήσεις [*Sponge Fishermen Recruitment*] 10/4/1904–11/4/1905.

8. Ναυτολογήσεις και άλλα συμβολαιογραφικά σπογγαλιευτικά έγγραφα [*Sponge Fishermen Recruitment and Other Sponge-Fishing Notarial Documents*] 8/1/1910–5/5/1912.

9. Ψήφισμα Δημογεροντίας-αλλαγή καθεστώτος. Συμβολαιογραφικές πράξεις [*Elders' Council Resolution: Regime Change. Notarial Deeds*] 1/5/1912–17/2/1917.

10. Notarial Documents: πιστοποιητικά και δηλώσεις ιδιοκτησίας πλοίων [*Certificates and Vessel Ownership Declarations*] 17/7/1915–15/1/1917.

11. Σπογγαλιευτικά, ποικίλα συμβολαιογραφικά [*Sponge-Fishing Agreements, Various Notarial Documents*] 3/9/1919–25/1/1920.

12. Συμβολαιογραφικά σπογγαλιευτικά έγγραφα [*Sponge-Fishing Notarial Documents*] 27/3/1919–22/5/1919.

13. Ναυτολογήσεις, εκκινήσεις και λοιπά συμβολαιογραφικά έγγραφα [*Sponge Fishermen Recruitment, Departures and Other Notarial Documents*] 1920–1930.

14. Σπογγαλιευτικά έγγραφα και λοιπές συμβολαιογραφικές πράξεις [*Sponge-Fishing Documents and Other Notarial Deeds*] 9/4/1920–6/6/1920.

15. Πωλήσεις σκαφών, εκκινήσεις και λοιπές συμβολαιογραφικές πράξεις [*Vessel Sales, Departures, and Other Notarial Deeds*] 6/6/1920–1/12/1920.

16. Συμβολαιογραφικές πράξεις [*Notarial Deeds*] 28/4/1921–19/5/1921.

17. Πωλητήρια λέμβων και λοιπές συμβολαιογραφικές πράξεις [*Bills of Boat Sales and Other Notarial Deeds*] 14/10/1921–29/11/1924.

18. Ναυτολογήσεις και λοιπές συμβολαιογραφικές πράξεις [*Sponge Fishermen Recruitment and Other Notarial Deeds*] 22/1/1924–27/3/1925.

19. Προνομιούχες εκκινήσεις συμβόλαια και δηλώσεις προνομιούχων εκκινήσεων [*Preferential Departure Contracts and Preferential Departure Declarations*] 5/5/1925–25/5/1927.

20. Συμβολαιογραφικές πράξεις [*Notarial Deeds*] 1929–1947.

D.   *Sponge Imports – Exports*

1. Εισαγωγές-εξαγωγές σπόγγων [*Sponge Imports – Exports*] 1946–1949.
2. Εισαγωγές-εξαγωγές σπόγγων [*Sponge Imports – Exports*] 1947–1949.
3. Σπογγαλιευτικά [*Sponge-Fishing Documents*] 1944–1950.
4. Λιμενικά δικαιώματα σπογγαλιευτικών [*Port Fees of Sponge-Fishing Vessels*]. 1949, εισαγωγές σπόγγων [*Sponge Imports*] 1947.
5. Εισαγωγές-εξαγωγές σπόγγων [*Sponge Imports – Exports*] 1954–1956.
6. Εισαγωγές-εξαγωγές σπόγγων [*Sponge Imports – Exports*] 1956–1957.
7. Αγορές, εξαγωγές, πωλήσεις σπόγγων [*Sponge Purchases, Exports, Sales*] 1957–1959.
8. Εισαγωγές-εξαγωγές σπόγγων [*Sponge Imports – Exports*] 1959–1961.
9. Εισαγωγές, εξαγωγές σπόγγων [*Sponge Imports, Exports*] 1938–1948.

E.   *Vessels*

1. Πιστοποιητικά ιδιοκτησίας πλοίων και λέμβων [*Vessel and Boat Ownership Certificates*] 8/1/1902–21/4/1905.
2. Ιδιοκτησίες πλοίων και λέμβων [*Vessel and Boat Ownership*] 22/4/905–19/12/1909.

3. Πιστοποιήσεις ιδιοκτησίας σκαφών, οικοδομικές άδειες [*Vessel Ownership Certificates, Building Permits*] 5/10/1911−28/12/1915.

4. Πωλητήρια πλοίων [*Bills of sale*] 5/2/1924−24/3/1925.

5. Βιβλίο πωλητηρίων, ενοικιάσεων σκαφών και ιδιοκτησίες πλοίων [*Book of Bills of Sale, Rental Agreements and Vessel Ownerships*] 24/3/1925−12/5/1926

6. Κατάλογος αγοραπωλησιών σκαφών [*Buying and Selling List*] 15/5/1926−12/2/1929.

7. Συμβολαιογραφικές σπογγαλιευτικές πράξεις [*Sponge-Fishing Notarial Deeds*] 14/2/1929−1/2/1932.

8. Ευρετήριο πωλήσεων σκαφών [*Vessel Sale Directory*] 27/4/1945−11/8/1947.

Elders' Council and Municipal Council [MC] Minutes

1. Πρακτικά Δημογεροντίας [*Minutes of the Elders' Council*] 1863−1884.

2. Πρακτικά Δημογεροντίας, συμβολαιογραφικές πράξεις [*Minutes of the Elders' Council, Notarial Deeds*] 5/2/1864−26/2/1885.

3. Πρακτικά ψηφίσματα [*Resolution Minutes*] 1879−1884.

4. Ποικίλα Δημογεροντίας [*Elders' Council Various Documents*] 1881−1884.

5. Πρακτικά και αλληλογραφία Δημογεροντίας [*Elders' Council Minutes and Correspondence*] 1/2/1884−26/1/1885.

6. Ψηφίσματα λαϊκών συνελεύσεων και άλλα πρακτικά [*Resolutions of Public Assemblies and Other Minutes*] 1884−1948.

7. Πρακτικά Δημογεροντίας και Δ.Σ. [*Elders' Council and MC Minutes*] 11/2/1885−11/10/1885 7a. Πρακτικά σπογγαλιευτικά κ.ά. [*Minutes of Sponge-Fishing Issues, etc.*] 28/2/1887−6/10/1887.

8. Πρακτικά διάφορα, αλληλογραφία Δημογεροντίας [*Minutes-Various, Elders' Council Correspondence*] 1/2/1884−2/12/1892.

9. Πρακτικά Δημογεροντίας και λοιπά συμβολαιογραφικά [*Elders' Council Minutes and Other Notarial Documents*] 30/12/1892−24/12/1893.

10. Ψηφίσματα λαϊκών συνελεύσεων [*Resolutions of Public Assemblies and Other Minutes*] 8/1/1893−4/1/1907.

11. Ψηφίσματα και δημοψηφίσματα λαϊκών συνελεύσεων [*Resolutions and Referenda of Public Assemblies and Other Minutes*] 1894−1906.

12. Πρακτικά Δ.Σ. [*MC Minutes*] 14/6/1896−3/2/1898.

13. Πρακτικά Δημογεροντίας [*Elders' Council Minutes*] 7/2/1898−26/12/1903.

14. Πρακτικά Δημογεροντίας [*Elders' Council Minutes*] 1/2/1899−28/12/1899.

15. Πρακτικά Δ.Σ., και σπογγαλιευτικά πρακτικά [*MC Minutes and Sponge-Fishing Minutes*] 29/2/1899−20/6/1900.

16. Πρακτικά Δ.Σ. [*MC Minutes*] 19/2/1902−30/10/1906.

17. Πρακτικά Δημογεροντίας και λοιπά συμβολαιογραφικά [*Elders' Council Minutes and Other Notarial Documents*] 2/1/1904−23/2/1905.

18. Πρακτικά Δ.Σ., κανονισμοί, συμβολαιογραφικές πράξεις [MC Minutes, Regulations, Notarial Deeds] 7/9/1906–4/3/1908.

19. Κτηματικά πρακτικά και λοιπές αποφάσεις Δημογεροντίας [Real Estate Minutes and Other Elders' Council Decisions] 7/3/1908–4/9/1909.

20. Δημοψηφίσματα, Προϋπολογισμός, Πρακτικά Δ.Σ. [Referenda, Budget, MC Minutes] 25/6/1909–3/2/1913 20a. Πρακτικά Δημογεροντίας και Δ.Σ. [Elders' Council and MC Minutes] 23/10/1910–12/4/1912.

21. Ψηφίσματα Δημογεροντίας-αλλαγή καθεστώτος. Συμβολαιογραφικές πράξεις [Elders' Council Resolution – Regime Change. Notarial Deeds] 29/4/1912–24/9/1913.

22. Πρακτικά Δ.Σ. [MC Minutes] 4/5/1912–2/6/1912.

23. Πρακτικά Εφοροδημαρχίας, Εφορίας Σχολείων και Κανονισμός των Σχολείων [Municipal Minutes, School Service and School Regulation] 21/7/1912–16/7/1919.

24. Πρακτικά Δ.Σ. [MC Minutes] 17/2/1915–25/5/1918.

25. Πρακτικά Δ.Σ. και Κανονισμοί [MC Minutes and Regulations] 4/3/1915–12/7/1916.

26. Πρακτικά Δ.Σ. [MC Minutes] 31/1/1916–24/1/1920.

27. Πρακτικά Δ.Σ., κανονισμοί, συμβολαιογραφικές πράξεις [MC Minutes, Regulations, Notarial Deeds] 28/10/1916–14/3/1927.

28. Πρακτικά Δ.Σ. [MC Minutes] 20/2/1917–7/12/1922.

29. Πρακτικά Δ.Σ. [MC Minutes] 31/5/1919–3/8/1920.

30. Πρακτικά Εφοροδημαρχίας και κανονισμοί εκπαιδευτικού χαρακτήρα [Municipal Minutes and Education-Related Regulations] 6/8/1923–15/11/1934.

31. Πρακτικά και ψηφίσματα [Minutes and Resolutions] 8/1/1924 and 19/9/1929.

32. Πρακτικά Δ.Σ. [MC Minutes] 29/12/1924–19/1/1925.

33. Πρακτικά Δ.Σ. και άλλα αντίστοιχα [MC Minutes and Other Corresponding Documents] 19/1/1925–1/12/1927.

34. Εκλογικοί κατάλογοι [Electoral Rolls] 1935.

35. Αποφάσεις του Ιταλού Επιτρόπου [Italian Commissioner Decisions] 1938–1941.

36. Διάφορα πιστοποιητικά και μαρτυρικές καταθέσεις από και προς τη Δημαρχία [Various Certificates and Testimonials from and to the Municipal Authority] 1922–1926.

37. Πιστοποιητικά και αιτήσεις γεννήσεως [Birth Certificates and Requests] 23/11/1948–16/12/1948.

38. Πρωτόκολλο ληξιαρχικών πράξεων [Civil Status Record Registry] 7/9/1949–26/9/1949.

39. Πρακτικά και αλληλογραφία Οικονομικής Επιτροπής [Financial Committee Minutes and Correspondence] 4/2/1902–23/6/1904.

40. Αποφάσεις του Βασιλικού Επιτρόπου στη Δημαρχία Καλύμνου και των Δημάρχων [Decisions of the Royal Commissioner to the Municipal Authority of Kalymnos, and of the Mayors], 31/12/1927–2/11/1934.

41. Διοικητικές Διαταγές του Ιταλού Κυβερνητικού Επιτρόπου [Administrative Orders of the Italian Governmental Commissioner] 1935–1937.

42. Αποφάσεις του Ιταλού Κυβερνητικού Επιτρόπου [*Decisions of the Italian Governmental Commissioner*] 3/4/1935–30/8/1940, and Πρωτόκολλο Πιστοποιητικών Δημαρχίας [*Certificate Registry of the Municipal Authority*] 10/5/1950–17/8/1950.

43. Διαταγές Κυβερνητικού Επιτρόπου [*Governmental Commissioner Orders*] 1935–1942.

44. Αποφάσεις Βασ. Επιτρόπου [*Governmental Commissioner Decisions*] 27/5/1937–21/6/1938.

45. Πρακτικά ειδικής επιτροπής διανομής τροφίμων και φαρμάκων [*Minutes of the Special Committee for the Distribution of Food and Medication*] 7/5/1944–21/8/1944 and Πρωτόκολλο εισερχομένων και εξερχόμενων εγγράφων της επιτροπής [*Committee Registry of Incoming and Outgoing Documents*] 16/12/1946–29/3/1947.

Land Property

1. Πρακτικά Επιτροπής Κτηματικών Υποθέσεων [*Real Estate Minutes of the Real Estate Committee*] 14/6/1899–15/8/1899 and 1/2/1902–1/11/1902.

2. Πρωτόκολλο αλληλογραφίας Δημαρχίας [*Correspondence Registry of the Municipal Authority*] 25/5/1916–28/9/1916 and Πρακτικά κτηματικών διαφορών του Σωματείου Κτηματικών Διαφορών [*Land Dispute Minutes of the Land Dispute Association*] 25/6/1917–29/11/1923.

3. Πρακτικά Δ.Σ. [*MC Minutes*] 9/9/1920–22/9/1922.

4. Κτηματικά Πρακτικά [*Real Estate Minutes*] 23/2/1925–20/11/1926 and 1/6/1929–23/3/1932.

5. Ενοικίαση αγροτεμαχίων Ψερίμου [*Parcel Lease on the Island of Pserimos*] 1931–1932.

Various

1. Statutes of the Agricultural Credit Union "Η Ένωση Παραγωγών Εσπεριδοειδών Βαθέος-Καλύμνου" [*"The Association of Citrus Fruit Producers of Vathy-Kalymnos"*], April 1946.

2. Πρακτικά Συνεδριάσεων Διοικητικού Συμβουλίου, Φιλαρμονικής [*Meeting Minutes of the Administrative Board, Philharmonic Band*] 18/11/1964–6/3/1968.

3. Πρακτικά και οικονομικά του Βουβάλειου Παρθεναγωγείου [*Minutes and Financial Records of the Vouvaleion All-Girl School*] 1923 1924.

4. Επιτροπή δημοσίων έργων [*Public Works Committee*] 30/12/1914–26/8/1915.

5. Κατάλογος δημοτών [*Register of Municipality Citizens*] [1936?].

6. Πρωτόκολλο αλληλογραφίας: εισερχόμενων και εξερχόμενων [*Correspondence Registry: Incoming and Outgoing Letters*] 28/9/1953–2/2/1954.

7. Πρωτόκολλο εισερχομένων και εξερχόμενων ληξιαρχικών επιστολών [Registry of Incoming and Outcoming Civil Status Letters] 13/12/1951–10/9/1953

Bibliography

Greek

Α' Πανελλήνιον Σπογγαλιευτικόν Συνέδριον [*Ρόδος 24–27 Φεβρουάριου 1949*]. *Εισηγήσεις και Πρακτικά, Γενική Διοίκησις Δωδεκανήσου* [*The First Colloquium on the Sponge Fishery, Rhodes 24–27 February 1949, Papers and Minutes*] Γενική Διοίκησις Δωδεκανήσου [*General Administration of the Dodecanese*], Rhodes 1951.

Σωτήριος Ι. Αγαπητίδης, *Η εργασία εις την σπογγαλιείαν* [Sotirios I. Agapitidis, *Working in the Sponge Fishery*], Athens 1938.

Σωτήριος Ι. Αγαπητίδης, "Ο πληθυσμός της Δωδεκανήσου", *Δωδεκανησιακή Επιθεώρησις* ["The Population of Dodecanese", *Dodekanisiaki Epitheorisis*] 2–4 [1948], pp. 83–89.

Σωτήριος Ι. Αγαπητίδης, "Γενική Εισήγησις εις το Α' Σπογγαλιευτικόν Συνέδριον", *Α' Πανελλήνιον Σπογγαλιευτικόν Συνέδριον* [Ρόδος 24–27 Φεβρουαρίου 1949] ["General Statement to the First Colloquium on the Sponge-Fishery", Rhodes 24–27 February 1949. *Papers and Minutes, General Administration of the Dodecanese*], Rhodes 1951, pp. 17–25.

Σωτήριος Ι. Αγαπητίδης, "Μεταπολεμικαί εξελίξεις εις την ελληνικήν σπογγαλιείαν", *Δωδεκάνησος* ["Post-War Developments in the Greek Sponge Fishery", *Dodekanissos*] 6 (1957), pp. 39–44.

Σωτήριος Ι. Αγαπητίδης, "Ο πληθυσμός της Δωδεκανήσου", *Νισυριακά* ["The Population of Dodecanese", *Nisyriaka*] 3 (1969), pp. 5–22.

Σωτήριος Ι. Αγαπητίδης, "Η οικονομική οργάνωση των σπογγαλιευτικών συγκροτημάτων – ειδικότερα στη Σύμη", *Τα Συμαϊκά* ["The Economic Organization of Sponge-Fishing Groups – Particularly on Symi", *Ta Symaika*] 3 (1977), pp. 180–202.

Σωτήριος Ι. Αγαπητίδης, "Πληθυσμιακές εξελίξεις στα Δωδεκάνησα", *Δωδεκανησιακά Χρονικά* ["Population Developments in the Dodecanese", *Dodekanisiaka Chronika*] 11 (1986), pp. 9–34.

Χριστίνα Αγριαντώνη, "Βιομηχανία", στο Κώστας Κωστής, Σωκράτης Πετμεζάς (επιμ.), *Η ανάπτυξη της ελληνικής οικονομίας κατά τον 19ο αιώνα (1830–1914)* [Christina Agriantoni, "Industry", in Kostas Kostis, Sokratis Petmezas (eds.), *The Development of Greek Economy in the 19th Century (1830–1914)*], Athens 2006, pp. 219–251.

Χριστίνα Αγριαντώνη, "Προς τη βιομηχανική τεχνολογία: οι συντεταγμένες της μεγάλης τομής" ["Towards Industrial Technology: Coordinates of the Great Breakthrough"], Proceedings of the Three-Day Working Meeting on the History of Greek Techniques, Patras 21–23 October 1988, ΠΤΙ/ΕΤΒΑ [Cultural-Technological Foundation of the Greek Bank for Industrial Development], Athens 1991, pp. 219–229.

Μαρί Ελιζαμπέτ Αντμάν, *Βία και πονηριά, Άντρες και γυναίκες σ' ένα ελληνικό χωριό* [Marie-Elisabeth Handman, *Violence and Artfulness, Men and Women in a Greek Village*], Athens 1987.

[Anonymous], "Σπογγαλιεία", *Αθηναΐς* ["Sponge Fishery", *Athinais*] 2/23 (1877), pp. 183–184.

[Anonymous], "Τα Δωδεκάνησα", *Ημερολόγιον Σκόκου* ["Ta Dodekanissa", *Imerologion Skokou*] 29 (1914), pp. 321–333.

[Anonymous], "Έτος πρώτο – 1904 – του Αναγνωστηρίου", *Καλυμνιακά Χρονικά* ["First Year – 1904 – of the Reading Room", *Kalymniaka Chronika*] 6 (1986), pp. 11–18.

Γιώργης Βαλέτας, *Επίτομη Ιστορία της Νεοελληνικής Λογοτεχνίας* [Giorgis Valetas, *Abridged History of Modern Greek Literature*], Athens 1966.

Λίνα Βεντούρα, *Έλληνες μετανάστες στο Βέλγιο* [Lina Ventoura, *Greek Immigrants in Belgium*], Athens 1999.

Γεώργιος Θ. Βεργωτής, "Περί την ιστορίαν του Αναγνωστηρίου Σύμης η "Αίγλη"", *Τα Συμαϊκά* [Georgios Th. Vergotis, "On the History of Symi's Reading Room "Aegli"", *Ta Symaika*] 1 (1972), pp. 123–138.

Jules Verne, *Twenty Thousand Leagues under the Sea*, 1994, Project Gutenberg (1st edition: Jules Verne, *Vingt mille lieues sous les mers*, Paris 1870).

Ιάκωβος Τ. Βισβίζης, "Ναξιακά νοταριακά έγγραφα των τελευταίων χρόνων του Δουκάτου του Αιγαίου (1538–1577)", *Επετηρίς του Αρχείου της Ιστορίας του Ελληνικού Δικαίου* [Iakovos T. Visvizis, "Naxos Notarial Documents from the Final years of the Duchy of the Aegean (1538–1577)", *Archive of the History of Greek Law Yearbook*] 4 (1951), pp. 1–166.

Ιάκωβος Τ. Βισβίζης, "Το κληρονομικόν δικαίωμα των συζύγων επί ατέκνου γάμου εις την Πάρον κατά τον 18ον αιώνα", *Επετηρίς του Αρχείου της Ιστορίας του Ελληνικού Δικαίου* ["The inheritance right of husbands in a childless marriage on Paros in the 18th century", *Archive of the History of Greek Law Yearbook*] 8 (1958), pp. 135–203.

Κωνσταντίνος Βλάμος, *Τ' Αλατσάτα* [Konstantinos Vlamos, *The Alatsata*], Thessaloniki 1946.

Βασιλική Γαλάνη-Μουτάφη, "Προίκα και κοινωνική οργάνωση στη Σάμο στα μέσα του 19ου αιώνα", *Αντιπελάργηση. Τιμητικός τόμος για τον Νικόλαο Α. Δημητρίου* [Vassiliki Galani-Moutafi, "Dowry and Societal Organization on Samos in the Mid-19th Century", *Antipelargisi. Honorary Volume to Nikolaos A. Dimitriou*], Athens 1992, pp. 59–85.

Μανουήλ Γεδεών, "Η Μητρόπολις Λέρου και Καλύμνου", *Εκκλησιαστική Αλήθεια* [Manouil Gedeon, "The Metropolis of Leros and Kalymnos", *Ekklisiastiki Alitheia*] 9 (1888–1889), pp. 106–107, 118–120.

Γιάννης Γεράκης, *Σφουγγαράδικες ιστορίες από την Κάλυμνο του 1900* [Giannis Gerakis, *Sponge-Fishing Stories from Kalymnos in 1900*], Athens 1999.

Δημήτριος Γερούκαλης, "Φαινομενολογία, προφίλ προσωπικότητας των δυτών και κλινική εικόνα της νόσου των δυτών υπό το πρίσμα της θεωρίας των καταστροφών", *Καλυμνιακά Χρονικά* [Dimitrios Geroukalis, "Phenomenology: Divers' Personality Profiles and Clinical Picture of the Divers' Disease in the scope of Catastrophe Theory", *Kalymniaka Chronika*], 9 (1990), pp. 390–394.

Γεώργιος Ελευθ. *Γεωργάς, Μελέτη περί σπογγαλιείας, σπόγγων και σπογγεμπορίου από των αρχαιοτάτων χρόνων μέχρι σήμερον* [Georgios Elefth. Georgas, *Study of the Sponge Fishery, Sponges and Sponge Trade from Ancient Times to the Present*], Piraeus 1937.

Κατερίνα Γιαννάτου, "Η Ειρήνη η Τουμπλού" Katerina Giannatou, *Καλυμνιακά Χρονικά* ["Irene the Toumplou", *Kalymniaka Chronika*] 13 (1999), pp. 101–104.

Κατερίνα Γιαννάτου, "Αποκριά στην παλιά Κάλυμνο", *Καλυμνιακά Χρονικά* ["Mardi Gras at the Old Kalymnos", *Kalymniaka Chronika*] 17 (2007), pp. 359–364.

Κατερίνα Γιαννάτου, "Η μάνα Καλυμνιά", *Καλυμνιακά Χρονικά* ["The Kalymnian Mother", *Kalymniaka Chronika*] 17 (2007), pp. 391–394.

Σοφία Γιαννάτου, "Η Πόθια", *Καλυμνιακά Χρονικά* ["Pothia", *Kalymniaka Chronika*] 15 (2003), pp. 255–258.

Στυλιανός Γονατάς, Απομνημονεύματα [Stylianos Gonatas, *Memoirs*], Athens 1958.

Αλεξάνδρα Γουλάκη-Βουτυρά, *Το εργαστήριο μαρμαρογλυπτικής του Ιωάννη Χαλεπά* [Alexandra Goulaki-Voutyra, *Marble Sculpting Workshop of Ioannis Chalepas*], Thessaloniki 1989.

Αλεξάνδρα Γουλάκη-Βουτυρά, "Τηνιακοί Μαρμαράδες στην Αθήνα του Όθωνα", *Τηνιακά* ["Marble Sculptors from Tenos to Otto's Athens", *Tiniaka*] 1 (1996), pp. 261–281.

Κωνσταντίνος Γουργιώτης, "Όροι εργασίας εις την σπογγαλιείαν", Α´ Πανελλήνιον Σπογγαλιευτικόν Συνέδριον [Ρόδος 24–27 Φεβρουαρίου 1949]. Εισηγήσεις και Πρακτικά, Γενική Διοίκησις Δωδεκανήσου [Konstantinos Gourgiotis, "Working Conditions in the Sponge Fishery", 1st Colloquium on the Sponge Fishery (Rhodes 24–27 February 1949). Papers and Minutes, General Administration of the Dodecanese], Rhodes 1951, pp. 73–88.

Μιχαήλ Γρηγορόπουλος, *Η νήσος Σύμη, πραγματεία υπό γεωγραφικήν, ιστορικήν και στατιστικήν έποψιν* [Michael Grigoropoulos, *The Island of Symi, Treatise from a Geographical, Historical and Statistical Perspective*], Athens 1877.

Ελένη Γύζη, "Ο Γλύπτης Μιχαήλ Κόκκινος", *Καλυμνιακά Σύμμεικτα* [Eleni Gyzi, "Sculptor Michail Kokkinos", *Kalymniaka Symmeikta*] 1 (1993), pp. 18–20.

Κώστας Δαμιανίδης, "Μέθοδοι σπογγαλιείας", Αφιέρωμα: Η Ελληνική σπογγαλιεία, *Η Καθημερινή, Επτά Ημέρες* [Damianidis, K. "Sponge-Fishing Methods in the Greek Sponge Fishery", *I Kathimerini*: Feature Section *Epta Imeres*], 13/9/1998, pp. 13–15.

Κώστας Δαμιανίδης, "Τα σπογγαλιευτικά σκάφη", *Αφιέρωμα: Η Ελληνική σπογγαλιεία, Η Καθημερινή, Επτά Ημέρες* [Damianidis, K. "Sponge-Fishing Vessels in the Greek Sponge Fishery", *I Kathimerini*: Feature Section *Epta Imeres*], 13/9/1998, pp. 18–20.

Κώστας Δαμιανίδης, "Greek Sponge Fishing Vessels", in Κώστας Δαμιανίδης (ed.), *Ναυπηγική και πλοία στην Ανατολική Μεσόγειο κατά τον 18ο και 19ο αιώνα* [*Shipbuilding and Ships in the Eastern Mediterranean in the 18th and 19th Centuries*], Conference Minutes, Chios 1999, pp. 253–263.

Κώστας Δαμιανίδης, Μουσείο Ναυτικής Παράδοσης και Σπογγαλιείας Νέας Κουτάλης [Museum of Maritime Tradition and Sponge-Fishing of Nea Koutali], Limnos 2006.

Κώστας Δαφνής (επιμ.), *Αρχείον Ιωάννου Καποδίστρια*, τ. Η', Εταιρεία Κερκυραϊκών Σπουδών [Kostas Dafnis (ed.), *Archive of Ioannis Kapodistrias*, vol. VIII, Society for Corfiot Studies], Corfu 1987.

Δημήτρης Δημητρόπουλος, "Αστικές λειτουργίες στις νησιωτικές κοινωνίες των Κυκλάδων (17ος–αρχές 19ου αιώνα)", Πρακτικά Επιστημονικού Συμποσίου Ελληνικός Αστικός Χώρος, Εταιρεία Σπουδών Νεοελληνικού Πολιτισμού και Γενικής Παιδείας [Dimitris Dimitropoulos, "Urban Functions in the Insular Societies of Cyclades", Minutes of Scientific Symposium "Greek Urban Space", Etaireia Spoudon Neoellinikou Politismou kai Genikis Paidias – Society for Neohellenic Culture and General Education Studies], Athens 2004, pp. 101–118.

Δημήτρης Δημητρόπουλος, *Μαρτυρίες για τον πληθυσμό των νησιών του Αιγαίου, 15ος–αρχές 19ου αιώνα*, *Τετράδια Εργασίας ΚΝΕ/ΕΙΕ* [*Testimonies on the Aegean Islands' Population from the 15th to Early 19th Century*, Research Notebooks INR/NHRF] Athens 2004.

Ίων Δραγούμης, "Οι σφουγγαράδες", *Εκλεκτά Μυθιστορήματα* [Ion Dragoumis, "The Sponge Fishermen", *Eklekta Mythistorimata*] 12 (1935), pp. 3–11.

Γεράσιμος Δ. Δρακίδης, *Λεύκωμα των Δωδεκανήσων* [Gerasimos D. Drakidis, *Almanac of the Dodecanese*], Athens 1913.

Νικόλας Μ. Δράκος, *Κάλυμνος, Φουρτούνες σωρό-Μπουνάτσες αργά και πού* [Nikolas M. Drakos, *Rough Seas Aplenty – Dead Calm Seas Few and Far Between*], Athens 1987.

Ντίνος Κ. Δράκος, "Από τη ζωή του Νικ. Βουβάλη", *Καλυμνιακά Χρονικά* [Dinos K. Drakos, "From the Life of Nik. Vouvalis", *Kalymniaka Chronika*] 5 (1985), pp. 37–38.

Δωδεκάνησος. Τετράτομος μελέτη του Υπουργείου Ανοικοδομήσεως και συνεργατών του υπό την διεύθυνσιν του κ. Κ. Α. Δοξιάδη [*Dodecanese. Study in Four Volumes by the Ministry for Reconstruction and Affiliates under the Direction of Mr K. A. Doxiadis*], Ministry for Reconstruction Publication Series, Athens 1947.

Έκθεσις περί γεωργίας, βιομηχανίας, ναυτιλίας της προξενικής περιφερείας Ρόδου ιδία διά το έτος 1910, Δελτίον του επί των Εξωτερικών Β. Υπουργείου [*Report on Agriculture, Industry, Maritime Affairs of the Consular Precinct of Rhodes for the Year 1910*, Bulletin of the Ministry for Foreign Affairs], vol. 1, Athens 1911.

Ε.Σ.Υ.Ε, *Γενική απογραφή του πληθυσμού της Δωδεκανήσου ενεργηθείσα την 19ην Οκτωβρίου 1947* [*National Statistical Service of Greece, General Census of the Dodecanesian Population Conducted on October 19th, 1947*].

Μαρία Ζαΐρη, "Ναυτιλιακές δραστηριότητες στην Κάλυμνο" *Καλυμνιακά Χρονικά* [Maria Zairi, "Maritime Activities on Kalymnos", *Kalymniaka Chronika*] 8 (1989), pp. 195–212.

Μαρία Ζαΐρη, "Από την ιστορία του πρώτου ημιγυμνασίου θηλέων στην Πόθια (1921)", *Καλυμνιακά Χρονικά* ["From the History of the First Semi-Secondary School for Girls in Pothia (1921)"], *Kalymniaka Chronika* 13 (1999), pp. 165–178.

Μαρία Ζαΐρη, "Ρωσίας ενθυμήματα", *Καλυμνιακά Χρονικά* ["Mementos from Russia", *Kalymniaka Chronika*] 15 (2003), pp. 266–267.

Μαρία Ζαΐρη, "Οι αποθήκες των σφουγγαριών", *Καλυμνιακά Χρονικά* ["Sponge Warehouses", *Kalymniaka Chronika*] 15 (2003), pp. 417–419.

Μιχαήλ Ν. Ζαΐρης, "Μιχαήλ Θέμελη Ολυμπίτης", *Καλυμνιακά Χρονικά* [Michail N. Zairis, "Michail Themeli Olympitis", *Kalymniaka Chronika*] 9 (1990), pp. 85–92.

Τάσος Ζάππας, Ψαράδες [Tassos Zappas, *Fishermen*], Athens 1973.

Ελένη Κ. Ζαχαρίου, "Η έννοια της ξενητειάς στη ζωή του Δωδεκανησίου σπογγαλιέως", *Ελληνική Δημιουργία* [Eleni K. Zachariou, "The Concept of 'Living in Foreign Parts' in the Life of the Dodecanese Sponge Fisherman", *Elliniki Dimiourgia*] 10/106 (1952), pp. 41–45.

Ιωάννης και Παναγιώτης Ζέπος [Ioannis and Panagiotis Zepos], *Jus Graecoromanorum*, vol. 8, Athens 1931.

Γιάννης Κλ. Ζερβός, *Μοιραίο σκάφανδρο και τ' ανάθεμα της μηχανής* [Giannis Kl. Zervos, *Fateful Scaphander and the Anathema of the Machine* (novel)], Athens 1959.

Γιάννης Κλ. Ζερβός, *Ιστορικά Σημειώματα* [*Historical Notes*], Athens 1961.

Γιάννης Κλ. Ζερβός, "Νικόλαος Εμμ. Βουβάλης", *Καλυμνιακά Χρονικά* ["Nikolaos Em. Vouvalis", *Kalymniaka Chronika*] 5 (1985), pp. 12–24.

Γιάννης Κλ. Ζερβός, "Σακελλάρης Μαγκλής", *Καλυμνιακά Σύμμεικτα* ["Sakellaris Magklis", *Kalymniaka Symmeikta*] 2 (1995), pp. 18–19.

Δανιήλ Α. Ζερβός, "Μια περιγραφή της Καλύμνου του 1862 και ένα πολιτικό κείμενο του 1908", *Καλυμνιακά Χρονικά* [Daniil A. Zervos, "A 1862 Description of Kalymnos and a Political Text of 1908"], *Kalymniaka Chronika* 18 (2009), pp. 85–125.

Σκεύος Γ. Ζερβός, "Η νόσος των γυμνών σπογγαλιέων", *Ανακοίνωση στο Β' Πανελλήνιο Ιατρικό Συνέδριο* [Skevos G. Zervos, "The Disease of Naked Sponge Fishermen", Paper presented at the 2nd *Panhellenic Medical Conference*, Athens 1903], pp. 1–6.

Σκεύος Ζερβός, "Η νόσος των γυμνών σπογγαλιέων ή "νόσος Σκεύου Γ. Ζερβού"", *Καλυμνιακά Χρονικά* [Skevos Zervos, "Sponge Divers' Disease or 'Skevos Zervos Disease'"], *Kalymniaka Chronika* 18 [2009], pp. 241–247.

Αλέξης Ζήρας, "Κώστας Παρορίτης, Παρουσίαση-Ανθολόγηση", *Η παλαιότερη πεζογραφία μας* [Alexis Ziras, "Kostas Paroritis, Presentation-Selection of Stories", *I palaioteri pezografia mas*], 1900–1914, vol. III, Sokoli, Athens 1997, pp. 366–421.

Π. Ζώτος, *Έκθεσις περί της ανά τας αφρικανικάς ακτάς διά σκαφάνδρου σπογγαλιείας* [P. Zotos, *Report on the Scaphander Diving Suit Sponge Fishery across the African Coasts*], Athens 1904.

Ημερολόγιο της Νομαρχίας του Αρχιπελάγους [*Yearbook of the Archipelago Province*], 1304 AH (1886/1887).

Τριαντάφυλλος Θεοδωρίδης, "Μιχαήλ Κόκκινος, ο γλύπτης – ο άνθρωπος – ο πατριώτης", *Καλυμνιακά Σύμμεικτα* [Triantafyllos Theodoridis, "Michail Kokkinos: Sculptor – Human Being – Patriot", *Kalymniaka Symmeikta*] 1 (1993), pp. 21–24.

Θεόδωρος Καβάσιλας, "Αξεθώριαστες εικόνες απ' τα παλιά ...", *Καλυμνιακά Χρονικά* [Theodoros Kavasilas, "Unfading Images from the Past ...", *Kalymniaka Chronika*] 6 (1986), pp. 313–320.

Ιάκωβος Ν. Καζάβης, *Οι Δωδεκανήσιοι* [Iakovos N.Kazavis, *The Dodecanesians*], New York 1950.

Μητροφάνης Καλαφατάς, "Χειμερινός Όνειρος", *Καλυμνιακά Χρονικά* [Mitrophanis Kalafatas, "Winter Dream", *Kalymniaka Chronika*] 13 (1999), pp. 259–287.

Ελένη Καλαφάτη, "Η πολεοδομία της Επανάστασης: Ναύπλιο 1822–1830", *Τα Ιστορικά* [Eleni Kalafati, "The Urban Planning of the Revolution: Nafplio 1822–1830", *Ta Istorika*] 2 (1984), pp. 265–282.

Κανονισμός της Δημογεροντίας της νήσου Καλύμνου 1894, Αναγνωστήριον Καλύμνου "Αι Μούσαι" [*Regulation of the Elder Council of the Island of Kalymnos 1894*, ed. Anagnostirion Kalymnou "E Moussɛ"], Kalymnos 2000.

Θεμελίνα Καπελλά, *Καλύμνικοι αντίλαλοι* [Themelina Kapella, *Kalymnian Echoes*], Athens 1981.

Θεμελίνα Καπελλά, "Η ιστορία του Αναγνωστηρίου", *Καλυμνιακά Χρονικά* ["The History of the Reading Room", *Kalymniaka Chronika*] 1 (1982), pp. 26–28.

Θεμελίνα Καπελλά, "Τα παράπονα των γυναικών της Καλύμνου [από την καταγραφή του Καρόλου Ντίτεριχ]", *Καλυμνιακά Χρονικά* ["The Complaints of the Women of Kalymnos [Taken from the Account of Karl Dieterich]", *Kalymniaka Chronika*], 4 (1984), pp. 43–47.

Θεμελίνα Καπελλά, "Ο αγώνας των γυναικών στο 1935 και ο πετροπόλεμος", *Καλυμνιακά Χρονικά* ["The Fight of the Women in 1935 and the Rock War", *Kalymniaka Chronika*] 6 (1986), pp. 87–102.

Θεμελίνα Καπελλά, "Καλλιόπη Νομ. Καλαβρού", *Καλυμνιακά Χρονικά* ["Kalliope Nom. Kalavrou", *Kalymniaka Chronika*] 6 (1986), pp. 305–306.

Θεμελίνα Καπελλά, *Ιστορικές μνήμες Καλύμνου* [*Historical Remembrances of Kalymnos*], Athens 1997.

Θεμελίνα Καπελλά, *Λαογραφικές Σελίδες Καλύμνου* [*Folklore Pages of Kalymnos*], Athens 1997.

Θεμελίνα Καπελλά, "Ο χορός του 'μηχανικού'", ["The Dance of the 'Mechanic'"], Feature: Greek Sponge Fishery, *I Kathimerini*: Feature Section *Epta Imeres*, 13/9/1998, p. 30.

Θεμελίνα Καπελλά, "Ποκινήματα, αγιασμός, αναχώρηση" ["Preparation, Sanctification, Departure"], Feature: Greek Sponge Fishery, *I Kathimerini*: Feature Section *Epta Imeres*, 13/9/1998, pp. 28–30.

Αλέκα Καραδήμου-Γερόλυμπου, *Μεταξύ Ανατολής και Δύσης. Βορειοελλαδικές πόλεις στην περίοδο των οθωμανικών μεταρρυθμίσεων* [Aleka Karadimou-Gerolympou, *Between East and West. Northern Greek Cities in the Era of Ottoman Reforms*], Athens 1997.

Γιάννης Α. Καραμήτσος, *Ύδρα, νήσος εντελής δρυόπων* [Giannis A. Karamitsos, *Hydra, An Entirely Dryopian Island*], Hydra 1998.

Αλέξανδρος Καρανικόλας, "Νότιες Σποράδες. Σελίδες από την ιστορία των προνομίων τους", *Παρνασσός* [Alexandros Karanikolas, "The Southern Sporades. Pages on the History of Their Privileges", *Parnassos*] 13 (1971), pp. 3–29.

Σωτήριος Αλ. Καρανικόλας, *Τα σεβάσματα της λατρείας των Συμαίων* [Sotirios Al. Karanikolas, *The Objects of Worship of the People of Symi*], vol. I, Piraeus 1962.

Νικήτας Σκ. Καραφυλλάκης, "Πηαίνετε α παίξετε", *Καλυμνιακά Χρονικά* [Nikitas Sk. Karafyllakis, "Go play", *Kalymniaka Chronika*] 14 (2001), pp. 290–327.

"Κάρολος Φλέγελ", Αφιέρωμα στα *Καλυμνιακά Χρονικά* ["Charles (Carl) Flegel", Feature article in *Kalymniaka Chronika*] 3 (1982), pp. 25–54.

Κωνσταντίνος Γ. Καταγάς, "Το καλύμνιο μέλι", *Καλυμνιακά Χρονικά* [Konstantinos G. Katagas, "Kalymnian Honey", *Kalymniaka Chronika*] 17 (2007), pp. 21–28.

Bernard Kayser, *Ανθρωπογεωγραφία της Ελλάδος*, T. Τσαβέας (μτφρ.) [*Anthropogeography of Greece*, Trans. T. Tsaveas], Athens 1968.

Ερατοσθένης Καψωμένος, "Η μυθολογία του Αιγαίου στη νεοελληνική λογοτεχνία" [Eratosthenis Kapsomenos, "The Mythology of the Aegean Sea in Modern Greek Literature"], in Αστέριος Αργυρίου (επιμ.), *Η Ελλάδα των νησιών από τη Φραγκοκρατία ως σήμερα* [Asterios Argyriou (ed.), *Greece of the Islands from the Frankish Rule to Today*], vol. I, Athens 2004, pp. 399–415.

Θέμελης Κινδύνης, *Η νήσος Κάλυμνος* [Themelis Kindynis, *The Island of Kalymnos*], Athens 1879.

Μιχαήλ Ιορδ. Κινδύνης, "Τάρπον Σπρινκς Φλώριδα", *Καλυμνιακά Χρονικά* [Michail Iord. Kindynis, "Tarpon Springs, Florida", *Kalymniaka Chronika*] 3 (1982), pp. 162–164.

Χριστίνα Κομπιτσάκη, "Ο ναός της Κοίμησης της Θεοτόκου Χώρας Καλύμνου", *Καλυμνιακά Χρονικά* [Christina Kompitsaki, "The Church of the Assumption of Mary in Chora, Kalymnos", *Kalymniaka Chronika*] 9 (1990), pp. 196–203.

Γιάννης Κορδάτος, *Ιστορία της νεοελληνικής λογοτεχνίας (από το 1453 ως το 1961)* [Giannis Kordatos, *History of Modern Greek Literature (1453 to 1961)*], vol. I, Athens 1962.

Αναστασία Κορκόλη, Παρασκευή Βέργου, "Οι τρεις Καλύμνιοι ζωγράφοι και η αγιογράφηση της Μητρόπολης Καλύμνου", *Καλυμνιακά Χρονικά* [Anastasia Korkoli, Paraskevi Vergou, "The Three Kalymnian Painters and the Iconography of Kalymnos' Metropolis", *Kalymniaka Chronika*] 7 (1988), pp. 349–365.

Γιώργης Ν. Κουκούλης, *Η Κάλυμνα των Επιγραφών* [Giorgis N. Koukoulis, *Kalymnos of the Epigraphs*], Athens 1980.

Γιώργης Ν. Κουκούλης, "Νικόλας Θ. Τηλιακός, Το χρονικό του 1869 [τον καιρό των Τουρκώ]", *Καλυμνιακά Χρονικά* [Giorgis N. Koukoulis, "Nikolas Th. Tiliakos, The Chronicle of 1869 [in the Time of the Turks]", *Kalymniaka Chronika*] 3 (1982), pp. 7–21.

Γιώργης Ν. Κουκούλης, "Η συμβολή της Καλύμνου στους αγώνες για τα προνόμια", *Καλυμνιακά Χρονικά* ["The Contribution of Kalymnos in the Struggle for Privileges", *Kalymniaka Chronika*] 4 (1984), pp. 23–35.

Γιώργης Ν. Κουκούλης, "Δύο έγγραφα της Δημογεροντίας Καλύμνου προς τη Δημογεροντία Σύμης" ["Two documents from the Elders' Council of Kalymnos to the Elders' Council of Symi"], *Kalymniaka Chronika* 6 (1986), pp. 45–60.

Γιώργης Ν. Κουκούλης, "Η Κάλυμνος στους αγώνες κατά της απογραφής του πληθυσμού (1885–1888)", *Καλυμνιακά Χρονικά* ["Kalymnos in the Struggles against the Population Census [1885–1888]", *Kalymniaka Chronika*] 7 (1988), pp. 39–62.

Γεωργία Κουλικούρδη, *Αίγινα I* [Georgia Koulikourdi, *Aegina I*], Athens 1990.

Στέφανος Κουμανούδης, *Συναγωγή νέων λέξεων υπό των λογίων πλασθεισών από της Αλώσεως μέχρι των καθ' ημάς χρόνων* [Stefanos Koumanoudis, *Collection of New Words Introduced by Scholars from the Fall of Constantinople to the Present*], vol. II, Athens 1900.

Theodoros A. Kriezis, "Η σπογγαλιεία", Οικονομικός Ταχυδρόμος, ["Sponge Fishery", *Oikonomikos Tachydromos*], 14/8/1932, p. 3.

Θεόδωρος Αντ. Κριεζής, *Η σπογγαλιεία* [Theodoros Ant. Kriezis, *The Sponge Fishery*], Athens 1937.

Ελένη Κυπραίου, "Η γυναίκα της Καλύμνου", *Καλυμνιακά Χρονικά* [Eleni Kypraiou, "The Woman of Kalymnos", *Kalymniaka Chronika*] 18 (2009), pp. 369–375.

Ανδρέας Κυρκιλίτσης, "Η σπογγαλιευτική πίστις και χρηματοδότησις", Α' Πανελλήνιον Σπογγαλιευτικόν Συνέδριον [Ρόδος 24–27 Φεβρουαρίου 1949]. *Εισηγήσεις και Πρακτικά, Γενική Διοίκησις Δωδεκανήσου* [Andreas Kyrkilitsis, "Sponge-Fishing Credit and Funding", 1st Colloquium on Sponge Fishery [Rhodes 24–27 February 1949]. *Papers and Minutes, General Administration of the Dodecanese*], Rhodes 1951, pp. 43–56.

Ηλέκτρα Κωστοπούλου, *Η Λέρος στην Οθωμανική Αυτοκρατορία. Σελίδες από τα βιβλία της Δημογεροντίας* [Ilektra Kostopoulou, *Leros in the Ottoman Empire: Pages from the Books of the Demogerontia*], Athens 2005.

Αλέξανδρος Λεμονίδης, *Το εμπόριον της Τουρκίας* [Alexandros Lemonidis, *The Commerce of Turkey*], Constantinople 1849.

Μιλτιάδης Ιακ. Λογοθέτης, *Οι πρωτοπόροι του δωδεκανησιακού εμπορίου, Οικονομική Βιβλιοθήκη Εμπορικού και Βιομηχανικού Επιμελητηρίου Ρόδου* [Miltiadis I. Logothetis, *The Pioneers of the Dodecanesian Trade*, Economic Library of the Chamber of Commerce And Industry Of Rhodes], Athens 1968.

Μιλτιάδης Ιακ. Λογοθέτης, *Οι πρωτεργάτες του λιμανιού της Νισύρου στα τελευταία χρόνια της Τουρκοκρατίας (1885–1912)*, [*The Pioneers of Nisyros Port in the Final Years of the Turkish Rule (1885–1912)*], Athens 1981.

Μιλτιάδης Ιακ. Λογοθέτης, "Το εμπόριο στις Νότιες Σποράδες (Δωδεκάνησα) κατά τα τελευταία χρόνια της Τουρκοκρατίας", *Δωδεκανησιακά Χρονικά* ["Commerce in the Southern Sporades (Dodecanese) in the Last Years of Turkish Rule ", *Dodekanisiaka Chronika*] 9 (1983), pp. 137–149.

Μιλτιάδης Ιακ. Λογοθέτης, "Πληροφορίες για την οικονομία και κοινωνία της Δωδεκανήσου στα τέλη του 19ου αιώνα από τα ημερολόγια της Νομαρχίας Αρχιπελάγους", *Δωδεκανησιακά Χρονικά* ["Information on the Economy and the Society on Dodecanese Islands in Late 19th Century, Retrieved from the Yearbooks of the Archipelago Province", *Dodekanisiaka Chronika*] 11 (1986), pp. 91–117.

Μαρία Α. Μαγκλή, "Αικατερίνη Βουβάλη", *Καλυμνιακά Χρονικά* [Maria A. Magkli, "Aikaterini Vouvali", *Kalymniaka Chronika*] 5 (1985), pp. 57–61.

Μαρία Μαγκλή, Θεμελίνα Καπελλά, *Λαογραφικά Καλύμνου*, Λύκειο των Ελληνίδων [Maria Magkli, Themelina Kapella, *Kalymnos Folkore*, Lykio ton Ellinidon], n.d.

Αντώνης Μαΐλης, "Στο Τάρπον Σπρινκς", *Η Καθημερινή*, *Επτά Ημέρες*, [Antonis Mailis, "At Tarpon Springs", *I Kathimerini*: Feature Section *Epta Imeres*], vol. XIII, Δωδεκάνησα [*Dodekanissa*] Athens 1996, pp. 37–38.

Χρύσα Α. Μαλτέζου, "Η παρουσία της γυναίκας στις νοταριακές πράξεις της περιόδου της Βενετοκρατίας", *Κρητολογία* [Chrysa A. Maltezou, "The Presence of Women in Notarial Acts in the Period of Venetian Rule", *Cretologia*] 16–19 (1983–1984), pp. 62–79.

Γιάννης Μαρίνος, "Πώς άρχισε η μετανάστευση από την Κάλυμνο στην Αυστραλία", *Καλυμνιακά Χρονικά* [Giannis Marinos, "How Immigration from Kalymnos to Australia Began", *Kalymniaka Chronika*] 15 (2003), pp. 429–433.

Ειρήνη Μαρίνου, "Η λειτουργία των μοτίβων στα παραμύθια και στις παραδόσεις της Καλύμνου", *Καλυμνιακά Χρονικά* [Eirini Marinou, "The Function of Patterns in Tales and Traditions of Kalymnos", *Kalymniaka Chronika*] 13 (1999), pp. 77–87.

Διονύσης Μαυρόγιαννης, "Το συμμετοχικό σπογγαλιευτικό σύστημα της Καλύμνου: θεσμικό πλαίσιο, οικονομικοί μηχανισμοί, κοινωνικός μετασχηματισμός", *Καλυμνιακά Χρονικά* [Dionysios Mavrogiannis, "The Participatory Sponge-Fishing System on Kalymnos: Institutional Framework, Financial Mechanisms, Social Transformation", *Kalymniaka Chronika*] 13 (1999), pp. 241–248.

Παντελής Μιχ. Μαύρος, "Ο πατριωτισμός των Καλυμνίων και οι συντελεστές του Εθνικού φρονήματός των", *Καλυμνιακά Χρονικά* ["The Patriotism of Kalymnians and the Factors of their National Beliefs", *Kalymniaka Chronika*] 3 (1982), pp. 107–109.

Μεγάλη Ελληνική Εγκυκλοπαίδεια [*Great Greek Encyclopaedia*], vol. I, Athens 1926.

Κώστας Μηνέττος, "Νικόλαος Καλλισπέρης, ο αγωνιστής και πολιτικός", *Καλυμνιακά Χρονικά* [Kostas Minettos, "Nikolaos Kallisperis, the Fighter and Politician", *Kalymniaka Chronika*] 13 (1999), pp. 179–184.

Μιχαήλειον Σπίτι Στοργής, Στέγη Θηλέων Καλύμνου, Ημερολόγιον 1973 [*Michailion House of Loving Care, All-Girls Housing of Kalymnos*, 1973 Diary], n.p.

Κ. Μιχαηλίδης, "Παρατηρήσεις πάνω σε τρεις πόλεις νησιών του Αιγαίου", *Αρχιτεκτονικά Θέματα* [K. Michailidis, "Observations on Three Towns of Aegean Islands", *Architektonika Themata*] 8 (1974), pp. 136–144.

Μιχαήλ Γ. Μιχαηλίδης-Νουάρος, *Νομικά έθιμα της νήσου Καρπάθου της Δωδεκανήσου* [M. G. Michailidis-Nouaros, *Legal Customs of the Dodecanese Island of Karpathos*], Athens 1926.

Βασίλης Μοσκόβης, "Μιχάλης Κόκκινος", *Καλυμνιακά Σύμμεικτα* [Vassilis Moskovis, "Michalis Kokkinos", *Kalymniaka Symmeikta*] 1 [1993], pp. 15–17.

Νίκος Μπακουνάκης, *Πάτρα: 1828–1860. Μια ελληνική πρωτεύουσα στον 19ο αιώνα* [Nikos Bakounakis, *Patra: 1828–1860: A Greek Capital City in the 19th Century*], Athens 1988.

Επαμ. Μπαλούμης, "Εθνικο-κοινωνικά στον Αν. Καρκαβίτσα", *Διαβάζω* ["Ethno-social Elements in An. Karkavitsas", *Diavazo*] 306 (1993), pp. 46–54.

Γιάννης Μπασκόζος, "Ανδρέας Καρκαβίτσας: Από την ηθογραφία στο ρεαλισμό", *Διαβάζω* [Giannis Baskozos, "Andreas Karkavitsas: From Ethography to Realism", *Diavazo*] 306 (1993), pp. 57–60.

Ρίκα Μπενβενίστε, "Μνήμη και ιστοριογραφία" [Rika Benveniste, "Memory and Historiography"] in R. Benveniste, Th. Paradellis (eds.), *Διαδρομές και τόποι της μνήμης. Ιστορικές και ανθρωπολογικές προσεγγίσεις* [*Paths and Places of Memory: Historical and Anthropological Approaches*], Athens 1999, pp. 11–26.

Νίκη Γρ. Μπιλλήρη, *Η Κάλυμνός μας* [Niki Gr. Billiri, *Our Kalymnos*], Athens 1982.

Νίκη Γρ. Μπιλλήρη, *Της θάλασσας και της στεριάς* [*Of Sea and Land*], Athens 1986.

Νίκη Γρ. Μπιλλήρη, *Σφουγγαράδες από την Κάλυμνο* [*Sponge Fishermen from Kalymnos*], Athens 1995.

Μαρία Μπογδάνου-Ηλιοπούλου, Αγγελική Φετοκάκη-Σαραντίδη, *Κάλυμνος, Ελληνική Παραδοσιακή Αρχιτεκτονική* [Maria Bogdanou-Iliopoulou, Angeliki Fetokaki-Sarantide, *Kalymnos, Greek Traditional Architecture*], Athens 1984.

Ευδοκία Ολυμπίτου, "Κάλυμνος" [Evdokia Olympitou, "Kalymnos"], in Κατερίνα Κορρέ-Ζωγράφου, Ευδοκία Ολυμπίτου, *Άνθρωποι και παραδοσιακά επαγγέλματα στο Αιγαίο* [Katerina Korre-Zografou, Evdokia Olympitou, *Men and Traditional Professions in the Aegean Sea*], Athens 2003, pp. 241–269.

Ευδοκία Ολυμπίτου, "Η εισαγωγή του καταδυτικού σκαφάνδρου στη σπογγαλιεία της Καλύμνου", *Τα Ιστορικά* ["The Introduction of the Sponge-Fishing Scaphander Diving Suit in the Sponge Fishery of Kalymnos", *Ta Istorika*] 38 (2003), pp. 163–186.

Ευδοκία Ολυμπίτου, "Σχεδιάζοντας το ταξίδι: Σπογγαλιευτικά συμφωνητικά και εργασιακές σχέσεις των πληρωμάτων στην Κάλυμνο, 19ος–20ός αι.", *Πρακτικά του Β' Ευρωπαϊκού Συνεδρίου Νεοελληνικών Σπουδών με θέμα* "Η Ελλάδα των νησιών από τη Φραγκοκρατία ως σήμερα" ["Planning the Voyage: Sponge-Fishing Agreements and Crew Work Relationships on Kalymnos, in the 19th and 20th Centuries", *Minutes from the 2nd European Congress of Modern Greek Studies: Greece of the Islands from the Frankish Rule to Today*], vol. II, Athens 2004, pp. 401–414.

Ευδοκία Ολυμπίτου, "Από την ορεινή Χώρα στην παραλιακή Σκάλα. Παρατηρήσεις για τη διαμόρφωση μιας νησιωτικής πόλης", *Ιόνιος Λόγος* ["From the Mountainous Chora to the Seaside Skala: Observations on the Configuration of an Island Town", *Ionios Logos*] 1 (2007).

Ευδοκία Ολυμπίτου, "Ψαρεύοντας στο Αιγαίο τον 19ο αιώνα" ["Fishing in the Aegean in the 19th Century"], in Dimitris Dimitropoulos, Evdokia Olympitou (eds.), *Ψαρεύοντας στις ελληνικές θάλασσες. Από τις μαρτυρίες του παρελθόντος στη σύγχρονη πραγματικότητα* [*Fishing in the Greek Seas: From Testimonies of the Past to Modern Reality, Research Notebooks* 33, ΙΝΕ/ΕΙΕ], Athens 2010, pp. 139–154.

Ευδοκία Ολυμπίτου, "Σπογγαλιευτική δραστηριότητα και κοινωνική συγκρότηση στο νησί της Καλύμνου, 19ος–20ός αιώνας", Μνήμων ["Sponge-Fishing Activity and Social Composition on the Island of Kalymnos, in the 19th and 20th Centuries", *Mnimon*] 31 (2010), pp. 247–266.

Walter Ong, *Προφορικότητα και Εγγραματοσύνη. Η Εκτεχνολόγηση του Λόγου*, Κώστας Χατζηκυριάκου [μτφρ.] [*Orality and Literacy. The Technologizing of the Word*, translated by Kostas Chatzikyriakou], Heraklion 1997.

Ιωάννης Σκεύου Ορφανός, "Η νήσος Κάλυμνος", *Καλυμνιακά Χρονικά* [Ioannis Skevou Orfanos, "The Island of Kalymnos", *Kalymniaka Chronika*] 17 (2007), pp. 93–97.

Βασίλης Παναγιωτόπουλος, "Από το Ναύπλιο στην Τριπολιτσά: Η σημασία της μεταφοράς μιας περιφερειακής πρωτεύουσας τον 18ο αιώνα", *Ο Ερανιστής* [Vassilis Panagiotopoulos, "From Nafplio to Tripolitsa: The Importance of the Transfer of a Regional Capital City in the 18th Century", *O Eranistis*] 11 (1974), pp. 41–56.

Νίκος Παπάζογλου, "Επεξεργασία και εμπόριο", Αφιέρωμα: Η Ελληνική σπογγαλιεία, Η Καθημερινή, *Επτά Ημέρες*, [Nikos Papazoglou, "Processing and Trade", Greek Sponge Fishery, *I Kathmerini*: Feature Section Epta Imeres], 13/9/1998, pp. 9–12.

Αντ. Παπακωνσταντίνου, "Σπογγαλιευτική και αλιευτική δραστηριότητα (Από τη σκοπιά της Αγροτικής Τράπεζας)", *Καλυμνιακά Χρονικά* [Ant. Papakonstantinou, "Sponge Fishing and Fishing Activity (From the Perspective of the ATE)", *Kalymniaka Chronika*] 2 (1981), pp. 164–167.

Αθανάσιος Παπάς, "Μια προσωπογραφία του Σακελλάρη Μαγκλή", *Καλυμνιακά Χρονικά* [Athanasios Papas, "Portrait of Sakellaris Magklis", *Kalymniaka Chronika*] 6 (1986), pp. 271–278.

Thierry Paquot, *Η τέχνη της σιέστας*, Μαρία Παγουλάτου (μτφρ.) [*The Art of the Siesta*, Trans. Maria Pagoulatou], Athens 2009.

Γιάννης Θεοφ. Πατέλλης, "Ο αγνοημένος", *Καλυμνιακά Χρονικά* [Giannis Theof. Patellis, "The Missing One", *Kalymniaka Chronika*] 3 (1982), pp. 27–29.

Γιάννης Θεοφ. Πατέλλης, "Επιστημονική δράση", Αφιέρωμα στον Σκεύο Ζερβό, Καλυμνιακά Χρονικά ["Scientific Action", in Tribute to Skevos Zervos, *Kalymniaka Chronika*] 9 (1990), pp. 24–32.

Γιάννης Θεοφ. Πατέλλης, "Σφουγγάρι και σφουγγαράδες", Αφιέρωμα: Η Ελληνική σπογγαλιεία, Η Καθημερινή, Επτά Ημέρες ["Sponge and Sponge-Fishermen", *I Kathimerini: Feature Section Epta Imeres*], 13/9/1998, pp. 4–6.

Γιάννης Θεοφ. Πατέλλης, "Η δημόσια υγεία στην Κάλυμνο την εποχή της Δημογεροντίας", *Καλυμνιακά Χρονικά* ["Public health in Kalymnos", *Kalymniaka Chronika*] 13 (1999), pp. 159–164.

Γιάννης Θεοφ. Πατέλλης, "Ο θεσμός της Δημογεροντίας στα Δωδεκάνησα. Το παράδειγμα της Καλύμνου", *Καλυμνιακά Χρονικά* ["The Institution of Demogerontia in the Dodecanese: The Example of Kalymnos", *Kalymniaka Chronika*] 15 (2003), pp. 57–65.

Γιάννης Θεοφ. Πατέλλης, "Ιωάννης Σκεύου Ορφανός", *Καλυμνιακά Χρονικά* ["Ioannis Skevou Orfanos", *Kalymniaka Chronika*] 17 (2007), pp. 85–92.

Αδαμάντιος Ε. Παχουντάκης, *Η σπογγαλιεία εν Αιγύπτω* [Adamantios E. Pachountakis, *Sponge Fishing in Egypt*], Alexandria 1905.

Μαρίνα Πετρονώτη, "Συμβολή στη μελέτη της οικονομικής αυτονομίας των γυναικών στα νησιά Κάλυμνο, Σάμο και Κάρπαθο", *Καρπαθιακαί Μελέται* [Marina Petronoti, "Contribution to the Study of the Financial Autonomy of Women on the Islands of Kalymnos, Samos and Karpathos", *Karpathiakai Meletai*] 1 (1984), pp. 243–267.

Γεώργιος Ν. Πιζάνιας, "Η συμβολή της Καλυμνιάς Σεβαστής Καλλισπέρη στην ελληνική παι- δεία", *Καλυμνιακά Χρονικά* [Georgios N. Pizanias, "The Contribution of Kalymnian Sevasti Kallisperi to Greek Education", *Kalymniaka Chronika*] 4 (1984), pp. 64–68.

Νικόλαος Σ. *Πιζάνιας, Η Κάλυμνος από πλουτολογικής, δημογραφικής, ιδία δε δημοσιονομικής απόψεως* [Nikolaos S. Pizanias, *Kalymnos from the Perspective of Plutology, Demography, and especially Finance*], Athens 1935.

Νικόλαος Σ. Πιζάνιας, *Για μια καινούργια Κάλυμνο. Σκοπός και καθήκοντα μιας συγχρονισμένης δημοτικής διοικήσεως* [*For a New Kalymnos: Objectives and Duties of a Synchronized Municipal Administration*], Athens 1950.

Νικόλαος Σ. Πιζάνιας, *Διά την ανασυγκρότησιν της σπογγαλιείας της Δωδεκανήσου* [*For the Reform of the Sponge Fishery in the Dodecanese*], Rhodes 1950.

Νικόλαος Σ. Πιζάνιας, "Η οργάνωσις της σπογγαλιευτικής επιχειρήσεως [τεχνικώς-οικο- νομικώς]", *Α' Πανελλήνιον Σπογγαλιευτικόν Συνέδριον* [Ρόδος 24–27 Φεβρουαρίου 1949]. Εισηγήσεις και Πρακτικά, Γενική Διοίκησις Δωδεκανήσου ["The Organization of the Sponge-Fishing Enterprise [on a Financial Technical Level]", *The First Colloquium on the Sponge Fishery*, Rhodes 24–27 February 1949, Papers and Minutes, General Administration of the Dodecanese], Rhodes 1951, pp. 27–42.

Νικόλαος Σ. *Πιζάνιας, Φυσικό και τεχνητό σφουγγάρι* [*Natural and Artificial Sponge*], Kalymnos 1952.

Εμμανουήλ Πρωτοψάλτης, "Η τύχη των Νοτίων Σποράδων κατά την Επανάστασιν και μετ' αυτήν", *Καρπαθιακαί Μελέται* [Emmanouil Protopsaltis, "The Fortune of Southern Sporades During the Revolution and Thereafter", *Karpathiakai Meletai*] 2 (1981), pp. 290–307.

Ιάκωβος Ρ. Ραγκαβής, *Τα Ελληνικά ήτοι περιγραφή γεωγραφική, ιστορική, αρχαιολογική και στατιστική της αρχαίας και νέας Ελλάδος* [Iakovos R. Ragavis, *Greek: Geographical, Historical, Archaeological and Statistical Description of Ancient and Modern Greece*], vol. 3, Athens 1854.

Νίκη Ρεΐση-Γλυνάτση, "Βουβάλειο Παρθεναγωγείο Κοιτίδα πνευματικής ζωής στην Κάλυμνο", *Καλυμνιακά Χρονικά* ["Vouvaleio All-Girls' School, Cradle of Kalymnos Intellectual Life", *Kalymniaka Chronika*] 15 (2003), pp. 406–414.

Διονύσιος Ν. Ρεΐσης, *Περιγραφή της νήσου Καλύμνου* [Dionysios N. Reisis, *Description of the Island of Kalymnos*], Athens 1913.

Λουδοβίκος Ρος [Ludwig Ross], "Νησιωτικά ταξείδια [*Inselreisen*] Κάλυμνος – Τέλενδος. Κατά μετάφρασιν υπό Μ. Μιχαηλίδου Νουάρου", *Δωδεκανησιακή Επιθεώρησις* [Ludwig Ross, "Island Travels: Kalymnos-Telendos". Trans. M. Michailidou Nouarou, *Dodekanisiaki Epitheorisi*] 8 (1947), pp. 334–337.

Bernard Russell. "Η σπογγαλιεία της Καλύμνου", *Σπουδαί* ["The Sponge Fishery of Kalymnos", *Spoudai*] 1 (1970), pp. 2–32 [1st publication: "Kalymnian Sponge Diving", *Human Biology* 39/2 (1967), pp. 103–130].

François Russo. *Εισαγωγή στην ιστορία των τεχνικών*, Χριστίνα Αγριαντώνη [μτφρ.] [*Introduction à l'histoire des techniques*, Trans. Christina Agriantoni] Athens 1993.

Γ. Σ., "Μανόλης Αριστοτέλη Μαγκλής", *Καλυμνιακά Χρονικά* [G. R., "Manolis Aristotelis Magklis", *Kalymniaka Chronika*] 4 (1984), pp. 241–242.

Παναγιώτης Σαβοριανάκης, *Νησιωτικές κοινωνίες στο Αιγαίο. Η περίπτωση των Ελλήνων της Ρόδου και της Κω (18ος–19ος αι.)* [Panagiotis Savorianakis, *Insular Societies in the Aegean: Greeks on Rhodes and Kos (18th–19th Centuries)*], Athens, n.d.

Γεώργιος Μ. Σακελλαρίδης. "Αλιεία, Σπογγαλιεία", *Καλυμνιακά Χρονικά* [Georgios M. Sakellaridis, "Fishery, Sponge Fishery", *Kalymniaka Chronika*] 2 (1981), pp. 167–175.

Γεώργιος Μ. Σακελλαρίδης, "Προβλήματα και προοπτικές αλιείας και σπογγαλιείας", *Καλυμνιακά Χρονικά* ["Problems and Perspectives of Fishery and Sponge Fishery", *Kalymniaka Chronika*] 3 (1982), pp. 166–170.

Γεώργιος Μ. Σακελλαρίδης, "Η πληθυσμιακή εξέλιξη της Καλύμνου και τα αίτιά της", *Καλυμνιακά Χρονικά* ["The Population Increase in Kalymnos and its Causes", *Kalymniaka Chronika*] 4 [1984], pp. 69–73.

Γεώργιος Μ. Σακελλαρίδης, "Antonio Ritelli", *Καλυμνιακά Χρονικά* [*Kalymniaka Chronika*] 6 (1986), pp. 151–169.

Γεώργιος Μ. Σακελλαρίδης, "Αυτοδιοίκηση στα χρόνια της σκλαβιάς", *Καλυμνιακά Χρονικά* ["Self-Government in Times of Servitude", *Kalymniaka Chronika*] 6 (1986), pp. 61–68.

Γεώργιος Μ. Σακελλαρίδης, "Η Ελληνική Επαρχία. Η σπογγαλιεία εις την Κάλυμνον", *Καλυμνιακά Χρονικά* ["Greek Provinces: The Sponge Fishery on Kalymnos", *Kalymniaka Chronika*] 6 (1986), pp. 207–208.

Γεώργιος Μ. Σακελλαρίδης, "Σχολιάζοντας την επικαιρότητα. Σπογγαλιεία, Βιοτεχνία-Οικοτεχνία", *Καλυμνιακά Χρονικά* ["Commenting on Current Affairs, Sponge Fishery, Craft Industry-Cottage Industry", *Kalymniaka Chronika*] 6 (1986), pp. 393–415.

Γεώργιος Μ. Σακελλαρίδης, "Το λυκαυγές της λύτρωσης (Μεταβατική περίοδος 8.9.1943–31.3.1947)", *Καλυμνιακά Χρονικά* ["The Twilight of Salvation. (Transitional Period 8/9/1943–31/3/1947", *Kalymniaka Chronika*] 7 (1988), pp. 80–93.

Γεώργιος Μ. Σακελλαρίδης, "Μιχαήλ Νεοκλέους Καλαβρός", *Καλυμνιακά Χρονικά* ["Michail Neokleous Kalavros", *Kalymniaka Chronika*] 7 (1988), pp. 125–139.

Γεώργιος Μ. Σακελλαρίδης, "Η οικονομική εξέλιξη της Καλύμνου στα σαράντα πρώτα χρόνια του ελευθέρου μας βίου [Διαπιστώσεις και προοπτικές]", *Καλυμνιακά Χρονικά*

["The Economic Evolution of Kalymnos in the First Forty Years of Our Free Life [Observations and Perspectives]", *Kalymniaka Chronika*] 8 (1989), pp. 127–149.

Γεώργιος Μ. Σακελλαρίδης, "Η εξέλιξη και διαμόρφωση του πληθυσμού της Καλύμνου", *Καλυμνιακά Χρονικά* ["The Development and Configuration of the Population of Kalymnos", *Kalymniaka Chronika*] 9 (1990), pp. 395–405.

Νίκος Σβορώνος, "Κοινωνικές δομές και πολιτιστική ανάπτυξη των πόλεων στον ελληνικό χώρο κατά την Τουρκοκρατία" [Nikos Svoronos, "Social Structures and Cultural Development of Towns in the Greek Area under Turkish Rule"], *in Αμητός εις μνήμην Φώτη Αποστολόπουλου* [*Amitos: In Memory of Fotis Apostolopoulos*], Athens 1984, pp. 330–337.

Χρίστος Σερμπέτης, "Η αλιευτική επιχείρησις εις την Ελλάδα", *Τεχνικά Χρονικά* [Christos Serbetis, "The Sponge-Fishing Industry in Greece", *Technika Chronika*] 24/279 (1947), pp. 30–37.

Γεώργιος Σεφέρης, *Δοκιμές* [Georgios Seferis, *Essays*], vol. I, Athens 1981.

Κυριάκος Σιμόπουλος, *Ξένοι Ταξιδιώτες στην Ελλάδα 1700–1800* [Kyriakos Simopoulos, *Foreign Travelers in Greece 1700–1800*], vol. II, Athens 1995.

Μιχάλης Ευστ. Σκανδαλίδης, "Κοινά διαλεκτικά Καλύμνου-Κω [Β]", *Καλυμνιακά Χρονικά* [Michalis Efst. Skandalidis, "Common Dialectics of Kalymnos – Kos [B]", *Kalymniaka Chronika*] 17 (2007), pp. 331–357.

Έρη Σταυροπούλου, "Ανδρέας Καρκαβίτσας, Παρουσίαση-Ανθολόγηση", *Η παλαιότερη πεζογραφία μας* ["Andreas Karkavitsas, Presentation of a Selection of Stories", *I palaioteri pezografia mas*], 1880–1900, vol. VIII, Sokoli, Athens 1997, pp. 174–228.

Μαρία Συναρέλλη, *Δρόμοι και λιμάνια στην Ελλάδα* [Maria Synarelli, *Roads and Ports in Greece, 1830–1880*], 1830–1880, Athens 1989.

Αθηνά Ταρσούλη, *Δωδεκάνησα* [Athina Tarsouli, *Dodecanese*], vol. 2, Athens 1948.

Ιπποκράτης Ταυλάριος, "Περί της νήσου Καλύμνου", *Πανδώρα* [Hippocrates Tavlarios, "About the Island of Kalymnos", *Pandora*] 12 (1861–1862), pp. 518–522.

Αναστάσιος Τζαμτζής, *Η ναυτιλία του Πηλίου στην Τουρκοκρατία* [Anastasios Tzamtzis, *Maritime Shipping in Pelion under Turkish Rule*], Athens n.d.

Έντουαρτ Π. Τόμσον, *Χρόνος, εργασιακή πειθαρχία και βιομηχανικός καπιταλισμός*, Βασ. Τομανάς [μτφρ.] [Eduard P. Thompson, *Time, Work-Discipline and Industrial Capitalism*. Translation, V. Tomanas], Athens 1983.

Κώστας Τριανταφύλλου, "Ο νέος μεγάλος ναός στην Πάτρα του Πολιούχου της Αγίου Ανδρέα", *Πελοποννησιακή Πρωτοχρονιά* [Kostas Triantafyllou, "The New Large Church of the Patron Saint of Patra, Saint Andrew", *Peloponnissiaki Protochronia*] (1962), pp. 306–309.

Σακελλάρης Ν. Τρικοίλης, "Καλύμνικα βαφτιστικά ονόματα", *Καλυμνιακά Χρονικά* [Sakellaris N. Trikoilis, "Kalymnian Christian Names", *Kalymniaka Chronika*] 13 (1999), pp. 25–38.

Σακελλάρης Ν. Τρικοίλης, ""Το δελφίνι του Δάμου Καλυμνίων". Ο διπλός συμβολισμός: Απόλλων-Θάλασσα", *Καλυμνιακά Χρονικά* [Sakellaris N. Trikoilis, "'The Dolphin of Damos Kalymnou' and its Double Symbolism: Apollo-Sea", *Kalymniaka Chronika*] 14 (2001), pp. 9–21.

Σακελλάρης Ν. Τρικοίλης,"Κοινωνική διαστρωμάτωση στην Κάλυμνο του 18ου και 19ου αιώνα", *Καλυμνιακά Χρονικά* ["Social Stratification on Kalymnos in the 18th and 19th Centuries", *Kalymniaka Chronika*] 17 (2007), pp. 49–64.

Σακελλάρης Ν. Τρικοίλης, Νεότερη ιστορία της Καλύμνου. Κοινωνική διαστρωμάτωση [*Modern History of Kalymnos: Social Stratification*], Athens 2007.

Ζαχαρίας Ν. Τσιρπανλής, "Στην Κάλυμνο του 1935. Συλλήψεις και εκπατρισμοί", *Καλυμνιακά Χρονικά* ["On the Kalymnos of 1935. Arrests and Expatriations", *Kalymniaka Chronika*] 7 (1988), pp. 153–189.

Ζαχαρίας Ν. Τσιρπανλής, *Η Ρόδος και οι νότιες Σποράδες στα χρόνια των Ιωαννιτών Ιπποτών (14ος–16ος αι.): συλλογή ιστορικών μελετών* [*Rhodes and the Southern Sporades in the Time of the Knights of the Order of Saint John (14th–16th Century): Collection of Historical Studies*], Rhodes 1991.

Θεόφιλος Μ. Τσουκαλάς, "Ἀναφορά στον Λέρνης Ιερεμία Πατελλάκη (1819–1844)", *Καλυμνιακά Χρονικά* [Theofilos M. Tsoukalas, "Report to Ieremias Patellakis of Lerne (1819–1844)", *Kalymniaka Chronika*] 13 (1999), pp. 147–158.

Χ. Φ., "Φωνή υπέρ των σπογγαλιέων" [Ch. F., "Voice in Favour of the Sponge Fishermen"], Γεώργιος Ν. Τασούδης (επιμ.), *Ἄρθρα και μελέται Χρυσάνθου Αρχιεπισκόπου Αθηνών του από Τραπεζούντος 1911–1949* [Georgios N. Tassoudis (ed.), *Articles and Studies by the Archbishop of Trabzon, Chrysanthos, 1911–1949*], vol. 3, Athens 1977, pp. 47–49.

Αγγελική Φενερλή, "Ο καλλωπισμός της πόλης. Ένας πρωτότυπος συμμετοχικός τρόπος χρηματοδότησης δημοσίων κτιρίων στην Ερμούπολη (19ος αι.)", *Πρακτικά του Β' Διεθνούς Συνεδρίου: Η πόλη στους νεότερους χρόνους* [Angeliki Fenerli, "Beautification of the Town: An Innovative Participatory Means of Funding Public Buildings in Hermoupolis [19th century]"], in *Minutes of the 2nd International Convention* "Η πόλη στους νεότερους χρόνους" ["The Town in Modern Times"], Athens 2000, pp. 173–182.

Κάρολος Φλέγελ, *Η νήσος Κάλυμνος* [Carl Flegel, The Island of Kalymnos], Constantinople 1896.

Κάρολος Φλέγελ, "Η Α.Θ. Παναγιότης ο Οικουμενικός Πατριάρχης Άνθιμος ο Ζ' εν Καλύμνω" ["His Holiness the Ecumenical Patriarch Anthimos VII in Kalymnos"], Samos 1896.

Κάρολος Φλέγελ, "Το σπογγαλιευτικό ζήτημα της Μεσογείου (Χανιά, 1903)", *Καλυμνιακά Χρονικά* ["The Sponge-Fishing Issue of the Mediterranean Sea (Chania, 1903)", *Kalymniaka Chronika*] 5 (1985), pp. 203–230.

Κάρολος Φλέγελ, "Τα Δωδεκάνησα ή Νότιες Σποράδες από ένα υπόμνημα των αρχών του αιώνα", Κυριάκος Κων. Χατζηδάκης [μτφρ.-σχόλια], *Καλυμνιακά Χρονικά* ["The Dodecanese, or the Southern Sporades from Memo of the Beginning of this Century". Translation and annotation, Kyriakos K. Chatzidakis, *Kalymniaka Chronika*] 12 (1997), pp. 54–72.

Αλέκος Φλωράκης, *Σχέδια τηνιακής μαρμαρογλυπτικής* [Alekos Florakis, *Designs of Marble Sculpting at Tinos*], Athens 1993.

Αλέκος Φλωράκης, "Τηνιακοί μαρμαρογλύπτες στη Σμύρνη", *Μικρασιατικά Χρονικά* ["Marble Sculptors from Tinos to Smyrna", *Mikrasiatika Chronika*] 20 (1998), pp. 261–310.

Ιπποκράτης Φραγκόπουλος, *Ιστορία της Καλύμνου* [Ippokratis Fragopoulos, *History of Kalymnos*], Athens 1995.

Στέλιος Φώκος, *Κώστας Παρορίτης. Εισαγωγή στη ζωή και το έργο του* [Stelios Fokos, *Kostas Paroritis: Introduction to His Life and Work*], Athens 1979.

Mario Vitti, *Ιστορία της νεοελληνικής λογοτεχνίας* [*History of Modern Greek Literature*], Athens 1978.

Mario Vitti, *Η γενιά του Τριάντα, Ιδεολογία και μορφή* [*Generation of the '30s: Ideology and Form*], Athens 1995.

Δημοσθένης Χαβιαράς, Περί σπόγγων και σπογγαλιείας από των αρχαιοτάτων χρόνων μέχρι των καθ' ημάς [Dimosthenis Chaviaras, *On Sponges and Sponge Fishing from Ancient Times to the Present*], Athens 1916.

Δημοσθένης Χαβιαράς, "Τινά περί σπογγαλιείας", *Συμιακός* ["On the Sponge Fishery", *Symiakos*] 5 (2010), Republished by Κωνσταντίνος Σκόκος, *Εθνικόν ημερολόγιον, χρονογραφικόν, φιλολογικόν και γελοιογραφικόν* [Konstantinos Skokos, *National Journal: Chronological, Philological and Satyrical*], vol. XII, 1903, pp. 411–415.

Νικήτας Χαβιαράς, "Συμαίων γυμνών σπογγαλιέων φρικτά επεισόδια", *Τα Συμαϊκά* [Nikitas Chaviaras, "Horrible Accidents Suffered by Symiot Naked Sponge Divers", *Ta Symaika*] 3 (1977), pp. 285–293.

Φανερωμένη Χαλκιδιού-Σκυλλά, *Ή σφουγγάρι ή τομάρι. Η ζωή των σφουγγαράδων της Καλύμνου μέσα από αληθινές μαρτυρίες* [Faneromeni Chalkidiou-Skylla, *Either Sponge or Corpse. The Life of the Sponge Fishermen of Kalymnos through Real Testimonies*], Kalymnos 2009.

Ιωάννης Π. Χαλκίτης, "Συμβολή στην ιστορία του Δήμου Καλυμνίων", *Καλυμνιακά Χρονικά* ["Contribution to the History of the Municipality of Kalymnians", *Kalymniaka Chronika*] 5 (1985), pp. 236–242.

Ιωάννης Π. Χαλκίτης, "Συμβολή στην ιστορία της Εκκλησίας της Καλύμνου. Η ουσιαστική συμμετοχή του λαού της Καλύμνου στη ζωή της ορθοδόξου τοπικής εκκλησίας του", *Καλυμνιακά Χρονικά* ["Contribution to the History of the Kalymnian Church: The Meaningful Participation of the People of Kalymnos in the Life of their Local Orthodox Church", *Kalymniaka Chronika*] 6 (1986), pp. 127–137.

Ιωάννης Π. Χαλκίτης, "Συμβολή στην ιστορία του Δήμου Καλυμνίων. Συμπλήρωμα στο χρονικό της διαιρέσεως του ενιαίου Δήμου της Καλύμνου σε δύο Δήμους: τον Δήμο Παραλίας-Λιμένος και τον Δήμο Χώρας", *Καλυμνιακά Χρονικά* ["Contribution to the History of the Municipality of Kalymnians: Supplement to the Chronicle of the Single Municipality Separation into Municipality of Beach-Port and Municipality of Chora", *Kalymniaka Chronika*] 6 (1986), pp. 145–158.

Ιωάννης Π. Χαλκίτης, "Συμβολή στην ιστορία της Εκκλησίας της Καλύμνου. Α' εκατονταετηρίς από της ανυψώσεως της Επισκοπής Λέρνης εις Μητρόπολιν Λέρου και Καλύμνου Νοέμβριος 1888–Νοέμβριος 1988", *Καλυμνιακά Χρονικά* ["Contribution to the History of the Church of Kalymnos. 1st Centenary from the Erection of Lerni Diocese as Metropolis of Leros and Kalymnos, November 1888–November 1988", *Kalymniaka Chronika*] 7 (1988), pp. 106–111.

Γεώργιος Χρ. Χαραμαντάς, πρεσβύτερος, *Επισκοπική Ιστορία της Εκκλησίας της Καλύμνου* [Georgios Chr. Charmantas, senior, *Episcopal History of the Church of Kalymnos*], Kalymnos 1983.

Γεώργιος Χρ. Χαραμαντάς, πρεσβύτερος [ed.], "Λουδοβίκος Ρος [Ludwig Ross], "Νησιωτικά ταξίδια. Κάλυμνος-Τέλενδος. Εικοστή πρώτη επιστολή"", *Καλυμνιακά Σύμμεικτα* [Ludwig Ross, "Island Trips: Kalymnos-Telendos 21st Letter", *Kalymniaka Symmeikta*] 1 (1993), pp. 71–74.

Γεώργιος Χρ. Χαραμαντάς, πρεσβύτερος [ed.], "Ιπποκράτη Δ. Ταυλάριου, "Περί της νήσου Καλύμνου"", *Καλυμνιακά Σύμμεικτα* ["Ippokrati D. Tavlariou, "About the Island of Kalymnos"", *Kalymniaka Symmeikta*] 1 (1993), pp. 75–80.

Γεώργιος Χρ. Χαραμαντάς, πρεσβύτερος, "Σακελλάριος Αντ. Μαγκλής [1844–1886]", *Καλυμνιακά Σύμμεικτα* ["Sakellarios Ant. Maglis [1844–1886]", *Kalymniaka Symmeikta*] 2 (1995), pp. 28–31.

Γεώργιος Χρ. Χαραμαντάς, πρεσβύτερος, *Χώρα, η πρωτεύουσα της νήσου Καλύμνου. Κομμάτια και σελίδες από την ιστορία της και την παράδοσή της* [*Chora, the Capital of Kalymnos Island. Pieces and Pages of its History and Traditions*], Athens 2000.

Γεώργιος Χρ. Χαραμαντάς, πρεσβύτερος, *Ένα γνήσιο λαϊκό ποίημα για τον ήρωα της Καλύμνου Μανόλη Καζώνη γραμμένο από τον Μανόλη Θεοδώρου Τρουμουλιάρη* [*An Original Popular Poem for the Hero of Kalymnos, Manolis Kazonis, Written by Manolis Theodorou Troumouliaris*], Athens 2002.

Γεώργιος Χαριτάκης, *Οικονομική Επετηρίς της Ελλάδος* [Georgios Charitakis, *Financial Yearbook of Greece*], Athens 1937.

Βίλμα Χαστάογλου, "Από τις "Σκάλες" του Λεβάντε στις σύγχρονες εμπορικές προκυμαίες", Πρακτικά του Β' Διεθνούς Συνεδρίου: Η πόλη στους νεότερους χρόνους [Vilma Hastaoglou, "From the "Skalas" of Levante to the Modern Commercial Docks", in the Minutes of the 2nd International Convention: [The City in Modern Times], Athens 2000, pp. 51–68.

Κυριάκος Κ. Χατζηδάκης, "Ο αγώνας για την κατάργηση των σκαφάντρων και ο Κάρολος Φλέγελ", *Καλυμνιακά Χρονικά* [Kyriakos Kon. Chatzidakis, "The Fight to Abolish the Scaphander Diving Suits and Carl Flegel", *Kalymniaka Chronika*] 3 (1982), pp. 30–43.

Κυριάκος Κ. Χατζηδάκης, "Από την έρευνα των αρχείων της Δημογεροντίας Καλύμνου" *Καλυμνιακά Χρονικά* ["From Research in the Archives of the Elders of Kalymnos", *Kalymniaka Chronika*] 5 (1985), pp. 275–282.

Κυριάκος Κ. Χατζηδάκης, "Η Κάλυμνος στα τέλη της Τουρκοκρατίας", *Καλυμνιακά Χρονικά* ["Kalymnos towards the End of Turkish Rule", *Kalymniaka Chronika*] 8 (1989), pp. 59–90.

Κυριάκος Κ. Χατζηδάκης, "Κάλυμνος, 1851", *Καλυμνιακά Χρονικά* ["Kalymnos, 1851", *Kalymniaka Chronika*] 12 (1997), pp. 38–44.

Κυριάκος Κ. Χατζηδάκης, "Η σπογγαλιεία στις Νότιες Σποράδες στα μέσα του 19ου αιώνα", *Καλυμνιακά Χρονικά* ["Sponge Fishery in the Southern Sporades in the Mid-19th Century", *Kalymniaka Chronika*] 13 (1999), pp. 229–240.

Κυριάκος Κ. Χατζηδάκης, "Από τον αγώνα για την προάσπιση των προνομίων στις Νότιες Σποράδες. Το λιμεναρχικό ζήτημα στην Κάλυμνο (1897–1899)", *Καλυμνιακά Χρονικά* ["From the Fight for the Defence of the Privileges of Southern Sporades. The Port Authorities Issue on Kalymnos" (1897–18990), *Kalymniaka Chronika*] 17 [2007], pp. 99–172.

Γιάννης Αντ. Χειλάς, "Χα[τ]ζής-Χα[τ]ζή[δ]ες και Χα[τ]ζήαινες", *Καλυμνιακά Χρονικά* [Giannis Ant. Cheilas, "Cha[t]zis, Cha[t]zides and Cha[t]ziaines", *Kalymniaka Chronika*] 13 (1999), pp. 95–98.

Γιάννης Αντ. Χειλάς, *Το έπος των σφουγγαράδων της Καλύμνου* [*The Epic Saga of Kalymnos' Sponge Fishermen*], Athens 2000.

Γιάννης Αντ. Χειλάς, "Που να σε φάει το ψάρι", *Καλυμνιακά Χρονικά* ["May the Fish Eat You", *Kalymniaka Chronika*] 18 (2009), pp. 275–287.

Literature in Other Languages

James M. Acheson, "Anthropology of Fishing", *Annual Review of Anthropology* 10 (1981), pp. 275–316.

Léon Arnou, *Manuel de l'épicier. Produits alimentaires et conserves, denrées coloniales, boissons et spiritueux ... etc.*, Paris 1904.

Athanasios N. Bernardakis, *Le présent et l'avenir de la Grèce*, Paris 1870.

Paul Bert, *La pression barométrique. Recherches de Physiologie Expérimentale*, Paris 1879.

C. D. Booth, Isabelle B. Booth, *Italy's Aegean Possessions*, London 1928.

Jean-Pierre Boude, "Les pêches méditerranéennes", *Études Internationales* 18 (1987), pp. 83–105.

Arthur E. Boycott, G. C. C. Damant, J. S. Haldane, "The Prevention of Compressed-air Illness", *The Journal of Hygiene* 8 (1908), pp. 343–443.

Arthur E. Boycott, G. C. C. Damant, J. S. Haldane, "Prevention de la maladie de décompression", Alain Foret (Preface and translation), Montpellier 2008.

Rogers Brubaker, Frederick Cooper, "Beyond 'Identity'", *Theory and Society* 29/1 [2000], pp. 1–47.

M. Cabirol, *Scaphandre, appareil de plongeur Cabirol*, Paris 1870.

Joao de Pina Cabral, "'Matriarcat et rôles conjugaux dans le Nord-Ouest du Portugal", *Recherches en anthropologie au Portugal* 4 (1992), pp. 37–51.

Roxane Caftanzoglou, "Kalymnos: Contribution à la connaissance d'une société", Mémoire de maitrise d'ethnologie spécialisée, [Unpublished Master's Thesis], Paris 1978.

John Campbell, *Honour, Family and Patronage: A Study of Institutions and Moral Values in a Greek Mountain Community*, Oxford 1964.

Miltiadis Carabokyro, *Etude sur la pêche des éponges. Les pays spongifères de l'Empire et le scaphandre*, Constantinople 1886.

Michael Catsaras, *Les hématomyelies des pêcheurs d'éponges de l'Archipel*, Paris 1888.

Michael Catsaras, "Recherches cliniques et expérimentales sur les accidents survenant par l'emploie des scaphandres", *Archives de Neurologie* 17/49–51 (1889), pp. 392–437.

M. B. C. Collas, *La Turquie en 1861*, Paris 1861.

Colonies françaises et pays de protectorat a l'Exposition universelle de 1889. Guide publié par la Société des études coloniales et maritimes, Paris 1889.

Jacques Henri Coriol, *La plongée en apnée*, Paris 4 2006.

Ernest J. J. Cresswell, *Sponges: Their Nature, History Modes of Fishing, Varieties, Cultivation, etc.*, London 19[20].

David Mc Cullough, *The Great Bridge: The Epic Story of the Building of the Brooklyn Bridge*, New York 1972.

Alexandras Dagkas, *Le mouvement social dans le Sud-Est européen pendant le xxᵉ siècle: Questions de classe, questions de culture*, Thessaloniki 2008.

Dona Lee Davis, Jane Nadel-Klein, "Gender, Culture and the Sea: Contemporary Theoretical Approach" in Carolyn E. Sachs (eds.), *Women Working in the Environment*, Washington 1997, pp. 49–61.

Auguste Denayrouze, *Manuel du matelot plongeur, et instructions sur l'appareil plongeur Rouquayrol-Denayrouze, basse pression*, Paris 1867.

Gaston Deschamps, *La Grèce d'aujourd'hui*, Paris 1894.

Dictionnaire Encyclopédique des sciences médicales, vol. 7, Paris 1870.

Karl Dieterich, *Sprache und Volksüberlieferungen der südlichen Sporaden im Vergleich mit denen der übrigen Inseln des ägäischen Meeres*, Vienna 1908.

Nicholas Doumanis, Nicholas G. Pappas, "Grand History in Small Places: Social Protest on Castellorizo (1934)", *Journal of Modern Greek Studies* 15/1 (1997), pp. 103–123.

Jill Dubisch, "Greek Women: Sacred or Profane", *Journal of Modern Greek Studies* 1/1 (1983), pp. 185–202.

Louis Figuier, *Les merveilles de la science, ou Description populaire des inventions modernes*, vol. 4, Paris 1870.

Carl (Charles) Flegel, *La question des pêcheurs d'éponges de la Méditerranée*, Cairo 1902.

Carl (Charles) Flegel, "The Abuse of the Scaphander in the Sponge Fisheries", *Bulletin of the Bureau of Fisheries* 28 (1908), Washington 1910, pp. 514–543.

Heidrun Friese, "Ainsi soit l'île. Images de la colonisation de Lampedusa: Récits historiques, récits indigènes", *Genèses* 19 (1995), pp. 148–156.

Elda Gaino, Roberto Pronzato, "Epidemie e pesca intensive minacciano la sopravvivenza delle spugne commerciali del bacino mediterraneo", *Bollettino dei musei e degli istituti biologici dell'Universita di Genova* 56–57 (1992), pp. 209–224.

Alphonse Gal, *Des dangers du travail dans l'air comprimé et des moyens de les prévenir*, Montpellier 1872.

Aliette Geistdoerfer, "De l'origine des marins. La genèse mythique d'une spécialisation technique", *Techniques et Culture* 43–44 (2004), pp. 2–14.

Alain Gilli, Patrick Maillard, *Plongée dans le monde de spongiaires: Guide des éponges de Méditerranée*, Marseilles 2000.

P. A. Hennique, *Les Caboteurs et pêcheurs de la côte de Tunisie: Pêche des éponges*, Paris 1888.

Michael Herzfeld, *The Poetics of Manhood: Contest and Identity in a Cretan Mountain Village*, Princeton 1985.

Michael N. Kalafatas, *The Bellstone: The Greek Sponge Divers of the Aegean: One American's Journey Home*, Brandeis University Press, Hannover 2003.

Roger E. Kasperson, *The Dodecanese: Diversity and Unity in Island Politics*, Chicago 1966.

Habib Kazdaghli, "Communautés méditerranéennes de Tunisie. Les Grecs du Millet-i-rum a l'assimilation française (xviiᵉ–xxᵉ siècles)", *Revue des mondes musulmans et de la Méditerranée* 95–98 (2002), pp. 449–476.

Habib Kazdaghli, "Les Grecs de Sfax à l'heure des choix", unpublished paper for scientific meeting: "Παραδοσιακές καλλιέργειες και προϊόντα στο Αιγαίο και τη Μεσόγειο" ["Traditional crops and products in the Aegean and the Mediterranean Sea"], 11–12 July 2003, Σεμινάρια της Ερμούπολης [Seminars of Hermoupolis] IHR/NHRF and Faculté des Lettres, Université de Manouba Tunisia.

Emile Y. Kolodny, *La population des îles de la Grèce: Essai de géographie insulaire en Méditerranée orientale*, vol. 1, Aix-en-Provence 1974.

Liberty Kovacs, *Liberty's Quest*, Bandon 2008.

Pierre Lemonnier, "Technologie ou Anthropologie des Techniques?", Ο αγροτικός κόσμος στον μεσογειακό χώρο [The Agricultural World in the Mediterranean Space], *Conference Minutes of the Greek-French Conference*, Athens, 1988, pp. 334–337.

André Leroi-Gourhan, *Evolution et techniques. 1. L'homme et la matière*, Paris, 1971.

Jacques Lordat, *Essai sur l'iconologie médicale ou sur les rapports d'utilité qui existent entre l'art du dessin et l'étude de la médecine*, Montpellier, 1833.

Louis Ch. Lortet, *La Syrie d'aujourd'hui, Le tour du monde*, Montpellier, 1875.

Bronislaw Malinowski, *Magic, Science, Religion and other Essays*, New York 1954.

Alfred Leroy de Méricourt, "Considérations sur l'hygiène des pêcheurs d'éponge", *Annales d'hygiène publique et de médecine légale* 31 (1869), pp. 274–286.

Ministère de la Marine, *Revue Maritime et coloniale*, vol. 107, Paris 1900.

Cleveland Moffett, *Careers of Danger and Daring*, The Century & Co, New York 1901.

Michel Mollat, "Les attitudes des gens de mer devant le danger et devant la mort", *Ethnologie Française* 9 (1979), pp. 191–200.

Jacques Momot, "L'histoire des technique et la plongée en scaphandre autonome", *Revue d'histoire des sciences et de leurs applications* 17 (1964), pp. 251–257.

Charles T. Newton, *Travels and Discoveries in the Levant*, vol. 1, London 1865 (A Greek translation was published in *Kalymniaka Chronika* 6 (1986), pp. 201–206).

Ali Fuat Oreng, *Yakindonem Tarihimizde Rodos ve Oniki Ada*, Istanbul 2006.

Efthymios Papataxiarchis, "A Hypothesis on the 1965–1977 Transition in the Socio-Economic Structure of the Sponge Fishing Industry in Kalymnos", (Doctoral thesis), Department of Social Anthropology, London School of Economics.

John J. Poggie, Jr., "Deferred Gratification as an Adaptive Characteristic for Small-scale Fishermen", *Ethos* 6/2 (1978), pp. 114–123.

Edward Potts, *Fresh Water Sponges: A Monograph*, Academy of Natural Sciences, Philadelphia 1887.

Roberto Pronzato, "Sponge-Fishing, Disease and Farming in the Mediterranean Sea", *Aquatic Conservation: Marine and Freshwater Ecosystems* 9 (1999), pp. 485–493.

Roberto Pronzato, Renata Manconi, "Mediterranean Commercial Sponges: Over 5000 Years of Natural History and Cultural Heritage", *Marine Ecology* 29 (2008), pp. 146–166.

Jean Rieucau, "Océan et continent, deux espaces vécus en mutation chez les gens de mer", *Annales de Géographie* 98/549 (1989), pp. 516–537.

Joseph Slabey Roucek, "Economic Geography of Greece", *Economic Geography* 11 (1935), pp. 91–104.

Bernard Russell, "Kalymnos: The Island of the Sponge Fishermen", *Annals of the New York Academy of Sciences* 268 [1976], pp. 289–307.

Bernard Russell, "The Fisherman and His Wife", in William Mernard, Jane Schieber (eds.), *Oceans: Our Continuing Frontier*, California 1976, pp. 304–309.

Bernard Russell, "Paratsoukli: Institutionalized Nicknaming in Rural Greece", *Ethnologia Europaea* II–III (1968–1969), pp. 65–74.

Peter L. Simmonds, *The Commercial Products of the Sea or, Marine Contributions to Food, Industry and Art*, London 1878.

Société des Nations, Conférence International du Travail, Geneva 1926.

Leon Sonrel, *Le Fond de la mer*, Paris 4 1880.

"Sponge fishing", *Scientific American* 5 (1849), pp. 33–40.

Jeanne Z. Stephanopoli, *Les îles de l' Egée. Leurs privileges*, Athens 1912.

Charles Stewart, "Hegemony or Rationality? The Position of the Supernatural in Modern Greece", *Journal of Modern Greek Studies* 7/1 (1989), pp. 77–104.

Martin Strohmeier, "Economy and Society in the Aegean Province of the Ottoman Empire, 1840–1912", *Turkish Historical Review* 1 (2010), pp. 164–195.

David E. Sutton, "'Tradition and Modernity': Kalymnian Constructions of Identity and Otherness", *Journal of Modern Greek Studies* 12/2 (1994), pp. 239–260.

David E. Sutton, "Local Names, Foreign Claims: Family Inheritance and National Heritage on a Greek Island", *American Ethnologist* 24/2 (1997), pp. 415–437.

David E. Sutton, "'He's too cold': Children and the Limits of Culture on a Greek Island", *Anthropology and Humanism* 23 (1998), pp. 127–138.

David E. Sutton, *Memories Cast in Stone. The Relevance of the Past on Everyday Life*, New York and Oxford 1998.

David E. Sutton, "Re-scripting Women's Collective Action: Nationalist Writing and the Politics of Gendered Memory", *Identities* 5/4 (1999), pp. 469–500.

David E. Sutton, "Greeks of Kalymnos", in Carol Ember, Melvin Ember (eds), *The Encyclopedia of Sex and Gender: Men and Women in the World's Cultures*, vol. 1, New York 2004, pp. 417–424.

David E. Sutton, "Tradition and Modernity Revisited: Existential Memory Work on a Greek Island", *History and Memory* 20/2 (2008), pp. 84–105.

Susan Buck Sutton, "What is a 'Village' in a Nation of Migrants?", *Journal of Modern Greek Studies* 6/2 (1988), pp. 187–215.

Gustave Tallent, *Cloche à plongeur et scaphandre*, Imprimerie Administrative, Melun 1899.

Jules Toutain, *La Tunisie au début du xxe siècle*, F. R. de Rudeval, Paris 1904.

Michael D. Volonakis, *The Island of Roses and Her Eleven Sisters or, The Dodecanese from the Earliest Times to the Present Day*, London 1922.

Eleni Voultsiadou, T. Dailianis, C. Antoniadou, D. Vafidis, C. Dounas and C. Chintiroglou, "Aegean Bath Sponges: Historical Data and Current Status", *Reviews in Fisheries Science* 19 (2011), pp. 34–51.

Faith Warm, *Bitter Sea: The Real Story of Greek Sponge Diving*, South Woodham Ferrers, London 2000.

Henry V. Wilson, *The Sponges,* Cambridge USA 1904.

Skevos Zervos, Paris Roussos, *White Book. The Dodecanese: Resolutions and Documents Concerning the Dodecanese 1912–1919*, London 1919.

Skevos Zervos, *Les anémones de la mer dans la pathologie de l'homme, L'Hellénopolype*, Paris 1937.

Index